THE CANADIAN YEARBOOK OF INTERNATIONAL LAW

2009

ANNUAIRE CANADIEN DE DROIT INTERNATIONAL

The Canadian Yearbook of International Law

VOLUME XLVII   2009   TOME XLVII

Annuaire canadien de Droit international

Published under the auspices of
THE CANADIAN BRANCH, INTERNATIONAL LAW ASSOCIATION
AND
THE CANADIAN COUNCIL ON INTERNATIONAL LAW

Publié sous les auspices de
LA SECTION CANADIENNE DE L'ASSOCIATION DE DROIT INTERNATIONAL
ET
LE CONSEIL CANADIEN DE DROIT INTERNATIONAL

UBCPress·Vancouver·Toronto

Printed in Canada on acid-free paper

ISBN 978-0-7748-1987-9
ISSN 0069-0058

Canadian Cataloguing in Publication Data

The National Library of Canada has catalogued this publication as follows:

The Canadian yearbook of international law — Annuaire canadien de droit international

Annual.
Text in English and French.
"Published under the auspices of the Canadian Branch, International Law Association and the Canadian Council on International Law."
ISSN 0069-0058

1. International Law — Periodicals.
I. International Law Association. Canadian Branch.
II. Title: Annuaire canadien de droit international.
JC 21.C3   341'.05   C75-34558-6E

Données de catalogage avant publication (Canada)

Annuaire canadien de droit international — The Canadian yearbook of international law

Annuel.
Textes en anglais et en français.
"Publié sous les auspices de la Branche canadienne de l'Association de droit international et le Conseil canadien de droit international."
ISSN 0069-0058

1. Droit international — Périodiques.
I. Association de droit international. Section canadienne.
II. Conseil canadien de droit international.
III. Titre: The Canadian yearbook of international law.
JC 21.C3   341'.05   C75-34558-6E

UBC Press
University of British Columbia
2029 West Mall
Vancouver, BC V6T 1Z2
(604) 822-5959
www.ubcpress.ca

Contents / Matière

Cases / Jurisprudence

Book Reviews / Recensions de livres

THE CANADIAN YEARBOOK OF INTERNATIONAL LAW

2009

ANNUAIRE CANADIEN DE DROIT INTERNATIONAL

Pushing the Boundaries:
Rethinking International Law
in Light of Cosmopolitan Obligations
to Developing Countries

GRAHAM MAYEDA

INTRODUCTION

Increasingly, traditional international law is proving inadequate for dealing with issues facing developing countries — it does not offer them sufficient tools for promoting their sustainable development policies, it pits them against powerful developed countries, and it is generally incompatible with a cosmopolitan theory of justice. It is time to rethink the foundations of international law to rectify these inadequacies.

A number of specific subfields of international law have already begun to challenge the basic principles underlying international law and the rules for generating this law. In the area of international environmental law, practitioners have been proposing innovative ways of converting "soft law" and emerging norms of sustainable development into important tools for promoting the protection of the environment. For example, Vaughn Lowe has argued that emerging principles of international law are "interstitial norms" that can help to "fill in the gaps" where primary norms of international law come into conflict.[1] Philippe Sands has argued that treaty law and custom are basically on the same level and should be

---

Graham Mayeda is an associate professor in the Faculty of Law, Common Law Section at the University of Ottawa. He would like to thank John Currie for his helpful comments on this article. He would also like to thank the participants of the Scholarship Roundtable on the Law and Politics of International Cooperation, sponsored by the Center for International and Comparative Law at Duke University and organized by Curt Bradley and Larry Helfer, for their comments and suggestions.

1 Vaughn Lowe, "The Politics of Law-Making: Are the Method and Character of Norm Creation Changing," in Michael Byers, ed., *The Role of Law in International Politics: Essays on International Relations and International Law* (Oxford: Oxford University Press, 2000) at 213.

used reciprocally to interpret one another.[2] Finally, John Jackson argues that globalization challenges "the underlying logic and legitimacy of international law norms."[3] He suggests that traditional international legal concepts such as sovereignty need to be rethought to deal with the increasing need for cooperation in particular areas of international regulation such as international trade.[4] He suggests we should create new norms of "good governance" for international organizations and make changes to the way that international law, including both treaty and customary law, is interpreted. In his view, the approach of the Vienna Convention on the Law of Treaties to the interpretation of international law is a barrier to dealing with issues raised by globalization and the ever-closer association of states in international legal regimes.[5]

I pick up on some of the ideas of Jackson, Sands, and Lowe and apply them to issues of international development. Based on my work with international investment agreements, I will suggest areas of customary international law that need to be further developed in order to take better account of the concerns of developing countries. In particular, I will suggest that principles of equity, which Thomas Franck and others have identified as being animated by ideas of distributive justice,[6] need to be further developed to provide developing countries with the flexibility they need to promote their sustainable development goals without running afoul of international obligations. Also, I will address some of the rules regarding the creation, interpretation, and application of customary international law norms in order to allow emerging norms of sustainable development, the right to development, and so on to be applied more effectively by international tribunals. Finally, I will suggest ways in which the process of international law-making must become more responsive to the needs of individuals — the beneficiaries of

---

2 Philippe Sands, "Sustainable Development: Treaty, Custom, and the Cross-Fertilization of International Law," in Alan Boyle and David Freestone, eds., *International Law and Sustainable Development* (Oxford: Oxford University Press, 2001).

3 John Jackson, *Sovereignty, the WTO and Changing Fundamentals of International Law* (Cambridge: Cambridge University Press, 2006) at 77.

4 *Ibid.* at 265.

5 *Ibid.* at 268. Vienna Convention on the Law of Treaties, 23 May 1969, 155 U.N.T.S. 331 (entered into force 27 January 1980) [Vienna Convention].

6 Thomas Franck, *Fairness in International Law and Institutions* (Oxford: Clarendon Press, 1995).

international legal protection of human rights and the environment — rather than simply favouring the interests of states. My approach will be philosophical and theoretical, beginning from notions of cosmopolitan justice. However, I will also provide practical examples drawn from international investment law and the international law of development more generally.

THE COSMOPOLITAN ROOTS OF INTERNATIONAL COOPERATION

When one searches for the philosophical foundation of international cooperation, one does not necessarily arrive at cosmopolitanism. Cosmopolitanism is generally considered to be based on individualism rather than on the collectivism of cooperation, since the norms of cosmopolitanism are based on a recognition of the worth of each human being in virtue of her humanity. Seyla Benhabib emphasizes the individualistic nature of cosmopolitan norms when she describes cosmopolitan justice:

Cosmopolitan norms of justice, whatever the conditions of their legal origination, accrue to individuals as moral and legal persons in a worldwide civil society. Even if cosmopolitan norms arise through treaty-like obligations, such as the UN Charter can be considered to be for signatory states, their peculiarity is that they endow *individuals* rather than states and their agents with certain rights and claims.[7]

However, I suggest that cosmopolitanism can still be the basis of norms of cooperation despite its traditional individualist perspective. In my view, cosmopolitanism is actually based on our experience of communal life — we respect all others because they are part of our experiential community. This suggests that Immanuel Kant was a bit off track when he developed the implications of cosmopolitan justice for international law in "Perpetual Peace: A Philosophical Sketch" based on the conception of the freedom of the individual.[8] Moreover, it suggests that if we return to the original insight that animated cosmopolitan thinkers — the value of community — we

---

7 Seyla Benhabib, *Another Cosmopolitanism* (Oxford: Oxford University Press, 2006) at 16. On the individualistic basis of traditional cosmopolitanism, see also Thomas W. Pogge, *World Poverty and Human Rights: Cosmopolitan Responsibilities and Reforms* (Cambridge: Polity Press, 2002) at 169–70.

8 Immanuel Kant, "Perpetual Peace: A Philosophical Sketch," in Immanuel Kant, *Kant: Political Writings*, edited by Hans Reiss (Cambridge: Cambridge University Press, 1991), 93.

will find that it provides a useful normative framework for an international law of cooperation.

In Cicero's *De Officii*, the classical statement of cosmopolitanism that has inspired many subsequent thinkers, Cicero states that the duty of justice is to be fulfilled in accordance with the norm of cosmopolitanism,[9] which is based on a recognition of our common humanity:

[F]or one man to take something from another and to increase his own advantage at the cost of another's disadvantage is more contrary to nature than death, than poverty, than pain and than anything else that may happen to his body or external possessions. In the first place, it destroys the common life and fellowship of men: for if we are so minded that any one man will use theft or violence against another for his own profit, then necessarily the thing that is most of all in accordance with nature will be shattered, that is, the fellowship of the human race.[10]

In itself, the recognition of common humanity does not entail individualism, since the commonality of our humanity may be developed through community rather than in distinguishing ourselves from it. Modern interpretations of Cicero have given cosmopolitanism an individualistic interpretation. For instance, Martha Nussbaum argues that the mantra of the classical cosmopolitan that each person is a "citizen of the world" was intended to emphasize individual identity over group identity. In her view, Cicero, as a good Stoic, saw cosmopolitanism as involving a rejection of local group loyalties.[11] She explains that for Diogenes the Cynic, "[t]he life of

---

9   Cicero distinguishes between duties of justice and duties of material aid: "Of the three [sources of duty] that remain the most wide-reaching one is the reasoning by which the fellowship of men with one another, and the communal life, are held together. There are two parts of this: justice, the most illustrious of the virtues, on account of which men are called 'good'; and the beneficence connected with it, which may be called either kindness or liberality." M.T. Griffin and E.M. Atkins, eds., *Cicero: On Duties* (Cambridge: Cambridge University Press, 1991) at I:20. For a discussion of the distinction between the two, see Martha C. Nussbaum, "Duties of Justice, Duties of Material Aid: Cicero's Problematic Legacy," in Angela Kallhoff, ed., *Martha C. Nussbaum: Ethics and Political Philosophy*, volume 4 of the Münsteraner Volesungen zur Philosophie (Münster: Lit Verlag, 2001), 3.

10   Cicero, cited in Griffin and Atkins, *supra* note 9 at III:21.

11   Diogenes the Cynic, in Diogenes Laertius, *Lives of Eminent Philosophers*, Book VI (Cambridge, MA: Harvard University Press, 1957) at 63.

the world citizen is, in effect ... a kind of exile — from the comfort of local truths, from the warm nestling feeling of local loyalties, from the absorbing drama of pride in oneself and one's own."[12]

Interpretations of cosmopolitanism since Cicero have given it an increasingly individualistic twist. Immanuel Kant, for instance, justified cosmopolitanism on the basis of human rationality — reason demands perpetual peace, and cosmopolitanism is the only way of achieving it. He states: "[R]eason, as the highest legislative moral power, absolutely condemns war as a test of rights and sets up peace as an immediate duty."[13] He deduces from this dictate of reason that states should form a confederation of republics — which would ensure perpetual peace because in a democratic republic individuals would never vote to endanger themselves by going to war,[14] and the eventual alliances between the republics and the closer economic ties that would result would make war perpetually unappealing:

[T]he *spirit of commerce* sooner or later takes hold of every people, and it cannot exist side by side with war. And of all the powers (or means) at the disposal of the power of the state, *financial power* can probably be relied on most. Thus states find themselves compelled to promote the noble cause of peace, though not exactly from motives of morality.[15]

Kant's cosmopolitanism is individualistic because it is derived, not from a shared experience of community, but, rather, discovered through the employment of each individual's rational faculty, which demands peace. This individualistic and rationalist strain of cosmopolitanism continues in many modern iterations. For instance, Charles Beitz sees modern cosmopolitanism as the "application to

---

[12] Martha C. Nussbaum, "Kant and Cosmopolitanism," in James Bohman and Matthias Lutz-Bachmann, eds., *Perpetual Peace: Essays on Kant's Cosmopolitan Ideal* (Cambridge, MA: MIT Press, 1997), 25 at 35.

[13] Kant, "Perpetual Peace," *supra* note 8 at 104.

[14] Kant says, "[i]f, as is inevitably the case under this [that is, a Republican] constitution, the consent of the citizens is required to decide whether or not war is to be declared, it is very natural that they will have great hesitation in embarking on so dangerous an enterprise. For this would mean calling down on themselves all the miseries of war, such as doing the fighting themselves, supplying the costs of the war from their own resources, painfully making good the ensuing devastation, and, as the crowning evil, having to take upon themselves a burden of debt which will embitter peace itself and which can never be paid off on account of the constant threat of new wars" (*ibid.* at 100).

[15] *Ibid.* at 114 [emphasis in original].

the global level of the individualist moral egalitarianism of the Enlightenment."[16] He describes it in an individualistic way as follows:

[Cosmopolitan liberalism] applies to the whole world the maxim that choices about what policies we should prefer, or what institutions we should establish, should be based on an impartial consideration of the claims of each person who would be affected. In contrast to social liberalism, cosmopolitan liberalism accords no ethical privilege to state-level societies. It aims to identify principles that are acceptable when each *person's* prospects, rather than the prospects of each society or people, are taken fairly into account.[17]

However, an exclusively individualistic interpretation of cosmopolitanism is unwarranted. Cicero was at pains to emphasize the connection between the Stoic and his community. In his portrayal, the Stoic cosmopolitan recognizes the importance and utility of local communities for enriching our lives,[18] and he likewise recognizes the value of a broader community centred on a common human rationality.[19] Indeed, a cosmopolitan is placed in a series of concentric circles that define increasingly broad communities:

The first circle is drawn around the self; the next takes in one's immediate family; then follows the extended family; then, in order, one's neighbors or local group, one's fellow city dwellers, and one's fellow countrymen. Outside all these circles is the largest one, that of humanity as a whole. [20]

Cicero himself places high value on community, although he sees this community as based on the common capacity for rationality shared by all humans:

The same nature, by the power of reason, unites one man to another for the fellowship both of common speech and of life, creating above all a particular love for his offspring. It drives him to desire that men should meet together and congregate, and that he should join them himself; and for the same reason to devote himself to providing whatever may contribute

---

[16] Charles R. Beitz, "Social and Cosmopolitan Liberalism" (1999) 75(3) International Affairs 515 at 518.

[17] *Ibid.* at 519.

[18] Nussbaum, *supra* note 12 at 32.

[19] *Ibid.* at 29.

[20] *Ibid.* at 32–33. Cicero also uses the circle metaphor, see Griffin and Atkins, *supra* note 9 at I:50–53.

to the comfort and sustenance not only of himself, but also of his wife, his children, and others whom he holds dear and ought to protect.[21]

In the following sections, I explore how, despite the modern individualistic interpretation, cosmopolitanism can provide the basis for an international law based on cooperation — that is, based on our experience of the relations between people and the responsibility that this experience entails.

THE PHENOMENOLOGY OF INJUSTICE

In the exposition of his cosmopolitan vision, *Perpetual Peace: A Philosophical Sketch*, Kant points out that "a violation of rights in *one* part of the world is felt *everywhere*."[22] By this statement, he meant to support the cosmopolitan view that international justice is about injustices to individuals and not just about injustices to states. However, what Kant's comment also indicates is that underlying cosmopolitanism is a phenomenology of injustice based on community and cooperation that is waiting to be uncovered. Indeed, Kant's quote suggests that we recognize our duties to others to the degree that we "feel" or experience the violation of another's rights, even if the person injured is in a distant place. If such feelings exist, as I will demonstrate they do, perhaps they are the basis of our understanding of cosmopolitan obligations to others. If so, the phenomenon of cosmopolitan obligation may provide a normative basis for cosmopolitanism that is neither individualist nor collectivist. To find such a normative basis would be beneficial because it would avoid the dichotomy between an international law paradigm based on human rights,[23] which is individualistic,[24] and a paradigm based on states,[25] which is purely collectivist. In turn, this allows us to use

---

[21] *Ibid.* at I:12.

[22] Kant, "Perpetual Peace," *supra* note 8 at 107–8 [emphasis in original].

[23] For an explanation of the philosophical foundation of human rights, see Henry Shue, *Basic Rights: Subsistence, Affluence and U.S. Foreign Policy* (Princeton, NJ: Princeton University Press, 1980).

[24] Of course, the individualism of the human rights paradigm is contested by those who advocate for third-generation human rights such as economic, social, and cultural rights, the right to self-determination, the right to development, and so on. See Karel Vasak and Philip Alston, eds., *The International Dimensions of Human Rights* (Westport, CT: Greenwood Press, 1982).

[25] For a classical explanation of the normative foundations of a state-based international legal system, see Anthony D'Amato, *International Law: Process and Prospect*

individualist paradigms such as international human rights and collectivist paradigms such as state sovereignty flexibly — the individual and the state simply become historically emergent concepts rather than ideal concepts that unify whole fields of international law. To put this another way, a phenomenological understanding of international obligation allows individualist mechanisms such as human rights and collectivist concepts such as the state to be used *where practical* in order to achieve international justice rather than being the *controlling concept* underlying our whole way of understanding international law. However, before expanding on such benefits, I turn first to a description of the phenomenon of "publicity" that supplies the normative content of cosmopolitanism.

Do we have any inherent feeling of repulsion when harm is caused to others — even others in far away places? In my view, we do. As human beings, we have the capacity to experience harm to those with whom we are not in close community — that is, our capacity to experience harms extends beyond harm to our family, friends, and neighbours. As a result of the individualistic orientation of contemporary Western philosophy, the inter-relational or inter-subjective nature of the phenomenon of cosmopolitanism has not been extensively explored. It has been obscured behind individualistic concepts and ideas of moral obligation such as Kantian natural rights theory (in which the freedom of the individual is the basis of his moral worth, and the goal of morality is to ensure that individuals are treated as having equal moral worth)[26] or utilitarianism (in which the aggregate utility of all individuals is maximized).[27] Due to the persistent neglect of inter-subjective approaches to moral obligation, I turn briefly to contemporary Japanese philosophy in order to help establish the phenomenological nature of

---

(Dobbs Ferry, NY: Transnational Publishers, 1987). D'Amato sees international law as based on the idea of enforceability. For him, domestic law is characterized by the fact that it can be enforced by the state, and he demonstrates that an equally effective enforcement system exists at the international level — "reciprocal entitlement violation" — whereby international law is enforced by the reciprocal violation of entitlements, a sort of tit-for-tat process. Given that such an enforcement mechanism exists, international law is just as much law as domestic law (at 13–26).

26 See Immanuel Kant, *The Metaphysics of Morals*, in H.S. Reiss, ed., *Kant: Political Writings* (Cambridge: Cambridge University Press, 1991), 133 at 137.

27 For example, see Henry Sidgwick, *The Methods of Ethics*, 7th edition (London: MacMillan, 1962) at 411.

cosmopolitan inter-subjectivity, since it, like many East Asian philosophical traditions, has explored inter-subjectivity in great depth.

Watsuji Tetsuro (1889–1960), who was one of Japan's pre-eminent modern philosophers and phenomenologists, explains in his famous book *Rinrigaku* (*Ethics*) that our ethical obligations to others are based on our experience of them rather than on some abstract rational understanding of duty or obligation.[28] However, this experience is not a physical experience of the presence of another. Rather, our ethical obligations are based on a phenomenon that he calls "publicity." This phenomenon contrasts the "public" with the "private." The private is what we want to hide, while the public is what we want others to know. Publicity is not based on the physical presence of two (or more) people face to face. Watsuji explains that something is not private simply because no one has seen it, nor is something public because others have experienced it directly (that is, physically). Rather, things are private or public depending on how we intend them to be experienced by others. For instance, when I leave the door to my office open, what I do there is "public" even though no one has walked by during the last twenty minutes. Everything I do is public as long as I keep the door open and there is the potential for interactions with others. Thus, as Watsuji explains, when we say that something is public, we do not mean that any given individual has become conscious of it. Rather, we mean that the information has been "disclosed to the public."[29] Publicity is thus the expression of what Watsuji calls the "spatiality" of human existence, which is the openness of human existence that creates a "public space" and provides the possibility that information will be disclosed or "revealed"[30] such that everyone can come to know it.[31]

According to Watsuji, publicity manifests itself through communication, and it is dependent on the various methods of communication that we set up around us: roads, radio, television, newspapers, postal services, and so on:

In ancient societies, what was to be communicated was written on a stone or a plate and displayed at important points of traffic flow. Or else, persons

---

28 Watsuji Tetsuro, *Watsuji Tetsuro's* Rinrigaku: *Ethics in Japan*, translated by Yamamoto Seisaku and Robert E. Carter (Albany, NY: SUNY, 1996).

29 *Ibid.* at 149.

30 *Ibid.* at 146–47.

31 *Ibid.* at 150.

were dispatched on foot to spread information to the public. This illustrates the intention of those concerned to inform all possible persons ...

A typical source of public information in the modern world is the press. The notice board that in ancient times consisted of "written words" has today developed into newspapers. Similarly, spreading information by speaking while strolling around consisted of "words circulated through the voice," whose form has developed into radio broadcasting. The press discloses information to the public by means of these two forms of communication. Its aim is to inform as many persons as possible, and that goal is now nearly achieved. The possibility of full participation that was once merely nominal has now become actual.[32]

There is no fixed size to "public" and "private." This is because the size and identity of the group of those to whom we reveal information can change.[33] Sometimes what is private is limited to the individual, but things can equally be private if only our family or friends know about it. Moreover, not just individuals, but even groups of people, can keep something private. For instance, a neighbourhood may be trying to hide from others that it is secretly cutting down public trees, or even a whole country can try to conceal its practice of torturing terrorism suspects even though the torture is carried out on behalf of a democratic state.[34] Thus, any given public entity — be it an individual or a group — can be a private being and vice versa.[35] Watsuji points out that historically publicity stopped at the level of the nation — little was known about what went on beyond the borders of a country. This is particularly true of the history of Japan, which, being physically isolated from the rest of the world, considered itself to be the world in its totality.[36]

This exposition of what Watsuji means by "publicity" demonstrates that proximity and distance cannot be used to determine the nature of our ethical obligations to others.[37] True, we might have different obligations to those who are in our private realm as compared to

---

[32] *Ibid.* at 149–50.

[33] For publication as "revelation," see *ibid.* at 147.

[34] *Ibid.* at 147.

[35] *Ibid.*

[36] *Ibid.* at 148.

[37] For a utilitarian justification of why our ethical obligations are not limited by distance, see Peter Singer, "Famine, Affluence and Morality" (1972) 1(3) Philosophy and Public Affairs 229.

the public. However, publicity is not determined by distance, nor is it defined by the number of people who are aware of information. Rather, the private is distinguished from the public by the possibility of acquiring the information, if one desires to obtain it. If information remains private — that is, inaccessible to us — then we cannot have an ethical responsibility to act on it. Yet, as the information becomes public, we may well have an obligation to act on it. Politicians recognize this distinction since they are constantly loath to admit to the knowledge of unsavoury and unethical behaviour in order to avoid any public perception that they had a duty to prevent it.

It follows from Watsuji's explanation of publicity as the possibility of accessing information about others that the spatial limits of individuals are far broader than we think in daily life. They are not limited by our physical being but, instead, extend to the limits of the information that a person can access. For instance, it is possible to experience disasters in far away places because of the possibility of gathering information from that place. Watsuji illustrates this notion with the example of being cut off from information from distant places during natural disasters. For instance, an earthquake occurs, the radio or television goes dead, we no longer have news from the disaster area, and we experience this lack of news — this lack of publicity — as a wound:[38]

When a certain event is prohibited from being described in a newspaper or magazine, the words *reporting* this event are prohibited from being spatially dispersed throughout several million copies. This prohibition stops the spread of a report to the public. The means of reporting are not restricted to a newspaper or a magazine. Instead, the telephone, letters, dialogue, and so forth can play a role in spreading the news of this event to a considerable extent. When the telephone, the mail service, and so on are interrupted in their function, and even transportation facilities are destroyed, then the report of this event is likely to be limited to a specific locality. Consequently, if a certain area were to be cut off from the services of communication — news reports, transportation, and so forth — then the people in this region would be cut off from the wider public. In this case, however, as far as physical space is concerned there is no change. As extended, the greater public suffers damage. No matter how distant this region is, whether it is a remote place in the mountains or a secluded island,

[38] Watsuji, *supra* note 28 at 159.

it is usually quite removed from the intense contact of communication, transportation, and the like. If this contact is interrupted against the will of the local people, then this event itself comes to emerge as an event of the gravest public concern. The interruption of contact is felt as physical damage by that society, so to speak.[39]

It is clear from this example that for Watsuji publicity is based on "communication" or "news" and not on the physical boundaries of our being. Indeed, we have constant evidence that publicity is an informational, rather than a physical, phenomenon. For instance, charities and non-governmental organizations take advantage of the phenomenon of publicity as access to information in their advertisements, which depend on public images of suffering in physically distant places in order to expand the sphere of our public awareness, thereby increasing the sphere of our public obligation.

The phenomenon of publicity that Watsuji describes explains why it is that we have an intuitive sense of different types of obligations to family members in comparison to strangers. We have little access to information about strangers and even less information about those in other countries. We obtain some information about large-scale goings on in other countries — massacres, wars, rebellions, and so on. But as the scale decreases from nation, to city, to village, to neighbourhood, to family, to individual, we have little if any access to specific information. Thus, the sphere of our subjective spatiality does not extend to encompass individuals in other countries, and so we feel no obligation to them.

The next question is: What are the ethical implications of Watsuji's phenomenological analysis of publicity? We might have an experience of the suffering of others in distant places, but how does this experience give rise to an obligation to do something about it? For phenomenologists such as Watsuji, there is no need to explain how an ethical obligation arises because the experience of the other whose rights are being violated or who is being harmed is precisely an experience of this suffering. It is not some anonymous contact with another. For instance, in Watsuji's example of how we experience being cut off from a place that is suffering natural disaster, he describes this experience as the experience of physical damage — a wound. Such an experience naturally requires us to take responsibility for our experience. Emmanuel Levinas, another phenomenologist, says that we are "accused" by the gaze of the other — that is,

---

[39] *Ibid.* at 158–59.

we are forced by the gaze of another suffering to take responsibility — to answer for our role in the suffering, to give voice to it, and to alleviate it.[40] Or, as Albert Camus said, we are naturally required to "take the victim's side."[41]

Rationalist approaches to ethics have tried to capture our natural response to being confronted with the suffering of others. For instance, Immanuel Kant felt that we must prevent others from suffering if the suffering is the result of a violation of the essence of their humanity as free beings. However, such rationalist interpretations have been criticized both for being essentialist and for reducing human worth to an inappropriate metric such as "freedom" or "happiness."[42] A phenomenologist overcomes these intellectualizations of basic experience, thereby also overcoming the objections to rationalist ethics. Of course, one could argue that phenomenologists are also essentialists, as they presume a universal response to an experience of the suffering of others. Indeed, empirically, it is obvious that not everyone feels accused when faced with another's suffering, nor does everyone feel the necessity of taking responsibility for the suffering of others. However, this challenge is easily dismissed — people often use rationalizations to justify their inaction and to dull the impact of the appeal of the other, but this does not itself deny the phenomenology of experiencing another's suffering — it does not deny the content of the experience. In other words, phenomenological analysis is not denied by an empirical observation of the lack of impact of an appeal. Phenomenology describes the experiential structure of an appeal, although this structure might in reality be ignored by a person who is distracted or self-involved and so on. When a person stands before

---

40 On accusation, see Emmanuel Levinas, *Otherwise Than Being or Beyond Essence*, translated by Alphonso Lingis (The Hague: Martinus Nijhoff, 1981) at 124. For my gloss on Levinas, see Graham Mayeda, "Who Do You Think You Are? When Should the Law Let You Be Who You Want to Be?" in Laurie Shrage, ed., *"You've Changed": Sex Reassignment and Personal Identity* (Oxford: Oxford University Press, 2009), 194 at 202-3.

41 Albert Camus, *The Plague* (New York: Alfred A. Knopf, 1960) at 230. As Henry Shue explains, "[t]he honouring of basic rights is an active alliance with those who would otherwise be helpless against natural and social forces too strong for them." Henry Shue, *Basic Rights: Subsistence, Affluence, and U.S. Foreign Policy* (Princeton, NJ: Princeton University Press, 1996).

42 For a feminist critique of Kant's rationalist approach, see Robin May Schott, "The Gender of Enlightenment," in James Schmidt, ed., *What Is Enlightenment?* (Berkeley: University of California Press, 1996) at 478.

you and says: "Help me!" or "I need help!" how can one deny that one is being called upon to respond? It is not the perspective of the person accused that determines the experience — rather, the experience is constituted between the two people interacting.

Having briefly explained the phenomenological analysis of publicity and the ethical response it engenders, the next question is: How is this phenomenological understanding of responsibility relevant to international law? The first step to answering this question is to explain how publicity manifests itself at the international level. For if we first identify the phenomenon of publicity at the international level, it follows that there must also be an experience of international responsibility. In my view, publicity manifests itself today at the international level as "globalization."

GLOBALIZATION AS THE PHENOMENOLOGICAL BASIS OF COSMOPOLITANISM

If cosmopolitanism is to be interpreted phenomenologically as based in our experience of community, it leads us to question what the modern phenomenological basis of cosmopolitan justice is. The answer is globalization.[43] Globalization is the modern experience of our community with others.

Globalization may seem like a strange choice as a phenomenon to represent our experience of community. For instance, many left wing critics think of globalization in terms of what Antonio Negri and Michael Hardt call "empire," which they consider a sort of anonymous network of institutions that force individuals to comply with global capitalist structure.[44] Far from being "public," global

---

[43] For various discussions of the meaning and significance of globalization, see Jagdish Bhagwati, *In Defense of Globalization* (Oxford: Oxford University Press, 2004); Thomas L. Friedman, *The Lexus and the Olive Tree: Understanding Globalization* (New York: Farrar, Straus, Giroux, 1999); Joseph E. Stiglitz, *Globalization and Its Discontents* (New York: Norton, 2002); and Martin Wolf, *Why Globalization Works* (New Haven: Yale University Press, 2004).

[44] Antonio Negri and Michael Hardt, *Empire* (Cambridge, MA: Harvard University Press, 2000), state that globalization operates by means of "governance without government," which "indicate[s] the structural logic, at times imperceptible but always and increasingly effective, that sweeps all actors within the order of the whole" (at 14). The modern concept of "empire" is distinguished from the ancient by "the recognition that only an established power, overdetermined with respect to and relatively autonomous from the sovereign nation-states, is capable of functioning as the center of the new world order, exercising over it an effective regulation and, when necessary, coercion" (at 14–15).

systems of capital and global institutions operate by means of impersonal arteries of political and economic power. Even advocates of economic globalization think of it as a series of impersonal transactions. For instance, Joseph Stiglitz defines economic globalization as "the closer economic integration of the countries of the world through the increased flow of goods and services, capital, and even labor."[45] Thus, globalization is rarely understood to be based on the phenomenon of "publicity" that I elaborated earlier.

However, other definitions of globalization are clearly based on the notion of publicity developed in the earlier sections. For instance, Jan Aart Scholte sees globalization as the "destruction of territorialism."[46] Such a definition emphasizes the decreasing importance of the nation state as the unit of international significance. John Jackson emphasizes the complementary aspect of decreasing emphasis on territorialism, namely the "conditions of interdependence in world economic and political relationships, which means that events or circumstances in one part of the world can have remarkably large and often swift effects in other distant parts of the world."[47] Thomas Friedman describes the extent of our interconnection as follows:

The globalization system ... has one overarching feature — integration. The world has become an increasingly interwoven place, and today, whether you are a company or a country, your threats and opportunities increasingly derive from who you are connected to. This globalization system is also characterized by a single word: the *Web*. So in the broadest sense we have gone from a system built around division and walls to a system increasingly built around integration and webs.[48]

And as Michael Trebilcock points out, some critics of globalization go even further. In their view, globalization has not just created closer relations between those in distant places, but it has, in fact, created a "global monoculture."[49] If this is true, it becomes clear

---

[45] Stiglitz, *supra* note 43 at 4.

[46] Jan Aart Scholte, *Globalizaton: A Critical Introduction* (New York: St. Martin's Press, 2000).

[47] Jackson, *supra* note 3 at 8–9.

[48] Thomas L. Friedman, *The Lexus and the Olive Tree* (New York: Anchor Books, 2000) at 8.

[49] Michael Trebilcock, "Critiquing the Critics of Economic Globalization" (2005) 1 J. Int'l L. & Int'l Relations 213 at 213.

that globalization results in ever-greater overlap in values, experiences, and information — that is, globalization is a manifestation of the phenomenon of publicity.

The latter approaches to globalization illustrate aspects of the phenomenon of publicity and recognize the normative content of this phenomenon. For instance, it is now commonplace to observe that developments in technology have dramatically changed the accessibility of information about people in distant places. As Jackson points out, "[i]deas and even products (for example, designs, advertisements, and documents) move at the speed of light between continents, often at a cost of mere pennies. A few keystrokes on a computer can move millions of dollars. Telephone calls from London to the United States are reputed to cost less than it costs to call from inner London to its suburbs, and the marginal cost of transcontinental telephone calls (not including the capital cost of the transmittal techniques) is often fractions of 1 cent."[50] However, the phenomenon is not limited to individuals — states, too, have increasing access to information collected by other states. For example, many states have agreements to share security information, customs and immigration details, and so on.[51]

The increasing access to information about those in distant places that globalization allows permits us to feel a connection to them and to experience in a direct way (although not face to face) the suffering of others. Natural disasters that take place in distant parts of the world are quickly known in even the far corners of the globe. The same goes for political instability, violations of human rights, armed conflicts, and so on. All of these experiences are met with "humanitarian responses" — be they state-based programs or privately organized. One might argue that many disasters are ignored,[52]

---

[50] Jackson, *supra* note 3 at 10.

[51] An illustration of the detrimental effects of such agreements is the case of Maher Arar. Arar was arrested by the US government while he was in Kennedy Airport in New York travelling to Tunisia on a vacation. The arrest occurred based on false information supplied by the Royal Canadian Mounted Police to the Americans. Arar was imprisoned in New York, interrogated, and then flown to Jordan and finally Syria, where he was detained for ten months in Syria and tortured. He was released in 2003 by the Syrian government, which had concluded that he had no connection to terrorism. For the details of the case, see Commission of Inquiry into the Actions of Canadian Officials in Relation to Maher Arar (Arar Commission), *Report of the Events Relating to Maher Arar*, 3 volumes (Canada, 2006).

[52] Rwanda and Somalia are only examples of the long list of disasters and atrocities committed by humans that are not faced head on by the international community.

and this ignorance indicates that our increased access to information about people in far away places does not seem to entail a moral recognition of obligation. However, the fact that we choose to ignore our moral obligations — that is, that we choose to ignore the wound in the social fabric that Watsuji discussed earlier — merely points out either our human capacity for wilful blindness or our ability to ignore our experience of moral obligation. In either case, both wilful blindness and denial point to our experience of the distress of others, just as our devoting billions of dollars towards health-related research does not successfully cover over our recognition of our mortality.[53]

Moreover, the normative content of globalization is evident equally in the reactions of opponents to economic globalization and the arguments of proponents. Both recognize the impact of the increasing inter-relationship between people in the "globalized" world, although they differ on their assessment of this impact. Indeed, both sides recognize that we live in a world where most people are cosmopolitans, sometimes in spite of themselves — we are familiar with the customs, political controversies, norms, and values of people in far distant places in ways that were previously impossible. This cosmopolitanism is based, as I have tried to show, on our concrete experience of publicity — an implicit connection with those in distant places — rather than on an abstract idea of the equal worth of individual humans, which is the traditional moral basis of cosmopolitanism. What are the legal consequences of our experience of community through globalization? In the next section, I answer this question.

UNFOLDING THE NORMATIVE CONTENT OF GLOBALIZATION AS A PHENOMENON OF PUBLICITY: COOPERATIVE COSMOPOLITANISM

One of the great advantages of recognizing the phenomenon of publicity as the normative basis of cosmopolitanism is that it overcomes the traditional dichotomy between a state-based international law regime and a system based on the recognition of individual rights. While my interpretation of cosmopolitanism retains one of the features of traditional cosmopolitanism — namely that the self-interest of states should not be the foundation

---

[53] On the bad faith inherent in everyday human existence in regard to the denial of human finitude, see Martin Heidegger, *Sein und Zeit* (Tübingen: Niemeyer Verlag, 1927).

of international law[54] — it is also innovative in that it does not see the only alternative as a system based on individualism such as the system of international human rights. Instead, in accordance with our experience of cosmopolitanism as a form of publicity, it is our relationships to others — our connection with them — a connection not defined solely by the state as a collectivity — that should be the basis of international law. Hence cooperation, which is the active component of the experience of togetherness that underlies cosmopolitan experience, is the operationalization of inter-subjective cosmopolitanism. Thus, publicity at the international level, which takes the form of globalization, entails a form of cooperative cosmopolitanism in which we collectively acknowledge the harm caused by states and individuals to those in other states.

What are the sorts of norms of international law that emerge from a recognition that globalization, as a form of publicity at the international level, is the phenomenological basis of cosmopolitanism? The following are some suggestions:

- looking behind the veil of state-based issues;
- de-emphasizing state practice and *opinio juris* as a basis for establishing international legal norms;
- recognizing an increased role for equity in international law;[55]
- taking responsibility for nationals causing harm in other states; and
- taking responsibility for harms to individuals in other states.

How do these norms relate to cosmopolitanism? First, one must recall that my version of cosmopolitanism is not centred on either the state or the individual. Instead, it is based on each person's recognition of the harm done to the collectivity (which, thanks to globalization, has been expanded to include people in far away places) through his or her experience of it (that is, its publicity) and the need to take responsibility for this harm, be it individually or on a collective basis through state action. This experience demands of us that we take some responsibility for our experience of

---

54 See Beitz, *supra* note 16 at 520–21.

55 As I will explain later in the article, by equity, I do not simply mean equity as a general principle of law or the *ex aequo et bono* jurisdiction of the International Court of Justice (Vienna Convention, *supra* note 5, Article 38(2)). Instead, I am referring to a general orientation of the law of equity towards contextual interpretation and application of legal rules.

harm to the collectivity. Thus, cooperative cosmopolitanism entails responsibility.

The emphasis on responsibility is common to many forms of phenomenological ethics. For instance, Confucian ethics is based on *ren,* which is often translated as human-heartedness or compassion. The responsibility that arises from a recognition of human-heartedness is expressed phenomenologically by Mencius (372–289 BCE), who states that if a person sees a child fall into the well, he will seek to help the child without thought of whether he will profit from saving her.[56] This example demonstrates that humans have the four "seeds" of virtue[57] — all of which are expressed experientially as "feelings" or "senses." It is through the cultivation of these feelings that a person can begin to lead an ethical life.[58] In the Western tradition, Emmanuel Levinas explains how responsibility arises from a concrete encounter with another. When we come face to face with another person who is suffering, the subjectivity of that person (that is, both the humanity behind the eyes and the uniqueness of their appeal) demand that we respond and take responsibility for this subjectivity.[59]

For what must we take responsibility? For the harm caused. What is this harm? Though the harm is often attributed by traditional international law to the state, it is usually experienced as a harm to real people — it is concrete harm. For instance, unlawful invasions harm real soldiers and civilians. Political instability harms the economic interests and the security of the person of nationals of the economically insecure state. Actions by companies abroad harm real people in those countries. Thus, we must take responsibility for these concrete harms to real people, rather than for these harms

---

56 *Mencius,* translated by D.C. Lau (New York: Penguin, 1970) at IIA:6, 82–83.

57 The four seeds are: a feeling of commiseration, a feeling of shame and dislike, a feeling of modesty, and a sense of right and wrong. Feng Yu-lan, *A History of Chinese Philosophy,* translated by Derk Bodde, 2 volumes (Princeton: Princeton University Press, 1952) at vol. I: 120–21).

58 See Tu Wei-ming, "The Value of the Human in Classical Confucian Thought," in Tu Wei-ming, *Confucian Thought: Selfhood as Creative Transformation* (Albany, NY: SUNY Press, 1995) 67 at 71.

59 Emmanuel Levinas, *Totality and Infinity: An Essay on Exteriority,* translated by Alphonso Lingis (Pittsburgh: Duquesne University Press, 1969) at 50–52. For an explanation of this text, see Mayeda, *supra* note 40. Of course, we often fail to take responsibility for our encounters, but the ability to deny responsibility does not deny the existence of it.

as seen through the lens of the state — that is, harms to individuals that can be attributed to states.[60]

Real, concrete people find themselves in real, concrete situations. They are not "people living in poverty" but, rather, this particular woman living in this place, with this culture, facing these specific challenges and circumstances. This means that the response to the concrete harm suffered by real, concrete people must take into account the context in which that harm arises. The emphasis on the concrete harms to concrete people living in specific circumstances follows from the experiential basis of our norm of cosmopolitan responsibility. When we hear of harm to people in a distant place, we experience it as a concrete harm to the social fabric, as Watsuji points out earlier. And, as with all experience, our experience of such harm is triggered by our ability to imagine the specific suffering of people facing a particular, concrete challenge. For instance, we feel a responsibility to help people who suffered harm in Hurricane Katrina because we can imagine the specific challenges they face — it is not some abstract, idealized harm for which we feel responsibility.

How do the values of responsibility, recognition of concrete harms, and the importance of context translate into the international legal norms that I listed at the beginning of this section? Looking behind the veil of international conflicts that are traditionally structured as conflicts between states follows from the importance of considering concrete harms in their context.[61] My contention is that we

---

60 Admittedly, international law seeks to do this to some degree through *erga omnes* obligations — obligations owed to the international legal community as a whole. A breach of such obligations allows any state to pursue a claim on behalf of the person whose rights have been infringed. See John Currie, *Public International Law* (Toronto: Irwin Law, 2001) at 368. As Currie points out, the limitation of this approach is that it "ultimately relies upon the will of states to take up and pursue a claim in which they may have no direct interest and which may well conflict with other pressing concerns, for example of a political nature" (*ibid.* at 369).

61 A limited example of this is the existence of international claims commissions that are convened after an armed conflict between states to provide remedies for individuals who have been harmed by an unlawful war. For a foundational work in this area, see Richard B. Lillich, *International Claims: Their Adjudication by National Commissions* (Syracuse: Syracuse University Press, 1962). For more recent articles, see Jann K. Kleffner, "Improving Compliance with International Humanitarian Law Through the Establishment of an International Complaints Mechanism" (2002) 15 Leiden J. Int'l L. 237; and Jann K. Kleffner and Liesbeth Zegveld, "Establishing an Individual Complaints Procedure for Violations of International Humanitarian Law" (2000) 3 Y.B. Int'l Hum. L. 381.

need to re-think the basis for recognizing international law by getting away from rigid notions of state practice and *opinio juris.* This follows both from the notion of individual responsibility and the fact that, as I suggested earlier, cooperative cosmopolitanism is neither individualist nor collectivist — rather, it sees the state and the collectivity as a means of putting into action our experience of responsibility. The recognition of an increased role for equity follows from recognizing that justice must respond to specific context. Not all specific cases fit into universally applicable rules, and equity recognizes that justice sometimes requires solutions to be crafted to meet the specific needs of specific people in specific circumstances. Finally, individuals must take responsibility for the behaviour of their nationals overseas for the simple reason that, as Kant said, "a violation of rights in *one* part of the world is felt *everywhere*,"[62] and our responsibility is engaged, on the one hand, because the capacity of failed or failing states limits their ability to protect their nationals and, on the other hand, because of the frequent complicity of our state in creating an international legal regime that facilitates infringements of rights by our nationals. Often, an individual's responsibility in this regard will be exercised through the mechanism of the state — individuals will collectively act to require their state to implement mechanisms for holding fellow nationals who are operating abroad responsible for their actions.

Finally, one cannot discuss cosmopolitan obligations without addressing the responsibility of individuals in one state for harms being committed in another state. Large-scale loss of life and the commission of international crimes such as genocide, war crimes, and so on — committed by, condoned by, or abetted through the inaction of the state in which it occurs — require a response. The difficulty, of course, is to determine what kind of responsibility is required: indirect sanctions (trade sanctions and so on) or direct intervention in another state? A further difficulty is setting the standard for intervention (is the trigger minor harm or only significant harm?) and determining if preventative action is permissible. These questions can only be resolved by opening our eyes to the context of intervention, which includes the context of historical colonialism and ongoing neo-colonialism.

In accordance with our experience of cosmopolitanism, it is our relationships to others — our connection with them, which is not defined solely by the state as a collectivity — that should be the basis

---

[62] Kant, *supra* note 22.

of international law. Hence cooperation, which is the active component of the experience of togetherness that underlies cosmopolitan experience, is the operationalization of inter-subjective cosmopolitanism.

THE LIMITS OF OUR OBLIGATIONS

Another potential drawback of my phenomenological analysis of the normative foundations of international law is the vagueness of the terms "responsibility" and the "harm" that entails this responsibility. The use of such terms naturally raises questions about what "harms" give rise to responsibility and what the limits of this responsibility are. If a person feels that by not being able to purchase a Mercedes Benz he is "harmed," are we obliged to take responsibility for it? If so, is sympathy a sufficient response or do we have to redistribute income to make the purchase possible? Utilitarians have tried to answer these questions in relation to international obligations. For instance, Peter Singer, in his famous 1972 article, stated that we are obliged to sacrifice our own well-being up to the point of marginal utility in order to satisfy the needs of others.[63] Richard Miller tried to temper such a radical viewpoint by arguing that we need only give to others to the point where further giving would pose a significant risk of worsening our life.[64] Non-utilitarians have also entered the fray, trying to find non-utilitarian criteria for understanding the bounds of our responsibility. Thus, Henry Shue, in *Basic Rights*, explains that a "basic right" is a right the enjoyment of which is essential for the enjoyment of other rights:

Basic rights ... are everyone's minimum reasonable demands upon the rest of humanity. They are the rational basis for justified demands the denial of which no self-respecting person can reasonably be expected to accept. Why should anything be so important? The reason is that rights are basic in the sense used here only if enjoyment of them is essential to the enjoyment of all other rights. This is what is distinctive about a basic right. When a right is genuinely basic, any attempt to enjoy any other right by sacrificing

---

[63] Singer, *supra* note 37. This means that we must help others until we reach the point at which our next action will harm us more than the failure to alleviate the other's suffering will harm her. This would entail giving away most of what we own — a radical proposal in the eyes of some.

[64] Richard Miller, "Beneficence, Duty and Distance" (2004) 32(4) Philosophy & Public Affairs 357 at 359.

the basic right would be quite literally self-defeating, cutting the ground from beneath itself.[65]

What these complex accounts are trying to capture is something reasonably intuitive — that some things in life are essential for us to be able to say we are living a human life while others are not.

Some have searched for a specific dividing line between those harms to others for which we are responsible and those for which we are not. David Miller has provided a particularly appealing account of the meaning of responsibility — one that could fit with my phenomenological analysis.[66] Miller first canvasses the possible candidates for a theory of responsibility and arrives at four options:

- *Principle of causal responsibility:* "To say that an agent is causally responsible for some state of affairs is simply to highlight the causal role-played [*sic*] by the agent in the genesis of that state of affairs."[67]
- *Principle of moral responsibility:* "Moral responsibility ... involves an appraisal of the agent's conduct ... [T]he agent's role in bringing about the outcome must be such that it leaves the agent liable to moral blame. That ... requires us to ask questions such as whether the agent intended the outcome, whether he foresaw it, whether his behaviour violated some standard of reasonable care, and so forth."[68]
- *Principle of capacity:* "[R]emedial responsibilities ought to be assigned according to the capacity of each agent to discharge them ... [W]e should give the responsibility to those who are best placed to do the remedying."[69]
- *Principle of community:* "[W]hen people are linked together by ties [such as family, collegial groups, nations, and so on] whether arising from shared activities and commitments, common identities, common histories, or other such sources, they also (justifiably) see themselves as having special responsibilities to one another."[70]

---

[65] Shue, *supra* note 41 at 19.

[66] David Miller, "Distributing Responsibilities," in Andrew Kuper, ed., *Global Responsibilities: Who Must Deliver on Human Rights?* (New York: Routledge, 2005), 95.

[67] *Ibid.* at 97.

[68] *Ibid.* at 98.

[69] *Ibid.* at 102.

[70] *Ibid.* at 103.

Miller finds that none of these principles alone is sufficient to capture what we intuitively understand as the nature of responsibility. Instead, he combines the four principles, explaining that different combinations of them explain who should take *immediate* responsibility for alleviating harm and who should take *final* responsibility. He concludes as follows:

[C]*apacity*, and to some extent *community*, are relevant principles when immediate responsibilities are being distributed, because these are criteria that tell us who is best able to relieve P's condition quickly and effectively. *Moral responsibility, causal responsibility*, and perhaps *community* again are invoked when final responsibilities are the issue.[71]

Miller concludes that what is really important is that each of the four principles of responsibility illustrate some *connection* between the agent and the patient, and, as long as one of the principles connects the two, responsibility can follow. Where two or more principles of connection apply, we must look at the strength of the various connections.[72]

Miller presents a very pragmatic and sensible approach to responsibility. It is compatible with the phenomenological explanation of responsibility because the four categories capture the various ways in which we experience our connection to those suffering in far away places. However, the deficiency of Miller's approach is that it views the relationship between agent and patient solely from the point of view of the agent. This is because Miller is presenting a theory of moral responsibility, which depends, he claims, on the view that "people should be held responsible for the harm that they do."[73] The phenomenological approach, however, considers the relationship between the two people — responsibility exists where publicity creates a link. Thus, Miller's approach inadequately captures the extent of responsibility we owe on the phenomenological approach.

I should first distinguish my approach from a purely victim-centred approach. Such an approach would assign responsibility on the basis of who is in the best position to bring effective relief to the victims.[74] However, my approach depends on a link between victims

---

[71] *Ibid.* at 109 [emphasis in original].

[72] *Ibid.* at 112.

[73] *Ibid.* at 107.

[74] Miller calls this a "forward-looking" theory (*ibid.* at 106).

and those responsible — an experiential link. It does not allow people to be used as a simple means of alleviating others' suffering. My approach also resembles Miller's principle of community. However, the basis of the responsibility I envision is not limited to connections that form the basis of my identity. The link I have uncovered is not based on my identity as a part of a family, neighbourhood, nation, or even common humanity. Instead, the link is based on concrete experience. This is clear from the fact that on the phenomenological view, the extent of my responsibility increases the more I explore the extent of the suffering of others. Likewise, the link is not purely the one described by theories of corrective justice.[75] Corrective justice is a moral theory of justice that depends on a causal and moral connection between agent and patient. According to corrective justice, when the damage done to another falls within the ambit of the risk I have unreasonably created, a link is established between me and the plaintiff, and I can be said to be legally responsible for the wrong and required to correct this wrong — that is, to compensate the plaintiff. Such a theory overlooks the phenomenology of responsibility, namely the experience of being accused and of being called to take responsibility for another's suffering. It abstracts our experience of responsibility behind a conceptual construct in which the link is not a concrete, experiential link but, rather, a distilled, impersonal legal one mediated through concepts such as the "ambit of the risk" and the "creation of unreasonable risk."

How, then, can I put appropriate limits on legal responsibility? In contrast to Miller, and in accordance with my phenomenological methodology, I prefer to provide a procedural rather than a substantive definition of the limits of obligation. When we experience the suffering of others, our responsibility is to listen, give voice to the suffering, and understand it to the degree we can. In voicing the harm that the other is suffering, we must try to put it into words that others will understand. We are responsible for those harms to others that, having tried to understand and articulate them, we can make others also recognize as harms.

This seems like a reasonableness test — my responsibility is limited by what I can explain to a reasonable person as a harm they would recognize. However, unlike the usual reasonableness test, which has been criticized by many for evaluating reasonableness in

---

[75] For an elaboration of the nature of corrective justice, see Ernest J. Weinrib, *The Idea of Private Law* (Cambridge, MA: Harvard University Press, 2005).

the abstract,[76] I am suggesting a contextualized concept of reasonableness — a judgment of reasonableness based on a real, good
faith attempt to inform oneself about the situation of the other and
to see the harm that she perceives as best one can from her perspective. However, again, such contextualized reasonableness standards
have been criticized since it is often difficult to enter into the context as experienced by another if we are familiar with our own
context and ignorant of the situation of others. It is for this reason
that self-critique is an essential aspect of ethics — one must bring
to light the barriers one brings to understanding the situation of
another. Of course, for most people, it is impossible in one's lifetime
to overcome all of these barriers. Thus, ethical behaviour must always be a mathematical limit function — something that we strive
to achieve by coming closer and closer to the limit, although we
may never reach it. However, as in calculus, we can come so close
to the limit of the function that we can have a pretty good idea of
where the other person is coming from.

To summarize, what are the limits of our obligation to others and
what harms are we obliged to take responsibility for? The limits of
our responsibility are determined by a process of understanding
the claim of another and critiquing the ideas and preconceptions
that hinder our ability to understand this claim. Or to put it another
way, we must make a good faith attempt to understand the context
in which another person is living and the standpoint from which
he is making his claim. If, having done this, we can make an account
of the harm the other is suffering that others familiar with the harm
and whose interests will be affected by acting on it accept, then we
should act. If we cannot make such an account, then our responsibility to understand is not exhausted (since the other person is
clearly still anguished), but our ability to act on this responsibility
is limited. Thus, we are responsible to everyone for all of the harms
they experience, but we are able to act to redress those harms only
if we are able to give an account of them that everyone (ideally)
could recognize and understand.[77] This account may involve some

---

[76] See Mayo Moran, *Rethinking the Reasonable Person: An Egalitarian Reconstruction of
the Objective Standard* (Oxford: Oxford University Press, 2003); and Supreme
Court of Canada Justice Ian Binnie's views on the drawbacks to concepts of
reasonableness in *R. v. Grant*, 2009 SCC 32 at paras. 169–74.

[77] Immanuel Kant spoke of the need to judge by placing oneself in the place of
others and imagining how they would judge. This would be an abstract way of
assessing what "everyone" could recognize and understand. Another way of

of the concepts of responsibility that Miller outlined earlier. But it is not limited to these concepts — if it is possible to give an account of harm that we all recognize as unacceptable, then we all must take responsibility for alleviating the harm.

On this account, states and individuals fall out of the picture. Neither is solely responsible. The state and the individual are merely two ways of taking collective responsibility for the suffering of others. Indeed, some sources of suffering are so great that both the state in which the individual lives and the state of the person perpetrating the harm should be engaged to prevent it. Others, however, can be mitigated through other strategies.

Does such a view justify intervention in other states — an interpretation of the duty to protect that requires intervention when grave harms are being done within the boundaries of another sovereign state? To answer this question is to confuse responsibility, as I am articulating it, with a reasonable solution. It does not make sense to me to speak of an absolute prohibition on intervention in other states. Yes, we are responsible for the harms that states perpetrate against their nationals or that sub-national groups perpetrate on each other. However, this responsibility does not necessarily justify intervention. The justification of such intervention depends on the degree to which we can articulate, understand, and evaluate the harm that would result from a breach of another state's sovereignty, since we are also responsible for this type of harm. When states intervene in the affairs of others, they can seriously undermine the ability of that state to stabilize legal, political, and social situations, as has occurred in Iraq and Afghanistan. Here, self-critique, which is an important part of the responsibility I articulated earlier, comes into play. An assessment of the justice of intervention necessarily involves critical self-reflection on the motives for intervention.

---

approaching it, and the way that I prefer, is to concretize this approach. A harm would be one that all would recognize if it violated some of the basic requirements for participating in a meaningful way in the formation of the norms of the society in which we live. In concrete terms, this means judging from the perspective of all those who will be affected by the judgment, which, in turn, means, in an ideal situation, consulting the relevant groups of affected individuals (for more details, see Graham Mayeda, "Between Principle and Pragmatism: The Decline of Principled Reasoning in the Jurisprudence of the McLachlin Court," in Sheila McIntyre and Sanda Rodgers, eds., *The Supreme Court of Canada and the Achievement of Social Justice: Commitment, Retrenchment or Retreat* (Markham, ON: Supreme Court Law Review and LexisNexisCanada, 2010) 41 also published in (2010) 50 S.C.L.R. (2d) 41.

In general, these motives are not altruistic, and if the motivation is not simply the prevention of harm to citizens of another state but, rather, the promotion of political and economic interests, then it is suspect. I will address this issue further in the next section.

CRITICISM OF MY VIEW AND COMPATIBILITY WITH TRADITIONAL ACCOUNTS OF THE BASIS OF INTERNATIONAL LEGAL OBLIGATION

One of the major objections to my approach to the normative foundation of international law might be the positivist's observation that none of the actions of international legal institutions to date reflect my phenomenological account of the normative foundations of international law. Most of these traditional accounts begin from the presumption that international law arose from the interactions between states. If we start from this point of view, then the recognition of the international legal personality of individuals and the incorporation of individual rights into a state-based system seems to be a revolution. Anthony D'Amato expresses this revolution as follows:

The idea of international human rights is so explosive, so revolutionary, that even as an idea it has yet to be assimilated into the collective consciousness. For, ultimately, human rights in international law means that the state is *not* the sole entity that possesses rights, it is not the alpha and omega of international law. Instead, individual persons have direct claims under international law. And more revolutionary than that, individuals under international law may have direct claims against their own states.[78]

However, the lack of recognition of cosmopolitan responsibility in traditional international law is not so perplexing if one simply admits that international law has never been ethical — that is, its institutions and norms have never been based on human experience. Instead, it has been dominated by political interests and ideas that are capable of being rationally justified even if their effect is to deny moral responsibility. However, the phenomenological analysis that reveals the inter-relatedness of our existence and the consequent demand for cooperation presses more urgently on us in a globalized world — the constant contact we have with others suffering nearby and in distant places is forcing us to see through the rationalizations of selfish behaviour that have hitherto been

---

[78] D'Amato, *supra* note 25 at 89.

tolerated in international law. Thomas Franck recognizes this idea in *Fairness in International Law and Institutions* when he explains the cause of the shift in international law since the end of the Second World War:

Another reason for the exponential growth of international law in recent years is a prismatic change in the way in which humanity perceives itself. The challenge of space exploration has joined with the depletion and degradation of the earth's environment — its forests, ozone layer, fisheries, lakes, streams, and ground water resources — to entice or compel individuals and governments to think in terms of our common destiny: to counter humanity as a single gifted but greedy species, sharing a common, finite, and endangered speck of the universe.[79]

As I have stated, positivist understandings of the legal character of international law have failed to question the normative foundations of this law. They observe that laws govern the conduct of states towards each other, they note that international laws increasingly govern the relation between states and individuals or between individuals of different nationalities, and they seek to describe these newly emerging rules. My approach has been normative, and, hence, the descriptions provided by positivists are necessarily inadequate. For instance, John Jackson expresses a typical positivist (and functionalist) analysis of the origin of international legal rules, stating that through empirical observation, we can simply identify what the policy objective (or objectives) is of international law norms and see this policy as supplying the normative content of international law. My response to this, however, is to ask whether we are justified in continuing to promote the particular policy that underlies the law.

I believe that there is some support for my normative analysis of international law if we look at other normative views of international law. If we look to the institutions created to implement these views, we see that there is implicit recognition of my phenomenological analysis of the normative basis of international law. One popular view about the normative basis of international law is that it is, like contract law, based on the freely given consent of states to an agreement made between them.[80] However, both in international law as

---

79 Thomas M. Franck, *Fairness in International Law and Institutions* (Oxford: Clarendon Press, 1995) at 6.

80 See Lori F. Damrosch et al., *International Law: Cases and Materials*, 4th edition (St. Paul MN: West Group, 2001) at 58; Oscar Schachter, *International Law in*

in domestic private law, it has been recognized that there are circumstances in which it is unfair to hold people or states to their bargains. The law of equity, which exists in a highly developed form in domestic legal systems, but only at a more formative stage at the international level, allows that parties to an agreement may not have foreseen a particular set of future circumstances when entering the agreement, or their consent may be the result of coercion or, more generally, enforcement of the agreement might breach a general norm of fairness. The existence of rules of equity supports my view that justice demands a contextual analysis of a situation, and the phenomenological approach derives its normative force precisely from an actual recognition of the concrete situation in which parties find themselves. For this reason, I am emboldened to think that pre-existing normative theories of international law that accept rules of equity as fundamental legal principles implicitly recognize the phenomenological approach, although their use of a rationalist rather than a phenomenological lens has obscured some of the fundamental, animating principles of international law.

Finally, one important potential criticism of my explanation of the normative foundation of cosmopolitanism is that it conflates legality with morality. Immanuel Kant was very careful to carve out the sub-set of legal norms that the state is justified in enforcing through force from the broader set of moral norms. Likewise, liberals of all stripes have sought to define the minimum set of legal and/or political norms that are necessary in order to allow individuals with different moral views and ideas about the nature of the good life to co-exist. Where does my project fit? Its purpose is, like that of Kant and other liberals, to expose the moral foundations of a just society and then to demonstrate what kind of legal rules this just society would have to have in order to actualize its moral foundation. However, in contrast to Kant and other liberals, the fundamental norm underlying a just social order is not the equality of individual citizens but, rather, our experience of responsibility for others. In reality, this experience is not an experience of equal responsibility for all — it differs based on our proximity to others.

Theory and Practice (Dordrecht: Martinus Nijhoff, 1991) at 35–37; Ian Brownlie, *Principles of Public International Law*, 6th edition (Oxford: Oxford University Press, 2003) at 3; Anthony C. Arend, *Legal Rules and International Society* (Oxford: Oxford University Press, 1999) at 87; Joost Pauwelyn, *Conflict of Norms in Public International Law: How WTO Law Relates to Other Rules of International Law* (Cambridge: Cambridge University Press, 2003) at 133 and 328.

But when we begin to unfold the nature of our experience of even this minimal responsibility for those in far away places, we find that its content is the sort of cooperative cosmopolitanism that I have laid out. Thus, to use the distinctions drawn by Thomas Pogge, I have articulated a moral cosmopolitanism as opposed to a legal cosmopolitanism,[81] and I have then tried to extrapolate from the ethical principles that follow from this moral cosmopolitanism the types of legal institutions that we are obliged to have in place to actualize the norms of cosmopolitanism as I have conceived it.

How does my very broad conception of responsibility and its limits fit with legal concepts of responsibility? Behind such a question may lurk the concern that I seem to have collapsed law and morality, which legal theorists in the European and North American tradition have attempted to disaggregate. These theorists begin from the presumption that law is about coercing behaviour, and the concept of legal responsibility, as distinct from that of moral responsibility, identifies the kinds of activities for which the state is justified in using its monopoly on force to change my behaviour (or, at least, to prevent its recurrence). However, a phenomenological concept of legality does not begin from such a presumption. Instead, it presumes that certain structures of experience underlie our concept of responsibility, and it seeks to describe these structures.[82] Responsibility is one of these structures. I then tried to explain how legal responsibility is differentiated from moral responsibility by the fact that legal responsibilities must be articulated in language acceptable to all people who, having critiqued their own biases and made a good faith effort to understand the suffering of others, can recognize the harm as one for which there is collective responsibility. The extent of our moral obligations is not limited in the way legal obligation is — it is not limited by the requirement of articulation in terms acceptable to the community.[83]

---

[81] Pogge distinguishes "legal cosmopolitanism" from "moral cosmopolitanism." The former "is committed to a concrete political ideal of a global order under which all persons have equivalent legal rights and duties – are fellow citizens of a universal republic," while the latter "holds that all persons stand in certain moral relations to one another" (Pogge, *supra* note 7 at 169).

[82] I say "structures" rather than simply "experiences" in order to avoid the objection, discussed earlier, that not everyone has the same subjective experience of responsibility when faced with the suffering of another.

[83] My approach is somewhat similar to that of Jürgen Habermas, whose theory of law depends on the uncovering of certain basic structures of language oriented

Having addressed some traditional accounts of the normative basis of international law and some criticisms of my phenomenological approach, I turn now to some of the specific reforms to international law that follow from my articulation of a cooperative cosmopolitanism.

SPECIFIC REFORMS TO INTERNATIONAL LAW IN LIGHT OF COOPERATIVE COSMOPOLITANISM

Earlier, I suggested that my phenomenological approach to cosmo-politanism gives rise to the five following general obligations:

- looking behind the veil of state-based issues;
- de-emphasizing state practice and *opinio juris* as a basis for establishing international legal norms;
- recognizing an increased role for equity in international law;
- taking responsibility for nationals causing harm overseas; and
- taking responsibility for harms to individuals in other states.

What are some of the practical ramifications of these obligations?

LOOKING BEHIND THE VEIL OF STATE-BASED ISSUES

Traditional Westphalian sovereignty is on its way out, having been criticized on many sides.[84] As John Jackson has noted in his recent book, international law is shifting from a sovereignty-based model to what he calls "sovereignty-modern," in which states are not the sole holders of power. Instead, he argues that international law must increasingly deal with issues about how to distribute power among governmental and non-governmental actors, and, in his view, we now live in a world in which traditional concepts of sovereignty are no longer useful for distributing this power.[85] Recognition of cooperative cosmopolitanism as the normative basis of international law can

---

towards mutual understanding and the articulation of a procedure for reaching consensus through discussion in the political forum that respects these basic socio-linguistic rules.

[84] See, for instance, Alfred van Staden and Hans Vollard, "The Erosion of State Sovereignty: Towards a Post-Territorial World? in Gerald Kreijen et al., eds., *State Sovereignty and International Governance* (Oxford: Oxford University Press, 2000), 165; Antony Anghie, *Imperialism, Sovereignty and the Making of International Law* (Cambridge: Cambridge University Press, 2005).

[85] Jackson, *supra* note 3 at 77.

help us to understand why the fiction of Westphalian sovereignty is not adequate for ensuring international responsibility for harm, but, more than this, it can also help us to understand why we must "pierce the veil" of the state to deal with certain international wrongs. Or as Philip Allott has written, it is time to "[overcome] artificial separation of the national and the international realms, removing the anomalous exclusion of non-governmental transnational events and transactions."[86]

Why does cooperative cosmopolitanism require us to give up on state-based sovereignty? Often, state-based claims do not fully capture the nature of the harm. First, in a purely state-based system, states frequently do not adopt harms to their nationals nor do they seek redress for these harms. Or to put this idea another way, states cannot always be trusted to protect the human rights of their nationals.[87] For instance, Canada refuses to recognize and adopt the historical wrong to its Aboriginal peoples, and, as a result, it has refused to vote in favour of the Declaration on the Rights of Indigenous Peoples, and, in refusing to implement the Kyoto Protocol, which it signed and ratified, it has refused to acknowledge its obligation to protect its own citizens and those of other states from the effect of global warming.[88] Second, even if states adopt the claims of their nationals, framing the dispute in terms of states may fail to capture the full nature and complexity of the harm to individuals, and this, in turn, may lead to courts failing to take account of the context when resolving the dispute.

For instance, in *Compañía de Aguas del Aconquija S.A. v. Argentina,* a tribunal for the International Center for Settlement of Investment Disputes (ICSID) dealt with a claim by a French company that an Argentine province had infringed the France-Argentina Bilateral Investment Treaty by failing to treat the company in a fair and equitable way.[89] The provincial government had repeatedly attempted to renegotiate the concession agreement between the

---

86 Philip Allott, "The Concept of International Law," in Michael Byers, ed., *The Role of Law in International Politics* (Oxford: Oxford University Press, 2000) at 88.

87 *Ibid.* at 249.

88 Declaration on the Rights of Indigenous Peoples, UN GAOR, 61st session, 13 September 2007, UN Doc. A/RES/61/295; Kyoto Protocol to the UN Framework Convention on Climate Change, December 1997, 37 I.L.M. 32 (1998).

89 *Compañía de Aguas del Aconquija S.A. v. Argentina* (2007), (International Centre for Settlement of Investment Disputes), Investment Treaty Arbitration <http://ita.law.uvic.ca/documents/VivendiAwardEnglish.pdf>.

company — a water utility — and Argentina. The concession agreement had resulted from the privatization of Argentina's water utilities during the Menem presidency — a privatization project that had resulted in a doubling of the price of water overnight and that had led to a general dissatisfaction with the idea of privatization. The ICSID tribunal failed to "pierce the veil" of the issue — it never addressed the issue of the human right to water or the important role of the state in ensuring access to water at a reasonable rate, nor did it appropriately assess the urgency of the financial crisis that Argentina was facing at the time and the role that this crisis played in the province's efforts to renegotiate the concession agreement. Instead, the tribunal considered the state only in terms of a party to a contract — the bilateral investment treaty. As a result, it found in favour of the foreign investor, primarily on the basis that once a state enters into a concession agreement, it is bound to ensure that the agreement is honoured and that the expectations of the investor are not disrupted *despite any harm honouring such an agreement might cause to its nationals* during a financial crisis. This is a good example of how a failure to look behind the formal dispute to the harms that underlie it can lead to injustice.[90]

Why should investment tribunals go to the trouble of looking behind the formal legal issues brought to the table by states and foreign investors? As Jackson points out, one reason is that human rights must be protected in order to ensure the property rights that are the foundation of international economic transactions:

[T]here is a complementarity or at least symbiosis between certain rights and the good operation of markets. Markets depend on information, so freedom of speech or the press may be critical. Market participants must travel, so the protection of individual freedom from arrest or other barriers to travel is important. Ownership rights for property (including foreign investments) are obviously important. Due process type procedures (right

---

90 For a criticism of the decision rendered in this case, see Graham Mayeda, "Bilateral Investment Treaties between Developed and Developing Countries: Dancing with the Devil? A Case Commentary on the Vivendi, Sempra and Enron Awards" (2008) 4(2) McGill Int'l J. Sustainable Development L. and Pol'y 119; and Graham Mayeda, "Investing in Development: The Role of Democracy and Accountability in International Investment Law" (2009) 46(4) Alberta Law Review 1009. On criticism of the application of the principle of fair and equitable treatment in other cases involving the Argentine financial crisis, see Graham Mayeda, "Playing Fair: The Meaning of Fair and Equitable Treatment in Bilateral Investment Treaties (BITs)" (2007) 41(2) Journal of World Trade 273.

of appeal), as well as fair notice and transparency (and other "good governance" norms), are likely to be relevant.[91]

Jackson goes on to ask "whether international institutions and norms for trade and economic transactions should explicitly recognize some of this necessary function of rights."[92] My answer is that cooperative cosmopolitanism demands it. It demands that we see the importance of securing basic rights for international economic transactions to occur. However, it also demands that we consider how the international rules set out for facilitating trade and investment can themselves threaten these basic rights and exclude large groups of people from participation in economic transactions. Indeed, Amartya Sen has argued that participation in economic transactions is itself a fundamental freedom, and international trade and investment law should have an eye to ensuring that this freedom is available to all.[93] Traditional international legal conceptions of sovereignty obscure these issues, because they generally require disputes to be framed as disputes between states or else as disputes between powerful economic organizations (investors, most of which are companies) and states (in an investor-state system).[94] Those mechanisms that exist for states to espouse the claims of their nationals or of nationals of other states offer only partial relief to this general trend.

Does cooperative cosmopolitanism require that we completely give up on state-based sovereignty? No. Sometimes, these harms can be best dealt with through the mechanism of the sovereign state: when harms to individuals or groups within a state are recognized as harms to the state itself — that is, when the state adopts the harms done to its nationals as harms to itself — it becomes easier to recognize that the harm potentially outstrips the interests of an individual. For instance, if a state adopts the infringement of the human rights of an individual as a harm to the state, it is acknowledging that similar harms threaten fundamental legal and moral values of the state — that is, they threaten the legal and

---

[91] Mayeda, "Playing Fair," *supra* note 90 at 252.

[92] *Ibid.*

[93] Amartya Sen, *Development As Freedom* (New York: Anchor, 1999) at 10 and 38–39.

[94] Indeed, as Vaughn Lowe has noted, corporations play an increasingly important role in international law (Lowe, *supra* note 1 at 225), and, consequently, admitting them into the realm of international legal persons still poses the danger of obscuring and marginalizing individuals and groups of individuals.

moral fabric of the state. In such cases, traditional concepts of sovereignty and of international law are able to adequately capture the kind of harm that is being complained of.

DE-EMPHASIZING STATE PRACTICE AND *OPINIO JURIS* AS A BASIS FOR ESTABLISHING INTERNATIONAL LEGAL NORMS

Many international law scholars have indicated the difficulties posed by the very restricted way in which international law is traditionally recognized. For instance, Vaughan Lowe points to the fact that non-state actors are increasingly involved in the creation of international legal norms,[95] and, as a result, the restriction of international law to state-based disputes is anachronistic. As well, difficulties arise from the increasingly complex set of human interactions that international law is asked to regulate. These interactions raise questions about how to apply long-standing principles such as sovereignty to modern contexts. The application of traditional rules of international law becomes even more difficult when we take into account globalization — the increasing publicity of international legal events. Our acute awareness of the inter-relationship between individuals, nations, and the natural world is creating a different context from that in which international law — historically, the domain of states and their sovereigns — emerged. It is no longer possible to ignore the fact that harms conducted in other countries are of concern to us at home.

Acknowledging the importance of context, Lowe suggests that today international law is increasingly shaped by "interstitial norms" — norms that are not primary rules of law, but which help to contextualize the application and interpretation of primary norms.[96] These norms "emerge" from the international legal system rather than being created by states,[97] and they emerge in this somewhat mysterious way primarily as a consequence of the far greater array of actors that are involved at the international level today than was the case in the past.[98] Lowe uses the example of sustainable development. In his view, sustainable development is not an emerging norm

---

[95] *Ibid.* See also Philip Alston, ed., *Non-State Actors and Human Rights* (Oxford: Oxford University Press, 2005).

[96] For another description of the "gap-filling" function of general legal principles, see Pauwelyn, *supra* note 80 at 127–30.

[97] *Ibid.* at 219.

[98] *Ibid.*

of international law if the standard for discovering such a norm is the traditional standard of state practice and *opinio juris*. Indeed, he states that sustainable development is not capable of being such a norm.[99] However, in his view, sustainable development still plays an important role in reconciling the competing and conflicting interests of various areas of law (for instance, the demands of development and environmental protection). As such, it has the status of an interstitial norm that inserts itself between competing international legal norms to help resolve conflicts between them:

[These norms] do not instruct persons subject to the legal system to do or abstain from doing anything, or confer powers, in the way that primary norms do. They direct the manner in which competing or conflicting norms that do have their own normativity should interact in practice.

Lowe's use of the concept of "interstitial norms" is an illustration of the creative ways in which international lawyers are trying to account for the increasingly complex interactions between different areas of international policy that frequently conflict — for example, areas such as trade and the environment.

Others have suggested that the metaphor or model of constitutionalism is an appropriate way of conceptualizing the changing role of international legal norms. David Schneiderman, for instance, sees the norms of international economic organizations such as the World Trade Organization and the more diffuse norms of international investment law as a set of "constitutional" norms that "aim to institutionalize a model of constitutional government intended primarily to facilitate the free flow of goods, services, capital, and persons unimpeded across the borders of national states."[100] He is critical of the increasing rigidity implied by constitutionalism, preferring instead that courts and governments "stay out of the way" and, instead, "create the conditions for economic development."[101] Law should perform "an enabling function, generating a framework for action and the release of private energies."[102]

In my view, both of these approaches capture something that is essentially correct about the changes in international law brought

---

[99] *Ibid.* at 216.

[100] David Schneiderman, *Constitutionalizing Economic Globalization: Investment Rules and Democracy's Promise* (Cambridge: Cambridge University Press, 2008) at 2.

[101] *Ibid.* at 20.

[102] *Ibid.* at 228.

about by globalization, but they do not capture it fully. With regard to Lowe, he is right to argue that certain norms provide the framework — the principles — for interpreting other norms. However, I conceive of these norms as "meta" norms rather than as second-order, interstitial norms. They may operate "interstitially" — that is, the role they play may be to resolve issues at the intersection of different areas of law. But these norms are justified on the basis of the ultimate normative foundation of international law — cooperative cosmopolitanism. Interstitial norms — norms that emerge without the support of traditional authors of international law — should be derived from the norm of cooperative cosmopolitanism. The result of this is that adjudication must proceed in a way that is similar to the method described by Ronald Dworkin, who sees constitutional interpretation as purposive — difficult decisions can be resolved through a principled interpretation of the constitution that takes into account the political consensus current in the public domain at the time the decision is being rendered. Judges ask themselves what the purpose of the right is — or put another way, what principle the assertion of the right serves — in order to interpret the law.[103] In my view, international law should be understood as the unfolding of the principle of cosmopolitan responsibility for harms to others. Its concrete content will be articulated through civil society debates about the application of cosmopolitan responsibility in specific cases.

The idea that certain "meta norms" help us to clarify conflicts between international legal rules is often misunderstood by international lawyers as a declaration that the meta norms are, like *jus cogens* norms, binding on states independent of their direct consent. However, this is to confuse principle with a legal norm. Joost Pauwelyn seems to make just such an error in *Conflict of Norms in Public International Law*,[104] where he equates what he calls "meta-principles" or "necessary principles"[105] with *jus cogens:*

[T]he so-called "necessary" principles ... could, from an institutional point of view, be said to be of a higher value than all other norms of international law. Indeed, without these "necessary" principles (think, for example,

---

[103] For a description of this method, see Ronald Dworkin, "Law's Ambitions for Itself" (1985) 71 Virginia Law Review 173. On my criticisms of Dworkin and my gloss on his principled approach, see Mayeda, *supra* note 77.

[104] Pauwelyn, *supra* note 80.

[105] *Ibid.* at 125.

of the *pacta sunt servanda* principle), there would be no such other norms at all ... In this sense, some of those "necessary" principles could even be described as norms part of *jus cogens*.[106]

The principle of cooperative cosmopolitanism is not a necessary principle of international law in this sense. It is a principle that describes our experience of our relationship with others from which we can derive certain legal norms to regulate this relationship. Yet it is not itself a legal norm. Moreover, the meta-principles to which I am referring cannot be over-ridden by specific norms of international law, as is the case with international law in which, as Pauwelyn states, a treaty or customary norm that derogates from a general principle of law can prevail over this principle. My principles are not "secondary" sources of international law in the way that Pauwelyn's principles are.[107]

In regard to Schneiderman's critique of constitutionalism, I am agnostic about whether the formality and rigidity of constitutionalism as Schneiderman conceives it is beneficial. However, what I do object to is his view that the animating norm of international law should be to "help mobilize the ... economy in directions that promoted popular understandings of the public good" — that is, to "release ... public and private energies."[108] Such libertarianism is, I think, contrary to the responsibility that is entailed by cooperative cosmopolitanism. We all stand accused by the mere fact of another's suffering, and we must therefore all take responsibility for it in some way.

How can the process for creating international law be understood so as to best reflect cooperative cosmopolitanism? I will answer this question by first canvassing the possibilities. Jackson suggests a number of ways of reconceptualizing the formation of international law in order to meet the challenges of globalization:

- *International institutions:* We could recognize that certain international institutions can create basic norms of international law in their areas of competence;[109]

[106] *Ibid.* at 127.

[107] *Ibid.*

[108] *Ibid.* at 229.

[109] This is the flip side of Schneiderman's constitutionalism, which claims that these institutions — especially economic institutions — are already creating constitutional norms. Schneiderman is likely right in this regard, as the Security Council has been making law for the last twenty years or so.

- *Evolution of sovereignty:* The concept of sovereignty could be altered (Jackson suggests this would be done by juridical institutions), thus resulting in a change in the basis of international norm formation;
- *Acquis communautaire:* We could recognize new sources of international law based on "international community." Governments and non-government entities could be involved in the description of these norms.
- *Recognize a norm of "interdependence":* If we recognize a norm of interdependence, this could supplement other norms such as sovereignty.[110]

In essence, I have been arguing for the fourth point. In my view, cooperative cosmopolitanism is the normative basis of international law, and, as a result, cooperation or interdependence should be an operative principle helping states and tribunals to interpret international responsibility and apply international norms. However, I do not agree with Jackson that this norm would simply supplement traditional concepts of sovereignty.[111] Although sovereignty often undermines some of the other norms such as contextualization that emerge from our experience of interdependence — an experience that provides the normative force of cosmopolitanism — it still has uses. Sovereignty should be seen as one method for actualizing our responsibility — given the power imbalance between states, corporations, and individuals, it can often be effective for states to adopt and defend the wrongs of their nationals. Thus, sovereignty is a limited recognition of cooperative cosmopolitan obligations.

RECOGNIZING AN INCREASED ROLE FOR EQUITY IN
INTERNATIONAL LAW

Most legal systems realize that the mechanical application of rules can lead to injustice. As a result, principles of equity broadly construed have developed that allow tribunals to take into account the specific nature of the dispute between the parties and the context in which this dispute arises.[112] The principles of equity are highly

---

[110] *Ibid.* at 263–64.

[111] *Ibid.* at 264.

[112] By "broadly construed," I mean "equity" in a broad sense, not just in the sense of principles that developed in the courts of equity that were incorporated into

developed in common law jurisdictions. For instance, in contract law, the principles of equity allow a party to avoid the performance of a contract if that party is fundamentally mistaken about an implied assumption of the contract. Similarly, if there is severe inequality in bargaining power, the contract can be declared void. As well, the doctrine of frustration allows a party to avoid its obligations under a contract if the performance is frustrated by events subsequent to the formation of the contract. Similar principles of equity exist in international law and apply to the interpretation and application of treaties. Both the Vienna Convention on the Interpretation of Treaties and customary international law permit countries to avoid their treaty obligations when the enforcement of such an obligation becomes manifestly unfair.[113]

In *Fairness in International Law and Institutions,* Thomas Franck argues that there are two principles of justice at work in international law: legitimacy, by which he means procedural fairness, and distributive justice.[114] In his view, principles of equity in international law are based on distributive justice.[115] However, Franck overlooks the important justice concerns that are raised by legitimacy itself. As we have seen, the cosmopolitan foundations of international law require that we take into account the context in which the dispute between parties has arisen. The legitimacy of international law depends not simply on the fairness by which its rules are created and applied in an abstract sense but also on the concrete application of the law. Thus, equity, whose principles regulate the application of law to specific cases where general rules result in inequity, is justified by the fundamental norm underlying international law. This means that equity — and the ability to deal fairly and justly with concrete situations — is a fundamental basis of the

---

the common law when the courts of equity and common law courts in England were merged.

[113] For instance, see the Vienna Convention, *supra* note 5, Articles 48(1) ("error"), Article 61(1) ("supervening impossibility of performance"), Article 62(1) ("fundamental change of circumstance"). See also Article 25 of the Draft Articles on State Responsibility, UN GAOR, 56th Sess., Supp. No. 10, UN Doc. A/56/10 (2001) at 43 on *force majeure* as an example of customary international law rules of equity.

[114] Franck, *supra* note 6 at 26.

[115] *Ibid.* at 47. Here, Franck states: "One (at resent the most highly developed) approach to a inquiry into the justice of international law is to study the emerging role of *equity* in the jurisprudence of international tribunals."

legitimacy of international law. Indeed, the principles of equity recognized by states form part of international law.[116]

The principles of equity are of particular importance in regard to developing countries. Judge Weeramantry recognized the diverse components that make up the law of sustainable development. For instance, he stated in the *Case Concerning Gabcíkovo-Nagymaros Project (Hungary v. Slovakia)* that "[t]he components of the principle [of sustainable development] come from well-established areas of international law — human rights, State responsibility, environmental law, economic and industrial law, equity, territorial sovereignty, abuse of rights, good neighbourliness — to mention a few."[117] Elsewhere, Weeramantry explains the fundamental role that equity plays in international law:

At its most general level, equity has been seen as the source of that dynamism which is necessary for legal development. Thus, in the words of the eminent comparativist Puig Brutau, "equity is one of the names under which is concealed the creative force which animates the life of the law."

At the level of international law, that creativity is well illustrated when one considers that equity has been the source that has given international law the concept of international mandates and trusts, of good faith, of *pacta sunt servanda*, of *jus cogens*, of unjust enrichment, of *rebus sic stantibus* and of abuse of rights. No doubt, the future holds for it a similarly vital creative role.[118]

It is easy to think of examples in which the interpretation and application of the principles of equity have had a direct impact on developing countries. The most recent example is in the interpretation of international investment agreements. Two recent decisions of the ICSID tribunals have interpreted and applied the

---

[116] As Thomas Franck notes, equitable principles are common to all legal systems and became part of international law by means of Article 38(1)(c) of the Statute of the Permanent Court of International Justice ((1926), P.C.I.J. 7 (Ser. D) No. 1), which allows the court to employ "general principles of law recognized by civilized nations" (*ibid.* at 48). See also Oscar Schachter, "International Law in Theory and in Practice: General Course in Public International Law" (1982) 1(78) Rec. des Cours 9 at 74.

[117] *Case Concerning Gabcíkovo-Nagymaros Project (Hungary v. Slovakia)*, [1997] I.C.J. Rep. 7 at 95 [*Gabcíkovo-Nagymaros*].

[118] *Case Concerning Maritime Delimitation in the Area between Greenland and Jan Mayen (Denmark v. Norway)*, Order of 13 June 1993, [1993] I.C.J. Rep. 38 at paras. 16-17 (Judge Weeramantry, separate opinion) [*Maritime Delimitation* case].

doctrine of necessity with widely differing results.[119] In *CMS Gas Transmission Co. v. The Argentine Republic*, the tribunal held that the collapse of the Argentine economy in the latter 1990s and early part of this millennium did not constitute a grave enough situation to justify the state in taking measures to control the price of natural gas, which resulted in losses to foreign investors in the gas industry.[120] Thus, neither the customary international law defence of necessity nor the non-precluded measures clause in the US-Argentina Bilateral Investment Treaty (a treaty-based defence similar to necessity) absolved Argentina of international wrongdoing.[121] Similar decisions were reached in *Enron Corp. et al. v. The Argentine Republic*[122] and *Sempra Energy International v. Argentine Republic*,[123]

[119] For the elements of the customary international law defence of necessity, see Article 25 of the International Law Commission's Draft Articles on State Responsibility, which describes the defence as follows:

1. Necessity may not be invoked by a State as a ground for precluding the wrongfulness of an act not in conformity with an international obligation of that State unless that act:

   a. is the only way for the State to safeguard an essential interest against a grave and imminent peril; and

   b. does not seriously impair an essential interest of the State or States towards which the obligation exists, or of the international community as a whole.

2. In any case, necessity may not be invoked by a State as a ground for precluding wrongfulness if:

   a. the international obligation in question excludes the possibility of invoking necessity; or

   b. the State has contributed to the situation of necessity.

[120] *CMS Gas Transmission Co. v. The Argentine Republic*, 44 I.L.M. 1205 (2005) (International Centre for Settlement of Investment Disputes (ICSID)) (Award of 12 May 2005) at para. 320 [*CMS Gas*].

[121] For discussion of whether the customary international law standard or the treaty standard ought to apply, see *CMS Gas Transmission Co. v. The Argentine Republic* (2007), (ICSID) (Annulment Decision of 25 September 2007) [*CMS Annulment Committee*] arguing that the treaty provision created *lex specialis* that displaced the international law standard; and José E. Alvarez and Kathryn Khamsi, "The Argentine Crisis and Foreign Investors: A Glimpse into the Heart of the Investment Regime," IILJ Working Paper no. 2008/5, International Investment Law Journal, <http://www.iilj.org>, arguing that given the state of international law at the time the bilateral investment treaty was drafted, the non-precluded measures clause was intended to reflect custom (at 46).

[122] *Enron Corp. et al. v. The Argentine Republic* (2007) (ICSID), Investment Treaty Arbitration, <http://ita.law.uvic.ca/documents/Enron-Award.pdf> [*Enron*].

[123] *Sempra Energy International v. Argentine Republic*, (2007) (ICSID), Investment Treaty Arbitration, <http://ita.law.uvic.ca/documents/SempraAward.pdf> [*Sempra*].

in which the tribunals held that the financial crisis did not threaten "the very existence of the State of its independence."[124] However, the tribunal in *LG & E Energy Corp et al. v. The Argentine Republic* held that a situation of necessity existed, since Argentina was faced with "an extremely serious threat to its existence, its political and economic survival, to the possibility of maintaining its essential services in operation, and to the preservation of its internal peace."[125] As such, a defence under the non-precluded measures clause of the treaty was available,[126] although the tribunal noted that a defence would also have been available at international law.[127]

As can be seen from these cases, although the defence of necessity has not been applied in many investment cases, it has the potential to be a decisive factor. The different assessments of the *LG & E, CMS Gas, Enron,* and *Sempra* tribunals demonstrates two things: the tribunal must be competent and have sufficient expert evidence to assess the context in which it is being asked to render a decision, and the scope and application of the defence of necessity should be clarified and, in my view, expanded. Financial crises — especially ones that dramatically affect the well-being of people in developing countries — must be recognized as legitimate exceptions to the performance of certain international obligations of a financial nature. When we take into account the inequality of bargaining power between developing countries and their developed country partners in bilateral trade and investment agreements, as well as the role of developed countries in contributing to international financial instability,[128] it becomes evident how important it is to provide competent tribunals with tools for looking behind the veil of legal rules to assess the fairness of the situation.

---

124 *Enron, supra* note 122 at para. 306; and *Sempra, supra* note 123 at para. 348.

125 *LG & E Energy Corp et al. v. The Argentine Republic,* 46 I.L.M. 36 (2006) (ICSID) (Decision on Liability of 3 October 2006) at para. 257 [*LG & E*].

126 *Ibid.* at paras. 229 and 245.

127 *Ibid.* at 245.

128 For an assessment of the ethical significance of developed country responsibility for creating this instability, see Thomas Pogge, who argues that the fact that developed and developing countries share a common international institutional framework means that developed countries are responsible for harms in developing countries created by this framework (Thomas W. Pogge, *World Poverty and Human Rights: Cosmopolitan Responsibilities and Reforms* (Cambridge: Polity Press, 2002)).

TAKING RESPONSIBILITY FOR NATIONALS CAUSING HARM IN OTHER COUNTRIES

It follows from the norm of cooperative cosmopolitanism that we must all take responsibility for the wrongs perpetrated by our co-nationals abroad. This can be done through voluntary corporate social responsibility initiatives of corporations operating abroad. However, it also requires individuals to advocate for collective action to control their fellow nationals. This means that at times, the state mechanism must be used — that is, states should legislate to ensure accountability of their nationals. This can be done through creating domestic causes of action for extra-territorial harms. It can also involve creating enforceable standards of corporate social responsibility, developing monitoring processes to support developing countries that are unable to undertake this monitoring due to lack of resources, providing technical support for developing countries to regulate foreign investors, and negotiating international agreements such as international investment agreements that allow for a state's nationals to be held accountable for wrongs committed in another state.

It may seem counter-intuitive that it is *states* that should be the mechanism for ensuring that nationals of one state behave responsibly in another. But as I mentioned at the beginning of this article, a phenomenological conception of cosmopolitan obligations does not ignore the historical emergence of states or the fact that traditional international law is based on states as the unit of legal responsibility. Moreover, state action, if it reflects the democratically expressed collective will of individuals in that state, can be an effective means for these individuals to act on this responsibility.

The responsibility for nationals causing harm in another jurisdiction is in practice asymmetrical, and it transforms into the responsibility of developed country states to take responsibility for the nationals operating in developing countries that lack effective institutions for protecting their citizens. As Thomas Pogge has pointed out, the justification for this asymmetrical responsibility results from three factors:

- the institutional order that we share has been shaped by the rich and imposed on the poor, and this order creates radical inequality between developed and developing countries;
- in the past and still today, developed countries exclude developing countries from the use of natural resources, thereby

diverting a disproportionate amount of these resources to nationals of developed countries; and
- the inequality that exists between the rich and the poor today results from a common violent history in which developed countries have by and large benefited from grievous wrongs to developing countries, which were their former colonies (or neo-colonies).[129]

In his view, these three factors have led "to the conclusion that the existing radical inequality is unjust, that coercively upholding it violates a negative duty, and that we have urgent moral reason to eradicate world poverty."[130] However, I believe that they lead equally to a responsibility to prevent the continuation of this unjust oppression as perpetuated by nationals of developed countries.

These responsibilities are already recognized in international human rights law. For instance, John Ruggie, the special representative on business and human rights, traces what he calls a "duty to protect" to international human rights documents, which require "states to 'ensure' (or some functionally equivalent verb) the enjoyment or realization of [internationally recognized human] rights by rights holders."[131] Ruggie goes on to limit legal liability of states, claiming:

The State duty to protect is a standard of conduct, and not a standard of result. That is, States are not held responsible for corporate-related human rights abuse per se, but may be considered in breach of their obligations where they fail to take appropriate steps to prevent it and to investigate, punish and redress it when it occurs.[132]

He goes on to state that international law does not require as a matter of law that states regulate their nationals abroad:

The extraterritorial dimension of the duty to protect remains unsettled in international law. Current guidance from international human rights

---

129 Thomas Pogge, *World Poverty and Human Rights* (Cambridge: Polity, 2008) at 199–204.

130 *Ibid.* at 204.

131 *Business and Human Rights: Towards Operationalizing the "Protect, Respect and Remedy*, Report of the Special Representative on Business and Human Rights, GA Doc. A/HRC/11/13 (22 April 2009) at para. 13.

132 *Ibid.* at para. 14.

bodies suggests that States are not required to regulate the extraterritorial activities of businesses incorporated in their jurisdiction, nor are they generally prohibited from doing so provided there is a recognized jurisdictional basis, and that an overall test of reasonableness is met.[133]

In these paragraphs, Ruggie is using the term "responsible" in its international law sense. This interpretation of the legal concept of responsibility is compatible with my notion of cosmopolitan responsibility, namely that states must take steps to prevent, investigate, punish, and redress wrongs to others by transnational corporations. Nevertheless, I would take a step further — it follows from cosmopolitan norms that states *must* regulate the extraterritorial activities of their nationals operating abroad if the state in which they operate lacks the capacity to do so. This follows from the requirement of international cooperation in the prevention of harm to others, but it recognizes limits to state intervention where the state hosting the national of another state has the capacity to prevent, investigate, and punish any harm committed by another. Moreover, it is not up to a state that wishes to intervene to determine unilaterally if another state lacks the capacity to protect its nationals. The standard must be developed and applied cooperatively by states in consultation with each other and with civil society.

Given the extensive literature on corporate social responsibility, I will not go into detail on the forms that responsibility for overseas wrongs of nationals of developed countries can take.[134] However,

---

[133] *Ibid.* at para. 15.

[134] For articles on this subject, see Steven R. Ratner, "Corporations and Human Rights: A Theory of Legal Responsibility" (2001) 111 Yale L.J. 443 (on the imposition of international corporate social responsibility obligations directly on corporations); Simon Chesterman, "Oil and Water: Regulating the Behavior of Multinational Corporations through Law" (2004) 36 N.Y.U. J. Int'l L. & Pol. 307; Sarah Joseph, *Corporations and Transnational Human Rights Litigation* (Oxford: Hart, 2004); Jedrzej George Frynas and Scott Pegg, eds., *Transnational Corporations and Human Rights* (Houndmills: Palgrave Macmillan, 2003); Nicola Jägers, *Corporate Human Rights Obligations: In Search of Accountability* (Antwerpen: Intersentia, 2002); Carlos M. Vázquez, "Direct vs. Indirect Obligations of Corporations under International Law" (2005) 43 Colum. J. Transnat'l L. 927; Surya Deva, "Human Rights Violations by Multinational Corporations and International Law: Where from Here?" (2003) 19 Conn. J. Int'l L. 1; Mahmood Monshipouri, Claude E. Welch, Jr., and Evan T. Kennedy, "Multinational Corporations and the Ethics of Global Responsibility: Problems and Possibilities" (2003) 25 Hum. Rts. Q. 965; Elliot J. Schrage, "Judging Corporate Accountability in the Global Economy" (2003) 42 Colum. J. Transnat'l L. 153; Logan

it should be recognized that voluntary mechanisms for ensuring corporate social responsibility have been largely ineffective in protecting abuses by transnational corporations and that such mechanisms fall short of the responsibility states bear to those in other countries.[135]

TAKING RESPONSIBILITY FOR HARMS TO INDIVIDUALS IN OTHER STATES

How can the phenomenon of publicity help us to resolve the many issues surrounding responsibility for harm committed to nationals of other states in those states? As I mentioned earlier, a phenomenological approach requires us to take into account the context in which a person lives. This context is necessary for understanding the harm they are suffering. Many harms committed by states against their nationals or sanctioned by them either explicitly or through omission have multiple causes — they are violations of human or environmental rights, but they are compounded by the colonial context in which they arise. Again, the framework laid out by Pogge takes this into account. The actions of states that harm their nationals or permit this harm are often related to the effects of an institutional order shaped by other countries, especially rich and powerful ones. This is as true today as it was in the colonial period. In my view, the way in which the actions of states and international bodies benefit from, and compound, the inequalities between these states should be one of the principle determinants for assessing the

---

Michael Breed, "Regulating Our Twenty-First-Century Ambassadors: A New Approach to Corporate Liability for Human Rights Violations Abroad" (2002) 42 Va. J. Int'l L. 1005; Anita Ramasastry, "Corporate Complicity: From Nuremberg to Rangoon: An Examination of Forced Labor Cases and Their Impact on the Liability of Multinational Corporations" (2002) 20 Berkeley J. Int'l L. 91; Beth Stephens, "The Amorality of Profit: Transnational Corporations and Human Rights" (2002) 20 Berkeley J. Int'l L. 45; John Christopher Anderson, "Respecting Human Rights: Multinational Corporations Strike Out" (2000) 2 U. Pa. J. Lab. & Employment L. 463; Diane Marie Amann, "Capital Punishment: Corporate Criminal Liability for Gross Violations of Human Rights" (2001) 24 Hastings Int'l & Comp. L. Rev. 327.

135 On the importance of building host-state capacity as opposed to relying on voluntary corporate social responsibility regimes, see Thomas F. McInerney, "Putting Regulation before Responsibility: Then Limits of Voluntary Corporate Social Responsibility," GWU Law School Public Law and Legal Theory Research Paper (2005), 123, <http://papers.ssrn.com/sol3/papers.cfm?abstract_id=658081#>.

appropriateness of a proposed intervention to prevent harm in another state.

As Thomas Weiss has pointed out, whether we are talking about humanitarian intervention or the emerging doctrine of responsibility to protect does "not [change] the underlying political dynamics. Military overstretch and the prioritization of strategic concerns to the virtual exclusion of humanitarian ones is the sad reality of a post-9/11 world."[136] As developing countries have pointed out, the preference for military rather than non-military intervention demonstrates a failure to understand the "deeper structural causes of conflict."[137] And while prevention is almost always better than a reactive response,[138] many Northern scholars who advocate prevention focus on *military intervention* to prevent harm.[139]

The major flaw in the conception of the responsibility to protect that leads to overlooking context is that it is too state-based. In articulating the idea, the International Commission on Intervention and State Sovereignty characterized the responsibility as a responsibility of states to prevent harm to their own citizens.[140] This view overlooks the fact that it is individuals who have a responsibility not to harm others — the state is merely an organizational tool for collective action. Second, the commission derives a responsibility of the "broader community of states" if a state is unable or unwilling to protect its nationals. Again, the responsibility is not that of the community of states but, rather, of the community of individuals who are witness to the harm others are suffering. However, not only does the commission fail to look behind the veil of the state, it also fails to recognize how the state is not necessarily the appropriate

---

[136] Thomas G. Weiss, "R2P after 9/11 and the World Summit" (2006) 24 Wis. Int'l L.J. 741 at 758.

[137] Greg Puley on behalf of Africa Peace Forum, African Women's Development and Communication Network, Africa Institute of South Africa and Project Ploughshares, *The Responsibility to Protect: East, West, and Southern African Perspectives on Preventing and Responding to Humanitarian Crises* (Waterloo, ON: Project Ploughshare, 2005) at 3.

[138] *Ibid.* at 4.

[139] See, for instance, Anne-Marie Slaughter, "A Duty to Prevent" (2004) 83 Foreign Affairs 136; Allen Buchanan and Robert O. Keohane, "The Preventive Use of Force: A Cosmopolitan Institutional Proposal" (2004) 18(1) Ethics and International Affairs 1. For a criticism of this view, see Weiss, *supra* note 136 at 752.

[140] International Commission on Intervention and State Sovereignty, *The Responsibility to Protect* (Ottawa: Government of Canada, 2001) at 2.15 (p. 13) and 2.29–2.30 (p. 17).

mechanism for dealing with harms because some states are symbols of historical colonialism or of ongoing neo-colonialism. And while the precautionary principle articulated by the commission attempts to deal with some of these factors[141] — in particular, the requirement of "right intention" aims at ensuring that colonial intentions are not the motivation for intervention[142] — it does not address the need for fundamental changes in the structure of international institutions in order to address the role that past or ongoing colonialism plays in creating the harm the interveners seek to address. As developing countries have pointed out, what is really needed to prevent humanitarian disasters is to:

- improve developing country capacity to promote political and economic justice, good governance, and preventive diplomacy;[143]
- improve regional capacity to deal with conflicts;[144]
- improve developing country capacity to analyze threats to peace and security and to develop local solutions for dealing with them;[145]
- allow decisions about intervention to be taken as close as possible to the conflict;[146] and
- incorporate civil society into decision making.[147]

These are just some of the useful suggestions for ensuring that our understanding of the suffering of those in other countries at the hands of their state occurs with an appreciation of the context in which the suffering occurs. Likewise, this contextual analysis will help ensure that solutions to humanitarian disasters are developed contextually rather than on the basis of an abstract legal principle or doctrine.

---

[141] According to the commission, the precautionary principle includes four elements: right intention, the use of force must be the last resort, the means used must be proportional to the humanitarian objective sought to be achieved, and there must be a reasonable prospect of halting or averting the harm sought to be alleviated (*ibid.* at 4.32–4.43 (pp. 35–37)).

[142] *Ibid.* at 4.33 (p. 35).

[143] Puley et al., *supra* note 137 at 23.

[144] *Ibid.*

[145] *Ibid.* at 25.

[146] *Ibid.* at 24.

[147] *Ibid.* at 25.

CONCLUSION

I have not intended my description and promotion of cooperative cosmopolitanism as the ideal normative basis of international law to supplant the sovereignty-based system of international law that exists today. To do so would undermine my descriptive phenomenological method, replacing it with a purely idealistic normative analysis much as Kant undertakes in "Perpetual Peace." Instead, I have tried to demonstrate that it has always been the case that the relations between people are regulated by our experience of the harms that others suffer and, thus, that international relations are merely a special case of the general obligation to take responsibility for these harms. The traditional Westphalian sovereignty-based international law system and the limited changes it has undergone with the advent of the United Nations only partially reflect this responsibility. In a world in which states were generally undemocratic and hostile to each other, the system of sovereignty and the limitations on the creation of international law were rational means of preventing harm. But today, we live in a world in which we have greater opportunities to access and understand the suffering that others experience, and the hostile relations between states are increasingly mitigated by the close economic, political, and social ties that bring us together. As a result, it is possible to use the norms derived from the phenomenon of publicity to generate specific norms of international responsibility that provide a principled foundation for international relations of all sorts.

In the foregoing, I have tried to demonstrate the phenomenological basis of my normative analysis, and I have extracted from this analysis several norms that are compatible with the basic experience of responsibility that we feel for others — that is, horror at their suffering. The norm that emerged — a norm of collective responsibility that I have called cooperative (as opposed to an individualistic) cosmopolitanism is "cosmopolitan" in the sense that it is based on our experience and understanding of the suffering of those in far-away places, and it is cooperative in the sense of being an obligation shared by all that must often be realized collectively and cooperatively.

When we deploy the normative content of our experience of cosmopolitan responsibility, we come to appreciate the importance of contextual analysis, which points to the specific, concrete harms suffered by particular people. We begin to look beyond our assumptions and presumptions as we gather more information about the nature of other's suffering, and we see the necessity of self-critique

— of questioning the ideas and values that we have provisionally held that appear to no longer adequately account for our experience of the concrete suffering of others. The more we pay heed to this suffering, the more we understand the importance of giving voice to others and helping them express their needs in ways that can be understood by others. The five principles of international law that I have articulated, namely

- looking behind the veil of state-based issues;
- de-emphasizing state practice and *opinio juris* as a basis for establishing international legal norms;
- recognizing an increased role for equity in international law;
- taking responsibility for nationals causing harm abroad; and
- taking responsibility for harms to individuals in other states,

follow from the need to understand the context of others' suffering, the importance of critiquing sclerotic conceptions of international law, and the inevitability of taking responsibility for the harms we now recognize and understand. These five general principles, which may not be an exhaustive list of the principles that can be developed through a phenomenological analysis, can be translated into more specific norms in the context of different areas of international relations. I have touched briefly on international investment law, the law of sustainable development, our duty to regulate our co-nationals operating abroad, and our responsibility to protect the nationals of other states from harm in those states. But these principles can also be elaborated in other areas of international law.

Sommaire

Repousser les frontières: repenser le droit international à la lumière d'obligations cosmopolites envers les pays en voie de développement

Cet article préconise une modification des fondements normatifs du droit international afin d'atténuer la marginalisation historique des pays en voie de développement. L'auteur décrit une forme de responsabilité collective appelée "cosmopolitisme coopératif" qui exige que les individus et les États assument leur responsabilité pour des préjudices subis au-delà de leurs frontières. Le cosmopolitisme coopératif comprend des obligations partagées par tous, assumées de manière collective et coopérative. Se fondant sur une approche phénoménologique et à l'aide d'exemples de domaines du droit international qui ont des répercussions négatives disproportionnées sur les pays en voie de développement (en particulier le droit international des investissements), l'article propose cinq modifications au droit international afin de tenir davantage compte de nos obligations cosmopolites: (1) élargissement du champ d'application du droit international au-delà des questions relatives à l'État; (2) atténuation de l'importance de la pratique des États et de l'opinio juris dans l'élaboration du droit international; (3) reconnaissance du rôle croissant de l'équité en droit international; (4) élargissement de la responsabilité des États pour les préjudices attribuables à leurs ressortissants à l'étranger; et (5) formulation d'une compréhension cosmopolite de la responsabilité en matière de protection des ressortissants étrangers.

Summary

Pushing the Boundaries: Rethinking International Law in Light of Cosmopolitan Obligations to Developing Countries

This article argues for a change in the normative assumptions of international law so as to attenuate the historical marginalization of developing countries. It describes a form of collective responsibility called "cooperative cosmopolitanism" that requires individuals and states to take responsibility for harms to those beyond their borders. Cooperative cosmopolitanism entails obligations shared by all that are realized collectively and cooperatively. Taking a phenomenological approach and relying on examples of areas of international law (especially international investment law) that have a disproportionately negative impact on developing countries, the article suggests five ways in which international law should evolve in order to take better account of our cosmopolitan obligations: (1) widening the ambit of international law beyond state-based issues; (2) de-emphasizing state practice and opinio juris as criteria for creating international law; (3) recognizing an increased role for equity in international law; (4) broadening state responsibility to include harms caused by their nationals abroad; and (5) articulating a cosmopolitan understanding of the responsibility to protect foreign nationals.

Le traitement jurisprudentiel du trafic de migrants en droit comparé: Un désaveu des dispositions législatives canadiennes

LOUIS-PHILIPPE JANNARD

L a mondialisation et l'émergence de phénomènes transnationaux posent de nombreux défis aux États. En termes de mobilité, les impacts de la mondialisation, combinés au développement de nouvelles technologies de communication et de transport, incitent un nombre grandissant de personnes à migrer afin d'améliorer leur situation, créant de nouvelles pressions aux frontières du Nord global.[1] À ces migrants économiques s'ajoutent les réfugiés qui fuient la persécution et sont à la recherche d'une protection internationale. En réponse à ces phénomènes, les États cherchent à renforcer le contrôle de leur espace national en s'appuyant sur leur mission traditionnelle: assurer la "sécurité" du pays. Cette tentative s'inscrit dans le processus de sécurisation de la sphère publique, par lequel un enjeu politique devient un enjeu "sécuritaire." En matière de migrations internationales, la sécurisation justifie de nombreuses mesures visant à "reprendre" le contrôle des frontières, contrôle qui se présente dès lors comme un enjeu de souveraineté étatique.[2]

Louis-Philippe Jannard est coordonnateur de la Chaire Hans et Tamar Oppenheimer en droit international public de l'Université McGill. L'auteur remercie François Crépeau, professeur titulaire de la chaire du même nom, ainsi qu'Idil Atak, LL.D. (2010, Université de Montréal), pour leurs précieux conseils. Il tient également à souligner la contribution d'Estibalitz Jimenez Calvo dont la thèse de doctorat a identifié cette piste de recherche, et la contribution de la *Foundation for Legal Research* sans laquelle cette recherche n'aurait pu être possible.

[1] Commission globale sur les migrations internationales, *Les migrations dans un monde interconnecté: nouvelles perspectives d'action* (Genève: Commission globale sur les migrations internationales, 2005) à la p. 12 et s.

[2] François Crépeau et Delphine Nakache, "Controlling Irregular Migration in Canada. Reconciling Security Concerns with Human Rights Protection" (2006) 12 I.R.P.P. Choices 1 à la p. 4.

Le durcissement des politiques migratoires, entraîné par la multiplication de ce type de mesures, diminue d'autant les possibilités
légales de migration. Il se crée ainsi un environnement propice aux
migrations irrégulières et, incidemment, au trafic de migrants.[3]

La communauté internationale et le Canada ont opté pour une
approche résolument sécuritaire pour faire face aux migrations
irrégulières,[4] bien que l'idée qu'elles menacent la souveraineté ou
la sécurité d'un pays ne s'avère qu'en de rares occasions.[5] Pourtant,
les migrations irrégulières comportent surtout des risques pour les
migrants eux-mêmes.[6] De plus, "[s]'ils ne sont pas mis en œuvre
avec discernement, les efforts pour empêcher la migration irrégulière peuvent compromettre davantage le bien-être [des] migrants."
Le contexte actuel ne répond pas à cette dernière préoccupation:
la sécurité étatique prime la sécurité de ces derniers. Au Canada,
l'adoption de mesures préventives et dissuasives visant à décourager
la venue d'étrangers a effectivement provoqué un accroissement
de leur vulnérabilité et une érosion de leurs droits, et ce, à toutes
les étapes du processus de migration.[7]

L'approche sécuritaire teinte aussi fortement la lutte contre le
trafic de migrants. En décembre 2000, la communauté internationale se dote d'un instrument juridique pour lutter contre ce phénomène. Il s'agit du Protocole contre le trafic illicite de migrants
par terre, air et mer[8] qui se rapporte à la Convention des Nations
Unies contre la criminalité transnationale organisée.[9] Abordant le

---

3 *Ibid.*

4 *Ibid;* Jef Huysmans, "The European Union and the Securitization of Migration"
   (2000) 38 J.C.M.S. 751; Khalid Koser, *Irregular Migration, State Security and Human Security* (Genève: Global Commission on International Migration, 2005) à
   la p. 13.

5 Koser, *supra* note 4 à la p. 10.

6 Commission globale sur les migrations internationales, *supra* note 1 aux pp.
   36–37; Tom Obokata, "Smuggling of Human Beings from a Human Rights
   Perspective: Obligations of Non-State and State Actors under International
   Human Rights Law" (2005) 17 I.J.R.L. 394.

7 Crépeau et Nakache, *supra* note 2 à la p. 12 et s.

8 Protocole contre le trafic illicite de migrants par terre, air et mer, additionnel à
   la Convention des Nations Unies contre la criminalité transnationale organisée,
   15 décembre 2000, UN Doc. A/55/383 (Annexe III) (entrée en vigueur: 28
   janvier 2004), art. 3 [Protocole contre le trafic illicite de migrants].

9 Convention des Nations Unies contre la criminalité transnationale organisée,
   15 décembre 2000, UN Doc. A/55/383 (Annexe I) (entrée en vigueur: 29
   septembre 2003).

phénomène sous l'angle de la criminalité organisée, il définit le trafic de migrants comme "le fait d'assurer, afin d'en tirer, directement ou indirectement, un avantage financier ou un autre avantage matériel, l'entrée illégale dans un État Partie d'une personne qui n'est ni un ressortissant ni un résident permanent de cet État."[10] Au Canada, l'article 117(1) de la Loi sur l'immigration et la protection des réfugiés (LIPR) crée une infraction similaire. Il stipule que "[c]ommet une infraction quiconque sciemment organise l'entrée au Canada d'une ou plusieurs personnes non munies des documents — passeport, visa ou autre — requis par la présente loi ou incite, aide ou encourage une telle personne à entrer au Canada."[11] Les pénalités associées à ce crime augmentent considérablement lors de l'entrée en vigueur de la LIPR en 2002. La peine maximale passe alors de dix ans de réclusion à l'emprisonnement à perpétuité.[12] Mentionnons que le trafic de migrants se distingue de la traite d'êtres humains, infraction qui implique l'exploitation d'un individu, inscrite à la fois dans la LIPR et dans le Code criminel.[13] La traite d'êtres humains fait aussi l'objet d'un instrument international particulier.[14]

L'adoption de pénalités aussi sévères, voire excessives,[15] laisse supposer un traitement conséquent des trafiquants par les tribunaux. Pourtant, les peines imposées de 2002 à 2004 ne correspondent pas à l'échelle prévue par la loi.[16] Alors que le resserrement des frontières affecte indûment les droits des migrants et des réfugiés, les trafiquants semblent bénéficier d'une relative clémence. De plus, la recherche d'un avantage financier ou matériel, qui

---

[10] Protocole contre le trafic illicite de migrants, *supra* note 8, art. 3.

[11] Loi sur l'immigration et la protection des réfugiés, L.C. 2001, c. 27 [LIPR].

[12] *Ibid.*, art. 117; Loi sur l'immigration, L.R.C. 1985, c. I (abrogée), art. 94.

[13] LIPR, *supra* note 11, art. 118; Code criminel, L.R.C. (1985), c. C-46, art. 279.01 à 279.04.

[14] Protocole visant à prévenir, réprimer et punir la traite des personnes, en particulier des femmes et des enfants, additionnel à la Convention des Nations Unies contre la criminalité transnationale organisée, 15 décembre 2000, en ligne: UNODC <http://www.unodc.org/documents/treaties/UNTOC/Publications/TOC Convention/TOCebook-f.pdf> (entrée en vigueur: 25 décembre 2003).

[15] Crépeau et Nakache, *supra* note 2 à la p. 17.

[16] Estibalitz Jimenez Calvo, *Le combat du trafic des migrants au Canada: contrôle migratoire d'abord, lutte au crime organisé ensuite*, thèse de doctorat, École de criminologie, Université de Montréal, 2006 [non publiée] à la p. 304 et s.

constitue un des éléments essentiels de l'infraction selon les termes du Protocole contre le trafic illicite de migrants, est exclue du libellé de l'infraction contenu dans la LIPR. Elle viserait ainsi toute forme d'aide à la migration irrégulière, et non seulement celle provenant d'un groupe criminel organisé. Ce constat suscite le questionnement suivant: contre qui se dirigent réellement les dispositions criminalisant le trafic de migrants? Les trafiquants ou les migrants? Nous démontrerons que les dispositions législatives canadiennes sont inadéquates: elles cherchent moins à réprimer une activité criminelle présumée dangereuse qu'à contribuer à dissuader l'immigration irrégulière. Nous ne remettons pas en question le droit souverain des États de contrôler l'entrée et la présence d'étrangers sur leur territoire. Néanmoins, en considérant, d'une part, les impacts incertains de l'immigration irrégulière sur les sociétés d'accueil et, d'autre part, les conséquences négatives — et démontrées — du resserrement des contrôles migratoires sur les migrants, il nous apparaît légitime de questionner l'opportunité de ce resserrement.[17]

Dans la première partie, nous analyserons la jurisprudence canadienne récente relative au trafic de migrants. Plus précisément, nous examinerons de quelles façons les dispositions de la LIPR, lorsqu'appliquées par les tribunaux judiciaires et administratifs, affectent les trafiquants et les migrants. Dans la deuxième partie, nous comparerons ces résultats avec les pratiques françaises, britanniques, américaines et australiennes. Nous étudierons, d'une part, les dispositions législatives et leurs impacts sur les trafiquants et les migrants, ainsi que le traitement jurisprudentiel du trafic de migrants dans ces quatre pays, d'autre part. Nous proposerons des modifications législatives en conclusion.

Le traitement jurisprudentiel du trafic de migrants au Canada: impacts différenciés pour les trafiquants et les migrants

DES DISPOSITIONS PÉNALES INADÉQUATES, QUI AFFECTENT INDÛMENT LES MIGRANTS

Nous examinerons ici l'application des dispositions criminalisant le trafic de migrants par les tribunaux canadiens. Nous constaterons que si les trafiquants reçoivent des peines peu élevées, les juges

---

[17] Au sujet des impacts de l'immigration irrégulière sur les sociétés d'accueil et du resserrement des impacts des politiques migratoires sur les migrants, voir Stephen

appliquent ces dispositions de façon inégale. De plus, les migrants subissent les contrecoups d'une définition incomplète de l'infraction.

Malgré un discours alarmiste, un traitement mesuré des trafiquants

L'article 117 de la LIPR prévoit de lourdes peines, qui s'articulent principalement en fonction du nombre de migrants trafiqués.[18] Lorsque l'infraction vise moins de dix personnes, son auteur est passible d'une amende maximale de cinq cent mille dollars et d'un emprisonnement maximal de dix ans, ou de l'une de ces peines. En cas de récidive, l'amende maximale augmente à un million de dollars et la peine d'emprisonnement maximale à quatorze ans. Lorsque l'infraction implique un groupe de dix personnes ou plus, les sanctions maximales sont une amende d'un million de dollars et l'emprisonnement à perpétuité.[19]

En adoptant de telles sanctions, le législateur transmet un message sans équivoque: le trafic de migrants constitue un crime d'une gravité considérable, comparable aux crimes de génocide et contre l'humanité, punis par des sanctions similaires.[20]

Le discours très négatif des tribunaux

Dans une analyse portant sur les décisions rendues entre 2002 et 2004, Jimenez constate un fort consensus parmi les tribunaux. On y présente le trafic de migrants comme un crime sérieux, comportant de nombreux impacts économiques, sociopolitiques et humains.[21] Un examen attentif de la jurisprudence récente révèle un argumentaire semblable.

Premièrement, selon plusieurs magistrats, la gravité du crime justifie une peine dissuasive. On présente le trafic de migrants comme

---

H. Legomsky, "Portraits of the Undocumented Immigrant: A Dialogue" (2009) 44 Ga L. Rev. 1 à la p. 7 et s. L'auteur y affirme que les données empiriques portant sur les impacts de l'immigration clandestine sur la société d'accueil demeurent incertaines, alors que les effets des politiques sur les individus se catégorisent plus facilement comme positifs ou négatifs. L'auteur penche donc pour les politiques plus clémentes à l'égard des migrants.

[18] LIPR, *supra* note 11, art. 117.

[19] *Ibid.*

[20] Loi sur les crimes contre l'humanité et les crimes de guerre, L.C. 2000, ch. 24, art. 4.

[21] Jimenez, *supra* note 16 à la p. 307.

un "crime extrêmement sérieux"[22] qui requiert une peine de prison ferme afin de "sanctionner de manière non équivoque ce type de comportement."[23]

The public needs to know that Canada is serious about protecting its national borders ... Sentences imposed by the courts for flagrant and organized penetrations of these borders must reflect that reality.[24]

Dans *R. v. Min,* le juge affirme qu'il est impératif que les cours punissent ce type d'infractions et qu'elles démontrent que les criminels seront sévèrement sanctionnés.[25] Dans *R. v. Tewana,* on souligne qu'un des principes importants pour déterminer la sentence est le caractère dissuasif de la peine, surtout lorsque l'accusé recherche un avantage financier.[26] Des arguments semblables se retrouvent dans les décisions *R. c. Savaresse-Belapatino* et *R. v. Wasiluk.*[27]

De plus, l'augmentation de la pénalité maximale associée au trafic de migrants refléterait l'intention du législateur selon laquelle la gravité du trafic de migrants nécessite une répression plus sévère.[28]

---

[22] *R. v. Enayatollah,* [2005] O.J. n° 5910, au para. 23 (Ont. Ct. J.) [*Enayatollah*].

[23] *R. c. Bejashvili,* [2007] J.Q. n° 16210, au para. 26 (C.Q. crim. & pén.) [*Bejashvili*].

[24] *R. v. Lin,* [2005] CanLII 51782 (Provincial Court of Newfoundland and Labrador), p. 14–15 [nous soulignons]. Dans cette affaire, Lin est accusé en vertu de l'article 126 de la LIPR, disposition qui prévoit que "[c]ommet une infraction quiconque, sciemment, incite, aide ou encourage ou tente d'inciter, d'aider ou d'encourager une personne à faire des présentations erronées sur un fait important quant à un objet pertinent ou de réticence sur ce fait, et de ce fait entraîne ou risque d'entraîner une erreur dans l'application de la présente loi." En l'espèce, l'accusé a aidé cinq immigrants chinois à faire de fausses présentations dans le but d'entrer au Canada. Il prétendait être le professeur et accompagnateur d'un groupe de cinq étudiants "coréens" en visite au Canada. Bien que Lin ne soit pas accusé de trafic de migrants en vertu de l'article 117, nous considérons ce cas puisqu'il y a similitude entre les actes perpétrés et le trafic de migrants. Voir également *R. c. Savaresse-Belapatino,* [2008] J.Q. n° 5345 (Cour du Québec, chambre criminelle), au para. 48 [*Savaresse-Belapatino*].

[25] *R. v. Min,* [2005] N.B.J. n° 602 (New Brunswick Provincial Court), au para. 49 et 101 [*Min*].

[26] *R. v. Tewana,* [2006] O.J. n° 4676, aux para. 81–83 (Ont. Ct. J.) [*Tewana*].

[27] *Savaresse-Belapatino, supra* note 24 au para. 3; *R. v. Wasiluk,* [2005] O.J. n° 4148, au para. 15 (Ont. Ct. J.) [*Wasiluk*].

[28] Jimenez, *supra* note 16 aux pp. 307–8. Voir *Décret fixant au 28 juin 2002 la date d'entrée en vigueur de certaines dispositions de la Loi,* TR/2002-97, Gaz. C. 2002. II.136 (édition spéciale); Loi sur l'immigration, *supra* note 12, art. 94.

The Crown also submits that the recent enactment of the Immigration Refugee Protection Act, increasing the maximum penalty, pursuant to Section 117(1) ... is not only reflective of the seriousness with which the legislature views these types of activities, but the need to increase the penalties for these types of offences ...

I concur with the Crown's submissions to that effect.[29]

Dans *R. v. Bajraktari*, le juge considère ces changements législatifs d'un même œil. "*I consider this as a strong indication from Parliament as to the seriousness with which it views this type of offence,*" affirme-t-il.[30]

Deuxièmement, les magistrats exposent les nombreuses implications du trafic de migrants afin de motiver les sanctions.[31] Le phénomène aurait de nombreux impacts négatifs: il mine l'intégrité des systèmes d'immigration canadien et étrangers, érode l'appui du public en faveur de la protection des réfugiés et représente une injustice envers les migrants "légitimes." Il compromet la sécurité nationale et la souveraineté territoriale du Canada, et entache sa réputation internationale.[32]

On mentionne les atteintes à l'intégrité du système canadien d'immigration dans les décisions *R. c. Savaresso-Belapatino, R. v. Tewana, R. v. Min* et *Singh c. Canada (Ministre de la Citoyenneté et de l'Immigration)*.[33] Dans les affaires *R. c. Bejashvili* et *R. v. Tewana*, les juges considèrent le trafic de migrants comme une menace à la sécurité nationale.[34] Dans *R. c. Wasiluk*, on évoque même des liens entre l'immigration irrégulière et le terrorisme, ainsi que l'importance de mieux contrôler les frontières à la suite des attentats du 11 septembre 2001.[35] Selon les jugements *R. c. Savaresso-Belapatino* et *R. v. Min*, le trafic de migrants porte atteinte à la souveraineté territoriale du Canada: les pays doivent avoir le contrôle de leurs frontières et des personnes qui les traversent.[36]

---

[29] *Wasiluk, supra* note 27 aux para. 23–24.

[30] *R. v. Bajraktari*, [2006] O.J. n° 2720 (Ontario Court of Justice), au para. 11 [*Bajraktari*].

[31] *Jimenez, supra* note 16 à la p. 309 et s.

[32] *Enayatollah, supra* note 22 au para. 23. Voir également *R. v. Dhalla*, [2007] CanLII 11719, au para. 17 (Ont. Sup. Ct. J.) [*Dhalla*].

[33] *Savaresso-Belapatino, supra* note 24 au para. 44; *Tewana, supra* note 26 au para. 83; *Min, supra* note 25 aux para. 97–99; *Singh (Ministre de la Citoyenneté et de l'Immigration)*, (2006) D.S.A.I. n° 1085 au para. 7 [*Singh*].

[34] *Bejashvili, supra* note 23 au para. 16; *Tewana, supra* note 26 au para. 83.

[35] *Wasiluk, supra* note 27 au paras. 19–20.

[36] *Savaresso-Belapatino, supra* note 24 au para. 45; *Min, supra* note 25 au para. 85.

Troisièmement, certains juges expriment leurs inquiétudes quant au sort réservé aux migrants qui recourent à des passeurs.[37] Certains magistrats déplorent les impacts négatifs du resserrement des contrôles frontaliers dû au trafic de migrants sur les citoyens canadiens et le mouvement des personnes.[38] Ils ne mentionnent toutefois pas les conséquences de ce resserrement sur le trafic de migrants en tant que tel, soit l'augmentation du recours aux passeurs pour traverser des frontières de plus en plus fermées.[39]

Les peines peu élevées imposées aux trafiquants

Bien que les tribunaux insistent sur la nécessité de dissuader le trafic de migrants par l'imposition de sentences élevées, les peines prononcées contredisent cet objectif.[40] Dans l'échantillon de six décisions examiné par Jimenez, les peines s'échelonnent de 160 heures de services communautaires pour avoir fait traverser la frontière canado-américaine à soixante-cinq migrants jusqu'à trois ans d'emprisonnement pour un récidiviste ayant trafiqué quarante personnes aux États-Unis par le Canada.[41] L'auteure tire une double conclusion de ce constat. D'une part, les sentences ne reflètent pas la sévérité attendue par le Parlement et les tribunaux. D'autre part, il n'y a pas de corrélation entre la perception de la gravité du phénomène et les peines infligées.[42]

Pour ce qui est des dix décisions repérées pour la période qui s'étend de janvier 2005 jusqu'à juillet 2009, les peines varient entre quatre-vingt-dix jours de prison à purger de façon intermittente et sept ans de réclusion.[43] Aucune amende n'est imposée. Deux condamnés doivent réaliser, en plus de leur peine d'emprisonnement, cent heures de travail communautaire.

---

[37] *Bajraktari, supra* note 30 au para. 18; *Enayatollah, supra* note 22 au para. 23; *Singh, supra* note 33 au para. 7.

[38] *Dhalla, supra* note 32 au para. 17; *Enayatollah, supra* note 22 au para. 23.

[39] Crépeau et Nakache, *supra* note 2 à la p. 17.

[40] Jimenez, *supra* note 16 à la p. 328.

[41] *Ibid.* à la p. 328 et s.

[42] *Ibid.* aux pp. 334–35.

[43] *Bejashvili, supra* note 23; *Savaresse-Belapatino, supra* note 24; *R. v. Alzehrani,* [2008] O.J. n⁰ 4422 (Ont. Sup. Ct. J.) [*Alzehrani*]; *Bajraktari, supra* note 30; *Enayatollah, supra* note 22; *R. v. Hallal,* [2006] O.J. n⁰ 2026 (Ont. Ct. J.) [*Hallal*]; *Min, supra* note 25; *R. v. Ng,* [2008] B.C.J. n⁰ 2576 (B.C. C.A.) [*Ng*]; *Tewana, supra* note 26; *Wasiluk, supra* note 27.

Tableau 1

LES SENTENCES IMPOSÉES AU CANADA,
JANVIER 2005 À JUILLET 2009.

Intitulé (année)	Description de l'accusation [article]	Sentence imposée
R. v. Alzehrani (2008)	Les accusés ont comploté en vue de trafiquer dix-sept migrants, en sept occasions, des États-Unis vers le Canada et du Canada vers les États-Unis [LIPR, 117(1)].	Alzehrani: quatre ans et demi de prison. Gashaj (co-accusé): quatre ans de prison.
R. v. Bajraktari (2006)	En cinq occasions, environ vingt migrants sont entrés illégalement au Canada [non précisé].	Deux ans et demi de prison.
R. c. Bejashvili (2007)	L'accusé a aidé une personne à entrer au Canada sans les documents requis [LIPR, 117(1)] et a fait des présentations erronées [LIPR, 127(a)].	Trois mois de prison.
R. v. Enayatollah (2007)	L'accusé a comploté en vue de trafiquer huit migrants du Canada vers les États-Unis [Code criminel, 465(1)(c)] et a participé aux activités d'une organisation criminelle dans le but d'augmenter sa capacité à faire passer illégalement des migrants aux États-Unis [Code criminel, 467.1].	90 jours de prison, à purger de façon intermittente.
R. v. Hallal (2006)	L'accusé a comploté dans le but de trafiquer trente migrants du Canada vers les États-Unis, en dix opérations [Code criminel, 465(1)(c)].	Dix-huit mois de prison.
R. v. Min (2005)	Les accusés ont trafiqué moins de dix migrants entre le Canada et les États-Unis, à deux reprises [non précisé].	Min: sept ans de prison. Yang: cinq ans de prison.
R. v. Ng (2008)	L'accusé a aidé une personne à entrer au Canada en sachant qu'elle n'avait pas les documents nécessaires [LIPR, 117(1)] et a aidé une personne à faire des présentations erronées [LIPR, 126].	Neuf mois de prison (à cela s'ajoutent dix-huit mois pour des infractions reliées à la prostitution).

Tableau 1 (suite)

R. c. Savaresse-Belapatino (2008)	Les co-accusés ont comploté pour faire entrer illégalement entre 150 et 500 personnes au Canada [LIPR, 117(1)].	Savaresse-Belapatino: trois ans de prison. Hurtado Ortiz: douze mois de prison.
R. v. Tewana (2006)	L'accusé a comploté pour violer les lois américaines sur l'immigration, soit faire entrer illégalement 120 migrants [non précisé].	Trois ans de prison.
R. v. Wasiluk (2005)	Les accusés ont trafiqué trente migrants, en quatre occasions [LIPR, 117(1)].	Quatorze mois d'emprisonnement conditionnel (assignation à résidence et couvre-feu) et cent heures de travail communautaire.

La pénalité maximale consiste en sept ans de réclusion, imposée dans l'affaire *R. v. Min*.[44] L'accusé principal avait déjà purgé une peine de quatre ans de prison pour une infraction similaire en 2001, ce dont le juge tient compte pour calculer la nouvelle sanction.[45] En l'espèce, Min est condamné pour deux infractions, la deuxième ayant eu lieu alors qu'on l'avait déjà mis en accusation pour la première. Son co-accusé, Yang, reçoit une peine de cinq ans de prison pour les deux mêmes délits. La troisième peine la plus élevée est de quatre ans et demi de prison dans la décision *R. v. Alzehrani*.[46] Dans ce cas, une des opérations avait causé la mort d'un des migrants. Le co-accusé Gashaj avait abandonné huit migrants dans une camionnette lors d'une opération avortée et a été condamné à quatre ans de prison, soit la quatrième peine en importance.[47] Si l'on fait exception de ces cas, caractérisés par d'importants facteurs aggravants, la peine moyenne est de 17,5 mois

---

[44] *Min, supra* note 25.

[45] *Ibid.* au para. 113.

[46] *Alzehrani, supra* note 43.

[47] *Ibid.;* É.-U., Immigration and Customs Enforcement, *ICE investigation lead to human smuggling sentences in Canadian Court*, 6 février 2009, en ligne: ICE <http://www.ice.gov/pi/nr/0902/090206toronto.htm>.

d'emprisonnement et la peine maximale, de trois ans. En considérant l'ensemble des cas, la peine d'emprisonnement moyenne n'est que de 29,6 mois, soit un peu moins de deux ans et demi de prison.[48] Le constat établi par Jimenez pour les années 2002 à 2004 se confirme. D'une part, cette moyenne ne correspond pas aux discours des tribunaux judiciaires et demeure nettement inférieure aux peines prévues par la LIPR. D'autre part, il n'y a pas de corrélation entre la gravité supposée du crime et les décisions des juges. Le traitement jurisprudentiel du trafic de migrants s'inscrit donc en faux avec la sévérité des discours législatif et judiciaire. Cette apparente contradiction pourrait s'expliquer par le fait que ces mesures visent moins à lutter contre une forme dangereuse de criminalité — qui justifierait de semblables pénalités — qu'à contribuer à dissuader l'immigration irrégulière. Au fond, les juges ne sont pas dupes de leur propre discours: ils sentent bien que, hormis la négligence criminelle menant à des blessures ou à la mort, l'acte de franchir une frontière ne constitue pas un crime au sens "classique" du terme, puisqu'il n'y a ni atteinte aux biens ni aux personnes.

Le peu d'influence du nombre de migrants trafiqués sur les sentences

Selon les termes de la LIPR, le nombre de migrants trafiqués constitue le premier facteur permettant de juger de la gravité de l'infraction. En effet, les pénalités se modulent principalement en fonction de cet élément, que nous utiliserons afin d'analyser les décisions. Nous considérerons également les circonstances atténuantes et aggravantes, précisées à l'article 121 de la Loi, dont le juge doit tenir compte lorsqu'il impose une sentence. Il s'agit de la survenance de mort ou l'infliction de blessures, l'implication d'une organisation criminelle, la recherche de profit, ainsi que la soumission du migrant à des traitements dégradants ou inhumains.[49] Nos observations se limiteront aux cas repérés pour les années 2005 à 2009.

Dans deux cas, *R. c. Bejashvili* et *R. v. Ng*, les accusés sont reconnus coupables du trafic d'une seule personne et sont respectivement condamnés à trois et neuf mois d'emprisonnement.[50] Dans

---

[48] Dans ces dix décisions, quatorze peines d'emprisonnement sont prononcées. Nous avons additionné la longueur, en mois, des peines de réclusion imposées et divisé cette somme le nombre de peines considérées (14).

[49] LIPR, *supra* note 11, art. 121.

[50] *Bejashvili, supra* note 23; *Ng, supra* note 43.

le premier cas, deux circonstances atténuantes jouent en faveur de l'accusé: aucun gain monétaire n'a été réalisé et la personne trafiquée a été acceptée en tant que réfugié.

Dans la décision *R. v. Enayatollah,* l'opération de trafic sur laquelle porte l'accusation implique huit migrants.[51] L'accusé doit purger quatre-vingt-dix jours de prison de façon intermittente. Dans deux affaires, entre dix et vingt migrants sont trafiqués.[52] Les sentences divergent grandement. Dans *R. v. Min,* le juge impose aux co-accusés des peines d'emprisonnement de sept et cinq ans pour le trafic de moins de vingt migrants en deux opérations — le nombre exact n'étant pas spécifié. Min, un récidiviste, et Yang, qui avait déjà été condamné aux États-Unis pour une infraction similaire, ont commis la deuxième infraction alors qu'ils attendaient leur procès pour la première infraction, ce qui explique la sévérité des peines. Dans *R. v. Alzehrani,* les co-accusés sont jugés pour le trafic de dix-sept personnes en sept épisodes et reçoivent des peines de prison de quatre ans et demi et quatre ans. Lors d'une des opérations menées par Alzehrani, un migrant meurt noyé. À la lumière de ce fait, la sanction imposée — quatre ans et demi — semble plutôt faible. Dans un autre ordre d'idées, le juge précise, dans ce jugement, les critères d'interprétation de l'article 117(1) de la LIPR.[53]

---

51 *Enayatollah, supra* note 22.

52 *Alzehrani, supra* note 43; *Min, supra* note 25.

53 *Alzehrani, supra* note 43 aux para. 7–11. Il s'agit d'une infraction d'intention spécifique qui requiert la connaissance que la personne aidée n'a pas les documents requis par la loi. Quatre éléments doivent être démontrés: (1) La personne trafiquée n'a pas les documents requis pour entrer au Canada; (2) La personne venait au Canada; (3) L'accusé organise, incite, aide ou encourage cette personne à entrer au Canada; et (4) L'accusé savait que cette personne ne possédait pas les documents nécessaires. Le juge commente ainsi ces critères, au para. 64: "*The Crown submitted that interpreting the legislation and applying the law in the manner I have done will make it virtually impossible to successfully prosecute those engaged in human smuggling. I recognize the difficulty, particularly when the individuals being smuggled are not apprehended or when the charge is conspiracy and the underlying crime itself is not completed. I do not understand why s. 117 of IRPA is limited to the smuggling of persons across the border who are without the required documents, as opposed to simply smuggling people across the border for whatever reason. However, if the manner in which the legislation is drafted makes it difficult to prosecute wrongdoers (which it does), and the wrongdoing is serious (which it is), the remedy lies in legislative reform, not by judicial interpretation that violates the plain meaning of the existing statutory language.*" En l'espèce, l'application de ces critères écarte vingt-trois des trente chefs d'accusation. Le nombre de migrants trafiqués par ces personnes pourrait donc être sensiblement plus élevé.

Dans trois jugements, entre vingt et trente migrants sont trafiqués.[54] La longueur des peines prononcées varie de quatorze mois d'emprisonnement conditionnel à deux ans et demi de prison. Dans *Bajraktari*, la sentence tient compte de plusieurs circonstances atténuantes et aggravantes. D'une part, l'accusé a rapidement plaidé coupable. D'autre part, le juge considère le rôle de l'accusé dans le transport et l'organisation ainsi que la recherche de profits pour imposer une peine d'emprisonnement de deux ans et demi. Dans *Hallal*, le juge invoque plusieurs facteurs aggravants pour justifier une sentence de dix-huit mois de prison. Il s'agit du niveau d'implication de l'accusé, du degré de planification et de la recherche de profits. Dans l'affaire *Wasiluk*, les accusés ont participé au trafic de trente migrants et écopent d'une peine d'emprisonnement conditionnel de quatorze mois et cent heures de travail communautaire. Les conditions sont, pour les sept premiers mois, une assignation à résidence en tout temps, sauf pour quelques activités. Pendant les sept derniers mois, les accusés doivent observer un couvre-feu de 23h à 6h. Le juge considère le rôle limité des accusés comme un facteur atténuant et la recherche de profit comme une circonstance aggravante.

Deux affaires concernent le trafic de plus de cent personnes.[55] Les trafiquants reçoivent des peines d'emprisonnement de trois ans, tandis qu'un co-accusé doit purger une peine de douze mois de prison. Dans *R. v. Savaresse-Belapatino*, le juge considère en tant que facteurs aggravants le degré d'organisation et le nombre élevé de migrants impliqués. Pour le principal accusé, il souligne son rôle parmi les têtes dirigeantes des opérations ainsi que la recherche de profits. Le co-accusé reçoit une peine de douze mois de prison en raison d'une implication moindre. Dans l'affaire *Tewana*, la recherche de profit constitue le principal facteur aggravant tandis que le juge voit comme des circonstances atténuantes l'aveu de culpabilité et la longueur de la détention provisoire.

Cette analyse permet d'apprécier les peines imposées avec plus d'exactitude. D'une part, le nombre de migrants trafiqués semble n'avoir qu'une faible influence sur la longueur des sentences. Tandis que quatorze mois d'emprisonnement conditionnel sont imposés dans l'affaire *Wasiluk* pour le trafic de trente personnes, Bajraktari écope de deux ans et demi pour le même nombre de

---

[54] *Bajraktari*, *supra* note 30; *Hallal*, *supra* note 43; *Wasiluk*, *supra* note 27.

[55] *Savaresse-Belapatino*, *supra* note 24; *Tewana*, *supra* note 26.

migrants.[56] Ng reçoit une peine de neuf mois d'emprisonnement pour le trafic d'un individu, alors qu'Enayatollah doit purger trois mois d'emprisonnement de façon intermittente pour le trafic de huit migrants.[57]

D'autre part, les juges donnent un poids variable aux circonstances atténuantes et aggravantes. Dans *R. v. Min*, deux récidivistes reçoivent des peines de sept et cinq ans.[58] Dans *R. v. Alzehrani*, le principal accusé est responsable de la mort d'un migrant et reçoit une peine de quatre ans et demi de prison. Il s'agit dans les deux cas du trafic de moins de vingt personnes.

La criminalisation de toute forme d'aide à la migration

La définition du Protocole contre le trafic illicite de migrants fait de la recherche d'un avantage financier ou matériel un élément constitutif de l'infraction.[59] De plus, l'article 6(1) précise que les États Parties confèrent "le caractère d'infraction pénale, lorsque les actes ont été commis intentionnellement et *pour en tirer, directement ou indirectement, un avantage financier ou autre avantage matériel* ... au trafic illicite de migrants."[60] Contrairement au droit international, la LIPR fait de cet élément un simple facteur à considérer lors de l'imposition de la peine.[61] Cette omission, qui a pour effet de criminaliser toute forme d'aide à la migration, a suscité plusieurs inquiétudes. On craignait que les organisations motivées par des considérations humanitaires devraient s'abstenir d'apporter leur aide aux migrants, et ce, même s'il s'agissait de réfugiés, afin de ne pas faire l'objet de poursuites judiciaires.

Lors des débats parlementaires précédant l'adoption de la Loi, la ministre de la Citoyenneté et de l'Immigration répondait à ces appréhensions en invoquant l'article 117(4) de la LIPR, qui requiert le consentement du procureur général pour engager des poursuites pénales relatives au trafic de migrants.[62] Elle affirmait que le ministre de la Justice n'intenterait pas de poursuite à l'encontre des travailleurs humanitaires qui aideraient un migrant clandestin

---

56 *Wasiluk, supra* note 27; *Bajraktari, supra* note 30.

57 *Ng, supra* note 43; *Enayatollah, supra* note 22.

58 *Min, supra* note 25.

59 Protocole contre le trafic illicite de migrants, *supra* note 8, art. 3.

60 *Ibid.*, art. 6(1) [nous soulignons].

61 LIPR, *supra* note 11, art. 121.

62 *Ibid.*

pour des raisons humanitaires. Ce pouvoir a toutefois été délégué au Service des poursuites pénales du Canada,[63] avec les conséquences suivantes.

Des travailleurs humanitaires menacés de poursuites pénales

Le Conseil canadien pour les réfugiés (CCR) a lancé, en novembre 2007, une "campagne d'opposition à la criminalisation de l'aide aux réfugiés" en réponse à l'arrestation et la mise en accusation, le 26 septembre 2007, d'une représentante d'un organisme d'aide aux réfugiés.[64] Janet Hinshaw-Thomas accompagnait alors douze demandeurs d'asile d'origine haïtienne à la frontière canado-américaine, qui ont d'ailleurs été admis pour poursuivre leur demande. Bien qu'elle n'agissait ni de façon clandestine ni dans le but d'en tirer un avantage quelconque, elle a été mise en détention. Les accusations portées contre elle, en vertu de l'article 117 de la LIPR, ont finalement été abandonnées sans explication le 8 novembre 2007. Malgré le retrait des accusations, cet événement a néanmoins été ressenti par plusieurs comme un avertissement. D'ailleurs, une seconde travailleuse humanitaire américaine, Margaret de Rivera, a été menacée de poursuites pénales en vertu des mêmes dispositions par des agents frontaliers. Elle accompagnait alors deux Haïtiens au poste de St-Stephen, au Nouveau-Brunswick.[65]

R. c. Bejashvili: la criminalisation de l'aide aux réfugiés

Dans un cas précis, une personne venue en aide à un réfugié a écopé d'une peine de prison. En effet, dans l'affaire *R. c. Bejashvili*, une femme est condamnée à trois mois de prison pour avoir aidé une personne à entrer illégalement au Canada, bien qu'aucun profit n'ait été réalisé et que la demande de statut de réfugié de la personne aidée ait été acceptée.[66] Rappelons que l'article 31 de la Convention relative au statut des réfugiés interdit l'application de sanctions pénales aux réfugiés en raison de l'entrée ou du séjour

---

[63] Conseil canadien pour les réfugiés, *Campagne d'opposition à la criminalisation de l'aide aux réfugiés,* (sans date), en ligne: Conseil canadien pour les réfugiés <http://www.ccrweb.ca/aideretencourager/index.htm>.

[64] *Ibid.*

[65] Conseil canadien pour les réfugiés, *De nouvelles menaces d'accusation pour avoir aider [sic] des réfugiés,* (17 janvier 2008), en ligne: Conseil canadien pour les réfugiés <http://www.ccrweb.ca/fra/media/communi/17jano8.html>.

[66] *Bejashvili, supra* note 23.

irréguliers.[67] Comment l'aide à un "non-crime" pourrait-elle constituer un délit?

Bref, la définition canadienne du trafic de migrants, en excluant la recherche d'un avantage financier ou autre, a eu pour effet de criminaliser l'aide des personnes qui assistent les migrants vulnérables, tels que les demandeurs d'asile et les réfugiés, pour des raisons humanitaires.

En définitive, les dispositions de la LIPR criminalisant le trafic de migrants se révèlent inadéquates. D'abord, les tribunaux imposent des sentences bien en deçà des peines maximales prévues par la loi, qui semble ainsi surestimer — volontairement — la gravité du crime. Ensuite, les juges donnent relativement peu d'importance au nombre de migrants trafiqués, au profit d'autres critères auxquels ils confèrent un poids variable. Enfin, elles ont pour effet de criminaliser toute forme d'aide à la migration. Il en résulte des impacts différenciés pour les trafiquants, d'une part, et les migrants et les demandeurs d'asile, d'autre part. Tandis que les premiers se voient imposer un traitement somme toute mesuré, les seconds subissent les contrecoups d'une aide humanitaire devenue criminelle. Ce phénomène empêche les demandeurs d'asile d'accéder à la protection internationale prévue par la Convention relative au statut des réfugiés et met leur vie et leur intégrité physique en danger. Dans la répression du trafic de migrants apparaît en filigrane la lutte contre l'immigration irrégulière.

UNE PRATIQUE ADMINISTRATIVE QUI CONFIRME CES IMPACTS DIFFÉRENCIÉS

Nous analyserons ici la jurisprudence de la Commission de l'immigration et du statut de réfugié (CISR) relative au trafic de migrants. Si les trafiquants bénéficient d'une relative clémence de la part des commissaires, les demandeurs d'asile ayant eu recours aux trafiquants pour parvenir au Canada voient leur crédibilité entachée.

La relative clémence des tribunaux administratifs à l'égard des trafiquants

L'article 37(1)(b) de la LIPR stipule qu'emporte interdiction de territoire le fait de s'être livré, "dans le cadre de la criminalité

---

[67] Convention relative au statut des réfugiés, 28 juillet 1951, 1989 R.T.N.U. 137, R.T. Can. 1969 n⁰ 6, art. 31 (entrée en vigueur: 22 avril 1954).

transnationale, à des activités telles le passage de clandestins."[68] Au moins deux personnes arrêtées pour trafic de migrants ont ainsi été interdites de territoire pour la période 2005–09.[69] Notons qu'un de ces individus, arrêté par la Gendarmerie royale du Canada (GRC) vers le 6 septembre 2006 et ensuite détenu par l'Agence des services frontaliers du Canada (ASFC), a été renvoyé le 14 septembre 2006, à la suite d'une décision de la CISR. Bien qu'il ait été soupçonné d'avoir aidé une quinzaine de personnes à traverser illégalement la frontière canado-américaine, il n'a pas fait l'objet de poursuites criminelles.[70] Jimenez a repéré deux cas similaires dans lesquels des trafiquants ont été expulsés du Canada en vertu de la même disposition, toujours sans être poursuivis.[71] L'autre individu visé par une interdiction de territoire en raison de trafic de migrants avait préalablement purgé une peine de neuf mois de prison, suivie de deux années de probation.[72]

L'article 36(1) de la LIPR crée une autre catégorie d'interdiction de territoire pour grande criminalité. L'alinéa (b) prévoit qu'emporte interdiction de territoire le fait d'"être déclaré coupable, à l'extérieur du Canada, d'une infraction qui, commise au Canada, constituerait une infraction à une loi fédérale punissable d'un emprisonnement maximal d'au moins dix ans."[73] L'infraction d'organisation d'entrée illégale au Canada, décrite à l'article 117(1) de la même loi, correspond à ces critères. Pour la période 2005–09, au moins six personnes ont fait l'objet d'interdictions de territoire en raison de condamnations antérieures pour trafic de migrants, notamment aux États-Unis.[74] Parmi ces six cas, la CISR a décidé, à trois reprises, de surseoir aux mesures de renvoi en raison de motifs

---

[68] LIPR, *supra* note 11, art. 37(1)(b).

[69] *Canada (Ministre de la Sécurité publique et de la Protection civile) c. Chung*, [2007] D.S.A.I. nᵒ 506 [*Chung*]; *Patel c. Canada (Ministre de la Citoyenneté et de l'Immigration)*, [2007] D.S.A.I. nᵒ 2368 [*Patel*].

[70] *Chung, supra* note 69.

[71] Jimenez, *supra* note 16 aux pp. 301–5.

[72] *Patel, supra* note 69.

[73] LIPR, *supra* note 11, art. 36(1)(b).

[74] *Chahal v. Canada (Minister of Citizenship and Immigration)*, [2005] D.S.A.I. nᵒ 1171 [*Chahal*]; *Gonzalez c. Canada (Ministre de la Citoyenneté et de l'Immigration)*, [2006] D.S.A.I. nᵒ 168; *Lee v. Canada (Minister of Citizenship and Immigration)*, [2008] D.S.A.I. nᵒ 1738 [*Lee*]; *Saravanapavananthan c. Canada (Ministre de la Citoyenneté et de l'Immigration)*, [2005] D.S.A.I. nᵒ 881; *Singh, supra* note 33; *Thiagarajah c. Canada (Ministre de la Citoyenneté et de l'Immigration)*, [2008] D.S.A.I. nᵒ 2071 [*Thiagarajah*].

humanitaires divers (conditions médicales, intérêt supérieur de l'enfant).[75]

Les décisions de la CISR tendent à renforcer l'argument selon lequel le traitement des trafiquants par les tribunaux canadiens ne correspond pas à la gravité de l'infraction décrite dans les discours judiciaire et législatif. D'une part, dans l'affaire *Canada (Ministre de la Sécurité publique et de la Protection civile) c. Chung*, les autorités décident d'expulser l'individu soupçonné de trafic de migrants au Canada sans le poursuivre.[76] Le simple renvoi constituerait-il une peine suffisante? À tout le moins, cette sanction ne saurait équivaloir à la peine maximale d'emprisonnement prévue par la loi.[77] D'autre part, les personnes frappées d'une interdiction de territoire en raison de condamnations antérieures à l'étranger pour trafic de migrants connaissent, lorsqu'ils demandent un sursis aux mesures de renvoi, un "taux de réussite" assez élevé. En l'occurrence, il s'agit de trois décisions favorables sur six.

La crédibilité entachée des migrants ayant eu recours aux trafiquants

Le recours aux trafiquants pour parvenir au Canada semble miner la crédibilité des demandeurs d'asile ayant utilisé les services de passeurs, notamment lorsqu'ils doivent établir leur identité. Dans *G.L.Y. (Re)*,[78] un demandeur d'asile originaire du Nigéria serait arrivé au Canada avec le concours d'une personne qui désirait simplement l'aider à échapper à sa situation. Cette personne aurait entrepris les démarches nécessaires — achat d'un faux passeport et d'un billet d'avion — et l'aurait accompagné jusqu'au Canada, par pure compassion.[79] Ce sont les seuls détails que fournit le demandeur d'asile, qui par ailleurs se montre "hésitant, vague et évasif"[80] dans ses réponses. Le tribunal juge cette histoire "invraisemblable."[81] Le commissaire précise:

La Section de la protection des réfugiés est un tribunal spécialisé, et le tribunal sait pertinemment qu'il existe des réseaux de passeurs qui font le

---

75 *Chahal, supra* note 74; *Lee, supra* note 74; *Thiagarajah, supra* note 74.

76 *Chung, supra* note 69.

77 LIPR, *supra* note 11, art. 117(3).

78 *G.L.Y. (Re)*, [2005] D.S.P.R. n° 845.

79 *Ibid.* aux para. 12–13.

80 *Ibid.* au para. 6.

81 *Ibid.* au para. 12.

trafic d'êtres humains, qui gagnent de l'argent, qui sont des criminels, qui protègent leurs arrières et qui disent aux clandestins de ne rien dire, de ne pas révéler leur identité et ainsi de suite. Le tribunal ne prête donc pas foi à l'épopée de M. XXXXX, et cela nuit à la crédibilité du demandeur d'asile parce qu'il faut de l'argent pour se procurer un billet d'avion et un faux passeport.[82]

Le demandeur d'asile présente, pour prouver son identité, un acte de naissance et une carte d'identité délivrée par son employeur. Le commissaire ne leur prête aucune valeur puisque, affirme-t-il, ce dernier aurait pu se procurer de faux documents auprès du réseau de trafiquants qui l'a amené au Canada.[83]

Bien qu'il ne s'agisse pas du seul élément qui discrédite le demandeur d'asile, le recours à un trafiquant mine sa crédibilité de façon importante. Dans *R.H.G. (Re)*,[84] les demandeuses d'asile, une mère et sa fillette de quatre ans, originaires de Chine, sont déboutées "parce qu'elles n'ont pas réussi à établir leur identité."[85] Encore une fois, le recours à un trafiquant ne constitue pas le seul élément qui justifie une décision négative, puisque "de sérieuses incohérences et omissions"[86] jettent un doute sur la crédibilité des demandeuses. Toutefois, l'implication d'un passeur et la disponibilité de documents contrefaits jouent en leur défaveur:

Dans les cas où le demandeur, comme en l'espèce, arrive au Canada avec un faux passeport canadien, sous la direction, sinon la domination, d'un passeur de clandestins, je suis convaincu qu'il revient à la [section de la protection des réfugiés] d'examiner *de manière critique* les autres documents au sujet de l'identité du demandeur et ses réponses à des questions au sujet de ces documents.[87]

Le commissaire examine ensuite les pièces d'identité soumises, notamment le *hukou*, une pièce d'identité délivrée par les autorités chinoises, et la carte d'identité de résident. Il n'accorde aucune "valeur probante" au *hukou*, notamment en raison d'une

---

[82] *Ibid.* au para. 13.

[83] *Ibid.* au para. 11.

[84] *R.H.G. (Re)*, [2006] D.S.P.R. nº 253.

[85] *Ibid.* au para. 4.

[86] *Ibid.* au para. 14.

[87] *Ibid.* au para. 25 [nous soulignons].

irrégularité grave propre au document, mais aussi du recours de la demandeuse à un réseau de passeurs et de la disponibilité de faux documents.[88] Il mentionne à nouveau le recours à un réseau de passeurs pour refuser d'accepter la carte d'identité de résident en tant que pièce d'identité valable.[89]

Dans *P.H.Q. (Re)*,[90] la disponibilité de documents frauduleux fournis par "des organisations criminelles, des agences de voyage [*sic*] et des fonctionnaires ... mêlés de très près au trafic juteux qui consiste à envoyer des gens à l'étranger,"[91] attestée par une preuve documentaire, nuit à la crédibilité du demandeur. En l'espèce, le commissaire décide d'exclure certains documents, notamment un mandat d'arrestation, en raison d'incohérences et de contradictions dans les explications du demandeur.

Dans *P.Z.Y. (Re)*,[92] une ressortissante chinoise dit craindre d'être persécutée parce qu'elle pratique le Falun Gong. Le commissaire estime qu'elle manque de crédibilité puisqu'elle ne peut fournir d'explication satisfaisante quant à sa participation "à l'organisation du mouvement et à l'enseignement de ses principes."[93] Le recours à un passeur discrédite la demandeuse:

> La revendicatrice est arrivée au Canada avec l'aide d'un passeur de clandestins ... Selon son propre témoignage, le passeur lui a donné des instructions ... Les documents [soumis au tribunal] montrent que les passeurs apprennent aux revendicateurs à inventer les détails de leur revendication et à désinformer.[94]

Dans ces quatre décisions, les commissaires considèrent le recours à un trafiquant comme un élément qui entache la crédibilité des demandeurs d'asile. Il ne s'agit pas du principal argument qui justifie le rejet de ces demandes, mais d'un fait qui renforce le manque de crédibilité constaté à la lumière d'autres preuves. Cette situation comporterait néanmoins des conséquences négatives pour le réfugié à qui l'on refuserait la protection internationale pour ce motif et qui pourrait ainsi être renvoyé vers la persécution.

---

88 *Ibid.* au para. 40.

89 *Ibid.* au para. 46.

90 *P.H.Q. (Re)*, [2002] D.S.S.R. n⁰ 434.

91 *Ibid.*, au para. 30.

92 *P.Z.Y. (Re)*, [2001] D.S.S.R. n⁰ 461.

93 *Ibid.* au para. 4.

94 *Ibid.*

En résumé, les commissaires de la CISR ne semblent pas s'inquiéter outre mesure du fait que des individus reconnus coupables de trafic de migrants demeurent au pays, tandis que d'autres trafiquants sont renvoyés sans subir de procès. Par contre, on questionne la crédibilité des demandeurs d'asile ayant eu recours aux services de passeurs pour parvenir au Canada. Ce constat corrobore les impacts différenciés décrits plus haut et tend à confirmer nos inquiétudes quant aux objectifs de la lutte contre le trafic de migrants.

LA PRATIQUE ÉTRANGÈRE: DES LOIS ET JURISPRUDENCES GÉNÉRALEMENT PLUS MESURÉES POUR LES TRAFIQUANTS, MAIS NON POUR LES MIGRANTS

DES LOIS PLUS MESURÉES À L'ÉGARD DES TRAFIQUANTS, MAIS QUI AFFECTENT INDÛMENT LES MIGRANTS

Nous observerons ici les lois française, britannique, américaine et australienne relatives au trafic de migrants. Si elles prévoient des peines maximales mieux proportionnées que la LIPR, l'absence de recherche d'un avantage financier comme élément constitutif de l'infraction connaît des impacts similaires à ceux de la loi canadienne pour les migrants, notamment en France.

Des sanctions maximales généralement inférieures pour les trafiquants

Dans l'ensemble, les lois étrangères prescrivent des sanctions plus basses que la LIPR. Tandis qu'au Canada la peine de prison maximale pour une première infraction impliquant moins de dix personnes — soit dix ans de prison[95] — se compare à ce que prévoient les lois australienne (dix ans),[96] américaine (dix ans)[97] et britannique (quatorze ans),[98] aucune loi étrangère ne sanctionne le trafic d'un groupe de plus de dix personnes par la prison à perpétuité. Une telle peine n'est prévue qu'en cas de mort d'un migrant, aux États-Unis.[99]

---

[95] LIPR, *supra* note 11, art. 117.

[96] Migration Act 1958, art. 233(1)(a) [Migration Act 1958]. Cet article prévoit une pénalité de dix ans d'emprisonnement lorsqu'il s'agit d'un groupe de moins de cinq personnes.

[97] Federal Immigration and Nationality Act, 8 U.S.C. §1324 [Nationality Act].

[98] Immigration Act, R.-U. 1971, *c.* 77, art. 25(1) [Immigration Act 1971].

[99] Nationality Act, *supra* note 97 au 1324(a)(1)(B)(iv).

France

En France, le trafic de migrants constitue une infraction en vertu de l'article L622–1 du Code de l'entrée et du séjour des étrangers et du droit d'asile, qui punit l'aide à l'entrée et au séjour irréguliers par une peine maximale d'emprisonnement de cinq ans et une amende de trente mille euros (un peu plus de 40 500 $ canadiens).[100] En vertu de l'article L622–3, le juge peut imposer des peines complémentaires telles que l'interdiction de séjour en France, la suspension du permis de conduire, la confiscation de la chose qui a servi à commettre l'infraction ainsi que l'interdiction de l'activité professionnelle ou sociale lors de laquelle l'infraction a été commise.[101]

La loi française prévoit cinq facteurs aggravants qui, lorsque constatés, peuvent entraîner jusqu'à dix ans d'emprisonnement et 750 000 euros d'amende (un peu plus d'un million de dollars canadiens). Les facteurs aggravants sont la perpétration de l'infraction en bande organisée, l'exposition de l'étranger à un risque immédiat de mort ou de blessures graves, la soumission de l'étranger à des conditions incompatibles avec la dignité humaine, la commission de l'acte au moyen d'une habilitation de circulation en zone réservée d'un aéroport ou d'un port ainsi que l'éloignement d'un mineur de son milieu familial ou traditionnel.[102] Les peines prescrites par la loi française ne se modulent donc pas en fonction du nombre de migrants trafiqués, mais selon certains facteurs aggravants.

Royaume-Uni

Au Royaume-Uni, le Immigration Act prévoit une peine d'emprisonnement maximale de quatorze ans ou une amende, ou les deux.[103]

---

[100] Code de l'entrée et du séjour des étrangers et du droit d'asile, art. L622–1 [Code de l'entrée et du séjour]: "Toute personne qui aura, par aide directe ou indirecte, facilité ou tenté de faciliter l'entrée, la circulation ou le séjour irréguliers, d'un étranger en France sera punie d'un emprisonnement de cinq ans et d'une amende de 30 000 Euros."

[101] *Ibid.*, art. L622–8.

[102] *Ibid.*, art. L622–5.

[103] Immigration Act 1971, *supra* note 98, art. 25: "*(1) A person commits an offence if he (a) does an act which facilitates the commission of a breach of immigration law by an individual who is not a citizen of the European Union ... (2) In subsection (1) "immigration law" means a law which has effect in a member State and which controls, in respect of some or all persons who are not nationals of the State, entitlement to (a) enter the State, (b) transit across the State, or (c) be in the State."*

La loi ne spécifie aucun facteur aggravant. Toutefois, la division criminelle de la Cour d'appel a identifié certains facteurs à considérer lors du choix de la sentence.[104] Selon ce jugement, la pénalité appropriée pour tous les cas de trafic de migrants est la réclusion, sauf pour les "infractions les plus mineures."[105] Parmi les facteurs aggravants identifiés, notons la recherche d'un avantage financier, des infractions répétées et des condamnations antérieures, le degré de planification, d'organisation et d'élaboration, le nombre de migrants impliqués ainsi que le trafic d'un étranger plutôt que celui d'un époux ou d'un membre de la famille rapprochée. La pénalité maximale prévue par la loi britannique est donc la même pour tout type d'infraction, peu importe le nombre de personnes impliquées ou la présence de facteurs aggravants.

Fait intéressant et unique dans les juridictions examinées, l'article 25A(1) criminalise tout acte facilitant la venue d'une personne qui prétend être un demandeur d'asile commis dans le but d'en tirer un avantage financier.[106] Cette infraction est passible des mêmes peines que le trafic de migrants.

États-Unis

La loi américaine contient deux infractions similaires. Première-ment, lorsqu'on fait entrer un étranger, *peu importe qu'il ait reçu ou non l'autorisation d'entrer aux États-Unis*, à un endroit autre qu'un point d'entrée désigné,[107] la loi prévoit une peine maximale de dix ans d'emprisonnement ou une amende, ou les deux, et ce, pour chaque étranger trafiqué.[108] Pour quiconque transporte ou abrite un étranger en situation irrégulière, ou encourage un étranger à entrer illégalement aux États-Unis, un maximum de cinq ans de prison ainsi qu'une amende sont prévus.[109] Si ces derniers actes sont accomplis dans le but d'en tirer un avantage financier, ce sont

---

[104] *R. v. Le and Stark*, [1999] 1 Cr. App. R. (S) 422 [*Le and Stark*].

[105] *Ibid.*, traduction libre de "most minor offences."

[106] Immigration Act 1971, *supra* note 98, art. 25A.

[107] Nationality Act, *supra* note 97 au 1324(a)(1)(A): "*Any person who (i) knowing that a person is an alien, brings to or attempts to bring to the United States in any manner whatsoever such person at a place other than a designated port of entry or place other than as designated by the Commissioner, regardless of whether such alien has received prior official authorization to come to, enter, or reside in the United States and regardless of any future official action which may be taken with respect to such alien*" [nous soulignons].

[108] *Ibid.* au para. 1324(a)(1)(B)(i).

[109] *Ibid.* aux para. 1324(a)(1)(A)(ii), (iii) et (iv).

plutôt dix ans de prison.[110] Lorsque l'étranger subit des blessures graves ou si sa vie est mise en danger lors d'un de ces actes, la durée maximale de la réclusion augmente à vingt ans tandis que l'empri-sonnement à perpétuité est prescrit en cas de mort.[111]

Deuxièmement, lorsqu'on fait entrer un étranger *qui n'en a pas reçu l'autorisation,* la peine maximale prévue est d'un an de prison ou une amende, ou les deux.[112] Toutefois, selon l'alinéa (a)(2)(B) (iii), lorsque l'étranger n'est pas immédiatement amené devant un agent d'immigration, la pénalité maximale consiste en dix ans de réclusion pour une première ou une seconde infraction.[113] L'alinéa (a)(2)(B)(ii) prévoit que lorsque cet acte est perpétré dans un but lucratif, il existe une peine minimale de trois ans de réclusion ainsi qu'une peine maximale de dix ans pour les deux premières infractions.[114] Pour toute autre infraction supplémentaire à chacun de ces alinéas, la loi prévoit une peine minimale de cinq ans et une peine maximale de quinze ans.[115] Selon les décisions *United States v. Ortega-Torres* et *United States v. Gonzalez-Torres,* chaque étranger trafiqué doit être considéré comme une infraction.[116]

---

[110] *Ibid.* au para. 1324(a)(1)(B)(i).

[111] *Ibid.* aux para. 1324(a)(1)(B)(iii) et (iv).

[112] *Ibid.* au para. 1324(a)(2): "*Any person who, knowing or in reckless disregard of the fact that an alien has not received prior official authorization to come to, enter, or reside in the United States, brings to or attempts to bring to the United States in any manner whatsoever, such alien, regardless of any official action which may later be taken with respect to such alien shall, for each alien in respect to whom a violation of this paragraph occurs (A) be fined in accordance with title 18 or imprisoned not more than one year, or both*" [nous soulignons].

[113] *Ibid.* au para. 1324(a)(2)(B): "*in the case of (i) an offense committed with the intent or with reason to believe that the alien unlawfully brought into the United States will commit an offense against the United States or any State punishable by imprisonment for more than 1 year, (ii) an offense done for the purpose of commercial advantage or private financial gain, or (iii) an offense in which the alien is not upon arrival immediately brought and presented to an appropriate immigration officer at a designated port of entry, be fined under title 18 and shall be imprisoned, in the case of a first or second violation of subparagraph (B)(iii), not more than 10 years, in the case of a first or second violation of subparagraph (B)(i) or (B)(ii), not less than 3 nor more than 10 years, and for any other violation, not less than 5 nor more than 15 years.*"

[114] *Ibid.*

[115] *Ibid.*

[116] *United States v. Ortega-Torres,* [1999] 174 F.3d 1199, 1201 (11e Cir. 1999): "*The use of the terms "each alien" and "violation" together in the introductory sentence of § 1324(a)(2) make clear that courts should count each alien as a separate violation for sentencing purposes.*"; *United States v. Gonzalez-Torres,* [2002] 309 F.3d 594, 601–602

Pour ces deux infractions, la durée de la peine de prison peut être haussée de dix ans s'il y a combinaison de certains éléments, soit (1) lorsque l'infraction *"was part of an ongoing commercial organization or enterprise"*; (2) il s'agit d'un groupe de dix étrangers ou plus; et (3) le transport comportait des risques pour la vie des étrangers, ou les étrangers trafiqués posaient de sérieux risques de santé publique.[117]

La loi américaine prévoit donc des peines relativement sévères. Cependant, les directives émises par le United States Sentencing Commission (USSC), dont la fonction principale est d'élaborer des politiques afin d'assurer l'imposition de sentences cohérentes dans l'ensemble du pays, sont nettement plus clémentes.[118] Ces directives prescrivent des peines d'abord calculées en *offense levels* qui sont ensuite converties en mois d'emprisonnement à l'aide d'une charte. Le *offense level* de base pour l'infraction de trafic de migrants est douze, ce qui correspond à une peine d'emprisonnement variant entre dix et seize mois. Les directives prévoient également des augmentations et diminutions du *offense level* en fonction de certains facteurs. Parmi les circonstances aggravantes, notons un nombre élevé des migrants trafiqués,[119] une condamnation précédente en vertu des dispositions relatives à l'immigration, le trafic d'un mineur non accompagné, l'utilisation ou la possession d'une arme, la présence d'un risque de mort ou de blessures graves lors du trafic, des actes ayant causé la mort ou des blessures graves ainsi que la détention involontaire sous la menace ou la coercition. Le trafic pour une raison autre que le profit et le trafic d'un époux ou d'un enfant constituent les seuls facteurs atténuants.

(9e Cir. 2002): *"The text of the statute unequivocally provides that penalties are to be assessed for "each alien in respect to whom a violation of this paragraph occurs." Nonetheless, Torres alleges that the penalty provision was not intended to apply to "each alien," but rather, was intended to apply to "each conviction." This position is directly contrary to the plain language of the statute and its legislative history."*

[117] *Ibid.* au para. 1324(a)(4).

[118] É.-U., United States Sentencing Commission (USSC), *Guidelines Manual*, novembre 2008, §2L1.1. Ces directives s'appliquent également aux sentences prononcées en vertu de 8 U.S.C. §1327, disposition qui criminalise le trafic de certains étrangers interdits de territoire.

[119] *Ibid.* Tandis que le trafic de cinq migrants ou moins n'entraîne pas d'augmentation du *offense level*, le trafic de six à vingt-quatre migrants correspond un *offense level* de quinze, soit une peine de dix-huit à vingt-quatre mois de prison.

Australie

En Australie, lorsqu'il s'agit de l'entrée clandestine de moins de cinq personnes, l'infraction est punissable, au maximum, de dix ans de prison ou d'une amende de 110 000 $ australiens (environ 102 000 $ canadiens), ou les deux.[120] Si le groupe comprend plus de cinq personnes, la loi prescrit une peine maximale de vingt ans de réclusion ou une amende de 220 000 $ australiens (environ 204 000 $ canadiens), ou les deux.[121] Dans ce cas, l'article 233C du Migration Act prévoit une peine minimale de cinq ans, sans possibilité de libération conditionnelle avant trois ans.[122] La loi australienne ne prévoit aucun facteur aggravant. Ainsi, la peine maximale de prison varie seulement en fonction du nombre de migrants trafiqués.

Tableau 2
COMPARAISON DES PEINES D'EMPRISONNEMENT
MAXIMALES SELON LE NOMBRE DE MIGRANTS TRAFIQUÉS,
POUR UNE PREMIÈRE INFRACTION.[1]

Pays	*Moins de dix personnes*	*Dix personnes ou plus*
Canada	Dix ans	Prison à perpétuité
France	Cinq ans	Cinq ans
Royaume-Uni	Quatorze ans	Quatorze ans
États-Unis	Dix ans (une ou deux personnes)	Quinze ans (trois personnes ou plus)
Australie	Dix ans (moins de cinq personnes)	Vingt ans (cinq personnes ou plus)

1 Pour les États-Unis, les peines indiquées sont celles prévues à l'article 1324(a)(2), puisque cette disposition s'apparente davantage aux infractions créées par les lois canadienne, australienne, française et britannique. La loi américaine prévoit que chaque étranger trafiqué constitue une infraction à la loi. Voir USSC, *supra* note 118.

---

120 Migration Act 1958, *supra* note 96, art. 233(1): "*A person shall not take any part in (a) the bringing or coming to Australia of a non-citizen under circumstances from which it might reasonably have been inferred that the non-citizen intended to enter Australia in contravention of this Act.*"

121 *Ibid.*, art. 232A.

122 *Ibid.*, art. 233C(2) et (3). Cette peine minimale a été ajoutée en 2001 par le Border Protection (Validation and Enforcement Powers) Act, 2001, n° 126.

L'examen du tableau précédent révèle que pour le trafic de moins de dix personnes, seule la loi britannique prévoit une peine plus sévère que la LIPR, tandis que la législation française prescrit une peine inférieure. La même sanction est prévue en Australie et aux États-Unis. Pour le trafic d'un groupe de dix personnes ou plus, seule la LIPR prévoit la réclusion à perpétuité. La loi australienne sanctionne sévèrement cet acte, et les dispositions françaises, britanniques et américaines prévoient respectivement des peines de cinq, quatorze et quinze ans.

Des lois aux effets indus sur les migrants

L'absence de recherche d'un avantage financier en tant qu'élément constitutif de l'infraction

À l'instar de la loi canadienne, les lois étrangères ne font pas de la recherche d'un avantage financier ou matériel un élément constitutif de l'infraction de trafic de migrants, et ce, bien que les cinq pays aient ratifié le Protocole contre le trafic illicite de migrants.[123] Rappelons que la LIPR criminalise tout type de trafic, qu'il ait été commis dans le but d'en tirer un profit ou non. Elle prévoit simplement que le tribunal doit tenir compte de cet aspect lors de l'imposition de la peine.[124] La recherche de profit ne constitue pas non plus un élément de l'infraction dans les lois australienne, française, britannique et américaine. Au Royaume-Uni, elle constitue une composante essentielle uniquement s'il s'agit du trafic de demandeurs d'asile.[125] Sinon, la jurisprudence britannique a fait de cet aspect un facteur aggravant dont le juge doit tenir compte pour déterminer la sentence.[126] La législation américaine prévoit une peine minimale de trois ans de réclusion lorsque l'acte est commis dans le but d'en tirer un avantage financier.[127] La pénalité maximale passe alors d'un an à dix ans d'emprisonnement.[128] Les lois française et australienne demeurent silencieuses à ce sujet.

[123] Nations Unies, Collection des traités, *12 .b Protocole contre le trafic illicite de migrants par terre, air et mer, additionnel à la Convention des Nations Unies contre la criminalité transnationale organisée*, en ligne: Collection des traités <http://www.treaties. un.org/Pages/ViewDetails.aspx?src=TREATY&mtdsg_no=XVIII-12-b&chapter =18&lang=fr&clang=_fr>.

[124] LIPR, *supra* note 11, art. 121(1)(c).

[125] Immigration Act 1971, *supra* note 98, art. 25A.

[126] *Le and Stark, supra* note 104.

[127] Nationality Act, *supra* note 97 au 1324(a)(2)(B).

[128] *Ibid.* au 1324(a)(2).

La législation française contient toutefois une exemption importante qui comble, en partie, cette lacune. Elle prévoit que l'aide au
séjour irrégulier ne peut donner lieu à des poursuites pénales
lorsqu'elle est le fait des ascendants ou descendants de l'étranger
(ou de leur conjoint), des frères et sœurs de l'étranger (ou de leur
conjoint) ou du conjoint de l'étranger.[129] Elle ne peut non plus
donner lieu à des poursuites "lorsque l'acte reproché était, face à
un danger actuel ou imminent, nécessaire à la sauvegarde de la vie
ou de l'intégrité physique de l'étranger," sauf s'il y a disproportion
entre les moyens employés et la menace.[130] Il n'existe aucune
exemption similaire dans les autres pays. Aux États-Unis, aider un
époux ou un enfant ne constitue qu'une circonstance atténuante,[131]
de même que selon la jurisprudence du Royaume-Uni.[132]

La création d'un "délit de solidarité": l'exemple français

En France, malgré l'existence de cette exemption, le "délit de solidarité" suscite plusieurs inquiétudes et débats. Un rapport de
l'Observatoire pour la protection des défenseurs des droits de
l'Homme fait état des craintes ressenties par les défenseurs des
droits des migrants.[133] Ce rapport affirme que:

> Les cas recensés d'arrestations, voire de poursuites, de personnes ayant
> porté assistance à des étrangers en situation irrégulière, soit dans le cadre
> de leur travail associatif soit à titre bénévole, permettent de conclure à
> l'existence en France d'un climat défavorable à la défense des droits des
> étrangers conduisant à une instrumentalisation de la loi à l'encontre des
> associations et des individus actifs dans ce domaine.[134]

Comme au Canada, l'exclusion de la recherche d'avantages financiers ou autres de la définition du trafic de migrants mène à
l'intimidation des organisations humanitaires qui œuvrent auprès

---

[129] Code de l'entrée et du séjour, *supra* note 100, L622–4(1) et (2).

[130] *Ibid.*, art. L622–4(3).

[131] USSC, *supra* note 118 au para. 2L1.1(b)(1).

[132] *Le and Stark, supra* note 104.

[133] Observatoire pour la protection des défenseurs des droits de l'Homme, *Délit de solidarité. Stigmatisation, répression et intimidation des défenseurs des droits des migrants*, (juin 2009), en ligne: Fédération internationale des ligues des droits de l'Homme <http://www.fidh.org/IMG/pdf/obsfra11062009.pdf>.

[134] *Ibid.* à la p. 76.

des migrants. Le Groupe d'information et de soutien des immigrés (GISTI), une association spécialiste du droit des étrangers en France, a d'ailleurs dressé une liste non exhaustive "des condamnations prononcées, depuis 1986, contre des personnes qui ont apporté une aide à des étrangers, la plupart du temps en les hébergeant."[135] On y recense trente-deux cas, entre 1986 et 2008. Cette liste ne contient que les cas de poursuites ayant entraîné une condamnation. Ne sont donc pas inclus les cas de poursuites ayant abouti à un non-lieu ou les simples placements en garde à vue, qui constituent la majorité des cas recensés par le rapport de l'Observatoire pour la protection des défenseurs des droits de l'Homme.[136] Plus récemment, une Française a été accusée d'aider et d'encourager l'immigration illégale pour avoir hébergé son futur mari dont le visa était expiré depuis dix-huit mois.[137] Le GISTI conclut "qu'en France la solidarité est un délit et que ceux qui agissent par humanité peuvent être poursuivis et même condamnés."[138]

Somme toute, les lois étrangères relatives au trafic de migrants contiennent des pénalités maximales relativement moins sévères que la loi canadienne, sans toutefois qu'il n'y ait d'écart important — la législation française mise à part. À l'opposé, un point commun se dégage de la comparaison des lois étrangères et canadienne: l'exclusion de la recherche d'un avantage financier. L'exemple français corrobore les impacts négatifs de cette omission sur les organisations humanitaires qui viennent en aide aux migrants, et conséquemment sur les migrants eux-mêmes.

LA PRATIQUE CONTRASTÉE DES TRIBUNAUX ÉTRANGERS

Dans cette partie, nous confronterons la pratique des tribunaux judiciaires canadiens avec la pratique des tribunaux étrangers. Elles se distinguent de deux façons. D'une part, en Australie, malgré des dispositions similaires pour une infraction impliquant un petit groupe de personnes, les juges imposent des peines plus élevées. D'autre part, la longueur moyenne des peines d'emprisonnement

---

[135] Groupe d'information et de soutien des immigrés, *Délit de solidarité: Besson ment!*, (31 juillet 2009), en ligne: GISTI <http://www.gisti.org/spip.php?article1399>.

[136] Observatoire pour la protection des défenseurs des droits de l'Homme, *supra* note 133 aux pp. 16–17

[137] Migration Policy Group, "Migration News Sheet," (juin 2009) à la p. 8.

[138] Groupe d'information et de soutien des immigrés, *Délit de solidarité: la réalité*, (2009) Plein droit n⁰ 83, Cahier de jurisprudence, II.

en France, au Royaume-Uni et aux États-Unis demeure plus faible qu'au Canada. Néanmoins, les pratiques des tribunaux de ces pays se rapprochent toutes de la pratique canadienne dans la mesure où les peines imposées demeurent largement inférieures à ce que prescrivent les textes législatifs.

Des peines plus sévères en Australie

Tout d'abord, soulignons que le nombre de condamnations pour trafic de migrants en vertu des articles 232A et 233(1)(a) du Migration Act 1958 demeure assez faible. Les statistiques officielles font état de dix-sept condamnations pour les années 2001–02 à 2004–05,[139] et nous avons repéré neuf cas de 2006 à 2009 (qui concernent parfois plusieurs accusés).[140] Tandis que le nombre peu élevé de cas semble indiquer que le trafic illicite de migrants constitue un problème de faible importance en Australie, l'analyse des sentences prononcées à l'encontre des trafiquants dénote une tout autre perception de la part des tribunaux.

Pour les accusations portées en vertu de l'article 233(1)(a), qui s'applique au trafic d'un groupe de moins de cinq personnes et prévoit une peine maximale de dix ans d'emprisonnement,[141] la

---

139 Australia, Commonwealth, Department of Immigration and Multicultural and Indigenous Affairs, *Managing the Border. Immigration Compliance 2004–2005*, Canberra: Australian Government Publishing Service, 2005 [*Australia Managing the Border*].

140 *Chaudhry v. R.*, [2007] WASCA 37 (Supreme Court of Western Australia) [*Chaudhay*]; *R. v. Achmad Olong*, [2008] SCC 20002647 (Northern Territory Supreme Court) [*Achmad Olong*]; Australia, Commonwealth, Australian Embassy in Indonesia, *Indonesian Jailed for People Smuggling*, (6 avril 2009), en ligne: Australian Embassy in Indonesia <http://www.indonesia.embassy.gov.au/jakt/MR09_034.html>; Australia, Commonwealth Director of Public Prosecution, *Annual Report 2006–07*, 2007 aux pp. 29–30; Australia, Commonwealth Director of Public Prosecution, *Annual Report 2005–06*, 2006 aux pp. 29–30; Australia, Commonwealth, Minister for Immigration and Citizenship, *Australia Jails 11 People Smuggler* (9 juillet 2009), en ligne: Minister for Immigration and Citizenship <http://www.minister.immi.gov.au/media/media-releases/2009/ceo9064.htm>; Australia, Commonwealth, Minister for Immigration and Citizenship, *Third People Smuggler Jailed* (18 avril 2009), en ligne: Minister for Immigration and Citizenship <http://www.minister.immi.gov.au/media/media-releases/2009/ceo9036.htm>; Australia, Commonwealth, Minister for Immigration and Citizenship, *Jailing of People Smuggler Sends Strong Message* (16 mars 2009), en ligne: Minister for Immigration and Citizenship <http://www.minister.immi.gov.au/media/media-releases/2009/ceo9025.htm>.

141 Migration Act 1958, *supra* note 96, art. 233(1)(a).

plupart des peines varient de deux à trois ans de réclusion.[142] La peine la plus faible est de deux ans, avec libération après trois mois, pour le trafic de trois personnes.[143] La sentence la plus sévère est de huit ans. Elle se compose de deux peines de quatre ans devant être servies cumulativement, c'est-à-dire l'une à la suite de l'autre.[144] En l'espèce, l'accusé avait participé à la venue d'un non-citoyen dans deux cas distincts.

L'article 232A prévoit une peine maximale de vingt ans d'emprisonnement pour le trafic d'un groupe de cinq personnes ou plus.[145] Rappelons que depuis 2001, l'article 233C requiert une peine minimale de cinq ans pour cette infraction. La plupart des peines prononcées en vertu de cette disposition oscillent de cinq à six ans de réclusion.[146] La sanction la plus faible est de trois ans dans l'affaire *Kadem v. R.* L'accusé avait plaidé coupable d'avoir facilité la

---

[142] *Al-Hashimi v. R.*, [2004] WASCA 61 (Court of Criminal Appeal of Western Australia): deux ans et demi; *Chaudhry, supra* note 140: huit ans de prison; *R. v. Feng Lin*, [2001] NSWCCA 7 (New South Wales Court of Criminal Appeal): trois ans de prison; l'affaire *Subramaniam Karuppiah* citée dans Australia, Commonwealth Director of Public Prosecution, *Annual Report 2006–07, supra* note 140 à la p. 29: deux ans et demi de prison; l'affaire *Logambal Kupusamy*, citée dans Australia, Commonwealth Director of Public Prosecution, *Annual Report 2006–07, supra* note 140 à la p. 30: deux ans de prison avec libération après trois mois.

[143] Australia, Commonwealth Director of Public Prosecution, *Annual Report 2006–07, supra* note 140 à la p. 30.

[144] *Chaudhry, supra* note 140; Australia, Commonwealth Director of Public Prosecution, *Annual Report 2005–06, supra* note 140.

[145] Migration Act 1958, *supra* note 96, art. 232A.

[146] *Asfoor v. R.*, [2005] WASCA 126 (Supreme Court of Western Australia) et Australia, Commonwealth Director of Public Prosecution, *Annual Report 2005–06, supra* note 140 à la p. 27: dix ans de prison; *Cita v. R.*, [2001] WASCA 5 133 (Court of Criminal Appeal of Western Australia) [*Cita*]: cinq et sept ans de prison (deux accusés); *Kadem v. R.*, [2002] WASCA 133 (Court of Criminal Appeal of Western Australia) [*Kadem*]: trois ans de prison. Dans la même affaire, le capitaine du navire a reçu une sentence de sept ans de prison et trois membres d'équipage quatre ans de réclusion chacun (au para. 39); *R. v. Al-Jenabi*, [2004] NTSC 44 (Northern Territory Supreme Court): huit ans d'emprisonnement; *R. v. Daoed*, [2005] QCA 458 (Supreme Court of Queensland) [*Daoed*]: neuf ans d'emprisonnement; *R. v. Disun*, [2003] WASCA 47 (Supreme Court of Western Australia) [*Disun*]: sept et quatre ans de prison (deux accusés); *SRBBBB v. Minister for Immigration and Multicultural and Indigenous Affairs*, [2003] AATA 1066 (Administrative Appeals Tribunal of Australia): trois ans et demi de prison; *SRCCCC v. Minister for Immigration and Multicultural and Indigenous Affairs*, [2004] AATA 315 (Administrative Appeals Tribunal of Australia): trois ans et demi de prison; *SZLDG v. Minister for Immigration and Multicultural and*

venue d'un groupe de 353 immigrants illégaux, dont il faisait partie.[147] La sentence la plus sévère s'élève à dix ans dans l'affaire *Asfoor v. R.*, pour le trafic de plus de huit cent personnes.[148]

Les sentences australiennes sont donc nettement plus élevées que les peines prononcées par les tribunaux canadiens, et ce, malgré des pénalités maximales relativement similaires et un nombre comparable de condamnations. Cette différence s'explique de deux façons.

Une première explication réside dans le nombre parfois très élevé de migrants impliqués dans les opérations de trafic. Un rapide examen des affaires où des accusations ont été portées en vertu de l'article 232A dévoile des chiffres étonnants. Dans l'affaire *Asfoor*, il s'agit de plus de huit cent migrants.[149] Dans *Cita v. R.*, Cita et son co-accusé sont reconnus coupables, respectivement, du trafic de 282 et 180 migrants.[150] Dans *Kadem v. R.*, il s'agit du trafic de 353 personnes.[151] Dans *R. v. Daoed*, l'accusé a participé à la venue de plus de quatre cent migrants, dont plusieurs sont morts noyés.[152] Dans *R. v. Disun*, 433 migrants tentaient de parvenir en Australie.[153] Dans *R. v. Achmad Olong*, l'accusé a facilité la venue de plus de 350 individus.[154] Malgré un faible nombre d'opérations de trafic de migrants, chacune concerne souvent des dizaines, voire des centaines

---

Indigenous Affairs, [2008] FCA 11 (Federal Court of Australia): huit ans d'emprisonnement; *Achmad Olong*, *supra* note 140: cinq ans de prison; l'affaire *Loe* citée dans Australia, Commonwealth Director of Public Prosecution, *Annual Report 2001–02*, 2002 à la p. 66: six ans d'emprisonnement; l'affaire *Mehmet Seriban* citée dans Australia, Commonwealth Director of Public Prosecution, *Annual Report 2005–06*, *supra* note 140 aux pp. 29–30: cinq ans et demi de prison; l'affaire *Man Pombili*, citée dans Australia, *Third People Smuggler Jailed*, *supra* note 140: six ans de prison; l'affaire *Abdul Hamid* citée dans Australia, *Jailing of People Smuggler Sends Strong Message*, *supra* note 140: six ans de prison; l'affaire *Amosh Ndolo* citée dans Australia, *Indonesian Jailed for People Smuggling*, *supra* note 140: cinq ans d'emprisonnement; l'affaire des onze Indonésiens citée dans Australia, *Australia Jails 11 People Smuggler*, *supra* note 140: cinq ans de prison (huit accusés) et cinq ans et demi (trois accusés).

147 *Kadem*, *supra* note 146.

148 Australia, *Annual Report 2005–06*, *supra* note 140 à la p. 27.

149 *Ibid.*

150 *Cita*, *supra* note 146.

151 *Kadem*, *supra* note 146.

152 *Daoed*, *supra* note 146.

153 *Disun*, *supra* note 146.

154 *Achmad Olong*, *supra* note 140.

d'individu. L'utilisation de bateaux, fréquente pour atteindre ce pays géographiquement isolé, permet le trafic de groupes aussi grands.[155] En comparaison, les opérations de trafic de migrants au Canada concernent rarement plus de cent migrants. Il s'agit plus fréquemment de quelques dizaines de migrants trafiqués en plusieurs épisodes.[156]

Une seconde explication se trouve dans la loi. En effet, depuis 2001, quiconque est reconnu coupable d'une infraction aux termes de l'article 232A du Migration Act encourt une peine minimale de cinq ans d'emprisonnement.[157] Ce durcissement à l'égard du trafic de migrants s'inscrit dans une politique défavorable à l'immigration, progressivement mise en place depuis 1989 en réaction au nombre grandissant de *boat people* tentant de rejoindre les côtes australiennes.[158] L'incident du MV *Tampa*, en 2001, a nourri cette hostilité envers l'immigration en donnant lieu à l'adoption de plusieurs lois visant à renforcer le contrôle des frontières — et, incidemment, diminuer les droits des étrangers.[159] Cette tendance, dans laquelle

---

[155] Australia, Commonwealth, Department of Immigration and Citizenship, "Fact sheet 73—People Smuggling" (20 mai 2009), en ligne: Department of Immigration and Citizenship <http://www.immi.gov.au/media/fact-sheets/73smuggling.htm>; *Australia Managing the Border, supra* note 139 à la p. 27 et s.

[156] Voir Tableau 1 et Jimenez Calvo, *supra* note 16 aux pp. 330–31.

[157] Migration Act 1958, *supra* note 96, art.233C; Border Protection (Validation and Enforcement Powers) Act, *supra* note 122, Schedule 2 — Amendment of the Migration Act 1958.

[158] Jennifer Hyndman et Alison Mountz, "Another Brick in the Wall? Neo-*Refoulement* and the Externalization of Asylum by Australia and Europe" (2008) 43 Government and Opposition aux pp. 249 et 256; Pierre-Olivier Savoie et Olivia Le Fort, "Quel habeas corpus pour les demandeurs d'asile? Le Canada, les États-Unis, la Suisse et l'Australie face à leurs obligations internationales" dans Daniel Dormoy et Habib Slim, dir., *Réfugiés, immigration clandestine et centres de rétention des immigrés clandestins en droit international* (Bruxelles: Éditions de l'Université de Bruxelles, 2008) à la p. 93.

[159] Savoie et le Fort, *supra* note 158 à la p. 94. En août 2001, un navire norvégien, le MV *Tampa*, vient au secours d'un groupe de 433 demandeurs d'asile provenant d'Afghanistan et du Sri Lanka dont le vaisseau, battant pavillon indonésien, commence à sombrer. Bien qu'en eaux territoriales australiennes, le gouvernement australien refuse d'accueillir ces demandeurs d'asile et engage des discussions avec l'Indonésie et la Norvège. Devant le refus du capitaine du MV Tampa de faire demi-tour, le gouvernement australien charge l'armée de s'emparer du navire. Les demandeurs d'asile seront finalement dirigés vers Nauru et la Nouvelle-Zélande. Voir Andreas Schloenhardt, *Migrant Smuggling: Illegal Migration and Organised Crime in Australia and the Asia Pacific Region* (Boston: Martinus Nijhoff, 2003) aux pp. 84–85.

s'inscrit la peine d'emprisonnement minimale de cinq ans pour les trafiquants, trouverait-elle sa source dans l'absence de charte protégeant les droits fondamentaux?

Des sentences inférieures en France, aux États-Unis et au Royaume-Uni

Comparativement, en France, au Royaume-Uni et aux États-Unis, les peines demeurent généralement plus faibles qu'au Canada.

France

Parmi la jurisprudence de la Chambre criminelle de la Cour de cassation étudiée, la majorité des peines varient entre dix mois et trois ans, mais sanctionnent fréquemment d'autres crimes, tels que la production de faux documents.[160] La peine d'emprisonnement

---

[160] Cass. crim., 13 mai 2009, n° 08–84.074: sept ans de prison et interdiction définitive de territoire; Cass. crim., 1er avril 2009, n° 08–85.979: dix-huit mois d'emprisonnement; Cass. crim., 18 mars 2009, n° 08–85.119: trois mille euros d'amende et deux ans d'interdiction d'exercer la profession d'avocat; Cass. crim., 17 mars 2009, n° 08–84.226: un an de prison et 7500 euros d'amende; Cass. crim., 21 janvier 2009, n° 08–82.460: un an de prison et trois ans d'interdiction de territoire; Cass. crim., 9 octobre 2007, n° 06–89.439: quatre mois de prison; Cass. crim., 7 mars 2009, n° 06–83.435: cinq ans d'emprisonnement et cent mille euros d'amende; Cass. crim., 11 janvier 2006, n° 05–83.995: sept ans de prison et cinquante mille euros d'amende; Cass. crim., 28 septembre 2005, n° 04–84.584: quatre ans de prison, quinze mille euros d'amende et dix ans d'interdiction de territoire; Cass. crim., 24 mai 2005, n° 04–86.343: deux ans de prison et quarante-cinq mille euros d'amende; Cass. crim., 6 octobre 2004, n° 03–86.556: trois ans de prison et trois ans d'interdiction des droits civiques; Cass. crim., 31 mars 2004, n° 03–84.979: quatre mois de prison; Cass. crim., 18 février 2004, n° 03–85.291: dix-huit mois de prison; Cass. crim., 21 janvier 2004, n° 03–80.328: deux ans de prison et deux ans d'interdiction professionnelle; Cass. crim., 10 décembre 2003, n° 03–80.328: quatre ans de prison et dix ans d'interdiction de territoire; Cass. crim., 13 novembre 2003, n° 03–83.359: deux ans de prison et trois mille euros d'amende; Cass. crim., 30 septembre, n° 02–83.183: dix mois de prison; Cass. crim., 15 janvier 2003, n° 02–81.008: neuf mois de prison et dix ans d'interdiction de territoire; Cass. crim., 4 décembre 2002, n° 02–83.381: trois ans de prison, quinze mille euros d'amende et sept ans d'interdiction de territoire; Cass. crim., 8 octobre 2002, n° 01–88.421: un mois de prison et dix mille francs d'amende; Cass. crim., 11 septembre 2002, n° 02–80.654: trois ans de prison et trois ans d'interdiction; Cass. crim., 26 juin 2002, n° 01–88.445: cinq mois de prison; Cass. crim., 30 avril 2002, n° 01–85.106: quatre mois de prison et quinze mille francs d'amende; Cass. crim., 28 février 2001, n° 00–81.597: quatre ans de prison, quinze mille francs d'amende et dix ans d'interdiction de territoire; Cass. crim., 27 février 2001, n° 00–84.284: six mois de prison et vingt mille francs d'amende.

Tableau 3

LES SENTENCES IMPOSÉES POUR AIDE À L'ENTRÉE ET AU SÉJOUR
IRRÉGULIERS EN FRANCE, 2000 À 2006.

Années	*2000*	*2001*	*2002*	*2003*	*2004*	*2005*	*2006*
Condamnations (n)	4153	4250	4940	5884	4847	4454	4564
Peines de prison (n)	3121	3222	3651	4241	3856	3636	3694
Proportion des peines de prison (%)	75.1	75.8	73.9	72.1	79.6	81.6	80.9
Sentence moyenne (mois)	5.7	6.5	5.8	6.1	6	6.2	6
Amendes (n)	109	104	129	120	151	132	188
Proportion d'amendes (%)	2.6	2.5	2.6	2	3.1	3	4.1
Amende moyenne (euros)	813	800	1092	883	798	964	959
Interdictions de territoire (n)	848	845	1054	1401	683	558	547
Proportion des interdictions de territoire (%)	20.4	19.9	21.3	23.8	14.1	12.5	11.9

la plus élevée est de sept ans, assortie à une interdiction définitive
de territoire, pour aide à l'entrée et au séjour irréguliers en bande
organisée.[161] La sanction la plus faible est un mois d'emprisonnement et dix mille francs d'amende.[162]

À première vue, la jurisprudence de la Cour de cassation révèle
une action judiciaire plus sévère qu'au Canada. Constat que démen-
tent toutefois les statistiques officielles.[163]

D'abord, la peine d'emprisonnement moyenne pour aide à l'entrée ou au séjour irréguliers varie entre 5,7 et 6,5 mois pour les
années 2000 à 2006, ce qui est clairement inférieur aux cinq ans
prévus par la loi.[164] La prison est imposée dans une proportion de
cas qui tend à augmenter depuis 2004, mais qui dépasse peu la
barre des 80 %. Ensuite, si à la lecture de la jurisprudence de la

---

[161] Cass. crim., 13 mai 2009, n° 08–84.074.

[162] Cass. crim., 8 octobre 2002, n° 01–88.421.

[163] France, Ministère de la Justice, *Annuaire statistique de la justice Édition 2008*, La
Documentation française, (2009) aux pp. 199–200; France, Ministère de la
Justice, *Annuaire statistique de la justice Édition 2006*, La Documentation fran-
çaise, (2006) aux pp. 197–98.

[164] Code de l'entrée et du séjour, *supra* note 100.

Cour de cassation l'imposition d'amende semble plus fréquente qu'au Canada, elle ne concerne qu'entre 2% et 4,1% de cas. L'amende moyenne varie entre 798 et 1092 euros. Enfin, les tribunaux accompagnent souvent les sanctions d'une interdiction de territoire, mais semblent y recourir de moins en moins fréquemment.

États-Unis

Les statistiques compilées par le USSC offrent un tableau assez complet des peines imposées pour le trafic de migrants par les tribunaux fédéraux américains.[165]

Tableau 4

LES SENTENCES MOYENNES ET MÉDIANES D'EMPRISONNEMENT
PRONONCÉES EN VERTU DE 8 U.S.C. §§1324 ET 1327,
AUX ÉTATS-UNIS, 2001 À 2008.

Année	Nombre de cas	Sentence moyenne (mois)	Sentence médiane (mois)
2001	1694	13.5	12
2002	1700	14.3	12
2003	2208	14.8	12
2004	1566	16.3	12.7
2004 post *Blakely*	713	14.8	14
2005	848	15	13
2005 post *Booker*	2304	15.6	12
2006	3433	15.9	12
2007	3352	16.1	13
2008	3522	16.3	13

[165] É.-U., United States Sentencing Commission, *Sourcebook of Federal Sentencing Statistics, Table 50—Mean and Median Sentences of Offenders Sentenced under Immigration Guidelines by Departure Status*, (2001–2008), en ligne: United States Sentencing Commission <http://www.ussc.gov/annrpts.htm>. Le 24 juin 2004, dans l'affaire *Blakely v. Washington*, [2004] 542 U.S. 296, la Cour suprême des États-Unis invalide une sentence imposée en vertu de la loi de l'État de Washington créant des directives d'imposition de peines (*sentencing guidelines*). L'imposition d'une peine plus élevée en vertu de cette loi viole le droit à un procès devant jury prévu par le sixième amendement. Cette décision a été appliquée à l'affaire *United States v. Booker*, [2005] 543 U.S. 220, le 12 janvier 2005, où la

La peine d'emprisonnement moyenne oscille entre 13,5 mois et 16,8 mois et tend à augmenter, de même que le nombre de cas. Ces données sont nettement inférieures aux peines maximales prescrites par la loi.[166] De plus, de 2001 jusqu'à 2009, les sentences moyennes sont presque systématiquement plus faibles que ce que prescrivent les directives.[167] Notons que la sentence médiane ne varie presque pas, ce qui démontre que les sentences prononcées demeurent similaires au fil des ans. L'augmentation de la moyenne indiquerait alors que de plus en plus de cas graves de trafic, caractérisés par des circonstances aggravantes, sont découverts.

Royaume-Uni

L'examen de la jurisprudence de la division criminelle de la Cour d'appel de 2001 à 2009 indique que la longueur de la majorité des peines d'emprisonnement varie entre dix mois et quatre ans et demi.[168] La peine de prison la plus courte est de deux

---

même instance détermine que l'application obligatoire des directives fédérales viole le droit prévu par le sixième amendement. Pour remédier à cette situation, elle invalide les dispositions prévoyant l'application obligatoire des directives qui deviennent ainsi simplement consultatives. Voir É.-U., United States Sentencing Commission, *2005 Sourcebook of Federal Sentencing Statistics*, (sans date), en ligne: United States Sentencing Commission <http://www.ussc.gov/ANNRPT/2005/SBTOC05.htm>.

[166] Nationality Act, *supra* note 97 au para. 1324.

[167] É.-U., United States Sentencing Commission, *Preliminary Quarterly Data Report*, 2009 à la p. 35; É.-U., United States Sentencing Commission, *Final Quarterly Data Report, Fiscal Year 2006*, 2007 à la p. 34.

[168] *R. v. Aras*, [2005] EWCA Crim 3617: douze mois et quatre ans et demi de prison (deux accusés); *R. v. Daloub*, [2007] EWCA Crim 2373: deux ans et demi de prison; *R. v. Dickinson*, [2001] EWCA Crim 1114: deux ans et demi, quatre ans et demi, trois ans de prison (trois accusés); *R. v. Green*, [2006] EWCA Crim 990: vingt-sept mois de prison; *R. v. Haismand and Others*, [2003] ECWA Crim 2246: un an, quatre ans de prison (deux accusés); *R. v. Javahrifard & R. v. Miller*, [2005] ECWA Crim 3231: trois ans de prison; *R. v. Kalonga*, [2004] ECWA Crim 1250: huit mois de prison; *R. v. Loja*, [2007] ECWA Crim 106: trois ans et demi de prison; *R. v. Mall*, [2004] ECWA Crim 585: cinq ans de prison; *R. v. Patel*, [2007] ECWA Crim 184: quatre ans de prison; *R. v. Sackey*, [2004] ECWA Crim 556: deux ans de prison; *R. v. Saini, R. v. Kalyan & R. v. Deo*, [2004] ECWA Crim 1900: sept ans et demi, quatre ans, trois ans et demi (trois accusés); *R. v. Shahzad*, [2006] ECWA Crim 3064: vingt mois de réclusion; *R. v. Singh*, [2005] ECWA Crim 2126 [*Singh*]: neuf mois, quatre ans, deux mois de prison (trois accusés); *R. v. Tipu and Another*, [2006] ECWA Crim 1859: huit ans, quatre ans (deux accusés); *R. v. Torto*, [2006] ECWA Crim 2268: sept ans de prison; *R. v. Tsepnis*, [2004] ECWA Crim 229: deux ans de prison; *R. v. Ulcay & R. v. Toygun*, [2007]

Tableau 5
LES SENTENCES D'EMPRISONNEMENT IMPOSÉES
POUR ASSISTANCE À L'ENTRÉE D'UN IMMIGRANT ILLÉGAL PAR LES
MAGISTRATES' COURTS (MC) ET LE *CROWN'S COURT* (CC),
EN ANGLETERRE ET AU PAYS-DE-GALLES, 2001 À 2007.[1]

Années	*2001*	*2002*	*2003*	*2004*	*2005*	*2006*	*2007*
Sentences MC-CC (n)	258	449	379	419	810	860	564
Sentences d'emprison-nement MC-CC (n)	220	390	333	363	756	793	497
Proportion de sentences d'emprisonnement MC-CC (%)	85.3	86.9	87.9	86.6	93.3	92.2	88
Moyenne des sentences d'emprisonnement MC-CC (mois)	14.1	13.1	12.5	13.5	9.6	7.4	7
Sentences d'emprison-nement MC (n)	80	121	55	51	309	463	259
Moyenne des sentences d'emprisonnement MC (mois)	3	3	5	5	3.4	3	3.3
Sentences d'emprison-nement CC (n)	130	269	278	312	447	330	238
Moyenne des sentences d'emprisonnement CC (mois)	22	16	14	15	13.9	13	11

1 Ces données n'incluent pas les sentences prononcées en Écosse et en Irlande du Nord.

mois[169] tandis que la plus longue est de douze ans.[170] Ces données sont globalement similaires aux sanctions imposées par les tribunaux canadiens. Cependant, les statistiques officielles révèlent un tout autre portrait.[171]

ECWA Crim 2379 [*Ulcay & Toygun*]: douze ans et sept ans de prison (deux accusés); *R. v. Uluc*, [2001] ECWA Crim 2991: dix-huit mois de prison; *R. v. Vaitekunas*, [2006] ECWA Crim 2922: deux ans, deux ans et demi (deux accusés); *R. v. Vuemba-Luzamba*, [2006] ECWA Crim 579: quatorze mois, seize mois (deux accusés); *R. v. Woop*, [2002] ECWA Crim 58: cinq ans de prison.

169 *Singh, supra* note 168.

170 *Ulcay & Toygun, supra* note 168.

171 R.-U., Home Office, *Criminal Statistics, England and Wales, 2005, Supplementary Tables, Volume 2, Persons sentenced to immediate custody at the crown court by sex, length*

Malgré une augmentation de la peine maximale pour trafic de migrants[172] et une hausse considérable du nombre de condamnations, nous constatons, de 2001 à 2007, une baisse de la longueur

of sentence and average sentence length, 2007, en ligne: Home Office <http://www. homeoffice.gov.uk/rds/crimstats05.html>; R.-U., Home Office, *Criminal Statistics, England and Wales, 2005, Supplementary Tables, Volume 1, Persons sentenced to immediate custody at magistrates' courts by sex, length of sentence and average sentence length*, 2007, en ligne: Home Office <http://www.homeoffice.gov.uk/rds/ crimstats05.html>; R.-U., Home Office, *Criminal Statistics, England and Wales, 2005, Supplementary Tables, Volume 5, Proceedings at all Courts*, 2007, en ligne: Home Office <http://www.homeoffice.gov.uk/rds/crimstats05.html>; R.-U., Home Office, *Criminal Statistics, England and Wales, 2004, Supplementary Tables, Volume 5, Proceedings at all courts*, 2005, en ligne: Home Office <http://www. homeoffice.gov.uk/rds/crimstats04.html>; R.-U., Home Office, *Criminal Statistics, England and Wales, 2004, Supplementary Tables, Volume 2, Persons sentenced to immediate custody at the Crown Court by offense, sex, length of sentence and average sentence length*, 2005, en ligne: Home Office <http://www.homeoffice.gov.uk/ rds/crimstats04.html>; R.-U., Home Office, *Criminal Statistics, England and Wales, 2004, Supplementary Tables, Volume 1, Persons sentenced to immediate custody at magistrates' courts by sex, length of sentence and average sentence length*, 2005, en ligne: Home Office <http://www.homeoffice.gov.uk/rds/crimstats04.html>; R.-U., Home Office, *Criminal Statistics, England and Wales, 2003, Supplementary Tables, Volume 2, Persons sentenced to immediate custody at the Crown Court by offense, sex, length of sentence and average sentence length & Annex A*, 2004, en ligne: Home Office <http://www.homeoffice.gov.uk/rds/crimstats03.html>; R.-U., Home Office, *Criminal Statistics, England and Wales, 2003, Supplementary Tables, Volume 1, Persons sentenced to immediate custody at magistrates' courts by sex, length of sentence and average sentence length*, 2004, en ligne: Home Office <http://www. homeoffice.gov.uk/rds/crimstats03.html>; R.-U., Home Office, *Criminal Statistics, England and Wales, 2002, Supplementary Tables, Volume 2, Persons sentenced to immediate custody at the Crown Court by offense, sex, length of sentence and average sentence length & Annex A*, 2003, en ligne: Home Office <http://www.homeoffice.gov. uk/rds/crimstats02.html>; R.-U., Home Office, *Criminal Statistics, England and Wales, 2002, Supplementary Tables, Volume 1, Persons sentenced to immediate custody at magistrates' courts by sex, length of sentence and average sentence length*, 2003, en ligne: Home Office <http://www.homeoffice.gov.uk/rds/crimstats02.html>; R.-U., Home Office, *Criminal Statistics, England and Wales, Supplementary Tables 2001 Vol. 1, Proceedings in magistrates' court*, London, National Statistics, 2002; R.-U., Home Office, *Criminal Statistics, England and Wales, Supplementary Tables 2001 Vol. 2, Proceedings in the Crown Court*, London, National Statistics, 2002; R.-U., Ministry of Justice, *Criminal Statistics annual report (NS)*, 31 juillet 2009, en ligne: Ministry of Justice <http://www.justice.gov.uk/publications/criminal annual.htm>; R.-U., Ministry of Justice, *Criminal statistics annual report (NS) 2006, Volume 5, Proceedings at all courts*, 1er avril 2009, en ligne: Ministry of Justice <http://www.justice.gov.uk/publications/criminalannual2006.htm>.

[172] De sept à dix ans en 1999 et de dix à quatorze ans en 2002: *Immigration and Asylum Act* (R-U.), 1999, *c. 33*, art. 29; *Nationality, Immigration and Asylum Act* (R.-U.), 2002, *c. 41*, art. 143.

moyenne des peines de réclusion, qui diminue de 14,1 mois à sept mois. Cette diminution correspond à une baisse de la longueur moyenne des peines d'emprisonnement imposées par le *Crown's Court*, qui diminue de moitié, de vingt-deux mois à onze mois. Ces données sont clairement inférieures à la peine maximale de réclusion — quatorze ans — prévue par la loi. Notons également une augmentation du nombre de causes entendues par les *magistrates' courts*, qui, contrairement au *Crown's Court*, s'occupent d'infractions mineures.[173] La durée moyenne des sentences d'emprisonnement prononcées par cette instance reste relativement stable, sauf pour les années 2003 et 2004. La proportion de sentences d'emprisonnement imposées augmente légèrement.

Bref, les sentences prononcées par les tribunaux français, états-uniens et britanniques sont inférieures à celles imposées par les juges canadiens. Pourtant, les condamnations pour trafic de migrants se comptent par milliers dans ces pays pour la période 2001–09, contrairement à seize au Canada. Il apparaît paradoxal que des peines plus sévères soient imposées là où le trafic semble constituer un problème de moindre importance. S'agirait-il de différences entre les types de trafic de migrants qui affectent d'un côté le Canada, et ces trois pays de l'autre? Les opérations de trafic vers le Canada exigeraient-elles un plus haut degré de perfectionnement que le trafic vers la France, les États-Unis ou l'Angleterre, ce qui en ferait un crime appelant des pénalités plus sévères? Malheureusement, les faits contenus dans les décisions de la Cour de cassation française et de la division criminelle de la Cour d'appel du Royaume-Uni examinées plus haut ne sauraient être représentatifs des opérations de trafic dans ces pays, puisque les peines prononcées par ces instances sont beaucoup plus élevées que la moyenne de l'ensemble des tribunaux. Nous ne pouvons donc les utiliser pour dresser un portrait fidèle du trafic de migrants vers ces pays et le comparer avec les opérations de trafic au Canada.

En définitive, la comparaison des décisions des tribunaux canadiens et étrangers révèle une pratique contrastée. D'une part, les magistrats australiens imposent des peines plus élevées qu'au Canada. D'autre part, les juges de la France, du Royaume-Uni et des

---

[173] La juridiction des *Magistrates' Court* se limite aux délits mineurs dont les sanctions sont inférieures à six mois d'emprisonnement ou cinq mille livres d'amende. Voir R.-U., Her Majesty's Courts Service, *Magistrates and Magistrates' Court*, 2 avril 2009, en ligne: Her Majesty's Courts Service <http://www.hmcourts-service.gov.uk/infoabout/magistrates/index.htm>.

États-Unis prononcent des sentences nettement moindres. En regard du nombre de condamnations, ce constat est contradictoire dans la mesure où les condamnations pour trafic de migrants se comptent par milliers dans ces trois pays, alors qu'il est plutôt faible au Canada et en Australie. La pratique des tribunaux canadiens correspond toutefois à la pratique des tribunaux étrangers dans la mesure où les juges infligent des peines franchement inférieures à ce que prévoit la loi.

CONCLUSION

En conclusion, les dispositions de la LIPR ne correspondent pas au droit international, qui requiert la recherche d'un avantage financier ou matériel pour qualifier le trafic de migrants d'infraction criminelle. Elles ne sont pas appliquées par les tribunaux canadiens qui prononcent des sentences bien en deçà des sanctions maximales. À l'étranger, les lois prévoient des peines maximales inférieures, et la pratique des tribunaux, bien que contrastée, demeure généralement plus clémente qu'au Canada. À la lumière de ces constats, des modifications législatives s'avèrent nécessaires.

D'abord, la définition de l'infraction devrait inclure la recherche d'un avantage financier ou matériel, dans le but d'éviter la criminalisation du personnel des organisations d'aide aux migrants et aux demandeurs d'asile. Ensuite, les peines maximales devraient être revues à la baisse afin de refléter la gravité réelle du crime. De plus, l'échelle de peines ne devrait pas se moduler uniquement selon le nombre de migrants trafiqués, mais en fonction de circonstances aggravantes telles que la présence de dangers pour la vie ou la santé des migrants, la soumission des migrants à des conditions dégradantes ou inhumaines, l'infliction de blessures, l'utilisation ou la possession d'arme ainsi que l'implication d'une organisation criminelle. Enfin, l'ajout de peines complémentaires permettrait d'adapter les sentences imposées aux circonstances particulières des différents incidents. Ainsi, la loi serait conséquente avec la pratique des tribunaux canadiens et les standards internationaux, tout en répondant aux besoins de répression et de dissuasion lorsque l'infraction comporte des circonstances qui appellent une sanction plus sévère. Le recours à des sanctions excessives pour punir le trafic de migrants reflète moins le désir de lutter contre une forme dangereuse de criminalité organisée — ce qui justifierait de telles peines — que celui de contribuer à dissuader l'immigration irrégulière. Ce type de mesures comporte des conséquences néfastes pour les migrants et les réfugiés qui, face au resserrement des politiques migratoires, doivent emprunter des routes toujours plus risquées.

Summary

Comparative Jurisprudential Treatment of Migrant Smuggling: A Disavowal of Canadian Legislation

The tightening of migration policies has resulted in a decrease in the legal opportunities for migration, thus fostering migrant smuggling. In 2002, Canada drastically increased the penalties associated with this phenomenon. These provisions are inadequate: they aim at preventing irregular migration rather than suppressing an alleged serious criminal activity. On the one hand, these provisions do not match the jurisprudential treatment of migrant smuggling in Canada and are inconsistent with foreign legislation and jurisprudence — the gravity of the crime is overrated. On the other hand, they are not in conformity with international law. By excluding the seeking of financial benefit from the definition of the prohibited activity, the legislation targets any form of help to undocumented migrants rather than specifically targeting migrant smuggling.

Sommaire

Le traitement jurisprudentiel du trafic de migrants en droit comparé: Un désaveu des dispositions législatives canadiennes

Le durcissement des politiques migratoires a diminué les possibilités légales de migration, créant ainsi un environnement propice au trafic de migrants. En 2002, le Canada a drastiquement augmenté les pénalités associées à ce phénomène. Ces dispositions sont inadéquates: elles cherchent moins à réprimer une activité criminelle présumée dangereuse qu'à dissuader l'immigration irrégulière. D'une part, les dispositions législatives s'inscrivent en faux avec le traitement jurisprudentiel du trafic de migrants au Canada, et ne correspondent ni aux lois ni à la jurisprudence étrangères: on surestime la gravité du crime. D'autre part, elles ne se conforment pas au droit international. En excluant la recherche d'un avantage financier de la définition canadienne de l'infraction, on privilégie la lutte à toute forme d'aide à la migration irrégulière, et non seulement au trafic de migrants.

Where Precision Is the Aim: Locating the Targeted Killing Policies of the United States and Israel within International Humanitarian Law

MICHAEL ELLIOT

INTRODUCTION

As a body of law, the purpose of which is to regulate an undertaking as varied, pervasive, and grave as warfare, international humanitarian law inevitably faces challenges. Currently, one of those challenges is the incorporation and treatment of terrorism within the existing framework. Although not a new phenomenon, in the last decade terrorism, and its place within international humanitarian law, has gained an increased focus and, with that, a new significance. In particular, the responses of Israel and the United States to the terrorist threat have underlined the difficulties posed by terrorism to international humanitarian law as well as the importance of resolving them.

The problems that terrorism creates for international humanitarian law are considerable, and it is beyond the scope of this article to address them all. Rather, this article will focus on the increasing resort to targeted killing as a state response. As international humanitarian law now stands, the lawfulness of targeted killing in this context remains unclear. What is clear is that targeted killing, persistently practised by both the United States and Israel, demands attention within the existing framework of international humanitarian law if that law is to remain relevant and effective in this context. This article will therefore consider two issues: whether targeted killing in the context of state responses to terrorism should be recognized as lawful under international humanitarian law and, if it should, how this recognition is to be achieved.

Michael Elliot is an LL.B. candidate at Dalhousie Law School in Halifax. The author is very grateful to William Fenrick for his encouragement and assistance in the writing of this article.

99

In an attempt to respond adequately to these issues, it is necessary to have an understanding of the context in which the targeted killing policies of Israel and the United States are pursued. The first part of this article will therefore examine what terrorism encompasses and some of the fundamental problems that it presents to international humanitarian law. As will be shown, the problems are considerable and have led some to demand that a new legal regime be constructed to govern state-terrorist conflicts. The second part will focus on targeted killing and how it is defined. It will also look at the current policies of targeted killing operated by Israel and the United States. The third part will then attempt to show how targeted killing fits within international humanitarian law. More specifically, it will demonstrate that in this context, as international humanitarian law currently stands, targeted killing is neither explicitly lawful nor explicitly unlawful.

The fourth part of this article focuses on the issue of whether targeted killing should be recognized as lawful under international humanitarian law. This article will argue that there are strong reasons why it should be. These take into account the fact that targeted killing can provide states with an effective means of combating terrorism; that states are currently engaging in targeted killing; that targeted killing can militate against certain objectionable consequences of the present application of international humanitarian law in the context of state-terrorist conflicts; and that targeted killing accords with the underlying principles of this body of law.

Having established that international humanitarian law should recognize targeted killing as lawful, the fifth part of the article will proceed to examine how such recognition should be achieved. It will do so by studying the 2006 Supreme Court of Israel decision in *Public Committee against Torture in Israel v. the Government of Israel* (*PCATI* case) as an example of an attempt to fit targeted killing in the context of state-terrorist conflicts within the existing legal framework.[1] In particular, it will consider two aspects of the court's judgment: (1) its categorization of terrorists; and (2) its imposition of the "least harmful means" requirement. It will argue that the former exposes the problems that accompany recognizing targeted killing as lawful by interpreting the prevailing legal rules in such a way as to tailor them to the context. It will further argue that the latter, in resorting to an underlying principle of international

---

1 *Public Committee against Torture in Israel et al. v. Government of Israel et al.*, Case no. HCJ 769/02, 13 December 2006 [*PCATI* case].

humanitarian law and adapting its articulation to the particular circumstances in which targeted killing occurs, presents the preferable means by which to recognize targeted killing as lawful in state-terrorist conflicts.

TERRORISM AND INTERNATIONAL HUMANITARIAN LAW

TERRORISM AS A CONCEPT

Terrorism, insofar as it refers to groups using violence to achieve political objectives, is not a new concept.[2] The French Revolution and even Britain's Glorious Revolution would arguably qualify as examples, and there are certainly many others.[3] Moreover, since at least the 1920s, many states have recognized terrorism to be a transnational problem.[4] In the last forty years, however, terrorism has substantially increased at least in scale, if not in frequency.[5] This increase may be attributed to a number of factors. The growth of mass media has facilitated terrorists' ability to attract widely based publicity.[6] Resources have become more readily available, which has led to terrorist organizations being able to exist on a significantly larger scale.[7] Moreover, while the underlying causes, particularly ideology, remain largely the same, they may now be spread to potential recruits with relative ease.[8] The global environment, in particular with its accelerated process of state creation, which has resulted in weaker states that struggle to govern effectively, also appears to have created a context in which large-scale terrorism can

---

[2] I recognize that its use in the context of the Israeli-Palestinian conflict is particularly charged. However, without intending to characterize all Palestinian resistance as "terrorism," my hesitation to apply the term does not extend to those militant groups that choose to direct violence at the civilian population and to the extent that certain Palestinian groups pursue this "tactic" and present many of the difficulties focused on by this article, the term seems appropriate.

[3] Arunabha Bhoumik, "Democratic Responses to Terrorism: A Comparative Study of the United States, Israel, and India" (2005) 33 Denv. J. Int'l L. & Pol'y 285 at 285.

[4] Reuven Young, "Defining Terrorism: The Evolution of Terrorism as a Legal Concept in International Law and Its Influence on Definitions in Domestic Legislation" (2006) 29 B.C. Int'l & Comp. L. Rev. 23 at 24–25.

[5] Bhoumik, *supra* note 3 at 286.

[6] *Ibid.*

[7] David Glazier, "Playing by the Rules: Combating Al Qaeda within the Law of War" (2009) 51 William and Mary L. Rev. 957 at 966.

[8] Bhoumik, *supra* note 3 at 286.

flourish by allowing terrorist organizations to identify more successfully areas in which they can operate with little interference.[9]
With this increase in scale has come, for the purpose of this
article, two significant changes. In the past, targets were more often
military or political; now, indiscriminate killing appears to be the
goal rather than simply a consequence.[10] Moreover, terrorist organizations are not generally located within a single definable state.
Rather, they are "an amorphous, largely invisible mass," with cells
in almost every country.[11] As a term, "terrorism" is value-laden and,
to a significant extent, defies definition.[12] This article will not attempt its own definition but will simply use the term to refer to
groups evidencing the two characteristics that present particular
difficulties to the traditional international humanitarian law framework: the operation against the civilian population and the state-less,
transnational aspect of undertakings and membership.

INTERNATIONAL HUMANITARIAN LAW FRAMEWORK

As a body of law, international humanitarian law, which encompasses international treaty law and customary international law,
applies to armed conflicts. It does not purport to regulate the resort
to military force but simply its use. It therefore applies to armed
conflicts regardless of whether they are otherwise recognized as
lawful under international law.[13] It is largely accepted that international humanitarian law was primarily designed to regulate warfare as it is more traditionally conceived — between two or more
states, with each side relying on recognizable and defined armed

9 Roy S. Schondorf, "Extra-State Armed Conflicts: Is There a Need for a New Legal
   Regime?" (2004) 37 N.Y.U. J. Int'l L. & Pol. 1 at 8.

10 Emanuel Gross, "The Laws of War Waged between Democratic States and Terrorist Organizations: Real or Illusive?" (2003) 15 Fla. J. Int'l L. 389 at 423.

11 *Ibid.* at 392.

12 Bhoumik, *supra* note 3 at 287. The difficulty in defining what constitutes "ter-
   rorism" is evident in the fact that although various international conventions
   prohibit certain "terrorist" activities, they have yet to come up with a generally
   accepted definition of the term itself (see, for example, 1997 International
   Convention for the Suppression of Terrorist Bombings, 2149 U.N.T.S. 284, 37
   I.L.M. 249 (1998); 1999 International Convention for the Suppression of the
   Financing of Terrorism, UN Doc. A/RES/54/109, 39 I.L.M. 270 (2000); 2005
   International Convention for the Suppression of Acts of Nuclear Terrorism, UN
   Doc. A/RES/59/290 (2005)).

13 Solon Solomon, "Targeted Killings and the Soldiers' Right to Life" (2007) 14
   ILSA J Int'l & Comp L. 99 at 106.

forces.[14] The four Geneva Conventions, which form a substantial part of the textual basis of international humanitarian law, were developed following the Second World War at a time when inter-state warfare was the focus as well as, arguably, the more common type of conflict.[15]

The two Additional Geneva Protocols, which were developed as supplements to the Geneva Conventions in 1977, provide more scope for non-traditional warfare. Additional Protocol II regulates non-international armed conflict.[16] Additional Protocol I, which applies to international armed conflict, includes within its application, by way of Article 1(4), "armed conflicts in which peoples are fighting against colonial domination and alien occupation and against racist régimes in the exercise of their right of self-determination."[17] The reach of this particular provision remains unclear, but it has not to this point been applied to terrorism as conceived in this article.

International humanitarian law has continued to develop, and be extended, not simply through the formulation of subsequent treaties but also through custom. The Geneva Conventions, for example, now are generally accepted to be declaratory of customary international law.[18] Doubt remains, however, as to the status of at least some of the provisions contained in the Additional Protocols,

---

[14] Marko Milanovic, "Lessons for Human Rights and Humanitarian Law in the War on Terror: Comparing *Hamdan* and the Israeli *Targeted Killings* Case" (2007) 89(866) Int'l Rev. of the Red Cross 373 at 393; Schondorf, *supra* note 9 at 2; Daniel Statman, "Targeted Killing" (2004) 5 Theoretical Inq. L. 179 at 179; Dale Stephens and Angeline Lewis, "The Targeting of Civilian Contractors in Armed Conflict" (2006) 9 Y.B. Int'l Humanitarian L. 25 at 26.

[15] Schondorf, *supra* note 9 at 2. Geneva Convention for the Amelioration of the Condition of the Wounded and Sick in Armed Forces in the Field, 12 August 1949, 6 U.S.T. 3114, 75 U.N.T.S. 31; Geneva Convention for the Amelioration of the Condition of Wounded, Sick and Shipwrecked Members of the Armed Forces at Sea, 12 August 1949, 6 U.S.T. 3217, 75 U.N.T.S. 85 [Geneva Convention II]; Geneva Convention Relative to the Treatment of Prisoners of War, 12 August 1949, 6 UST 3316, 75 U.N.T.S. 135 [Geneva Convention III]; Geneva Convention Relative to the Protection of Civilian Persons in Time of War, 12 August 1949, 6 U.S.T. 3516, 75 U.N.T.S. 287.

[16] Protocol Additional to the Geneva Conventions of 12 August 1949, and Relating to the Protection of Victims of Non-International Armed Conflicts, 8 June 1977, 1125 U.N.T.S. 609 [Additional Protocol II].

[17] Protocol Additional to the Geneva Conventions of 12 August 1949, and Relating to the Protection of Victims of International Armed Conflicts, 8 July, 1977, 1125 U.N.T.S. 3, Article 1(4) [Additional Protocol I].

[18] Dieter Fleck, ed., *The Handbook of International Humanitarian Law*, 2nd edition (Oxford: Oxford University Press, 2008) at 27–28.

which have not reached the near-universal status of the Geneva Conventions.[19] Although many of the provisions are now recognized as having achieved the status of customary international law, they are recognized on an individual basis rather than by virtue of their inclusion in the Additional Protocols. Significantly, neither the United States nor Israel is among their signatories,[20] which means that, if their provisions are to apply to either of those states, they must be recognized as declaratory of customary international law. Even more significantly for this article, Article 1(4) of Additional Protocol I was an especially controversial provision and is at least one of the reasons for the refusal of the United States and Israel to ratify the protocol.[21] As such, this provision is unlikely to be considered customary international law and should therefore not apply to either of those states' conflicts with terrorist organizations.[22]

TERRORISM WITHIN A LEGAL FRAMEWORK

Before proceeding to examine responses to terrorism within international humanitarian law, there is a threshold issue: international humanitarian law must apply to these responses. There is, in fact, no consensus as to a single existing framework within which terrorism fits. Nor, arguably, should there be, given the difficulty of defining it as a concept and the range of activities to which the term is applied. Even within the (relatively) narrow realm within which this article conceives of it, however, difficulties arise with attempts to locate terrorism within the available legal frameworks.

The two frameworks commonly proposed are those of criminal justice/law enforcement and of war. The dual nature of most terrorist acts provides a basis for inclusion in either model. Certain characteristics would seem to make the criminal justice/law enforcement model more apt. For example, the strategy of terrorists in picking relatively easy, high value targets is more typical of criminals than of combatants.[23] Moreover, terrorists do not seek to use over-

---

19 *Ibid.* at 29–30.

20 *Ibid.*

21 Orna Ben-Naftali and Karen Michaeli, "'We Must Not Make a Scarecrow of the Law': A Legal Analysis of the Israeli Policy of Targeted Killings" (2003) 36 Cornell Int'l L.J. 233 at 256.

22 *Ibid.*

23 Gregory E. Maggs, "Assessing the Legality of Counterterrorism Measures without Characterizing Them as Law Enforcement of Military Action" (2007) 80 Temp. L. Rev. 661 at 696.

whelming force against their enemy's strengths with the aim of attaining a clear and incapacitating victory.[24] In other respects, however, terrorist organizations appear more suited to the laws regulating armed forces. The weapons that they use, the magnitude and persistence of their acts, their basic motivations, and the size of their operations are better suited to the military model.[25] The fact that terrorists often seek credit for their acts also suggest that the military, not criminal justice, model is the more appropriate.[26]

Before 11 September 2001, criminal law was the generally accepted response paradigm.[27] Attempting to deal with terrorism on this basis, states enacted various anti-terrorism statutes. The United States's Omnibus Diplomatic Security and Anti-Terrorism Act, which made terrorist acts against Americans abroad a federal crime and permitted arrest overseas for trial in American courts, is one example of such a statute.[28] Israel's Prevention of Terrorism Ordinance, which makes management or membership in a terrorist organization punishable by imprisonment, is another.[29] Given the transnational aspect of terrorism, states have also recognized the importance of inter-state cooperation in combating it. Currently, thirteen global treaties address specific terrorist acts, typically calling for their criminalization and imposing the "no safe haven" rule by creating a legal obligation for nations to cooperate in responding within the criminal law paradigm.[30]

As a framework, the criminal law system offers significant advantages. In particular, its use of sanctions is more compatible with the rule of law and democratic values than is the resort to military force.[31] These sanctions have the value of representing moral condemnation in a way that the military model cannot.[32] Moreover,

---

[24] *Ibid.* at 696–97.

[25] *Ibid.*

[26] *Ibid.*

[27] Michael N. Schmitt, "The Rule of Law in Conflict and Post-Conflict Situations: U.S. Security Strategies: A Legal Assessment" (2004) 27 Harv. J.L. & Pub. Pol'y 737 at 738.

[28] Omnibus Diplomatic Security and Anti-Terrorism Act of 1986, Pub. L. No. 99–399, 3071(a)-(c), 100 Stat. 853; see also Bhoumik, *supra* note 3 at 312.

[29] Prevention of Terrorism Ordinance, 1 L.S.I. 76, (1948); see also Bhoumik *supra* note 3 at 324.

[30] Glazier, *supra* note 7 at 967.

[31] Bhoumik, *supra* note 3 at 299.

[32] *Ibid.* at 299.

criminal justice is relatively open to accountability and is less subject to political preferences.[33] In the international context, criminal justice has the added benefit of conferring a sense of legitimacy upon the state reaction.[34] Where the terrorist threat is as dispersed as it is with Al-Qaeda, this is particularly important in that it encourages the international cooperation upon which effective response relies.

Given these characteristics, where the terrorism addressed is on a relatively small scale, the criminal justice system would seem the more appropriate framework. Where terrorist organizations operate on a larger scale, however, at least two problems become evident. The first is that there is a substantial risk that basic democratic values will gradually be eroded as the interests of national security shift the balancing analysis. The issue is not simply whether the terrorist problem is preventable but, rather, whether it is preventable within a democratic framework.[35]

It is at least in part the democratic commitment to principles such as due process and freedom of movement, of expression, and of association that makes the solution so difficult.[36] The risk when this solution is pursued within the democratic framework is that those central commitments may begin to slacken. Rules of evidence and procedure may be relaxed, interrogation techniques may be "enhanced,"[37] while police powers may be increased in an attempt to deal with the distinct characteristics of terrorism.[38] A prolonged ability to detain suspects without charge and without counsel is a relatively common feature of such regimes, as illustrated by the Americans' activities in Guantanamo, Cuba.[39] It has been suggested, in fact, that it is through the domestic response to terrorism that the erosion of democratic principles has been most evident in Western democracies.[40] It seems that democratic societies are as yet

---

[33] *Ibid.* at 298–99.

[34] Glazier, *supra* note 7 at 970.

[35] Bhoumik, *supra* note 3 at 291.

[36] *Ibid.*

[37] Glazier, *supra* note 7 at 982.

[38] Bhoumik, *supra* note 3 at 294.

[39] *Ibid.*

[40] *Ibid.* The effect on civil rights is not limited to Western democracies. Russia, for example, has been engaged in rolling back the recently renewed right to jury trials for suspected terrorists (see Glazier, *supra* note 7 at 982–83).

unable to provide total security against terrorism while maintaining the openness that is fundamental to democracy.[41] The choice of expediency over principle presents a slippery slope.[42]

The second problem is simply lack of effectiveness. It appears that emergency and anti-terrorism legislation has had little or no discernable impact on the violence perpetrated.[43] Part of the ineffectiveness of this paradigm stems from the functional characteristics of criminal justice. It tends to be reactive rather than preventive.[44] Mere intention is generally not sufficient — an act must have been committed. Moreover, sentence length is tied to the severity of the crime, which means that any criminal proceedings initiated in a preventive effort will likely result in relatively short-term sanctions.[45]

The problems posed to the criminal justice system become more apparent when one considers the characteristics of terrorism. For reasons discussed, terrorism is not a normal crime. It tends to be highly organized and is politically motivated.[46] The threat of potential criminal sanctions is unlikely to have much, if any, effect.[47] Moreover, the larger terrorist organizations are widely dispersed rather than located domestically. These organizations are not merely spread out, they are also substantial — Al-Qaeda, for example, is said to have trained tens of thousands of fighters in their Afghan camps.[48] Simply put, it seems too great a task for domestic law enforcement agencies, even with inter-state cooperation, to combat effectively such large, complex, and polymorphous organizations, especially where they have resources and weapons that rival those of some states.[49]

While criminal justice does continue to provide a mechanism for state responses to terrorism, therefore, its limitations have been increasingly exposed. As a result, there has been a growing tolerance

---

[41] *Ibid.* at 296.

[42] Glazier, *supra* note 7 at 982–83.

[43] Bhoumik, *supra* note 3 at 293.

[44] *Ibid.* at 300.

[45] Glazier, *supra* note 7 at 970.

[46] Bhoumik, *supra* note 3 at 300.

[47] *Ibid.*

[48] Glazier, *supra* note 7 at 966.

[49] Vincent-Joel Proulx, "If the Hat Fits, Wear It, If the Turban Fits, Run for your Life: Reflections on the Indefinite Detention and Targeted Killing of Suspected Terrorists" (2005) 56 Hastings L.J. 801 at 810.

of military action, at least in regard to large-scale terrorism, to complement the criminal justice response.[50] Israel, the United States, Russia, Turkey, and the United Kingdom are all combating terrorism through both criminal proceedings and military force.[51] The resort to military force is not simply a consequence of the perceived insufficiency of law enforcement in the context of large-scale terrorism. It makes sense to address the terrorist organizations' functional capabilities, rather than simply their violent acts, and therefore to respond on a broader scale.[52] Moreover, because terrorism is no longer predominantly secular or nationalistic, nor necessarily dependent upon state support, diplomacy and economic sanctions are largely ineffective.[53] As a result, the laws governing war have assumed a growing relevance in this context. Just as the laws designed to govern times of peace, which are not designed to deal with large-scale violence,[54] grant too little power to the state, however, the laws that regulate war may grant too much.[55] Furthermore, although the application of these laws solves many of the problems presented to the criminal justice framework by terrorism, it poses new ones.

International humanitarian law applies to armed conflicts. The first hurdle that must therefore be overcome is that, in order for international humanitarian law to apply, the interaction must qualify as an "armed conflict." The fact that this threshold must be crossed carries consequences. The escalation of a conflict will favour states, in the sense that, once the threshold has been crossed, it is only their powers that are increased — those of the state enemy, the terrorists, are not.[56] From this imbalance, it follows that states have an incentive to increase the level of violence, at least to the point that it will meet the threshold requirements.

What those threshold requirements are, however, remains somewhat unclear. Neither the Geneva Conventions nor the Additional Protocols define "armed conflict." The term has nonetheless received some attention, in particular, from the Appeals Chamber of

---

[50] Schmitt, *supra* note 27 at 747.

[51] Maggs, *supra* note 23 at 662.

[52] Bhoumik, *supra* note 3 at 295.

[53] Schmitt, *supra* note 27 at 745.

[54] Schondorf, *supra* note 9 at 19.

[55] Maggs, *supra* note 23 at 697.

[56] Schmitt, *supra* note 27 at 23.

the International Criminal Tribunal for the Former Yugoslavia (ICTY) in *Prosecutor v. Tadic,* in which "armed conflict" is defined as occurring where "there is resort to armed force between States or protracted armed violence between governmental authorities and organized armed groups or between such groups within a state."[57] This definition neither expressly includes nor excludes state-terrorist conflicts, although state conflicts with terrorist organizations may qualify.[58] Whether the American conflict with Al-Qaeda is an "armed conflict" no matter where such conflict occurs is highly controversial, but at least in certain areas, such as Afghanistan, it does appear to qualify, while the characterization of the Israeli-Palestinian conflict as an "armed conflict" in the *PCATI* case was not especially controversial, given the intensity and protracted nature of the violence that occurred.[59]

Assuming that the necessary threshold is met, the next and more difficult problem presents itself: is the armed conflict international or non-international? There is no simple answer to this question because the terms of both legal frameworks do not actually contemplate these sorts of conflicts, nor does a general agreement appear to have been reached as to the more appropriate characterization. The principal impediment to characterizing armed conflicts between one or more states and a terrorist organization as international is that international armed conflicts are considered to apply only to inter-state conflicts.[60] Where one of the parties is not a state, as is the case with terrorist organizations, the armed conflict cannot be characterized as international. This, in any event, was the reasoning of the Supreme Court of the United States in *Hamdan v. Rumsfeld,* which in this respect at least, has been considered the proper interpretation.[61]

Nonetheless, there is an exception to the requirement that for an armed conflict to be "international" it must be between opposing

---

[57] *Prosecutor v. Tadic,* Decision on the Defense Motion for Interlocutory Appeal on Jurisdiction, Case no. IT-94-1, P 70 (2 October 1995), reprinted in 35 I.L.M. 32 (1996) [*Tadic*].

[58] Schondorf, *supra* note 9 at 11.

[59] Milanovic, *supra* note 14 at 382.

[60] *Ibid.* at 392. See also Geneva Conventions, *supra* note 15, Common Article 2, which states that the conventions shall apply to armed conflict "between two or more of the High Contracting Parties."

[61] *Ibid. Hamdan v. Rumsfeld,* 548 U.S. 557 (2006), 126 S. Ct. 2749 (Supreme Court of the United States).

states: Article 1 (4) of Additional Protocol I, which extends the reach of international armed conflict to what are essentially national liberation movements. Although it seems that this provision was not originally intended to have an especially wide field of application, its scope has broadened.[62] It would certainly appear sufficient to cover many activities otherwise characterized as "terrorism." The principal problem with its application to the conflicts with which this article is concerned, however, is, as noted earlier, the fact that it is highly doubtful that the article qualifies as customary international law. As neither the United States nor Israel has ratified Additional Protocol I, Article 1 (4) cannot be employed to extend the application of the law of international armed conflict to the conflicts between Israel and Hamas or the United States and Al-Qaeda. There would seem, therefore, to be no sound legal basis for characterizing either such conflict as international.

The consequence of this, according to the reasoning of *Hamdan,* is that such conflicts must be non-international.[63] Non-international armed conflicts fall under Common Article 3 of the Geneva Conventions and Additional Protocol II. According to Additional Protocol II, Article 1, non-international armed conflicts are those that do not fall within Additional Protocol I and

> which take place in the territory of a High Contracting Party between its armed forces and dissident armed forces or other organized armed groups which, under responsible command, exercise such control over a part of its territory as to enable them to carry out sustained and concerted military operations and to implement this Protocol.[64]

Non-international armed conflicts are subject to a different, and more limited, legal regime than are international armed conflicts.[65] This relative lack of regulation is perhaps unsurprising given the competing interest represented by territorial sovereignty. It is, moreover, augmented by customary international law, which has incorporated many of the provisions applicable to international armed conflicts into the law governing non-international armed

---

62 Fleck, *supra* note 18 at 48.

63 Milanovic, *supra* note 14 at 392.

64 Additional Protocol II, *supra* note 16, Article 1.

65 Fleck, *supra* note 18 at 56. By way of illustration, Additional Protocol II has a mere fifteen substantive articles, while Additional Protocol I contains over eighty.

conflicts.[66] In addition to customary international law, each party involved in an internal armed conflict is bound, at a minimum, to apply the fundamental humanitarian provisions of international law, Common Article 3 and Additional Protocol II.[67] However, although these provisions ensure that internal armed conflicts remain governed by international humanitarian law, they nonetheless do not amount to the breadth of regulation to which international armed conflicts are subject.

The difficulty here, however, is not the relatively minimal regulation imposed upon non-international armed conflicts but, rather, the fact that they must be internal. That is, the international humanitarian law framework applies to such armed conflicts if they occur within a state.[68] This fact was not enough to prevent the Supreme Court of the United States from characterizing that country's conflict with Al-Qaeda as a non-international armed conflict. If the scope of the framework's application was recognized, however, it should have been. Since 11 September 2001, the United States has used military force against Al-Qaeda in, at least, Afghanistan, Pakistan, and Yemen, exercised belligerent rights on the high seas, and detained and tried captured enemies in Cuba.[69] To find such a conflict to be regulated by non-international armed conflict law, which was designed for, and was supposed only to apply to, internal conflicts is a considerable stretch.[70]

---

[66] Jean-Marie Henckaerts, "Study on Customary International Humanitarian Law: A Contribution to the Understanding and Respect for the Rule of Law in Armed Conflict" (2005) 87(857) Int'l Rev. of the Red Cross 175.

[67] Fleck, *supra* note 18 at 55.

[68] *Ibid.* at 54. Geneva Conventions *supra* note 15, Common Article 3 reads: "In the case of armed conflict not of an international character *occurring in the territory* of one of the High Contracting Parties" [emphasis added].

[69] Glazier, *supra* note 7 at 993.

[70] It is worth noting that Common Article 3 does not explicitly stipulate that non-international armed conflicts are *only* those that occur within the territory of a state, and it has been suggested that they should in fact encompass all armed conflicts that do not qualify as international (see, for example, Ben-Naftali and Michaeli, *supra* note 21 at 256). However, as is clear from the drafting history of Common Article 3, its purpose was to extend the protection of international humanitarian law to internal conflicts specifically (see Lindsay Moir, *The Law of Internal Armed Conflict* (Cambridge: Cambridge University Press, 2002) at 23–29). Moreover, the general perception of its reach has recognized its limitation to armed conflicts that are internal in scope (Milanovic, *supra* note 14 at 379).

It was not a stretch that the Supreme Court of Israel was willing to make in the *PCATI* case, even though there is somewhat more of a basis for considering the conflict with which it dealt to be internal in nature, considering the comparatively localized nature of the terrorist threat to which Israel was responding. Instead, the court concluded that the armed conflict was in fact international.[71] It did so, however, not on the basis of Article 1(4) of Additional Protocol I, which, as discussed, is the single textual basis for such a conclusion. In fact, the court declined to provide much justification for its conclusion in this respect, which is particularly unsatisfactory given that it is the first time that the court has held the conflict to be international.[72]

Having concluded that the armed conflict is international in nature, the Supreme Court of Israel nonetheless failed to recognize the applicability of the law of belligerent occupation, which, under Geneva Convention IV, is regulated by international humanitarian law. Israel, according to the International Court of Justice, is the belligerent occupier of the Occupied Territories.[73] However, Israel has refused to recognize itself as occupying foreign territory, primarily on the basis that Jordan and Egypt have relinquished their territorial sovereignty of the West Bank and Gaza Strip.[74]

It is possible that a purposive interpretation of the law of belligerent occupation would recognize its applicability to the ongoing Israeli conflict.[75] There can be no doubt, however, that the status of the Occupied Territories is currently unclear and that the effective control exercised by Israel regularly changes.[76] Even if the law of belligerent occupation is available to regulate the conflict at the moment, there can be no assurance that this availability will

---

[71] *PCATI* case, *supra* note 1 at para. 21.

[72] Milanovic, *supra* note 14 at 384.

[73] *Ibid.* at 383.

[74] *Legal Consequences of the Construction of a Wall in the Occupied Palestinian Territory,* Advisory Opinion, 9 July 2004, [2004] I.C.J. Rep. 136 at paras. 90–101.

[75] Milanovic, *supra* note 14 at 383.

[76] Mustafa Mari, "The Israeli Disengagement from the Gaza Strip: An End of the Occupation?" (2005) 8 Y.B. Int'l Humanitarian L. 356; Yuval Shany, "Faraway, So Close: The Legal Status of Gaza after Israel's Disengagement" (2005) 8 Y.B. Int'l Humanitarian L. 369. Moreover, the fact that the occupation has lasted so long (over forty years) raises questions as to whether this is the type of belligerent occupation contemplated by Geneva Convention IV (Milanovic, *supra* note 14 at 383).

continue. Moreover, as is evident in the case of the United States, such law is not of more general value since it is not applicable to many of the armed conflicts that occur between states and terrorist organizations.

The problems with fitting state responses to terrorism within international humanitarian law, which include whether the requisite level of violence has been reached to constitute an armed conflict and, further, whether this armed conflict is to be classed as international or non-international, therefore persist. Resolving the issues simply by resorting to the framework that is the most humanitarian, as appears to have been done in the *PCATI* case by applying international, not non-international, armed conflict law, may be understandable, but it is nonetheless conceptually misguided, as well as being legally unsubstantiated.[77] This is not to suggest that these conflicts are therefore to be considered unregulated by international humanitarian law: the fact that the fit is poor does not mean that the existing framework ceases to be applicable. Where the difficulties go to the very basic structure of the law, however, it does mean that there is cause to re-consider how that law is to be constructed so as to remain effective in this context.

The development of customary international law offers the potential to construct a legal framework that is better able to regulate the particular characteristics of these types of armed conflicts or at least to plaster over the cracks that they expose within the existing structure. To this point, however, it has not been used for this purpose. Customary international law has instead been primarily concerned with extending the reach of the existing rules to otherwise unregulated circumstances, such as those of non-international armed conflict.[78] Its principal value, therefore, is with respect to ensuring that activities do not occur in a "legal void" merely because the instruments of international law would not otherwise apply. It is not as helpful in resolving the difficulties presented to those instruments by circumstances ill-suited to the existing laws that they codify.[79] Moreover, because customary international law is heavily

---

[77] Roy S. Schondorf, "The Targeted Killings Judgment: A Preliminary Assessment" (2007) 5 J. Int'l Crim. Just. 301 at 306.

[78] Henckaerts, *supra* note 66 at 189.

[79] See, for example, *ibid* at 190, where it is noted that state practice has offered little in the way of help in resolving the difficulties that arise in the characterization of combatants and civilians, a deficiency that is of particular importance for the focus of this article.

based on the rules established by treaties, those treaties and the legal structure that they impose remain at the core of international humanitarian law. As a result, customary international law, although relevant, is not as useful as might be hoped in resolving the problems presented by state-terrorist conflicts.

Given the difficulties involved in positioning terrorism within the basic categories of international humanitarian law, it is unsurprising that further difficulties arise when its legal norms are actually applied. Law that is tailored for circumstances other than those to which it is applied will likely find itself a poor fit. Moreover, because there are few historical examples of such armed conflicts to draw upon, and states have not reached a common position, there is currently no consistent practice to bolster the assistance offered by the more generic customary international humanitarian law provisions.[80]

The recognition of the difficulties presented to the existing framework of international humanitarian law by state-terrorist armed conflicts has caused many, including United States administration lawyers, to consider it inadequate and to conclude that a new legal regime is necessary.[81] Since there is no new legal regime currently in existence, however, this tendency has led to concern that rejecting international humanitarian law's applicability will result in a legal void, allowing states to operate without the restraints of any law at all.[82] This evidently unacceptable result is unlikely, however, as even in the absence of a clear and existing legal framework, customary norms are to be applied to all types of armed conflicts, and the underlying principles of international law will continue to govern state actions.[83] Nonetheless, significant consequences flow from rejecting international humanitarian law's applicability in this context. There is good reason to believe that those universal norms and principles, sufficient perhaps for minor gaps

---

[80] Schondorf, *supra* note 9 at 54.

[81] Gross, *supra* note 10; Amos Guiora, "Terrorism on Trial": Targeted Killing as Active Self-Defense" (2005) 37 Case W. Res. J. Int'l L. 319; Nathan G. Printer, Jr., "The Use of Force against Non-State Actors under International Law: An Analysis of the U.S. Predator Strike in Yemen" (2003) 8 UCLA J. Int'l L. & Aff. 331; Maggs, *supra* note 23; Richard D. Rosen, "Targeting Enemy Forces in the War on Terror: Preserving Civilian Immunity" (2009) 42 Vand. J. Transnat'l L. 683; Schondorf, *supra* note 9; Statman, *supra* note 14.

[82] Schondorf, *supra* note 9 at 54.

[83] *Ibid.* at 54 and 57.

in the law, will be inadequate to regulate effectively state behaviour in the context of an armed conflict as a whole. The actions of the United States with respect to detainees is evidence of the fact that, in areas where existing law is perceived to be inapplicable, the residual norms and principles lack, at the very least, the requisite specificity and concreteness to be effective.[84]

It would appear, then, that at least so long as there is no new legal regime, neither choice — either to accept or to reject international humanitarian law — is particularly attractive. However, it is only if one regards international humanitarian law as a strict and inflexible set of rules that its applicability to state-terrorist armed conflicts becomes so problematic. It is this article's position that international humanitarian law should not be so reduced but, rather, be recognized as being capable of adapting to remain a relevant and effective legal framework in this context. It is in this light that state policies of targeted killing are to be examined not only as evidencing a number of the difficulties to which a strict application of the existing rules of international humanitarian law may give rise but also as demonstrating how this law may maintain its relevance and effectiveness through resort to its underlying principles.

The Policy of Targeted Killing and Its Definition

TARGETED KILLING AS A POLICY

It is generally safe to assume that states that engage in the liquidation of their enemies will deny that they are doing so.[85] In November 2000, however, Israel openly admitted to a policy of targeted killing.[86] The policy is implemented by the Israel Defense Forces, which, it seems, have pursued it with some regularity and at least some success. According to the Israeli human rights organization B'Tselem, targeted killing has resulted in the deaths of 238 targeted Palestinians between September 2000 and March 2010. It has also, however, caused the deaths of 170 Palestinian civilians.[87] Questions have been raised as to how careful the Israelis have been

---

[84] Bhoumik, *supra* note 3 at 320.

[85] Orna Ben-Naftali, "A Judgment in the Shadow of International Criminal Law" (2007) 5 J. Int'l Crim. Just. 322 at 324.

[86] *Ibid.*

[87] B'Tselem, Statistics: Fatalities, <http://www.btselem.org/english/statistics/casualties.asp>.

in confining targeted killing to the "armed conflict" context rather than to the law enforcement context.[88] For the most part, however, the targeted killing seems to be limited to countering the terrorists within the area of armed conflict and, hence, within the sphere of international humanitarian law's application. It has nonetheless received widespread condemnation.[89]

Ironically enough, some of this condemnation was initially from the United States, despite the fact that the United States has arguably engaged in targeted killings since at least the 1980s. In 1986, President Ronald Reagan authorized the bombing of Colonel Muammar Qadhafi's Libyan compound.[90] During the Gulf War of 1991, President George H.W. Bush authorized the bombing of Saddam Hussein's presidential palace in Baghdad.[91] In 1998, President Bill Clinton authorized the firing of over seventy cruise missiles at Al-Qaeda camps in Afghanistan in an attempt to kill Osama bin Laden and his lieutenants.[92]

Such apparent hypocrisy suggests that it was not so much the killing attempts to which the United States objected but, rather, the willingness to admit to them — in each of its own examples, the United States refused to admit that any particular individual had been targeted.[93] This stance changed under the presidency of George W. Bush. It was, for example, a mission specifically targeting Saddam Hussein that marked the beginning of the Iraq War in 2003.[94] After 11 September 2001, the United States adopted two targeted killing programs. One of these is a Predator drone program operated by the US military. The government has openly admitted that it is an official policy and limited it to the war zones of Afghanistan and

---

88 "Yemen/US: Take Steps to Avoid Airstrike Tragedy: Civilian Deaths in US-Assisted Raid Underscore Risks of Military Force in Counterterror Measures," Human Rights Watch (8 March 2010), <http://www.hrw.org/en/news/2010/03/08/yemenus-take-steps-avoid-airstrike-tragedies>.

89 Kristen Eichensher, "On Target? The Israeli Supreme Court and the Expansion of Targeted Killings" (2007) 116 Yale L.J. 1873 at 1873.

90 Jonathan Ulrich, "The Gloves Were Never On: Defining the President's Authority to Order Targeted Killing in the War against Terrorism" (2005) 45 Va. J. Int'l L. 1029 at 1030.

91 *Ibid.* at 1038.

92 *Ibid.* at 1039.

93 *Ibid.* at 1040.

94 *Ibid.* at 1041.

Iraq.[95] As such, it involves many of the same issues as the Israeli program and will therefore not be dealt with in this article.[96] Instead, this article will focus upon the second United States Predator drone program, to which the United States government has as yet not admitted but which nonetheless appears to function under the guise of a targeted killing policy.

This second Predator drone program is operated not by the United States military but, rather, by the Central Intelligence Agency (CIA). Exactly what it entails is difficult to determine, as a government shroud of secrecy significantly impedes the gathering of information on the program, but the significant attention it has garnered has meant that certain features appear clear.[97] According to press reports, shortly after 11 September 2001, President Bush delegated trigger authority to the director of the CIA to kill Al-Qaeda members virtually anywhere.[98] The director, in turn, delegated this authority to the head of the CIA's Counterterrorist Center.[99] Since then, the program has been operating at a "rapid pace," which has actually increased since President Barack Obama came into office.[100] Although he has publicly insisted on a clean break from the counterterrorism policies of the Bush administration,[101] it appears that on his first full day in office he authorized two strikes.[102] During his first ten months in office, President Obama authorized more strikes

---

[95] Jane Mayer, "The Predator War: What Are the Risks of the C.I.A.'s Covert Drone Program?" *New Yorker* (26 October 2009), <http://www.newyorker.com/reporting/2009/10/26/091026fa_fact_mayer#ixzz0eDwTOWu4>.

[96] There is some suggestion that the two versions are more inter-related than the US government would have us believe (for example, it is possible that even with respect to the military program, the decisions to fire are being made at the CIA headquarters in Langley) (see Mary Ellen O'Connell, "Unlawful Killing with Combat Drones: A Case Study of Pakistan, 2004–2009," in Simon Bronitt, ed., *Shooting to Kill: The Law Governing Lethal Force in Context* [forthcoming] at 6–7). The extent to which they are in fact interrelated is currently unclear, however, and I will therefore focus on the CIA program, which, regardless of the interrelation, is the more problematic of the two.

[97] Richard Murphy and Afsheen John Radsan, "Due Process and Targeted Killing of Terrorists" (2009) 32 Cardozo L. Rev. 405 at 412.

[98] *Ibid.* at 413.

[99] *Ibid.*

[100] Mayer, *supra* note 95.

[101] Murphy and Radsan, *supra* note 97 at 414.

[102] *Ibid.* at 407.

than President Bush did in his final three years.[103] Most of these have been directed at the remote regions of Pakistan and, although accurate estimates are difficult given that it continues to be a "covert" policy, it is believed to have resulted in somewhere between 326 and 538 deaths.[104]

Since the CIA program continues to exist under the government stamp of secrecy, is operated by an intelligence service rather than the military, and is used in areas that are not otherwise "battlefields," it exists in a particularly grey area of the law. The ramifications of this feature of its existence will be discussed later in the article.

METHOD OF TARGETED KILLING: PRECISION STRIKES AND
PREDATOR DRONES

The resort to targeted killing as a policy reflects the increasing use of precision attacks in warfare.[105] Precision, in this respect, encompasses not simply accuracy but also "the ability to locate and identify a target, strike it accurately in a timely fashion, and determine whether desired effects have been achieved or re-strike is needed."[106] As a result of improvements in technology, doctrine, and tactics, precision attacks have become a viable and efficient practice for modern armed forces.[107] If properly employed, they risk less collateral damage as well as limiting the need for re-strikes.[108]

Predator drones, which are a type of unmanned combat air vehicle, are designed to facilitate, to some extent, the ultimate in precision attacks. It is probable that drones were invented either during or directly following the Second World War.[109] They were first used on a large scale by the Americans during the Vietnam War to conduct reconnaissance.[110] They continued to be used for reconnaissance purposes during the conflicts in the Balkans during the 1990s.[111] In 2000, however, the United States was at last ready to

---

103 Mayer, *supra* note 95.

104 *Ibid.*

105 Michael N. Schmitt, "Precision Attack and International Humanitarian Law" (2005) 87(859) Int'l Rev. of the Red Cross 445 at 453.

106 *Ibid.* at 446.

107 *Ibid.*

108 *Ibid.* at 453.

109 O'Connell, *supra* note 96 at 3.

110 *Ibid.*

111 *Ibid.*

employ them as a launch for missiles.[112] It is now estimated that the United States currently possesses 25,000 drones of one sort or another, of which roughly 100 are the Predator drones typically used in the targeted killing policies that are the focus of this article.[113]

In general, modern militaries will have at least one ground-based pilot to fly the drone, as well as an operator who uses the advanced sensors with which the drone is equipped to scan for targets (since the CIA program remains covert, the precise process employed is unclear, but it is presumably patterned at least to some extent on that of the military).[114] Since they travel at relatively slow speeds and have a flight time of up to twenty-four hours, Predator drones are able to hover over an area for prolonged periods of time.[115] Along with sensors, drones are generally equipped with high-resolution cameras, allowing their operators to view objects on the ground in detail during both day and night.[116] Once targets have been identified and selected, the drone operator is able to launch a missile from the drone.[117] These missiles are themselves equipped with cameras, allowing the operator to observe the target from the time that the missile is launched until impact.[118] If doubts arise following the launching of the missiles, the missiles may be remotely diverted by the operator.[119] Given these capabilities, the value of Predator drones to states in combating dispersed and evasive terrorist organizations is evident. This value, however, at least insofar as international humanitarian law is concerned, is contingent upon targeted killing being a lawful practice.

THE DEFINITION OF TARGETED KILLING

The first difficulty in addressing targeted killing is defining it. In particular, it must be distinguished from the two practices with

---

[112] *Ibid.*

[113] *Ibid.* The United States also has fifteen Reaper drones, which are similar to Predator drones, but are newer and more heavily armed.

[114] Marc Garlasco et al., "Precisely Wrong: Gaza Civilians Killed by Israeli Drone-Launched Missiles," Human Rights Watch (30 June 2009), <http://www.hrw.org/en/reports/2009/06/30/precisely-wrong> at 4.

[115] *Ibid.*

[116] *Ibid.*

[117] *Ibid.*

[118] *Ibid.*

[119] *Ibid.*

which it is commonly associated, at least by its opponents: extra-judicial killing and assassination. The need to distinguish targeted killing from these two practices stems from the fact that both are illegal. Extra-judicial killing has been defined as "an unlawful and deliberate killing carried out by order of a government or with its acquiescence reflecting a policy to eliminate individuals even though arrest is an option."[120] It is unlawful in accordance with international human rights law, which, under Article 6(1) of the International Covenant on Civil and Political Rights, states that "[e]very human being has the inherent right to life. This right shall be protected by law. No one shall be arbitrarily deprived of his life."[121] Pursuant to this provision, extra-judicial killing is illegal because it sanctions the use of lethal force without the guarantees of due process or the requirements of immanency and absolute necessity.[122]

The illegality of extra-judicial killing emphasizes the importance of correctly identifying the legal framework applicable to a state's conflict with a terrorist organization. If it is the criminal justice framework, "targeted killing" is simply another name for "extra-judicial killing" and is therefore illegal. As discussed in the first part of this article, however, the criminal justice framework will not always be the appropriate model — at a certain point, the conflict reaches the threshold of an "armed conflict." It is nonetheless worth emphasizing that this threshold must be met if targeted killing is to be legal.[123] This is particularly true when considering the CIA program, given the fact that it does not appear to be limited to war zones.

Even under international humanitarian law, further distinction is required. State-sponsored assassination, typically associated with the killing of a political leader or statesman, is prohibited, even

---

120 Guiora, *supra* note 81 at 329.

121 International Covenant on Civil and Political Rights, 16 December 1966, S. Treaty Doc. no. 95–20 (1978), 999 U.N.T.S. 171, Article 6(1).

122 Jason W. Fisher, "Targeted Killing, Norms, and International Law" (2007) 45 Colum. J. Transnat'l L. 711 at 719.

123 Where international humanitarian law applies, it operates as the *lex specialis* but, as such, does not preclude the applicability of international human rights law. The impact of the inter-relationship between these two bodies of law in this context will be further developed in the fifth part of this article, but for now it is worth emphasizing that, even where the armed conflict threshold is met, international human rights law may nonetheless remain relevant and shape the lawfulness of targeted killing.

during war.[124] There is, however, little consensus as to a particular definition of "assassination" for this purpose.[125] There are two provisions of note in this context. Under Article 23(b) of the Annex to the Convention IV Respecting the Laws and Customs of War on Land, it is "especially forbidden ... to kill or wound treacherously individuals belonging to the host nation or army."[126] The term "treacherously" is not defined, but Article 37(1) of Additional Protocol I helpfully suggests its own clarification of the concept by prohibiting any killing "by resort to perfidy."[127] "Perfidy" is defined as "acts inviting the confidence of an adversary to lead him to believe that he is entitled to, or is obliged to accord, protection under the rules of international law applicable in armed conflict, with intent to betray that confidence."[128]

Neither provision has been interpreted to preclude the use of stealth or surprise but, rather, to proscribe such deceptive means as the faking of non-combatant status or a willingness to surrender to kill another.[129] As a result, targeted killing as practised by Israel and the United Staes, insofar as it does not employ such deceptive means — and there is no suggestion that it does — does not constitute assassination as prohibited by international humanitarian law. Before continuing to consider its legality as a separate concept, however, it should be noted that targeted killing is to some extent already legally confined: where killing a targeted individual occurs within the law enforcement context or through the employment of treacherous or perfidious means, that killing will be unlawful.

Having established that in order for targeted killing to be legal, it cannot constitute extra-judicial killing and assassination, the next task is to provide an accurate definition of what it does constitute. This article will adopt the description proffered by Nils Melzer in *Targeted Killing in International Law*, as a use of lethal force by a

---

[124] Nathan Canestaro, "American Law and Policy on Assassinations of Foreign Leaders: The Practicality of Maintaining the Status Quo" (2003) 26 B.C. Int'l & Comp. L. Rev. 1 at 11.

[125] *Ibid.* at 4.

[126] Convention IV Respecting the Laws and Customs of War on Land and Its Annex: Regulations Concerning the Laws and Customs of War on Land, 18 October 1907, paras. 22, 23(b), <http://www.icrc.org/IHL.nsf/52d68d14de6160eoc1 2563daoo5fdb1b/1d1726425f6955aec125641eoo38bfd6?OpenDocument>.

[127] Additional Protocol I, *supra* note 17, Article 37(1).

[128] *Ibid.*

[129] Ulrich, *supra* note 90 at 1051–52.

subject of international law that is directed against an individually selected person who is not in custody and that is intentional (rather than negligent or reckless), premeditated (rather than merely voluntary), and deliberate (meaning that "the death of the targeted person [is] the actual aim of the operation, as opposed to deprivations of life which, although intentional and premeditated, remain the incidental result of an operation pursuing other aims").[130] The question then becomes whether this practice is in fact legal under international humanitarian law.

THE LEGALITY OF TARGETED KILLING UNDER INTERNATIONAL HUMANITARIAN LAW

If the paradigm governing the conflict between states and terrorism is found to be that of war, it would seem clear that deliberate and even selective killing of terrorists would be legal. War is largely premised on the idea that the killing of those who represent the military force of the respective parties is both necessary and acceptable. Once again, however, the problems posed to international humanitarian law by terrorism mean that the legality of targeted killing in this context is by no means evident. In fact, the decision of the *PCATI* case has been criticized for starting from the premise that targeted killing can ever be legal in such circumstances.[131]

At the heart of the debate is the characterization of the individual terrorists who are the subjects of the targeted killings. International humanitarian law as it is traditionally conceived contemplates two categories of individuals: combatants and civilians. Those who meet the requirements of a combatant are legitimate objects of attack.[132] Civilians, in contrast, are generally immune from direct attack.[133] The one exception to this rule is "for such time as they are directly participating in hostilities."[134] Neither category, however,

---

130 Nils Melzer, *Targeted Killing in International Law* (Oxford: Oxford University Press, 2008) at 3–4. This definition could conceivably encompass killings that would fall within the parameters of extra-judicial killings and assassinations. It is necessary therefore to emphasize that such killings would be excluded from its reach for the purposes of this article.

131 Helen Keller and Magdelena Forowicz, "A Tightrope Walk between Legality and Legitimacy: An Analysis of the Israeli Supreme Court's Judgment on Targeted Killing" (2008) 21 Leiden J. Int'l L. 189.

132 Printer, Jr., *supra* note 81 at 377.

133 Additional Protocol I, *supra* note 17, Article 51(2).

134 *Ibid.* Article 51(3).

is well adapted to the circumstances of individual terrorists, which has led some to demand the recognition of a third category, generally referred to as "unlawful combatants."[135] Under international humanitarian law, an individual's primary status — that is, "combatant" or "civilian" — determines the protection afforded that individual and the legal consequences of his or her conduct.[136] The distinction between combatants and civilians lies at the heart of the law regulating warfare.[137] Given this fact, it might be helpful if that distinction was clear-cut. Unfortunately, but perhaps inevitably given the complexities of warfare, it is not.

As an international legal term, "combatant" refers to a person authorized by international law to fight in accordance with international law governing armed conflict.[138] There are several advantages for states such as Israel and the United States to classifying terrorists as "combatants." It would make killing them, perhaps even without first attempting capture, legal in a broader set of circumstances.[139] It would also justify detaining those who are captured for the duration of hostilities. Furthermore, although they would be protected from abuse during that time, there is no express legal limitation on the subject or duration of interrogations of combatants, nor do they have a right to counsel during such questioning.[140] There are, however, drawbacks to states in classifying terrorists as "combatants," most notably the legitimacy it confers upon their aims and actions.[141]

The current framework of international humanitarian law, however, renders moot speculation as to whether the benefits of classifying terrorists as "combatants" outweigh the costs. For an individual to be classed as a "combatant" under international humanitarian law, certain conditions must be met. These conditions, replicated in each of the first three Geneva Conventions, include: (1) command by a person responsible for his subordinates; (2) a fixed distinctive emblem recognizable at a distance; (3) carrying

---

[135] Gross, *supra* note 10 at 417; Glazier, *supra* note 7 at 997; Murphy and Radsan, *supra* note 97 at 419.

[136] Fleck, *supra* note 18 at 79.

[137] Ben-Naftali, *supra* note 21 at 265.

[138] Fleck, *supra* note 18 at 81.

[139] Glazier, *supra* note 7 at 1001.

[140] *Ibid.* at 1001–2.

[141] *Ibid.* at 1002.

arms openly; and (4) conducting operations in accordance with the laws and customs of war.[142] Members of terrorist organizations quite evidently do not meet these conditions. As was pointed out in the *PCATI* case, they have no fixed emblem recognizable at a distance, nor do they conduct their operations in accordance with the laws and customs of war.[143] As international humanitarian law currently stands, therefore, terrorists are not combatants. It appears to follow, unless a third category is recognized and at least for now one is not,[144] that terrorists must therefore be civilians. "Civilians" are not defined under the instruments of international humanitarian law, nor does state practice or international jurisprudence provide a clear definition.[145] The consensus seems to be instead that they are to be defined negatively — those who are not combatants are civilians.[146]

This result is in some ways an attractive one to states that are countering terrorism. It means that terrorists would not have the right to participate in hostilities and would therefore not be immune from domestic law.[147] Acts of violence would therefore remain domestic crimes, and terrorists would suffer the stigma of being mere criminals.[148] However, civilians are generally immune from attack. Moreover, as discussed earlier, there are constraints on detaining and interrogating criminals.

Regardless of the particular consequences, however, classifying terrorists as "civilians" seems conceptually flawed. In armed conflicts, in which all of those who represent the armed forces of either side are combatants, it is logical to define civilians negatively as "all others." However, state-terrorist encounters do not represent this type of armed conflict. Members of terrorist organizations do represent the armed forces of one side of the conflict, but they do not qualify as combatants. Yet it seems conceptually misguided to conclude therefore that it is an armed conflict between a state and

---

[142] Geneva Convention I, *supra* note 15, Article 13(2); Geneva Convention II, *supra* note 15, Article 13(2); Geneva Convention III, *supra* note 15, Article 4(2).

[143] *PCATI* case, *supra* note 1 at para. 24.

[144] Fleck, *supra* note 18 at 83.

[145] Nils Melzer, *The ICRC's Clarification Process on the Notion of Direct Participation in Hostilities under International Humanitarian Law*, <http://www.themissing.icrc. org/web/eng/siteengo.nsf/html/direct-participation-article-020709> at 2.

[146] *Ibid.* at 4; see also *PCATI* case, *supra* note 1 at para. 24.

[147] Glazier, *supra* note 7 at 1004.

[148] *Ibid.* at 1004.

civilians (who are not within that state).[149] This would be to say, in effect, that a state-terrorist clash is not simply not a "fair fight" but, rather, that it is not a fight at all. Clearly, this is not the case, and it would likely be found even by the terrorists to be not just inaccurate but also a little insulting.

The exception to civilian immunity, which lasts "for such time as they take a direct part in hostilities," may provide a solution, but it does not provide an especially satisfactory one, as discussed in the fifth section of this article. It is a particularly difficult exception to define and is highly dependent on the context. It is not defined in the instruments of international humanitarian law, and much (written) state practice is deliberately vague.[150] In the *Tadic* case, the ICTY considered the exception unnecessary to define, preferring to leave it open for determination on a case-by-case basis.[151] However, such vagueness is problematic when the consequences of misinterpretation are so significant — that is, the fact that an attack will have been launched against a civilian, which is a war crime under the Statute of the International Criminal Court.[152] It would therefore seem inadvisable to rest an entire armed conflict upon the interpretation of such an exception.

Understanding that terrorists do not fit within any of the categories currently recognized by international humanitarian law suggests that it may be a mistake to base the legality of targeted killing simply upon the classification of terrorists: there is no classification applicable or at least none that has been generally accepted. A better approach would be to determine instead whether targeted killing should be lawful under international humanitarian law and, if it should be, how that legality is to be achieved. It is these two questions that are the focus of the next two sections of this article.

Should International Humanitarian Law Recognize Targeted Killing as Lawful

As international humanitarian law currently stands, the practice by states of targeted killing in their conflicts with terrorist organizations exists in a legal no man's land. The prevailing legal framework

---

[149] Schondorf, *supra* note 77 at 306.

[150] Stephens, *supra* note 14 at 36.

[151] *Tadic, supra* note 57 at 616.

[152] Statute of the International Criminal Court, opened for signature 17 July 1998, 2187 U.N.T.S. 3 (entered force 1 July 2002), Article 8 on war crimes.

presents as many questions as it does answers. Where the law is unclear to the point that many have rejected it as irrelevant, it should not be relied upon as the sole authority with respect to lawfulness. Rather, the answer to whether targeted killing in this context is lawful under international humanitarian law should be pursued through an examination of two more fundamental issues: whether international humanitarian law should recognize targeted killing as lawful, and, if so, in what manner such recognition is to be achieved.

In answering the first of these two questions, this article will consider four issues: whether targeted killing is effective in combating terrorist organizations; what is the relevance of the current targeted killing policies of Israel and the United States; what are the potentially counter-productive effects that international humanitarian law may produce when applied to state-terrorist armed conflicts and the extent to which targeted killing may militate against these effects; and whether targeted killing accords with the principles underlying international humanitarian law.

THE EFFECTIVENESS OF TARGETED KILLING

Targeted killing, if successful, results in the death of at least the target, who is generally identified as a threat through intelligence gathering that may be difficult to verify. Almost inevitably, despite the developments in technology, it results in the deaths of bystanders as well. It therefore involves great risk of harm, with no guarantee that its object will be achieved. There are numerous examples of targeted killing attempts that have failed to accomplish their aims and that have resulted in unnecessary death and destruction.[153] In addition to the very serious immediate consequences, targeted killing may also achieve effects that are, in the longer term, counter-productive. It may provoke retaliation, and it may spur recruitment by making martyrs of those killed.[154] It can also promote a greater degree of cooperation between otherwise adversarial terrorist organizations, uniting them against a common enemy.[155]

Despite these risks, studies suggest that targeted killing can in fact be an effective counter-terrorist practice.[156] In his article "Targeted

---

[153] "Yemen/US," *supra* note 88.

[154] Fisher, *supra* note 122 at 735.

[155] *Ibid.*

[156] *Ibid.* at 736.

Killing, Norms, and International Law," W. Jason Fisher provides four reasons why this might be the case. First, and most obviously, it can prevent terrorist acts by eliminating those who commit them.[157] Second, it may strike at the core structure of terrorist organizations by "removing" its leadership.[158] The United States has claimed that targeted killing has resulted in the deaths of eight of Al-Qaeda's top twenty leaders and, in 2009 alone, more than a dozen of its senior leaders.[159] Although there is usually reason to doubt the accuracy of such American claims, there is nonetheless evidence that targeted killing can be successful in killing terrorist leaders.[160] Third, by engaging the concentration and energy of the terrorists, the threat can reduce their attack capabilities.[161] Fourth, it can serve as a deterrent, in that those eager for the martyrdom of a suicide bomber and especially those who are not, may not be quite so enthused about death as a targeted kill.[162] To these potential consequences may be added the demoralizing effect upon the organizations' members, given the ability of the practice to locate and kill in almost any circumstance.[163] Furthermore, targeted killing restricts the terrorists' movements since leaving hiding places may render them vulnerable.[164] Due to its reliance on informants, targeted killing can also spread distrust and discord among terrorist ranks.[165]

The fact that targeted killing, when used in appropriate circumstances, can be an effective means of combating terrorism does not alone justify its recognition as lawful under international humanitarian law. It is, however, a factor. Laws of war have historically been grounded in their consistency with military efficiency: to be considered as a viable legal instrument in times of war by those to whom it applies, international humanitarian law cannot completely impede states from engaging in effective means of warfare.[166] This is

---

[157] *Ibid.* at 734.

[158] *Ibid.*

[159] Mayer, *supra* note 95.

[160] *Ibid.*

[161] Fisher, *supra* note 122 at 734.

[162] *Ibid.* at 735.

[163] Statman, *supra* note 14 at 191.

[164] *Ibid.*

[165] Mayer, *supra* note 95.

[166] Hays Parks, "The Protection of Civilians from Air Warfare" (1998) 27 Israel Y.B. Human Rights 71.

particularly so when one party, in this case the terrorist organization, refuses to comply with such law. When one looks at the existing framework, however, international humanitarian law risks doing just that.

THE RELEVANCE OF THE CURRENT TARGETED KILLING POLICIES OF ISRAEL AND THE UNITED STATES

Given that targeted killing provides an effective means by which states may combat terrorist organizations, it is unsurprising that states should pursue it as a policy. The fact that states are engaging in targeted killing on a regular basis is an important consideration in the inquiry into whether targeted killing should be recognized as lawful for the simple reason that international humanitarian law is international law. There are two characteristics inherent to international law that are of particular relevance: the multiple sources from which the law may originate and the difficulty and complexity of enforcing compliance with it.

Within the international context, there exists no single, formal norm-creating authority.[167] Rather, international law finds its source principally in three categories: treaties, customs, and general principles of law.[168] This lack of uniformity, at least in origin, has a number of consequences. Of specific relevance for this article is that the pattern of creating and recognizing international legal obligations to an extent depends on the structure of international relations.[169] Thus the fact that both Israel and the United States are pursuing a policy of targeted killing poses, rather paradoxically, an immediate problem to those who suggest that it should not be recognized as a lawful practice. As stated, custom is a source of international law. In order for custom to attain the status of customary international law, two elements must be present: state practice (*usus*) and a belief that such practice is required, prohibited, or allowed as a matter of law (*opinio juris*).[170] Following the *PCATI* case, Israel clearly considers targeted killing to be allowed as a matter of law. Given that the CIA program continues to operate in "secrecy,"

---

167 Stephane Beaulac, "An Inquiry into the International Rule of Law" European University Institute Max Weber Programme 2007/14 at 9.

168 *Ibid.* at 10.

169 Paul B. Stephan, "Unilateral Recourse to Military Force against Terrorist Attacks" (2009) 10 Chi. J. Int'l L. 91 at 93.

170 Henckaerts, *supra* note 66 at 178.

the stance of the United States on this point is somewhat more ambiguous, although at least in certain contexts, given its admission to the military version of its targeted killing policy, the United States also appears to consider it lawful.

The state practice requirement encompasses, significantly in the case of targeted killing, the use of certain weapons and the treatment of categories of persons.[171] However, the state practice must be virtually uniform, extensive, and representative.[172] The practice and perception of every state with an interest in the legal issue is to be accorded equal value in determining whether a custom is formed.[173] The fact that a number of other states are currently acquiring drones suggests that a state practice is developing.[174] However, the debate surrounding the policies of targeted killing pursued by Israel and the United States indicates that this requirement is not yet met and that targeted killing has not therefore achieved customary international law status, at least for now.

The persistence of Israel and the United States in pursuing targeted killings nonetheless has implications for the legality of the practice. Some contend that it should result in targeted killing becoming recognized as an international norm, which, in this context, is a collective understanding about the proper behaviour of actors.[175] International norms denote those norms that command a broad degree of support within the system of states and which shape states' interests and policies.[176] As such, international norms, though not qualifying as international law, have significant implications for its legal rules, either supporting or undercutting them.[177] Although there is no easy means by which such norms may be identified, the argument has at least been made that targeted killing has achieved the qualities requisite to such recognition.[178] There is,

---

[171] *Ibid.* at 179.

[172] *Ibid.* at 180.

[173] Beaulac, *supra* note 167 at 17–18.

[174] These include both state and non-state actors: Brazil, Georgia, China, Pakistan, Russia, Iran, and Hamas are all said to have acquired drones, and although they are not all openly engaged in targeted killing as a policy, they presumably might be in the near future (O'Connell, *supra* note 96 at 5).

[175] Fisher, *supra* note 122 at 715.

[176] *Ibid.*

[177] *Ibid.*

[178] *Ibid.*

therefore, a basis for finding that targeted killing is increasingly moving in the direction of legality as contemplated by international law. Even if it has not reached that level as a practice unto itself, its implementation by Israel and the United States poses a problem to its characterization as unlawful under international law. This problem stems from the difficulties encountered when an effort to enforce compliance with international law is attempted.

What is generally perceived to be the great weakness of international law is not that it derives from a variety of sources but, rather, that its rules are not enforced through a central body.[179] For the most part, there appears to be a general consensus that international law is backed by sufficiently effective sanctions to constitute law: it is simply the case that those sanctions are enforced through mechanisms not commonly present within the domestic context.[180] War and reprisals remain the primary enforcement instruments of international law, although over time other coercive measures have been added.[181] In certain contexts, for example, the community of states may intervene through its cooperative organs to respond to serious and continuing violations of international humanitarian law.[182] The fact remains, however, that the mechanisms by which international law is enforced, though generally effective, lack many of the coercive measures of domestic law. As a result, international law enforcement still functions to a significant degree through "self-judging and self-help."[183] Its claim to be law is, arguably, based ultimately upon belief,[184] and its existence as a viable legal system thus rests largely on continued and widespread general compliance.[185]

---

[179] Fleck, *supra* note 18 at 675 (as noted there, there are examples where this is not the case, including with respect to the maintenance of international peace and security, which is enforced by the Security Council under Chapter VII of the UN Charter, but these are very much the exception).

[180] Mary Ellen O'Connell, *The Power and Purpose of International Law: Insights from the Theory and Practice of Enforcement* (Oxford: Oxford University Press, 2008) at 7; Duncan B. Hollis, "Why State Consent Still Matters: Non-State Actors, Treaties, and the Changing Sources of International Law" (2005) 23 Berkeley J. Int'l L. 137.

[181] *Ibid.*

[182] Fleck, *supra* note 18 at 685.

[183] O'Connell, *supra* note 180 at 7–8.

[184] *Ibid.* at 9. This perspective is supported by the fact that those judicial institutions that exist are limited to what is essentially voluntary jurisdiction (Simon Chesterman, "An International Rule of Law?" (2008) 56 Am. J. Comp. L. 331 at 357).

[185] *Ibid.* at 12.

Where that general compliance is no longer certain, there is something to be said for reconsidering the current legal framework. This is particularly true when it is states such as the United States that are refusing compliance. While sovereign equality may be one of the fundamental principles of international law, it cannot be said to constitute an accurate description of the factual distribution of power.[186] Although the standing of the United States within the international community may be waning, few question that it maintains a dominant position, and Israel is more than a mere makeweight. In a context that lacks an ultimate enforcement mechanism for its legal rules, the persistent practices of those — or, in this situation, at least one of them — in whom much of the power resides present a significant impediment to the imposition of compliance.

The unique characteristics of international law as law do not make the answer to the legality of targeted killing any easier. They do, however, condition the context in which that answer is developed. The determined pursuit by Israel and the United States of targeted killing as a policy in itself provides some basis for recognizing it as lawful. At the very least, it raises doubts as to the effectiveness of declaring it unlawful.

Given the limitations of international law, it would seem better to recognize targeted killing as lawful and then regulate its employment rather than to deny its legality and allow it to continue unregulated. Given that there is no indication that either the United States or Israel is decreasing its resort to targeted killing, recognizing its lawfulness would allow international humanitarian law to define it and to delineate the context in which it may be practised.[187] The importance of defining the boundaries of targeted killing in this context is underlined by the fact that the United States and Israel are not the only actors who are collecting drones.

Targeted killing by any state poses "frightening risks of error and abuse."[188] This is particularly so when pursued in the clandestine manner of the CIA Predator drone program. As mentioned, this program is not limited to war zones but could operate anywhere. Moreover, so long as it remains covert, there will, quite rightly, be concerns over accountability respecting its employment.[189] The

---

[186] Karl M. Meessen, "Unilateral Recourse to Military Force against Terrorist Attacks" (2003) 28 Yale J. Int'l L. 341 at 354.

[187] Fisher, *supra* note 122 at 753.

[188] Murphy and Radsan, *supra* note 97 at 408.

[189] Bhoumik, *supra* note 3 at 302.

distinction between targeted killing and extra-judicial killing may be fairly clear within war zones, but it is not so clear when the operations are conducted beyond what may be clearly seen to be such.

While recognizing and more carefully defining targeted killing will not necessarily prevent abuse of its potential, not doing so will almost certainly lead to its being continued. Insisting on a legal framework that makes any action unlawful will lead states to reject the framework as a whole.[190] This is particularly so when the action is an effective means of combating what has been identified by United States security strategies as the defining threat to the country.[191] Even for a country as powerful as the United States, there are interests served by submitting to the legal constraints of international law, provided that those constraints do not entirely deny to it actions that it considers necessary. On a broad level, the United States may regard the increased likelihood that future adversaries will be bound by international law as valuable.[192] Moreover, the legal rules of international law can provide a consistent resolution of the issues it raises that would otherwise be unavailable to the United States.[193]

In this particular context, there is an added advantage to the United States and Israel in being seen to comply with the law: maintaining the moral high ground in countering terrorism is an integral factor in recruiting allies.[194] With the terrorist threat dispersed into many non-hostile states, international cooperation is a key requirement if the response is to be effective.[195] At the moment, the United States, at least, has alienated the international community by pursuing Al-Qaeda without due regard for the applicable legal framework or, for that matter, international opinion.[196] Legal compliance is a way in which the "just party" status may be reclaimed, and the United States can thereby achieve the international cooperation that is so important.[197]

So long as the US policy of targeted killing is condemned as a whole, there is no incentive for it to restrict the policy's use. If its

---

[190] Schondorf, *supra* note 9 at 22.

[191] Schmitt, *supra* note 27 at 745.

[192] Stephan, *supra* note 169 at 97. The potential value of this may be seen in the fact that so many other states are acquiring drones.

[193] *Ibid.* at 99.

[194] Canestaro, *supra* note 124 at 32.

[195] Glazier, *supra* note 7 at 962.

[196] *Ibid.* at 964.

[197] *Ibid.* at 962.

actions are criticized irrespective of the context in which the targeted killing is practised, the choice becomes either to cease the practice altogether or pursue it unfettered despite concerns as to its legality. The United States has clearly chosen the latter. It can therefore perceive little difference between having an open policy conducted by its military and having the CIA, which is not a part of its armed forces and therefore without the right to use force during armed combat, operate a targeted killing policy that is pursued regardless of the consent of the state in which the targeted killing strikes are employed or of the occurrence of armed conflict.[198]

Explicitly recognizing that targeted killing may be lawful in certain circumstances and within certain legal confines would alter the choice to be made. Adding the ability to abide by the law while pursuing a targeted killing policy would not only provide a means by which the United States could achieve at least some of its objectives lawfully, it would also give meaning to the condemnation of those actions that stray outside of the legal confines. The difference between an open military targeted killing policy and a covert CIA targeted killing policy would no longer be perceived by the US government as irrelevant: it would take on genuine significance because only the latter would be unlawful.

Legal rules do not always precede factual developments.[199] Even if the status of targeted killing under international humanitarian law is unclear, it need not remain so. Recognizing targeted killing as lawful would allow its scope to be confined and would encourage states' compliance. Denying its legality, in contrast, risks allowing it to continue unconstrained and achieving in time the status of a custom, but as a result not of principled legal rules but, rather, of unrestrained state practice.

THE ABILITY OF TARGETED KILLING TO MITIGATE
THE COUNTER-PRODUCTIVE EFFECTS OF INTERNATIONAL
HUMANITARIAN LAW

As may be clear by now, states' refusal to prioritize compliance with international humanitarian law with respect to terrorism may in part be attributed to the way in which it applies to their military

---

[198] Many of the Predator drone strikes operated by the CIA in Pakistan, for example, were without the authorization of the Pakistani government and during a time when no armed conflict was occurring in that country (see O'Connell, *supra* note 96 at 8 and 16).

[199] Meessen, *supra* note 186 at 342.

responses to that threat. It is not simply that the law does not comfortably accommodate these types of armed conflicts within its present application. In certain respects, its application may actually run counter to its underlying humanitarian purposes. As will be shown, targeted killing has the potential to mitigate these effects, which is in itself a strong argument that it should be recognized as lawful.

According to one scholar, the current legal framework regulating state-terrorist armed conflicts is "fundamentally defective."[200] Although this assessment may seem exaggerated, international humanitarian law, when strictly applied as it now stands to state responses to terrorism, does create objectionable consequences. The two consequences addressed by this article are closely related: the encouragement of non-compliance and the increase in civilian casualties. As discussed under the third part of this article, an individual's primary status — that is, "combatant" or "civilian" — determines the protection afforded that individual and the legal consequences of his or her conduct.[201] Those that meet the requirements of a combatant are legitimate objects of attack.[202] Civilians, in contrast, are generally immune from direct attack.[203]

Since international humanitarian law requires that certain conditions, among them compliance with the laws and customs of war, be met if one is to be classified as a combatant and thus a legitimate target, avoiding such status is not difficult — basically, one needs only not to comply with the law. Since not complying with the law is perhaps paramount among terrorists' many strengths as a military force, international humanitarian law, in this respect at least, seems to play into the hands of the terrorists. Fundamentally defective or not, a body of law that grants protected status on the basis of its violation can hardly expect universal compliance. Highly desirable though the status of combatant may be in certain circumstances, its attraction will inevitably pale when accompanied by an increased likelihood of death as a legitimate target.

The incoherence of international humanitarian law's application in this context is further evident in the requirement that a distinctive emblem be worn. Once again, this is not an especially difficult

---

[200] Rosen, *supra* note 81 at 691.

[201] Fleck, *supra* note 18 at 79.

[202] Printer, Jr., *supra* note 81 at 377.

[203] Additional Protocol I, *supra* note 17, Article 51 (2).

condition to avoid for those who rely on blending in with, rather than standing out from, the civilian population. Although the requirement is a law of war, it is generally regarded as pertaining to one's right to the status of a prisoner of war rather than to one's legitimacy as a target.[204] However, the deprivation of combatant privilege, which international humanitarian law imposes on those who fail to distinguish themselves when they are required to do so,[205] is unlikely to be an effective threat in this context, given that terrorists have already conceded this and embraced the result by refusing to comply with the laws and customs of war. International humanitarian law, then, deprives terrorists of a privilege that they have already willingly surrendered by refusing to obey the laws of war.

Bizarrely, then, by violating international humanitarian law, members of terrorist organizations are able to ensure, without foregoing anything they would not otherwise have lost by virtue of their operations, that they are not legitimate targets under that law, unless, and then only for so long as, those members directly participate in hostilities.[206] There is no reason that the terrorists cannot meet the

---

[204] Additional Protocol I, *supra* note 17, art. 44; Jean-Marie Henckaerts and Louise Doswald-Beck, *Customary International Humanitarian Law* (Cambridge: Cambridge University Press, 2005) at 15–16 and 384–89.

[205] Should Additional Protocol I, *supra* note 17, Article 44(4) be applicable, and for it to be so in this context it would have to be recognized as declaratory of customary international law, international humanitarian law would soften even that blow—those who violate the distinction requirement imposed by Additional Protocol I, Article 44(3), would forfeit the right to the protection accorded a prisoner of war, but "nevertheless be given protections equivalent in all respects to those accorded to prisoners of war by the Third Convention and by this Protocol." For further discussion of the implications of this provision, see Glazier, *supra* note 7.

[206] Bizarrely, or perhaps not. Rosen, *supra* note 81, argues that the Additional Protocols were in fact developed to negate the superiority of Western nations, in particular the United States and Israel (at 688). According to Rosen, "third world" states, as well as Soviet bloc members, garnered the majority of the voting delegates and were therefore able to shape Additional Protocol I in an effort to level the playing field in their conflicts with the West (at 724–26). As Additional Protocol I has not been ratified by either Israel or the United States, this perspective, while interesting, is not integral to the arguments of this article, as the relevant provisions of Additional Protocol I must also have achieved customary international law status. Moreover, it is the Geneva Conventions that impose the conditions on combatants (Additional Protocol I is less clear on this point), and there is no indication these were drafted to mitigate the superiority of Western nations.

requirements of international humanitarian law. Hamas and Al-Qaeda, for example, could come up with uniforms — presumably their use of distinctive garb need not be limited to ceremonial photographs — and could thus meet the "distinctive emblem" condition.[207] The present state of international humanitarian law simply provides an incentive not to meet its own requirements: it is in the very act of disregarding the law that they attain the benefit of its most fundamental protection.[208]

The failure of terrorists to act in accordance with the law does not negate the states' responsibility to comply with it. International humanitarian law does not require that all parties to the conflict agree on its application and observe its rules in order to apply. Moreover, although originally based upon treaties, much of international humanitarian law has achieved customary international law status.[209] Thus, in ignoring the rules of international humanitarian law, terrorist organizations need not be concerned that their actions will result in international humanitarian law no longer applying to the states with which they are in conflict.

Nonetheless, reciprocity in observance of those rules, though not necessary for compliance, is generally integral to the extent to which they are respected.[210] It is reciprocity that is commonly perceived to be a principal source of the value of international humanitarian law as law.[211] Strictly applied, therefore, international humanitarian law not only provides incentives for terrorist organizations to ignore its most fundamental norms: it risks that states, in engaging with those organizations through military means, will come to devalue international humanitarian law as a regulatory framework. For those who consider targeted killing unlawful, both Israel and the United States must be said to have already done so.

The failure by international humanitarian law to impose an effective obligation upon terrorists to obey the laws and customs of war, including the requirement to distinguish themselves,[212] has at

---

207 Rosen, *supra* note 81 at 375.

208 *Ibid.* at 376.

209 Fleck, *supra* note 18 at 27–30.

210 Printer, Jr., *supra* note 81 at 365.

211 Maj W. Hays Parks, "Crimes in Hostilites," *Marine Corps Gazette* (August 1976) at 21–22.

212 It is worth emphasizing that the requirement to distinguish oneself is not necessarily limited to the period during which one is engaged in hostilities (which is itself a broader concept than "directly participating"). Even Additional Protocol

least one other important consequence beyond encouraging non-compliance: it puts civilians at risk. Terrorists surround themselves with civilians.[213] In fact, employing the protection offered by civilians may be said to be a tactic lying at the very centre of their operations.[214] In addition to blending into the civilian population, terrorists place civilians in control of their facilities.[215] They also avail themselves of the protection of civilian objects by,[216] among other means, using churches, mosques, and schools to store weapons.[217]

Such an abuse of the protection afforded "true" civilians and civilian objects would seem to leave states with a choice either to refrain from direct attacks or to engage in them despite the severe risk to civilians. However, because international humanitarian law only becomes relevant once a threshold of violence is met, which will involve direct attacks, on a broad level this is not really a choice at all. States must be engaging in at least some direct attacks for this law to be applicable. The aim of international humanitarian law should therefore be to mitigate the effects of those attacks. In general, its requirements of military necessity, proportionality, and distinction reflect this aim.[218] In the context of state-terrorist conflicts, however, the manner in which the law of distinction is formulated risks exacerbating, rather than mitigating, these effects.

The principle of distinction places the burden upon the attacking party, which, in this case, is the state, to distinguish between those who are legitimate objects of attack (combatants) and those who are not (civilians).[219] This burden is unvarying. The requirement that combatants distinguish themselves, however, is not. Article 44(3) of Additional Protocol I, although generally interpreted only to apply to the self-determination struggles falling within Article 1(4), nonetheless recognizes that

---

I, *supra* note 17, Article 44(3), which relaxes the requirement of distinction (though, as noted later in this article, it does not apply to the two armed conflicts focused upon), recognizes that in general it extends to "military operation[s] preparatory to an attack."

[213] Guiora, *supra* note 81 at 329.

[214] Rosen, *supra* note 81 at 734.

[215] *Ibid.* at 742–43.

[216] Additional Protocol I, *supra* note 17, Article 52(1).

[217] Rosen, *supra* note 81 at 742.

[218] Schondorf, *supra* note 9 at 56.

[219] Additional Protocol I, *supra* note 17, Article 48.

there are situations in armed conflicts where, owing to the nature of the hostilities an armed combatant cannot so distinguish himself, he shall retain his status as a combatant, provided that, in such situations, he carries his arms openly: (a) during each military engagement, and (b) during such time as he is visible to the adversary while he is engaged in a military deployment preceding the launching of an attack in which he is to participate.[220]

As terrorists are unlikely to qualify as combatants, this exception to the general requirement that combatants distinguish themselves further underlines the fact that the principal responsibility to distinguish under international humanitarian law lies with the attacker. In traditional warfare, this is logical, particularly given that holding responsible the individual who has already been attacked serves little purpose — disapproving military tribunals would not be his or her most pressing concern. In traditional warfare, however, the legitimate objects of attack are not usually doing their utmost to obscure the distinction that must be made. It is because terrorists are so intent on imbedding themselves within the civilian population that this assignment of responsibility results in a potentially objectionable result: it effectively assigns the blame for any resulting civilian casualties to the state.

This assignment of blame occurs despite the fact that the decision to direct an attack, presuming that the terrorists themselves are legitimate targets, is itself not a breach of the law (again, providing the other requirements, particularly proportionality, are met). It further reinforces the usefulness of the terrorists' tactic: those states held by law to be responsible for significant civilian casualties generally receive widespread international condemnation.[221] Without trying to suggest that all "wins" weigh equally in the balance, international humanitarian law in effect nonetheless creates a "win-win" scenario for the terrorists: either self-preservation or a propaganda coup.[222]

---

[220] *Ibid.*, Article 44(3). Note, however, that as Israel and the United States did not accede to this instrument, it is not applicable in this context and cannot therefore absolve terrorists of their responsibility to distinguish themselves from civilians (Ben-Naftali, *supra* note 21 at 266).

[221] Rosen, *supra* note 81 at 748.

[222] The 2002 battle of Jenin between Palestinian forces responsible for several terrorist attacks and the Israel Defense Forces illustrates this effect. See Rosen, *supra* note 81 at 753–55 for a more detailed account, and at 752–69 for a number of similar examples.

International humanitarian law exists to mitigate the suffering that results from armed conflict.[223] It does not exist to "level the playing field."[224] The fact that terrorists would stand little hope of success were they to refrain from operating within heavily populated areas is irrelevant to international humanitarian law. Acknowledging this fact, international humanitarian law should assign the ultimate responsibility, and with it the blame, for endangering the civilian population, to those to whom it really belongs: the terrorists.[225] There are other mechanisms — in particular, the requirement of proportionality — that serve to hold responsible the states whose attacks result in unnecessary suffering. Yet international humanitarian law essentially places the blame that results from civilian deaths upon the attacking state. As a result of the propaganda opportunities that this presents, it can have the effect of increasing, rather than limiting, those deaths.[226]

Identifying the current defects of international humanitarian law is not in itself sufficient to establish that targeted killing should be recognized under it as lawful. It does suggest, however, that a method of engaging in those direct attacks that can counter some of the potential problems has value beyond simple military effectiveness. Targeted killing seems to be such a method because of its precision and, thus, its ability to ensure that direct attacks are discriminatory. Moreover, as the degree of precision increases, the ability at least to limit the resulting civilian deaths increases and, with it, will come a corresponding decrease in propaganda opportunities. The protection afforded to terrorists, including that which may result from their refusal to comply with the laws and customs of war, will no longer appear so assured when strikes are possible in so many contexts. As this protection decreases, the incentives to ignore the laws and customs of war should also decrease.

---

[223] Gross, *supra* note 10 at 405.

[224] Rosen, *supra* note 81 at 685.

[225] Printer, Jr., *supra* note 81 at 376. It is not that the terrorists should bear sole responsibility, as the attacking state would continue to be responsible for distinguishing between lawful and unlawful targets, but simply that the terrorists should bear the ultimate responsibility.

[226] There is something to be said for holding anyone who will actually listen responsible for civilian deaths. What is important for this article's purposes is that the negative consequences from this assignment of blame may be mitigated by the practice of targeted killing.

TARGETED KILLING ACCORDS WITH THE UNDERLYING PRINCIPLES
OF INTERNATIONAL HUMANITARIAN LAW

Assuming that targeted killing is an effective means by which states may counter terrorist organizations; that recognizing it as lawful and delineating the degree to which it is lawful, rather than denying its legality and allowing it to continue unregulated, is a worthwhile goal; and that targeted killing can alleviate some of the counterproductive effects of international humanitarian law's application in this particular context, targeted killing should nonetheless not be recognized as lawful if it does not accord with the underlying principles of this body of law. As will be shown, however, targeted killing, if properly practised, does accord with those principles.

The principal purposes of international humanitarian law are the protection of the victims of armed conflict and the regulation of the conduct of hostilities.[227] As such, its existence is to a certain extent a recognition of the normative context in which it operates. Under domestic law, the use of force is generally prohibited, but within the international arena it is legal, provided certain criteria are present.[228] International humanitarian law therefore recognizes the inevitability of armed conflict and attempts to balance the principle of military necessity and the demands of humanity so as to minimize the suffering inflicted.[229]

Given that international humanitarian law represents a compromise, in that it acknowledges if not the value, then at least the reality, of military requirements, it is not enough simply to object to targeted killing on the basis that it results in death. International humanitarian law does recognize the lawfulness of killing.[230] The real issue is whether, in the particular context, targeted killing strikes the appropriate balance between military necessity and the principle of humanity. Resolution of this issue, in turn, depends upon whether targeted killing is in accordance with the foundational principles of international humanitarian law: humanity, necessity, proportionality, distinction, and the prohibition against causing unnecessary suffering.[231]

---

227 Melzer, *supra* note 145 at 1.
228 That is, it is legal under international humanitarian law: even where the resort to force is unjustified under *jus ad bellum,* its use may nonetheless be lawful under international humanitarian law.
229 Melzer, *supra* note 145 at 1.
230 Ben-Naftali and Michaeli, *supra* note 21 at 280.
231 Schondorf, *supra* note 9 at 56.

It has been suggested that targeted killing is in fact "the most natural application" of those principles within the context of state response to terrorism.[232] As will be shown, it at least has the potential to be so. Targeted killing, to some extent by definition, is a more discriminating means of warfare than other, more conventional offensive measures.[233] It is premised upon the idea that those practising it can distinguish between civilians and terrorists. It is thus a means by which to focus military action upon those against whom that action is (intended to be) directed. The continuing development of the technology employed allows for that focus to be increasingly accurate and, importantly, increasingly verifiable.[234] Consequently, when properly employed, targeted killing is a manifestation of the principle of distinction as a military practice.[235]

Linked to its reflection of the distinction principle is the fact that targeted killing can also be more "humane" than other military measures. As a result of the terrorists' immersion within civilian populations, assuming that some military response is justified, the alternative is an invasion of the sheltering community.[236] It would seem to follow, and incidents have shown that it does follow, that the fighting that would erupt would lead to considerably more death and injury, much of it inflicted upon civilians.[237] As such, targeted killing provides the potential to preserve civilian lives.

It also provides the potential to preserve combatant lives. Although these do not weigh in the analysis in the same manner, or to the same degree, as those of civilians, modern military ethics do dictate that they be a relevant factor in military decisions.[238] A solution that achieves the same military result in a way that causes fewer combatant deaths, provided that it does not result in increased harm to civilians, must be preferable.[239] Since targeted killing acts as an alternative to military invasion, it can achieve such a result.

---

[232] Statman, *supra* note 14 at 180.

[233] Ulrich, *supra* note 90 at 1063.

[234] Schmitt, *supra* note 105 at 453.

[235] Although international humanitarian law is not a reflection of morality in the way that criminal codes might be, it is worth noting that there are persuasive arguments as to why targeted killing is in fact morally preferable to other military practices currently recognized as lawful (see Statman, *supra* note 14).

[236] Statman, *supra* note 14 at 186.

[237] Solomon, *supra* note 13 at 103.

[238] *Ibid.* at 109.

[239] *Ibid.* at 115–16.

Insofar as targeted killing minimizes the number of deaths, both of civilians and of combatants, which result from military responses to terrorism, it reflects principles of humanity and the prohibition of suffering. Ensuring that targeted killing, when actually carried out, does in fact reflect these principles depends in part on whether it also corresponds to the principles of proportionality and military necessity. Since this is a highly contextualized inquiry, it will be addressed in the next section, which examines how international humanitarian law is to go about regulating targeted killing. The question posed by this section, then — whether targeted killing should be recognized as lawful under international humanitarian law — may now be answered: it should. It is currently employed by states that show no indication of ceasing its use; it provides an effective means by which states may respond to the threat of terrorist organizations; it alleviates certain inconsistencies within international humanitarian law; and, when properly employed, it is a more accurate reflection of the principles underpinning international humanitarian law than other available measures. It is, therefore, in the interest of international humanitarian law to recognize targeted killing as lawful.

HOW SHOULD INTERNATIONAL HUMANITARIAN LAW RECOGNIZE TARGETED KILLING AS LAWFUL

It is one thing to say that a practice such as targeted killing should be recognized as lawful under the existing legal framework, and it is another to determine how that framework should be applied to regulate the practice. This article does not attempt to propose the precise means of regulation or to identify the particular way in which such regulation should be achieved. Rather, it will simply assert that not all ways are equal. More specifically, it will argue that the regulation of targeted killing, given that it exists in the context of the uncomfortable fit of states' military responses to terrorism within international humanitarian law, must find its origins in the fundamental principles on which that law is premised, and not in the prevailing legal rules through which those principles are applied.

The need to ground the regulatory framework of targeted killing within the principles, rather than the existing rules, of international humanitarian law is illustrated by the Supreme Court of Israel judgment in the *PCATI* case. In particular, it may be seen in two aspects of the decision: the categorization of terrorists as "directly participating" civilians and the "least harmful means" requirement. The former is an example of an attempt to adapt the prevailing rules to the particular characteristics of terrorists and terrorist organizations. As will be shown, this instrumental approach is problematic and should not be the primary means by which recognition is achieved. The latter, in contrast, is an example of an apparently new rule that can be justified as an expression of an underlying principle — that of military necessity — within the context of terrorism in general and targeted killing in particular. As such, it provides a method by which international humanitarian law may be tailored to regulate more effectively state-terrorist armed conflicts, without risking problematic consequences when applied to other types of conflicts.

SUPREME COURT OF ISRAEL'S CATEGORIZATION OF "TERRORISTS"

As discussed, it is a difficult task to determine into which category terrorists fit under the existing rules of international humanitarian law. The Supreme Court of Israel followed the reasoning detailed in the third section of this article to find that terrorists are civilians: since they do not meet the specific requirements imposed by international humanitarian law, they cannot be combatants, and, under the generally accepted dichotomous approach, it necessarily follows that they are therefore civilians.[240] This is perfectly logical reasoning and compliant with existing international humanitarian law.[241]

However, having found the conflict between Israel and the Palestinian terrorists to be an international armed conflict and thereby holding its own armed forces to be combatants in war, it may be presumed that the court was, quite reasonably, reluctant to hold all members of the opposing side to be immune from attack.[242] It was thus left with two options: to recognize a new category of so-called "unlawful combatants" or to find a way of ensuring that terrorists fall within the exception to the guarantee of civilian immunity from attack, which is "for such time as they take a direct part in hostilities."[243] The court preferred the latter approach. Although Israel is not a party to Additional Protocol I, the fact that this particular provision was said to have achieved customary international law

---

[240] *PCATI* case, *supra* note 1 at para. 26.

[241] William J. Fenrick, "The Targeted Killings Judgment and the Scope of Direct Participation in Hostilities" (2007) 5 J. Int'l Crim. Just. 332 at 336.

[242] *PCATI* case, *supra* note 1 at para. 16.

[243] Additional Protocol I, *supra* note 17, Article 51(3).

status allowed the court to find it applicable.[244] The task then became shaping its application to the context.

Civilians do not generally have the right to take up arms and engage in hostilities under the same conditions as combatants — the only situation in which such a right exists is in a *levée en masse*.[245] However, international humanitarian law does not specifically prohibit direct participation by civilians nor is such participation an international crime.[246] Rather, international humanitarian law simply deprives civilians who take a direct part in hostilities, not of civilian status, but of civilian immunity "for such time" as they do so.

There are three components to the exception: "for such time," "takes direct part," and "hostilities." Unhelpfully, none of these components has been defined in treaty law[247] or in state practice.[248] Accordingly, there is great uncertainty as to their exact meaning, and what is more, there does not seem to be a general consensus within scholarly opinion.[249] The court was therefore left with some room to manoeuvre in how it applied the exception to the particular context with which it had to deal. Such room was not needed insofar as the term "hostilities" was concerned. The court's conclusion that "hostilities" are "acts which by their nature and objective are intended to cause damage to the army," state, or civilian population was not especially controversial.[250] Moreover, it evidently applied to the terrorists at issue.

More controversial were its interpretations of "takes a direct part" and "for such time." The court adopted a broad approach to "takes a direct part." The "direct" aspect was said not to be

narrowed merely to the person committing the physical act of attack. Those who have sent him, as well, take a "direct part." The same goes for the person who decided upon the act, and the person who planned it. It is not to be said about them that they are taking an indirect part in hostilities. Their contribution is direct.[251]

[244] *PCATI* case, *supra* note 1 at para. 30.

[245] Fleck, *supra* note 18 at 239; Geneva Convention II, *supra* note 15, Article 4A(6).

[246] Fleck, *supra* note 18 at 261.

[247] Keller, *supra* note 131 at 203.

[248] *Ibid.* at 205.

[249] *Ibid.*

[250] *PCATI* case, *supra* note 1 at para. 33.

[251] *Ibid.* at para. 37.

The court, in effect, interpreted "takes a direct part" to mean "performs the function of a combatant."[252] As such, it would extend to those who transport, supervise, or provide services to the unlawful combatants, regardless of their distance from the battlefield.[253] It would not, however, reach so far as to include the selling of food or medicine to the unlawful combatants or to granting logistical, strategic, or monetary support.[254]

The court took a similarly broad approach to "for such time." The real dilemma that this component poses in the context of terrorism is that terrorists tend to be repeat offenders (excepting, of course, those who take on the suicide bombing assignments). The "revolving door" phenomenon, whereby terrorists can prepare for each attack under immunity, with the "for such time" qualification providing terrorists with, as the Israeli court uniquely puts it, the "'horns of the altar' to grasp," was not acceptable and to be avoided.[255] Inevitably, this component, like the component "takes a direct part," will require case-by-case evaluation, but the court did state that a member of a terrorist organization who commits a "chain of hostilities" within that context will lose "his immunity from attack 'for such time' as he is committing the chain of acts."[256]

In effect, the court took a "functional" approach to interpreting the exception: terrorists have a civilian status but a combatant function.[257] The result of this interpretation is that terrorists are not entitled either to the privileges of a combatant, including prisoner of war status and immunity from domestic prosecution, or to the immunity of a civilian.[258] Slightly less clear is what is required under this interpretation to remove oneself from this characterization, but it seems that the court adopted what has been called the "affirmative disengagement approach."[259] Under this approach, terrorists must proactively distance themselves from the terrorist organization of which they are members.[260]

---

[252] *Ibid.* at para. 35.

[253] *Ibid.*

[254] *Ibid.*

[255] *Ibid.* at para. 40.

[256] *Ibid.* at para. 39.

[257] Keller and Forowicz, *supra* note 131 at 200.

[258] *Ibid.*

[259] *Ibid.* at 211–12.

[260] *Ibid.* at 211.

The general consensus is that the court's interpretation of the "directly participating" exception was expansive,[261] which does not mean that it is unjustifiable under the existing framework of international humanitarian law.[262] The court's approach to each of the components is not an unreasonable reading and is supported by references to academic opinion. It seems to be accepted as being compliant with international humanitarian law.[263] The problem with the court's approach to classifying terrorists concerns not so much the result it reached but, rather, the method by which the court reached it. The protection of non-combatants, particularly civilians, is a central aim of international law.[264] The single exception to that protection should not be interpreted so as to provide a suitable result in circumstances that have already been shown to present difficulties to the fundamental structure of international humanitarian law. The interpretation may be justifiable, but it is not principled: the court has simply used the vagueness of the exception to shape its understanding so as to reach the result considered necessary in this specific context.

Where to draw the line with respect to when civilians are "taking a direct part in hostilities" and when they are not has become a highly significant and contentious issue in modern warfare.[265] When the distinction was originally made between combatants and civilians, civilian contributions to the war effort were generally distanced from the battlefields. Traditionally, only a small minority actually became involved in combat.[266] That is no longer the case. Battlefields have increasingly been shifted into civilian population centres, which has led to more frequent and extensive intermingling of civilians with armed actors and military operations.

Also significant is the developing trend of outsourcing traditional military functions, which has resulted in engaging private contractors, civilian intelligence personnel, and other civilian government employees in the reality of armed conflict. Private

---

[261] *Ibid.* at 204; Orna Ben-Naftali and Karen Michaeli, "International Decisions: *Public Committee Against Torture v. Government of Israel*" (2007) 101 A.J.I.L. 459 at 465; Eichensher, *supra* note 89 at 1875; Schondorf, *supra* note 77 at 307.

[262] Fenrick, *supra* note 241 at 336.

[263] Keller, *supra* note 131 at 204.

[264] Rosen, *supra* note 81 at 685.

[265] Stephens, *supra* note 14 at 26.

[266] Melzer, *supra* note 145 at 1.

contractors are a source of particular difficulty to the traditional dichotomy between combatants and civilians, as the range of military activities that they perform is virtually unlimited.[267] They may now be said to play an indispensable role in many states' ability to use military force,[268] including that of the United States.[269]

To permit the increasing civilianization of warfare while simultaneously providing virtually blanket immunity for the civilians undertaking those roles, whether they are terrorists or contractors, seems absurd.[270] The Supreme Court of Israel evidently found it untenable, at least in the context of terrorists. It is equally untenable, however, to allow civilianization to erode the protection of civilians who are in fact, not simply in status, civilians. For those civilians, the "direct part" exception must be read as just that — an exception. As such, it should be narrowly interpreted.[271] This narrow interpretation would also accord with the stipulation of Article 50(1) of Additional Protocol I that in situations of doubt the individual should be presumed to be a civilian.[272] The focus then should be on whether individuals pose an immediate and severe threat.[273] Factors such as a strict and direct causal link between the act and the expected harm, and not the function, should be emphasized.[274]

The court's interpretation, however, resulted from its almost exclusive focus on one end of the "directly participating" spectrum — civilians who belong to a like-minded group engaged full-time in combatant-like activity.[275] As asserted, there are very different issues when the individual takes a direct part at most only occasion-

---

[267] Stephens, *supra* note 14 at 46.

[268] *Ibid.* at 29.

[269] *Ibid.*

[270] *Ibid.* at 47.

[271] Ben-Naftali, *supra* note 21 at 278.

[272] Additional Protocol I, *supra* note 16, Article 50(1); Keller, *supra* note 131 at 220.

[273] Ben-Naftali and Michaeli, *supra* note 21 at 278–79.

[274] Melzer, *supra* note 145 at 6.

[275] This is likely because of the question that was before the court (see Fenrick, *supra* note 241 at 337); the institutional limitations of any court will affect decisions and would have in this case, but as this article is considering the *PCATI* case as an effort at accommodating targeted killing within international humanitarian law, the limitations of the court are not as relevant as the result and the manner in which it was reached.

ally in hostilities,[276] which is a fact that the court did acknowledge.[277] Yet it does not seem advisable, nor is it consistent, to have one test for certain "false" civilians and another for "true" civilians.

Once applied outside the context of targeted killing, then, the court's approach dangerously weakens civilian protections.[278] Requiring only behaviour that is similar to that of combatants risks the consideration of civilians acting in self-defence to be performing a combatant-like function and thereby vulnerable to direct attack.[279] At the very least, it affords a wide margin of error in this respect.[280] The duration for which that vulnerability lasts is also of concern. No standard by which that time is measured was provided by the court,[281] but it is certainly beyond the hours immediately surrounding the attack to which it had been traditionally limited.[282]

The scope and extent of the court's interpretation are still uncertain.[283] As a result, its full effects, if applied outside the context in which it was made, cannot now be known. This is particularly so because its implications extend beyond simply whether individuals may lawfully be the objects of direct attack, encompassing such issues as their detention and prosecution under domestic law.[284] International humanitarian law is, however, "built upon the assumption that civilians do not take a direct part in hostilities."[285] It would therefore seem clear that the effects of such an expansive interpretation of what it means to "take a direct part" would be such as to erode the most basic protections afforded civilians under international humanitarian law.

Given that this body of law faces considerable difficulties in regulating armed conflicts between states and terrorist organizations, erosion is to some extent inevitable when the existing rules are interpreted in such an instrumental manner. Where the outer limits of law are in sight, such as in this case, it is preferable to return

276 Fenrick, *supra* note 241 at 338.

277 *PCATI* case, *supra* note 1 at para. 40.

278 Eichensher, *supra* note 89 at 1876.

279 Keller, *supra* note 127 at 210.

280 *Ibid.*

281 Ben-Naftali, *supra* note 85 at 329.

282 Eichensher, *supra* note 89 at 1876.

283 Stephens, *supra* note 14 at 44.

284 Schondorf, *supra* note 77 at 307.

285 Fleck, *supra* note 18 at 261.

to the law's origins than to strain it to the point that it begins to lose its shape. The value of returning to those origins — in this case, the foundational principles of international humanitarian law — will be shown in the subsequent discussion of the "least harmful means" requirement.

Before proceeding to this discussion, however, and acknowledging that it is easier to criticize than to construct, I should at least address what I consider to be a better approach than that of the Supreme Court of Israel: recognizing a third category. This is a highly controversial approach and not without its own problems. However, it is arguable that in some sense the expansive interpretation of the "directly participating" exception actually creates a third category, in effect if not in name.[286] Explicitly acknowledging the third category and freeing the law from the constraints of the existing two-category approach would allow the legal rules to be more effectively tailored to the particular circumstances, while avoiding the weakening of those rules that currently prevail.

The particular circumstances, it should be noted, are not simply those of the terrorists — the CIA operators manning the Predator drones are themselves unlawful combatants.[287] They are not trained in the law of armed conflict; they are not bound by the Uniform Code of Military Justice to respect the laws and customs of war;[288] and, although apparently and bizarrely, some do wear military uniforms during their shifts at the controls in their US offices,[289] they do not generally meet the distinctive emblem requirement.[290] Only lawful combatants have the right to use force during an armed conflict, yet the CIA operators regularly fire missiles at targeted individuals.[291] Recognizing a new category would not therefore necessarily mean simply caving to US demands: it could place stricter restrictions than those that currently exist, and are ineffective, on the way in which the United States operates its targeted killing policies.

---

[286] Ben-Naftali and Michaeli, *supra* note 261 at 464.

[287] John J. Klein, "Problematic Nexus: Where Unmanned Combat Air Vehicles and the Law of Armed Conflict Meet," Air and Space Power Journal, 22 July 2003, <http://www.airpower.maxwell.af.mil/airchronicles/cc/klein.html>.

[288] O'Connell, *supra* note 96 at 8.

[289] Mayer, *supra* note 95.

[290] O'Connell, *supra* note 96 at 8.

[291] *Ibid.*

The principal concern with a new category is that its recognition will create, and exist in, a legal void.[292] International humanitarian law, however, has already shown itself to be flexible enough to incorporate the "freedom fighters" who sprang from the phenomenon of colonialization, albeit within the existing two-category approach.[293] Moreover, considering the actions of the United States with respect to captured terrorists, it seems more likely that it is the refusal to admit a third category, rather than a recognition thereof, which will result in the treatment of terrorists occurring within a legal void.[294]

The principle of distinction, upon which the categories are based, is important because it draws a line between objects that may be attacked lawfully and those that may not. For international humanitarian law to apply, as discussed, members of terrorist organizations must presumably be legitimate objects of a direct attack. A new category would therefore reflect the underlying reason for distinction, while avoiding the considerable difficulties and undesirable consequences of attempting to insert terrorists into one of the existing two categories. It would also perhaps be the most important step in restoring, at least on the part of the United States, compliance with the rule of law.[295]

Moreover, the legal implications of characterizing terrorists should be the result of a principled consideration of their standing, not simply an unintended by-product of the current law. The court's expansive interpretation of the "directly participating" exception effectively entailed denying terrorists the legal benefits of either category: they are not entitled either to the privileges of combatants or to the protections of civilians.[296] It is quite likely that many would consider this to be the appropriate result, but, even if it is, it should be arrived at because of careful regard for what legal standing their status warrants rather than as a consequence of their failure to fit comfortably within existing categories.

---

292 Curtis A. Bradley, "The United States, Israel and Unlawful Combatants" (2009) 12 Green Bag 2d 397 at 407.

293 Gross, *supra* note 9 at 420.

294 Margaret L. Satterthwaite, "Symposium on the New Face of Armed Conflict: Enemy Combatants after *Hamdan v. Rumsfeld:* Rendered Meaningless: Extraordinary Rendition and the Rule of Law" (2007) 75 Geo. Wash. L. Rev. 1333 at 1395.

295 Glazier, *supra* note 7 at 997.

296 Ben-Naftali and Michaeli, *supra* note 261 at 464.

THE LEAST HARMFUL MEANS REQUIREMENT

The "least harmful means" requirement was one of four imposed by the Supreme Court of Israel upon any targeted killing conducted.[297] It prohibits targeted killing where a less harmful means, including arrest, interrogation, and trial, may be employed.[298] It is only when the risk of other means "involves a risk so great to the lives of the soldiers" or if the "harm to nearby innocent civilians might be greater than caused by refraining" from targeted killing that targeted killing may be justified.[299] In effect, it simply prohibits the infliction of greater harm upon civilians who are "directly participating" than is strictly necessary for the removal of the military threat that they pose in concrete circumstances.[300]

The "least harmful means" requirement, along with the three other requirements, has been hailed as an "important and unprecedented development in limiting the legality of targeted killing."[301] Less discernable than its use, however, is its source. The court was disappointingly unclear as to how it was arrived at as a requirement, which has led to some confusion as to its origin. It has been suggested that the "least harmful means" requirement has been drawn from human rights law,[302] occupation law,[303] or even domestic Israeli law.[304] The source employed by the court may or may not be conclusively identified, but what is important for the requirement's recognition as a legally valid stipulation depends not on the court's reasoning but, rather, on whether the requirement may be objectively derived from the recognized principles of international

---

[297] The other three requirements were: (1) that well-based, convincing, and verified information provide the basis for categorizing a civilian as falling into one of the discussed categories, with the burden of proof on the army being heavy; (2) that a thorough and independent investigation be performed (retroactively) regarding the precision of the target's identification and the circumstances of the attack; and (3) that any resulting harm to civilians be proportional to the military advantage (*PCATI* case, *supra* note 1 at para. 40).

[298] *Ibid.* at para. 40.

[299] *Ibid.*

[300] Nils Melzer, "Targeted Killing or Less Harmful Means?—Israel's High Court Judgment on Targeted Killing and the Restrictive Function of Military Necessity" (2006) 9 Y.B Int'l Humanitarian L. 96.

[301] Keller, *supra* note 131 at 213.

[302] Milanovic, *supra* note 14 at 390.

[303] Ben-Naftali, *supra* note 85 at 330.

[304] Schondorf, *supra* note 77 at 309.

humanitarian law.[305] As will be shown, it can be so derived, in particular from the principle of military necessity.

Military necessity is generally recognized as a fundamental principle in international humanitarian law.[306] As has been discussed, international humanitarian law seeks to balance military necessity and the demands of humanity.[307] In this sense, military necessity acts in a permissive capacity. It is the justifying factor in international humanitarian law that permits resort to measures that meet the needs existing in the extreme circumstances of armed conflict.[308] As a result, it is often perceived to stand in opposition to the values that international humanitarian law seeks to protect.[309] To the particularly discouraged, it seems to appear that when "ideals of humanity [have] clashed with military necessity, as inevitably occurred in all areas critical to protecting civilians, they encountered an immovable force."[310]

Notwithstanding this view, there is another, restrictive aspect to military necessity. As a principle, it is fundamental to the notion of limited war upon which international humanitarian law is premised.[311] In effect, it prohibits any degree or type of force that is in excess of what is required to accomplish a legitimate purpose in the concrete circumstances.[312] It requires that parties cause no more death, injury, or destruction than the circumstances demand to achieve that purpose.[313] It thus provides "the oldest and most effective restraint ever imposed on warfare."[314]

Military necessity is expressed as a basic rule of international humanitarian law under Article 35(1) of Additional Protocol I, which states that in "any armed conflict, the right of the Parties to the conflict to choose methods or means of warfare is not unlimited." Otherwise, it is not generally given independent expression

---

[305] Melzer, *supra* note 300 at 95.

[306] *Ibid.* at 97–99.

[307] Fleck, *supra* note 18 at 38.

[308] Melzer, *supra* note 300 at 104.

[309] *Ibid.* at 100.

[310] Chris af Jochnick and Roger Normand, "The Legitimation of Violence: A Critical History of the Laws of War" (1994) 35 Harvard Int. L.J. 49–95 at 68.

[311] Printer, Jr., *supra* note 81 at 360.

[312] Melzer, *supra* note 300 at 108.

[313] *Ibid.* at 111.

[314] *Ibid.* at 100.

within the positive legal rules of international humanitarian law for the simple reason that it is already incorporated therein.[315] In this sense, military necessity is an inherent condition for the lawfulness acknowledged by these rules.[316]

Yet the importance of military necessity is not limited to its shaping of the existing international humanitarian law rules presently in existence. Inevitably, these rules do not explicitly cover every circumstance. Military necessity therefore further serves to reduce lawful military action from that which international humanitarian law does not prohibit in the abstract to that which is reasonably required in the concrete circumstances.[317] It is in this sense that the "least harmful means" requirement may be justified.

There is no international humanitarian law provision that limits the lawfulness of killing combatants or "directly participating" civilians to circumstances in which they may not be arrested or detained.[318] Yet the fact that it does not prohibit direct attacks against combatants and civilians does not necessarily amount to an express authorization to kill such persons at any time or in any place.[319] Unnecessary killing remains wrong.[320] The wide variety of operational and contextual circumstances that arise in armed conflict, however, means that the required standard of necessity imposed by the principle varies. In large-scale confrontations, it may only require "reasonableness," but, as the confrontations gradually move away from the large scale, the standard slides closer to that of absolute necessity.[321]

Military necessity, then, provides a means by which international humanitarian law, even if it possesses no precise rule to directly regulate the activity, may be adapted to effectively ensure that the activity does not exceed that which is lawful in the particular circumstances. Essentially, military necessity is an instrument to tailor international humanitarian law to that which it regulates. It is in

---

[315] Glazier, *supra* note 7 at 997. An exception to this general lack of independent expression is Additional Protocol I, Art. 35(2) and (3), which prohibit, *inter alia*, the use of weapons that cause "superfluous injury."

[316] Melzer, *supra* note 300 at 110.

[317] *Ibid.* at 108.

[318] Milanovic, *supra* note 14 at 390.

[319] Melzer, *supra* note 300 at 109.

[320] Thomas Hurka, "Proportionality in the Morality of War" (2005) 33 Phil & Pub. Aff. 34 at 36.

[321] *Ibid.* at 112.

this context that the "least harmful means" requirement should be viewed. Targeted killing does not take place in large-scale confrontations. It is instead a mechanism by which one, generally more powerful, party, the state, conducts operations against selected enemy individuals who are members of another party.[322] Nor does targeted killing occur within the extreme conditions of a typical battlefield but, rather, in situations conducive to a greater degree of planning and consideration. There is therefore no reason for it to be subject to the broader conception of military necessity that regulates the battlefield of more traditional, symmetrical warfare, in which careful measurement and planning are not always so feasible.

If the "least harmful means" requirement is seen in this light, the question then becomes how well it gives expression to military necessity within the context of targeted killing. That is, under the conditions in which targeted killing occurs, is the requirement that targeted killing be lawful only when alternative measures risk a greater harm an accurate reflection of the principle of military necessity? This article asserts that it is for two distinct, but closely related, reasons. The first reason is that the "least harmful means" requirement represents a balance between the two legal frameworks that state responses to terrorism appear to straddle: those of war and those of crime. It is unlikely that the complex and diverse threat posed by terrorist organizations can be effectively combated within either legal framework alone.[323] The debate over whether the criminal justice/law enforcement or military model is preferable stems from the fact that while both can be useful, they can also present disadvantages. Clearly, an approach drawing upon multiple legal systems would be preferable.[324] The measures taken should be shaped by the particular nature of terrorism, which implies that no single way will be wholly appropriate.[325] International humanitarian law governs armed conflicts but not necessarily to the exclusion of all other bodies of law. Notably, although it is *lex specialis* with respect to armed conflicts, it is supplemented by international human rights law.[326] It should therefore not be seen in isolation but, rather, as a

---

[322] *Ibid.*

[323] Proulx, *supra* note 49 at 810.

[324] *Ibid.*

[325] Gross, *supra* note 10 at 456–57.

[326] Louise Doswald-Beck, "The Right to Life in Armed Conflict: Does International Humanitarian Law Provide All the Answers?" (2006) 88(864) International

body of law that can interact with, and be shaped by, other bodies of law where necessary. In this case, the other body of law is criminal law.

The "least harmful means" requirement, in imposing the condition that arrest and trial must be the preferred recourse where possible, recognizes the fact that targeted killing occurs in circumstances that are to some extent comparable to peacetime policing.[327] Targeted killing is a more calculated and considered form of action than that which occurs in the extreme conditions of a battlefield. There is usually an opportunity to consider other means of nullifying the threat posed, and, therefore, the need to deliberate as to the necessity of inflicting a significant amount of damage is that much greater.

Just because international humanitarian law exists to regulate warfare does not mean that it should accept that, once its framework has been recognized as applicable, all types of killing are lawful. In fact, it quite clearly does not. The distinction between combatants and civilians is premised on the idea that only certain types of killing are lawful. These two categories may be sufficient to distinguish between killing that is lawful and that which is not in more traditional, symmetrical warfare, but, as has been shown, they are not so in state-terrorist armed conflicts. Thus, the "least harmful means" requirement delineates the circumstances in which killing may be lawful under the conditions of this particular type of armed conflict.

Although the requirement does recognize the "criminal law" aspect of targeted killing, it is nonetheless rooted within the context, and governing law, of war. Killing terrorists is still lawful. To require anything else would be largely to deny the fact that international humanitarian law regulates warfare. It is simply that in these circumstances, killing is lawful under more restricted conditions than those regulating other types of warfare.

The second reason for recognizing the value of the "least harmful means" requirement is that it largely reflects state practice. In general, military and intelligence officials consider targeted killing to be a last resort.[328] In a conflict in which information is often of

---

Review of the Red Cross 882; as mentioned, it has been suggested that human rights law was in fact the court's source for the "least harmful means" requirement (Milanovic, *supra* note 14 at 390).

[327] Melzer, *supra* note 300 at 112.

[328] Ulrich, *supra* note 90 at 1056.

paramount importance, it is of considerably greater value to states to obtain information from terrorists rather than simply to kill them. It is only where capturing terrorists would be too dangerous or logistically impossible that targeted killing becomes the chosen method.[329]

Furthermore, targeted killing strikes are delivered by drones rather than by manned aircraft, which means that the level of precision demanded should be higher. Manned aircraft generally have a minimum operating altitude due to understandable concerns about being shot down.[330] This can result in difficulty in properly identifying legitimate targets as well as in reducing awareness of the surrounding geographical and physical context in which attacks are conducted.[331] Drones, however, are not manned and may therefore be flown at lower altitudes without risk to their pilots.[332] When they are used in targeted killing, therefore, it is reasonable to hold their operators to a greater degree of accountability for any mistakes that may have been made. An ability to acquire an accurate and detailed picture of the context means that it should be possible to discover when alternative means are available.

The "least harmful means" requirement thus recognizes and reflects not only the legal context in which targeted killing occurs but also the practical context. It is in states' interests to make arrests where possible, and they have the technology to ensure, at least to a greater extent than feasible in more conventional methods of warfare, that direct attacks are a last resort. As such, "least harmful means" presents a viable and appropriately sophisticated legal

---

[329] *Ibid.*

[330] Klein, *supra* note 287.

[331] See, for example, the *International Criminal Tribunal for the Former Yugoslavia: Final Report to the Prosecutor by the Committee Established to Review the NATO Bombing Campaign against the Federal Republic of Yugoslavia,* 39 I.L.M. 1257 (2000), in particular, the report on "The Attack on the Djakovica Convoy on 14/4/99," which describes the difficulties arising from the operating height of manned aircraft (at 1276).

[332] It may be the case that certain factors, such as the involvement of "mission essential" equipment that is considered too valuable to risk destruction, will prevent lower altitude in some contexts (Klein, *supra* note 287), but otherwise the risk of losing the US $4.5 million that a Predator drone is said to cost (O'Connell, *supra* note 96) should not prevent even the most cold-hearted from operating the drones at a lower altitude, given that states may be held liable to compensate financially those who suffer unjustifiable damage at the hands of those states.

stipulation to regulate a practice that otherwise offers genuine challenges to those rules that currently exist within international humanitarian law.

In contrast to the Supreme Court of Israel's characterization of terrorists, the "least harmful means" requirement is not derived from the existing legal rules of international humanitarian law. As a result, it does not risk eroding, or re-shaping, those rules in an attempt to apply international humanitarian law to regulate a type of armed conflict for which it was not designed. Instead, it gives expression to a principle underlying the law, that of military necessity, but tailors it to the particular circumstances of targeted killing and, more generally, to state conflicts with terrorist organizations.

The fact that the principles underlying international humanitarian law govern all actions that occur within the context of the armed conflict that it regulates does not mean that there is no need to give those principles expression through concrete rules. In fact, that is precisely what international humanitarian law does. The values encompassed by those principles represent a broad spectrum, while the norms that international humanitarian law articulates draw a relatively identifiable line.[333] The importance of delineating that line through expressing those principles has been shown, and it is that much greater when attempting to regulate a practice that struggles to fit within the existing framework.[334] Thus, while the court's characterization of terrorists arguably frustrates a fundamental principle of international humanitarian law, the "least harmful means" requirement ensures that a different fundamental principle is expressed and given scope within the context in which it is applied. In doing so, it is an example of the way in which international humanitarian law may remain a relevant and effective legal framework in regulating state conflicts with terrorist organizations, despite the conceptual difficulties that those conflicts appear to present.

Conclusion

The increasing resort by states to military force in their efforts to counter terrorist organizations and the threat such organizations

---

[333] Daniel Munoz-Rojas and Jean-Jaques Fresard, "The Roots of Behaviour in War: Understanding and Preventing IHL Violations" (2004) 853 Int'l Rev. Red Cross 204.

[334] *Ibid.*

present demands an increasing role for international humanitarian law in regulating those efforts. The fact remains, however, that as a legal framework international humanitarian law was not designed to regulate the type of asymmetrical armed conflicts that result. Consequently, its application encounters conceptual difficulties at even the most basic level. This does not mean, however, that it lacks the capacity to provide an effective framework for regulating those conflicts.

After 11 September 2001, United States administration lawyers considered the laws of war as a "relic," unsuited to the challenge that terrorism presented.[335] Yet that is to misunderstand what international humanitarian law is or, at least, what it can be. International humanitarian law is not simply a body of rules, which must be applied mechanically, if at all. Rather, it is the expression of principles that apply regardless of the type of conflict. Although they have found their current articulation in a set of rules designed for a different type, they may nonetheless provide the means by which this particular type of conflict can be regulated effectively.

The targeted killing policies of Israel and the United States are evidence of the potential problems that arise when attempting to apply strictly the prevailing legal rules of international humanitarian law. As a result of the particular circumstances in which such policies occur, they do not fit comfortably within the existing legal framework. Nonetheless, attempting to manipulate the current rules so as to apply them despite the evident conceptual difficulties in doing so, and the potentially problematic consequences that may result, should not be the preferred means of ensuring that international humanitarian law regulates these policies. Instead, resort should be made to the principles underlying international humanitarian law to ensure that, as law, it remains both relevant and effective. The "least harmful means" requirement illustrates that applying the principles, not simply the existing rules, of international humanitarian law not only prevents compromising the current framework but also allows for the fashioning of rules that are properly adapted to the circumstances that they are to regulate. In doing so, it presents a target at which it is actually worth aiming.

---

[335] Glazier, *supra* note 7 at 959.

Sommaire

Préciser l'objectif: Peut-on réconcilier les politiques d'assassinats ciblés des États-Unis et d'Israël avec le droit international humanitaire?

D'après la pratique étatique, l'assassinat ciblé est de plus en plus vu comme une stratégie viable et efficace pour combattre la menace posée par des organisations terroristes. Étant donné son rôle accru dans les conflits armés récents, il est particulièrement important que le droit international humanitaire (DIH) puisse fournir un cadre juridique dans lequel peut s'inscrire cette pratique. Tel qu'actuellement conçu, toutefois, le DIH est mal adapté à la nature particulière des conflits armés entre les États et les organisations terroristes en général, et, plus spécifiquement, à la pratique d'assassinats ciblés. Cet article passe en revue la décision de la Cour suprême d'Israël dans Public Committee against Torture in Israel *v.* Government of Israel, *qui sert d'exemple de tentative de réconciliation de l'assassinat ciblé et le DIH. Ce jugement met l'accent sur la qualification de "terroriste" et sur l'imposition de l'exigence des "moyens les moins préjudiciables." Tandis que ce premier met en relief, selon l'auteur, les difficultés associées à une telle tentative de réconciliation, ce dernier souligne les avantages de s'appuyer sur les principes fondamentaux du DIH, dans ce cas le principe de la nécessité militaire. L'auteur conclut que ce sont ces principes, plutôt que les règles existantes, qui doivent servir de mécanisme de réconciliation de l'assassinat ciblé et le DIH.*

Summary

Where Precision Is the Aim: Locating the Targeted Killing Policies of the United States and Israel within International Humanitarian Law

If state practice is any indication, targeted killing is increasingly becoming regarded as a viable and effective response to the threat posed by terrorist organizations. Its growing role in armed conflict makes it particularly important that international humanitarian law (IHL) prove capable of providing an effective framework within which this practice may be governed. As it is currently conceived, however, IHL has shown itself ill-suited to the particular nature of armed conflicts between states and terrorist organizations on a broad level and, more specifically, to the practice of targeted killing. This article examines the decision of the Israeli Supreme Court in Public

Committee against Torture in Israel v. Government of Israel *as an example of an effort to fit targeted killing within IHL, focusing on its characterization of "terrorists" and its imposition of the "least harmful means" requirement. The author suggests that, while the former exposes the difficulty of reconciling this development in armed conflict with existing rules, the latter demonstrates the benefits of relying on fundamental principles of IHL, in this case that of military necessity. The article concludes by contending that it is these principles, rather than existing rules, that should be viewed as the appropriate mechanism by which to accommodate targeted killing within IHL.*

Trading Away Women's Rights:
A Feminist Critique of the
Canada–Colombia Free Trade Agreement

GREGG ERAUW

INTRODUCTION

International investment agreements (IIAs) and free trade agreements (FTAs) with investment chapters are often advanced as a means to alleviate poverty, promote human rights, and strengthen democracy around the world.[1] However, opponents of international investment have argued that the provisions of these agreements only provide heightened protection for the rights of foreign investors that invest in a state party, while providing few, if any, obligations on such investors in the respect of human rights.[2] In addition, critics have argued that these investment agreements can deter state parties from implementing social policy that advances the public interest and protects the human rights of its citizens from the negative impacts of a foreign investor's activity.[3] This latter phenomenon

Gregg Erauw, B.A. (Hons) (WLU), M.A. (McMaster), J.D. candidate (Ottawa). Sincere thanks to Penelope Simons in the Faculty of Law at the University of Ottawa and Stefanie Ligori for their endless encouragement, guidance, and editorial input in the production of this article.

[1] Government of Canada, *Canada Concludes Negotiations for Free Trade, Labour Cooperation and Environment Agreements with Colombia*, News Release no.135 (7 June 2008), Government of Canada, <http://news.gc.ca/web/article-eng.do?nid=403869>.

[2] UN Human Rights Council (UNHRC), *Protect Respect and Remedy: A Framework for Business and Human Rights: Report of the Special Representative of the Secretary-General on the Issue of Human Rights and Transnational Corporations and Other Business Entities*, UN Doc. A/HRC/8/5 (2008) at para. 12–13.

[3] Penelope Simons, cited in Canada, Standing Committee on International Trade, *Human Rights, the Environment and Free Trade with Colombia* (June 2008) at 65. See also UNHRC, *supra* note 2; M. Sornarajah, *The International Law of Foreign Investment* (Cambridge: Cambridge University Press, 2004).

is particularly problematic when a state party to an investment agreement is engaged in an armed conflict in which human rights abuses and breaches of humanitarian law occur with impunity.[4] In these cases, the "governance gap" that exists between the state's ability to control protected corporate activity and manage the adverse effects of economic activity becomes all the more apparent.[5] These issues and their specific impact on Colombian women are of key concern with respect to the recently signed Canada–Colombia Free Trade Agreement (CCFTA).[6]

This article seeks to critically examine the proposed CCFTA using a feminist approach to international investment law and argues that the implementation of the CCFTA, combined with the current social, economic, and political dynamics in Colombia, will have a disproportionate impact on the rights of Colombian women. The first part of the article will provide a brief overview of the feminist approach to international law and international investment law and will discuss the importance of this approach in the analysis of the CCFTA. The second part will discuss the state of women's rights in Colombia, and the third part will examine the specific impact that the CCFTA's investment, dispute settlement, and labour rights provisions will have on Colombian women. Finally, the fourth part of the article will provide recommendations for addressing the CCFTA's adverse impact on Colombian women.

---

4   Georgette Gagnon, Audrey Macklin, and Penelope Simons, *Deconstructing Engagement: Corporate Self-Regulation in Conflict Zones: Implications for Human Rights and Canadian Public Policy*, University of Toronto Public Law Research Paper no. 04-07 (2003) at 12, Social Science Research Network, <http://ssrn.com/abstract=557002 or DOI: 10.2139/ssrn.557002>.

5   UNHRC, *supra* note 2 at para. 3; and *ibid.* at 1.

6   Canada–Colombia Free Trade Agreement, 21 November 2008, Department of Foreign Affairs and International Trade, <http://www.international.gc.ca/trade-agreements-accords-commerciaux/agr-acc/colombia-colombie/can-colombia-toc-tdm-can-colombie.aspx> [CCFTA]. At the time of writing, the CCFTA had not yet come into force, but its implementing statute was passed by Canada's Parliament and received Royal Assent on 29 June 2010. The CCFTA will come into force once Colombia has completed its ratification process. It is also important to note that the fact that the agreement is titled a "free-trade" agreement, rather than an "investment" agreement, is a misnomer. The article will later demonstrate that trade is not the major reason behind adopting the CCFTA, but, rather, it is to spur investment in oil, gas, and mining projects in Colombia by Canadian enterprises, which will be protected by the investor rights provisions in Chapter 8 of the CCFTA.

THE FEMINIST APPROACH TO INTERNATIONAL INVESTMENT LAW

WOMEN IN THE GLOBAL ECONOMY

In no country in the world are women economically, socially, politically, legally, and culturally equal to men in similar situations.[7] The best illustration of these disparities is in the global economy, where, although women represent half of the population, they "do two-thirds of the world's work, receive 10 percent of the world's income, and own only 1 percent of the means of production."[8] Furthermore, "[w]hile women actually work more hours than men in almost all societies, their work is under-remunerated and undervalued because most of it takes place outside the market economy, in households or subsistence sectors."[9] J. Ann Tickner explains that "earning lower wages and owning an insignificant proportion of the world's capital puts women at an enormous disadvantage in terms of power and wealth and thus contributes to their economic insecurity."[10] For feminists, this economic insecurity "can only be understood in the context of patriarchal structures ... which have the effect of consigning women to households or low-paying jobs."[11] One such patriarchal structure is rooted in international investment law.

THE FEMINIST CRITIQUE OF INTERNATIONAL LAW AND INTERNATIONAL INVESTMENT LAW

In international law, "sex and gender are an integral part ... in the sense that men and maleness are built into its structure."[12] This is primarily because "it remains true that a category of elite men monopolize all secular, religious, national and international institutional forms of power. This monopoly means that men's interests are defined and accepted as apparently objective and neutral categories, to the ultimate benefit of all men."[13] For example, feminists

---

7 Hilary Charlesworth and Christine Chinkin, *The Boundaries of International Law: A Feminist Analysis* (Manchester: Manchester University Press, 2000) at 4.

8 Martha C. Ward, *A World Full of Women* (Boston: Allyn and Bacon, 1996) at 224, cited in Richard H. Robbins, *Global Problems and the Culture of Capitalism*, 4th edition (Boston: Pearson Education, 2008) at 349.

9 J. Ann Tickner, "You Just Don't Understand: Troubled Engagements between Feminists and IR Theorists" (1997) 41 Int'l Studies Q. 611 at 626.

10 J. Ann Tickner, *Gender in International Relations: Feminist Perspectives on Achieving Global Security* (New York: Columbia University Press, 1992) at 75.

11 Tickner, *supra* note 9 at 627-28.

12 Charlesworth and Chinkin, *supra* note 7 at 19.

13 *Ibid.* at 4.

argue that the international legal system perpetuates a number of dichotomies that have a significant impact on women.[14] As Hilary Charlesworth explains, "[i]nternational legal discourse rests on a series of distinctions; for example, objective/subjective, legal/political, logic/emotion, order/anarchy, mind/body, culture/nature, action/passivity, public/private, protector/protected, independence/dependence."[15] Charlesworth further explains that these dichotomies are gendered such that the first term identifies "male" characteristics and the second "female" and that international law typically values the "male" characteristics more than the "female."[16] In particular, the dichotomy of public/private is problematic because traditionally there is a state-centric focus and privileging of sovereignty that overlooks internal inequalities, such as poverty and the economic inequality between men and women in the domestic or private realm. It is a division that draws a line "between the 'public' world of politics, government, and the state and the 'private' world of home, hearth and family."[17] In liberal thought, which is the conceptual basis for international investment agreements such as the CCFTA, the private realm is to be free from regulation and intrusion. As Anne Orford describes,

[l]iberalism was premised on the idea that all propertied men were born free and equal, meaning that the governance of one such man by another could only be legitimate by agreement. That agreement, imagined as a contract, created two opposed realms — the public realm, where men agreed to be governed by the state, and the private realm, where the state could not interfere with a man's liberty. The liberal state could not legitimately regulate behaviour understood to be properly in the realm of individual liberty. The protection of economic, social and cultural rights in

---

[14] See *ibid.* at 50. Feminism should not be seen as a single homogenous method or viewpoint. Feminists' critiques (or feminisms) vary. They include liberal feminism, radical feminism, third-world feminism, and post-modern feminism, to name a few. This article will draw on various feminist viewpoints in order to critique the CCFTA. Such an approach is called "situated-judgment" and employs different feminist analytical strategies in order to challenge international law's silence(s) towards women depending on the context and the level of analysis.

[15] Hilary Charlesworth, "Feminist Methods in International Law" (1999) 93 Am. J. Int'l L. 379 at 382.

[16] *Ibid.*

[17] *Ibid.*

turn draws on a tradition that sees the state as the principle source of power that must be constrained and harnessed.[18]

Furthermore, feminists would argue that the maintenance of the public/private distinction and the lack of regulation in the private realm often obscures and legitimizes men's domination over women.[19] In international investment law, IIAs and FTAs reinforce this distinction and its aforementioned inequality by not recognizing that the distribution of wealth and goods is structured along gender lines.[20]

A liberal argument in support of IIAs and FTAs is that international investment law can promote equality because it is premised on the principle of non-discrimination, which ensures "that the protection and benefits bestowed by the particular legal system are universally available to the subjects of that system."[21] The purpose of the international investment law regime and investment agreements is to protect from expropriation the property interests of investors and companies producing and manufacturing goods in foreign countries.[22] Agreements such as the CCFTA, which have "non-discrimination" provisions, claim to be "gender neutral." Gender neutral means that IIAs and FTAs are not specifically aimed at either men or women and are assumed to affect both sexes equally. However, as the evidence later in this article suggests, FTAs with investment chapters such as the CCFTA are more "gender blind" than gender neutral. Gender blind means that they ignore different gender roles, responsibilities, and capabilities and that a given policy is based on information derived from men's activities and/or assumes that those affected by the policy have the same needs and interests.[23] Considering the description of the socio-economic status of women in Colombia that follows in this article

---

[18] Anne Orford, "Contesting Globalization: A Feminist Perspective on the Future of Human Rights" (1998) 8 Transnat'l L. & Contemp. Probs. 171 at 175.

[19] Charlesworth and Chinkin, *supra* note 7 at 44.

[20] *Ibid.* at 39.

[21] David Kinley and Adam McBeth, "Human Rights, Trade and Multinational Corporations," in R. Sullivan, ed., *Business and Human Rights: Dilemmas and Solutions* (Sheffield: Greenleaf Publishing, 2003) at 57.

[22] John Currie, Craig Forcese, and Valerie Oosterveld, *International Law: Doctrine, Practice and Theory* (Toronto: Irwin Law, 2007) at 693.

[23] Heather Gibb, *Gender and Regional Trade Agreements* (paper produced for the thirteenth Meeting of the APEC Women Leaders Network, 12 May 2008) at 13

— where women work predominantly within the household, subsistence sectors, and outside of the market economy — their concerns and structural position in the global economy is ignored in international investment law and the legal framework of the CCFTA. International investment law and the CCFTA's ignorance of gender, in general, is also illustrative of how the discipline has flourished at the expense of women and that this silence on gender is "as important as its positive rules and rhetorical structures."[24] The silence with respect to gender disparities in the global economy and in Colombia does nothing but reinforce the systemic socio-economic inequality of Colombian women.

WHY FEMINISM MATTERS

In analyzing the CCFTA, feminism offers an approach that challenges the gendered assumptions upon which IIAs and FTAs are conceived and built. Furthermore, feminism helps investigate the gender silences within these agreements in order to discover and problematize their gender impacts. Where agreements claim to have a general application and to be neutral and impartial despite glaring gender inequality, feminism provides a tool for investigation. Therefore, employing the category of "women" can be a valuable method of highlighting the marginalization of women as well as questioning masculine norms that may be perpetuating structural violence upon them.[25] Specifically, when we consider the socio-economic position of women in a country with ongoing internal conflict, such as Colombia, IIAs and FTAs such as the CCFTA can contribute to their inequality by assuming that men and women have the same needs and interests and that the distribution of wealth in Colombia is not gendered.

SITUATION OF COLOMBIAN WOMEN

Colombia continues to be embroiled in a decades-long internal conflict, which is rife with violations of international humanitarian law and international human rights law.[26] Critics of the proposed

---

[unpublished] North-South Institute, <http://www.nsi-ins.ca/english/pdf/Gender_RTA.pdf>.

[24] Charlesworth and Chinkin, *supra* note 7 at 49.

[25] *Ibid.* at 2 and 60.

[26] See UNHRC, *Report of the UNHCHR on the Situation of Human Rights in Colombia*, UN Doc. A/HRC/10/32 (9 March 2009). See also Amnesty International,

CCFTA have stated their concern that by entering into the agreement with Colombia, Canada would be providing tacit approval of these violations and that its investors may be complicit beneficiaries of human rights abuses in Colombia.[27] Furthermore, there is a concern that with the protections afforded to Canadian investors under the agreement, along with the encouragement of investment in the mining and extractive sector, the CCFTA will have a detrimental impact on Colombians.

HUMAN RIGHTS ABUSES OF WOMEN IN COLOMBIA

Colombian women will be particularly affected by the CCFTA since the gendered human rights abuses that they face render them more vulnerable. Colombia is home to the second largest internally displaced population in the world, second only to the Sudan.[28] Currently, there are an estimated four million people internally displaced in Colombia, and, of those displaced persons, 74 percent are women and children.[29] This number is significant because displaced persons in Colombia often lack registration and identity documents, which makes it difficult for them to access basic government assistance, employment, healthcare, and education.[30]

In April 2009, the Colombian Constitutional Court affirmed that there was an "explicit link between displacement and sexual violence, and concluded that the conflict had a disproportionate impact on women."[31] The United Nations High Commissioner for Refugees (UNHCR) has also noted that displaced girls are more vulnerable to sexual exploitation and pregnancy than other teenagers in

---

Amnesty International Report 2009: State of the World's Human Rights, Amnesty International, <http://report2009.amnesty.org/en/regions/americas/colombia>.

27 MiningWatch Canada et al., *Land and Conflict — Resource Extraction, Human Rights, and Corporate Social Responsibility: Canadian Companies in Colombia* (Ottawa: Inter Pares, 2009) at 1, Inter Pares, <http://www.interpares.ca/en/publications/pdf/Land_and_Conflict.pdf>.

28 Refugees International, *Colombia: Displaced Women Demand Their Rights* (16 November 2009) at 1, Refugees International, <http://www.refintl.org/sites/default/files/111609_COL_displaced.pdf>.

29 MiningWatch Canada et al., *supra* note 27 at 5.

30 UN High Commissioner for Refugees (UNHCR), *The State of the World's Refugees 2006: Human Displacement in the New Millennium* (Oxford: Oxford University Press, 2006) at 170, UNHCR, <http://www.unhcr.org/4444afce0.html>.

31 Amnesty International, *supra* note 26.

Colombia.[32] As part of Colombia's internal conflict, guerrilla groups, paramilitaries, and government forces have been competing for political and economic control and wealth by displacing Colombians in order to appropriate lands rich in resources. In particular, these armed groups have used sexual violence as a weapon to effectively displace inhabitants from such lands. One report from the Colombian government's Ombudsman Office stated that 18 percent of displaced women identified sexual assault as a direct cause of their displacement.[33] However, sexual violence as a cause of displacement may also be under-reported because "women are ashamed to report incidents when attempting to register as displaced."[34]

Unfortunately for displaced Colombian women, perpetrators of sexual violence continue to carryout their activities with a great degree of impunity. In 2008, the Constitutional Court ordered the Colombian attorney-general's office to investigate 182 cases of sexual violence against displaced women, yet to date no one has been brought to justice for these offences nor has there been any progress in the investigation.[35] In addition, of the total number of cases, 58 percent were attributed to paramilitary forces, 23 percent to government security forces, 8 percent to insurgent groups, and the remainder to unknown perpetrators in Colombia's internal conflict.[36]

Due to the difficulty that displaced women face in obtaining government assistance and access to social services, many women are pressured into prostitution in order to feed their families. The risk is particularly acute for women who are forced to flee when armed groups in the conflict have killed their husbands or partners.[37] Thus, the social conditions that displaced women face places them at risk of further persecution through sexual violence. For example, displaced women in Chocó told Refugees International that,

almost every displaced woman they knew felt pressured into transactional sex in order for their family to survive, and there has also been a recent

[32] UNHCR, *supra* note 30 at 170.

[33] Refugees International, *supra* note 28 at 1.

[34] *Ibid.* at 2.

[35] UNHRC, *supra* note 26 at para. 61.

[36] Oxfam International, *Sexual Violence in Colombia: Instrument of War*, Briefing Paper (2009) at 14, Oxfam International, <http://www.oxfam.org/sites/www.oxfam.org/files/bp-sexual-violence-colombia.pdf>.

[37] Refugees International, *supra* note 28 at 2.

increase in trafficking of women for prostitution at the border with Panama ... Many displaced women can find informal employment as domestic workers, but pay is low (averaging only $50 per month) and work is insecure.[38]

Therefore, due to the intersectionality of their social location, displaced women in Colombia, as compared to men, experience economic insecurity differently and face unique risks in the context of economic, political, and social instability. In this way, any activity under the CCFTA that may cause displacement would serve to further the inequality of women in Colombia.

WOMEN'S SOCIO-ECONOMIC RIGHTS IN COLOMBIA

Poverty is also a problem in Colombia and contributes to the denial of the economic and social rights of women. Fifty-four percent of women, compared to a national average of 46 percent of the total population, live below the poverty line. Women also have an unemployment rate that is 8 percent higher than their male counterparts.[39] Of those persons living in poverty in Colombia, 68.2 percent live in rural areas where the armed conflict is most prevalent.[40] In addition, "rural poverty is of particular concern given that poverty and exclusion in rural areas has traditionally been one of the root causes of socio-political violence in the country and continues to be an important conflict accelerator."[41] Overall, Colombia's socio-economic conditions can be characterized as having significant inequalities.

Socio-economic inequalities are further demonstrated in land-ownership, where it was "found that 0.4 percent of landholders (15,273 holdings) account for 61.2 percent of registered agricultural land, while 97 percent (3.5 million landholders) share only 24.2 percent.[42] The organization ABColombia has noted that the concentration of land ownership is a direct result of internal

---

38 *Ibid.*

39 Oxfam International, *supra* note 36 at 8.

40 Canada, Standing Committee on International Trade, *supra* note 3 at 9.

41 ABColombia, *Poverty, Inequality and Drugs*, ABColombia, <http://www.abcolombia.org.uk/mainpage.asp?mainid=76>.

42 Center for International Policy, "Do Wealthy Colombian's Pay Their Taxes?" (3 August 2004) Center for International Policy, <http://www.ciponline.org/colombia/040804cip.htm>.

displacement in Colombia and further entrenches poverty in the
country:

Concentration of land ownership has increased over recent years, fuelled
by the forced displacement of rural communities: it is estimated that around
6 million hectares of land have been abandoned by people fleeing the
conflict. Unequal landownership deprives rural farmers of a livelihood
and so perpetuates income inequality. Additionally, by reducing the land
available for small-scale farmers to produce food for subsistence, unequal
landownership contributes to food insecurity, with resulting health problems including malnutrition, anaemia, calcium deficiencies, and deficiencies in calorie intake.[43]

To the extent that the disparity of landownership is a function of
internal displacement processes, it can be inferred that since women
and children account for 74 percent of the displaced people in Colombia, they are significantly affected by the landholdings disparity.
In order to limit the socio-economic disparities and promote
greater economic equality in Colombia, trade unions have been an
important mechanism for advocating for the rights of workers in
Colombia. However, the most recent statistics from the National
Trade Union School on the violence against women trade unionists
indicate that thirteen female trade union leaders were killed in the
first eleven months of 2006, fifteen in 2005, and sixteen in 2004.[44]
In 2009, a total of forty-five trade unionists were assassinated in
Colombia.[45]

---

43 ABColombia, *supra* note 41.

44 Helda Martínez, "Rights-Colombia: Defending Women's Defenders," *Inter Press
Service News Agency* (9 June 2008), Inter Press Service News Agency, <http://
ipsnews.net/news.asp?idnews=42720>.

45 Canadian Union of Public Employees (CUPE), *Forty-Five Colombian Union Leaders
Assassinated in 2009*, News Release (10 March 2010), CUPE, <http://cupe.ca/
trade/canada-colombia-trade-deal-report>. This is a decrease from 2008, when
forty-nine trade unionists were murdered, but still higher than in 2007 when
thirty-nine were killed. As of 14 September 2010, there were thirty-six trade
unionists murdered in Colombia, compared to twenty-six at the same time in
2009. One of the arguments advanced in favour of the CCFTA at the Standing
Committee on International Trade was that the human rights situation in Colombia was improving because total trade unionist deaths in 2007 decreased
from the seventy-two murders reported in 2006. For the 2006, 2007, and 2008
figures, see Canada, Standing Committee on International Trade, *supra* note 3
at 6; and Bill Conroy, *Labor Activists Say U.S.-Colombia Free Trade Agreement Will Be
Signed in Blood If Approved,* News Bulletin (30 September 2007), NarcoNews,

THE INTERSECTION BETWEEN HUMAN RIGHTS ABUSES AGAINST
WOMEN, THE CCFTA, AND FOREIGN INVESTORS

The internal conflict fuelling human rights abuses in Colombia occurs in rural areas that are rich in oil and gold. The left-wing guerrillas, paramilitaries, and government security forces battle for control over these limited resources in order to gain social, economic, and political power, in so doing they forcefully displace Colombians. As stated by Gauri Sreenivasan, in her testimony to the Standing Committee on International Trade,

[t]he overlap between [conflict and natural resources] is sobering. Colombian regions that are rich in minerals and oils have been marked by violence. They are the source of 87% of forced displacements, 82% of violations of human rights and international humanitarian law, and 83% of assassinations of trade union leaders in the country.[46]

Of further concern is that this violence could be exacerbated under the CCFTA. The president of Colombia, Álvaro Uribe, has commented that he hopes the CCFTA will "help spur oil, gas and mining exploration across half of Colombia's territory."[47] This level of investment would have serious implications for those individuals, particularly women, who have already suffered disproportionate displacement while living in rural areas rich in natural resources. Canadian investors currently have a significant amount of business in Colombia, with Canadian mining corporations accounting for 52 percent of all mining activity.[48] Furthermore, it is expected that the protections afforded to corporations under the CCFTA's investor provisions will provide the impetus for an influx of investment that will exacerbate the conflict as armed groups compete to claim

---

<http://www.narconews.com/Issue47/article2807.html>. For the figures reported on 14 September 2010, see Kirsten Begg, *Trade Unionist Murders Up in 2010* (14 September 2010), Colombia Reports, <http://colombiareports.com/colombia-news/news/11837-trade-unionist-murders-up-in-2010.html>.

46 Canada, Standing Committee on International Trade, *supra* note 3 at 33.

47 Mylene Bruneau, Council on Hemispheric Affairs, "Canada-Colombia Free Trade Agreement Could Be a Lose-Lose Deal" (1 May 2009), Council on Hemispheric Affairs, <http://www.coha.org/canada-colombia-free-trade-agreement-could-be-a-lose-lose-deal>.

48 MiningWatch Canada et al., *supra* note 27 at 11.

resource-rich land desired by foreign investors.[49] It is also important to note that increased mega-mining projects in Colombia can also displace artisanal miners and farmers through the environmental, health, and economic affects of investor activity in Colombia's mining sector.

Considering the state of women's rights in Colombia, there exists a serious risk that Canadian corporations could benefit from past human rights abuses through the use of misappropriated land as well as be complicit in ongoing human rights abuses should they operate and profit in Colombia's conflict zone. In addition, the clear failure of the state of Colombia to protect women from human rights abuses can create a serious problem for foreign investors that may be looked to as the sole provider and decision maker in a community where it has invested.

The Colombian context presents especially difficult challenges for companies making investments to be able to protect or respect human rights standards and contribute positively to the overall human rights situation. Indeed, the high level of violence and the continued presence of paramilitaries in areas of high investment raise serious concerns that Canadian investment risks contributing to, or exacerbating, the violence and risks benefiting from, or being complicit with, the human rights abuses and massive displacement that continue to occur. In such circumstances, "where the state is not willing or able to protect human rights, the obligation on corporations to respect human rights becomes more critical while, at the same time more difficult to define and fulfil."[50]

Since women in Colombia face a disproportionate risk of displacement and physical violence and face higher rates of poverty and work predominately in the informal economy, they risk further exploitation under the impact of the CCFTA. Where women are already marginalized due to the social, economic, and political conditions in Colombia, the CCFTA enters into an environment that has great gender disparities and, without specific attention to women's rights, risks exacerbating and contributing to inequality. Advocates of investment agreements have argued that the benefit

---

[49] The CCFTA provisions mentioned include: the rules on non-discrimination, national treatment (Article 803), most-favoured-nation treatment (Article 804), restrictions on performance requirements (Article 807), rules on expropriation and compensation (Article 811), and the investor-state dispute settlement clause (Article 819).

[50] MiningWatch Canada et al., *supra* note 27 at 1.

of the CCFTA is that it will promote prosperity and equality and help eliminate human rights abuses by advancing democracy and eliminating poverty.[51] The next section, however, illustrates the deficiencies of international investment law by examining specific provisions of the CCFTA and how its current conception, structure, and enforcement provide little protection for women.

THE FEMINIST APPROACH AND THE EFFECT OF SPECIFIC CCFTA PROVISIONS ON COLOMBIAN WOMEN

In international investment law, the needs of women are ignored in a number of ways. According to Fiona Beveridge, the core values of international investment law, such as non-discrimination on the grounds of nationality and equality before the law, are based on a dichotomy between market and state that has been problematized by feminists as a concept that delegitimizes state intervention and positions social interests as being opposed to market interests.[52] For example, when looking at the investor-state dispute settlement provisions of agreements such as the CCFTA, there is a possibility that a government's attempts to transcend the systemic inequality of women (or other disadvantaged groups for that matter) through the implementation of laws and regulations on social policy could be seen as a violation of the national treatment, most-favoured-nation treatment, or performance requirements provisions of the CCFTA, and, therefore, the government would be in non-compliance under the agreement and subject to penalties. Furthermore, while international investment law may, on the one hand, offer formal accommodation of gender-based claims (that is, Article 2201.3 of the CCFTA, which permits a defence of social policy that is neces-sary for human life and health), through the expression of its core values in the agreement it simultaneously strengthens a "dichotom-ous view of international economic relations, which serves to devalue

---

[51] See Canada, Standing Committee on International Trade, *supra* note 3 at 19, 22, 23, 29, and 65. The advocates that I refer to include individuals that gave testimony to this effect to the Standing Committee on International Trade. They include Álvaro Uribe, president of Colombia; Thomas D'Aquino, chief executive officer and president of the Canadian Council of Chief Executives; Jean-Michel Laurin, vice-president of global business policy for Canadian Manufacturers and Exporters; and Brian Zeiler-Kligman, policy analyst for the Canadian Chamber of Commerce.

[52] Fiona Beveridge, "Feminist Perspectives in International Economic Law," in Doris Buss and Ambreena Manji, eds., *International Law: Modern Feminist Approaches* (Portland: Hart Publishing, 2005) 173 at 190.

such claims."[53] This reinforced dichotomy will be explored and critiqued later in this article, during the discussion on Article 819 and Article 2201.3 that concern the dispute settlement provisions of the CCFTA.

Of additional concern to feminists is that neither the main text nor the side agreements of the CCFTA mention women or the rights of women. This is significant because the evidence in the previous section illustrates that investment affects men and women differently. While FTAs such as the CCFTA appear on the surface to be gender neutral and impartial, and therefore treat their subjects equally, such neutrality is a misconception. On the contrary, these agreements are in fact silent with respect to women's rights. They ignore women's specific socio-economic needs and interests and perpetuate their marginalization. Furthermore, the legal framework of the CCFTA provisions, which is discussed later in this article, reinforces the socio-economic gender hierarchy, constricts government attempts to alleviate historical disadvantage through substantive policy measures, and imposes no obligations on foreign investors to ensure that their investment activities do not have an adverse impact on the rights of Colombian women.

INVESTMENT PROVISIONS: CHAPTER 8

The CCFTA investment provisions are significant because the current level of trade between Canada and Colombia is a small fraction compared to the current level of investment, as well as the expected level of investment, that flows from Canada to Colombia. In 2009, trade totalled $1.33 billion between Canada and Colombia, while Canadian exports accounted for $601 million.[54] In contrast, Canadian direct investment in Colombia totalled $773 million in 2009.[55] However, in 2007, the Canadian Embassy in Bogotá estimated that the current stock of Canadian investment in Colombia

---

53 *Ibid.* at 191.

54 Office of the Chief Economist, *Merchandise Trade by Country (Customs Basis)*, Department of Foreign Affairs and International Trade, <http://www.international.gc.ca/economist-economiste/assets/pdfs/PFACT_Annual_Merchandise_Trade_by_Country-ENG.pdf>. All funds are in Canadian dollars, unless otherwise specified.

55 Office of the Chief Economist, *Outward FDI Stocks by Country*, Department of Foreign Affairs and International Trade, <http://www.international.gc.ca/economist-economiste/assets/pdfs/FDI_stocks-Outward_by_Country-ENG.pdf>.

was significantly higher at $3 billion.[56] These figures illustrate that
the level of investment is what the CCFTA is most concerned about,
despite it being titled a "free trade" agreement. Earlier-mentioned
statements from the president of Colombia also demonstrate that
attracting foreign investment is his primary objective in signing and
ratifying the CCFTA. The investment provisions of the CCFTA include national treatment,[57] most-favoured-nation treatment,[58]
performance requirements,[59] expropriation,[60] and corporate social
responsibility.[61]

ARTICLES 803 AND 804: NATIONAL TREATMENT AND
MOST-FAVOURED NATION TREATMENT

The national treatment clause, Article 803 of the CCFTA, affirms
that investors from either state party are to have their investments
treated no less favourably than local investors in like circumstances
with respect to the establishment, acquisition, expansion, management, conduct, operation, and sale or other disposition of investments in its territory.[62] In other words, Canadian corporations and
their investments are to be treated no less favourably than Colombian ones. The most-favoured nation clause, Article 804 of the
CCFTA, states that investors from either state party are to have their
investments treated no less favourably than investors of a non-party
in like circumstances with respect to the establishment, acquisition,
expansion, management, conduct, operation, and sale or other
disposition of investments in its territory.[63] Therefore, Canadian
corporations are to have their investments treated no less favourably
than Colombia treats other foreign investors in its territory.

---

[56] Department of Foreign Affairs and International Trade, *Economic Analysis of
Prospective Free Trade Agreement(s) between Canada and the Countries of the
Andean Community* (June 2007) at 11, Department of Foreign Affairs and
International Trade, <http://www.international.gc.ca/trade-agreements-accords-
commerciaux/assets/pdfs/FINAL_And_Econ_Anal_Ju_22_2007-App-en.pdf>.

[57] CCFTA, *supra* note 6 at 803.

[58] *Ibid.* at 804.

[59] *Ibid.* at 807.

[60] *Ibid.* at 811.

[61] *Ibid.* at 816.

[62] *Ibid.* at 803.

[63] *Ibid.* at 804.

These two articles are also known as non-discrimination clauses. The purpose of these provisions is rooted in the minimum standards of protection that are owed by states to aliens (foreigners) under customary international law.[64] However, in the latter part of the twentieth century, protection has shifted from agreements between states that protect the civil rights of aliens to agreements that protect the rights of foreign investors.[65]

In light of the socio-economic position of Colombian women mentioned earlier, as well as the socio-economic position of women globally, where women receive 10 percent of the world's income and own only 1 percent of the means of production,[66] there is a clear gender disparity that alerts us to the fact that the investor is predominately male. Furthermore, the feminist perspective that international law and international investment law has "maleness" built into its structure is demonstrated by the security that investors receive in the CCFTA's non-discrimination provisions. These provisions, Articles 803 and 804, legally reinforce and preserve systemic socio-economic inequality based on gender where women's inequality is the product of domination of women by men.[67]

Articles 803 and 804 ensure the domination of men over women by maintaining the dichotomy between market and social concerns. The best illustration of this relationship is how investors are protected under the CCFTA from the redistributive capacity of the state. For example, Articles 803 and 804 do not allow for specific exceptions to the prohibition on discrimination against foreign investors when the state is trying to pursue policy objectives, such as human rights.[68] Rather, state parties must rely on either reservations or the general exceptions provision (Article 2201.3) and hope that an arbitration panel will recognize the validity of human rights policies. Unfortunately, as the case of *Compañia de Aguas del Aconquija S.A. and Vivendi Universal S.A. v. Argentine Republic*, which is

---

64 Luke Eric Peterson, *Human Rights and Bilateral Investment Treaties: Mapping the Role of Human Rights Law within Investor-State Arbitration* (Montreal: International Centre for Human Rights and Democratic Development, 2009) at 10, Rights & Democracy, <http://www.dd-rd.ca/site/_PDF/publications/globalization/HIRA-volume3-ENG.pdf>.

65 *Ibid.* at 11.

66 Robbins, *supra* note 8.

67 Catherine MacKinnon, *Feminism Unmodified: Discourses on Life and Law* (Cambridge, MA: Harvard University Press, 1987) at 39, cited in Charlesworth and Chinkin, *supra* note 7 at 42.

68 I credit Penelope Simons for bringing this point to my attention.

discussed later in this article, demonstrates, using reservations or general exceptions provisions do not always guarantee that an arbitration panel will recognize the government's policy in the pursuit of human rights as non-discriminatory treatment against investors. The impact is that the CCFTA's non-discrimination provisions restrain a government's ability to pursue policies that seek to achieve equality of outcomes, thereby ensuring that the male position as investor and possessor of global wealth is secured, while women remain socially and economically marginalized.

Women in Colombia are further disadvantaged by the CCFTA because the investment provisions, while protecting investor rights, impose no obligations on these actors to protect or promote the rights of Colombian women affected by the adverse impacts of foreign investment. This arrangement privileges the interests and needs of men that own the means of production but ignores the interests and needs of those people subjected to the adverse impacts of foreign investment. Since human rights violations against women already occur with a great degree of impunity in Colombia, the establishment of additional protections for investors under Articles 803 and 804 further protects the investment interests of men and contributes to a culture of impunity. For example, if the government of Colombia develops a social policy that attempts to constrain the adverse impact of a foreign investment project on women, this could be seen as a "restriction on their investment" or "unjustifiable discrimination," and the investor can have its interests protected under the investor-state dispute settlement provisions of the CCFTA.

The legal rules established in Articles 803 and 804 that treat investors equally are also problematic because they ignore the structural impediments faced by women in Colombia and the global economy. These non-discrimination provisions, much like the anti-discrimination provisions in domestic legislation, require women to conform to a male-defined world because the provisions are only enforced with respect to individual cases of discrimination, thus failing to address structural inequality.[69] Anti-discrimination provisions "can at most solve a limited number of discrete problems without addressing their underlying causes."[70] Furthermore, the principle of equal treatment cannot adequately transform a world in which the distribution of goods is structured along gendered

---

[69] Charlesworth and Chinkin, *supra* note 7 at 39.

[70] Nicola Lacey, "Legislation against Sex Discrimination: Questions from a Feminist Perspective" (1987) 14 J.L. & Soc'y 411 at 415, cited in *ibid.*

lines because equal treatment "assumes a world of autonomous individuals starting a race or making free choices [that] has no cutting edge against the fact that men and women are simply running different races."[71] In order for women to be taken into account or equally benefit from non-discrimination provisions under the CCFTA, women would have to have the same needs, interests, values, and priorities as investors. Essentially, women would have to run the same race as men. However, because of their socio-economic position, this experience is not plausible. In addition, even if women had the same needs and interests as men, it would only give women "access to a world already constituted by men and with the parameters determined by them."[72]

ARTICLE 807: PERFORMANCE REQUIREMENTS

The clause on performance requirements, Article 807 of the CCFTA, provides that neither state party may impose or enforce a performance requirement on an investor. In particular, Article 807 prohibits a state party from requiring an investor to: export a given level or percentage of goods or services; achieve a given level or percentage of domestic content; purchase, use, or accord a particular good produced or sold by people in its territory; restrict sales of an investor's goods or services or specify the volume or value of exports; or specify the market to which a good or service produced by the investment is supplied.[73] Considering that Colombian women tend to hold less secure employment and are more likely to live in poverty, the government of Colombia may wish to address this disadvantage by establishing new social policy, which attempts to secure equality of outcomes for men and women. However, under the CCFTA a problem arises if this new policy in any way infringes on the rights of Canadian investors. By denying an investor a particular benefit or requiring them to bare some of the obligations or cost of the social policy, there is a risk that the state investor dispute settlement provision of the CCFTA could be invoked by the investor.[74] A claim from a foreign investor could arise where the investor feels that the concerned policy imposes performance requirements. For example, if the government decides to promote small- and medium-sized

71 *Ibid.*

72 *Ibid.*

73 CCFTA, *supra* note 6 at 807.

74 Peterson, *supra* note 64 at 39.

enterprises (SMEs) operated by female entrepreneurs in Colombia by requiring foreign investors to purchase local supplies, services, or goods from these SMEs, it would be contrary to the restrictions on performance requirements under Article 807 of the CCFTA, and the dispute settlement provision could be engaged by the investor.

Restrictions on performance requirements eliminate the Colombian government's opportunity to use foreign direct investment to meet specific domestic economic objectives, such as hiring local workers.[75] The ramification of Article 807 is that it impedes a state party's range of options in developing public policy and, in particular, policy that promotes substantive socio-economic equality domestically through affirmative action. When an investor is protected from sharing the burden of eliminating systemic inequality, while benefiting from a legal arrangement that reinforces inequality, the status quo is maintained, and the domination of men over women continues with legal authorization.

ARTICLE 811: EXPROPRIATION

Article 811 of the CCFTA provides that a state party cannot nationalize or expropriate a covered investment either directly or indirectly unless it occurs for a public purpose and is conducted in a non-discriminatory manner, with prompt, adequate, and effective compensation at fair market value in accordance with the due process of law.[76] The irony of this provision is that investors have the opportunity to receive fair and just compensation for an infringement of their investment rights, while the expropriation of women's undervalued and underpaid labour allows foreign investors to accumulate the wealth they now seek to protect under the CCFTA. Furthermore, the predominance of investment by Canadian investors in the oil, gas, and mining sectors has led to mining activity occurring on lands expropriated from Colombians during the forced displacement of inhabitants by paramilitaries, guerrillas, and military threats.[77] Expropriations by these latter groups have not occurred with the protections that investors receive under Article

---

[75] Tony Vanduzer, Penelope Simons, and Graham Mayeda, "Modeling International Investment Agreements for Economic Development," in V. Qualo, ed., *Bilateralism and Development: Emerging Trade Patterns* (London: Cameron May, 2008) at 384.

[76] CCFTA, *supra* note 6 at 811.

[77] See MiningWatch Canada et al., *supra* note 27 at 6 and 43.

811, specifically when they occur for a public purpose and are conducted in a non-discriminatory manner, with prompt, effective, and adequate compensation, and in accordance with the due process of law.[78]

ARTICLE 816: CORPORATE SOCIAL RESPONSIBILITY

Article 816 of the CCFTA includes a unique corporate social responsibility provision that "[e]ach Party should encourage enterprises ... to voluntarily incorporate internationally recognized standards of corporate social responsibility in their internal policies"[79] to address issues such as "labour, the environment, human rights, community relations and anti-corruption."[80] While Article 816 is new to Canadian investment agreements and is a significant step forward in recognizing that investment has consequences for human health, labour rights, and the environment, the corporate social responsibility provision of the CCFTA remains insufficient. This insufficiency is primarily a result of Article 816 being only applicable to state parties and not to investors specifically as well as the fact that it is strictly voluntary and merely a best efforts provision that is unenforceable.[81] In particular, Article 816 suffers from the same deficiencies as other international corporate social responsibility codes and guidelines.[82] Some of the criticisms of these guidelines are that they are vague and have poorly defined language, are aspirational and drafted in permissive language, as well as recognize a commitment to the law of the host state rather than international law.[83] Essentially, this means that nothing will change under the CCFTA with respect to corporate social responsibility and the impact

---

[78] *Ibid.*

[79] CCFTA, *supra* note 6 at 816.

[80] *Ibid.*

[81] Canadian Council for International Co-operation (CCIC) et al., *Making a Bad Situation Worse: An Analysis of the Text of the Canada-Colombia Free Trade Agreement* (Ottawa: CCIC, 2009) at 18, Make Poverty History, <http://www.makepoverty history.ca/en/colombia/ analysis>.

[82] For example, the Global Sullivan Principles of Social Responsibility, the International Code of Ethics for Canadian Business, the Voluntary Principles on Security and Human Rights, the Organisation for Economic Co-operation and Development Guidelines for Multinational Enterprises, and the Global Compact.

[83] Penelope Simons, "Corporate Voluntarism and Human Rights: The Adequacy and Effectiveness of Voluntary Self-Regulation Regimes" (2004) 59 Relations industrielles/Industrial Relations 101 at 109–11.

of investment on women. The adverse impacts of Canadian investment are illustrated in the following section with an examination
of current corporate mining activity in Colombia and how the rights
of Colombian women are impacted when corporate social responsibility is not enforced.

One of the primary objectives of the CCFTA, as articulated by
Colombia's president, is to spur mining and oil extraction investment in over half of the country's resource-rich rural areas.[84] This
proposed influx of investment creates various problems for women
in Colombia. First, the internal conflict could be fuelled further
with armed groups competing for land rich in natural resources,
thereby displacing more people in Colombia, of which women are
already a disproportionate part. According to a 2006 United Nations' report,

> [t]he conflict [has been] complicated by interests in the ... exploitation
> of huge deposits of oil and other mineral resources found across the
> country's major regions. Struggle for and control of flow of income or
> rents from these economies provided additional sources for financing of
> the armed conflict, as well as the motivations and strategies for continuing
> it. The interests involved range from the local, through the national, to
> the transnational ... It seems that the possession of land has become one
> of the objectives of the paramilitary forces. Various sources report that
> disappearances perpetrated against the civilian population in rural areas
> may be aimed at causing terror and displacement, and the unlawful ap-
> propriation of land and other property.[85]

Armed groups are also able to appropriate land by use of force
or threat of force, making owners sign transfers and deeds to land
under duress and for little compensation.[86] Even if displacement
is a result of Colombia's armed conflict, lands obtained by foreign
investors for economic activity will likely be the result of such forced
displacement, thereby making such investors complicit beneficiaries
of the human rights violations.[87]

---

[84] Bruneau, *supra* note 47.

[85] UNHRC, *Report of the Working Group on Enforced or Involuntary Disappearances,
Addendum, Mission to Columbia (5–13 July 2005)*, UN Doc. E/CN.4/2006/56/
Add.1 (17 January 2006) at para. 13 and 56, cited in MiningWatch Canada at
al., *supra* note 27 at 6.

[86] *Ibid.*

[87] *Ibid.*

Second, transnational corporate activity can have impacts on women's economic, social, and cultural rights. For example, in Cajamarca, Colombia, where subsistence agriculture is most prevalent and poverty widespread, the arrival of AngloGold Ashanti, a South African gold mining company, had a significant impact on the employment of women in the town. Initially when the mine opened, four hundred workers were hired. Although not many of the workers hired were women, some of the women were offered jobs in the mines as drilling supervisors. Unfortunately, when the female workers got pregnant, they were fired from their positions.[88] In addition, non-governmental organization (NGO) officials from the area of Cajamarca have stated that historically prostitution, alcohol, and drugs accompany mining activity and that when Anglo-Gold Ashanti came to town the number of prostitutes increased substantially once the mine opened.[89] Foreign investor activity in the mining sector can also have a significant impact on traditional industries such as subsistence farming, where the mining of land renders farming impossible. AngloGold Ashanti has also been accused of causing water shortages and widespread pollution by using cyanide in the leaching process, which particularly affects the health of children, seniors, and pregnant women.[90] Once the land has been mined and individuals can no longer subsist off of the land, many women and girls are forced by members of their own family to become prostitutes in order to make ends meet.

The negative impact of mining from foreign investors is further demonstrated by the effect that Canadian mining has had on food security in Colombia. Two Canadian corporations operating in Colombia, Greystar and B2Gold, have been implicated in preventing peasant farmers from accessing necessary crop inputs, such as seeds, fertilizer, and herbicides. This interference prevents farmers from getting their crops to market, which leads to unemployment, underemployment, and displacement because of increased food insecurity.[91] In addition, once the land is mined, it becomes virtually useless for any other productive purpose, including growing subsistence crops in the future. This occurs not only when the mine occupies

---

88 Helda Martínez, "Women Lead Opposition to Gold Mine," *Inter Press Service News Agency* (3 August 2009), Inter Press Service News Agency, <http://ipsnews.net/news.asp?idnews=47942>.

89 *Ibid.*

90 *Ibid.*

91 MiningWatch Canada at al., *supra* note 27 at 18.

productive land and withdraws it from food production but also when mining activity pollutes the water or diverts water supplies for the operation of the mine and undermines agricultural productivity.[92] Food insecurity affects women disproportionately because of the cultural norms that prioritize the nutrition of boys and men, leading women to forego eating so that the rest of their family does not go hungry.[93] If locals are not able to gain employment at the mine, which has become the primary employer in the town, they often have few, if any, options. This fact also hits women especially hard since mining is such a physically intensive occupation, where some workers have to haul heavy equipment up steep mountainsides, and women are often deemed unsuitable for the work.[94] An argument espoused by Canadian investors and those promoting the CCFTA is that investment activity will boost employment in Colombia.[95] However, if it displaces and renders useless industries that have sustained a community for hundreds of years (that is, subsistence agriculture and artisanal mining) — replacing it with a single employer that hires fewer workers in the community — little benefit has been created by the investment. Again in the case of Greystar, community leaders in California, Colombia, have stated that Greystar's investment and mining operations have eliminated unemployment, while, in reality, 90 percent of women of working age were unemployed.[96] Given the lack of employment opportunities with foreign mining corporations, investor activity has the potential of pressuring women into the informal economy. This renders women even more vulnerable, since working as domestic workers or prostitutes in order to obtain the necessities of life places them at an increased risk of violence and abuse.

The evidence illustrates that Canadian investors such as Greystar are currently contributing to the marginalization of women's rights in Colombia. With respect to Article 816 of the CCFTA and voluntary corporate social responsibility, this means that Greystar's activities will not change in Colombia once the CCFTA comes into force.

[92] *Ibid.*

[93] Charlesworth and Chinkin, *supra* note 7 at 7.

[94] Martínez, *supra* note 88.

[95] See Canada, Standing Committee on International Trade, *supra* note 3 at 22–23. Testimony of President Uribe, Thomas D'Aquino, and Jean-Michel Laurin supported this proposition.

[96] Juan Lucero, "California, Pueblo Indignado," editorial comment, *El Tiempo* (18 April 2005), quoted in MiningWatch Canada at al., *supra* note 27 at 17.

The culture of impunity combined with unenforceable corporate social responsibility standards do not provide an adequate impetus for changing corporate behaviour or for assurances that women's rights are protected from adverse investor activity.

ANNEX II: COLOMBIAN RESERVATIONS TO THE CCFTA

Annex II of the CCFTA provides that some broad sectors and policies may be exempt from certain CCFTA obligations and allows both the Colombian and Canadian governments future policy flexibility.[97] In Colombia's reservations, there is an exemption made for minorities and indigenous groups, that "Colombia reserves the right to adopt or maintain any measure according rights or preferences to socially or economically disadvantaged minorities and ethnic groups, including with respect to the communal lands held by ethnic groups in accordance with Art. 63 of the *Constitución Política de Colombia.*"[98] This reservation applies to Articles 803, 804, and 807 of the CCFTA. Such a reservation is important for the protection of indigenous and minority rights. However, it is concerning that there is no corresponding reservation for the rights or preferences of women who are also disadvantaged socially and economically in Colombia. This furthers the argument that a gendered hierarchy is maintained throughout the CCFTA to the detriment of women's specific socio-economic needs and interests. While male rights are taken into account, women's rights are ignored.

ARTICLE 819 AND ARTICLE 2201.3: THE INVESTOR-STATE DISPUTE SETTLEMENT PROVISIONS

Article 819 of the CCFTA allows an investor to bring a state party to binding international arbitration on its own initiative if it believes that the state has infringed on its rights under the Chapter 8 investment rules of national treatment, most-favoured-nation treatment, performance requirements, and expropriation.[99] There is an exemption to this rule, however, under Article 2201.3. Article 2201.3 provides the government with a defence if it can show that the measures that infringed an investor's rights were necessary to: protect human, animal, or plant life or health, ensure compliance

---

97 CCIC et al., *supra* note 81 at 17.

98 CCFTA, *supra* note 6 at Annex II—Colombia.

99 *Ibid.,* Article 819. Note that Article 816, the corporate social responsibility provision, is exempt from investor-state arbitration.

with laws and regulations that are not inconsistent with the CCFTA, or conserve living or non-living exhaustible natural resources.[100] These provisions pose a number of problems for the Colombian government. First, it is very costly for a developing country to defend against a claim from an investor in arbitration. Furthermore, if the investor is successful in the dispute, the Colombian government may be subject to a significant award of damages. Both of these possibilities can influence the decision of whether or not to introduce social policy initiatives in the public interest, leading to a regulatory chill. In 2007, for example, an international arbitration panel found that Argentina was liable to Vivendi Universal for US $105 million in damages, plus more than US $700,000 in legal costs. This occurred after the arbitration panel found that the Argentine province of Tucumán expropriated Vivendi's investment for the provision of water and sewage services in the province.[101]

Advocates of investment agreements such as the CCFTA point to the Chapter 22 general exceptions provisions that would allow for the Colombian government to meet particular social policy objectives even if they infringe on investor rights. Article 2201.3 states that:

For the purposes of Chapter Eight (Investment), subject to the requirement that such measures are not applied in a manner that constitute arbitrary or unjustifiable discrimination between investment or between investors, or a disguised restriction on international trade or investment, nothing in this Agreement shall be construed to prevent a Party from adopting or enforcing measures necessary:

(a) to protect human, animal or plant life or health, which the Parties understand to include environmental measures necessary to protect human, animal or plant life and health;

---

[100] *Ibid.*, Article 2201.3.

[101] See *Compañía de Aguas del Aconquija S.A. and Vivendi Universal S.A. v. Argentine Republic* (2007), Case no. ARB/97/3, International Centre for Settlement of Investment Disputes (ICSID). In its decision, ICSID awarded Vivendi US $105 million, plus interest against Argentina when the province of Tucumán had denied Vivendi fair and equitable treatment and expropriated Vivendi's investment for the provision of water and sewage services in the province. Vivendi's investment was protected under a bilateral investment treaty between France and Argentina. In addition, the arbitration tribunal awarded legal costs to Vivendi in the amount of US $701,961. In its defence, Argentina argued that it and the province were not liable because the water provided by Vivendi was a risk to human health. This is a defence that is similarly provided by Article 2201.3 of the CCFTA.

(b) to ensure compliance with laws and regulations that are not inconsistent with this Agreement; or

(c) for the conservation of living or non-living exhaustible natural resources.[102]

With the inclusion of this provision, supporters of investment agreements have argued that gender-sensitive policies enacted by the host government may be saved, even if the government policy infringes on investors rights in Chapter 8 of the CCFTA.[103] Yet, the inclusion of Article 2201.3 does not ensure that the issues of concern to women will be considered or that a gender analysis will take place even if this article is invoked as a defence by the Colombian government at arbitration. As Fiona Beveridge explains, the "general exceptions" styled provisions are inadequate in three respects. First, dispute settlement arbitration is usually an uncertain process, where the panel balances the competing claims by attempting to assess what constitutes "arbitrary or unjustifiable" under Article 2201.3.[104] One consequence of arguing a gender-based claim on the basis of this exception provision is that it can have what Beveridge calls a "chilling effect" on governments setting economic and social regulations:

The argument about "chilling" appears at heart to be an argument about legal certainty: that since the requirements of international trade law are set in the form of standards (most favoured nation, national treatment and proportionality, for example), there is an inherent uncertainty about which exceptions will be deemed acceptable and which unacceptable. This uncertainty can be regarded as a disincentive to governments to embark on regulatory paths which seem to raise a "risk" of being declared unlawful by such standards.[105]

In *Vivendi Universal v. Argentina,* for example, Argentina unsuccessfully relied on an exceptions provision of its bilateral investment

---

[102] CCFTA, *supra* note 6, Article 2201.3.

[103] Beveridge, *supra* note 52 at 185–6. In her article, Beveridge makes a feminist critique of the WTO Dispute Settlement Panel and Article XX of the General Agreement on Tariffs and Trade, 55 U.N.T.S. 194. I cite her analysis here since it is illustrative of the same principles that the CCFTA's Article 2201.3 is based. In addition, the fundamental international economic law principles and provision wording underpinning the WTO panel's defence, GATT Article XX, is the same as that under Article 2201.3 of the CCFTA.

[104] *Ibid.* at 186.

[105] *Ibid.* at 188.

agreement with France, which is similar to Article 2201.3 of the CCFTA. In its argument before the arbitration panel, Argentina argued and provided evidence that the quality of the water and sewage treatment being provided by Vivendi was a risk to human health and that this issue provided the province of Tucumán with a valid reason to expropriate Vivendi's investment. Unfortunately for Argentina and the province, the arbitration panel did not find this claim persuasive and found that the expropriation in the form of human health to be unacceptable in this case.

Second, Beveridge also notes that arbitrators on dispute settlement panels are trade and investment law specialists, not human rights specialists.[106] Therefore, it can be strongly asserted that they have a bias towards a claim that furthers investment rather than social policy and the adequate consideration or importance of human rights in the interpretation of the CCFTA. Third, Beveridge suggests that the interpretation of these agreements in favour of gender-based claims is severely restricted by the scope of the agreements themselves because it makes no reference to gender equality or to the advancement of women.[107]

CHAPTER 16 LABOUR PROVISIONS AND THE CANADA–COLOMBIA
LABOUR COOPERATION AGREEMENT

Although the CCFTA does not mention women in its text, human rights are mentioned in Chapter 16 of the CCFTA text and in the Canada–Colombia Agreement on Labour Cooperation (CCALC).[108] In both agreements, the mention of human rights is in reference to labour rights, which are foundational to international human rights.[109] Within the text of the CCFTA, Chapter 16 provides that Canada and Colombia, as members of the International Labour Organization (ILO), affirm their obligations and commitment to the ILO Declaration on Fundamental Principles and Rights at Work.[110] This declaration is "an expression of commitment by government, employers and workers' organizations to uphold basic

---

[106] *Ibid.* at 186.

[107] *Ibid.*

[108] Canada, Canada–Colombia Labour Cooperation Agreement, 21 November 2008, Human Resources and Skills Development, <http://www.hrsdc.gc.ca/eng/labour/labour_agreements/ccalc/index.shtml> [CCALC].

[109] Currie, *supra* note 22 at 545.

[110] CCFTA, *supra* note 6 at Chapter 16.

human values that are vital to our social and economic lives."[111] The four principles enumerated in the declaration are: freedom of association and collective bargaining; the elimination of all forms of forced labour; the abolition of child labour; and, finally, the elimination of discrimination in employment and occupation. The latter principle has a gender component and takes into account gender-based claims. Unfortunately, Chapter 16 of the CCFTA contains only general statements that are not enforceable standards and obligations in international investment law.[112]

In order to find the human rights provisions that are considered enforceable, one must look to the CCALC. Again, this agreement sets out obligations on Canada and Colombia to ensure that their statutes, regulations, and practices embody and provide protection for the following internationally recognized labour principles and rights: (1) freedom of association and the right to collective bargaining; (2) the elimination of all forms of forced or compulsory labour; (3) the effective abolition of child labour; (4) the elimination of discrimination with respect to employment; (5) acceptable conditions of minimum wages, hours of work, and health and safety; and (6) the provision of migrant workers with the same legal protections as domestic workers.[113] Despite the provision that requests "the elimination of discrimination in respect of employment," nowhere else can gender be inferred in the CCALC. Furthermore, the drawback of the side agreement is that these recognized labour principles and rights obligations do not require the state parties to raise labour standards. Rather, state parties are required to enforce domestic labour standards.[114] This is problematic in the case of Colombia, where labour rights are contravened with impunity and labour activists are subjected to violence, including extrajudicial murder.[115]

To its credit, the CCALC does have a complaints mechanism for the "enforcement" of its labour provisions. In the event of a violation of labour rights, a foreign investor, union, or an individual can bring a complaint under the labour complaint mechanism.[116]

---

[111] ILO Declaration on Fundamental Principles and Rights at Work, 1998, International Labour Organization, <http://www.ilo.org/declaration/thedeclaration/textdeclaration/lang--en/index.htm>.

[112] CCIC et al., *supra* note 81 at 12.

[113] CCALC, *supra* note 108 at Article 1.

[114] CCIC, *supra* note 81 at 13.

[115] UNHRC, *supra* note 26 at 23, 75, 76.

[116] CCALC, *supra* note 108 at Articles 10–20.

However, one of the flaws of the complaint mechanism is that a complaint can only move forward to an arbitration panel if: (1) one of the state-parties agrees to send it to an arbitration panel and (2) an ILO standard was violated as an "encouragement to trade with another party or as an encouragement for the establishment, acquisition, expansion or retention of investment in its territory."[117] Furthermore, the mechanism does not allow an individual to take a foreign investor to arbitration for rights violations. Rather, most complaints are settled at the "ministerial consultation" stage between the state parties without regard to the victim bringing the complaint. The penalties for non-compliance with ILO standards do not allow for sanctions or countervailing duties against the non-compliant state or for a remedy specifically for the victim of the infringement.[118] This is problematic for women because the settlement of complaints at the "ministerial consultation" phase keeps their concerns private and subject to mere political solutions, where the parties consulting about a woman's complaint are often men. Another problem with the CCALC is that since it is a side agreement it is not taken into account in the interpretation of the main text of the CCFTA. Instead, it is kept separate and maintains the false dichotomy between social concerns and economic policy.

Heather Gibb has argued that there are further limitations to the ILO standards espoused in agreements such as the CCALC. First, the ILO declaration does not take into account workers that are not engaged in a traditional employer-employee relationship. For example, the right to organize does not consider the large number of people, particularly Colombian women, who work predominately in the agricultural and informal sector.[119] In addition, the inclusion of the principle of "non-discrimination in employment" is also left undefined.[120] Moreover, workplace issues that are of concern to women beyond "non-discrimination in employment and occupation" are issues that are not mentioned in the CCALC or the CCFTA, such as maternity leave with pay and without loss of seniority, family health insurance, sexual harassment, physical abuse, reproductive

---

117 *Ibid.* at Article 2.

118 CCIC, *supra* note 81 at 15.

119 Heather Gibb, "Core Labor Standards: An Incremental Approach," in Richard Sandbrook, ed., *Civilizing Globalization: A Survival Guide* (Albany: SUNY, 2003) 61 at 63.

120 Kate E. Andrias, "Gender, Work and NAFTA Labor Side Agreement" (2003) 37 U.S.F. L. Rev. 521 at 544. The lack of definition was also an issue in the North American Agreement on Labour Cooperation.

rights, and equal pay for work of equal value.[121] The silence of the CCFTA and the CCALC on these women's rights risks their continued exploitation by Canadian investors.

Finally, in contrasting the investor-state arbitration dispute settlement provision and the complaints mechanism available under the CCALC for violations of labour rights, there is a clear privileging of investor rights compared to the human rights of those subjected to egregious investor or state actions. First, investors are able to take the state-party to investor-state arbitration without exhausting local remedies, while individuals bringing complaints under the CCALC mechanism are required to exhaust local remedies before bringing a claim. Second, an investor can initiate the arbitration process at its own behest, while under the CCALC mechanism complaints filed by an individual or organization require a state party to refer it to a review panel. Finally, remedies awarded for violations of an investor's rights are unlimited and are granted directly to the investor, while remedies granted under the CCALC mechanism are capped at $15 million and put into a fund that the defendant state party must use for "appropriate labour initiatives" rather than being granted directly to the claimant.[122] Essentially, the CCALC complaints mechanism demonstrates the old adage that "a right without a remedy is no right at all." The comparison between the enforcement of investor rights and labour rights also illustrate that women's needs and interests have second-class status. The rights of investors are secured through strong adjudicative forums and investment provisions, while individuals who have suffered the negative impact of investments, including and in particular women, are forced to rely on inadequate regimes and weak provisions that fail to provide individual remedies. This division maintains the disadvantaged socio-economic position of Colombian women through the CCFTA and the CCALC's gender bias.

LEARNING FROM EXPERIENCE? WOMEN'S RIGHTS UNDER THE NORTH AMERICAN FREE TRADE AGREEMENT (NAFTA) AND THE NORTH AMERICAN AGREEMENT ON LABOUR COOPERATION (NAALC)

There are some important lessons with respect to women's issues and women's rights to be taken from the sixteen years of NAFTA and its side labour rights agreement, the NAALC. A major problem is that, while in theory the CCALC gives women an opportunity to

[121] Gibb, *supra* note 119 at 63. See also *ibid.* at 545.

[122] CCALC, *supra* note 108 at Article 20(5).

challenge acts that are gender discriminatory in employment, in practice this often proves ineffective. For example, in the sixteen years under the NAALC labour complaints mechanism, there have been no complaints that have gone beyond the ministerial consultation phase to an arbitration panel.[123] In the NAALC experience, there have been cases involving women's rights in Mexico that have been all but ignored under the complaints mechanism. One case involved female workers at a Sony plant in Nuevo Laredo who were beaten and jailed for supporting an independent union. This case was "resolved" through the ministerial consultation mechanism between the United States and Mexico. The "solution" called only for public workshops in Mexico, but no female workers were reinstated nor was a union formed.[124] Another example was the case of *Auto Trim / Custom Trim / Breed*, where the inadequacy of Mexico's health and safety laws resulted in illness and birth defects among women workers.[125] Unfortunately, no penalties or recommendations for improvements were instituted under the NAALC process.[126] These examples illustrate a serious obstacle to getting women's rights recognized through a side labour agreement, especially when the state parties to the agreement are the ones that decide whether a complaint will go to arbitration or how a complaint is to be resolved. They also illustrate that any claims that women's rights could be promoted or enhanced through the CCALC are not persuasive, since the CCALC does not account for their structural inequality and unique needs or interests.

RECOMMENDATIONS

There is a wealth of recommendations that could be made to enhance the CCFTA to ensure women's concerns are met, and the following are some of the most promising options.

GENDER MAINSTREAMING

The incorporation of women's issues and the female perspective goes beyond the "add women and stir" approach.[127] According to

---

[123] CCIC, *supra* note 81 at 12.

[124] Andrias, *supra* note 120 at 550.

[125] *Case of Auto Trim de Mexico, S.A. de C.V., Matamoros, Tamaulipas, Mexico, and Custom Trim/Breed Mexicana, S.A. de C.V., Valle Hermoso, Tamaulipas, Mexico*, U.S. N.A.O. Case no. 2000-01.

[126] Andrias, *supra* note 120 at 550.

[127] Orford, *supra* note 18 at 193.

Vandana Shiva, gender mainstreaming is crucial in order to get to the core of the patriarchal underpinnings of the system and allow women's voices to be heard:

Gender analysis ... needs to take into account the patriarchal bias of paradigms or models, processes, policies and projects of global economic structures. It needs to take into account how women's concerns, priorities and perceptions are excluded in defining the economy, and excluded from how economic problems and solutions are proposed and interpreted.[128]

Furthermore, women need to be equitably involved in decision making. This can involve participation in a range of decision-making capacities, from the negotiation of such agreements, to being on arbitration panels.[129] As well, the recognition and consideration of social dimensions and the unique position of women in the global economy will also have to be incorporated into the text of IIAs and FTAs, including the CCFTA's main text and its labour provisions.[130] Finally, the engendering of agreements such as the CCFTA must be taken further to recognize the importance of other factors that have an impact on an individual's socio-economic and power disadvantage in the system. Therefore, an intersectional approach should be promoted: "Gender roles cannot be seen in isolation. Gender intersects and is intertwined with other factors such as race, class and ethnicity that affect or even determine the condition of men and women, their opportunities and choices."[131] Recognition and consideration of intersectionality helps ensure that investment and trade agreements do not disproportionately impact any one group. Finally, it is important to recognize the silences in international law that reproduce gendered outcomes and address these silences by "rebuilding the basic concepts of international law in a way that do not support or reinforce the domination of women by men."[132]

---

[128] Vandana Shiva, *Trading Our Lives Away: an Ecological and Gender Analysis of 'Free Trade' and the Wto* (New Delhi: Research Foundation for Science, 1995), cited in Marilee Karl, "Inseparable: The Crucial Role of Women in Food Security Revisited," *Women in Action* (11 July 2009) 9 at 15, ISIS International, <http://isiswomen.org/downloads/wia/wia-2009-1/1wia09_00aFeatures_Karl.pdf>.

[129] Beveridge, *supra* note 52 at 188–189.

[130] Ruth Pearson, "Feminist Responses to Economic Globalization: Some Examples of Past and Future Practice" (2003) 11 Gender and Development 25 at 30–31.

[131] Karl, *supra* note 128 at 15.

[132] Charlesworth and Chinkin, *supra* note 7 at 61.

HUMAN RIGHTS IMPACT ASSESSMENT

In order to limit the negative impact of investment projects on the already precarious situation of women in Colombia — in particular, women in rural areas where a majority of the natural resource extraction will occur, the CCFTA should require investors to conduct an independent human rights impact assessment (HRIA).[133] A HRIA, therefore, should be conducted prior to each investment project in order to determine, and possibly eliminate, any negative or adverse effects that the project might have on women. The HRIA should be done through a consultative and inclusive approach, where women farmers, female business owners, associations, and NGOs, can be involved in the assessment of investment projects. Foreign investors should also be mindful of the impact that the securitization of their operations will have on the community and women in particular.[134] For example, it is possible that the security personnel hired by foreign investors to protect their operations in Colombia may be from former paramilitary groups or the Colombian military that have previously terrorized the community and committed violence against women. Therefore, the CCFTA should require foreign investors to screen security forces and provide human rights training for them in order to eliminate these risks.

CORPORATE SOCIAL RESPONSIBILITY

A number of corporate social responsibility measures have been developed over the past ten years. However, it is recommended that the stricter UN draft *Norms on the Responsibilities of Transnational Corporations and Other Business Enterprises with Regard to Human Rights* (*UN Norms*) be incorporated by reference into the corporate social responsibility provision (Article 816) of the CCFTA.[135] The *UN*

---

[133] See International Centre for Human Rights and Democratic Development, *Human Rights Impact Assessments for Foreign Investment Projects: Learning from Community Experiences in the Philippines, Tibet, the Democratic Republic of Congo, Argentina, and Peru* (Montreal: Rights and Democracy, 2007), Rights & Democracy, <http://www.dd-rd.ca/site/_PDF/publications/globalization/hria/ full%20report_may_2007.pdf>. See also Canada, Standing Committee on International Trade, *supra* note 3 at 43–45.

[134] MiningWatch Canada at al., *supra* note 27 at 21.

[135] UNHRC, *Norms on the Responsibilities of Transnational Corporations and Other Business Enterprises with Regard to Human Rights,* UN Doc. E/CN.4/Sub.2/2003/12/Rev.2 (2003).

Norms will bring the CCFTA closer to alleviating some of the concerns discussed earlier with respect to the limitations on the current labour rights and principles included into the CCFTA and the CCALC. Furthermore, if adopted, it will "provide for potentially robust enforcement infrastructure and compliance mechanisms."[136] The *UN Norms* would also encourage foreign investors to respect human rights and take responsibility for their actions that have a negative impact on the rights of women. Additionally, the CCFTA should include provisions that ensure that the state parties are able to pursue social policy that would alleviate historical disadvantage or provide for affirmative action programs, without risk of an investor taking the state to binding arbitration. The inclusion of such a provision would be an additional protection of women's rights. To further advance this idea, a more robust complaints mechanism under the CCALC should be developed, where individuals can bring actions against a foreign investor for conduct that infringes on women's rights and have access to compensation where a violation is found.

CONCLUSION

This article has argued that the structure of international investment law and the CCFTA neglect to consider the unique position of women in Colombia and that this may have a detrimental impact on women when the CCFTA is implemented. Although the examination of the CCFTA in this article does not claim to be a definitive feminist analysis, it does highlight some of the adverse effects on women of a legal structure that claims to be gender neutral and non-discriminatory. By attempting to expose the silences of the CCFTA and international investment law to the concerns of women, this article has attempted to illustrate that the CCFTA is more gender blind than gender neutral and that such investment agreements demonstrate that international investment law reinforces gender hierarchy by marginalizing women. This was done primarily by looking at the potential negative implications for women developing out of the CCFTA's provisions of investment, dispute settlement procedures, and labour rights. These provisions included the possible displacement of more women in Colombia from Canadian mining operations in Colombia. In addition, it considered the impact on women of the Chapter 8 investment provisions of the

---

136 Gagnon, Macklin, and Simons, *supra* note 4 at 5.

CCFTA and the limitations to the dispute settlement provisions in considering gender-based claims. In particular, it was shown that these CCFTA provisions have the potential to push women into the less secure informal economy, contribute to their socio-economic inequality, and expose them to physical violence. Furthermore, the arguments that have been made by advocates for the CCFTA, such as the Article 2201.3 defence and the fact that the CCALC complaints mechanism will ensure that women's rights are protected, were demonstrated to be dubious in view of how these mechanisms are constructed and how they have worked in other IIAs and FTAs. Finally, several recommendations were made on how the CCFTA and international investment law can account for, and address, the marginalization of women and how it can minimize their exploitation in Colombia and in the global economy. These recommendations include: mainstreaming gender and recognition of intersectionality; incorporating a provision requiring human rights impact assessments (HRIA) for every investment project; and incorporating by reference the principles of the *UN Norms* into Article 816 of the CCFTA's corporate social responsibility provision. Moving forward, further research following up on some of the predictions, patterns, and issues identified in this article may be necessary once the CCFTA is in force. Such an activity would be beneficial in closing the gap between feminist theory and practice and would lend confidence to the value of using a feminist approach to international investment law.

Sommaire

L'échange des droits de la femme: Une critique féministe de l'Accord de libre échange Canada-Colombie

Le conflit interne en Colombie a donné lieu à des violations documentées des droits de la personne et du droit international humanitaire. En particulier, les femmes colombiennes et leurs droits fondamentaux ont été touchés de façon disproportionnée par le conflit. C'est dans ce contexte que l'Accord de libre échange Canada-Colombie (ALECC) *est proposé et il est préoccupant que les investisseurs canadiens pourraient perpétuer la violence ou devenir complices bénéficiaires de violations des droits de la personne en Colombie une fois l'*ALECC *ratifiée. Dans ce contexte, cet article adopte une approche féministe au droit international sur les investissements pour soutenir que les accords d'investissement internationaux et les accords de libre* *échange avec dispositions sur l'investissement (comme l'ALECC) maintiennent et renforcent la hiérarchie entre les sexes au détriment des droits socioéconomiques, des besoins et des intérêts des femmes. À la lumière d'une critique féministe des dispositions de l'ALECC sur la non-discrimination, la performance, l'expropriation, la responsabilité sociale, les réserves, l'arbitrage investisseur-État, et les exceptions générales, ainsi que de l'accord parallèle sur le travail, les conséquences du droit international sur les investissements pour les droits des femmes en Colombie et ailleurs deviennent apparentes. Afin de remédier à ces lacunes, des recommandations sont faites pour atténuer les préjudices potentiels du droit international des investissements et de l'ALECC sur les droits des femmes.*

Summary

Trading Away Women's Rights: A Feminist Critique of the Canada–Colombia Free Trade Agreement

The internal conflict in Colombia has resulted in documented violations of human rights and international humanitarian law. In particular, Colombian women and their human rights have been disproportionately impacted by the conflict. It is within this context that the Canada–Colombia Free Trade Agreement (CCFTA) *is being proposed, and there is serious concern that Canadian investors could perpetuate the violence or become complicit beneficiaries of human rights violations in Colombia once the* CCFTA *is ratified. Against this background, this article takes a feminist approach to international investment law to demonstrate that international investment agreements (IIAs) and free trade agreements with investment provisions (FTAs), such as the* CCFTA, *maintain and reinforce gender hierarchy to the detriment of women's socio-economic rights, needs, and interests. By engaging in a feminist critique of the* CCFTA's *provisions on non-discrimination, performance, expropriation, corporate social responsibility, reservations, investor-state arbitration, and general exceptions, as well as the labour side agreement, the ramifications of international investment law on Colombian women's rights and women's rights generally becomes apparent. In order to remedy these shortcomings, recommendations are made to alleviate the potential strain of international investment law and the* CCFTA *specifically on women's rights.*

The Protracted Bargain: Negotiating the Canada–China Foreign Investment Promotion and Protection Agreement

JUSTIN CARTER

INTRODUCTION

The nature of international investment has rapidly transformed over the last half-century. At the centre of this transformation has been the bilateral investment treaty (BIT), an international agreement between two countries that provides protections for home-country investors in the territory of the other contracting party. The current globalized trade and investment regime requires strong institutional support mechanisms for it to operate effectively and fairly. States of all levels of economic development have recognized this requirement and have accordingly embraced the BIT and its supporting dispute mechanisms as an important means in strengthening international investment frameworks.

Canada and China began negotiating their own BIT or Foreign Investment Promotion and Protection Agreement (FIPA) in 1994, and negotiations remain ongoing.[1] The implications of a successfully concluded Canada–China FIPA are clear. Once concluded, this agreement would arguably be Canada's most important FIPA,

---

Justin Carter is a research associate with the Institute of Asian Research at the University of British Columbia. This article was commissioned as part of the Asia Pacific Dispute Resolution Project (APDR) and was helped by a Major Collaborative Research Initiative (MCRI) grant, funded by the Social Sciences and Humanities Research Council of Canada (SSHRC). The author's sincere gratitude goes out to Dr. Pitman Potter, the APDR principal investigator, for making this project possible, as well as to the MCRI Program and SSHRC. Further gratitude is expressed to Dr. Andrew Newcombe for assisting the author with various parts of the analysis.

[1] Canada has opted to call its bilateral investment treaties (BITs) "foreign investment promotion and protection agreements" (FIPAs). There is no significance in this difference in language. For the purposes of this article, FIPA will be used only in relation to Canada's bilateral treaty program.

although such an assertion is not based on current indicators of Canadian investment in China. Recent Canadian foreign direct investment (FDI) has largely been in natural resources and financial services — two sectors whose admission of foreign investment is highly regulated in China.[2] As of the end of 2008, the total stock of Canadian FDI in China amounted to only CDN $3.58 billion,[3] which is only a third of the total stock of Canadian FDI in Hungary — a country with which Canada already has a FIPA.[4] Instead, the importance of a Canada–China FIPA resides in growth prospects for both Canadian investment in China as well as Chinese investment in Canada. While Chinese FDI in Canada has also remained relatively negligible, with total stock at the end of 2008 totalling CDN $2.75 billion, it is anticipated that Chinese investment will begin flowing into Canada at increased rates due to China's interest in Canada's natural resources.[5]

The original negotiations of the Canada–China FIPA were put on hold until after China's accession to the World Trade Organization (WTO), having resumed in 2004.[6] Since 2004, twelve rounds of negotiations have taken place, with the last round taking place in Beijing in January 2010. Considering how long the negotiations have gone on for and the fact that a successful conclusion has still eluded the two countries, on the surface it might seem that this delay reflects resoundingly different views in each country's normative preferences with respect to investment treaty provisions. This may not necessarily be the case, however, although the length of negotiations must surely reflect differences in certain on-the-table or off-the-table aspects of the negotiation process. After briefly examining the history of Canada and China's respective BIT programs, followed by a comparison of the two countries' approaches on various aspects of investment treaties, this article attempts to

---

2 Madanmohan Ghosh and Weimin Wang, *China and U.S. Outward FDI and Exports: Are China and India Special?* Industry Canada Working Paper no. 2007–05 (2007).

3 See Foreign Affairs and International Trade Canada, *Background on the Canada-China Foreign Investment Promotion and Protection Agreement (FIPA)*, Foreign Affairs and International Trade Canada, <http://www.international.gc.ca/trade-agreements-accords-commerciaux/agr-acc/fipa-apie/china-chine.aspx?lang=en&menu_id=13&menu=R> at para. 2.

4 See Statistics Canada, *Foreign Direct Investment Positions at Year End*, Statistics Canada, <http://www.statcan.gc.ca/daily-quotidien/090408/t090408a1-eng.htm>.

5 See Foreign Affairs and International Trade Canada, *supra* note 3 at para. 3.

6 *Ibid.* at para. 1.

expose some of these differences, while also addressing areas of convergence and complementarity.

Non-economic factors are also scrutinized in this analysis, with particular attention given to sustainability and human rights issues. While in scholarship, international investment law has traditionally been treated separately from human rights and other non-economic concerns, over recent years increased attention has been paid in developing and assessing the associated linkages.[7] Following this general methodology, opportunities for coordinating compliance between economic and non-economic norms within the context of the Canada–China FIPA are examined. Such implications are important considerations in relation to the Canada–China FIPA since increased Canada–China bilateral investment will only increase general awareness of these concerns.

THE BIT

Unlike the multilateral legal regime that oversees international trade through the auspices of the WTO,[8] international investment relies upon a web of international investment agreements alongside international legal norms to govern its legal framework.[9] The way

---

7   For a list of relevant works, see note 176 in this article.

8   For instance, the General Agreement on Tariffs and Trade, 14 April 1994, in Marrakesh Agreement Establishing the World Trade Organization, Annex 1A, 1867 U.N.T.S. 187, 33 I.L.M. 1153 (1994) (entered into force 15 April 1994) [WTO Agreement] [GATT]; General Agreement on Trade in Services, 1994, in WTO Agreement, Annex 1B, 284 (1999), 1869 U.N.T.S. 183, 33 I.L.M. 1167 (1994) (entered into force 15 April 1994) [GATS]; Agreement on Trade-Related Aspects of Intellectual Property Rights, 1994, in WTO Agreement, Annex 1C, 320 (1999), 1869 U.N.T.S. 299, 33 I.L.M. 1197 (1994) (entered into force 15 April 1994) [TRIPS Agreement]; and the many extra agreements, annexes, and schedules that make up the WTO regime.

9   From 1995 to 1998, the Organisation for Economic Co-operation and Development (OECD) attempted to negotiate a multilateral agreement on investment (MAI). Negotiations broke down, however, after states failed to reach consensus on a broad range of issues. The desire to reach a MAI was also pursued through the WTO's *Singapore Issues*, which expanded the Agreement on Trade-Related Investment Measures (TRIMS). However, this again failed due to reticence from developing countries. See generally Jürgen Kurtz, "A General Investment Agreement in the WTO? Lessons from Chapter 11 of NAFTA and the Multilateral Agreement on Investment" (2002) 23 U. Pennsylvania J. Int'l Econ. L.; C. Schittecatte, "The Politics of the MAI: On the Social Opposition of the MAI and Its Role in the Demise of the Negotiations" (2000) 1 J.W.I. 329; OECD, "The Multilateral Agreement on Investment (Report by the Chairman to the Negotiating

states receive and manage foreign investment markedly varies from country to country. Consequently, consensus over an agreed upon set of legal principles that define how and to what extent foreign investment should be protected from the sovereign acts of states has thus far eluded the international community. As a result, the BIT has become an important legal vehicle to govern international investment because it provides states with the opportunity to negotiate preferences with other states. While each BIT is different in content and scope, the modern BIT is generally speaking a reflection of liberal norms surrounding open markets, non-discrimination, and due process.

Without BITs, customary international legal norms and countries' domestic laws prevail in determining the legal nature of foreign investor-host state disputes. In order to overcome the associated deficiencies attached to this regime, BITs have become a desirable option for states, as they offer protections for home-country investors beyond those that are accorded by customary international law.[10] The minimal protections accorded to the investor through customary international law are limited to certain rights, which states are obligated to accord only after a particular investment has been admitted into its jurisdiction. These include minimum treatment standards and obligations surrounding compensation in the event of expropriation.[11] It remains silent on other areas of protection from discriminatory regulation such as national treatment and most-favoured nation (MFN) treatment. These two forms of investor rights are crucial in affording a foreign-invested enterprise equal footing *vis-à-vis* domestic and other foreign firms with respect to the application of law, regulation, and general government interference.

Group" (1998) 98 DAFFE/MAI, <http://www.oecd.org/daf/mai/pdf/ng/ng989fe.pdf>; and P. Muchlinski et al., eds., *The Oxford Handbook of International Investment Law* (New York: Oxford University Press, 2008).

10 See Statute of the International Court of Justice, Chapter XIV of the Charter of the United Nations, 26 June 1945, Can. T.S. 1945 No. 7. Article 38, para. 1 (b), refers to customary international law as "international custom, as evidence of a general practice accepted as law." See also Brian D. Lepard, *Customary International Law: A New Theory with Practical Applications* (New York: Cambridge University Press, 2010).

11 However, no common set of norms has developed over how compensation should be calculated. See Rudolf Dolzer and Christoph Schreuer, *Principles of International Investment Law* (New York: Oxford University Press, 2008) at 91. See notes 44 and 137 in this article for further discussion.

Other substantive obligations not represented in customary international law that are often conferred on states through BITs include the curtailment of performance requirements, the enhancement of transparency of laws and regulations, allowances for unrestricted capital transfers, and the unrestricted allowance of subrogation.

Another key deficiency associated with customary international law from the perspective of the investor is that disputes between a host government and an investor that believes it has been mistreated are often settled in the host country's domestic courts under domestic law. In most circumstances, this is not desirable to investors since even the most basic rights that are accorded under customary law often exist in conflict with local norms and practices and are subject to processes associated with *selective adaptation*.[12] Moreover, in many circumstances, the capacity of host-state court systems to provide fair and impartial proceedings outside of political influence is uncertain. The Convention on the Settlement of International Disputes between States and Nationals of Other States (ICSID Convention), which is a multilateral treaty formulated by the World Bank in 1966, has helped overcome this issue by providing an impartial dispute settlement process.[13] However, the convention has remained imperfect in remedying certain disputes, as this forum is used pursuant to the treaty only in circumstances when both the complainant and the respondent provide consent. Modern BIT investor-state dispute provisions often provide a way to overcome the procedural inadequacies for investors that customary international law and the ICSID Convention, as a stand-alone agreement, provide. These BITs expressly delineate procedural terms that guarantee investors access to international fora such as the International Centre for Settlement

---

[12] Selective adaptation "involves a dynamic by which international rule regimes are mediated by local cultural norms." See Pitman B. Potter, *Selective Adaptation in Comparative Perspective: Approaches to Understanding Reception of International Law under Conditions of Globalization*, Asia Pacific Dispute Resolution Programme, prepared for the Law and Society Association General Meeting (2007). For further discussion, see generally Ljiljana Biukovic, "Selective Adaptation of WTO Transparency Norms and Local Practices in China and Japan" (2008) 11 J. Int'l Econ. L. 803; and Pitman B. Potter, "Legal Reform in China: Institutions, Culture, and Selective Adaptation" (2004) 28 Law & Soc. Inquiry 465.

[13] Convention on the Settlement of International Disputes between States and Nationals of Other States, 18 March 1965, 17 U.S.T. 1270, T.I.A.S. 6090, 575 U.N.T.S. 159 (entered into force 14 October 1966). It is often known as the Washington Convention. The International Centre for Settlement of Investment Disputes (ICSID) was the institution established under guidance from the World Bank to oversee the convention and its dispute settlement procedures.

of Investment Disputes (ICSID), the United Nations Commission on International Trade Law (UNCITRAL), or ad hoc fora in their disputes with host governments. Besides providing "teeth" for an investment treaty, a BIT's procedural provisions ultimately work towards the promotion of investment,[14] as they diminish many of the aspects of investment risk involved in investing in offshore jurisdictions that have weak governance and legal systems.

While the substantive and procedural provisions of a BIT afford a certain degree of improvement in the expected costs and risks associated with a given investment decision, it should be mentioned that this is just one criterion in the evaluation of whether or not to pursue an investment in a given jurisdiction. Local economic conditions, supply-chain particularities, and general government policy decisions are examples of performance criteria that are likely weighed more heavily by investors.[15] Furthermore, the BIT is unable to mitigate general operating- and market-based risks that any investment decision encounters.

Ever since Germany and Pakistan entered into the first BIT in 1959, their use has grown exponentially — by the end of 2008, there were 2,676 BITs in existence.[16] The sheer diversity of states that have embraced these agreements suggests that their efficacy and flexibility is widely perceived as being beneficial, regardless of the level of economic development or political conviction. Countries have time and again chosen to trade off the relinquishment of state sovereignty for the economic benefits that BITs are perceived to bring. Despite the fact that BITs are considered symmetrical agreements between two parties, they are often perceived as being asymmetrical when they are between a capital-exporting state and

---

[14] It is uncertain the extent that BITs actually promote investment. The degree that investment will increase directly from the introduction of an investment agreement will reside in factors such as host country investment policies, pre-existing regulatory risks of the host country, the degree of protections afforded in a BIT, and whether or not one contracting party is a major capital exporter. For empirical studies on the efficacy of BITs in promoting investment, see Jeswald W. Salacuse and Nicholas P. Sullivan, "Do BITs Really Work?: An Evaluation of Bilateral Investment Treaties and Their Grand Bargain" (2005) 46 Harv. Int'l L.J. 67; and Eric Neumayer and Laura Spess, "Do Bilateral Investment Treaties Increase Foreign Direct Investment to Developing Countries" (2005) 22 World Development 1567.

[15] See Salucuse and Sullivan, *supra* note 14 at 15.

[16] See United Nations Conference on Trade and Development, *World Investment Report 2009: Transnational Corporations, Agricultural Production and Development* (2009) at 32.

a capital-importing state. When such a BIT is signed, the treaty's practical effect recurrently applies to the protection of investors of the developed country and the legal obligation of the developing country since investment will typically flow in one direction. This occurs because smaller developing countries generally do not have investors with the capacity to invest offshore. Nonetheless, BITs have overwhelmingly been signed between wealthier countries and lower-income countries, as these BITs provide the largest economic advantage for both contracting parties. However, while the capital importing-exporting paradigm has consistently held true over the half-century of BIT proliferation, there has been a movement over the last couple of decades that has seen developing countries entering into BITs among themselves.[17]

BACKGROUND ON CANADA'S FOREIGN INVESTMENT PROMOTION AND PROTECTION AGREEMENT PROGRAM

Canada was a relatively late starter with its own BIT program, having signed its first investment treaty with the Soviet Union when it followed similar overtures taken by a group of western European states in 1989.[18] While the treaty was significant for a host of reasons surrounding the loosening of rigid Cold War geopolitics, its relevance for Canadian investors was pale in comparison to the Canada–United States trade-and-investment dyad that was at the time also transforming. Parliamentary discourse surrounding Canada's involvement in free trade and investment agreements originated in 1982 when the Standing Senate Committee on Canada–United States relations recommended that the Canadian government begin negotiating a free-trade agreement with the United States.[19] Trade, and particularly investment liberalization, had for some time been a sensitive issue in the Canadian political psyche, which continued after the federal government officially launched negotiations for a

---

[17] Developing country-developing country BITs are too numerous to mention here. It is a trend that started in the 1980s, but it has made far greater strides over the last decade. For a full discussion, see Zachary Elkins et al., "Competing for Capital: The Diffusion of Bilateral Investment Treaties, 1960–2000" (2006) Social Science Research Network at 7.

[18] See the Canada-Soviet Union FIPA (1989). This has since become the Canada-Russian Federation FIPA post-dissolution of the Soviet Union.

[19] The Standing Senate Committee on Canada-United States Relations ran from 1976 to 1982 and produced three volumes of reports. See Parliament of Canada, *The Senate Today,* Government of Canada, <http://www.parl.gc.ca/information/about /process/Senate/ Senatetoday/invest-e.html>.

Canada–US Free Trade Agreement (FTA). Accordingly, the Canada-US FTA took a while to gain traction as a viable policy outcome for the Mulroney administration. After the agreement was signed by both Canada and the United States in 1988, and the ratification bill passed through the House of Commons, the Liberal-dominated Senate refused to pass the bill through the upper house without a federal election. After the Progressive Conservative Party got re-elected in 1988, the implementation legislation passed through both the lower and upper house, and, to much controversy, the Canada-US FTA was enacted and implemented into Canadian law.[20]

The Canada-US FTA, followed by its more expansive trilateral successor, the North American Free Trade Agreement (NAFTA),[21] became much more than agreements that sought to overcome trade barriers. Tariffs on American imports into Canada (and *vice versa*) were already far lower than the world average.[22] The implications of these agreements also stretched into the realm of investment, having included chapters on rights and protections for investors.[23] NAFTA added an extra level of protection, insofar as its dispute resolution provisions included allowances for international arbitration initiated by private actors.[24] Chapter 16 of the Canada-US FTA, followed by NAFTA Chapter 11, can be considered the most important bilateral

---

20 See Canada-US Free Trade Agreement, 2 January 1988, 27 I.L.M. 281 (entered into force 1 January 1989) [CUSFTA]. For a historical account, see generally John Sawatsky, *Mulroney: The Politics of Ambition* (Toronto: Macfarlane, Walter, and Ross, 1991); and Michael Hart, "Free Trade and Brian Mulroney's Economic Legacy," in R.B. Blake *Transforming the Nation: Canada and Brian Mulroney* (Montreal and Kingston: McGill-Queen's University Press, 2007).

21 See North American Free Trade Agreement between the Government of Canada, the Government of Mexico and the Government of the United States, 17 December 1992, Can. T.S. 1994 No. 2, 32 I.L.M. 289 (entered into force 1 January 1994) [NAFTA].

22 There is disagreement to the degree that pre-FTA tariffs actually inhibited trade between Canada and the United States. Prior to the treaty's entry into force, Canadian and US tariff levels were already significantly lower on each others' imports than the average for the rest of the world. However, Canada stood to gain significantly with respect to the United States pre-FTA import tariffs on imported manufactured Canadian goods. See Daniel Trefler, "The Long and Short of the Canada-U.S. Free Trade Agreement" (2004) [unpublished, archived at University of Toronto].

23 See CUSFTA, *supra* note 20, Chapter 16; and NAFTA, *supra* note 21, Chapter 11.

24 Cai Congyan, "China-US BIT Negotiations and the Future of Investment Treaty Regime: A Grand Bilateral Bargain with Multilateral Implications" (2009) 12 J. Int'l Econ. L. 457 at 464.

investment treaties ever to be entered into between two signatories in terms of the magnitude of investment they would go on to affect. Moreover, the Canada-US FTA represents the first trade or investment agreement that the two countries have signed with another developed country.

As of early 2010, Canada had entered into seven free-trade agreements besides NAFTA.[25] Of these agreements, only the Canada–Israel FTA and the Canada-European Free Trade Association FTA include an investment chapter inserted within their text or are not complemented by a FIPA.[26] While Canada has accomplished a lot in the way of trade liberalization over recent years with its FTAs, its FIPA program has been far more expansive. As of early 2010, Canada had signed and ratified FIPAs with twenty-four countries.[27] Therefore, including those investment provisions inserted within Canada's FTAs, Canada is currently a signatory to twenty-eight treaties that confer investor rights and protections as well as provide for dispute resolution mechanisms. The number of investment treaties that Canada, as well as other countries, has entered into compared to free-trade agreements reflects the absence of a multilateral treaty that covers international investment.

Canada's FIPA program has followed the path taken by many capital-exporting countries, having largely concentrated on entering into agreements with low-to-middle income countries,[28] the most

[25] These include the Canada-Jordan Free Trade Agreement (2009); the Canada-Columbia Free Trade Agreement (2008); the Canada-Peru Free Trade Agreement (2009); the Canada-Costa Rica Free Trade Agreement (2002); the Canada-Chile Free Trade Agreement (1997); and the Canada-Israel Free Trade Agreement (1997). This also includes the Canada-European Free Trade Association Free Trade Agreement (2009), which has limited scope and minimal obligations.

[26] The European Free Trade Association is comprised of Iceland, Liechtenstein, Norway, and Switzerland.

[27] Canada-foreign FIPA co-signatories are: Argentina (1991); Armenia (1997); Barbados (1996); Costa Rica (1998); Croatia (1997); Czech Republic (1990); Ecuador (1996); Egypt (1996); Hungary (1991); Jordan (2009); Latvia (1995); Lebanon (1997); Panama (1996); Peru (2006); Philippines (1995); Poland (1990); Romania (1996); Russian Federation (1989); Slovak Republic (1990); Thailand (1997); Trinidad and Tobago (1995); Ukraine (1994); Uruguay (1997); and Venezuela (1996). Canada also signed FIPAs with El Salvador (1999) and South Africa (1995), but these treaties have not been ratified.

[28] The average 2008 per capita gross domestic product for Canada's twenty-four ratified FIPA partners was US $9,567. Compiled using data from World Bank Development Indicators (2010), <http://databank.worldbank.org/ddp/home. do?Step=12&id=4&CNO=2>.

developed of which has included many of the former Soviet satellite countries immediately following the dissolution of the Soviet Union. In fact, aside from the Czech Republic (1990), Poland (1990), the Slovak Republic (1990), and the United States (Chapter 11, NAFTA), Canada has not pursued investment agreements with any of its partners in the Organisation for Economic Co-operation and Development (OECD).[29] The government of Canada identifies potential FIPA partners "primarily on the basis of commercial factors."[30] Designing selection criteria that identify and measure the applicability of foreign parties tends to focus on which jurisdictions Canadian investors would benefit the most from the protections of a FIPA. This involves an assessment of the potential economic benefits in relation to the existing vulnerability of Canadian investors. Selection criteria defined by the Department of Foreign Affairs and International Trade (DFAIT) include: (1) commercial and economic interests (current and potential Canadian investment); (2) existing investment protection (rule of law and levels of corruption); (3) the likelihood of engagement and reaching a desirable outcome; and (4) trade and foreign policy objectives. From the perspective of the Canadian government, there is little incentive to allocate the resources necessary to go through the process of negotiating, drafting, and implementing a BIT with another developed country because of the levels of transparency and integrity that already exist in the governance and court systems of what are consistently democratic states. As a result of these factors, Canada's FIPA program has been formulated around objectives pertaining to the protection of Canadian investment in foreign jurisdictions with little emphasis on the promotion of investment in Canada.[31]

---

29 However, the Czech Republic, Poland, and Slovakia were not OECD members when Canada-foreign FIPAs were signed with these countries.

30 See Foreign Affairs and International Trade Canada, *Canada's FIPA Program: Its Purpose, Objective, and Content* (2009), Foreign Affairs and International Trade Canada, <http://www.international.gc.ca/trade-agreements-accords-commerciaux/agr-acc/fipa-apie/fipa-purpose.aspx?lang=en>.

31 Investment promotion is also not included in the Canada FIPA model's substantive provisions. However, it has been included in the preambles of all agreements and in the text of some Canada-foreign FIPAs. For instance, Article II(1) of the Canada-Czech Republic FIPA states that "each contracting Party shall encourage the creation of favourable conditions for investors of the other Contracting Party to make investments in its territory." Although, Article II(3) goes on to expressly permit either party to use pre-establishment investment barriers, as long as it is applied equally to all states.

Canada's new FIPA model was drafted in 2003 and would go on to be used as a template in the negotiation of all future Canada-foreign FIPAs.[32] This was the first time that Canada publicized its investment treaty preferences for the world to see.[33] The updated FIPA model was compiled to "reflect, and incorporate the results of, its growing experience with the implementation and operation of the investment chapter in NAFTA," moving away from the OECD-based preferences of earlier FIPAs.[34] Thus, the FIPA model is a reflection not only of the text of the agreement but also of Canada's experience with cases pursuant to NAFTA Chapter 11.[35] As a result, Canada's FIPA model is larger and more comprehensive than preceding FIPAs including NAFTA Chapter 11, which is also emblematic of the highly complex factual and procedural aspects of modern investor-state disputes.

BACKGROUND ON CHINA'S BILATERAL INVESTMENT TREATY PROGRAM

China's BIT program commenced in 1982, less than four years after Deng Xiaoping's historical declaration during the third plenum when his rise to prominence as China's leader ushered in a new era of reform.[36] Polemicized at this time was Mao Zedong's heavy-industrial development model that prevailed up until his death in

---

[32] Canada's FIPA model contains five sections with fifty-two articles and four annexes. For a copy of the FIPA model, see Foreign Affairs and International Trade Canada, *supra* note 3.

[33] See Céline Lévesque, "Influences on the Canadian FIPA Model and the US Model BIT: NAFTA Chapter 11 and Beyond" (2006) 44 Can. Y.B. Int'l L. 249.

[34] See Foreign Affairs and International Trade Canada, *supra* note 3.

[35] In the late 1990s and early 2000s, a series of investor-state disputes pursuant to NAFTA Chapter 11 led many legislative members in both Canada and the United States to view the investment chapter as a legal instrument that curtailed each country's right to legitimately regulate. See Guillermo A. Alvarez, "The New Face of Investment Arbitration: NAFTA Chapter 11" (2003) 28 Yale J. Int'l L. 365. Cases against Canada that affected Canadian opinion on the matter include: *Ethyl Corporation v. Canada*, UNCITRAL (NAFTA), 38 I.L.M. 708 (Award on Jurisdiction, 24 June 1998); *Pope & Talbot Inc. v. Canada*, UNCITRAL (NAFTA) (Statement of Claim, 25 March 1999); and *S.D. Myers, Inc. v. Canada*, UNCITRAL (NAFTA), (Partial Award, 13 November 2000).

[36] See Guangyuan Yu, *Deng Xiaoping Shakes the World: An Eyewitness Account of China's Party Work Conference at the Third Plenum (November-December 1978)* (Norwalk: Eastbridge, 2004); and Barry Naughton, "Deng Xiaoping: The Economist" (1993) 135 China Quarterly 491.

the mid-1970s.[37] This model relied on a command economy that diverted resources away from consumption and into large-scale investment. Autarky and self-reliance were major canons of Maoist China during the pre-reform era, and, as such, the country had little interest in using its comparative advantage (that is, labour) combined with international trade to attain the gains from trade that would ultimately end up being necessary, during the post-reform period, in lifting China's economy out of perpetual stagnation. International investment was equally viewed with disapproval. At least up until the Sino-Soviet split of the late 1950s, the importation of Soviet capital would provide the technological foundation necessary to realize the limited economic gains that were in fact achieved.[38] For thirty years, Soviet assistance and limited technological licensing from the West would be the closest semblance of forcing investment in the Chinese economy.

China's pre-reform position towards customary international legal norms was also deeply ambivalent, which can be explained by its infrequent engagement with the international community.[39] The discursive elements of Chinese scholarship and policy promulgations with respect to public international law up until the early 1970s continued to coalesce around China's experience with nineteenth-century "unequal" treaties.[40] In 1971, the People's Republic of China

[37] See generally Barry Naughton, *The Chinese Economy: Transitions and Growth* (Cambridge, MA: MIT Press, 2007).

[38] See generally Lorenz Luthi, *The Sino-Soviet Split: Cold War in the Communist World* (Princeton, NJ: Princeton University Press, 2008); Immanuel Chung-Yueh Hsü, *The Rise of Modern China* (New York: Oxford University Press, 2000) at 671–88; and Jonathan Spence, *The Search for Modern China* (New York: W.W. Norton, 1999) at 584–86.

[39] See James C. Hsuing, "China's Recognition Practice and Its Implications in International Law," in Jerome A. Cohen, ed., *China's Practice of International Law* (Cambridge, MA: Harvard University Press, 1972), 14 at 15.

[40] See Hungdah Chiu, "Chinese Views of Unequal Treaties," in Jerome A. Cohen, ed., *China's Practice of International Law* (Cambridge, MA: Harvard University Press, 1972), 239 at 258–66. The Communist Chinese took a much more vociferous stance on the issue of unequal treaties but never provided a clear definition of what the term meant. A common view at the time is exemplified by Chinese scholar Chou Keng-sheng's definition — a definition that extends to most modern BITs. He espoused that "even those treaties which provide mutual benefit in form, but, due to the unequal economic position between two contracting parties, in fact yield unilateral benefits to one side and subject the other side only to exploitation, are neither treaties of mutual benefit nor equal international transactions." See his article "The Principle of Peaceful Coexistence from the Viewpoint of International Law" (1955) 6(41) Cheng-fa Yen-chiu (Political Legal Research) at footnote 85, in Hungdah Chiu's chapter.

(PRC) assumed the Republic of China's (Taiwan's) seat in the United Nations, and when it gained this forum to voice its own exposition of norms it did so in a manner that often supported Third World causes.[41] The issues of international investment, natural resource development, and permanent sovereignty had been consistently advanced by developing countries in the United Nations General Assembly for some time, even prior to the PRC's admission into the international body.[42] This discussion, which primarily focused on the right of sovereign nations to expropriate foreign investment pursuant to domestic laws, culminated with the New International Economic Order's (NIEO) movement during the early 1970s. The tenets surrounding the movement were embodied in resolution through the NIEO Declaration in 1973.[43]

[41] See Samuel S. Kim, "The People's Republic of China in the United Nations" (1974) 26 World Politics 299.

[42] See *Permanent Sovereignty over Natural Resources*, GA Res. 1803, UNGAOR, 17th Sess. (14 December 1962); *Permanent Sovereignty over Natural Resources*, GA Res. 2158, 21st Sess. (25 November 1966); *Permanent Sovereignty over Natural Resources*, GA Res. 2386, UNGAOR, 23rd Sess. (19 November 1968); *Permanent Sovereignty over Natural Resources of Developing Countries and Expansion of Domestic Sources of Accumulation for Economic Development*, GA Res. 2692, UNGAOR, 25th Sess. (11 December 1970); *Permanent Sovereignty over Natural Resources of Developing Countries*, GA Res. 3016, UNGAOR, 27th Sess. (18 December 1972); and *Permanent Sovereignty of Natural Resources*, GA Res. 3171, UNGAOR, 28th Sess. (17 December 1973).

[43] See *Declaration on the Establishment of a New International Economic Order*, GA Res. 3201, UNGAOR, 28th Sess. (1 May 1974) [NIEO Declaration]. See also *Charter of Economic Rights and Duties of States*, GA Res. 3281, UNGAOR, 29th Sess. (12 December 1974) [CERDS]. China's role in the assertion of developing country sovereign rights was mixed. For instance, it declined joining the "Group of 77" developing states. See Marc Lanteigne, *China and International Institutions: Alternate Paths to Global Power* (New York: Routledge, 2005) at 37. However, it did provide some support to the new international economic order (NIEO) movement. While the NIEO Declaration posits a reconciliatory interpretation of the common norms surrounding arbitration and international adjudication, it asserted the primacy of the sovereign in decision making and its domestic legal framework as the defining force in legal interpretation. Perhaps the largest break from customary international law in this document was the choice of language surrounding compensation, having discarded the compensatory cannons of the Hull Rule with a single attribute — "appropriate" compensation, according to the laws of the host nation. See Article 2.2 of CERDS, which states that every state has the right "to nationalize, expropriate, or transfer ownership of foreign property, in which case compensation should be paid by the State adopting such measures, taking into account its relevant laws and regulations in all circumstances that the State considers pertinent." See note 146 in this article for further discussion on compensation.

Juxtaposed against this backdrop was China's post-reform experience with international investment. China began to embrace foreign capital as a means to achieve the levels of economic development that had been strived for over the previous three decades. China's economic planners implemented a favourable taxation regime for foreign investors, which supplemented its affordable labour market as factors that promoted China's attractiveness for foreign investors.[44] In 1978, FDI in China was non-existent. By 2007, the total stock of FDI in China totalled US $747.7 billion.[45] A crucial factor in China's dramatic success over thirty years of economic reform has been the role that direct investment from foreign sources has played in transforming the country's productive capabilities. Without this investment, China's industrialization as we have come to know it would likely not have been achieved.

In order to both propel and complement domestic reforms pertaining to investment, China began its BIT program a full seven years before Canada, having entered into its first BIT with Sweden in 1982. It subsequently entered into investment agreements with capital-exporting states throughout the 1980s such as Germany (1983), the United Kingdom (1986), Japan (1988), and Australia (1988).[46] While these early treaties were representative of China's reformative transformation into a capital-importing state, the actual extent that these early treaties served in attracting foreign investment was arguably negligible, as the levels of protections granted to investors in these agreements were weak. To start with, "first-generation" Sino-foreign investment agreements completely ignored national treatment protections.[47] Considering the degree that inefficient state-owned enterprises (SOEs) dominated the Chinese industrial landscape at the time, embedding national treatment provisions into these agreements could have proven fatal to many of its domestic industries. Another aspect of China's first-generation BITs was that virtually all of them excluded procedural provisions that allow for investor-state dispute resolution mechanisms without host-state consent. This exclusion is significant because, as is discussed later, the substantive provisions of an investment

---

[44] See Zhaodong Jiang, "China's Tax Preferences to Foreign Investment: Policy, Culture, and Modern Concepts" 18 Nw. J. Int'l L. & Bus. 549.

[45] See National Bureau of Statistics, *China Statistical Yearbook 2008* (2009).

[46] China-Germany BIT was amended in 2003.

[47] See Cai, *supra* note 24 at 461. For further discussion on national treatment, see the later sections of this article.

agreement are essentially meaningless for investors if they also do not provide remedial recourse in the event of an alleged act of mistreatment. Host-state obligations were also limited in these early agreements, insofar as they allowed state sovereignty to remain unconstrained in the preservation of laws and regulations that governed the entry and operation of foreign investment.[48]

In the late 1990s, China's policy-makers began synthesizing more liberal norms into the text of China's newly negotiated BITs. This can be attributed to a variety of transformative aspects in China's domestic economy during this time that would go on to change the way it would perceive the purpose of its BIT program. For one, by the late-1990s, China's robust economic performance and international trade led to the development of surplus capital and growth in the country's foreign exchange reserves, which provided Chinese enterprises and an environment conducive to considering outward investment.[49] In addition, political and institutional influence played a role in that local and provincial governments often promoted outward investment with the hope that local companies would acquire technical and trade support.[50] Policy initiatives surrounding overseas investment were given further impetus through the central government's "go global" (*zou qu chu*) strategy, which was promulgated in 2000.[51] This policy was characterized by export tax rebates, foreign exchange assistance, and financial support for outward investment in specific targeted sectors.[52] Perhaps the most striking and controversial impetus behind China's outward advancement, however, has been the rapid growth in China's need for natural resources. China became a net importer of a variety of

---

[48] Alex Berger, "China's New Bilateral Investment Treaty Programme: Substance, Rational, and Implications for International Investment Law Making" (paper presented to the American Society of International Law International Economic Law Interest Group 2008 Biennial Conference, "The Politics of International Economic Law: The Next Four Years," Washington, DC, 2008).

[49] Kevin G. Cai, "Outward Foreign Direct Investment: A Novel Dimension of China's Integration into the Regional and Global Economy" (1999) 160 China Quarterly 856.

[50] See *ibid.* at 863.

[51] See Peter J. Buckley et al., "The Determinants of Chinese Outward Direct Investment" 38 J. Int'l Bus. Stud. 499; and Ping Deng, "Investing for Strategic Resources and Its Rationale: The Case of Outward FDI from Chinese Companies" 50 Business Horizons 71.

[52] See Buckley, *supra* note 51 at 504.

commodity classes during the 1990s, including oil in 1993.[53] In order to properly secure the natural resources vital in the continued expansion of its economy, SOEs, under government guidance, made strategic investments in offshore locations, largely in the form of mergers and acquisitions.[54] In doing so, China's SOEs found that the only locations available to invest in these types of projects were in developing countries that were often unstable, autocratic, or pariahs on the international scale. Nonetheless, by the early 2000s, China had become a substantial exporter of capital to other developing countries. During this process, it became apparent to Chinese policy-makers that its SOEs required more protections than could be conferred either through international law or through its pre-existing BITs.[55]

Lifting off from this new reality, China's new-generation BITs have gone on to afford investors considerably higher levels of protection than did its first-generation BITs.[56] This shift has involved a more liberalized approach that provides greater coverage in the definition of investments, broad absolute and relative standards of treatment, and procedural provisions that allow for binding third-party dispute resolution.[57] By early 2010, China had signed 126 BITs with ninety-nine having entered into force. The long list of Sino-foreign BITs makes evident a gradual evolution in Chinese policy-makers' preferences with respect to foreign investment. Likely catalyzed by its increased investment in the developing world, China has abjured in its attachment to its old restrictive standards, having embarked

---

53 See Stephanie Hanson, *China, Africa, and Oil* (2008), Council on Foreign Relations, <http://www.cfr.org/ publication/9557/>.

54 See Deng, *supra* note 51 at 73.

55 Not surprisingly, many of the China's initial second-generation BITs were with developing countries that it had some form of economic relationship with, largely with respect to investment in natural resources. Such treaties include: the China-Ethiopia BIT (1998); the Botswana-China BIT (2000); the China-Congo BIT (2000); the China-Iran BIT (2000); the China-Kenya BIT (2001); the China-Nigeria BIT (2001); the China-Sierra Leone BIT (2001); the China-Myanmar BIT (2001); and the China-Uganda BIT (2004). The average 2008 per capita gross domestic product for China's ninety-nine ratified FIPA partners was US $16,102, considerably higher than Canada's FIPA partners' $9,567. See World Bank Development Indicators, *supra* note 28.

56 The most liberal of which can be considered some of its most recent BITs: the China-Bosnia Herzegovina (2002); the China-Germany BIT (2003); the China-Netherlands BIT (2004); and the China-Finland BIT (2006). See note 72 in this article for further discussion.

57 See Berger, *supra* note 48 at 3.

on a BIT campaign that is more closely aligned with developing country standards. However, China's outward investment remains greatly overshadowed by the inward investment that continues to pour in from developed countries such as Canada. [58] If China plans around this dichotomy when it negotiates its BITs, it could realistically attempt to negotiate more liberal BITs with developing countries in order to enhance the protection of its investments in those jurisdictions, while taking a more restrictive approach when negotiating BITs with developed countries. However, this has not transpired, as China has followed a very consistent path in its current BIT program and has entered into some of its most progressive BITs with developed countries such as Germany (2003), the Netherlands (2004), and Finland (2006). China has taken an approach that signals stability and predictability for its investment climate, at least as it pertains to the text of the treaties that it signs. In 2003, China joined a number of developed countries, including Canada, in drafting its own BIT model. China now has a general template that highlights its preferences, although its most recent BITs have liberalized further beyond its model preferences.

Comparing Canadian and Chinese BIT Approaches

Canada and China's respective model investment treaties are used extensively in the following analysis. However, and as is demonstrated later, China's most recent approach to its BIT program has diverged somewhat from what is prescribed in its BIT model. Most-favoured nation (MFN) treatment provisions in the Canada–China FIPA will automatically refer many of the treaty's investor protections to the least restrictive provision of its kind in all Sino-foreign BITs regardless of what is actually prescribed in the treaty. Therefore, reference is made to the least restrictive provision that exists in China's BIT program. China's BITs have progressively become less restrictive, which means that it needs to consider what effect Canada–China FIPA provisions will have on prior Sino-foreign treaties. Conversely, it can be argued that Canada's FIPAs have become more restrictive, with older FIPAs conferring treatment that is more favourable than its most recent FIPAs.[59] Canada has

---

[58] In 2009, China's financial and capital account surplus was US $109.1 billion. See A. Batson, "China's Current Account Surplus Fell in 2009," *Wall Street Journal* (13 February 2009), <http://online.wsj.com/article/NA_WSJ_PUB: SB10001424052748704041504575046230753948598.html>.

[59] Andrew Newcombe, personal communication, 9 June 2010.

addressed this in its FIPA model with an exception clause that precludes MFN reference to previous treaties.[60] While model investment treaties are used as templates that depict preferences coming into negotiations, the final text of concluded agreements involving a contracting party might stray considerably from the text of its respective draft model. It needs to be kept in mind that BITs are *negotiated outcomes* and, as such, result from the bargaining of on-the-table preferences — a process that can be dramatically influenced by explicit or implicit off-the-table factors.

BITs are essentially win-win outcomes for both contracting parties, but this does not mean that subtle variations in preferences over legal effect and language will not preclude the emergence of irreconcilable difference. States often have ironclad preferences that cannot be negotiated away no matter what is offered from the other side of the table. This is especially important with respect to investment treaties because of MFN treatment clauses. States are careful when negotiating substantive provisions in their BITs because MFN provisions in third-party agreements could see negotiated substantive provisions in a new treaty apply to many, if not all, of its pre-existing and future BITs. In addition, states are often only willing to give up so much in the way of sovereignty in the name of reaching a conclusion in a BIT negotiation. If Party A is considering entering into investment treaty negotiations with Party B, and it perceives that the economic benefit from the treaty will fail to supersede the sovereign losses attached to the treaty, then it is likely that Party A will not so much as even enter into preliminary talks with the other party. If it does enter into discussions, it might take a restrictive stance on the extent that the BIT's provisions set out state obligations. However, such an approach could in turn affect the economic efficacy of the agreement since more restrictive clauses could end up doing little to enhance the promotion of an investment.

Another aspect of the bargaining process in BIT negotiations is the negotiating environment or off-the-table particularities. This can be considered the context in which negotiations take place. As has been discussed, the capital importing-exporting paradigm has provided significant context behind the dissemination of BITs worldwide. Negotiations of the these types of agreements are largely

---

[60] See Canada FIPA model, Annex III(1): "Article 4 shall not apply to treatment accorded under all bilateral or multilateral international agreements in force or signed prior to the date of entry into force of this Agreement."

one-sided in that preferences dictated by capital-exporting states, often in their model BITs, become essential terms in reaching successful conclusions because capital-importing states do not possess the relative power to say "no." This is not the case, however, with the Canada–China FIPA. As previously mentioned, investment between the two countries flows in a bi-directional manner, and each country has strong convictions in key areas of investment standards, notably with respect to national treatment. It is not in either country's interest to give up on one aspect of its treaty preferences without a reasonable *quid pro quo* in another aspect.

This begs the question as to whether other off-the-table aspects exist between the two countries that may affect the nature of negotiations. One consideration that should be looked into is the perceived importance of bilateral investment between the two countries. If bilateral investment is perceived to be more important for one country than for the other, then it can be reasonably assumed that patching out a FIPA would also be more meaningful for that country. A way to consider if any such asymmetries exist is to briefly examine the economic relationship between the two countries. While Canada's total international exports fell substantially between 2008 and 2009 due to the global recession, its exports to China increased 7 percent.[61] However, Canadian exports to China still remain relatively low, making up only 3 percent of Canada's total exports, albeit up from 2 percent in 2008.[62] The low magnitude of bilateral economic relations also applies to investment, with two-way investment flows remaining fairly negligible.[63] There has been a perception in Canada that the country's over-reliance on bilateral trade and investment with the United States could be detrimental to Canada's economic performance moving forward.[64] This perspective has viewed the furthering of Canada's access to Chinese markets as being inextricably important to Canada's overall economic strategy, and the Canada–China FIPA is a crucial component in this new

---

[61] Compiled using data from Trade Data Online, Industry Canada, <http://www.ic.gc.ca/eic/site/tdo-dcd.nsf/eng/Home>.

[62] *Ibid.*

[63] See Foreign Affairs and International Trade Canada, *supra* note 3.

[64] See generally Danielle Goldfarb, "Too Many Eggs in One Basket? Evaluating Canada's Need to Diversify Trade" (2006) 236 C.D. Howe Institute, Commentary; and Daryl Copeland, "Diversifying Canada's Dependence: Look East" (2003) 27 Asian Perspective 277.

rubric.[65] On the other hand, China's incessant thirst for primary inputs implies a heightened level of need for Chinese access to Canadian natural resources. It is difficult to measure one level of perceived necessity *vis-à-vis* another, but it is reasonable to suggest that Canada and China stand to gain equally from a concluded FIPA.

General foreign policy and bilateral relations play a key role in setting the off-the-table stage for trade treaty negotiations. In 2006, a policy shift by the Canadian federal government on its discourse over China human rights concerns saw a souring of relations between the two countries. The resulting political climate has since proven to be an obstacle in galvanizing accommodation and overcoming differences, although recent developments have seen an amelioration of this situation. Economic uncertainty in the United States and the drive to diversify Canada's outward economic strategy were the likely catalysts behind Ottawa's decision to pursue its recent rapprochement with China.[66] This decision has implications for the FIPA bargaining process in that China might be able to leverage to its advantage the new sense of urgency characterized in the Canadian approach. If Canada now indeed places more emphasis on the necessity for a concluded FIPA with China, then asymmetries in the bargaining process may become evident. Such asymmetries could "confer bargaining advantages" for the Chinese side in negotiations, whether such asymmetries are perceived or actually have an objective basis.[67]

The following comparative analysis of Canada and China's respective BIT provision preferences is not exhaustive, although it covers the five most important aspects of the investment treaty: (1) minimum standard of treatment; (2) national treatment; (3) MFN treatment; (4) expropriation; and (5) procedural protections. One important aspect of the modern BIT, for instance, that is not discussed in depth in this article is the provision that prohibits performance requirements that condition foreign investment on areas

---

65 See Foreign Affairs and International Trade Canada, *Expanding Canadian Access to Global Markets and Networks,* Foreign Affairs and International Trade Canada, <http://www.international.gc.ca/commerce/strategy-strategie/markets-marches.aspx>.

66 See China Daily, "Canadian PM's Visit to China Re-Energizes Ties," *China Daily* (9 December 2009), Xinhua, <http://www.chinadaily.com.cn/world/2009-12/09/content_9149242.htm>.

67 Richard Ned Lebow, *The Art of Bargaining* (Baltimore: Johns Hopkins University Press, 1996) at 116.

such as local-content requirements, export performance, foreign-exchange balancing requirements, and technology transfer. China's accession to the WTO has meant that it has had to fulfil its trade-related investment measures (TRIMs) obligations. While China's regulatory stance on these matters has theoretically shifted in compliance with WTO norms, areas of non-compliance resurface time and again.[68] Another important aspect that is not covered in a detailed manner is that of capital transfers and currency convertibility. Canadian and Chinese policies on capital transfer and currency convertibility rights for foreign investors do not differ all that much, although China has taken a precautionary stance on the issue of speculative investment and the associated sudden outflows of capital during times of crisis. Accordingly, China has embedded such concerns into previous BITs, allowing policy-makers to impose restrictions on transfers in the event of balance-of-payments threats.[69]

Finally, human rights and sustainability issues related to the Canada–China FIPA are also contemplated. While this BIT will be first and foremost an economic agreement between the two states, issues surrounding coordinated compliance need to be addressed in order to provide a meaningful analysis. The yet-to-be concluded treaty has many non-economic overtones that will continue to shape policy discourses surrounding the intersection of trade, human rights, and sustainability objectives in a Canada–China bilateral context.

SUBSTANTIVE PROVISIONS

Minimum Standard of Treatment

Treatment provisions are arguably the most important substantive provisions that exist in BITs, and have spurred much of the recent debate surrounding the interpretation of investment treaty provisions. Minimum standard of treatment is an absolute standard in that it accords investors fundamental rights or objective standards that are not based on comparison with other investors. There exists

---

[68] See United States Trade Representative, *2008 Report to Congress on China's WTO Compliance 2008* (2008) at 59–60. An example of this is that many US firms have voiced concerns that Chinese government officials often "encourage" technology transfer without actually formally requiring it.

[69] For instance, the China-Mexico BIT (2008). See Tian Feng, *Meiguo ban zhong mei shuangbian touzi xieding zhi yi*, JRJ.com, <http://finance.jrj.com.cn/2008/12/0104392922830.shtml>.

considerable evidence in claims and cases throughout the twentieth century that suggest that the contemporary foundations of minimum standard of treatment are firmly ingrained within the norms of customary international law.[70] Under traditional custom in international law, states are obligated to accord foreigners and their property a minimum standard of treatment once admitted into its territory.[71] In cases where a BIT does not exist between two countries, the minimum standard is the defining standard in diplomatic protection claims.[72] BITs have sought to solidify and expand upon customary minimum standard of treatment norms by including such terms as fair and equitable treatment, the disallowance of arbitrary or discriminatory measures,[73] full protection and security, compensation of extraordinary losses, and more favourable treatment clauses.[74]

The most important element of the minimum standard of treatment class of protections, *fair and equitable treatment,* has been the most frequently invoked standard in recent international investment disputes pursuant to the substantive provisions of a BIT.[75] Virtually

[70] See Peter Muchlinski et al., eds., *supra* note 9 at 264. The minimum standard in international law as we have come to know it can be viewed as the sum of the legal doctrines, incidents, cases, and decisions that took place throughout the nineteenth and the first half of the twentieth centuries. This includes the Russian Revolution (1917), *Neer v. Mexico* (1926), and the Mexican nationalization of American interests (1936), and the Hull Rule (1936). See Andreas H. Roth, *The Minimum Standard of International Law Applied to Aliens* (Leiden: A.W. Sijthoff, 1949); and *L.F.H. Neer and Pauline Neer v. United Mexican States,* Docket no. 136, General Claims Commission United States and Mexico (Opinion Rendered, 15 October 1926).

[71] See Dolzer and Schreuer, *supra* note 11 at 11–12.

[72] See Andrew Newcombe and Lluís Paradell, *Law and Practice of Investment Treaties: Standards of Treatment* (New York: Wolters Kluwer, 2009) at 233.

[73] Arbitrary or discriminatory measures, however, while technically being a relative standard because it relies upon a comparison between investors are often placed in minimum standard of treatment provisions within the nomenclature of international investment law. See *ibid.* at 235.

[74] See *ibid.* at 233.

[75] See Dolzer and Schreur, *supra* note 11 at 119; and Newcombe and Paradell, *supra* note 72 at 255. The full protection and security standard is the other primary element of minimum standard of treatment and is often included alongside fair and equitable treatment in BIT minimum standard provisions. Full protection and security has its roots in securing investor protection from physical violence, but it has evolved to guarantee protections from host-state laws and regulations that infringe upon investor rights. The responsibility for the state, however, is

all BITs, old and new, insert the words "fair and equitable treatment" into their substantive provisions one way or another. Some countries, such as China, [76] have used this term without providing any context whatsoever. This is similar to the language used in German, Dutch, and Swedish BITs. Other countries, such as Canada, place the significance of fair and equitable treatment standards directly in the realm of customary international law.[77] This approach defines fair and equitable treatment as that which has been established by international custom.

Notwithstanding the universality and the importance of fair and equitable treatment provisions in the modern BIT, the term has, as with many other treatment standards, remained amorphous and has shifted temporally.[78] Regardless of its elusive definition, most successful claims in international investment arbitration today are based on claims made by investors surrounding alleged violations of fair and equitable treatment.[79] While fair and equitable treatment has historically not been "a term of art in public international law"[80] and, up until recently, has not been viewed as providing a distinguishable set of legal prescriptions,[81] recent developments in its interpretation have circumscribed a clearer set of parameters in its application. For instance, the NAFTA Free Trade Commission

---

not one of strict liability. Instead, host states must use due diligence in assuring the protection and security of investors.

[76] See Table 1 in this article.

[77] Canada has consistently used this wording throughout its BIT and FTA-investment programs. The FIPA model wording is almost an exact mirror of the wording used in Canada's first FIPA with the Soviet Union. Article 3(1) of that agreement states that "investments or returns of investors of either Contracting Party shall at all times be accorded fair and equitable treatment in accordance with principles of international law and shall enjoy full protection and security in the territory of the other Contracting Party." NAFTA Article 1105(1) also uses this wording. The NAFTA FTA issued an interpretative statement relating NAFTA Article 1105(1) with the minimum treatment standards of customary international law. See *Waste Management, Inc. v. Mexico,* ICSID Case no. ARB(AF)/98/2 (Award, 30 April 2004) at para. 90 [*Waste Management II*].

[78] See Dolzer and Schreuer, *supra* note 11 at 119.

[79] *Ibid.* at 119.

[80] See Newcombe and Paradell, *supra* note 72 at 263.

[81] See Stephen Vasciannie, "The Fair and Equitable Treatment Standard in International Investment Law and Practice" (2000) 70 Brit. Y.B. Int'l L. 99; and OECD, *Fair and Equitable Treatment Standard in International Investment Law,* Working Papers on International Investment (2004).

(FTC), along with the governments of Canada, Mexico, and the United States, have through various submissions in NAFTA disputes reaffirmed the meaning of fair and equitable treatment in that "the concept [does] not require treatment in addition to or beyond that which is required by the customary international law minimum standard of treatment of aliens."[82] Canada has followed the United States' lead in confirming fair and equitable treatment's relation to customary international law standards. However, the United States in its BIT model proceeds further in its definition. Article 5(2), paragraph (a), states that "fair and equitable treatment includes the obligation not to deny justice in criminal, civil, or administrative adjudicatory proceedings in accordance with the principles of due process embodied in the leading legal systems of the world." However, decisions in disputes related to treaties that fall outside the NAFTA framework have interpreted fair and equitable treatment as "an independent treaty standard with an autonomous meaning."[83] This has implied that fair and equitable treatment standards exceed those accorded in customary law, although in jurisprudential practice, fundamental differences in the international minimum standard of treatment and fair and equitable treatment have not arisen.[84]

With all of the discussion surrounding fair and equitable treatment's relationship to customary international law, it is often easy to lose sight of what this standard of protection means for investors. Fair and equitable treatment's most cogent and effectual element is tied to an investor's legitimate expectations when investing in a given jurisdiction[85] and principles surrounding good faith. An investor's

---

82 See NAFTA Free Trade Commission (FTC), *Notes of Interpretation of Certain NAFTA Chapter 11 Provisions* (31 July 2001). The NAFTA FTC's interpretation of fair and equitable treatment is a binding interpretation.

83 See Newcombe and Paradell, *supra* note 72 at 264. For case examples, see *MTD Equity Sdn. Bhd. & MTD Chile S.A. v. Chile*, ICSID Case no. ARB/01/7 (Award, 25 May 2004); *Occidental Exploration and Production Company v. Ecuador*, LCIA Case no. UN3467 (Final Award, 1 July 2004); *LG&E International Inc. v. Argentina*, ICSID Case no. ARB/02/1 (Decision on Liability, 3 October 2006); *PSEG Global Inc. and Konya Ilgin Elektrik Üretim ve Ticaret Limited Sirketi v. Turkey*, ICSID Case no. ARB/02/5 (Award, 19 January 2007); and *Siemens A.G. v. Argentina*, ICSID Case no. ARB/02/8 (Award, 6 February 2007).

84 See Newcombe and Paradell, *supra* note 72 at 272.

85 See *Waste Management, Inc. v. Mexico (Waste Management II)*, ICSID Case no. ARB(AF)/00/3 (NAFTA) (Award, 30 April 2004); *S.D. Myers, Inc. v. Canada*, UNCITRAL (NAFTA) (Partial Award, 13 November 2000); and *Mondev International Ltd. v. United States*, ICSID Case no. ARB(AF)/99/2 (NAFTA) (Award, 11 October 2002).

legitimate expectations rely on the legal framework that is either "explicitly or implicitly implied by the host state" at the time of the investment admission.[86] This can take the form of any verbal or written representations or guarantees that an investor takes into account when deciding whether or not to invest in a jurisdiction. The notion that countries should act in good faith after the admission of investment reflects obligations surrounding transparency, regulatory fairness, and the prohibition of the abuse of authority.[87] While these tenets have increasingly been articulated in international fora due to the proliferation of BITs globally, it could be reasonably supposed that many of these aspects have become ingrained in customary aspects of international law through the overwhelming concordance of agreement that has taken place in institutions such as the WTO.[88]

China's BITs all contain fair and equitable treatment language, but, up until recently, a more accurate definition has never been provided.[89] Of late, China has been open to providing more detail. For example, the China-New Zealand FTA takes a detailed approach similar to that prescribed by the United States in its BIT model. Article 143(2) of the agreement states that "fair and equitable treatment includes the obligation to ensure that, having regard to the general principles of law, investors are not denied justice or treated unfairly or inequitably in any legal or administrative proceeding affecting the investment of the investor."[90]

China's view on fair and equitable treatment in relation to customary law has undergone a similar evolution to other aspects of its BIT program. As at least one scholar has noted, some Chinese jurists remain wary in regarding fair and equitable language in Sino-foreign BITs and the role that customary international law plays in the sovereign determination of China's existence.[91] Reflecting this

---

[86] See Dolzer and Schreuer, *supra* note 11 at 134. A legal framework is composed of legislation and treaties, guarantees contained in decrees, contractual obligations, and executive assurances.

[87] See Muchlinksi et al., eds., *supra* note 9 at 272–90.

[88] See *ibid.* at 278. The issue of transparency as a customary legal norm has arguably been shaped, *inter alia*, through provisions in the GATS, *supra* note 8, Article III and in GATT, *supra* note 8, Article X(2).

[89] See China BIT model, Article 3 in Table 1. See also Congyan, *supra* note 24 at 468.

[90] See China-New Zealand Free Trade Agreement (7 April 2008) (entered into force 1 October 2008).

[91] See Cai, *supra* note 24 at 468.

common domestic view, China has generally refrained from including "customary international law" in its investment treaties. However,
its stance on this matter has been one of piecemeal, perhaps be-
grudging, acceptance. This process has accelerated over recent
years, culminating with the investment chapter in the China-Peru
FTA, which prescribes fair and equitable treatment using almost
the exact wording from the earlier-mentioned NAFTA FTC's interpretation[92] as well as from Canada's FIPA model.[93] It can be considered that China's approach with fair and equitable treatment
now parallels that of Canada but goes even further in including
examples surrounding due process. It is unclear why China's approach has undergone this shift, but with respect to the Canada–
China FIPA negotiations this should be viewed as a development
conducive to reaching a negotiated conclusion (see Table 1).

National Treatment

National treatment provisions establish an obligation on the contracting parties to provide a relative or contingent standard of
treatment to investors and investments of the other contracting
party. It does not set out an absolute or minimum standard that
parties are required to adhere to. NAFTA Article 1102 prescribes
national treatment as the obligation for a contracting party to "accord to investors of another Party treatment no less favourable than
it accords, in like circumstances, to its own investors with respect to
the establishment, acquisition, expansion, management, conduct,
operation, and sale or other dispositions of investment." It can be
considered an "empty shell" that requires substantive content, as it
does not have any "intrinsic content" to assess the relative treatment
given to investors of a contracting party.[94]

Under commonly accepted norms of international investment
law, national treatment is a treaty-based obligation. While national treatment has become a core component of BITs worldwide, its
nature varies considerably from treaty to treaty and the degree of
non-discrimination guaranteed is often limited by an extensive list
of reservations and exceptions. National treatment provisions also
play a vital role in promoting investment, as its prohibition of

[92] See NAFTA Free Trade Commission, *supra* note 82.

[93] See Table 1 for the text of this provision. Translated text from the China BIT
model are taken from Dolzer and Schrueer, *supra* note 11.

[94] See Newcombe and Paradell, *supra* note 72 at 148–49.

Table 1
MINIMUM STANDARD OF TREATMENT

Canada FIPA Model	China BIT Model	China-Peru FTA (2009)
ARTICLE 5	**ARTICLE 3**	**ARTICLE 132**
(1) Each party shall accord to covered investments treatment in accordance with the customary international law minimum standard of treatment of aliens, including fair and equitable treatment and full protection and security.	(1) Investments of investors of each contracting party shall all the time be accorded fair and equitable treatment in the territory of the other contracting party.	(1) Each party shall accord fair and equitable treatment and full protection and security in accordance with customary international law in its territory to investment of investors of the other party.
(2) The concepts of "fair and equitable treatment" and "full protection and security" do not require treatment in addition to, or beyond, that which is required by the customary international law minimum standard of treatment of aliens.		(2) For greater certainty,
		(a) the concepts of "fair and equitable treatment" and "full protection and security" do not require additional treatment to that required under the minimum standard of treatment of aliens in accordance with the standard of customary international law;
		(b) a determination that there has been a breach of another provision of this agreement or another international agreement does not imply that the minimum standard of treatment of aliens has been breached;
		(c) "fair and equitable treatment" includes the prohibition against denial of justice in criminal, civil, or administrative proceedings in accordance with the general accepted principles of customary international law; and
		(d) the "full protection and security" standard does not imply, in any case, a better treatment to that accorded to nationals of the party where the investment has been made.

discrimination of foreign firms relative to domestic firms creates an operating environment for the foreign enterprise based on a "level playing field" of competition in the host country's marketplace. Unlike minimum standard of treatment, national treatment provisions are not embedded within BITs because of any deference to customary international legal norms. Host states pursue these provisions in their BITs based on economic objectives and in the evaluation of trade-offs between security or cultural preservation and the objective of realizing investment growth.

Developing an obligations-based framework that relies on a relative form of standard-setting requires an applicable and well-defined "comparator" to lay out the basis for mistreatment — that is a comparison must be made between the treatment of a foreign investor and a similarly situated domestic investor. Obvious difficulties arise here in that for a dispute to be launched pursuant to national treatment, an investor will be obligated to prove that discrimination has occurred based on nationality. This requires the identification of a domestic investor that operates in the same sector or the same geographic area depending on the context of mistreatment.

One important aspect of national treatment BIT provisions that is fundamentally important in the negotiations of the Canada–China FIPA is the way they approach the issue of admission of investment. The degree of risk involved in granting expansive national treatment protections, especially as it pertains to pre-established investment, explains why very few international investment treaties accord unfettered national treatment and establishment rights to investors. Canadian and US BITs use a pre-entry model that expands the obligation of contracting parties, so that they apply national treatment protections to both investments that have been established in accordance with domestic laws as well as investments that are seeking admission. Bilateral investment treaties that include pre-establishment national treatment provisions in their respective texts almost always have exception and reservation clauses based on each contracting party's preferences. Article 9(1) of Canada's FIPA model states that Articles 3 (national treatment), 4 (MFN treatment), 6 (senior management, boards of directors and entry of personnel), and 7 (performance requirements) shall not apply to "any existing non-conforming measure that is maintained by" a contracting party at the national or sub-national level. Canadian-foreign FIPAs often refer to an annexed schedule that lists exceptions and reservations, which is broken down either sectorally or according to a schedule of relevant federal statutes that have provisions outlining limitations and screening requirements for foreign investment.[95] During the era of China's early BITs, its domestic industries were still highly unproductive and were not in a position to compete against foreign investment enterprises that possessed an enormous

[95] The Schedule of Canada in the Canada-Jordan FIPA (2009) lists relevant statutes as: Investment Canada Act, R.S.C. 1985, c. 28 (1st Supp.) and Investment Canada Regulations, SOR/85–611 (measures that deal with the acquisition and establishment of businesses in Canada by foreigners or foreign entities); Canada Business Corporations Act, R.S.C. 1985, c. C44; Canada Corporations Act, R.S.C. 1970, c. C32; Canada Business Corporations Act (CBCA) Regulations, SOR/79–316 (measures pertaining to Canadian ownership levels); Citizenship Act, R.S.C. 1985, c. C-29; Foreign Ownership of Land Regulations, SOR/79–416 (measures pertaining to the foreign ownership of land); Air Canada Public Participation Act, R.S.C. 1985, c. C-29; Canadian Arsenals Limited Divestiture Authorization Act, S.C. 1986 c. 20; Eldorado Nuclear Limited Reorganization and Divestiture Act, S.C. 1988, c. 41; Nordion and Theratronics Divestiture Authorization Act, S.C. 1990, c. 4 (measures that establish limits on the non-residential ownership of shares in certain companies); Customs Act, R.S.C. 1985, c. 1 (2nd Supp.); Duty Free Shop Regulations, SOR/86–1072 (measures that establish residency requirements for duty free shop operations); Cultural Property Export and Import Act, R.S.C. 1985, c. C-51 (measures that outline restrictions on foreign participation in the import and export of cultural property); Patent Act, R.S.C. 1985, c. P-4; Patent Rules, C.R.C. 1978, c. 1250; Patent Cooperation Treaty Regulations, SOR/89–453 (measures that establish residency requirements for the registering of patents); Canada Petroleum Resources Act, R.S.C. 1985, c. 36 (2nd Supp.); Territorial Lands Act, R.S.C. 1985, c. T-7; Federal Real Property and Immovables Act, S.C. 1991, c. 50; Canada-Newfoundland Atlantic Accord Implementation Act, S.C. 1987, c. 3; Canada-Nova Scotia Offshore Petroleum Resources Accord Implementation Act, S.C. 1988, c. 28; Canada Oil and Gas Land Regulations, C.R.C. 1978, c. 1518 (measures establishing Canadian ownership requirements for oil and gas production rights and licences); Investment Canada Act, R.S.C. 1985, c. 28 (1st Supp.); Investment Canada Regulations, SOR/85–611; Policy on Non Resident Ownership in the Uranium Mining Sector, 1987 (measures pertaining to non-resident ownership in the uranium mining sector); Coastal Fisheries Protection Act, R.S.C. 1985, c. C33; Fisheries Act, R.S.C. 1985, c. F14; Coastal Fisheries Protection Regulations, C.R.C. 1978, c. 413; Policy on Foreign Investment in the Canadian Fisheries Sector, 1985; Commercial Fisheries Licensing Policy, 1996 (measures that deal with foreign fishing vessels and the foreign ownership of fish processing enterprises); Canada Transportation Act, S.C. 1996, c. 10; Aeronautics Act, R.S.C. 1985, c. A-2; Canadian Aviation Regulations — Part II and IV, 1996 (measures that restrict foreign participation in the air services sector or foreigners wishing to register or operate Canadian aircraft); Canada Shipping Act, R.S.C. 1985, c. S-9, Part I; and Marine Certification Regulations, SOR 97–391 (requirements for owning a ship on the Canadian register).

competitive advantage. Reflecting the need of the Chinese government to discriminate between domestic and foreign firms in certain instances, some early Sino-foreign BITs do not even mention national treatment.[96] Furthermore, when FDI entered into the country, government pressure and other factors meant that investment typically took the entry model of a joint venture with a Chinese partner.[97] This afforded Chinese industry the opportunity to gradually adjust to increased competition while also facilitating technology transfers and opening new markets to Chinese exports. Throughout the 1990s, however, dramatic restructuring, increased competition, and privatization reshaped Chinese industry.[98] In light of these changes, domestic Chinese industry was much better situated to compete against foreign firms that were increasingly looking to establish wholly owned foreign enterprises.[99] In addition, by the late 1990s, Chinese enterprises were beginning their pursuit of overseas investment. The previously discussed *zou qu chu* policy further ramified this new reality.[100] These factors and other shifting policies and structural aspects of the Chinese economy help explain the transition in China's approach to national treatment in its investment treaties.[101]

96 For instance, the original China-Finland (1983) and the China-Singapore BIT (1985) do not include national treatment in their substantive texts. The China-Finland BIT was renegotiated in 2006; the new agreement includes national treatment provisions.

97 See Paul W. Beamish, "The Characteristics of Joint Ventures in the People's Republic of China" (1993) 1 J. Int'l Marketing 29; and Xiaowen Tian, *Managing International Business in China* (New York: Cambridge University Press, 2007) at 30.

98 The adoption of the People's Republic of China Company Law of 1994 provided the legal framework necessary to transition state-owned enterprises (SOEs) into legal corporate entities. See Naughton, *supra* note 36 at 301–2.

99 This includes established equity joint ventures, whereby the foreign partner seeks to acquire the interests held by the Chinese partner. See Toshiyuki Arai, "Changing Trends in Japanese Direct Investment in China" (October 2004) China Law and Practice.

100 See Buckley et al., *supra* note 51.

101 Other policies include "grasping the large and letting go the small" (*zhuada fangxiao*), which was adopted in 1995 and then formally promulgated during the fifteenth Communist Party Congress in 1997. This saw the restructuring of thousands of SOEs of various sizes. Some were privatized, but many merged to increase competitiveness, although still remained under state control. By the end of 1996, approximately 70 percent of small SOEs had been privatized in some provinces. See Yuanzheng Cao, "From Federalism, Chinese Style to Privatization, Chinese Style" (1999) 7 Economics of Transition 103.

Sino-foreign investment treaties that have national treatment provisions included within their text are often qualified with language that refers the applicability of protections to parties' domestic laws.[102] This choice of wording amounts to little more than a best effort clause, insofar as China and the other contracting party have the ability to use or modify existing legislation or enact new laws in order to discriminate against certain types of foreign investment. However, China's BITs have undergone an evolution of their national treatment provisions that parallels the overall liberalization of the way that it approaches international investment. Much to the dismay of some Chinese scholars,[103] China now does not include the "subject to its laws" language in the national treatment provisions of some of its agreements.[104] The China-Finland BIT (2006), which follows this pattern, instead includes a protocol that qualifies many of the corpus's provisions. With respect to national treatment, the protocol states that the agreement's national treatment provisions "do not apply to any existing non-conforming measure maintained within its [*sic*] territory of the People's Republic of China or any amendment thereto provided that the amendment does not increase the non-conforming effect of such a measure from what it was immediately before the amendment took place."[105] In effect,

---

102 See China BIT model, Article 3(2), in Table 2 in this article.

103 See Cai, *supra* note 24 at 460. It is important to note that Cai does not necessarily subscribe to such views.

104 See the China-Bosnia Herzegovina (2002), Article 3(1); the China-Netherlands BIT (2004), Article 3(3); the China-Germany BIT (2003), Article 3(2); and the China-Finland BIT (2006), Article 3(2). While the relative bargaining position of Germany and the Netherlands might explain why national treatment provisions are liberal for Chinese standards, the fact that Bosnia Herzegovina was the first of such Sino-foreign treaties confirms that this is a policy projected from the leadership of the central government of the People's Republic of China.

105 It is interesting to note that this agreement only allows China to use nonconforming measures and not Finland. Essentially, China's policy-makers are still able to use existing laws and regulations against Finish investors, while Chinese investors are able to take advantage of the agreement's substantive provisions when investing in Finland on a basis that is no less favourable than domestic investors. The imbalance that exists here is perhaps representative of the special and differential treatment that European nations often give in good faith to developing countries with the idea that as their economies liberalize their economies will be better equipped to remove non-conforming measures. With respect to this, the protocol states that "the People's Republic of China will take all appropriate measures to progressively remove all non-conforming measures." For further discussion, see Berger, *supra* note 48 at 13.

this means that China cannot increase discriminatory treatment through the implementation of new non-conforming measures. While China has made considerable strides in how it approaches national treatment in its BITs, the hard line it has continued to take with respect to the admission of investment presents a significant obstacle in the negotiation of both the Canada–China FIPA and the China-US BIT. Over the past fifteen years, almost all of Canada's FIPAs have accorded pre-establishment rights to investors,[106] as have US-foreign BITs.[107] China's approach on this matter is done through its definition of what constitutes an investment. Article 1 of China's Model FIPA defines an "investment" as that which has been "invested" in the territory of the other contracting party.[108] This assigns any further reference to the term "investment" or "investor" in the text of the agreement as investment that is already established. In contrast, Canada simply defines an investment, *inter alia*, as an enterprise, an equity security of an enterprise, or a debt security of an enterprise.[109] On the issue of establishment, it is likely that negotiations will centre on the definition of investment and not the express wording of the relevant substantive provisions.

Another aspect of national treatment language that differs between the Canadian and the Chinese approaches is the inclusion of an express comparator. In NAFTA and the BITs that Canada and the United States are party to, national treatment provisions provide the express comparator, "in like circumstances," but a majority of international investment agreements do not have this included in their text.[110] This includes Sino-foreign BITs.[111] This should not

---

[106] The Canada-Ecuador FIPA (1997) even goes so far as to prescribe a standalone provision on the establishment of investment. Article II(3) states: "Each Contracting Party shall permit establishment of a new business enterprise or acquisition of an existing business enterprise or a share of such enterprise by investors or prospective investors of the other Contracting Party on a basis no less favourable than that which, in like circumstances, it permits such acquisition or establishment."

[107] However, it should be noted that, and perhaps indicative of its tough stance on pre-establishment rights with limited use of non-conforming measures, the United States has only successfully concluded one BIT since 2003 — the US-Uruguay BIT (2006).

[108] See Article 1(1) of the China BIT model.

[109] See section A of the Canada FIPA model.

[110] See Newcombe and Paradell, *supra* note 72 at 160.

[111] See Table 2 in this article for Canada and China's BIT model national treatment language.

present an occlusion in negotiations, however, as tribunal rulings have interpreted the very nature of national treatment and its anti-discriminatory purpose in a way that the absence of an express comparator clause "is arguably not legally significant."[112]

One considerable obstacle with respect to national treatment is the lack of transparency in China's laws and regulations. Canada's approach, which uses listed non-conforming measures and an express transparency provision to provide transparency for investors on either a sectoral or a statutory basis,[113] exists in stark contrast to China's generalist approach of merely stating that domestic laws and regulations supersede the rights conferred by the agreement. Generally speaking, there has been no move by China to explain which laws and regulations actually apply to the screening in the admission process of foreign investment, although it does publish a *Foreign Investment Industrial Guidance Catalogue* that respectively lists disallowed, admitted, and preferred categories of investment.[114] Considering the difficulties that China has had in compiling the official journal that lists all trade-related laws and regulations, as required in its WTO accession agreement,[115] it is likely that China is either unwilling or unable to consider the myriad of existing domestic legislation that might affect its reception of incoming investment and would prefer to continue with its ad hoc approach on the matter. It is presumable that Canadian negotiators have engaged extensively with the Chinese side on the issue of including a transparency clause and listing non-conforming domestic laws and regulations. The issue of transparency may continue to be a significant stumbling block in treaty negotiations (see Table 2).

MFN Treatment

MFN treatment has for some time been considered "the cornerstone of all modern economic treaties,"[116] and it defines the spirit

---

[112] See Newcombe and Paradell, *supra* note 72 at 161. For tribunal interpretations on the matter, see *Pope & Talbot Inc. v. Canada,* UNCITRAL (NAFTA) (Statement of Claim, 25 March 1999); and *S.D. Myers v. Canada,* UNCITRAL (NAFTA) (First Partial Award, 13 November 2000) 40 I.L.M. (2001).

[113] See Canada FIPA model, Article 19.

[114] See the Foreign Investment Industrial Guidance Catalogue (amended in 2007) in *China Law and Practice* (December 2007/January 2008).

[115] See United States Trade Representative, *supra* note 65 at 95–97.

[116] See Stanley K. Hornbeck, "The Most Favoured Nation Clause" (1909) 3 Am. J. Int'l L. 395, referred to in Scott Vesel, "Clearing a Path through a Tangled

Table 2

NATIONAL TREATMENT

Canada FIPA Model	China BIT Model	China-Finland BIT (2006)
ARTICLE 3	ARTICLE 3	ARTICLE 3
(1) Each party shall accord to investors of the other party treatment no less favourable than that it accords, in like circumstances, to its own investors with respect to the establishment, acquisition, expansion, management, conduct, operation, and sale or other disposition of investments in its territory.	(2) Without prejudice to its laws or regulations, each contracting party shall accord to investments and activities associated with such investments by investors of the other contracting party treatment not less favourable than that accorded to the investments and associated activities by its own investors.	(2) Each contracting party shall accord to investments by investors of the other contracting party treatment no less favourable than the treatment it accords to investments by its own investors with respect to the operation, management, maintenance, use, enjoyment, expansion, sale, or other disposal of investments that have been made.

of the current international trade regime through Article I of the General Agreement on Tariffs and Trade.[117] Its use has risen alongside norms surrounding the comity of nations, whereby cordial acts of reciprocity between states are viewed to strengthen the international system as a whole. For instance, MFN clauses have even found their way into consular and diplomatic agreements.[118] MFN treatment was extended into the realm of international investment law during the second half of the twentieth century through the proliferation of BITs.

While national treatment comparisons are done on a domestic-foreign basis, under MFN treatment the basis for comparison is foreign with foreign. Being a relative standard, MFN treatment provides no absolute definitions for what constitutes mistreatment but is instead operationalized in a similar manner to national treatment in that it outlines parameters for substantive content to be placed inside. The basic purpose behind MFN treatment is much the same as national treatment in that it prohibits nationality-based discrimination. As a result, treaty language surrounding MFN treatment is almost exactly identical to that of national treatment. For instance, NAFTA Article 1103(1) states that "[e]ach Party shall accord to investors of another Party treatment no less favorable than that it accords, in like circumstances, to investors of any other Party or of a non-Party with respect to the establishment, acquisition, expansion, management, conduct, operation, and sale or other disposition of investments."

Perhaps the most important aspect of MFN provisions in investment treaties is that its inclusion can provide uniformity across a nation's entire investment treaty portfolio. If a country enters into

---

Jurisprudence: Most-Favoured Nation Clauses and Dispute Settlement Provisions in Bilateral Investment Treaties" (2007) 32 Yale J. Int'l L. 125.

[117] GATT, *supra* note 8. Article I states: "With respect to customs duties and charges of any kind imposed on or in connection with importation or exportation or imposed on the international transfer of payments for imports or exports, and with respect to the method of levying such duties and charges, and with respect to all rules and formalities in connection with importation and exportation, and with respect to all matters referred to in paragraphs 2 and 4 of Article III, any advantage, favour, privilege or immunity granted by any contracting party to any product originating in or destined for any other country shall be accorded immediately and unconditionally to the like product originating in or destined for the territories of all other contracting parties" (footnotes omitted).

[118] See William J. Aceves, "The Vienna Convention on Consular Relations: A Study of Rights, Wrongs, and Remedies" (1998) 31 Vand. J. Int'l L. 257.

a BIT with a party on more favourable terms than it had with other parties, it must, by virtue of the spirit of MFN treatment, extend those same levels of substantive protections to all other BIT partners that have MFN provisions in the text of their agreements. It is to this extent that MFN treatment provisions are retrospective.[119] In terms of procedural protections, however, the application of MFN treatment has been less certain. Making this applicability more ambiguous is the fact that recent ICSID arbitrations have reached "sharply divergent results" on the matter.[120]

Canada's approach to MFN treatment in its FIPA model and in its recent BITs has been based on NAFTA's MFN provisions. Article 4(1) of Canada's FIPA model is virtually identical to the NAFTA language quoted earlier.[121] As with Canada-foreign FIPA national treatment provisions, MFN treatment in these agreements is done on a pre-establishment basis but is subject to the same exceptions and reservations to which national treatment provisions are subject. However, the earlier-mentioned Annex III clause that Canada puts in its newer FIPAs precluding MFN reference to previous treaties dramatically affects the scope of MFN coverage.[122] Canada and the United States learned a lot from their experience as respondents in NAFTA tribunal claims, and after a period of examining improvements that needed to be made, both countries revamped and released their new treaty models with provisions and exceptions that addressed these concerns. Since provisions in Canada's earlier FIPAs were either designed around the OECD framework or were verbatim replications of NAFTA Chapter 11 provisions, changes were made

---

[119] See Stephen W. Schill, "Tearing Down the Great Wall: The New Generation Investment Treaties of the People's Republic of China" (2007) 15 Cardozo J. Int'l & Comp. L. 73 at 100–1.

[120] See Hornbeck, *supra* note 116 at 126. The five ICSID cases that have tackled this issue are: *Maffezini v. Spain,* ICSID Case no. ARB/97/7 (Decision on Jurisdiction, 25 January, 2000) 5 ICSID (W. Bank) 396 (2000); *Siemens A. G. v. Argentina,* ICSID Case no. ARB/02/8 (Decision of Jurisdiction, 3 August 2004); *Salini Costruttori S.p.A. v. Jordan,* ICSID Case no. ARB/02/13 (Decision on Jurisdiction, 9 November 2004), 44 I.L.M. 573 (2005); *Plama Consortium v. Bulgaria,* ICSID Case no. ARB/03/24 (Decision on Jurisdiction, 8 February 2005), 44 I.L.M. 721 (2005); and *Gas Natural SDG v. Argentina,* ICSID Case no. ARB/03/10 (Decision of the Tribunal on Preliminary Questions on Jurisdiction, 17 June 2005).

[121] See Table 3 in this article for the text of the provision.

[122] See Canada FIPA model, *supra* note 60.

so that disputing investors would not be able to take advantage of loose substantive and procedural standards that could be interpreted in the disputant's favour. With reference to NAFTA claims, this was especially true with the minimum standard of treatment and specific procedural aspects, notably transparency.[123] Since the result of gap filling could be considered more restrictive from the perspective of the investor, it was necessary for Canada to include the Annex III clause, otherwise the FIPA model revisions would have been rendered useless essentially.

China uses a similar clause in its BITs, having consistently negotiated provisions that exclude MFN protections based on comparisons made with FTAs between China and third parties.[124] Such exclusions also apply to other non-BIT economic treaties (for example, taxation treaties).[125] China has signed FTAs with Peru (2009), New Zealand (2008), Costa Rica (2010), Pakistan (2006), and Chile (2005), as well as with the nations that collectively make up the Association of South-East Asian Nations (signed in 2002, but entered into force in 2010). However, of all these FTAs, only the China-Peru and the China-New Zealand FTAs include a chapter with substantive and procedural investment provisions. While these two chapters do include some innovative exceptions with respect to national treatment in the way of relinquishing certain obligations from contracting parties, there is no language in China's FTAs that suggests a greater degree of investor rights *vis-à-vis* what is contained in its BITs.[126] Perhaps the most plausible explanation regarding

---

[123] For a full explanation of what was learned from NAFTA and the NAFTA claims process, see Lévesque, *supra* note 33.

[124] As such, it should take no issue in Canada's insistence to include an Annex III type clause in the FIPA.

[125] Article 3(4) of China's BIT model says regarding Article 3(3) on MFN treatment that it "shall not be construed as to oblige one Contracting Party to extend to investors of the other Contracting Party the benefit of any treatment, preference, or privilege by virtue of: (a) any customs union, free trade zone, economic union, and any international agreement resulting in such unions, or similar institutions; (b) any international agreement or arrangement relating wholly or mainly to taxation; (c) any arrangements for facilitating small scale frontier trade in border areas."

[126] For instance, with respect to national treatment, Article 129(3) of the China-Peru FTA (2009) states that "the Parties reserve the right to adopt or maintain any measure that accords differential treatment to socially or economically disadvantaged minorities or ethnic groups."

this inclusion is that since its inception China's BIT program has borrowed many characteristics of its BITs from many European countries, including Germany.[127]

Finally, the issue of MFN in relation to the procedural protections of Sino-foreign BITs is also important to consider. As is discussed in greater detail later, Chinese BITs have been scant in prescribing dispute resolution mechanisms to substantive areas besides expropriation, except for some of its most recent BITs such as those with Germany and the Netherlands.[128] China has made it quite clear that it wants to avoid affording ubiquitous procedural protections across its treaty portfolio. For instance, it has made express exemptions surrounding investor-state dispute mechanisms and MFN applicability in some recent treaties.[129] It remains unclear, however, to what extent investors from the home states of some of China's earlier BITs could use MFN clauses to argue for procedural protections that are equal to those granted in either the China–Germany or the China–Netherlands BITs. With respect to the Canada–China FIPA, Canadian negotiators must keep these issues in mind when negotiating both the investor-state dispute provisions and the MFN provisions. A strong set of procedural provisions will reduce the need for Canadian investors to rely on MFN protections to access certain dispute resolution mechanisms and would render footnotes precluding the MFN treatment clause from procedural protections irrelevant. Of course, the inclusion of Canada's Annex III clause precluding MFN reference to past treaties would also render these aspects of past Sino-foreign BITs irrelevant (see Table 3).

---

127 For example, see Article 3(4) of the Germany-Ethiopia BIT (2005).

128 There has been significant discussion surrounding whether MFN treatment protections should extend beyond substantive and into the realm of procedural. If some of China's new agreements afford much greater access for investors to investment dispute mechanisms, then it is argued that MFN treatment should accord these same rights to investors in third-party agreements. See Aaron Chandler, "BITs, MFN Treatment and the PRC: The Impact of China's Ever–Evolving Bilateral Investment Treaty Practice" (2009) 43 Int'l L. 1301.

129 Article 131(2) of the China-Peru FTA (see Table 3 in this article) is footnoted with the following: "For greater certainty, treatment 'with respect to the establishment, acquisition, expansion, management, conduct, operation, and sale or other disposition of investments referred to in paragraphs 1 and 2 of Article 131 (Most-Favoured-Nation Treatment) does not encompass dispute settlement mechanisms, such as those in Article 138 (Settlement of Disputes between Parties) and Article 139 (Investor-State Dispute Settlement), that are provided for in international investment treaties or trade agreements."

Table 3
MFN TREATMENT

Canada FIPA Model	*China-Peru FTA*
ARTICLE 4	ARTICLE 131
(1) Each party shall accord to investors of the other party treatment no less favourable than that it accords, in like circumstances, to investors of a non-party with respect to the establishment, acquisition, expansion, management, conduct, operation, and sale or other disposition of investments in its territory.	(1) Each party shall accord to investors of the other party treatment no less favourable than that it accords, in like circumstances, to investors of any third state with respect to the establishment, acquisition, expansion, management, conduct, operation, and sale, or other disposition of investments in its territory.
(2) Each party shall accord to covered investments treatment no less favourable than that it accords, in like circumstances, to investments of investors of a non-party with respect to the establishment, acquisition, expansion, management, conduct, operation, and sale or other disposition of investments in its territory.	(2) Each party shall accord to investments of investors of the other party treatment no less favourable than that it accords, in like circumstances, to investments in its territory of investors of any third state with respect to the establishment, acquisition, expansion, management, conduct, operation, and sale, or other disposition of investments (see note 129 for the text's footnote on this provision).

Expropriation

Expropriation has been an important consideration in public international law for well over a century, having been represented in minimum standard norms and international treaties. The primary principle of international law — that states exert permanent sovereignty over their claims, territories, and natural resources — exists in tension with the principle that requires states to uphold the acquired rights of foreigners.[130] Expropriation of foreign-owned property, as has been interpreted customarily, is a reconciliation of

---

[130] See Newcombe and Paradell, *supra* note 72 at 321. See also *Norwegian Shipowners Claims (Norway v. United States)*, Permanent Court of Arbitration (Award of the Tribunal, 13 October 1922).

the requirements of these two principles. States can exercise their sovereign claim over any property that is located within its territory, including the private property of a foreigner, but they should do so in a manner that is consistent with international standards. Customary international legal norms emphasize four conditions that states are obligated to respect when they dispossess foreigners of their property: (1) that the dispossession fulfils public objectives; (2) that it is non-discriminatory; (3) that due process is exercised; and (4) that compensation is paid.[131] If even one of these conditions is not met in the event of expropriation, the act can be deemed illegal. The public interest condition requires the state to demonstrate that the expropriation was undertaken in the interest of a legitimate public need. For instance, an act of expropriating property with the aim of handing it over to a third party (that is, a domestic enterprise) does not fulfil this condition.[132] The non-discriminatory condition simply requires states to not expropriate foreign-owned property based on nationality, ethnicity, or religion. The due process condition, in its most straightforward form, requires states to comply with local laws and providing notice when executing the expropriation. Finally, the most important and controversial condition, compensation, will be covered in more depth later in this section.

There are two distinct categories that define how expropriation is exercised: direct and indirect expropriation. Direct expropriation involves an abnegation of a foreign investor's acquired rights combined with a corresponding acquisition of those rights by the host state or by any third party that is sanctioned by the host state.[133] This includes circumstances surrounding the nationalization of industries, wartime requisitions, and outright confiscation. While the concern for direct expropriation was significant during the 1960s and 1970s, its relevance today is limited since developing countries have become far more receptive to foreign investment.

---

[131] However, not all countries accept the due process rule as being part of customary international law. See Newcombe and Paradell, *supra* note 72 at 321 and 369.

[132] For such an example, see *Walter Fletcher Smith Claim (Cuba v. United States)*, II R.I.A.A. 915 (1929). This case covered the expropriation by a Cuban municipal government of Captain Smith's Mariano Beach property. In the award, the tribunal ruled that the "expropriation proceedings were not, in good faith, for the purpose of public utility." Moreover, the expropriated property went on "to be used by the defendant for purposes of amusement and private profit, without any reference to public utility."

[133] Newcombe and Paradell, *supra* note 72 at 324.

Accordingly, states with a record of dispossessing foreigners of their property and some communist states that have sought to overcome stigmas have often enacted domestic legislation that assures compensation in the event of expropriation.[134] More recently, however, accusations of expropriation by foreign investors against host states have generally focused more attention on indirect expropriation.[135] Indirect expropriation, which falls back on principles similar to those of the minimum treatment standard, has more recently overshadowed direct expropriation as the common form of investor-state disputes surrounding expropriation. The deprivation of investor rights that leads to such a claim can occur in a *de facto* form, both cumulatively (creeping expropriation) or abruptly, as the state interferes with property and other rights to such a degree that the firm can no longer reasonably operate.

Expropriation was a highly litigious and political issue throughout much of the twentieth century, culminating in the assertion of sovereign rights by developing countries in the early 1970s. China played a role in the campaign undertaken by developing countries to redefine customary rules surrounding the dispossession of foreign property, which was done through the auspices of the UN General Assembly — for example, the Declaration of the New International Economic Order (NIEO) and the subsequent Charter of Economic Rights and Duties of States (CERDS).[136] This movement took

---

[134] See M. Sornarajah, *The International Law on Foreign Investment* (Cambridge: Cambridge University Press, 2004) at 110. Article 5 of the People's Republic of China's (PRC) Law of Wholly Foreign-Owned Enterprises (2000) states: "The State will not nationalize or expropriate wholly foreign-owned enterprises. Under special circumstances, the State, based on the need of social and public interests, may expropriate wholly foreign-owned enterprises pursuant to legal procedures and give commensurate compensation." However, the Regulations for the Implementation of the PRC Law on Joint Ventures Using Chinese and Foreign Investment (2001) are vaguer on the issue and do not include a standalone provision. In Article 2, it merely states that such investments are "Chinese legal persons and are subject to the jurisdiction and protection of Chinese law."

[135] See OECD, *Indirect Expropriation and the 'Right to Regulate' in International Investment Law*, OECD Working Papers on International Investment no. 2004/4 (2005).

[136] Being UN General Assembly resolutions, the NIEO Declaration and CERDS, *supra* note 44, were non-binding and ended up having very limited relevance to overall balance of customary international law. However, they were bold assertions of sovereignty that generated significant political overtones that shaped the way international investment would be perceived by both developing and developed countries.

an opposing view on the Hull Rule's tenets of "prompt, adequate, and effective compensation" in the event of expropriation,[137] espousing the view that compensation for expropriation should be determined based on the domestic laws, and not according to a minimum international standard. It also sought to integrate core elements of the Calvo doctrine into their guiding set of principles surrounding sovereignty and expropriation.[138] The Calvo doctrine had since the late nineteenth century been a touchstone emphasized by developing countries, as it addressed the jurisdictional encroachment that was viewed as having been imposed on weaker states by stronger states through customary norms. This was particularly relevant to the issue of international investment, as developing states often felt that customary law burdened them with onerous and unfair obligations.[139] The key Calvo doctrine norms that were embedded within CERDS underscored the reaffirmation that states possess ultimate jurisdiction in disputes surrounding foreign nationals and their investments as well as that international intervention in such matters should only be considered after all local resources are exhausted.[140] Responses to the NIEO movement and the string

---

[137] The Hull Rule of "prompt, adequate, and effective" compensation was first articulated by United States secretary of state Cordell Hull in a letter he wrote to the Mexican president after the Mexican nationalization of American petroleum companies in 1936. See Cordell Hull, *Addresses and Statements by the Honorable Cordell Hull, Secretary of State of the United States of America: In Connection with His Trip to South American to Attend the Inter-American Conference for the Maintenance of Peace Held at Buenos Aries, Argentina, December 1–23, 1936* (Washington, DC: Government Printing Office, 1936). See also Rudolf Dolzer, "New Foundations of the Law of Expropriation of Alien Property" (1981) 75 Am. J. Int'l L. 553. The Hull Rule was the key guiding principle in customary international law on the issue of compensation until developing countries challenged its legitimacy during the 1960s and 1970s.

[138] See Carlos Calvo, *Derecho internacional teórico y práctico de Europa y América* (Paris: Amyot Librairie Diplomatique, 1868); and C. Calvo, *Le Droit International Théorique et Pratique*, 5th edition (Paris, 1896).

[139] See Charles N. Brower, "The Charter of Economic Rights and Duties of States: A Reflection or Rejection of International Law" (1975) 9 Int. L. 295.

[140] See CERDS, *supra* note 43, Article 2(2) subparagraph (a): "Each State has the right to regulate and exercise authority over foreign investment within its national jurisdiction in accordance with its laws and regulations and in conformity with its national objectives and priorities. No State shall be compelled to grant preferential treatment to foreign investment."

of expropriations that took place throughout the twentieth century up until the 1980s were catalysts behind the global proliferation of BITs during this time.[141] From the perspective of capital-importing countries that began taking a benign view of international investment, the BIT was an instrument used to assure investors from capital-exporting states that their economies were open for business and that they would no longer experience the levels of government interference that existed in years past. These BITs, including those entered into by many states that led the NIEO movement, contain content that is a significant departure from the tenets espoused in the NIEO Declaration and CERDS (see Tables 4 and 5).

While the international investment regime has moved on considerably from the NIEO era, dissonance remains on certain issues, notably compensation, although this too has moved further towards a uniform interpretation. Recent Sino-foreign BITs have shifted in the way compensation is defined, but they still do not use the Hull Rule tenets of prompt, adequate, and effective compensation. The language that it has chosen to use appears to be a move towards a compromise between the normative conditions of the Hull Rule, which has been considered "extortionate" as described by the Chinese side during negotiations of the China-US BIT,[142] and the desire of China to integrate its own long-standing norms into its BITs. Considering the level of similarity between the manner in which China has insisted in circumventing the Hull Rule and the actual standard the Hull Rule implies, this issue should not be fundamentally important for Canadian negotiators. Such thinking also applies to the way that China now defines compensation. Comparing the language used in its BIT model with that used in its most recent BITs suggests that China has shifted in its preference of using valuation methods that assess the book value of an investment's worth to the acceptance of fair market valuation.[143] However, it is unclear whether Canada's inclusion of going-concern value in its

---

[141] See Salacuse and Sullivan, *supra* note 14 at 68.

[142] See Wenhua Shan, *The Legal Framework of EU-China Investment Relations: A Critical Appraisal* (Oxford: Hart Publishing, 2005).

[143] See Table 4 on the China-Peru BIT, Article 133(2) on expropriation in this article,. Article 4(2) of the China-Finland BIT (2006) also uses this language. For further discussion on valuation methods of expropriations, see Henry T.C. Hu, "Compensation in Expropriations: A Preliminary Economic Analysis" (1979) 20 Va. J. Int'l L. 61.

Table 4
EXPROPRIATION

Canada FIPA Model	China BIT Model	China-Peru FTA
ARTICLE 13	ARTICLE 4	ARTICLE 133
(1) Neither party shall nationalize or expropriate a covered investment either directly, or indirectly through measures having an effect equivalent to nationalization or expropriation (hereinafter referred to as "expropriation"), except for a public purpose, in accordance with due process of law, in a non-discriminatory manner and on prompt, adequate, and effective compensation.	(1) Neither contracting party shall expropriate, nationalize, or take other similar measures (hereinafter referred to as "expropriation") against the investments of the investors of the other contracting party in its territory, unless the following conditions are met:	(1) Neither contracting party shall expropriate, nationalize, or take other similar measures (hereinafter referred to as "expropriation") against the investments of the investors of the other contracting party in its territory, unless the following conditions are met:
	(a) for the public interests;	(a) for the public interests;
	(b) under domestic legal procedure;	(b) under domestic legal procedure;
	(c) without discrimination; and	(c) without discrimination; and
	(d) against compensation.	(d) against compensation.
(2) Such compensation shall be equivalent to the fair market value of the expropriated investment immediately before the expropriation took place ("date of expropriation") and shall not reflect any change in value occurring because the intended expropriation had become known earlier. Valuation criteria shall include going concern value, asset value including declared tax value of tangible property, and other criteria, as appropriate, to determine fair market value.	(2) The compensation mentioned in paragraph 1 of this article shall be equivalent to the value of the expropriated investments immediately before the expropriation is taken of the impending	(2) The compensation mentioned in subparagraph 1 (d) of this article shall be equivalent to the fair market

value of the expropriated investments immediately before the expropriation took place ("the date of expropriation"), convertible, and freely transferable. The compensation shall be paid without unreasonable delay.

expropriation becomes public knowledge, whichever is earlier. The value shall be determined in accordance with generally recognized principles of valuation. The compensation shall include interest at a normal commercial rate from the date of expropriation until the date of payment. The compensation shall also include interest at a normal commercial rate from the date of expropriation until the date of payment. The compensation shall be made without delay, be effectively realizable, and freely transferable.

(3) Compensation shall be paid without delay and shall be fully realizable and freely transferable. Compensation shall be payable in a freely convertible currency and shall include interest at a commercially reasonable rate for that currency from the date of expropriation until date of payment.

(4) The investor affected shall have a right, under the law of the party making the expropriation, to prompt review, by a judicial or other independent authority of that party, of its case and of the valuation of its investment in accordance with the principles set out in this article.

(5) The provisions of this article shall not apply to the issuance of compulsory licenses granted in relation to intellectual property rights or to the revocation, limitation, or creation of intellectual property rights, to the extent that such issuance, revocation, limitation, or creation is consistent with the WTO Agreement.

Table 5
CANADA FIPA MODEL ANNEX B.13(1)

The parties confirm their shared understanding that:

(a) indirect expropriation results from a measure or series of measures of a party that have an effect equivalent to direct expropriation without formal transfer of title or outright seizure;

(b) the determination of whether a measure or series of measures of a party constitute an indirect expropriation requires a case-by-case, fact-based inquiry that considers, among other factors:

   (i) the economic impact of the measure or series of measures, although the sole fact that a measure or series of measures of a party has an adverse effect on the economic value of an investment does not establish that an indirect expropriation has occurred;
   (ii) the extent to which the measure or series of measures interfere with distinct, reasonable investment-backed expectations; and
   (iii) the character of the measure or series of measures;

(c) except in rare circumstances, such as when a measure or series of measures are so severe in light of their purpose that they cannot be reasonably viewed as having been adopted and applied in good faith, non-discriminatory measures of a party that are designed and applied to protect legitimate public welfare objectives, such as health, safety, and the environment, do not constitute indirect expropriation.

---

own valuation criteria[144] is compatible with China's current preferred valuation methods.[145]

Perhaps the largest area of concern regarding expropriation is in regard to the issue of indirect expropriation. The Canada FIPA model addresses indirect expropriation in greater detail than what is provided in the corpus's expropriation provision through an annexed clause.[146] China has not taken such an approach in its BITs, thus leaving a lot of room for interpretation as to what such an act might be. It would be in Canada's interests to persuade the Chinese side to include a similar annex in the Canada–China FIPA for the sake of certainty and predictability. One area of particular concern for investors in relation to indirect expropriation has to do with

---

[144] See Table 4 on Canada FIPA model, Article 13(2) in this article.

[145] The most commonly used method for determining market value in lawful expropriations has been the discounted cash flow method. See Dolzer and Schreuer, *supra* note 11 at 274.

[146] See Table 5 in this article.

intellectual property. While China has the same obligations under the WTO Agreement on Trade-Related Aspects of Intellectual Property Rights that other WTO signatories have, its new Anti-Monopoly Law (2008)[147] contains provisions related to intellectual property that concern North American investors.[148] Article 54 of the statute recognizes that while intellectual property rights are maintained in China, the abuse of such rights in acts that affect market competition can lead to compulsory licensing of the intellectual property in question. However, the Anti-Monopoly Law is not clear on what distinguishes a legitimate act of exercising intellectual property rights from unlawful acts.[149] The compulsory licensing of intellectual property would indeed interfere with an investor's "distinct, reasonable investment-backed expectations."[150] A Canada–China FIPA that includes meaningful language on expropriation such as Annex B (13) 1 would assist in providing legal remedies for Canadian investors concerned with the intellectual property provisions in China's Anti-Monopoly Law. It would also signal to China that onerous and unfair regulation could potentially be put under the microscope by Canadian investors and subject to challenge.

PROCEDURAL PROVISIONS

By far the most progressive impact that the modern BIT has had on the jurisprudence of international investment law has been the inclusion of clauses that call for binding dispute resolution mechanisms through the use of international arbitral fora. These include both state-state and investor-state dispute resolution mechanisms.[151] If the home state of an investor has not entered into an investment agreement with the host state of its overseas investment, the investor has no forum to rely on for recourse besides the host-state's

---

[147] See Anti-Monopoly Law of the People's Republic of China (promulgated by the Standing Commitee of the National People's Congress on 30 August 2007 and effective 1 August 2008). TRIPS Agreement, *supra* note 8.

[148] See the Economist Intelligence Unit, "Evaluating a Potential US-China Bilateral Investment Treaty" (prepared for the US-China Economic and Security Review Commission, 2010).

[149] See the American Chamber of Commerce in the People's Republic of China, *American Business in China 2009 White Paper* (2009) at 34.

[150] See Canada FIPA model, Annex B.13(1), subparagraph (b)ii.

[151] State-state disputes typically surround the clarification and interpretation of investment treaty provisions. This article will focus on investor-state dispute resolution provisions, as these are the most important procedural provisions to consider in such an analysis.

domestic court system should the investor feel mistreated. Customary international law is limited in affording investors recourse in international dispute settlement fora, which essentially guarantees that investor-state disputes that are not backed up by some form of agreement will be reviewed in the host-state's courts or arbitral bodies.[152] Forum shopping is also not an option, as conflict of laws and *forum non-conveniens* means that third parties for the most part will not accept jurisdiction for these types of disputes because they do not possess the closest degree of connection with the dispute at hand.

When host nations' domestic courts are called upon to settle investor-state disputes, impartiality cannot be guaranteed, making it a highly undesirable avenue for recourse from the viewpoint of the foreign investor. This is particularly important with respect to China, considering the lack of independence that has often been recognized to exist in its courts and its track record in dealing with disputes involving complainant foreign parties.[153] Domestic courts in many jurisdictions often do not have the capacity to deal with the technical and intricate aspects of international investment law.[154] Furthermore, host states have the ability to exercise sovereign immunity (*jure imperii*), which precludes the admissibility of a disputant's grievance.[155] Within the context of assimilation, international norms surrounding investment protections will often be overlooked in favour of localized practice rules and influence.[156] Investors view these aspects of a given jurisdiction's judiciary as a primary risk that will, depending on the degree of exposure to the regulatory influences of the state, be an important component in the performance criteria used to evaluate the desirability of a specific investment. When reasonable legal procedures do not exist to remedy disputes, investor rights and protections are meaningless. Procedural provisions of BITs that assure international arbitral dispute resolution mechanisms help overcome many of these risks.

---

[152] See Dolzer and Schreuer, *supra* note 11 at 214.

[153] See Jerome A. Cohen, "China's Legal Reform at the Crossroads" (2006) 169 Far Eastern Economic Review 23; and Keith E. Henderson, "Halfway Home and a Long Way to Go," in *Judicial Independence in China: Lessons for Global Rule of Law Promotion*, edited by Randall Peerenboom (New York: Cambridge University Press, 2010).

[154] See Dolzer and Schreuer, *supra* note 11 at 214.

[155] *Ibid.* at 215.

[156] For a broader discussion in the assimilation of various international legal norms in China, see Donald C. Clarke and James V. Feinerman, "Contradictions:

The degree of importance attached to the procedural provisions of a given BIT is largely determined by the level of judicial capacity and development in domestic court systems and arbitral fora of the treaty's contracting parties. Accordingly, a large part of the impetus behind the international movement to afford dispute resolution rights in BITs through the use of international fora was generated through the capital exporting/importing paradigm, whereby investors of capital-exporting states needed procedural protections in place in order to guarantee certain standards. While the large number of BITs entered into between developing countries over recent years has challenged this conventional modality with the inclusion of comprehensive dispute resolution provisions in many BITs between low-income countries, an overwhelming majority of investor-state disputes continue to be between investors of a developed country and the host government of a developing country.[157] In rare instances when developed countries enter into BITs among themselves, comprehensive international arbitral provisions are often not included, as some countries oppose the use of such provisions because they are deemed unnecessary.[158]

Consistent with China's conformance with other aspects of international investment law, it has taken a gradualist approach in contemplating international dispute settlement provisions in its investment treaties. During the 1980s, China negotiated BITs that gave cursory attention to procedural provisions. Those that allowed

---

Criminal Law and Human Rights in China" (1995) 141 China Quarterly 135; Pitman B. Potter, "The Chinese Legal System: Continuing Commitment to the Primacy of State Power" (1999) 159 China Quarterly 673; Sarah Biddulph, "The Production of Legal Norms: A Case Study of Administrative Detention in China" (2003) 20 U.C.L.A. Pacific Basin Journal 217; and Stanley Lubman, "Bird in a Cage: Chinese Law Reform after Twenty Years" (2000) 20 N.W.J. Int'l L. & Bus. 425.

[157] For a list of all pending and concluded ICSID cases, see <http://icsid.worldbank. org/ICSID /Front Servlet?requestType=CasesRH&actionVal=ListCases>.

[158] For instance, when Australia and the United States were negotiating their FTA, Australia convinced the United States that each country's pre-existing legal protections meant that such clauses were not required. In fact, after examining the political and regulatory consequences associated with NAFTA Chapter 11, the Australian side "simply refused to consider the inclusion of such an invest-or-state dispute resolution mechanism in its FTA." See Ann Capling and Kim Richard Nossal, "Blowback: Investor-State Dispute Mechanisms in International Trade Agreements" (2006) 19 Governance: An International Journal of Policy, Administration, and Institutions 151 at 152.

for the use of ad hoc tribunals to settle investor-state disputes only did so with limited consent in cases concerning the amount of compensation that should be paid in alleged acts of expropria-tion.[159] China acceded to the ICSID Convention in 1993 but main-tained limited consent with respect to investor-state disputes. This requires that separate consent must be agreed upon by China either in the pre-investment phase or during the actual dispute, which has limited the effectiveness these procedural provisions have had on protecting foreign investors.[160] Combined with the fact that direct expropriation and nationalization are not the frequent acts they once were, the requirement of a consent clause has meant that investment disputes involving China as the respondent invariably never end up in ICSID arbitration. More recently, China has been able to maintain a wide degree of separation from ICSID notwith-standing the more stringent procedural clauses provided in its most recent BITs. China's BIT program first began including compre-hensive investor-state dispute settlement clauses in the succession of BITs it entered into with mostly African nations in the early 2000s,[161] including provisions that allow for arbitration using the ICSID Convention, the ICSID Additional Facility Rules, or the UNCITRAL framework, whichever is selected by the disputing in-vestor. It expanded this approach with developed nations in con-cluded BITs with Germany, the Netherlands, and Finland,[162] having also removed the consent restriction in these treaties.[163]

---

[159] An example of this is the China-Denmark BIT (1985), which in Article 8(3) states that "if a dispute involving the amount of compensation resulting from expropriation mentioned in Article 4 cannot be settled within six months after resorting to the procedure specified in Paragraph 1 of this Article by the na-tional or company concerned it may be submitted to an international arbitral tribunal established by both parties."

[160] See generally Mark A. Cymrot, "Investment Disputes with China" (2006) 6 Disp. Resol. J. 80.

[161] See Schill, *supra* note 119 at 93.

[162] Although China's newer BITs allow for comprehensive dispute resolution mech-anisms, these BITs still require that such disputes to exhaust China's domestic administrative review procedures. See China-Finland BIT (2006), Article 9.

[163] Even with the procedural protections that these new BITs afford investors by way of guaranteed access to international tribunals, China has still not once been party to an investment dispute involving ICSID. See ICSID, *List of Cases*, <http://icsid.worldbank.org/ICSID/FrontServlet?requestType=CasesRH&acti onVal=ListCases>.

The limited scope in the procedural provisions of Chinese BITs over the past three decades has also meant that Chinese investors have only had access to the ICSID Convention under certain circumstances, pursuant to specific investment treaties. Consequently, there has only been one case of a Chinese investor using the ICSID forum to launch an investor-state claim.[164]

China's proclivity in distancing itself from international fora such as ICSID can be partly explained by its desire to have investment disputes involving foreign parties remedied through its own domestic arbitral fora. Most investment disputes in China are settled through either the China International Economic and Trade Arbitration Commission (CIETAC) or the Beijing Arbitration Commission. While these two institutions represent the robust arbitral "industry" that has grown inside China,[165] CIETAC, in particular, has been a target for criticism surrounding its ability to be partial and objective.[166] Furthermore, and notwithstanding recent reforms that have taken place, CIETAC panels are still adjudicated by Chinese nationals. In many instances, arbitrators possess close affiliations with officials in the Ministry of Commerce. CIETAC has also retained the authority to reject the arbitrators that are chosen by parties.[167]

Unfortunately for Canadian investors, ICSID-based investor-state dispute resolution protections remain elusive, even in cases that involve a partnering signatory to a FIPA that happens to be an ICSID member. This has not been because of any specific lack of political will on the federal level but, instead, reflects localized interpretations surrounding the desirability of Canada becoming a fully bound ICSID member combined with Canadian constitutional particularities. While Canada signed onto the ICSID Convention in 2006, it has not been able to ratify its involvement in the treaty since the convention does not contain a federalism clause.[168] This absence

---

164 See *Tza Yap Shum. v. The Republic of Peru*, ICSID ARB/07/6 (2007).

165 See Ellen Reinstein, "Finding a Happy Ending for Foreign Investors: The Enforcement of Arbitration Awards in the People's Republic of China" (2005) 16 Ind. Int'l & Comp. L. Rev. 37.

166 See generally Cymrot, *supra* note 160.

167 See *ibid.* at 85.

168 Canada is considered to possess a "dualist" legal regime, whereby international law needs to be translated into domestic law in order for it to have a legal basis. In terms of international treaties, the federal Parliament, and in many cases

requires that each province must pass legislation on top of federal legislation in order for the convention to have legal effect in Canada.[169] All modern Canada-foreign FIPAs and the Canadian FIPA model include ad hoc tribunal clauses that afford a pre-established "commission" comprised of cabinet-level representatives of the signatories to establish "any other body of rules" to be used in arbitration.[170] The Canada FIPA model, and all FIPAs since 1995, also afford disputing investors the right to submit their claims under the ICSID Convention (so long as both parties to the FIPA are also party to the convention), the ICSID Additional Facility Rules (in instances when only one FIPA co-signatory is party to the convention), or through the use of UNCITRAL arbitration rules. Until Canada implements the ICSID Convention, Canadian investors, as well as foreigners investing Canada, will have to rely on the ICSID Additional Facility Rules, UNCITRAL, or ad hoc methods, none of

---

provincial legislatures, are required to pass legislation in order for a given international treaty to be implemented. For a full discussion of the relationship between international law and domestic law in Canada, see Jutta Bunnée and Stephen J. Toope, "A Hesitant Embrace: The Application of International Law by Canadian Courts" (2003) 40 Can. Y.B. Int'l L. 3. Dualism exists in contrast to the "monist" regime, whereby international law is not required to be translated into domestic law. For instance, the ratification of international treaties in the United States merely requires for a ratification bill to pass through the Senate. Furthermore, the Executive Office of the United States is constitutionally permitted to enter into executive-congressional agreements that afford the executive to enter into international treaties without ratification, so long as pre-arranged conditions are reflected in the treaty provisions.

169 See Dierk Ullrich, "Inch by Inch: Canada Moves toward New Investment Protection Legislation," *Bar Talk* (June 2008), Canadian Bar Association: British Columbia Branch, <http://www.cba.org/BC/ bartalk_06_10/ 06_08/guest_ ullrich.aspx>. Provincial legislation is required as arbitral procedure is a matter of justice within jurisdiction of the province. Provinces that have enacted such legislation include: British Columbia's Settlement of International Disputes Act, S.B.C. 2006, C. 16; Newfoundland and Labrador's Settlement of International Disputes Act, S.N.L. 2006, c. S-13.3; Saskatchewan's Settlement of International Disputes Act, S.S. 2006, c. S-47.2; Ontario's Settlement of International Disputes Act, S.O. 1999, c. 12 schedule D; and the Northwest Territories' Settlement of International Disputes Act, S.N.W.T. 2009. See also Martin Valasek and Azim Hussain, "Investor-State Arbitration, Court Intervention, and the ICSID Convention in Canada," *Canadian Bar Association Bulletin* (December 2009), Canadian Bar Association, <http://www.cba.org/CBA/newsletters-sections/ pdf/ 11_09_intl-icsid.pdf>.

170 See Canada FIPA model, Article 27(1), subparagraph (d).

which prevent national courts from interfering in the arbitration process.[171]

In addressing NAFTA Chapter 11 concerns, Canada has included in its FIPA model and subsequent treaties some of the most comprehensive investor-state dispute resolution provisions that exist in BITs globally. These provisions differ considerably from standard Chinese preferences. Section C of the Canada FIPA model includes sixteen pages of text with extensive provisions that establish high levels of transparency in the procedural process. In contrast, China's investor-state procedural provisions are typically one or two pages in length. Perhaps some of Canada's most contrasting investor-state procedural preferences are those surrounding public access to *in camera* tribunal hearings and access to all documents apart from those that are designated confidential.[172] *Amicus curiae* clauses allowing third parties to file submissions to arbitration tribunals are also used by Canada.[173] Chinese BITs are of course silent on these matters. Clearly, the paucity in its BIT procedural provisions presents a significant divergence in preferences from what Canada includes in its FIPAs, which may have presented an area of significant disagreement in the bargaining process.[174] Since the United States follows the same NAFTA-based preferences as Canada, it is also in the process of bargaining around these differences in its own BIT negotiations with China. It is unlikely that either Canada or the United States would be willing to negotiate away these clauses. In the case of China, it is difficult to speculate on its level of flexibility on the matter of comprehensiveness and transparency. If it did indeed decide to acquiesce to Canadian and US interests on these matters, it would avoid having the same levels of transparency apply to its other investment treaties due to the exclusion clause that it puts in its BITs that precludes MFN rights from the procedural provisions of its investment agreements.[175]

---

[171] Pierre-Olivier Savoie, "ICSID: Prospects for Canadian Investors and Foreign Investors in Canada," *International Disputes Quarterly: Focus on Construction Arbitration* (Winter 2008), White and Case, <http://www.whitecase.com/idq/winter_2008_ca1_2/>.

[172] See Canada FIPA model, Article 38.

[173] See Canada FIPA model, Article 39.

[174] Andrew Newcombe, personal communication, 9 June 2010.

[175] See note 129 in this article.

HUMAN RIGHTS AND SUSTAINABILITY

The interaction between international investment and non-economic goals such as public welfare, human rights, and sustainability is increasingly being broached in discussion.[176] Establishing normative and institutional foundations of economic and non-economic standards associated with investment treaties requires the identification of conditions that are conducive to the coordinated compliance between multiple policy domains.[177] BITs are first and foremost economic treaties, but the inclusion of non-economic objectives in these agreements has been commonplace. For instance, all BITs contain varying degrees of non-economic objectives in their texts (that is, those objectives located within non-conforming measures — for instance, national security and cultural exceptions).

Sustainability concerns, for instance, are determined within an international investment context by social objectives surrounding environmental degradation and the deprivation of local rights in jurisdictions with weak forms of governance. Sustainability is of course an amorphous concept during the best of times and can even refer to strict economic imperatives, but, for the purposes of this discussion, it will be left within the realm of its non-economic attributes. The relevance of sustainability to BITs generally involves the practical consequences of a given treaty more so than its actual legal effect. For one, investment agreements and trade agreements, in general, can be viewed as having a net-positive effect on both the environment and public welfare through a more efficient allocation of resources. However, if left unmitigated, trade and investment liberalization can lead to deleterious environmental and social

---

176 For comprehensive work on this matter, see Emilie M. Hafner-Burton, *Forced to Be Good* (New York: Cornell University Press, 2009); Pierre-Marie Dupuy et al., eds., *Human Rights in International Investment Law and Arbitration* (New York: Oxford University Press, 2009); Howard Mann, *International Investment Agreements, Business and Human Rights: Key Issues and Opportunities* (2008), International Institute for Sustainable Development, <http://www.iisd.org/pdf/2008/iia_business_human_rights.pdf>; Ryan Suda, "The Effect of Bilateral Investment Treaties on Human Rights: Enforcement and Realization" (paper presented to the Symposium on Transnational Corporations and Human Rights, Global Working Papers, NYU Law, 2005); and Peter Muchlinksi, "Regulating Multinationals: Foreign Investment, Development and the Balance of Corporate and Home Country Rights and Responsibilities in a Globalizing World" (paper presented to the second Columbia International Investment Conference, 2007).

177 See Pitman B. Potter, "Co-ordinating Corporate Governance and Corporate Social Responsibility" (2009) 39 H.K.L.J. 677.

consequences should stakeholder input not be considered or in cases when laws and regulations prove insufficient in addressing complex externalities.

The assessment of these environmental trade-offs has been a key part of the Department of Foreign Affairs and International Trade's initial environmental assessment of its FIPAs, which follows the guidelines set forth in the 2001 Framework for Conducting Environmental Assessments of Trade Negotiations.[178] The scope of these assessments is limited to the projected economic and environmental effects of the agreement within Canada. It does not assess implications in the territory of the co-signatory. The report identifies key sectors where future Chinese FDI in Canada will likely target, including natural resources, information and communication technologies, pharmaceuticals, manufacturing, and agriculture. Although, it should be noted that what China ultimately needs from Canada for the time being are natural resources, the other sectors listed, while contributing robustly to the Canadian economy, will not likely be deeply penetrated by Chinese investment for some time. Furthermore, because Canada is home to nearly 60 percent of the world's mining companies,[179] some of Canada's investment into China should continue to target the extractive sector by way of joint venture, but this remains somewhat hampered by Chinese restrictions on foreign investment in natural resources.[180] Nonetheless, the potential environmental consequences of a Canada–China FIPA need to be considered in both countries if the treaty does

---

[178] See Department of Foreign Affairs and International Trade, *Framework for Conducting Environmental Assessments of Trade Negotiations* (February 2001), Foreign Affairs and International Trade, <http://www.international.gc.ca/trade-agreements-accords-commerciaux/assets/pdfs/FinalFramework-e.pdf>.

[179] See Natural Resources Canada, "Government of Canada Positions Mining Industry for Continued Success," *The NewsRoom* (11 May 2009), Natural Resources Canada, <http://news.gc.ca/web/article-eng.do?m=/index&nid=449359>.

[180] China continues to be the world's largest gold producer, and Canadian firms have developed a presence in China developing gold fields. However, China has taken a fairly restrictive approach on the admission of foreign investment in its natural resources sector, as all such investments are required to be done under the auspices of a joint venture with a Chinese entity. Furthermore, China has taken a highly restrictive approach in both the investment and international trade in rare earth metals mined in China. For Chinese laws and regulations relating to foreign investment in China's natural resources sector, see *inter alia*, the *PRC Mineral Resources Law* (enacted 19 March 1996); and *Measures for the Administration of Foreign-Invested Mineral* (promulgated by the Ministry of Commerce and Ministry of Land and Resources, 18 July 2008).

indeed lead to more mergers and acquisitions and especially to Greenfield investment in the extractive sectors of each country.

Regardless of the view that one takes on the purpose of the BIT, these agreements, along with international investment in general, have human rights implications that need to be considered. The discussion surrounding China's internalization of international human rights norms has been considerable.[181] Processes surrounding the primacy of the party-state and selective adaptation restrict the level of efficacy these norms have had on the implementation of domestic law and policy. Canadian investment in China reflects both impediments and opportunities in the advancement of international human rights norms inside China and in overcoming some of the barriers associated with the internal assimilation and the normative interpretation of international human rights norms. For instance, Canadian firms have in the past been called into question for their role in furthering party-state goals to the detriment of localized human rights concerns.[182]

On the other hand, Canadian and other foreign firms operating in China often do so by adhering to corporate social responsibility (CSR) standards that surpass local compliance obligations and CSR conformance standards.[183] Such efforts particularly apply to areas such as environmental performance and the upholding of workers' rights. While cases of lax-standard shopping by unscrupulous multinational enterprises may still exist, generally speaking, today's foreign firms enter into China and other developing countries upholding best practices that are ubiquitously employed throughout their global operations — that is, in many cases universal best practices are commonly applied by multinational enterprises under

---

[181] See Rights and Democracy, *Bilateral Human Rights Dialogue with China* (2001), Rights and Democracy, <http://www.ichrdd.ca/site/publications/index.php?id=1290&subsection=catalogue>; and Pitman B. Potter, "China and the International Legal System: Challenges of Participation" (2007) 191 China Quarterly 699.

[182] See the chapter "Tracking Dissent on the High Plateau: Communication Technology on the Gormo-Lhasa Railway," in Rights and Democracy, *Human Rights Impact Assessments for Foreign Projects Investment Projects,* International Centre for Human Rights and Democracy (2007). This chapter provides a critical examination into the human rights implications of Nortel's work in developing the telecommunications system for the Gormo-Lhasa Railroad.

[183] For a CSR analysis of big-box retailers, see Ans Kolk et al., "Corporate Social Responsibility in China: An Analysis of Domestic and Foreign Retailers' Sustainability Dimensions" (2008) Social Science Research Network.

guidance from the parent back in the home country, but considerations for local responsiveness are also made by overseas branches.[184] This process is bar setting, in that CSR practices conducted by foreign firms inform and transcribe these standards into the normative preferences of local communities. This effort, in turn, raises expectations for domestic enterprises that find themselves having to raise their own standards in order to compete in a changing marketplace. This process can be considered to have a net-positive benefit for societal objectives such as environmental performance and workers' rights even though certain aspects of a company's operations may indeed serve in upholding the legitimacy of the party-state.

While there exist certain practical consequences of the BIT in relation to human rights and sustainability, the inclusion of human rights and sustainability norms directly into the legal text of BITs and trade agreements is quite uncommon. Aside from the regular insertion of the word "sustainability" into the preambular language of investment treaties,[185] the closest semblance of anything meaningful has been the European Union's (EU) and the United States' inclusion of human rights norms in the legal text of their trade agreements, with the EU largely focusing on universal human rights such as political and civil freedoms, and the United States focusing on workers' and children's rights.[186] In both of these jurisdictions, the program of regulating human rights through international trade has been generally undertaken through a generalized system of preferences, which has been ingrained in law in both the US and the EU.[187] In terms of international investment, the United States

---

[184] See *ibid.* at 10–14.

[185] For instance, the preamble of the Canada-Jordan FIPA (2009) provides the following paragraph: "recognizing that the promotion and the protection of investments of investors of one Party in the territory of the other Party will be conducive to the stimulation of mutually beneficial business activity, to the development of economic cooperation between them and to the promotion of sustainable development."

[186] See generally Hafner-Burton, *supra* note 176.

[187] See the US Trade Act, U.S.C. 107–210 (enacted 6 August 2002); and the Human Rights and Democracy Clause in EU Agreements, EU Resolution no. P6_TA0056 (2006). The executive-congressional agreement in the US Trade Act permits the executive office to negotiate trade-related agreements without the requirement of Senate ratification should workers' rights clauses be included in the text of these treaties. It should be noted that the EU does not enter into investment treaties, as the jurisdiction for investment was left in the

has continuously promoted labour rights in its investment agreements. Article 13 of the US model BIT provides for labour rights surrounding the right of association and the right to organize and bargain collectively and promotes "acceptable conditions" of wage, hourly work, and occupational health and safety standards. It also affords a "prohibition" on any form of compulsory labour and child labour. It is unclear how these preferences might be affecting China–United States BIT negotiations.

The US BIT model and many US-foreign BITs apply the same "obligations" to environmental laws, as does Article 11 of the Canada FIPA model, which states: "The Parties recognise that it is inappropriate to encourage investment by relaxing domestic health, safety or environmental measures." BITs that include such clauses rely on state-state mechanisms for compliance, while emphasizing the state as the actor responsible for achieving non-economic objectives. If a contracting party in such a BIT feels as though the other contracting party has engaged in such encouragement, the complainant has the ability to request consultations with the derogating party, and the two parties "shall consult with a view of avoiding such discouragement."[188] It could be argued that such provisions, while not only diverging from the spirit of the modern investment treaty of having the investor as the addressor of treaty compliance, also provide limited capacity in actually achieving these putative goals. First, an admonition, a threat to withdraw from a treaty, or moral suasion levied in state-state consultations relies solely on coercive, and not legal, effect. This is in contrast to the programs of a generalized system of preferences in trade treaties that hold developing countries accountable through a legal application of punitive tariffs should they violate the terms of a generalized system of preferences. Second, it serves no purpose in addressing the pre-existing deficiencies associated with a country's domestic laws and regulations relating to environmental protection.

---

hands of the individual member states. Virtually, all EU members have avoided negotiating human rights or workers' rights language into their BITs. The exception is Finland, however, which has embedded workers' rights language in the preambles of some of its treaties. See, *inter alia*, the Finland-Guatemala BIT (2005). However, it is important to add that the same preambular language was not placed in the China-Finland BIT (2006).

188 Both the Canada FIPA model, Article 11, and the US BIT model, Article 13(1), use identical language.

Considering the scant attention that BITs have given to human rights and environmental obligations for states and investors, it might be regarded that such norms have been subordinated to the primacy of investment liberalization. With respect to this fact, it is important to address whether BITs constrain states' abilities to uphold domestic environmental and human rights objectives as well as the duties that other international treaties prescribe. BITs have since their inception balanced obligations heavily towards the agency of the host state, with no responsibilities borne by either investors or home countries,[189] which has implications for how human rights and sustainability norms are implemented into law or regulation by the state. Disputes pursuant to BITs are typically initiated solely at the discretion of investors, and, while the state negotiates, signs, and is ultimately obligated to the legal content of the investment treaty, it is the investor that renders its key components operational, insofar as it is the investor who interprets the text of these agreements and relates it to perceived acts of mistreatment by host states. This article has examined many of the key responsibilities that host states agree to upon entering into a BIT, including the rights afforded through the minimum standard of treatment and indirect expropriation. Pursuant to these rights, investors have a legitimate expectation of not being subject to burdensome, unnecessary, or discriminatory regulation. The question then arises whether the enactment or enforcement of human rights laws, labour rights laws, public health and safety laws, and environmental laws in the post-establishment phase of investment can lead to claims in breach of these standards. Canada, the United States, and Mexico have all experienced this first hand with virtually all of NAFTA's claims arguing some form of breach of NAFTA Article 1105 (minimum standard of treatment).[190]

Furthermore, states may encounter situations when certain human rights obligations associated with international treaties or

---

189 Peter Muchlinksi, "Regulating Multinationals: Foreign Investment, Development and the Balance of Corporate and Home Country Rights and Responsibilities in a Globalizing World" (paper presented for the second Columbia International Investment Conference, 2007).

190 As of 1 March 2007, 97 percent of claims had cited a breach of Article 1105. See Scott Sinclair, "NAFTA Chapter 11 Investor-State Disputes," Canadian Centre for Policy Alternatives (March 2007), <http://www.policyalternatives. ca/sites/default/files/uploads/publications/National_Office_Pubs/2005/ chapter11_january2005.pdf>.

customary international law come into conflict with obligations delineated in an investment treaty. Literature and interpretation of this matter has asserted that the enactment of such laws are legitimate and not in conflict with international investment treaty norms when they are done for *bona fide* purposes for the public good and are in no way conducted in a discriminatory manner.[191] It is advisable for countries to further their ability to regulate domestic non-economic concerns such as human rights and sustainability without fear of disputant reprisal through the express inclusion of public-good clauses that qualify post-establishment rights in the text of their BITs. Canada's FIPA program has taken this approach in providing allowances for environmental- and conservation-based regulatory initiatives that do not contravene indirect expropriation or minimum standard of treatment provisions.[192] Generally, however, these areas of conflict have not been adequately resolved in the international investment treaty regime, and more work needs to be undertaken in order to overcome some of the complexities of this problem.[193]

In summary, the Canada–China FIPA and bilateral investment treaties in general reflect cogent human rights and sustainability implications that signatories need to consider in both the negotiation and implementation phase. Specific concerns arise in the Canada–China context surrounding increased investment in the extractive industries of both countries and with respect to sensitive human rights issues in China. In terms of the bargaining process

---

[191] See Mann, *supra* note 176 at section 3.1.

[192] See the Canada FIPA model, Article 10(1), states: "Subject to the requirement that such measures are not applied in a manner that would constitute arbitrary or unjustifiable discrimination between investments or between investors, or a disguised restriction on international trade or investment, nothing in this Agreement shall be construed to prevent a Party from adopting or enforcing measures necessary: (a) to protect human, animal or plant life or health; (b) to ensure compliance with laws and regulations that are not inconsistent with the provisions of this Agreement; or (c) for the conservation of living or non-living exhaustible natural resources." Canada has employed this provision in its FIPA program in response to the string of NAFTA cases it was a respondent to, whereby complaints were made based on the enactment of environmental and health and safety regulation and the alleged infringement on the minimum standard of treatment rights. See *Pope & Talbot Inc. v. Canada, supra* note 112; and *S.D. Myers v. Canada, supra* note 112.

[193] For a general discussion of conflicting international human rights and investment protection norms in international investment treaties, see Suda, *supra* note 176.

of the treaty, Canada does not include the workers' rights clauses that the United States insists on including in all of its trade-related treaties. Taking into consideration Canada's relative level of power on the world stage, it would not be advisable for such preferences to be included in Canada's position anyway. It is likely that the United States is having its own difficulties in convincing the Chinese side to accept these provisions in their own negotiations, notably on the rights of association and to organize and bargain collectively. Furthermore, the level of efficacy such clauses carry is questionable. Thus, coordinating compliance within the text of the Canada–China FIPA may not be an explicitly realizable goal. However, further examination of the treaty's practical implications and consequences surrounding conformance through corporate responsibility and leadership could suggest enhanced results.

CONCLUSION

A Canada–China FIPA would provide Canadian companies with important legal support in their business operations in China. In terms of promoting investment between the two parties, this agreement indeed has the potential to bolster economic relations. The elusiveness in reaching such an agreement has been considered by some commentators as being a major obstacle in the expansion of Canada–China two-way investment.[194] This has occurred notwithstanding the prioritization of Canadian businesses and policy-makers to see increased two-way investment between the two countries.[195] However, reaching a successful conclusion in negotiations of the Canada–China FIPA should not be attributed to a lack of effort, with high-level officials from each country having met twelve times now over the course of the last six years. In that time, the federal government has invested considerable resources in an effort to finally put together a workable draft with their Chinese counterparts.

The significance of the treaty, and all the good intentions surrounding it, has not been enough to avert dissonance at the negotiating table. As has been explained, many areas of convergence and divergence exist between Canadian and Chinese approaches in their respective BIT programs, especially in light of the recent

---

[194] See Raaj Tiagi and Lu Zhou, *Canada's Economic Relations with China* (Vancouver: Fraser Institute, Studies in Chinese Economic Policy, 2009) at 81.

[195] See *ibid.* at 81.

advances China has made with respect to various substantive and procedural standards. For example, Canada has followed the United States in many aspects of its FIPA program, especially with the level of deference each country's investment treaties give to customary law and related concepts such as the Hull Rule. In contrast, China has frequently demonstrated ambivalence in the way it views customary international law in the investment treaty context. While this may have presented an insurmountable barrier a decade or two ago, China's BIT program has undergone an evolution, having culminated with its most recent treaties that contain provisions amenable to certain customary norms. This has presented an opportunity for reconciling the North American approach with the Chinese approach.

However, key differences do remain in some key areas. It is highly unlikely that China would be willing to enter into any treaty that prescribes national treatment on a pre-establishment basis. Canada's approach of listing all non-conforming measures and exceptions that qualify relative treatment provisions diverges considerably from China's subject-to-laws approach. For the time being, the best Canada might hope for with respect to this would be something similar to the protocol included in the China-Finland BIT, whereby each party agrees to not introduce non-conforming measures beyond those that existed at the time of signing the agreement even though specific measures might not be outlined in the treaty.[196] There also exist considerable differences in the way Canada and China each approach the issues of public access, transparency, and allowances for *amici* in the arbitration process. Canada has taken a highly comprehensive approach on these matters. Meanwhile, Chinese BITs only include the most basic procedural provisions, although recent Sino-foreign BITs do allow for the use of international arbitral fora at the discretion of the investor.[197] Given the comprehensiveness and length of Canada's procedural provisions compared to China's basic approach, this area might represent for negotiators the most frustrating and laborious part of the negotiating process.

While treaty preferences have played an important role in delaying the conclusion of the Canada–China FIPA, other off-the-table factors have also hampered the process. Canadian dialogue with China has been discordant over a broad range of issues for a number of

[196] See note 105 in this article.
[197] See note 162 in this article.

years following the federal government's decision to adjust its discourse on China's human rights. It can be assumed that reaching concordance within this difficult milieu is quite difficult. Recent developments have assuaged tensions, however, with the federal government having acquiesced and moved from its defiant platform. China's foreign minister Yang Jiechi said last year that Beijing is willing to put past "difficulties" aside, provided that each country "not interfere in [the] other country's internal affairs."[198] This reconciliation of differences presents an opportunity for negotiators, but we will have to wait until the next round of negotiations to see if tense relations were indeed the true impediment in concluding negotiations or if each country's preferences on various treaty aspects remain the key stumbling blocks.

Sommaire

Un processus prolongé: La négociation de l'Accord Canada–Chine sur la promotion et la protection des investissements étrangers

En 1994, le Canada et la Chine ont amorcé la négociation d'un accord sur la promotion et la protection des investissements étrangers (APIE). Après 16 ans et plusieurs séries de négociations, les deux États ne sont toujours pas en mesure de solidifier un traité viable. Se référant aux préférences de fond et de procédure de chaque pays (selon leurs modèles respectifs d'accords sur les investissements bilatéraux et leurs traités existants), cet article donne un aperçu des obstacles "sur la table" qui nuisent vraisemblablement aux négociations. Cette analyse indique qu'il existe des domaines de convergence entre les préférences de chaque pays, bien que des domaines importants de divergence persistent sur certaines questions clés. De plus, certains facteurs "hors-la-table" exacerbent le désaccord qui existe entre les préférences des deux pays, telles les conditions générales de leurs relations bilatérales. Un autre aspect qui est soulevé est l'idée de coordonner la conformité entre le commerce international et des droits de la personne dans le contexte de l'APIE Canada–Chine. Quoique les accords bilatéraux soient des accords économiques, d'importants éléments non-économiques affectent leurs effets pratiques et juridiques sur les différents acteurs concernés. Malgré les conséquences

---

[198] See Mike Blanchfield, "Canada-China Relations Improving, Growing: China Foreign Minister Yang Jiechi Met with Harper, Ignatieff," *Canwest News Services* (23 June 2009), Canada-China Business Council, <http://www.ccbc.com/Portals/0/CanWest.pdf>.

importantes de l'APIE Canada–Chine pour les droits de la personne et les politiques environnementales, on peut en déduire que ces facteurs auront peu d'influence sur le contenu de l'accord ultimement négocié.

Summary

The Protracted Bargain: Negotiating the Canada–China Foreign Investment Promotion and Protection Agreement

In 1994, Canada and China began negotiating a bilateral foreign investment promotion and protection agreement (FIPA). After sixteen years and multiple rounds of negotiations, the two states have not been able to solidify a workable treaty. By examining each country's substantive and procedural preferences in their respective bilateral investment treaty models and in past treaties, this article outlines some of the likely "on-the-table" obstacles in the negotiating process. The analysis indicates that there are areas of considerable convergence between each country's preferences, although significant areas of divergence exist on some key issues. Further confounding the disagreement that exists between the two countries are "off-the-table" factors such as general bilateral relations. One further aspect that is considered is the idea of coordinating compliance between international trade and human rights norms in the context of the Canada–China FIPA. While bilateral investment treaties are economic agreements, pronounced non-economic elements shape the practical and legal effect that these treaties have on various affected actors. Despite the important implications the Canada–China FIPA has for human rights and environmental policy concerns, it can be inferred that these factors will have little bearing on the actual negotiated outcome of the agreement.

Notes and Comments /
Notes et commentaires

———

Poursuivre le génocide, les crimes contre l'humanité et les crimes de guerre au Canada: Une analyse des éléments des crimes à la lumière de l'affaire *Munyaneza*

INTRODUCTION

Le 22 mai 2009, le juge André Denis de la Cour supérieure du Québec a reconnu Désiré Munyaneza coupable de sept chefs d'accusation de génocide, crimes contre l'humanité et crimes de guerre pour avoir participé à des meurtres et à des actes de violence sexuelle et de pillage au Rwanda en 1994.[1] Le 29 octobre 2009, M. Munyaneza a été condamné à la prison à vie sans possibilité de libération conditionnelle avant une période de vingt-cinq ans,[2] soit la sentence la plus sévère en vertu du droit canadien. La défense a porté en appel tant le verdict de culpabilité que la peine imposée.[3]

———

Fannie Lafontaine est professeure à la Faculté de droit de l'Université Laval et membre de l'Institut québécois des hautes études internationales. Certaines parties de ce commentaire reprennent, en la détaillant, une analyse en anglais parue dans le *Journal of International Criminal Justice*. L'auteure remercie Edith-Farah Elassal pour son temps et son talent.

[1] *R. c. Munyaneza* (2009), Q.C.C.S. 2201 [*Munyaneza*]. L'accusé a choisi, avec le consentement du Procureur général, d'être jugé sans jury par un juge d'une cour supérieure de juridiction criminelle conformément à l'art. 473(1) du Code criminel, L.R.C. 1985, c. C-46 [Code criminel].

[2] *R. c. Munyaneza* (2009), Q.C.C.S. 4865 [*Jugement sur la peine Munyaneza*].

[3] Au sujet de la décision de la Cour d'appel d'accorder la permission d'en appeler sur des questions mixtes de fait et de droit, voir *Munyaneza c. R* (2009), Q.C.C.A. 1279. La requête de la défense pour permission d'en appeler de la peine infligée le 29 octobre 2009 a été déférée à la formation de la Cour d'appel qui entendra l'appel de la condamnation: voir *Munyaneza c. R.* (2009), Q.C.C.A. 2326. Voir

Le jugement rendu dans l'affaire *Munyaneza* est historique d'un point de vue canadien. Cette première condamnation en vertu de la Loi sur les crimes contre l'humanité et les crimes de guerre[4] signale le retour possible — et souhaité — du Canada à une politique plus musclée à l'égard des criminels de guerre se trouvant sur son territoire.[5] L'un des principaux objectifs de la Loi sur les crimes de guerre est en effet d'améliorer et de renforcer la capacité du Canada à poursuivre et à punir les personnes présumées responsables de génocide, de crimes contre l'humanité et de crimes de guerre, soit ce qu'il est convenu d'appeler le "noyau dur" des crimes internationaux, et cela, peu importe où la commission des crimes a eu lieu.

Le jugement dans l'affaire *Munyaneza* a été soigneusement rédigé afin de limiter un éventuel renversement en appel, à tout le moins pour une question de droit. Les quelque deux cent pages de la décision se concentrent principalement sur la preuve à l'appui de l'acte d'accusation. En effet, le juge résume le témoignage et soupèse la crédibilité des soixante-six témoins (trente en poursuite, trente-six en défense, l'accusé n'a pas témoigné) qu'il a entendus au cours du procès, qui a duré plus de deux années, incluant les délibérations. Une annexe confidentielle contient des résumés plus détaillés des témoignages et protège l'identité de plusieurs témoins à qui l'anonymat a été accordé par le juge.

L'analyse juridique du juge Denis n'est pas infaillible. Celle-ci est toutefois bien mince, tant au regard de la longueur que le jugement y consacre, quelque vingt-cinq pages, qu'au regard de la profondeur

---

également *Requête pour permission d'en appeler de la sentence imposée*, C.A.Q. 500-10-004416-093, 23 novembre 2009.

4   Loi sur les crimes contre l'humanité et les crimes de guerre, L.C. 2000, c. 24 [Loi sur les crimes de guerre]. La Loi est entrée en vigueur le 23 octobre 2000.

5   Quelques jours après le jugement sur la peine dans l'affaire *Munyaneza*, des poursuites pénales ont été lancées contre M. Jacques Mungwarere pour des crimes qui auraient été commis pendant le génocide au Rwanda. Après l'acquittement de Irme Finta, confirmé par la Cour suprême du Canada en 1994, le Canada avait à toutes fins pratiques abandonné les poursuites pénales de criminels de guerre pour les remplacer par des mesures administratives et d'immigration. *R. c. Finta*, [1994] 1 R.C.S. 701 [*Finta*]. La plus connue des affaires d'immigration liée aux crimes de guerre — qui se comptent par dizaines — est celle concernant Léon Mugesera, dont l'expulsion du pays a été confirmée par la Cour suprême en 2005 : *Mugesera c. Canada (Ministre de la Citoyenneté et de l'Immigration*, [2005] 2 R.C.S. 100 [*Mugesera*]. L'arrêt de la Cour suprême dans cette affaire constitue un jugement phare en matière de crimes internationaux au Canada.

avec laquelle les questions juridiques sont étudiées. Elle définit les crimes de façon sommaire et le fait généralement en conformité avec le droit international applicable. La principale faiblesse du jugement réside sans doute dans l'application relativement défaillante du droit aux faits retenus par le juge. Bien que le droit relatif aux crimes internationaux soit relativement bien énoncé et que les faits soient longuement relatés, la discussion finale ne parvient pas à rattacher clairement les faits au droit. Il semble que le juge ait été si convaincu de la culpabilité de l'accusé au regard des faits qu'il n'a pas jugé nécessaire d'effectuer une qualification juridique précise de ceux-ci. Évidemment, cela a pour effet de rendre plus difficile toute contestation juridique de ses conclusions.[6]

Bien qu'elle ne passera pas à l'histoire pour la contribution qu'elle fait au droit substantiel en vertu de la Loi sur les crimes de guerre, la décision *Munyaneza* demeure néanmoins la première analyse de cette loi et des définitions qu'elle propose des infractions de droit international maintenant criminalisées dans le système juridique canadien. Cette décision offre ainsi une précieuse opportunité de discuter du régime juridique mis en place par la Loi, qui fait s'entrecroiser le droit international et le droit canadien, et plus particulièrement des éléments constitutifs des crimes, qui demeurent peu connus et peu analysés à ce jour au Canada.

Le texte qui suit se veut ainsi une analyse de certains des éléments du crime de génocide, des crimes contre l'humanité et des crimes de guerre qui ont été pertinents dans l'affaire *Munyaneza* et abordés dans le jugement. En premier lieu, nous élargirons un peu la discussion afin de traiter de deux éléments communs à tous ces crimes, soit la référence au droit international coutumier dans les définitions et la délicate question du droit applicable aux infractions sous-jacentes qui existent également en droit canadien. Par la suite, nous traiterons de certains éléments spécifiques à chacune des trois infractions définies dans la Loi. Cette analyse est essentielle non seulement pour l'appel de la décision *Munyaneza,* mais également — peut-être surtout — pour l'interprétation qui sera donnée des crimes prévus par la Loi dans les jugements futurs. Il s'agit d'un régime juridique nouveau, original et complexe. Une compréhension en profondeur de celui-ci en assurera un développement cohérent et respectueux tant de la lettre que de l'esprit de la Loi. La peine infligée à M. Munyaneza, de même que le régime

---

6 *Avis d'appel de la condamnation amendé et mis à jour,* C.A.Q. 500-10-004416-093, 19 novembre 2009, au para. 29, motif d'appel 12A [*Avis d'appel*].

des peines applicables en vertu de la Loi, seront aussi brièvement analysés. À cet égard, certaines questions portant sur l'interaction entre le Code criminel et la Loi feront l'objet d'une discussion. Soulignons que le juge Denis a conclu que M. Munyaneza avait personnellement commis les crimes reprochés. Par conséquent, les modes de participation aux infractions ne seront pas étudiés dans cet article.[7] Cela dit, les constats factuels du juge ne semblent pas tous permettre de conclure, en vertu du droit canadien, à une responsabilité de M. Munyaneza en tant qu'auteur principal des crimes reprochés.[8] Une discussion juridique plus approfondie des faits démontrant le degré de participation de l'accusé aux crimes aurait été souhaitable.[9] Il va sans dire que cette question est déterminante dans l'analyse des éléments constitutifs qui doivent fonder la responsabilité de l'accusé pour les infractions reprochées. En outre, puisque l'accusé n'a soulevé aucun motif d'exonération de responsabilité lors de son procès, nous ne discuterons pas des moyens de défense, justifications ou excuses disponibles en vertu de l'article 11 de la Loi. Enfin, les questions relatives à la procédure et à la preuve ne seront pas étudiées dans ce commentaire.[10] Ce dernier s'intéressera uniquement aux questions de droit substantiel soulevées par le jugement, lesquelles concernent les éléments constitutifs des crimes reprochés à l'accusé.

PRINCIPES GÉNÉRAUX RELATIFS AUX CRIMES

Dans l'arrêt *Finta*, la première affaire criminelle en matière de crimes de guerre au Canada, rendue sous l'ancien régime du Code criminel remplacé par la Loi sur les crimes de guerre, et la seule avant *Munyaneza*, la Cour suprême avait imposé à la poursuite la charge de prouver non seulement que l'accusé avait commis une infraction en vertu du droit international, mais aussi qu'il

---

7 Les deux parties avaient présenté des arguments à ce sujet. Pour une discussion au sujet des modes de participation aux infractions en vertu de la Loi, voir Fannie Lafontaine, "Parties to Offences under the *Canadian Crimes against Humanity and War Crimes Act*: An Analysis of Principal Liability and Complicity" (2009) 50 Les Cahiers de Droit 967.

8 Voir par exemple les para. 2059 (véhicules prêtés afin de faciliter la commission des exactions), 2060 (distribution d'armes aux *Interahamwe*), etc.

9 *Avis d'appel*, *supra* note 6 au para. 29. Cet aspect a été soulevé en tant que motif d'appel.

10 *Ibid.* Les arguments de la défense en appel se concentrent surtout sur des questions de fait ou sur des questions mixtes de fait et de droit.

avait commis une infraction au droit canadien. La Cour avait conclu que "[p]our qu'il soit déclaré coupable, l'accusé doit donc avoir commis un acte qui constituait à la fois un crime de guerre ou un crime contre l'humanité *et* aurait constitué une infraction aux lois du Canada en vigueur à l'époque de sa perpétration."[11] Voilà qui constituait certainement un fardeau très lourd pour la poursuite. La Loi sur les crimes de guerre modifie ce paysage juridique en criminalisant le "noyau dur" des crimes internationaux en tant qu'infractions autonomes en vertu du droit canadien.[12] Avant de discuter de certains éléments particuliers à chacun des crimes, il importe de traiter de deux points qui sont communs à tous les crimes et qui caractérisent le régime juridique mis en place par la Loi.

RÉFÉRENCE AU DROIT INTERNATIONAL COUTUMIER

Les États ont adopté différentes approches quant à la mise en œuvre du Statut de Rome de la Cour pénale internationale[13] et, plus particulièrement, quant à la répression des crimes internationaux. Une analyse des législations nationales de mise en œuvre permet de constater que certains États prévoient des définitions identiques à celles contenues dans le Statut de Rome, alors que d'autres prévoient des définitions plus larges ou, au contraire, plus strictes. Certains ne fournissent tout simplement pas de définition.[14]

L'approche canadienne est quelque peu difficile à classifier. La Loi sur les crimes de guerre réfère au Statut de Rome, mais uniquement en tant que moyen d'interprétation du droit international

---

11 *Finta, supra* note 5, au para. 182 [souligné dans la version originale].

12 La question de savoir si l'ancien art. 7(3.71) du Code criminel constituait un titre de compétence en soi ou créait les nouvelles infractions de crimes contre l'humanité et de crimes de guerre a été longuement discutée dans l'arrêt *Finta*. Essentiellement, la majorité était en accord avec l'opinion de la majorité de l'instance inférieure qui a estimé que cet article créait de nouvelles infractions, leur existence au regard des faits devant être décidée par le jury (aux para. 170 et s.). La minorité, quant à elle, était plutôt d'avis que cet article était purement attributif de compétence et devait donc être décidé par le juge du procès (aux para. 31 et s.).

13 Statut de Rome de la Cour pénale internationale (17 juillet 1998), 2187 R.T.N.U. 159 [Statut de Rome].

14 Pour un aperçu intéressant des conséquences de chacune de ces approches, voir Julio Bacio Terracino, "National Implementation of ICC Crimes: Impact on National Jurisdictions and the ICC" (2007) 5 Journal of International Criminal Justice 421.

coutumier. En effet, les articles 4 (3) et 6 (3) de la Loi, qui définissent les crimes internationaux, ne réfèrent pas au Statut de Rome. À titre d'exemple, le terme "génocide" est défini comme étant un "[f]ait — acte ou omission — commis dans l'intention de détruire, en tout ou en partie, un groupe identifiable de personnes et constituant, au moment et au lieu de la perpétration, un génocide selon le droit international coutumier ou le droit international conventionnel." Cette définition prévoit donc expressément certains éléments constitutifs du crime de génocide, à savoir (1) un acte ou une omission commis; (2) dans l'intention de détruire, en tout ou en partie; (3) un groupe identifiable de personnes. Toutefois, le contenu exact de ces éléments de même que celui d'autres éléments constitutifs du crime de génocide devra être déterminé conformément au droit international coutumier.

Une telle approche offre tout le dynamisme et la flexibilité voulus pour permettre une adaptation aux développements juridiques futurs. Cependant, l'identification du droit international coutumier applicable constitue une tâche difficile. C'est là que le Statut de Rome entre en jeu. La Loi sur les crimes de guerre prévoit que ce dernier permet d'identifier le contenu du droit international coutumier:

Il est entendu que, pour l'application du présent article, les crimes visés aux articles 6 et 7 et au paragraphe 2 de l'article 8 du Statut de Rome sont, au 17 juillet 1998, des crimes selon le droit international coutumier, et qu'ils peuvent l'être avant cette date, sans que soit limitée ou entravée de quelque manière que ce soit l'application des règles de droit international existantes ou en formation.[15]

Manifestement, le droit international coutumier peut être plus étendu ou, au contraire, plus limité que les définitions contenues dans le Statut de Rome. Néanmoins, les juges canadiens auront une marge de manœuvre limitée quant à l'interprétation du droit international coutumier. Il leur sera difficile d'interpréter le droit international coutumier comme étant plus restrictif que les dispositions du Statut de Rome en raison d'une déclaration législative sans équivoque les enjoignant d'interpréter le premier conformément aux secondes. Ce choix législatif, bien qu'imparfait car ne

---

[15] Loi sur les crimes de guerre, *supra* note 4, art. 6(4). Voir aussi art. 4(4) concernant les crimes commis au Canada. Ces articles du Statut de Rome sont reproduits en annexe de la Loi.

reflétant pas nécessairement avec fidélité le contenu du droit international coutumier, présente néanmoins le singulier avantage de guider le juge dans un domaine complexe du droit international. Il assure, de même, que les développements jurisprudentiels au Canada demeurent en ligne avec le Statut de Rome, en conformité avec le principe de complémentarité.[16] Cela étant dit, rien n'empêche le juge canadien d'interpréter le droit international coutumier de manière plus généreuse que le Statut de Rome. En effet, les articles précités sont clairs à l'effet qu'ils ne doivent pas avoir pour conséquence de "limite[r] ou entrave[r] de quelque manière que ce soit l'application des règles de droit international existantes ou en formation." Il convient de noter que l'article 6 (5) de la Loi donne une indication supplémentaire quant au contenu du droit international coutumier, en confirmant que les crimes contre l'humanité étaient des crimes avant 1945. Cette mention s'explique par l'historique jurisprudentiel canadien en matière de crimes contre l'humanité, qui laissait planer un doute à cet égard.[17]

Malgré l'absence de mention explicite des *Éléments des crimes* de la Cour pénale internationale (CPI)[18] dans la Loi sur les crimes de guerre — contrairement à la législation d'autres États[19] — il sera certainement possible pour un tribunal canadien d'y référer en tentant de définir les contours du droit international coutumier

---

[16] Statut de Rome, *supra* note 13, préambule, au para.10, art. 1 et 17.

[17] Dans l'affaire *Finta*, *supra* note 5, au lieu de conclure que le principe de non-rétroactivité n'avait pas été violé parce que ces crimes existaient en droit international coutumier, le juge Cory, au nom de la majorité, s'est appuyé sur l'opinion de Kelsen en précisant que la gravité des crimes permettait des poursuites rétroactives. L'art. 6(5) de la Loi vise à corriger cette affirmation juridique que nous pouvons qualifier d'inexacte relativement à l'état du droit tel qu'il existait avant la Seconde Guerre mondiale.

[18] *Éléments des crimes*, ICC-ASP/1/3 (part II-B), 9 septembre 2002 [*Éléments des crimes*]. Ce document, adopté par l'Assemblée des États parties de la CPI, énumère les éléments essentiels du génocide, des crimes contre l'humanité et des crimes de guerre au regard de chaque infraction sous-jacente les composant. L'art. 9 du Statut de Rome prévoit que: "Les éléments des crimes aident la Cour à interpréter et appliquer les art. 6, 7 et 8." Tel que mentionné ci-dessous, il existe une controverse au sein de la CPI concernant leur valeur obligatoire.

[19] La législation de la Nouvelle-Zélande, par exemple, prévoit que les crimes doivent être interprétés à la lumière des *Éléments*: International Crimes and International Criminal Court Act (2000), Public Act No 26, art. 12(4). La législation du Royaume-Uni prévoit essentiellement la même chose: International Criminal Court Act 2001 (R.-U.), 2001, c. 17, art. 50(2); International Criminal Court Act 2001 (Elements of Crimes) (No. 2) Regulations 2004.

pour un crime particulier. Le juge Denis dans l'affaire *Munyaneza* mentionne d'ailleurs brièvement leur existence.[20] Considérant que les décisions de la CPI — lesquelles s'appuieront très souvent sur les *Éléments*[21] — ne seront pas "écartées à la légère"[22] par les cours de justice canadiennes invitées à interpréter la Loi sur les crimes de guerre, les *Éléments des crimes* seront, du coup, indirectement appliqués au Canada. En effet, les juges canadiens pourraient théoriquement ne pas tenir compte des *Éléments* et adopter une position conforme au droit international coutumier lorsque ceux-ci s'en éloignent.[23] Toutefois, le contenu de la loi canadienne, précisant que les crimes prévus au Statut de Rome constituent des crimes en vertu du droit international coutumier, et la valeur qu'il convient d'accorder à la jurisprudence de la CPI, pourraient donner indirectement aux *Éléments des crimes* le statut de droit international coutumier dans la jurisprudence canadienne en ce qui concerne le génocide, les crimes contre l'humanité et les crimes de guerre. Quelques exemples de cette possibilité seront donnés ci-après. Que ce résultat soit en bout de ligne bel et bien conforme avec l'état actuel du droit international coutumier demeure cependant incertain. Le Tribunal pénal international pour l'ex-Yougoslavie a estimé, en effet, que certains des *Éléments* ne sont pas conformes au droit international coutumier.[24]

Nous notons en terminant sur cette question que bien que la référence au droit international *conventionnel* dans les définitions des crimes suscite quelques interrogations, elle n'aura de toute

---

[20] *Munyaneza, supra* note 1, au para. 86.

[21] Il y a un désaccord au sujet du statut juridique qu'il convient d'accorder aux *Éléments des crimes*. Voir par exemple *The Prosecutor v. Omar Hassan Ahmad Al Bashir*, ICC-02/05-01/09-3, Decision on the Prosecution's Application for a Warrant of Arrest against Omar Hassan Ahmad Al Bashir (4 mars 2009), aux para. 126-28 et dissidence de la Ušacka, au para. 17 (Cour pénale internationale (CPI), Ch. préliminaire I) [*Al Bashir*].

[22] *Mugesera, supra* note 5, aux para. 82 et 126. Voir aussi *Munyaneza, supra* note 1, par exemple aux para. 82, 87, 93, 95, 105, 114 et 146.

[23] Voir William A. Schabas, "Canada" dans Ben Brandon et Max du Plessis, dir., *The Prosecution of International Crimes: A Practical Guide to Prosecuting ICC Crimes in Commonwealth States* (Londres: Commonwealth Secretariat, 2005) à la p. 158.

[24] *Le Procureur c. Radislav Krstić*, IT-98-33-A, Arrêt (19 avril 2004), au para. 224 (Tribunal pénal international pour l'ex-Yougoslavie (TPIY), Ch. d'appel). Voir généralement Robert Cryer "Elements of Crimes ," dans Antonio Cassese *et al.*, dir., *The Oxford Companion to International Criminal Justice* (Oxford: Oxford University Press, 2009), aux pp. 308-9.

façon qu'une importance limitée dans l'interprétation qui sera faite des crimes en vertu de la Loi. En effet, le droit international conventionnel est défini ainsi à l'article 2 de la Loi: "Conventions, traités et autres ententes internationales en vigueur, auxquels le Canada est partie ou qu'il a accepté d'appliquer dans un conflit armé auquel il participe." Or, comme nous le verrons ci-dessous, la définition du génocide est la même en droit coutumier et en droit conventionnel. Quant aux crimes contre l'humanité, outre le Statut de Rome, il n'existe pas de traité international les criminalisant comme tels et seule une convention qui n'est pas encore en vigueur (et que le Canada n'a même pas signée) sur les disparitions forcées réfère au fait que ces infractions peuvent constituer des crimes contre l'humanité. Cette convention renvoie par ailleurs au "droit international applicable" pour la définition du crime, lequel est constitué, essentiellement, du droit international coutumier et du Statut de Rome.[25] La pertinence de la référence au droit international conventionnel pourrait être un peu plus grande pour les crimes de guerre, dans la mesure où une incertitude demeure peut-être quant au caractère coutumier de certaines infractions graves contenues dans le Protocole additionnel 1 de 1977 ou de certains crimes de guerre commis dans le cadre d'un conflit armé non-international et qui sont criminalisés par le Statut de Rome. Le Statut de Rome est en effet évidemment un traité pertinent selon l'article 2 de la Loi et ce, depuis la ratification de ce dernier par le Canada en juillet 2000. Par contre, tant pour le génocide que pour les crimes contre l'humanité et les crimes de guerre, cela est de peu d'utilité puisque, comme nous l'expliquions ci-dessus, le droit international *coutumier* est défini en référence au Statut de Rome dans la Loi et ce, à partir du 17 juillet 1998.

Par ailleurs, nous notons que les traités pertinents dans les poursuites pour génocide, crimes contre l'humanité et crimes de guerre devront, en vertu de l'article 2, avoir été ratifiés par le Canada et ce, même si ce dernier n'est pas impliqué dans le conflit ou les violations en cause. Ces traités devront par ailleurs également être applicables à ce conflit ou cette situation, c'est-à-dire, notamment, que les États ou les groupes parties au conflit dans le cadre duquel le crime est commis devront également les avoir ratifiés ou avoir accepté leurs dispositions. En effet, les définitions des crimes

---

[25] Convention internationale pour la protection de toutes les personnes contre les disparitions forcées, NU Doc. A/61/488 (pas encore entrée en vigueur), préambule et article 5.

contenues dans la Loi exigent que l'acte ou l'omission soit considéré comme un crime en droit international "au lieu de la perpétration." Cette démonstration liée au droit conventionnel constitue
un fardeau assez lourd et somme toute relativement inutile considérant l'adéquation fréquente expliquée ci-dessus entre ce dernier
et le droit coutumier. Enfin, nous notons que l'article 2 exige que
le traité ou la convention faisant partie du droit international
conventionnel soit *en vigueur*, mais le texte ne précise pas à quel
moment il doit l'être. Les définitions des crimes, qui exigent que
l'acte ou l'omission soit un crime en droit international "au moment
... de la perpétration," de même que l'interdiction de la criminalisation *ex post facto*, semblent indiquer que le traité doit être en vigueur au moins au moment de la perpétration de l'infraction. Même
si la formulation de l'article 2, reproduit *supra*, pourrait sembler
exiger qu'il soit également en vigueur lors de la poursuite (en anglais: "any convention ... that *is* in force"), l'évaluation du droit
applicable doit se faire au "moment de l'infraction," ce qui rend
juridiquement inutile l'état du droit conventionnel au moment de
l'inculpation ou du procès. Cette explication est conforme aux
principes d'interprétation en matière criminelle au Canada, selon
lesquels l'abrogation d'un texte de loi n'empêche pas les poursuites
et l'application de sanctions en vertu de celui-ci.[26] Ce débat revêt
par ailleurs peu d'importance en pratique, les traités pertinents
n'étant certes pas sur le point d'être abrogés. En conclusion, la
référence au droit international conventionnel dans les définitions
des infractions aura une importance limitée dans les poursuites en
vertu de la Loi, confirmant ainsi le profond ancrage de cette dernière dans la coutume internationale.

DROIT APPLICABLE AUX INFRACTIONS SOUS-JACENTES

Avant de discuter de la définition des crimes internationaux prévue
dans la Loi et de l'interprétation donnée par le juge Denis dans
l'affaire *Munyaneza*, il convient de se poser une question préalable,
qui est d'application générale aux trois grandes infractions prohibées par la Loi. Les éléments constitutifs de chacun de ces crimes
comprennent une infraction sous-jacente qui, accompagnée de
l'élément contextuel ou mental propre à chaque crime, peut constituer l'infraction internationale. Ainsi, la définition du génocide en
droit international coutumier, à laquelle la Loi réfère et qui est

---

[26] Loi d'interprétation, L.R.C. 1985, c. I-21, art. 43 d).

contenue dans la Convention sur la prévention et la répression du crime de génocide[27] et reprise dans le Statut de Rome,[28] prévoit certaines infractions, tels le meurtre, l'atteinte à l'intégrité physique ou mentale et les mesures visant à entraver les naissances au sein du groupe, qui, si elles sont accompagnées des autres éléments constitutifs (un groupe protégé et l'intention spécifique de détruire ce groupe), pourront constituer des actes de génocide. Il en est de même pour la définition des crimes contre l'humanité énumérant de nombreuses infractions sous-jacentes (meurtre, extermination, réduction en esclavage, déportation, violence sexuelle, torture, etc.[29]) qui, accompagnées de l'élément contextuel d'une attaque systématique ou généralisée contre une population civile et de l'élément mental requis, peuvent constituer des crimes contre l'humanité. Une longue énumération de conduites prohibées dans le contexte d'un conflit armé est également prévue dans la définition des crimes de guerre.[30]

Or, il existe en droit canadien des infractions équivalentes à certaines infractions sous-jacentes des crimes internationaux, soit le meurtre, la torture ou les violences sexuelles (quoique le crime d'"agression sexuelle" n'inclue vraisemblablement pas certains actes tels que l'esclavage sexuel, la prostitution forcée,[31] la grossesse forcée et la stérilisation forcée). Il convient alors de se demander quel régime juridique doit gouverner leur interprétation.

Dans *Munyaneza*, le juge Denis débute son analyse des infractions sous-jacentes du crime de génocide (il applique la même analyse aux crimes contre l'humanité et aux crimes de guerre) avec une analyse de l'expression "meurtre intentionnel." Il mentionne que "[cette] notion de 'meurtre intentionnel' n'existe pas au Code criminel canadien."[32] Il conclut alors qu' "[e]n utilisant dans la Loi un terme différent de celui du code criminel, le législateur canadien voulait faire référence à la définition de "meurtre intentionnel" retrouvée dans le droit international et sa jurisprudence."[33]

---

[27] Convention pour la prévention et la répression du crime de génocide, 78 R.T.N.U 277, 1948.

[28] Statut de Rome, *supra* note 13, art. 6.

[29] *Ibid.*, art. 7.

[30] *Ibid.*, art. 8.

[31] Code criminel, *supra* note 1, art. 212(1). Plus particulièrement le sous-alinéa (h) pourrait être un équivalent imparfait de la "prostitution forcée."

[32] *Munyaneza*, *supra* note 1 au para. 81.

[33] *Ibid.* au para. 82.

La conclusion du juge Denis en ce qui concerne l'applicabilité du droit international aux actes sous-jacents nous semble juste, mais le raisonnement qui la sous-tend est discutable. En effet, la Loi sur les crimes de guerre n'utilise pas, quant à la définition des crimes, "un terme différent de celui du code criminel" et l'expression "meurtre intentionnel" n'existe pas comme telle en droit international. Tout comme le Statut de Rome, la définition de crimes contre l'humanité prévue dans la Loi énumère le "meurtre" en tant qu'infraction sous-jacente. Le terme "meurtre" est également utilisé dans le Code criminel.[34] Les définitions de génocide et de crimes de guerre de la Loi n'énumèrent aucune infraction sous-jacente. Elles réfèrent plutôt au droit international coutumier, qui utilise quant à lui les termes "meurtre" pour le génocide et "homicide intentionnel" et "meurtre" pour les crimes de guerre.[35] L'expression "meurtre intentionnel" n'est donc aucunement utilisée en droit international. Le juge Denis semble confondre les termes utilisés dans l'Acte d'accusation (ou peut-être dans les dispositions relatives aux peines prévues dans la Loi), qui réfèrent à la notion de "meurtre intentionnel," avec ceux utilisés dans les définitions des crimes prévues par la Loi, qui n'en font pas mention. Cela étant dit, même si elle repose sur un raisonnement juridique déficient, la conclusion du juge Denis à l'effet que le droit international doive trouver application relativement aux définitions des infractions sous-jacentes constitutives du crime de génocide, des crimes contre l'humanité et des crimes de guerre est importante et elle est, à notre avis, exacte, pour les raisons suivantes.

Outre *Munyaneza*, il n'existe aucune autorité sur la question. L'arrêt *Mugesera* n'indique pas clairement à quel corpus législatif la Cour suprême réfère dans la définition qu'elle donne de l'infraction de "meurtre" en tant qu'infraction sous-jacente du crime contre l'humanité.[36] Les éléments constitutifs du meurtre que la Cour énumère sommairement pourraient être ceux d'un corpus législatif comme de l'autre. Néanmoins, il est possible de déduire que la Cour s'en remettrait au droit interne lorsque les crimes reprochés existent en vertu de celui-ci et au droit international lorsque ce ne serait pas le cas: "[n]otre droit interne ne définit d'ailleurs pas clairement la persécution, contrairement à l'assassinat par exemple."[37] Nous

---

[34] Code criminel, *supra* note 1, art. 229.

[35] Statut de Rome, *supra* note 13, art. 6(a), 8(2)(a)(i) et 8(2)(c)(i).

[36] Voir *Mugesera*, *supra* note 5 au para. 130.

[37] *Ibid.* au para. 139.

soumettons respectueusement que le fait d'appliquer le droit interne lorsque l'infraction reprochée existe en vertu de celui-ci, dans le cas du meurtre par exemple, et de s'en remettre aux principes développés par le droit international dans d'autres cas, créerait inévitablement une disparité indésirable dans la façon dont sont définis les crimes internationaux au Canada.

La Loi sur les crimes de guerre est silencieuse sur la question. L'article 2 (2) prévoit toutefois que, "[s]auf indication contraire, les termes de la présente loi s'entendent au sens du Code criminel." Il est pour le moins incertain que l'expression "les termes" devrait inclure les définitions d'infractions telles que le meurtre énoncées dans la Loi.

D'abord, il convient de remarquer que lorsque le législateur, dans la Loi sur les crimes de guerre, a décidé d'appliquer les dispositions du Code criminel en ce qui concerne le meurtre, il l'a fait de façon explicite. À titre d'exemple, les articles 4 (2) *a)* et 6 (2) *a)* de la Loi, qui traitent des peines applicables, prévoient:

Quiconque commet une infraction visée aux paragraphes (1) ou (1.1):

(a) est condamné à l'emprisonnement à perpétuité, si le *meurtre intentionnel* est à l'origine de l'infraction [nous soulignons].

Tel que l'a remarqué le juge Denis, l'expression "meurtre intentionnel" n'est pas utilisée dans le Code criminel. Par conséquent, l'article 2 (2) de la Loi sur les crimes de guerre, précédemment évoqué, ne peut trouver application. L'article 15 de la Loi, traitant de l'admissibilité à une libération conditionnelle, se lit quant à lui comme suit:

15. (1) Le bénéfice de la libération conditionnelle est subordonné, en cas de condamnation à l'emprisonnement à perpétuité en application des articles 4 ou 6:

a) si le meurtre commis avec préméditation et de propos délibéré est à l'origine de l'infraction, à l'accomplissement d'au moins vingt-cinq ans de la peine;

b) si le meurtre intentionnel mais non commis avec préméditation et de propos délibéré est à l'origine de l'infraction, à l'accomplissement d'au moins vingt-cinq ans de la peine, lorsque la personne a déjà été reconnue coupable:

(i) *soit d'une infraction visée aux articles 4 ou 6 qui a à son origine le meurtre intentionnel, commis ou non avec préméditation et de propos délibéré,*

(ii) *soit d'un homicide coupable constituant un meurtre, quelle que soit la description qu'en donne le Code criminel* [nous soulignons].

Le législateur distingue clairement le "meurtre intentionnel" en tant qu'infraction sous-jacente du crime de génocide, des crimes contre l'humanité et des crimes de guerre (1) du simple meurtre, tel que défini par le Code criminel (2). Une distinction similaire se retrouve à l'article 15 (2) b) de la Loi, qui précise que "la mention, [aux dispositions du Code criminel portant sur la peine], de meurtre au deuxième degré vaut mention d'une infraction visée aux articles 4 ou 6 de la présente loi, si le meurtre intentionnel mais non commis avec préméditation et de propos délibéré est à l'origine de l'infraction."[38] De tels distinctions et renvois n'auraient pas été nécessaires si le "meurtre intentionnel" devait toujours être interprété à la lumière du Code criminel.

L'utilisation, dans ces dispositions concernant les peines, de l'expression "meurtre intentionnel" en ce qui concerne les crimes internationaux peut s'expliquer par le fait que le meurtre est désigné de différentes façons dans les statuts internationaux. Tel que mentionné ci-dessus, parfois nommé "meurtre" (génocide et crimes contre l'humanité), parfois "homicide intentionnel" (crimes de guerre), l'appellation varie en fonction du crime international concerné. Ces termes ont été interprétés de façon similaire par les instances internationales.[39] L'utilisation de l'expression "meurtre intentionnel" dans les dispositions sur les peines de la Loi sur les crimes de guerre vise probablement — justement — à éviter une confusion avec le crime de meurtre prévu au Code criminel et à utiliser un terme unique pour cette infraction sous-jacente constitutive de tous les crimes internationaux. Nous rappelons que les définitions des crimes, elles, réfèrent aux termes utilisés en droit international coutumier.

Finalement, soulignons que les infractions sous-jacentes peuvent avoir un sens différent lorsqu'elles sont constitutives de l'un des crimes internationaux ou lorsqu'elles sont traitées comme des

---

38 Voir aussi Code criminel, *supra* note 1, art. 745. L'art. 26 de la Loi réfère aussi expressément au meurtre en vertu du Code criminel pour les crimes commis à l'étranger à l'égard d'un témoin de la CPI.

39 Par exemple *Le Procureur c. Milorad Krnojelac*, IT-97-25-T, Jugement (15 mars 2002), aux para. 323-24 (TPIY, Ch. pr. inst.); *Le Procureur c. Dario Kordić et Mario Čerkez*, IT-95-14/2-T, Jugement (26 février 2001), au para. 236 (TPIY, Ch. pr. inst.) [*Kordić et Čerkez*].

infractions autonomes. Le crime de torture peut servir à illustrer notre propos. L'article 269.1 du Code criminel codifie cette infraction en droit canadien. Cette disposition vise à mettre en œuvre les obligations du Canada en vertu de la Convention contre la torture.[40] Par conséquent, les exigences prévues au Code criminel sont essentiellement identiques à celles contenues dans la Convention. Toutefois, cette définition de la torture en tant qu'infraction autonome diffère de celle de la torture lorsqu'elle est constitutive d'un crime de guerre ou d'un crime contre l'humanité. Dans ces derniers contextes, les instances internationales ont adopté une définition large de la torture, qui n'exige pas que celle-ci soit le fait d'un agent étatique.[41] Les *Éléments des crimes* de la CPI privilégient la même approche.[42] En outre, les *Éléments* sont accompagnés d'une note précisant qu'"[il] est entendu qu'aucune intention spécifique n'a besoin d'être établie pour ce crime."[43] Voilà qui s'écarte significativement des définitions contenues dans la Convention contre la torture et dans le Code criminel, qui prévoient plutôt qu'un acte de torture doit être infligé avec une intention spécifique[44] et par

---

[40] Convention contre la torture et autres peines ou traitements cruels, inhumains ou dégradants, 10 décembre 1984, (1987) 1465 R.T.N.U. 85, art. 4 à 7 [Convention contre la torture].

[41] *Le Procureur c. Dragoljub Kunarac et al.*, IT-96-23-T & IT-96-23/1-T, Jugement (22 février 2001), au para. 496 (TPIY, Ch. pr. inst.), confirmé dans *Le Procureur c. Dragoljub Kunarac et al.*, IT-98-23 & IT-96-23/1-A, Arrêt (12 juin 2002), aux para. 145-48 (TPIY, Ch. d'app.) [*Kunarac*]; voir aussi *Le Procureur c. Miroslav Kvočka et al.*, IT-98-30/1-A, Arrêt (28 février 2005), au para. 284 (TPIY, Ch. d'app.); *Le Procureur c. Laurent Semanza*, ICTR-97-20-T, Jugement et sentence (15 mai 2003), aux para. 342-43 (Tribunal pénal international pour le Rwanda (TPIR), Ch. pr. inst.) [*Semanza*].

[42] *Éléments des crimes*, *supra* note 18, art. 7(1)(f), 8(2)(a)(ii)-1 et 8(2)(c)(i)-4.

[43] *Ibid.*, art. 7(1)(f). Par ailleurs, en vertu des *Éléments*, le crime de torture en tant que crime de guerre exige la preuve d'un but spécifique: art. 8(2)(a)(ii)-1 et 8(2)(c)(i)-4. Pour un aperçu intéressant des différents régimes juridiques applicables au crime de torture, voir Paola Gaeta, "When is the Involvement of State Officials a Requirement for the Crime of Torture?" (2008) 6 Journal of International Criminal Justice 183.

[44] Convention contre la torture, *supra* note 40, art. 1: "aux fins notamment d'obtenir d'elle ou d'une tierce personne des renseignements ou des aveux, de la punir d'un acte qu'elle ou une tierce personne a commis ou est soupçonnée d'avoir commis, de l'intimider ou de faire pression sur elle ou d'intimider ou de faire pression sur une tierce personne, ou pour tout autre motif fondé sur une forme de discrimination quelle qu'elle soit." Voir également Code criminel, *supra* note 1, art. 269.1(2)a) et b).

"un agent de la fonction publique ou toute autre personne agissant à titre officiel ou à son instigation ou avec son consentement exprès ou tacite."[45]

La Loi sur les crimes de guerre garantit que la torture, lorsqu'elle est constitutive d'un crime international, ne restera pas impunie au Canada. En référant au droit international coutumier et au Statut de Rome, la définition de la torture telle qu'entendue dans la Loi est par conséquent fondamentalement différente de celle prévue au Code criminel. Voilà qui confirme que *les infractions sous-jacentes du crime de génocide, des crimes contre l'humanité et des crimes de guerre doivent être interprétées à la lumière du droit international* tel qu'il s'est développé précisément au regard de ces crimes et ce, quelle que soit l'infraction sous-jacente concernée.

DÉFINITIONS DU CRIME DE GÉNOCIDE, DES CRIMES CONTRE L'HUMANITÉ ET DES CRIMES DE GUERRE

GÉNOCIDE

Certaines questions liées à la définition du crime

En n'énumérant pas les cinq actes prohibés ni les groupes protégés, la définition du crime de génocide prévue à la Loi sur les crimes de guerre, reproduite *supra,* prévoit que le droit international coutumier pourrait se développer en incluant d'autres actes prohibés ainsi que de nouveaux groupes protégés. Par ailleurs, il est intéressant de souligner que la version française de la loi — qui possède une valeur égale à la version anglaise[46] — ne contient pas la mention "comme tel" alors que la version anglaise contient les termes "*as such.*"[47] Cette exigence fait pourtant partie du droit international coutumier et est, par conséquent, partie intégrante de la définition du crime de génocide prévue dans la Loi, et cela malgré l'omission mystérieuse dans la version française.[48] Ce qualificatif a été inter-

---

45 Convention contre la torture, *supra* note 40, art. 1. L'art. 269.1 du Code criminel prévoit la même exigence.

46 Loi sur les langues officielles, L.R.C. 1985, c. 31, art. 13.

47 La définition française se lit ainsi: "'génocide' Fait — acte ou omission — commis dans l'intention de détruire, en tout ou en partie, un groupe identifiable de personnes et constituant, au moment et au lieu de la perpétration" alors que la version anglaise se lit comme suit: "'genocide' means an act or omission committed with intent to destroy, in whole or in part, an identifiable group of persons, *as such*, that, at the time and in the place of its commission" [nous soulignons].

48 Dans l'affaire *Munyaneza, supra* note 1, au para. 107, le juge Denis fait fi de cette omission et discute du sens de l'expression "comme tel."

prété par la jurisprudence des tribunaux *ad hoc* comme signifiant
que "l'acte doit avoir été commis à l'encontre d'un individu, parce
que cet individu était membre d'un groupe spécifique et en raison
même de son appartenance à ce groupe, ce qui signifie que la victime est le groupe lui-même et non pas seulement l'individu."[49]

Soulignons brièvement que l'article 318 du Code criminel prévoit
une infraction distincte pour quiconque "préconise ou fomente"
le génocide. Même si cette infraction a été interprétée par la Cour
suprême comme étant équivalente au crime international d'"incitation au génocide,"[50] la définition de génocide contenue dans le
Code criminel diffère de celle prévue par le droit international
coutumier et, conséquemment, de celle prévue dans la Loi. Elle est
plus large dans un sens, et plus stricte dans l'autre. Elle est plus
restreinte en ce qu'elle est limitée à des actes sous-jacents qui visent
la destruction *physique* des membres du groupe protégé, soit "le fait
de tuer des membres du groupe" et "le fait de soumettre délibérément le groupe à des conditions de vie propres à entraîner sa
destruction physique."[51] Ainsi, la définition exclut trois importantes
infractions sous-jacentes du crime en droit coutumier, soit l'"atteinte grave à l'intégrité physique ou mentale de membres du
groupe," les "mesures visant à entraver les naissances au sein du
groupe" et le "transfert forcé d'enfants du groupe à un autre
groupe." La définition est par ailleurs plus large car elle couvre des

49 *Le Procureur c. Eliézer Niyitegeka*, ICTR-96-14-T, Jugement portant condamnation
(16 mai 2003), au para. 410 (TPIR, Ch. pr. inst.). Voir aussi *Le Procureur c. Geor-
ges Rutaganda*, ICTR-96-3-T, Jugement et sentence (6 décembre 2009), au para.
60 (TPIR, Ch. pr. inst.); *Le Procureur c. Jean-Paul Akayesu*, ICTR-96-4-T, Jugement
(2 septembre 1998), au para. 521 (TPIR, Ch. pr. inst.) [*Akayesu*]; *Le Procureur c.
Alfred Musema*, ICTR-96-13, Jugement et sentence (27 janvier 2000), au para.
165 (TPIR, Ch. pr. inst.); *Prosecutor v. Radislav Krstić*, IT-98-33-T, Judgement (2
août 2001), au para. 561 (TPIY, Ch. pr. inst.) [*Krstić*]: "[T]he victims of genocide must be targeted *by reason* of their membership in a group ... The intent to
destroy a group as such, in whole or in part, presupposes that the victims were
chosen by reason of their membership in the group whose destruction was
sought. Mere knowledge of the victims' membership in a distinct group on the
part of the perpetrators is not sufficient to establish an intention to destroy the
group as such." [italiques dans la version originale]; *Le Procureur c. Goran Jelisić*,
IT-95-10-T, Jugement (14 décembre 1999), aux para. 67 et 79 (TPIY, Ch. pr.
inst.); *Affaire relative à l'application de la Convention pour la prévention et la répression
du crime de génocide (Bosnie-Herzégovine c. Serbie-et-Monténégro)*, Arrêt, [2007] C.I.J.
rec. 1, aux para. 187 et 193 [*Application de la Convention sur le génocide*].

50 *Mugesera*, *supra* note 5, aux para. 82 et s.

51 Code criminel, *supra* note 1, alinéas 318(2) a) et b).

facteurs distinctifs qui ne sont pas protégés par la définition en droit international coutumier, soit la "couleur" et l'"orientation sexuelle."[52] Toutefois, la définition n'inclut pas la protection des groupes "nationaux," et est, de cette manière, plus restreinte que la définition internationale.

En théorie, des personnes ayant participé à différents degrés à la commission d'un génocide pourraient donc être poursuivies au Canada en vertu de deux définitions différentes du même crime. De plus, le crime de "préconisation ou fomentation" du génocide, étant une infraction du Code criminel, relève de la compétence des procureurs généraux des provinces,[53] alors que les autres formes de commission du génocide sont de la compétence du Procureur général du Canada en vertu de la Loi.[54] À titre d'exemple, Désiré Munyaneza a été accusé par le Procureur général du Canada d'avoir, entre autres, par des actes de violence sexuelle, porté une atteinte grave à l'intégrité physique ou mentale de membres du groupe protégé comme acte constitutif de génocide. Cet acte de génocide n'est pas couvert par le crime d'incitation visé à l'article 318 du Code criminel. Par ailleurs, l'expulsion de Léon Mugesera du Canada était fondée sur des motifs raisonnables de croire que ce dernier avait "préconisé ou fomenté" le génocide, un crime prévu par l'article 318 du Code criminel. Si M. Mugesera était poursuivi au criminel pour ce crime, il le serait en vertu d'un régime procédural et substantiel complètement distinct de celui utilisé à l'encontre de son compatriote.

Ce cumul de définitions mine le rôle universel de la Loi sur les crimes de guerre en ce qui concerne la poursuite et la définition du "noyau dur" des crimes internationaux. Il est à noter, bien qu'il ne soit pas élaboré sur cette possibilité dans ce commentaire, que rien n'empêche la poursuite du crime prévu à l'article 318 du Code criminel en vertu de la Loi, celle-ci prévoyant le crime de conseil,[55] qui s'apparente à l'infraction inchoative d'"incitation au génocide," telle que développée par les tribunaux internationaux.

---

[52] Loi modifiant le Code criminel (propagande haineuse), L.C. 2004, ch. 14, art. 1. L'élément distinctif de l'orientation sexuelle a été ajouté en 2004.

[53] Code criminel, *supra* note 1, art. 2, sous "procureur général." Les alinéas b.1) à g) prévoient des exceptions pour les crimes principalement liés aux biens culturels, au terrorisme et à la fraude.

[54] Loi sur les crimes de guerre, *supra* note 4, art. 9(3).

[55] *Ibid.*, art. 4(1.1) et 6(1.1).

Cette possibilité devrait être explorée afin d'éviter la fracture inutile dans le régime substantiel et procédural s'appliquant à la poursuite de crimes internationaux créée par la coexistence d'infractions de génocide dans la Loi et dans le Code criminel.

Une question sera brièvement étudiée en ce qui concerne l'étude du crime de génocide effectuée par le juge Denis. Dans son analyse succincte de l'intention spécifique du crime (*dolus specialis*), il précise que "[1]'existence d'un plan ou d'une politique de destruction du groupe ne fait pas partie non plus des éléments essentiels de l'infraction."[56] Sans entrer dans les détails relatifs à cette question complexe, mentionnons qu'il existe une controverse relativement à la nécessité ou non d'établir l'existence d'un plan ou d'une politique. Même si les tribunaux ont conclu qu'il ne s'agit pas d'un élément juridique du crime de génocide,[57] certains auteurs estiment au contraire qu'une politique est toujours à la base de la commission du crime de génocide.[58] Les *Éléments des crimes* de la CPI prévoient par ailleurs un élément contextuel supplémentaire à la définition du génocide en exigeant que "[1]e comportement [se soit] inscrit dans le cadre d'une série manifeste de comportements analogues dirigés contre ce groupe."[59] La Chambre préliminaire dans l'affaire *Al Bashir* semble avoir interprété cette condition comme exigeant la preuve d'une politique de mise en œuvre d'un génocide en tant que condition préalable à l'intention génocidaire individuelle.[60] *Il s'agit là d'une situation où les Éléments pourraient avoir une*

---

56 *Munyaneza, supra* note 1, au para. 99.

57 *Le Procureur c. Goran Jelisić*, IT-95-10-A, Arrêt (5 juillet 2001), au para. 48 (TPIY, Ch. d'app.); *Le Procureur c. Clément Kayishema et Obed Ruzindana*, ICTR-95-1-T, Jugement (21 mai 1999), au para. 94 (TPIR, Ch. pr. inst.); *Application de la Convention sur le génocide, supra* note 49, au para 373.

58 Voir par exemple William A. Schabas, *Genocide in International Law*, 2ème édition (Cambridge: Cambridge University Press, 2009) à la p. 244. Voir l'analyse et les propositions dans Antonio Cassese, "Is Genocidal Policy a Requirement for the Crime of Genocide?" dans Paola Gaeta, dir., *The UN Genocide Convention: A Commentary* (Oxford: Oxford University Press, 2009) à la p. 128.

59 *Éléments des crimes, supra* note 18, art. 6(a)(4).

60 *Al Bashir, supra* note 21, aux para. 149-52; Claus Kreß, "The Crime of Genocide and Contextual Elements: A Comment on the ICC Pre-Trial Chamber's Decision in the *Al Bashir* Case" (2009) 7 Journal of International Criminal Justice 297. Cette conclusion n'a pas été revisitée dans la seconde décision de la Chambre préliminaire dans cette affaire: *The Prosecutor v. Omar Hassan Ahmad Al Bashir*, ICC-02/05-01/09, Second Decision on the Prosecution's Application for a Warrant of Arrest (12 juillet 2010), aux para. 13–17 (CPI, Ch. préliminaire I).

incidence indirecte sur l'interprétation que feront les tribunaux canadiens du droit international coutumier pour les crimes commis après le 17 juillet 1998 et ce, même si le régime du Statut de Rome s'écarte possiblement du droit international coutumier sur cette question. Une politique étatique ou organisationnelle pourrait donc indirectement devenir partie de la définition de génocide en vertu de la Loi.

Le juge Denis poursuit rapidement avec une analyse des actes sous-jacents du crime de génocide. Ces actes sont interprétés de la même façon lorsqu'ils sont constitutifs de crimes contre l'humanité et de crimes de guerre.[61] Par conséquent, l'analyse qui suit est également pertinente pour ces crimes.

Infractions sous-jacentes: meurtre et violence sexuelle

Meurtre

Tel que mentionné ci-dessus, le juge Denis débute son analyse des infractions sous-jacentes avec une discussion au sujet de l'expression "meurtre intentionnel." Il constate que cette expression n'existe pas en droit canadien et conclut alors:

En utilisant dans la Loi un terme différent de celui du code criminel, le législateur canadien voulait faire référence à la définition de "meurtre intentionnel" retrouvée dans le droit international et sa jurisprudence.

La différence est cependant bien mince. En droit international, on doit démontrer que:

(a) la personne est morte;
(b) l'accusé a causé la mort au moyen d'un acte ou d'une omission ou qu'il a contribué de façon substantielle à la mort;
(c) l'accusé avait l'intention de causer la mort de la victime ou de lui infliger des sévices graves qu'il savait susceptible de causer la mort.[62]

Nous avons discuté ci-dessus de l'applicabilité du droit international aux infractions sous-jacentes et de la justesse du raisonnement du juge Denis. Nous formulerons ici quelques remarques relatives à la conclusion du juge concernant la différence "bien mince" entre

---

[61] *Munyaneza, supra* note 1, aux para. 118, 121, 140 et 142.

[62] *Ibid.* aux para. 82 et 83, citant *Mugesera, supra* note 5, au para. 130 ainsi que *Le Procureur c. Brđanin*, IT-99-36-T, Jugement (1er septembre 2004) (Ch. pr. inst.) [*Brđanin*].

le droit canadien et le droit international au sujet de la définition de "meurtre."

En ce qui concerne l'*actus reus,* les exigences du droit international semblent être plus sévères que celles prévues en droit canadien. En effet, tel que le confirme le juge Denis, en droit international le lien de causalité entre le comportement de l'accusé et la mort requiert au minimum une "contribution substantielle" de la part de l'accusé. Par ailleurs, en droit canadien, le comportement doit plutôt avoir "contribué à la mort, de façon plus que mineure."[63] La Cour suprême a rejeté de façon explicite l'utilisation de l'expression "cause substantielle" pour décrire le lien de causalité requis pour toutes les infractions d'homicide et a indiqué que cette expression implique un "degré plus élevé de causalité juridique."[64] *Le meurtre en tant qu'acte constitutif du crime de génocide, de crimes contre l'humanité et de crimes de guerre exigera, par conséquent, une contribution plus importante de la part de l'accusé.* Le juge Denis n'a pas développé au sujet de la causalité, n'ayant apparemment aucun doute sur le fait que l'accusé avait tué directement de nombreux Tutsis à différentes occasions.[65]

En ce qui concerne la *mens rea,* le critère appliqué par le juge Denis, provenant de la jurisprudence des tribunaux *ad hoc,*[66] est presque identique à celui du meurtre prévu à l'article 229 a) (ii)

---

[63] *Smithers c. The Queen,* [1978] 1 R.C.S. 506. Dans l'arrêt *R. c. Nette,* [2001] 3 R.C.S. 488, au para. 71 [*Nette*], la Cour suprême n'a pas changé cette exigence mais a reformulé le critère de causalité dans les termes suivants: "une cause ayant contribué de façon appréciable," préférant cette formule à celle énoncée ci-dessus, qui avait aussi été exprimée de manière négative dans *Smithers,* soit une "cause ayant contribué d'une façon qui n'est pas négligeable ou insignifiante."

[64] *Nette, ibid.* aux para. 61, 64 et 66. L'exigence de causalité "substantielle" est pertinente pour les poursuites intentées en vertu de l'art. 231(5) et (6) du *Code criminel* permettant de condamner une personne pour meurtre au premier degré en l'absence de toute préméditation (*R. c. Harbottle,* [1993] 3 R.C.S. 306, confirmé dans *Nette*).

[65] *Munyaneza, supra* note 1, notamment aux para. 1949, 1951, 1955, 1958, 1963, 1964, 2065, 2067, 2069, 2074 et 2082.

[66] *Krstić, supra* note 49, au para. 485. Notons que dans quelques affaires, le critère appliqué se lit comme suit: "intention to kill or to cause serious bodily harm *which he/she should reasonably have known* might lead to death" [nous soulignons]. Cette description objective de la *mens rea* serait clairement en violation avec la *Charte canadienne des droits et libertés,* partie I de la *Loi constitutionnelle de 1982,* constituant l'annexe B de la *Loi de 1982 sur le Canada* (R.-U.), 1982, c.11, qui est entrée en vigueur le 17 avril 1982: *R. c. Vaillancourt,* [1987] 2 R.C.S. 636; *R. c. Martineau,* [1990] 2 R.C.S. 633.

du Code criminel. Cette disposition contient un élément d'insouciance quant à la question de savoir si l'accusé sait que la mort est "de nature" à s'ensuivre et qu'il lui est indifférent que la mort s'ensuive ou non (en anglais, *"he knows is likely to cause his death, and is reckless whether death ensues or not"*). La Cour suprême a cependant précisé qu'il s'agissait là d'un "léger assouplissement" à "l'intention de causer la mort."[67]

Il sera intéressant de voir si l'élément mental du "meurtre" sera interprété de façon similaire par la CPI. Rappelons que la Loi sur les crimes de guerre renvoie au Statut de Rome en précisant que les crimes qui y sont contenus sont, au 17 juillet 1998, des crimes selon le droit international coutumier. Or, le Statut de Rome semble exclure l'insouciance. L'insouciance peut se caractériser par la prévisibilité subjective par l'accusé de la probabilité ou de la possibilité de la survenance d'une conséquence et l'adoption d'une conduite sans s'en soucier. L'intention peut quant à elle se caractériser, relativement à une conséquence, soit par le désir que celle-ci survienne, soit par l'adoption d'une conduite avec la connaissance subjective d'un risque très élevé de survenance de la conséquence prohibée. En effet, l'intention peut également se démontrer par un élément de connaissance relatif à une conséquence. Toutefois, contrairement à l'insouciance, le degré de risque prévu par l'accusé avant de s'engager dans sa conduite est dans ce cas beaucoup plus élevé, soit certain ou quasi-certain.[68] La persévérance de l'accusé dans sa conduite en connaissance des conséquences pourra donc démontrer l'intention ou l'insouciance, en fonction du degré de risque de survenance de la conséquence.

L'article 30 (1) du Statut de Rome prévoit la règle générale applicable à tous les crimes: "Sauf disposition contraire, nul n'est pénalement responsable et ne peut être puni à raison d'un crime relevant de la compétence de la Cour que si l'élément matériel du crime est commis avec intention et connaissance." L'intention est définie de manière stricte et semble exclure l'insouciance telle que décrite ci-dessus. L'article 30 (2) b) prévoit en effet qu'il y a "intention au sens du présent article lorsque ... [r]elativement à une conséquence, une personne entend causer cette conséquence *ou est consciente que celle-ci adviendra* [*will* occurr] *dans le cours normal des événements*" [nous soulignons]. La Chambre préliminaire II dans

---

67 *R. c. Cooper*, [1993] 1 R.C.S. 146 aux pp. 154-55.

68 Voir discussion et autorités dans Lafontaine, "Parties to Offences," *supra* note 7.

l'affaire *Bemba* confirme que ces paragraphes envisagent deux types de "dol": celui qui implique la volonté de l'accusé de parvenir au résultat prohibé et celui qui n'exige pas que le suspect ait effectivement l'intention ou la volonté de faire survenir les éléments matériels du crime, mais exige qu'il sache que ces éléments seront le résultat presque inévitable (une "certitude virtuelle" ou une "certitude pratique") de ses actes ou omissions. La Chambre exclut explicitement l'insouciance, qu'elle définit comme la prévision de la survenance des conséquences comme une simple probabilité ou possibilité.[69]

Le terme "de nature à" (ou *"likely"* — probable — dans la version anglaise), utilisé dans le critère précédemment mentionné pour le meurtre en droit canadien, exige donc une prévisibilité d'un risque sensiblement moins élevé que la mort s'ensuive que celui exigé en vertu du Statut de Rome. La référence à l'insouciance, malgré la mention par la Cour suprême qu'il ne s'agit pas d'un critère très différent de l'intention, demeure moins strict que les exigences du Statut de Rome à cet égard. *Ainsi, les poursuites intentées en vertu de la loi canadienne qui impliqueront l'infraction sous-jacente de meurtre pour des crimes commis après le 17 juillet 1998 devront revoir les contours de l'élément mental requis, et cela conformément au standard plus élevé prévu dans le Statut de Rome.* Mentionnons finalement que la préméditation n'est pas un élément exigé pour l'infraction sous-jacente de meurtre,[70] mais, comme nous le verrons *infra*, il s'agit d'un facteur per-

---

[69] *Le Procureur c. Jean-Pierre Bemba Gombo*, ICC-01/05-01/08-424, Décision rendue en application des alinéas a) et b) de l'article 61–67 du Statut de Rome, relativement aux charges portées par le Procureur à l'encontre de Jean-Pierre Bemba Gombo (15 juin 2009), aux para. 357-69 (CPI, Ch. préliminaire II) [*Bemba*]. Pour exclure l'insouciance, la Chambre traite de *"recklessness"* mais, dans la version française de sa décision, elle utilise le terme "négligence" alors que le Code criminel canadien utilise le terme "insouciance" pour désigner la notion connue sous le nom de *"recklessness"* en anglais. Sa description du concept fait toutefois référence à l'insouciance telle qu'elle est comprise en droit canadien. Cette décision confirme en outre l'applicabilité de l'art. 30 au meurtre constitutif de crimes contre l'humanité, au para. 138; *contra* au sujet du degré de risque: *Le Procureur c. Thomas Lubanga Dyilo*, ICC-01/04-01/06-803, Décision sur la confirmation des charges (29 janvier 2007), aux para. 352-55 (ICC, Ch. préliminaire I). Voir discussion et autorités dans Lafontaine, "Parties to Offences," *supra* note 7.

[70] Malgré quelques hésitations initiales, l'opinion qui a prévalu exclut la préméditation en tant qu'élément constitutif du meurtre: voir par exemple *Le Procureur c. Tihomir Blaškić*, IT-95-14-T, Jugement (3 mars 2000), au para. 216 (TPIY, Ch. pr. inst.) [*Blaškić*]; *Kordić et Čerkez*, *supra* note 39, au para. 235; *Akayesu*, *supra*

tinent lors de la détermination de la peine, tant en droit international[71] qu'en droit canadien.[72]

Violence sexuelle

Quant aux autres actes sous-jacents du crime de génocide, le juge Denis concentre son analyse sur l'"atteinte grave à l'intégrité physique ou mentale," laquelle peut être causée, selon lui, par les actes suivants: "torture physique ou mentale; traitements inhumains ou dégradants; viol; violences sexuelles; persécution."[73] Bien qu'il commence son analyse avec l'infraction sous-jacente de traitements inhumains ou dégradants (étrangement définie en vertu de la jurisprudence traitant des crimes de guerre, exigeant de ce fait que les victimes soient des "personnes protégées"), ses conclusions factuelles se concentrent uniquement sur les actes de violence sexuelle allégués dans la preuve, qui feront par conséquent l'objet d'une analyse plus approfondie.

Le juge Denis, citant la décision *Akayesu*, mentionne que "[1]a jurisprudence internationale, qui en cela ne diffère pas de la jurisprudence canadienne, définit la violence sexuelle comme 'tout acte sexuel commis sur la personne d'autrui sous l'emprise de la coercition'."[74] Il dresse, par la suite, une liste non limitative d'actes constitutifs de violence sexuelle, à savoir "a) obliger une personne à se déshabiller en public; b) la pénétration sexuelle; c) le viol; d) l'attentat à la pudeur."[75] Cette énumération, malgré son caractère non limitatif, omet curieusement les nombreux actes de violence sexuelle maintenant codifiés dans le Statut de Rome.[76] Pour les fins

---

note 49, aux para. 588–89; *Krstić, supra* note 49, à la note de bas de page 1119; *Brđanin, supra* note 62, au para. 386. Aucune dérogation à l'art. 30 du Statut de Rome n'est possible en ce qui concerne le meurtre; ce crime doit être commis avec intention et connaissance, excluant toute exigence de préméditation.

71 La préméditation a été considérée comme un facteur aggravant lors de la détermination de la peine: voir par exemple *Le Procureur c. Jean Kambanda*, ICTR-97-23-S, Jugement portant condamnation (4 septembre 1998), aux para. 61-62 (TPIR, Ch. pr. inst.); *Le Procureur c. Omar Serushago*, ICTR-98-39-S, Sentence (5 février 1999), aux para. 27-30 (TPIR, Ch. pr. inst.); *Krstić, supra* note 49, au para. 711; *Blaškić, supra* note 70, au para. 793.

72 Voir Loi sur les crimes de guerre, *supra* note 4, art. 15.

73 *Munyaneza, supra* note 1, au para. 84.

74 *Ibid.*, au para. 95, citant *Akayesu, supra* note 49.

75 *Ibid.*, au para. 96.

76 Voir Statut de Rome, *supra* note 13, art. 7(1)(g), 8(2)(b)(xxii) et 8(2)(e)(vi).

de cet article, nous émettrons toutefois deux brefs commentaires au sujet de la définition de la notion de violence sexuelle.

Tout d'abord, malgré le caractère indéniablement historique de la décision rendue dans l'affaire *Akayesu*, l'utilisation du critère de la coercition en tant qu'élément constitutif du viol et de la violence sexuelle a été critiquée et renversée dans la jurisprudence subséquente. Dans l'affaire *Kunarac*, la Chambre d'appel a confirmé que l'absence de consentement de la victime était le critère approprié et qu'il reflétait davantage les différentes approches retenues dans les législations nationales tout en respectant le principe sous-jacent de l'autonomie sexuelle de l'individu.[77] Cette dernière interprétation, plutôt que celle retenue dans l'affaire *Munyaneza*, "ne diffère pas de la jurisprudence canadienne" en matière d'agression sexuelle.[78] Dans la mesure où ces développements font probablement partie du droit international coutumier, le juge Denis aurait dû en tenir compte. Il semble que le droit international coutumier est en effet vraisemblablement différent du critère initialement élaboré dans *Akayesu* et qu'il était différent aussi en 1994.

Les *Éléments des crimes* du Statut de Rome ont été rédigés avant l'arrêt de la Chambre d'appel dans l'affaire *Kunarac*. Ils mettent une emphase plus grande sur la coercition et la force en exigeant que les actes aient été commis "par la force ou en usant à l'encontre de ladite ou desdites ou de tierces personnes de la menace de la force ou de la coercition, telle que celle causée par la menace de violences, contraintes, détention, pressions psychologiques, abus de pouvoir, ou bien à la faveur d'un environnement coercitif, ou encore en profitant de l'incapacité de ladite personne de donner son libre consentement."[79] Le régime de la CPI s'écarte donc de façon discutable du droit international coutumier en exigeant la preuve de l'emploi de la force ou la menace à titre d'élément matériel constitutif des crimes de viol et de violence sexuelle au lieu de le considérer comme un élément dont la cour peut tenir compte lors de l'appréciation du consentement de la victime.[80] En effet,

---

[77] Robert Cryer et al., *An Introduction to International Criminal Law and Procedure*, (Cambridge: Cambridge University Press, 2007) à la p. 210. *Kunarac, supra* note 41.

[78] Julie Desrosiers, *L'agression sexuelle en droit canadien*, (Cowansville: Yvon Blais, 2009).

[79] *Éléments des Crimes, supra* note 18, art. 7(1)(g)-1 et 7(1)(g)-6.

[80] Nous notons que le test deviendra peut-être, en fin de compte, celui de l'absence de consentement: Règle 70 du *Règlement de procédure et de preuve* de la CPI,

la jurisprudence post-*Kunarac* a confirmé que l'absence de consentement pouvait être prouvée hors de tout doute raisonnable en démontrant l'existence de circonstances cœrcitives *"under which meaningful consent is not possible."*[81]

Il s'agit là d'un bel exemple de la situation délicate dans laquelle seront plongés les juges canadiens lorsque les *Éléments des crimes* ne reflètent pas adéquatement l'état du droit international coutumier. En s'appuyant sur la jurisprudence de la CPI, qui interprétera fort probablement le crime de viol à la lumière des *Éléments,* les juges canadiens risquent de s'éloigner de l'esprit et de la lettre des dispositions de la Loi sur les crimes de guerre qui prévoient que les crimes doivent être définis en conformité avec le droit international coutumier. Dans un tel cas, les *Éléments des crimes* devraient être écartés. Cependant, considérant la difficulté d'identifier le droit international coutumier, les *Éléments* risquent fort de devenir la norme coutumière appliquée au Canada en matière de crimes internationaux.

Une seconde remarque au sujet de la violence sexuelle concerne l'absence de définition du terme "viol" dans la décision rendue par le juge Denis, et cela malgré le fait que plusieurs de ses conclusions factuelles concernent cette forme de violence sexuelle. La Loi sur les crimes de guerre inclut l'acte de "violence sexuelle" dans sa définition de crime contre l'humanité.[82] La Loi ne réfère pas au viol, qui constitue, néanmoins, une infraction sous-jacente reconnue du crime de génocide, des crimes contre l'humanité et des crimes de guerre en droit international. Le "viol" fait notamment partie des actes à caractère sexuel énumérés à l'article 7 (1) g) du Statut de Rome qui représente selon la loi canadienne, doit-on le rappeler, l'état du droit international coutumier. En droit canadien, le crime de viol a été remplacé en 1983 par le terme "agression sexuelle," plus général et moins préjudiciable à un sexe.[83] La Loi sur les crimes

---

ICC-ASP/1/3; Max du Plessis, "ICC Crimes," dans Ben Brandon et Max du Plessis, dir., *The Prosecution of International Crimes: A Practical Guide to Prosecuting ICC Crimes in Commonwealth States* (Londres: Commonwealth Secretariat, 2005) 35 à la p. 50.

[81] *The Prosecutor v. Sylvestre Gacumbitsi,* ICTR-2001-64-A, Judgment (7 juillet 2006), au para. 155 (TPIR, Ch. d'app.).

[82] Loi sur les crimes de guerre, *supra* note 4, art. 4(3) et 6(3).

[83] Code criminel, *supra* note 1, art. 271. Pour une analyse des éléments constitutifs, voir *R. c. Chase,* [1987] 2 R.C.S. 293; *R. c. Ewanchuk,* [1999] 1 R.C.S. 330. Voir généralement, Desrosiers, *supra* note 78.

de guerre réintroduit, par conséquent, le crime de viol en droit canadien lors des poursuites pour crimes internationaux. Considérant que les infractions sous-jacentes de ces crimes doivent être interprétées à la lumière du droit international, comme il a été discuté ci-dessus, et considérant de toute façon l'absence de définition d'un tel crime en vertu du droit interne, il aurait été préférable d'en circonscrire les éléments constitutifs permettant d'établir les conditions préalables à un verdict de culpabilité.

Crimes contre l'humanité

La Loi sur les crimes de guerre modernise la définition des crimes contre l'humanité qui était contenue dans les anciennes dispositions du Code criminel, en y ajoutant notamment des actes sous-jacents qui ne s'y trouvaient pas, soit la violence sexuelle, l'emprisonnement et la torture. Les paragraphes 4(3) et 6(3) de la Loi prévoient la définition suivante:

Meurtre, extermination, réduction en esclavage, déportation, emprisonnement, torture, violence sexuelle, persécution ou autre fait — acte ou omission — inhumain, d'une part, commis contre une population civile ou un groupe identifiable de personnes et, d'autre part, qui constitue, au moment et au lieu de la perpétration, un crime contre l'humanité selon le droit international coutumier.

Pour des raisons qui n'ont pas été énoncées publiquement, les crimes sous-jacents qui sont prévus aux paragraphes (i) (disparitions forcées de personnes) et (j) (crime d'apartheid) de l'article 7(1) du Statut de Rome, n'ont pas été inclus aux articles 4(3) et 6(3) de la Loi.[84] Il ne s'agit probablement pas d'une coïncidence que le

---

[84] Il semble toutefois que rien n'empêcherait une poursuite au Canada pour ces crimes, du moins s'ils ont été commis après le 17 juillet 1998. En effet, la Loi indique que l'art. 7 du Statut de Rome constitue le droit international coutumier après cette date (art. 4(4) et 6(4)). De plus, la définition de crimes contre l'humanité dans la Loi contient une énumération non-exhaustive des infractions sous-jacentes constitutives de crimes contre l'humanité, en ce qu'elle y inclut tout "autre fait — acte ou omission — inhumain." Ainsi, il serait à notre avis fort possible de conclure qu'une disparition forcée commise, par exemple, en Colombie ou au Sri Lanka en 2009, constituerait un "autre acte inhumain" "qui constitue, au moment et au lieu de la perpétration, un crime contre l'humanité selon le droit international coutumier," ce dernier étant défini ici en référence à l'art. 7 du Statut de Rome.

Canada n'ait pas non plus ratifié les conventions internationales liées à ces graves violations des droits humains fondamentaux.[85] Nous aborderons deux questions relatives aux éléments constitutifs des crimes contre l'humanité.[86] En premier lieu, nous notons que la question controversée de l'exigence d'un plan ou d'une politique gouvernementale lors de l'attaque lancée contre une population civile devra peut-être être revisitée en droit canadien dans la jurisprudence interprétant la Loi sur les crimes de guerre. Dans l'affaire *Mugesera*, la Cour suprême du Canada a abordé cette question dans les termes suivants:

> Dans l'arrêt *Procureur c. Kunarac, Kovac and Vukovic* ... la Chambre d'appel du TPIY a statué que rien n'exige que l'attaque résulte d'une politique ou d'un plan gouvernemental ou autre ... Il semble que, *à l'heure actuelle, le droit international coutumier n'exige pas qu'une politique sous-tende l'attaque,* mais nous n'écartons pas la possibilité qu'il évolue et pose un jour cette condition (voir p. ex. l'al. 7(2)a) du Statut de Rome).[87]

En prévoyant dans la Loi sur les crimes de guerre que le Statut de Rome représente l'état du droit international coutumier, le législateur canadien a choisi implicitement d'exiger la preuve que

---

85 Convention internationale pour la protection de toutes les personnes contre les disparitions forcées, *supra* note 25 et Convention internationale sur l'élimination et la répression du crime d'apartheid, (1976) 1015 R.T.N.U. 243. Certains auteurs ont prudemment avancé que la position intrigante du Canada relativement au crime d'apartheid peut être expliquée par son *"unease with the grievances of the country's Aboriginal population".* William A. Schabas et Stéphane Beaulac, *International Human Rights and Canadian Law — Legal Commitment, Implementation and the Charter,* 3e éd. (Toronto: Thomson Carswell, 2007) à la p. 248. Il serait possible d'avancer, tout aussi prudemment, que la même chose pourrait être vraie en ce qui concerne le crime de disparition forcée. En juin 2009, le Canada a réitéré son intention de ne pas ratifier ce traité ainsi que d'autres traités: voir la réponse du Canada aux recommandations suivant l'Examen périodique universel du Conseil des droits de l'homme des Nations Unies, en ligne: Ministère du Patrimoine canadien <http://www.pch.gc.ca/pgm/pdp-hrp/inter/101-fra.cfm>.

86 Pour une analyse de la question avant l'entrée en vigueur de la Loi sur les crimes de guerre, voir Alain Joffe, "Les crimes contre l'humanité dans le Code criminel: Une contribution canadienne au droit international" (1995) 9 R.Q.D.I. 521; pour une analyse post-*Finta* mais pré-*Mugesera*, voir Madeleine J. Schwartz, "Prosecuting Crimes against Humanity in Canada: What Must Be Proved" (2002) 46 Crim. L.Q. 40.

87 *Mugesera, supra* note 5 aux para. 157–58 [nous soulignons].

l'attaque a été menée en application ou dans la poursuite d'une politique. En effet, l'article 7(2)(a) du Statut de Rome prévoit:

Par "attaque lancée contre une population civile," on entend le comportement qui consiste en la commission multiple d'actes visés au paragraphe 1 à l'encontre d'une population civile quelconque, *en application ou dans la poursuite de la politique d'un État ou d'une organisation ayant pour but une telle attaque* [nous soulignons].

L'arrêt de la Cour suprême dans l'affaire *Mugesera* a été rendu en application des anciennes dispositions du Code criminel, mais alors que la Loi sur les crimes de guerre avait déjà été adoptée. En fait, la Cour précise spécifiquement que les différences dans les définitions contenues à la Loi sur les crimes de guerre n'ont "aucune pertinence" pour les besoins de l'analyse qu'elle effectue.[88] Néanmoins, au regard de l'*actus reus*, l'interprétation donnée à la notion d'"attaque" dans cet arrêt s'éloigne de façon significative du choix du législateur dans la Loi sur les crimes de guerre relativement à l'exigence d'une politique d'un État ou d'une organisation.

Dans l'affaire *Munyaneza*, le juge Denis cite l'affaire *Kunarac* pour appuyer sa conclusion à l'effet que l'attaque n'a pas besoin d'être le résultat d'une politique gouvernementale.[89] Considérant que le comportement répréhensible a eu lieu en 1994 et que la Loi sur les crimes de guerre prévoit que le Statut de Rome constitue le droit international coutumier au 17 janvier 1998, son raisonnement est justifié. Cependant, *toutes poursuites futures pour des crimes ayant eu lieu après cette date devront ignorer tant les conclusions de l'arrêt Mugesera que de l'affaire Munyaneza relativement à l'exigence d'une politique, et cela peu importe si le Statut de Rome représente effectivement l'état du droit international coutumier à ce sujet.*

En second lieu, il importe de discuter brièvement de la *mens rea* requise pour le crime contre l'humanité, et plus précisément de l'élément de connaissance de l'attaque par l'accusé. Dans l'arrêt *Mugesera*, la Cour suprême résume cet élément ainsi:

Il est désormais bien établi que l'accusé doit non seulement avoir l'intention de commettre l'infraction sous-jacente, mais aussi connaître l'existence de l'attaque et savoir que son ou ses actes en font partie *ou qu'il court le risque que son ou ses actes en fassent partie*: voir p. ex. *Tadic*, Chambre

---

[88] *Ibid.* au para. 118.
[89] *Munyaneza, supra* note 1 au para. 114.

d'appel, par. 248; *Ruggiu*, par. 20; *Kunarac*, Chambre de première instance, par. 434; *Blaskic*, par. 251.
Il suffit que l'auteur de l'acte soit conscient du lien entre son ou ses actes et l'attaque. Il n'est pas nécessaire qu'il ait eu l'intention de s'en prendre à la population cible. Ses motifs importent peu, une fois démontré qu'il connaissait l'existence de l'attaque et *qu'il savait que son acte en faisait partie ou qu'il lui était indifférent que son acte se rattache à l'attaque*. *Kunarac*, Chambre d'appel, par. 103. Même si la personne a agi pour des raisons purement personnelles, l'acte peut constituer un crime contre l'humanité s'il est prouvé qu'elle possédait la connaissance requise.

...

Dans l'arrêt *Finta*, les juges majoritaires de notre Cour ont décidé que l'accusé devait avoir une connaissance subjective des circonstances qui faisaient de son acte un crime contre l'humanité (p. 819). Cette exigence demeure en ce sens que l'accusé doit être au courant de l'attaque et savoir que son ou ses actes en font partie *ou, du moins, courir le risque qu'ils en fassent partie.*[90]

L'élément de connaissance de l'attaque est donc double. L'accusé doit non seulement connaître l'existence de l'attaque, mais également savoir que ses actes en font partie ou, comme la Cour suprême le mentionne en s'appuyant sur une lignée de jurisprudence des tribunaux *ad hoc*, prendre un risque à cet égard. Le juge Denis, dans *Munyaneza*, reprend cette caractérisation de l'élément mental.[91]

Il convient de rappeler que l'article 30 du Statut de Rome prévoit que les crimes doivent être commis avec intention et connaissance. Le premier volet de l'élément mental, soit celui de la connaissance de l'existence de l'attaque, semble se rapporter aux circonstances faisant partie de l'infraction. Dans l'affaire *Bemba*, la Chambre préliminaire de la CPI se prononce ainsi concernant l'élément "connaissance" de l'attaque:

L'article 7(1) du Statut exige que l'auteur agisse "en connaissance" de l'attaque lancée contre la population civile. L'attaque doit être considérée comme une circonstance des crimes contre l'humanité et, partant, l'élément tenant à la "connaissance" est un aspect de l'élément psychologique visé à l'article 30(3) du Statut selon lequel "[i]l y a connaissance ...

---

[90] *Mugesera*, *supra* note 5 aux para. 173, 174 et 176 [nous soulignons].

[91] *Munyaneza*, *supra* note 1 au para. 113.

lorsqu'une personne est consciente qu'une circonstance existe ou qu'une conséquence adviendra dans le cours normal des événements.[92]

L'accusé doit donc être conscient, subjectivement, de l'existence de l'attaque contre la population civile. Il n'est pas nécessaire de prouver que l'auteur avait connaissance de toutes les caractéristiques de l'attaque.[93]

Par ailleurs, le second volet semble se rapporter davantage à une conséquence. La connaissance de l'accusé porte en effet sur le fait que les actes qu'il commet à l'encontre d'une victime font effectivement partie de l'attaque. À cet égard, les *Éléments des crimes* mentionnent ce qui suit, comme dernier élément essentiel de chaque infraction sous-jacente constitutive de crimes contre l'humanité: "L'auteur savait que ce comportement faisait partie d'une attaque généralisée ou systématique dirigée contre une population civile ou entendait qu'il en fasse partie."[94] Rappelons que les définitions données à l'article 30 du Statut de Rome excluent l'insouciance. Ainsi, bien que la Cour suprême ait été rassurante sur le fait que son interprétation des crimes contre l'humanité fondée sur les anciennes dispositions du Code criminel soit applicable à la définition en vertu de la Loi, il semble, encore une fois, qu'un aspect essentiel de l'infraction doive être réévalué à la lumière du Statut de Rome. En effet, on ne saura se contenter de l'insouciance de l'accusé quant à sa connaissance du fait que ses actes faisaient effectivement partie de l'attaque. L'accusé devra au minimum savoir que ses actes font certainement ou quasi-certainement partie de l'attaque. Ainsi, le Statut de Rome et les *Éléments* ne se contentent pas de l'insouciance *et l'accusé devra, dans une poursuite en vertu de la Loi pour des crimes commis après le 17 juillet 1998, avoir une connaissance subjective de l'attaque et avoir l'intention que ses gestes participent de cette attaque ou savoir qu'ils en font certainement ou quasi-certainement partie.*

Crimes de guerre

Les crimes de guerre ont été criminalisés dans une certaine mesure au Canada depuis la fin de la Seconde Guerre mondiale, par

---

[92] *Bemba, supra* note 69 au para. 87.

[93] Voir notamment *Éléments des crimes, supra* note 18, art. 7, 2ème paragraphe introductif.

[94] *Ibid.*, art. 7, 5 ème élément de chaque paragraphe.

le biais de la Loi sur les conventions de Genève,[95] en autant qu'ils constituaient des "infractions graves" aux dites conventions.[96] Aucune poursuite ne fut jamais entreprise au Canada sur la base de cette législation. Les amendements au Code criminel, en 1987, permettaient aussi aux tribunaux canadiens d'avoir compétence sur les crimes de guerre, qui étaient définis en référence au droit international coutumier et dans le contexte spécifique d'un conflit armé *international*. La Loi sur les crimes de guerre confirme l'intention du législateur canadien d'inclure un large éventail de crimes de guerre pouvant être poursuivis au Canada. Les paragraphes 4(3) et 6(3) de la Loi définissent ces crimes ainsi:

Fait — acte ou omission — commis au cours d'un conflit armé et constituant, au moment et au lieu de la perpétration, un crime de guerre selon le droit international coutumier ou le droit international conventionnel applicables à ces conflits, qu'il constitue ou non une transgression du droit en vigueur à ce moment et dans ce lieu.

Cette définition dépasse évidemment le strict cadre des "infractions graves" et inclut notamment les crimes de guerre commis lors d'un conflit ne présentant pas un caractère international, ce qui constitue également une évolution par rapport aux anciennes dispositions du Code criminel. Il ne fait, en effet, désormais plus de doute que ces crimes font partie du droit international coutumier. Le Statut de Rome à son article 8 (2) en codifie plus d'une quinzaine.

S'appuyant sur la jurisprudence du Tribunal pénal international pour le Rwanda (TPIR), le juge Denis a conclu que le conflit, ayant eu lieu au Rwanda en 1994, ne présentait pas un caractère international. Il a rappelé que tant le Canada que le Rwanda étaient parties aux quatre Conventions de Genève et leurs Protocoles additionnels en 1994 et a statué que l'article 4 du Statut du TPIR constituait le droit international coutumier à cette époque.[97]

---

95 Loi sur les Conventions de Genève, L.R.C. 1985, c. G-3. Voir également la *Loi sur les crimes de guerre*, L.C. 1946, c.73, qui a principalement servie de fondement législatif aux poursuites par le Canada de responsables de crimes de guerre en Europe après la Seconde Guerre mondiale. Pour un résumé des procès d'après-guerre, voir notamment William J. Fenrick, "The Prosecution of War Criminals in Canada" (1990) 12 Dal. L.J. 256 à la p. 286.

96 *Ibid*, art. 3.

97 *Munyaneza*, *supra* note 1 aux para. 132-35.

M. Munyaneza a été accusé de meurtre, de violence sexuelle et de pillage. Nous avons discuté du meurtre et de la violence sexuelle ci-dessus. La Défense soutient en appel que le juge Denis a erré en droit lors de la détermination du lien requis (*"nexus"*) entre les crimes et le conflit armé. Au sujet de la définition du crime de pillage, la Défense soumet de plus que le juge aurait dû retenir celle du Statut de Rome prohibant "[1]e pillage *d'une ville ou d'une localité*, même prise d'assaut".[98]

Bien que le juge ait pris en considération la jurisprudence existante au sujet du lien requis entre les crimes et le conflit armé, il est exact qu'il n'a pas élaboré sur cette question à la lumière des faits propres à l'espèce. Comme au regard d'autres questions en litige, son application du droit aux faits aurait pu être davantage systématique. Cela était particulièrement important en l'espèce pour deux raisons. Premièrement, la preuve pouvait ouvrir la porte à une argumentation présentant certains des crimes reprochés comme des crimes de droit commun, c'est-à-dire sans lien avec le conflit armé. Deuxièmement, une distinction entre le contexte génocidaire (détruire les Tutsis en tant que tels) et le conflit armé contre le Front patriotique rwandais (FPR) (justifiant les attaques contre les collaborateurs Tutsis) aurait été justifiée dans l'analyse du lien requis pour établir la présence de crimes de guerre.

Néanmoins, l'exposé du juge relatif au droit en vigueur est généralement exact et ce dernier ne semble avoir aucun doute sur le fait que les crimes ont été commis "dans le cadre" d'un conflit armé. En ce qui concerne le pillage, même si le Statut de Rome interdit le pillage d'une ville ou d'une localité, les *Éléments des crimes* ne semblent pas limiter le crime dans le sens souhaité par la Défense.[99] Les *Éléments* sont similaires aux principes énoncés par le juge Denis au paragraphe 146 du jugement. Les conclusions factuelles du juge[100] appuient un verdict de culpabilité pour le crime de pillage tel que défini même si, encore une fois, les explications juridiques et l'application aux faits auraient pu être davantage développées.

---

[98] Art. 8(2)(e)(v), Voir *Avis d'appel, supra* note 6, motifs d'appel 10 et 1-G [nous soulignons].

[99] *Éléments des crimes, supra* note 18, art. 8(2)(e)(v). Il a été dit que *"the reference to town, place and assault within the definition [in the Rome Statute] are highly confusing, legally redundant, and historically passé"*: voir James G. Stewart, "The Future of the Grave Breaches Regime: Segregate, Assimilate or Abandon?" (2009) 7 Journal of International Criminal Justice à la p. 871, note 66.

[100] Voir les para. 1943, 1944, 1945, 1948, 2061 et 2062.

CERTAINES QUESTIONS RELATIVES AUX PEINES EN VERTU DE LA LOI

Le juge Denis a condamné M. Munyaneza à l'emprisonnement à perpétuité pour les six chefs d'accusation de génocide, crimes contre l'humanité et crimes de guerre impliquant la commission de meurtres et de violence sexuelle. Il lui a, en outre, infligé une peine de huit années d'incarcération en raison de sa participation à des actes de pillage, constitutifs d'un crime de guerre, appliquant ainsi la coutume de doubler le temps passé en détention préventive (l'accusé a été arrêté le 19 octobre 2005, soit quatre ans avant le prononcé de la sentence).[101] Pour les crimes impliquant la commission de meurtres, le juge a conclu que ceux-ci avaient été commis avec préméditation et de propos délibéré. Il a, par conséquent, assorti la possibilité d'une libération conditionnelle à l'accomplissement d'une période de vingt-cinq années d'emprisonnement. En ce qui concerne les actes de violence sexuelle, cette période a été fixée à dix ans.

L'article 15 de la Loi sur les crimes de guerre, reproduit ci-dessus, prévoit que le bénéfice d'une libération conditionnelle, dans le cas d'une condamnation à vie, dépendra du caractère "prémédité et de propos délibéré" du meurtre à l'origine de l'infraction. Ces termes sont directement tirés du Code criminel, soit de l'article 231 (2), définissant la notion de meurtre au premier degré. Cela crée une situation pour le moins singulière dans la mesure où le "meurtre" en tant qu'infraction sous-jacente d'un crime international sera interprété en vertu du droit international, tel que discuté ci-dessus, alors que la question relative à la "préméditation et au propos délibéré" semble nécessiter une interprétation en vertu du droit canadien.[102] Puisque les questions relatives à la peine ont été

---

[101] *Jugement sur la peine Munyaneza, supra* note 2 au para. 63. Le juge Denis ne prend pas en considération la coutume de doubler le temps passé en détention préventive au moment de fixer l'admissibilité à une libération conditionnelle pour les crimes impliquant le meurtre et la violence sexuelle.

[102] *Arguments juridiques de la poursuivante*, No: 500-73-002500-052, au para. 38. Dans l'affaire *Munyaneza*, la Couronne s'est appuyée sur le droit international pour définir la notion de meurtre et sur le droit interne pour déterminer si celui-ci avait été commis "avec préméditation et de propos délibéré." Dans le *Jugement sur la peine Munyaneza, supra* note 2, le juge Denis n'élabore pas sur le droit qui devrait régir l'interprétation de l'expression "avec préméditation et de propos délibéré." Diverses dispositions dans la Loi sur les crimes de guerre indiquent que le "meurtre commis avec préméditation et de propos délibéré" devrait être considéré comme un "meurtre au premier degré": par exemple, art. 15(2)(a).

délibérément laissées à la discrétion des États dans le cadre du système mis en place à la CPI,[103] le recours à la législation nationale aux fins de détermination de la peine apparaît justifié, même si cela signifie qu'une même conduite sera analysée tour à tour en vertu du droit international et du droit national.

Le juge Denis semble appliquer le critère de la "préméditation et du propos délibéré" au crime de génocide et aux crimes contre l'humanité de façon générale,[104] au lieu de l'appliquer de manière plus précise à chaque infraction sous-jacente. Cette approche peut être critiquée en raison de la manière dont le droit canadien apprécie habituellement le caractère prémédité et délibéré d'une conduite, c'est-à-dire au regard d'un meurtre individuel précis. Cette façon de faire est aussi en désaccord avec les dispositions pertinentes de la Loi sur les crimes de guerre qui prévoient l'admissibilité à la libération conditionnelle. Cette dernière est fixée à vingt-cinq ans si "le meurtre commis avec préméditation et de propos délibéré *est à l'origine de l'infraction*"[105] impliquant ainsi que la "préméditation" doit être analysée en fonction des crimes sous-jacents à l'infraction internationale prohibée. L'approche du juge Denis rejoint toutefois celle adoptée dans certaines affaires internationales.[106] En effet, le critère canadien devra peut-être s'adapter à la nature des crimes en cause, souvent commis à grande échelle ou par des groupes d'individus agissant de concert, ce qui rend plus difficile l'analyse du caractère prémédité de chaque infraction sous-jacente.

CONCLUSION

La décision du juge Denis dans l'affaire *Munyaneza* nous donne l'occasion de constater que les définitions des crimes, qui réfèrent au droit international coutumier et, à des fins d'interprétation, au Statut de Rome, permettent que le droit interne puisse évoluer dans une harmonie souhaitable avec le droit international. L'interaction avec les principes existants de droit interne, y compris les dispositions relativement aux peines, n'est pas toujours sans heurts, mais les décisions qui seront rendues dans la foulée de l'affaire

---

[103] Voir Statut de Rome, *supra* note 13, art. 80.

[104] *Jugement sur la peine Munyaneza, supra* note 2 au para. 27.

[105] Voir par exemple, Loi sur les crimes de guerre, *supra* note 4, art. 15(1)(a) [nous soulignons].

[106] Par exemple *Semanza, supra* note 41 au para. 339.

Munyaneza contribueront certainement à créer une jurisprudence à la fois proprement canadienne et profondément ancrée dans le droit international.

Il reste à voir si le nouveau paysage juridique au Canada permettra de contrer l'effet discutable résultant de l'échec de la poursuite dans l'affaire *Finta*. Il nous faut espérer que la Loi sur les crimes de guerre aura une incidence positive sur la volonté quelque peu timide du gouvernement à poursuivre les criminels de guerre. Les États ont un rôle complémentaire à jouer aux instances internationales. Agir localement en faveur de l'objectif global de lutte contre l'impunité permettra au Canada de contribuer significativement au "développement durable" de la justice pénale internationale.[107] Le succès de la Loi dépendra ainsi tout autant de la force de ses dispositions et de l'interprétation qu'en feront les tribunaux que de la volonté politique d'utiliser pleinement cette loi à l'encontre des personnes ayant commis des crimes internationaux et qui se trouvent sur le territoire canadien.

FANNIE LAFONTAINE
Faculté de droit, Université Laval

Summary

Prosecuting Genocide, Crimes against Humanity, and War Crimes in Canada: An Analysis of the Elements of Crimes in Light of *Munyaneza*

The Munyaneza *decision represents the first judicial analysis of the Crimes against Humanity and War Crimes Act and of the international offences now criminalized in Canadian law. The new legal regime — which intertwines international and Canadian law in various respects — is original and complex and constitutes an important pillar in the global fight against impunity for the most serious international crimes. This article offers a*

---

107 Voir Fannie Lafontaine, "'Think Globally, Act Locally': Using Canada's Crimes Against Humanity and War Crimes Act for the 'Sustainable Development' of International Criminal Law," à paraître dans les *Travaux du 36e Congrès annuel du Conseil canadien de droit international portant sur La contribution du Canada au droit international*, Ottawa; Fannie Lafontaine et Edith-Farah Elassal, "La prison à vie pour Désiré Munyaneza — Vers un 'développement durable' de la justice pénale internationale" Le Devoir (2 novembre 2009).

critical analysis of the Munyaneza *judgment as it relates to the constitutive elements of genocide, crimes against humanity, and war crimes. It offers a discussion of some of the most challenging aspects of those crimes' definitions and aims to contribute to the development of future jurisprudence regarding these crimes that is coherent with the act's letter and purpose in international law. The sentencing scheme provided by the act is also briefly analyzed.*

Sommaire

Poursuivre le génocide, les crimes contre l'humanité et les crimes de guerre au Canada: Une analyse des éléments des crimes à la lumière de l'affaire *Munyaneza*

La décision Munyaneza *constitue la première analyse judiciaire de la* Loi sur les crimes contre l'humanité et les crimes de guerre *et des définitions qu'elle propose des infractions de droit international maintenant criminalisées dans le système juridique canadien. Il s'agit d'un régime juridique nouveau, original et complexe, qui fait s'entrecroiser le droit international et le droit canadien, et qui constitue un pilier important de l'entreprise globale de lutte contre l'impunité pour les crimes internationaux les plus graves. L'auteure propose une analyse critique du jugement* Munyaneza *en ce qui concerne les éléments constitutifs du crime de génocide, des crimes contre l'humanité et des crimes de guerre. Elle offre me discussion de certains des aspects les plus difficiles des définitions de ces crimes et vise à contribuer à ce que la jurisprudence future soit cohérente avec l'esprit et la lettre de la loi et avec le droit international. Le régime des peines applicables en vertu de la* Loi *est aussi brièvement analysé.*

Searching for Accountability: The Draft UN International Convention on the Regulation, Oversight, and Monitoring of Private Military and Security Companies

INTRODUCTION

On 13 July 2009, a United Nations Draft International Convention on the Regulation, Oversight and Monitoring of Private Military and Security Companies (Draft Convention)[1] was approved for distribution and comment by the cumbersomely titled Working Group on the Use of Mercenaries As a Means of Violating Human Rights and Impeding the Exercise of the Rights of Peoples to Self-Determination (UN Working Group) of the UN Office of the High Commissioner for Human Rights.[2] The existence of the Draft Convention itself appears to effectively render moot the perennial scholarly debate about whether private military and security contractors are presumptively mercenaries and, thus, illegal as such under international law. Indeed, the emphasis in recent years has shifted in both academic and policy circles to the question of how the international community and affected states should adapt to

The author is pleased to acknowledge the support of the Canadian Red Cross, the Liu Institute for Global Issues, the Department of Foreign Affairs and International Trade (Canada), and the Department of National Defence (Canada). This article does not necessarily represent the views of any of these organizations.

1 United Nations Office of the High Commissioner for Human Rights (UNHCR), Working Group on the Use of Mercenaries As a Means of Violating Human Rights and Impeding the Exercise of the Rights of Peoples to Self-Determination (UN Working Group), *Draft International Convention on the Regulation, Oversight and Monitoring of Private Military and Security Companies* (final draft for distribution, 13 July 2009) [Draft Convention].

2 For a brief history of the UN Working Group's efforts leading to the Draft Convention, see J. Chris Haile, "New U.N. Draft International Convention on the Regulation, Oversight and Monitoring of Private Military and Security Companies" (2009) 6(9) Int'l Government Contractor 70.

the reality of private military and security activity so as to ensure that risks associated with their conduct are managed, that oversight and accountability for wrongdoing is strengthened, and that greater transparency is brought to the industry and its regulation.

Just a few years ago, the preparation of a draft convention would have been dismissed as hopelessly naive by many observers. While the ultimate adoption of an international treaty addressing this controversial phenomenon remains a distant prospect, the Draft Convention has refocused attention on the legal response to the exponential growth of private military and security activity in the last decade, implicitly rejecting the sufficiency of industry self-regulation models and reliance on general provisions in domestic and international law. While some states have adopted specific laws and regulations dealing with this matter, there are vast differences among these practices and their effectiveness as well as among the approaches that are taken by so-called contracting states, territorial states, and home states.[3]

The creation of the Draft Convention also attests to persistent concerns about the scope of activities engaged in by private military and security companies in Iraq, Afghanistan, and elsewhere, including several high-profile allegations of indiscriminate killing of civilians and the use of contractors during problematic interrogations of detainees.[4] However, at the same time, national governments and their armed forces, international organizations, private companies, non-governmental organizations, and even some individuals continue to hire private military and security companies, viewing their services as indispensable to operating in complex security environments where state security is either absent or deemed insufficient for a variety of reasons. In rare instances, states have even required companies to hire their own private security contractors as a condition of operating in their territory. In short, because private military and security companies appear to be here to stay, the international community had best learn to more effectively deal with them.

The ambitious goal set by the UN Working Group is reportedly to consult with UN member states as well as researchers, interested non-governmental groups, and individuals to prepare an official draft treaty that would be tabled at the UN Human Rights Council

---

3 These terms are defined in the Draft Convention, *supra* note 1, Article 2(n)-(p).

4 See Benjamin Perrin, "Promoting Compliance of Private Security and Military Companies with International Humanitarian Law" (2006) 88 Int'l Rev. Red Cross 613, n. 5.

as early as September 2010. This article aims to contribute to the constructive debate surrounding the substantive content of the Draft Convention itself and identify areas for Canadian law and policy development on this topic. The first part of this article briefly summarizes the major elements of the Draft Convention on a thematic basis. Without purporting to be an exhaustive review, the second part critically evaluates several key aspects of the Draft Convention and exposes potentially significant concerns about the consistency of the current version with the general principles of international law. Finally, the third part makes policy recommendations for the government of Canada in light of the Draft Convention, given that Canada is a home state, contracting state, and, less significantly, a territorial state. These recommendations are made irrespective of progress made towards the negotiation and adoption of the Draft Convention.

OVERVIEW OF THE DRAFT CONVENTION

The stated purpose of the Draft Convention is to "reaffirm and strengthen the principle of State responsibility" in relation to the conduct of private military and security companies, which it defines as follows:

(a) A *Private Military and/or Security Company (PMSC)* is a corporate entity which provides on a compensatory basis military and/or security services, including investigation services, by physical persons and/or legal entities.

(b) *Military services* refer to specialized services related to military actions including strategic planning, intelligence, investigation, land, sea or air reconnaissance, flight operations of any type, manned or unmanned, satellite surveillance, military training and logistics, and material and technical support to armed forces, and other related activities.

(c) *Security services* refer to armed guarding or protection of buildings, installations, property and people, police training, material and technical support to police forces, elaboration and implementation of informational security measures and other related activities [emphasis in original][.]

The Draft Convention proposes a hybrid approach to address the activities that may be engaged in by private military and security companies. First, the Draft Convention takes the position that certain activities can never be carried out by private military and security companies and their personnel. Second, the Draft Convention sets out a regulatory framework to oversee and monitor permissible private military and security services. After first outlining the prohibited categories of conduct, the Draft Convention's regulatory regime is described.

The Draft Convention is, at least in part, similar to "suppression conventions" that oblige states to criminalize certain conduct under their domestic law, recognizing the possibility of extraterritorial jurisdiction and committing themselves to cooperate with one another in the enforcement of such offences through provisions dealing with extradition and mutual legal assistance.[5] Conduct that private military and security companies are *prohibited* from engaging in, as specified in the Draft Convention, includes:

- fundamental state functions:[6]
  - waging war and/or combat operations
  - taking prisoners
  - law-making
  - espionage
  - intelligence and police powers, especially the powers of arrest or detention including the interrogation of detainees;
- transfer of the [State's] right to use force and/or to carry out special operations[7] and any other "illegal or arbitrary use of force" by private military and security companies;[8]
- directly participating in armed conflicts, military actions or terrorist acts, whether international or non-international in character, in the territory of any state;[9]
- a wide range of conduct related to nuclear weapons, chemical weapons, bacteriological (biological) and toxin weapons, delivery

---

5   See Draft Convention, *supra* note 1, Articles 22–23 (jurisdiction), 24 (extradition), and 25 (mutual legal assistance).

6   *Ibid.*, Article 2(k) (definitional provision); see also Article 31(5). The term "intrinsically governmental" is alternatively used in Article 8 of the Draft Convention, *supra* note 1: "States parties shall define and limit the scope of activities of private military and/or security companies and specifically prohibit functions which are intrinsically governmental, including waging war and/or combat operations, taking prisoners, espionage, intelligence and police powers, especially the powers of arrest or detention, including the interrogation of detainees." This inconsistent use of language should be remedied.

7   *Ibid.*, Article 4(6).

8   *Ibid.*, Article 1(2).

9   *Ibid.*, Article 10.

systems, components or equipment as well as weapons likely to adversely affect the environment, including depleted uranium;[10]
- using firearms, ammunition, and equipment as well as methods of conducting fighting and special operations of such character as will cause excessive damage or unnecessary suffering or that are non-selective in their application or that otherwise violate international humanitarian law;[11]
- trafficking in firearms, their parts, components, or ammunition;[12]
- actions inconsistent with the principle not to interfere with the domestic affairs of the receiving country, not to intervene in the political process or in the conflicts in its territory, as well as to take all necessary measures to avoid harm to the citizens and damage to the environmental and industrial infrastructure, and objects of historical and cultural importance;[13]
- committing any of the listed offences ("Offences"):[14]
  - war crimes
  - crimes against humanity
  - genocide;
- violations of the International Covenant on Civil and Political Rights, in particular, violations of Articles 6 (right to life), 7 (prohibition of torture), 9 (security of person, prohibition of disappearances, arbitrary detention, and so on), and 12 (prohibition of forced expulsion and displacement);[15]
- violations of the Convention against Torture and Other Cruel, Inhuman or Degrading Treatment or Punishment;[16]
- violations of the International Convention for the Protection of All Persons from Enforced Disappearance;[17]

---

[10] *Ibid.*, Article 11(1)-(2).

[11] *Ibid.*, Article 11(3).

[12] *Ibid.*, Article 12(1).

[13] *Ibid.*, Article 18(4).

[14] *Ibid.*, Articles 22 and 28.

[15] International Covenant on Civil and Political Rights, 19 December 1966, 999 U.N.T.S. 171, Can. T.S. 1976 No. 4, 6 I.L.M. 368 (entered into force 23 March 1976).

[16] Convention against Torture and Other Cruel, Inhuman or Degrading Treatment or Punishment, 10 December 1984, 1465 U.N.T.S. 85, 23 I.L.M. 1027, 26 (entered into force 26 June 1987).

[17] International Convention for the Protection of All Persons from Enforced Disappearance, UN GAOR, 61st Sess., Annex, Agenda Item 68, UN Doc. A/Res/61/177 (2007).

- grave breaches of the 1949 Geneva Conventions and 1977 Additional Protocols to the Geneva Conventions;[18]
- reckless endangerment of civilian life and right to privacy and property;
- damage to, or destruction of, cultural heritage;
- serious harm to the environment; and
- other serious offences under international human rights law.

As mentioned earlier, apart from these prohibited activities, the Draft Convention proposes that a multi-part regulatory framework apply to the permissible private military and security services as well as to the investigation of alleged prohibited activities or failures to comply with regulatory standards set out in the Draft Convention. The Draft Convention's regulatory framework requires that state parties to the Draft Convention implement a domestic licensing regime both when "exporting" such services (that is, the "home state" or state party where the company is registered or incorporated)[19] and when "importing" services (that is, the "territorial state" where the services are delivered).[20] Additionally, "contracting states" have obligations under the Draft Convention. There is some inconsistency in the use of terminology in referring to this typology of states in the Draft Convention that should be remedied.

Under the Draft Convention, private military and security companies and their personnel would be subject to several regulatory requirements imposed by states parties, such as:

---

18 Geneva Convention (I) for the Amelioration of the Condition of the Wounded and Sick in Armed Forces in the Field, 12 August 1949, 75 U.N.T.S. 31 (entered into force 21 October 1950); Geneva Convention (II) for the Amelioration of the Condition of the Wounded, Sick, and Shipwrecked Members of Armed Forces at Sea, 12 August 1949, 75 U.N.T.S. 85 (entered into force 21 October 1950); Geneva Convention (III) Relative to the Treatment of Prisoners of War, 12 August 1949, 75 U.N.T.S. 135 (entered into force 21 October 1950); Geneva Convention (IV) Relative to the Protection of Civilian Persons in Time of War, 12 August 1949, 75 U.N.T.S. 287 (entered into force 21 October 1950); Protocol Additional to the Geneva Conventions of 12 August 1949, and Relating to the Protection of Victims of International Armed Conflicts (Protocol I), 8 June 1977, 16 I.L.M. 1391 (entered into force 7 December 1978); Protocol Additional to the Geneva Conventions of 12 August 1949, and Relating to the Protection of Victims of Non-International Armed Conflicts (Protocol II), 8 June 1977, 16 I.L.M. 1442 (entered into force 7 December 1978).

19 See Draft Convention, *supra* note 1, Articles 2(h) and 2(p).

20 See *ibid.*, Articles 2(i) and 2(o).

- obtaining a licence in both their home state and each territorial state in which they deliver services;[21]
- professional training, examination, and vetting "according to the applicable international standards for military and security services and for the use of specific equipment and firearms";[22]
- abiding by rules on the use of force;[23]
- respecting the sovereignty and laws of the country in which they are providing services;[24] and
- observing international humanitarian law as well as "norms and standards set out in the core international human rights instruments."[25]

In terms of enforcing the prohibition on certain private military and security services as well as promoting compliance with the regulatory standards established under the Draft Convention, a broad obligation on states parties would require them to "take such measures as are necessary to investigate, prosecute and punish violations of the present Convention, and to ensure effective remedies to victims."[26]

More specifically, the Draft Convention provides for the possibility of concurrent sanctions for wrongdoing by the personnel of private military and security companies as well as the corporate entities themselves. Individual personnel are subject to individual criminal responsibility for the offences listed earlier as well as for "arbitrary or abusive use of force,"[27] while the company's liability extends to civil, criminal, and/or administrative sanctions not only for the offences listed earlier but also for "human rights violations or criminal incidents," including having their corporate licences revoked.[28] The Draft Convention also provides that "States [P]arties may refer cases to the International Criminal Court [ICC]."[29]

---

21 *Ibid.*, Article 17(1),(3).
22 *Ibid.*, Article 18(3).
23 *Ibid.*, Article 19(1).
24 *Ibid.*, Article 18(4).
25 *Ibid.*, Article 18(5).
26 *Ibid.*, Article 21(2).
27 *Ibid.*, Article 20(2).
28 *Ibid.*, Articles 2(q) and 13.
29 *Ibid.*, Articles 26(2).

Beyond creating a domestic regulatory network to oversee and monitor private military companies that frequently operate transnationally, the Draft Convention proposes that a new international committee be established to investigate and report on allegations of misconduct by these companies. The Committee on the Regulation, Oversight, and Monitoring of Private Military and Security Companies (International Committee) would be comprised of independent experts nominated and selected by states parties in a detailed regime set out in Part VI of the Draft Convention. The UN Working Group drew its inspiration for the functioning of the International Committee from a committee established under the Convention on the Protection of the Rights of All Migrant Workers and Members of Their Families.[30]

CRITICAL COMMENTARY ON THE DRAFT CONVENTION

Alongside the development of the Draft Convention, the Montreux Document on Pertinent International Legal Obligations and Good Practices for States Related to Operations of Private Military and Security Companies during Armed Conflict (Montreux Document), which dates from 17 September 2008, is a non-legally binding document developed with the participation of seventeen governments including home states, territorial states, contracting states, and others.[31] While the Draft Convention is arguably too bold and expansive (for the reasons described later in this commentary), the Montreux Document is arguably too modest and restrictive (as it is merely a declaration of existing international law and good practices). Consequently, the UN Working Group would be well advised to use the Montreux Document's statement on existing international legal obligations as a foundation and then build on these obligations based on the views of the states that are most likely to be affected by the Draft Convention. In this way, the Draft Convention

---

[30] Convention on the Protection of the Rights of All Migrant Workers and Members of Their Families, 18 December 1990, 30 I.L.M. 1517 (entered into force 14 March 2003).

[31] Afghanistan, Angola, Australia, Austria, Canada, China, France, Germany, Iraq, Poland, Sierra Leone, South Africa, Sweden, Switzerland, Great Britain and Northern Ireland, Ukraine, and the United States. See Montreux Document on Pertinent International Legal Obligations and Good Practices for States Related to Operations of Private Military and Security Companies during Armed Conflict, UN General Assembly Doc. A/63/467–S/2008/636 (6 October 2008) [Montreux Document].

would do what all treaties endeavour to achieve: first, to codify the existing state of customary international law and, second, to progressively develop international law through a binding legal instrument.

From a structural perspective, the Draft Convention's hybrid approach of defining prohibited conduct by private military and security companies, coupled with a regulatory framework relying on domestic and international oversight, is, in itself, an acceptable model. While there are numerous issues that are raised with the Draft Convention, I will focus on three significant threshold issues that should be addressed in a revised Draft Convention:

- activities prohibited by private military and security companies;
- state responsibility for conduct of private military and security companies; and
- the ICC's referral mechanism for violations.

THE NEED FOR CLARIFICATION OF PROHIBITED ACTIVITIES

The Draft Convention is to be commended for attempting to enumerate the categories of activities that private military and security companies are forbidden from undertaking. However, the current list of prohibited activities is ill defined, vast, and requires greater precision. To illustrate some of the complexity involved, three issues are highlighted here: detention, directly participating in armed conflicts, and use of force.

Detention

A notable distinction between the Draft Convention and the Montreux Document relates to the extent to which private military and security companies may be involved in matters dealing with prisoners or detainees. While the Draft Convention expressly prohibits contractors from taking prisoners and exercising powers of arrest or detention, including the interrogation of detainees, the Montreux Document adopts a much narrower view. To begin with, the Montreux Document includes "prisoner detention" in its list of services that private military and security companies may perform but later clarifies that such private contractors are not permitted to "exercis[e] the power of the responsible officer over prisoner of war camps or places of internment of civilians in accordance with the Geneva Conventions."[32]

---

[32] *Ibid.* at 6–7.

Direct Participation in Hostilities

Under international humanitarian law, the protected status of a civilian subsists "unless and for such time as they take a direct part in hostilities."[33] A significant consequence of the suspension or loss of protected status is that the individual may legally be subject to attack as well as prosecuted under domestic law for criminal acts that do not necessarily violate international humanitarian law. As mentioned earlier, the Draft Convention prohibits private military and security companies from "directly participating in armed conflicts, military actions or terrorist acts, whether international or non-international in character, in the territory of any State."[34] While this language is very similar to the "direct participation in hostilities" concept in international humanitarian law, the Draft Convention is not clear in importing this standard. Recently, the International Committee of the Red Cross provided greater clarity on what constitutes "direct participation in hostilities."[35] As will be seen below, the concept of "direct participation in hostilities" is a helpful one to use as the bright line between permissible self-defence and improper use of force as well.

Use of Force

An element of inconsistency in the Draft Convention sees the recognition of "police powers" as a "fundamental State function"[36] that private military and security companies are prohibited from engaging in, while states parties must nevertheless "establish rules on the use of force and firearms by the personnel of private military and security companies" that are consistent with the 1990 UN Basic

---

33 See Protocol I, *supra* note 18, Articles 51(3).

34 Draft Convention, *supra* note 1, Article 10.

35 "Reports and Documents: Interpretive Guidance on the Notion of Direct Participation in Hostilities under International Humanitarian Law Adopted by the Assembly of the International Committee of the Red Cross on 26 February 2009" (2008) 90(872) Int'l Rev. Red Cross 991.

36 Draft Convention, *supra* note 1, Article 2(k) (definitional provision); see also Article 31(5). The term "intrinsically governmental" is alternatively used in Article 8 of the Draft Convention: "States parties shall define and limit the scope of activities of private military and/or security companies and specifically prohibit functions which are intrinsically governmental, including waging war and/or combat operations, taking prisoners, espionage, intelligence and police powers, especially the powers of arrest or detention, including the interrogation of detainees." This inconsistent use of language should be remedied.

Principles on the Use of Force and Firearms by Law Enforcement Officials.[37] While it is tempting to refer to the rules on use of force in policing as an analogy to the private military and security context, there are significant limitations to this approach. Self-defence, defence of others under your charge, and defence of property are appropriate concepts that the Draft Convention references to evaluate the propriety of the use of force by private security and military companies (such concepts are familiar to domestic criminal law across major legal systems of the word and typically include requirements of restraint and proportionality — they are not unique to a law enforcement context). However, beyond these appropriate basic principles on the use of force by civilians (that is, those not directly taking part in hostilities), the Draft Convention would permit private military and security personnel to engage in armed intervention to "prevent or put a stop to the commission of a serious crime that would involve or involves a grave threat to life or of serious bodily injury."[38] While it is easy to foresee circumstances where such intervention could have a positive outcome, it is a very slippery slope to recognize this form of non-state policing activity that the Draft Convention itself has arguably prohibited elsewhere.

Under international humanitarian law, civilians have a right to defend themselves (using necessary, proportionate, and reasonable force) against criminality, banditry, and even an imminent unlawful attack by a party to the armed conflict.[39] Consequently, private security and military companies and their personnel should be prohibited from "directly participating in hostilities" as defined under international humanitarian law applicable during international and non-international armed conflict. This concept already includes notions of allowable forms of self-defence and use of force by civilians. During periods of armed conflict, this model is arguably more appropriate than making reference to policing standards. Absent the existence of an armed conflict to trigger the applicability of international humanitarian law, however, it is appropriate for the

---

[37] See *ibid.*, at 18, note 4. *UN Basic Principles on the Use of Force and Firearms by Law Enforcement Officials*, 7 September 1990, Office of the United Nations High Commissioner for Human Rights, <http://www2.ohchr.org/english/law/firearms.htm>.

[38] *Ibid.*, Articles 19(4)(d).

[39] See Benjamin Perrin, "Private Security Companies and Humanitarian Organizations: Implications for International Humanitarian Law," in Benjamin Perrin, ed., *Edges of Conflict: Non-State Actors, Contemporary Armed Conflict and International Humanitarian Law* [forthcoming].

Draft Convention to recognize analogous rights to use force in defence of person and property, so long as the force used is necessary, proportionate, and reasonable in the circumstances.

VAGUENESS AND OVER-EXTENSION OF STATE RESPONSIBILITY

The Draft Convention frames the myriad of issues raised by private military and security companies in terms of state responsibility. While this is not surprising given that the document is a proposed international treaty, the emphasis placed on state responsibility does not represent a mere codification of existing customary international law rules or principles dealing generally with state responsibility for internationally wrongful acts — despite reference in the preamble of the Draft Articles on Responsibility of States for Internationally Wrongful Acts.[40] Rather, the Draft Convention would extend state responsibility for the conduct of private military and security companies in a significant and extremely broader manner.

The Draft Convention states: "Each State *[P]arty bears responsibility* for the military and security activities of private entities registered or operating in their jurisdiction, whether or not these entities are contracted by the State."[41] This is a vast extension of the attribution of state responsibility, going well beyond existing customary international law rules and principles in a manner that is vague and undefined. This flows from the apparent conceptual approach of the drafters that the focal point of pressure to address concerns about private military and security contractors is states. As a result, it is highly unlikely that major home states, territorial states, or contracting states will be willing to accept the Draft Convention in its current form.

In contrast to the Draft Convention, the Montreux Document's focus on state responsibility is explicitly an exercise in recalling "certain existing international legal obligations of States regarding private military and security companies."[42] It is far more specific and prudent in ascribing obligations to contracting states, territorial states, and home states than the Draft Convention and is a preferable starting point for expanding on obligations that may be specific to private military and security company activity.

---

[40] Draft Articles on Responsibility of States for Internationally Wrongful Acts, 12 December 2001, International Law Commission, <http://untreaty.un.org/ilc/texts/instruments/english/draft%20articles/9_6_2001.pdf>.

[41] Draft Convention, *supra* note 1, Article 4(2) [emphasis added].

[42] Montreux Document, *supra* note 31 at 7.

In my view, expanding state responsibility in the vast and ill-defined manner proposed in the Draft Convention is not likely to gain traction nor is it desirable. Instead, the Draft Convention should first codify existing rules governing state responsibility for home states, territorial states, and contracting states, drawing inspiration from the Montreux Document. The bulk of the Draft Convention then is directed towards securing the commitment of states parties to enact effective domestic legislation and regulatory regimes to license, investigate, and sanction private military and security companies and their personnel that run afoul of the agreed criminal and regulatory standards as well as to cooperate with other states parties in ensuring there is no gap in the regulatory network.

PROBLEMATIC REFERRAL MECHANISM OF THE ICC

As noted earlier, the Draft Convention provides that "States [P]arties may refer cases to the International Criminal Court."[43] This seemingly innocuous provision presents three significant problems that make it untenable in its present form: the first is largely political, while the second and third are legal problems. First, the provision itself would be unlikely to be supported by the United States (one of the most significant, if not the most significant, home state and contracting state for private military and security companies), unless the policy of the US government towards the ICC further improves. While the United States has agreed with the UN Security Council to refer the Darfur situation in Sudan to the ICC, this was an exceptional case. The United States has consistently opposed the jurisdiction of the ICC over US nationals, and its efforts to secure bilateral legal agreements with states parties to the Rome Statute of the International Criminal Court (Rome Statute) have been well documented.[44]

Second, the Draft Convention's ICC referral provision is even more problematic in the manner that it interfaces with the Rome Statute. After much debate about when the ICC may exercise jurisdiction over a situation, the Rome Statute itself limits the initiation of investigations by the ICC prosecutor to situations referred by either a state party, the UN Security Council, or *proprio motu* (on the prosecutor's own initiative), which are all subject to review by the

---

43 Draft Convention, *supra* note 1, Article 26(2).

44 Rome Statute of the International Criminal Court, United Nations Diplomatic Conference of Plenipotentiaries on the Establishment of an International Criminal Court, UN Doc. A/CONF.183/9 (17 July 1998) [Rome Statute].

ICC Pre-Trial Chamber. The Draft Convention contemplates the referral of "cases" (that is, presumably a single serious incident or more systematic misconduct committed by private military and security company personnel), but the Rome Statute rejected such a possibility — in part, due to concerns about politicized prosecutions, targeted prosecutions of individuals, and shielding of perpetrators who are associated with the referring state.[45] Thus, instead of this scenario, "situations" are referred to the ICC prosecutor (that is, geographic areas where crimes within the jurisdiction of the ICC have allegedly taken place on a large scale, with the authority to investigate and prosecute not only non-state actors but also military leaders and senior government officials). Additionally, the Draft Convention's list of offences goes far beyond those that the ICC has jurisdiction over (that is, genocide, war crimes, and crimes against humanity). Further, the ICC does not have jurisdiction over corporate entities but only over natural persons, so it would be unavailable as a judicial body to prosecute corporate entities themselves.

Third, there is an issue with the very existence of an ICC referral mechanism appearing in a treaty separate from the Rome Statute itself. At best, the Draft Convention's ICC referral provision is redundant in cases where a state is both party to the Draft Convention and to the Rome Statute — in which case, the legal authority for the ICC prosecutor to receive a referral of a matter is already covered in the Rome Statute. At worst, where a state is party to the Draft Convention but not to the Rome Statute, the Draft Convention's ICC referral provision would improperly purport to grant a privilege to such a state under a treaty to which it is not party. This is problematic at a minimum since it detracts from the legitimacy of the ICC's jurisdiction by allowing non-state parties to use the ICC as a vehicle to prosecute others, all the while shielding their own territory and nationals to at least a large extent from the jurisdiction of the ICC. Indeed, this has been a concern expressed over the UN Security Council's referral of the Darfur case. However, the Draft Convention raises the additional problem that while the Rome Statute at least expressly provides for the use of a UN Security Council referral, it does not expressly recognize the right of non-state parties to make such a referral. Undoubtedly, part of the

45 See Rod Rastan, "The Power of the Prosecutor in Initiating Prosecutions," a paper prepared for the Symposium on the International Criminal Court (3–4 February 2007, Beijing, China) at 4, International Centre for Criminal Law Reform and Criminal Justice Policy, <http://www.icclr.law.ubc.ca/Site%20Map/ICC/PoweroftheProsecutor.pdf>.

rationale for this decision is that states wishing to unilaterally refer matters to the ICC prosecutor should also bear the burden of adopting the Rome Statute as a whole. The Rome Statute itself recognizes that, apart from a referral by the UN Security Council, a non-state party must declare that it accepts the jurisdiction of the ICC in order for the tribunal to exercise jurisdiction over the alleged crimes that were neither committed in the territory of a state party to the Rome Statute or by nationals of a state party to the Rome Statute.[46] Owing to these objections, the UN Working Group would be well advised to remove the ICC's referral provision from the Draft Convention and leave the matter of ICC jurisdiction in the four corners of the Rome Statute where it has been agreed to by state parties to that treaty.

POLICY RECOMMENDATIONS FOR THE GOVERNMENT OF CANADA

While it is nowhere near as significant as the United States in its relation to private military and security company activities, Canada is nevertheless a territorial state, home state, and contracting state for private military and security services. The federal Criminal Code addresses self-defence, defence of others, and defence of property within the ambit of Canadian criminal jurisdiction,[47] the Firearms Act regulates the possession of firearms,[48] while provincial legislation requires private security companies to be licensed.[49] However, the government of Canada has yet to adopt legislation to address its role as an exporter of private military and security services or a contractor of such services abroad. A lack of sufficient oversight of private military and security companies is a cause for concern. The circulation of the Draft Convention and Canada's participation in the preparation of the Montreux Document provides a timely impetus for domestic policy development on this topic.

The Department of Foreign Affairs and International Trade and the Department of National Defence have both employed private military and security companies in Afghanistan and elsewhere. Activities performed by such companies under contract by federal departments overseas include: training of members of the Canadian Armed Forces (performed by Blackwater Worldwide, now

---

[46] See Rome Statute, *supra* note 44, Articles 12(3).

[47] Criminal Code, R.S.C. 1985, c. C-46, ss. 34–43.

[48] Firearms Act, S.C. 1995, c. 39.

[49] See, for example, Security Services Act, S.B.C. 2007, c. 30.

Xe Services LLC), the provision of armed perimeter security for Canadian diplomatic posts in multiple countries, and even armed close protection services for senior Canadian officials visiting Afghanistan, including Prime Minister Stephen Harper. In addition, there have been high profile incidents involving private military and security companies being incorporated or having their head offices in Canada. For example, Garda International made headlines when several of its private military and security personnel were abducted in Iraq. Unfortunately, most of this information has only been publicly disclosed due to media reports and requests under the Access to Information Act. Consequently, there has been a significant lack of transparency surrounding the practices of the federal government in contracting private military and security services.

The following preliminary recommendations are made for the government of Canada:

1. The Department of Foreign Affairs and International Trade should promote further diplomatic efforts to gain the support of other states for the principles set out in the Montreux Document while advancing this document's principles as a more credible starting point for a reformulated Draft Convention.

2. The government of Canada, in consultation with the Department of National Defence, the Department of Foreign Affairs and International Trade, and the Canadian International Development Agency, should adopt a transparent and clear policy on the use of private military and security companies contracted by federal departments and agencies or paid through contracts using federal public funds. Such a policy should, at a minimum,

   a. specify which activities are prohibited from being engaged in by private military and security companies;

   b. require that private military and security companies and their personnel be vetted for criminal records, prior contractual violations, or misconduct;

   c. ensure that private military and security personnel have the same minimum level of training in international humanitarian law and international human rights law as members of the Canadian Armed Forces;

   d. ensure that when private military and security personnel are armed, they comply with international standards on the carrying and use of firearms and local laws as well as any more stringent rules agreed to by contract;

e. ensure that private military and security personnel will be subject to local jurisdiction in the country they are operating and subject to extraterritorial jurisdiction under the Crimes Against Humanity and War Crimes Act;[50]

f. fully investigate any allegations of misconduct by private military and security contractors and fully cooperate with local investigations;

g. ensure contractual clauses are in place to suspend/remove individual contractors from duty and terminate contract (with penalties to the contractor) for improper conduct; and

h. disclose basic contractual details about all private military and security companies retained by the government of Canada in the annual reports to Parliament by the applicable government department or agency (that is, name of firm, the duration of contract, the geographic scope of contract, the dollar amount of contract, the number of personnel employed, the terms of reference of activities engaged in by the private military and security company).

3. Parliament should adopt legislation to regulate companies incorporated or registered in Canada that export private military and security services abroad. As a starting point, the Montreux Document's standards for home states should be considered — both the first part on pertinent legal obligations as well as the second part on good practices of home states, including:

a. ensuring respect for international humanitarian law and international human rights law;

b. investigating and prosecuting under the War Crimes and Crimes Against Humanities Act of serious international crimes committed by private military and security companies and their personnel;

c. clearly identifying the categories of services that may or may not be lawfully exported;

d. establishing a licensing system with clear criteria for granting, suspending, and revoking such licences;

e. authorizing the Governor General in Council to promulgate a list of entities and individuals that private military and security companies licensed in Canada are prohibited from providing services to (similar to US law); and

[50] Crimes Against Humanity and War Crimes Act, S.C. 2005, c. 24.

f. establishing a monitoring and compliance regime with criminal and civil liability.

Private military and security companies are a reality of modern
day conflict and complex security environments. International efforts to enhance their accountability are to be commended, but
these are only likely to be effective if they are carefully tailored and
able to marshal the support of affected states. Domestic legislation
will likely continue to play a leading role in implementing such
measures, and, as such, it is a worthwhile exercise for countries such
as Canada to adopt such measures as part of a broader international response to the proliferation of privatized military and security
activities.

BENJAMIN PERRIN
Faculty of Law, University of British Columbia

Sommaire

À la recherche de l'imputabilité: Le projet de l'ONU de la Convention internationale relative à la réglementation, à la supervision et
au contrôle des sociétés militaires et de sécurité privées

*La prolifération des sociétés militaires et de sécurité privées a attiré l'attention
publique et scientifique au cours de la dernière décennie. Ce commentaire
passe en revue le projet de l'ONU de la* Convention internationale relative à la réglementation, à la supervision et au contrôle des sociétés
militaires et de sécurité privées *(en date du 13 juillet 2009). Il traite
de l'importance du projet de convention, puis décrit l'approche adoptée pour
la réglementation de ce sujet controversé. Plusieurs éléments problématiques
du projet de convention sont identifiés, y compris la définition des activités
interdites, la responsabilité des États pour la conduite des sociétés militaires
et de sécurité privées, et la proposition d'un mécanisme de saisie de la Cour
pénale internationale. Enfin, indépendamment du progrès dans les négociations sur le projet de convention, quelques recommandations de politiques
spécifiques sont proposées pour le gouvernement du Canada, le Canada
étant pays d'origine et État contractant de services militaires et de sécurité
privés.*

Summary

Searching for Accountability: The Draft UN International Convention on the Regulation, Oversight and Monitoring of Private Military and Security Companies

The proliferation of private military and security companies has attracted significant public and scholarly attention during the last decade. This comment examines the United Nations Draft International Convention on the Regulation, Oversight and Monitoring of Private Military and Security Companies (Draft Convention). It discusses the significance of the Draft Convention and then describes the approach taken to the regulation of this controversial topic. Several problematic elements of the Draft Convention are identified including the definition of prohibited activities, State responsibility for the conduct of private military and security companies and the proposed International Criminal Court referral mechanism. Finally, specific policy recommendations are made for the government of Canada as a home state and contracting state of private military and security services, irrespective of the progress of negotiations on the Draft Convention.

The Definition of Damage Resulting from Transboundary Movements of Living Modified Organisms in Light of the Cartagena Protocol on Biosafety

INTRODUCTION

In *Case Concerning Gabcíkovo-Nagymaros Project (Hungary/Slovakia)*, the International Court of Justice found that "in the field of environmental protection, vigilance and prevention are required on account of the often irreversible character of damage to the environment and of the limitations inherent in the very mechanism of reparation of this type of damage."[1] However, despite the fact that for centuries humanity has not taken into account the effects of its actions on the environment, more recently a growing number of new norms have been developed that do take such things into consideration, including the 2001 Cartagena Protocol on Biosafety (Cartagena Protocol).[2]

The concept of risk and, more precisely, the concept of risk that has always been related to living modified organisms (LMOs) are dealt with in two areas.[3] The first of these concepts involves

---

The author was a member of a research project entitled International Production and Trade of Genetically Modified Organisms, Reference no. LE059A05, which was financed by the Council of Education of the Regional Government for Castilla y León. He wishes to thank Thérèse Leroux, professor at the Université de Montréal, for her support and advice during his work at the Centre de Recherche en Droit Public.

[1] *Case Concerning Gabcíkovo-Nagymaros Project (Hungary/Slovakia)*, 25 September 1997, [1997] ICJ Rep. 78.

[2] Cartagena Protocol on Biosafety, 29 January 2000, 39 I.L.M. 1027 (2000), <http://www.biodiv.org/biosafety/protocol.asp>. The list of state parties are available at <http://www.cbd.int/convention/parties/list.shtml> [Cartagena Protocol].

[3] R. Falkner, "Regulating Biotech Trade: The Cartagena Protocol on Biosafety" (2000) 76(2) International Affairs 299 at 300.

preventing or avoiding the realization of damages, even in a situation of scientific uncertainty, through the adoption of *a priori* measures. The second of these areas is aimed at reparation and compensation, if this harm or damage has already actually been carried out, through *a posteriori* mechanisms.

The Cartagena Protocol aims to achieve "an adequate level of protection in the field of the safe transfer, handling and use of living modified organisms resulting from the modern biotechnology."[4] It establishes, with respect to the first type of measures, a series of previsions that regulate the advance informed agreement procedure and the transmission of information to the biosafety clearing-house. In regard to the second group of measures, the Cartagena Protocol limits itself to establishing in Article 27 a mandate for the Conference of the Parties (COP), which should undertake a process in relation "to the appropriate elaboration of international rules and procedures in the field of liability and redress."[5]

During the negotiations about liability and redress for damages that led to the adoption of Article 27, the definition of damage emerged as a critical point of discussion. It is necessary here to take into account that the definition does not only need to be linked to the objective of the Cartagena Protocol, with respect to providing sufficient protection against damage to "the conservation and the sustainable use of biological diversity," but that it also needs to be coherently linked to the Convention on Biological Diversity (CBD) as well as to numerous other national and international instruments related to the protection of biodiversity.[6]

THE CONTROVERSIAL QUESTION OF LIABILITY AND REDRESS
FOR DAMAGES RELATED TO GENETICALLY MODIFIED ORGANISMS
(GMOs)

The majority of questions in relation to the risks related to GMOs were dealt with during the negotiations of the CBD. The text that was adopted by the CBD introduced rules in which three inter-related aspects were regulated: risks, possible damages, and restate-

---

4 Cartagena Protocol, *supra* note 2, Article 1 (Objective).

5 *Ibid.*, Article 27 (Liability and Redress).

6 Convention on Biological Diversity, Nairobi, 22 May 1992, 31 I.L.M. 818 (1992), <http://www.biodiv.org/convention/articles.asp> [CBD]. Currently, 191 states are parties to the CBD following the deposit of their ratification or accession instrument. See the status of ratifications and entry into force at <http://www.cbd.int/convention/parties/list.shtml>.

ment. Following these rules, Principle 13 of the Rio Declaration on Environment and Development provided the mandate: "States shall develop national law regarding liability and compensation for the victims of pollution and other environmental damage."[7] The elaboration of these principles, however, was followed by a series of difficult negotiations, which culminated in a new position in the regulation of the subject matter that involved the adoption of a compromise mandate in the Cartagena Protocol.

THE PROVISIONS OF THE CBD

Initially, the CDB established Article 8(g), which invited the contracting parties to set up, or maintain, the necessary measures to regulate, administer, or control risks to the environment that would derive from the use and liberation of LMOs resulting from biotechnology, while also taking into account the risks for human health. This rule was completed by Article 14.2, which charged the COP with the task of carrying out an examination of the question of liability and restatement in relation to the damages caused to biological diversity beyond the borders of each state.

Finally, along with Article 14.2, the CBD also established, among other rules regarding various aspects of biotechnology, Article 19.3. This rule contained a mandate to adopt a protocol that would regulate adequate procedures in the sphere of the transfer, manipulation, and use of LMOs produced by biotechnology, which could have adverse effects for the conservation and sustainable use of biological diversity.[8] The presence of Article 19.3 clearly reflected a compromise solution in which the signatories gave themselves a delay before adopting a regulation in the future.[9] The text contains

---

[7] Rio Declaration on Environment and Development, 13 June 1992, 31 I.L.M. 874 (1992), Annex I, <http://www.unep.org/Documents.Multilingual/Default.asp?documentID=78&articleID=1163>.

[8] CBD, *supra* note 6, Article 19.3.

[9] R. Falkner, "Negotiating the Biosafety Protocol: The International Process," in Chr. Bail, R. Falkner, and H. Marquard, eds., *The Cartagena Protocol on Biosafety: Reconciling Trade and Biotechnology with Environment and Development?* (London: Royal Institute of International Affairs and Earthscan Publications, 2002), 3 at 6; G. Henne and S. Fakir, "The Regime Building of the Convention on Biological Diversity on the Road to Nairobi" (1999) 3 Max Planck Y.B. U.N. L. 315 at 327; V. Koester, "The Biodiversity Convention Negotiation Process: And Some Comments on the Outcome," in E.M. Basse et al., ed., *Environmental Law: From International to National Law* (Copenhagen: GadJura, 1997), 205 at 222. The same article is also published in (1997) 27(3) Envt'l Pol'y & L. 175 at 181.

three aspects that have clearly shaped later negotiations.[10] However, it also reflects the agreement of transboundary movement of LMOs, which had negative consequences for the conservation and sustainable use of biodiversity.[11]

NEGOTIATIONS OVER THE CARTAGENA PROTOCOL

The awareness of the need and the forms of a possible protocol led to complex negotiations that continued over the next seven years at the heart of the Open-Ended Ad Hoc Working Group on Biosafety (BSWG), which was established by the first COP to the CBD.[12] Most authors agree that the most contentious points in the discussions, which eventually led to the breakdown of negotiations, were fundamentally related to establishing the scope of the protocol, the application of the advance informed agreement procedure, the problem of basic products, and the "highly conflictive question" of the relationship between this new instrument and other international agreements.[13] Aside from these issues, however, the question of liability and restatement for damages was also a significant cause of disagreement from the outset of the negotiations.[14]

R. Pomerance, "The Biosafety Protocol: Cartagena and Beyond" (2000) 8(3) N.Y.U. Envtl. L.J. 614 at 615.

[10] A. Gupta, *Framing "Biosafety" in an International Context,* Environment and Natural Resources Program Discussion Paper no. E-99-10 (Cambridge, MA: Kennedy School of Government, Harvard University, 1999) at 4.

[11] O. Rivera-Torres, "The Biosafety Protocol and the WTO" (2003) 26(2) B.C. Int'l & Comp. L. Rev. 263 at 271.

[12] W. Damena, "Liability and Redress," in Bail, Falkner, and Marquard, *supra* note 9, 366 at 368. S. Maljean-Dubois, "Le Protocole de Carthagène sur la biosécurité et le commerce international des organismes génétiquement modifiés (OGM)" (2001) 11(2) L'Observateur des Nations Unies 41 at 45. *Liability and Redress (Article 27). Terms of Reference for the Open-Ended Ad Hoc Group of Legal and Technical Experts on Liability and Redress in the Context of the Cartagena Protocol on Biosafety: Synthesis Report of Submissions Received from Parties, Other Governments and Organizations,"* Doc. UNEP/CBD/BS/COP-MOP/1/9 (31 October 2003) at 2, para. 8.

[13] *Report of the Extraordinary Meeting of the Conference of the Parties for the Adoption of the Protocol on Biosafety to the Convention on Biological Diversity,* Doc. UNEP/CBD/ ExCOP/1/3 (20 February 2000) at 27, para. 3 [*CBD Report*].

[14] S. Burgiel, "The Cartagena Protocol on Biosafety: Taking the Steps from Negotiation to Implementation" (2002) 11(1) R.E.C.I.E.L., 53 at 54; A. Cosbey and S. Burgiel, *The Cartagena Protocol on Biosafety: An Analysis of Results,* An IISD Briefing Note (Winnipeg: International Institute for Sustainable Development, 2000)

It was in the third meeting that negotiations finally began on the issues of liability and redress.[15] The representatives recognized that these issues were of crucial importance and should be considered in the future protocol. However, one member suggested that Article 14.2 of the CBD already provided a point of departure for future work in this area.[16] Finally, the BSWG adopted a text that included Article 27, which referred to liability and redress and contained various options that dealt with a great variety of possibilities.[17]

In the sixth meeting, there was an attempt to reach a compromise position based on a document presented by the president of the working group, Kate Cook, a member of the British delegation. This position was intended to be halfway between the polarized postures that were either in favour of a system of strong liability or called for the complete suppression of the article (zero option).[18] In the end, a text was approved requesting the parties to examine the modalities for the establishment and development of norms and procedures about liability and restatement. This was to be done within a period of four years from the first Meeting of the Parties (MOP).[19]

---

at 2; Rivera-Torres, *supra* note 11 at 272; G.W. Schweizer, "The Negotiation of the Cartagena Protocol on Biosafety" (1999–2000) 6(2) Environmental Lawyer 577 at 585; P.-T. Stoll, "Controlling the Risks of Genetically Modified Organisms: The Cartagena Protocol on Biosafety and the SPS Agreement" (2000) 10 Y.B.I.E.L. 82 at 87; S. Ladika, "Informal Talks Seen to Reaffirm Commitment of All Parties to Agree on Biosafety Protocol" (1999) 22(22) International Environment Reporter 785 at 786.

[15] K. Cook, "Liability: "No Liability, No Protocol,"" in Bail, Falkner, and Marquard, *supra* note 9, 371 at 378.

[16] *Report of the Third Meeting of the Open-Ended Ad Hoc Working Group on Biosafety*, Doc. UNEP/CBD/BSWG/3/6 (17 October 1997) at 10 and 11, para. 39.

[17] Secretariat of the Convention on Biological Diversity, *The Cartagena Protocol on Biosafety: A Record of the Negotiations* (Montreal: Secretariat of the Convention on Biological Diversity, 2003) at 82; Annex I, "Consolidated Text of Draft Articles 'Biosafety Protocol' Consolidated Text," Doc. UNEP/CBD/BSWG/3/6 (17 October 1997) at 88–90.

[18] "BSWG-6 Hightlights Tuesday, 16 February 1999" (1999) 9(112) Earth Negotiations Bulletin 2; Cook, *supra* note 15 at 377.

[19] Burgiel, *supra* note 14 at 55. P. Newell and R. Mackenzie, "The 2000 Cartagena Protocol on Biosafety: Legal and Political Dimensions" (2000) 10(4) Global Environmental Change: Human and Policy Dimension 313 at 315. The different versions revised by the Open-Ended Ad Hoc Working Group on Biosafety (BSWG) of the draft project are the following documents: Doc. UNEP/CBD/BSWG/6/L.2 and Doc. UNEP/CBD/BSWG/6/L.2/Rev.1. The final draft of the project is

This text proved to be a great success and was to remain unaltered during the next informal consultations that took place in Vienna and Montreal in September 1999 and January 2000 respectively. In the course of the extraordinary meeting of the COP, all remaining questions were dealt with, and all significant disagreements were overcome. Finally, on 29 January 2000, the text of the Cartagena Protocol was adopted.[20]

THE DEVELOPMENT OF ARTICLE 27 OF THE CARTAGENA PROTOCOL

The first COP to the CBD serving as the MOP to the Cartagena Protocol established, through Decision no. BS-I/8, an Open-Ended Ad Hoc Working Group of Legal and Technical Experts on Liability and Redress (WG-L&R), as laid out in Article 27 of the Cartagena Protocol.[21] During its third meeting, the WG-L&R focused on the channelling and limitation of liability, the canalization and limitation of liability, the mechanism of financial security, the settlement of claims, standing to bring claims, the complementary capacity-building measures, and the choice of the instrument.[22] At the end of this third meeting, the WG-L&R presented a blueprint of a decision of the COP-MOP on the international rules procedures in the field of liability and redress for damage resulting from the transboundary movement of LMOs.[23]

---

published in *Report of the Sixth Meeting of the Open-Ended Ad Hoc Working Group on Biosafety,* Doc. UNEP/ExCOP/1/2 (15 February 1999) at 32, Article 25.

20 *CBD Report, supra* note 13 at 33, para. 92; Falkner, *supra* note 9 at 22. Schweizer, *supra* note 14 at 580; S. Zarrilli, *International Trade in Genetically Modified Organisms and Multilateral Negotiations: A New Dilemma for Developing Countries* (Geneva: United Nations Conference on Trade and Development, 2000), Doc. UNCTAD/DITC/TNCD/1 (5 July 2000) at 19, para. 64, <http://www.unctad.org/en/docs/poditctncd1.en.pdf>.

21 See *Report of the First Meeting of the Conference of the Parties serving as the Meeting of the Parties to the Protocol on Biosafety,* Doc. UNEP/CBD/COP-MOP/1/15 (14 April 2004) at 102–4.

22 *Report of the Open-ended Ad Hoc Working Group of Legal and Technical Experts on Liability and Redress in the Context of the Cartagena Protocol on Biosafety on the Work of Its Third Meeting,* Doc. UNEP/CBD/BS/WG-L&R/3/3 (15 March 2007) at 6, paras. 34 and 36 [*OEWG Liability Report*].

23 *OEWG Liability Report, supra* note 22 at 14, Annex I, "Blueprint for a COP/MOP Decision on International Rules and Procedures in the Field of Liability and Redress for Damage Resulting from Transboundary Movements of Living Modified Organisms."

The WG-L&R further summarized the operational text and, with the aim of facilitating the work of the group, created two subgroups that were to work on the texts. The first of these subgroups focused on damages.[24] The second subgroup worked on the administrative focus and civil liability.[25] During the fifth meeting of the WG-L&R, more detailed work was completed in this area and the text was reduced by a considerable extent.[26] The most significant development during this session was the pledge by the companies supplying biotechnological agricultural products to assume a contractual obligation to repair any damages to the biological biodiversity that were caused by their products.[27] However, as had been the norm in previous negotiations about the protocol, it was necessary to continue work through a further meeting of the Friends of the Co-Chairs group in which the proposed norms and procedures could be negotiated in more detail.[28] The meeting was held in Bonn before the fourth meeting of the COP-MOP, and it succeeded in creating a document with a revised structure and with significant changes in different sections, including the section related to damages.[29]

---

[24] *Report of the Open-Ended Ad Hoc Working Group of Legal and Technical Expert on Liability and Redress in the Context of the Cartagena Protocol on Biosafety on the Work of Its Fourth Meeting*, Doc. UNEP/CBD/BS/WG-L&R/4/3 (13 November 2007) at 4, para. 18.

[25] *Ibid.*

[26] *Report of the Open-Ended Ad Hoc Working Group of Legal and Technical Expert on Liability and Redress in the Context of the Cartagena Protocol on Biosafety on the Work of Its Fifth Meeting*, Doc. UNEP/CBD/BS/WG-L&R/5/3 (25 March 2008) at 9, para. 56.

[27] This offer was made by Thomas Carrato of the Global Industry Coalition, on behalf of BASF, Bayer CropScience, Dow AgroSciences, DuPont/Pioneer, Monsanto and Syngenta. *Ibid.* at 7, para. 36.

[28] *Ibid.* at 13, para. 88. *Final Report of the Open-Ended Ad Hoc Working Group of Legal and Technical Experts on Liability and Redress in the Context of the Cartagena Protocol on Biosafety, Addendum on Proposed Operational Texts on Approaches and Options Identified Pertaining to Liability and Redress in the Context of Article 27 of the Biosafety Protocol: Outcomes of the Meeting of the Friends of the Co-Chairs, Bonn, 7–10 May 2008*, Doc. UNEP/CBD/BS/COP-MOP/4/11/Add.1 (11 May 2008) at 1, para. 1 [*Addendum on Operational Texts*].

[29] *Addendum on Operational Texts, supra* note 28 at 1, para. 2. *Report of the Fourth Meeting of the Conference of the Parties to the Convention on Biological Diversity serving as the Meeting of the Parties to the Cartagena Protocol on Biosafety*, Doc. UNEP/CBD/BS/COP-MOP/4/18 (10 June 2008) at 23 and 24, para. 154 [*Report of the Fourth Meeting*].

Finally, the fourth meeting of the COP-MOP, which was held during May 2008, approved Decision no. IV/12 in which a Group of the Friends of the Co-Chairs Concerning Liability and Redress in the Context of the Cartagena Protocol on Biosafety (GF-L&R) was established. This group had the mandate of finalizing the negotiation of the norms and procedures in this area in a meeting, which was held in February 2009.[30]

THE DEFINITION OF DAMAGE IN THE CONTEXT OF ARTICLE 27
OF THE CARTAGENA PROTOCOL

The development of rules related to liability and restatement for damages in accordance with the Cartagena Protocol requires a clear definition of "damage."[31] Unlike other international texts that deal extensively with damages, Article 27 only mentions the source of damage, referring to "damage resulting from transboundary movements" of LMOs.[32] As such, the concept and extent of damage needs to be defined in the context of the entire Cartagena Protocol.[33]

Closely linked to the definition of damage is a series of other questions such as whether the extent of damage as understood in Article 27 covers damage to the environment, to people, or to goods since the text of the Cartagena Protocol only makes reference to "adverse effects on the conservation and sustainable use of biological diversity."[34] Furthermore, it does not clarify what should be understood by "conservation and sustainable use." The question arises as to whether this reference to "damage to the conservation and sustainable use of biological diversity" is different from "damage to biological diversity" as contained in paragraph 3 of the preamble, and, furthermore, whether "taking into account risks to human health" implies the inclusion of personal damages such as

---

[30] *Report of the Fourth Meeting, supra* note 29 at 82, para. 1, Decision no. BS-IV/12 on Liability and Redress under the Cartagena Protocol on Biosafety.

[31] E. Duall, "A Liability and Redress Regime for Genetically Modified Organisms under the Cartagena Protocol" (2004) 36(1) Geo. Wash. Int"l L. Rev. 173 at 193.

[32] *Identification of Issues Relating to Liability and Redress for Damage Resulting from the Transboundary Movement of Living Modified Organisms,* Doc. UNEP/CBD/WS-L&R/1/2 (4 November 2002) at 5, para. 23 [*Identification of Issues*].

[33] *Ibid.* at 6, para. 6. Duall, *supra* note 31 at 194.

[34] See Cartagena Protocol, *supra* note 2 at Articles 1, 2.4, 4, 7.4, 10.6, 11.8, 12.1, 15.1, 16.2, 16.5(a), 17.1, 17.3(c), 17.4, 18.1, 21.6(c), 23.1(a), 26.1, and Annex III on Risk Assessment.

the costs of medical treatment in the concept of damage as recounted in the rules of the Cartagena Protocol. Similarly, it is necessary to clarify whether the reference in Article 26 to "socio-economic considerations arising from the impact of living modified organisms on the conservation and use of biological diversity" allows us to interpret these types of considerations within the notion of damage.[35]

Aside from the absence of a definition, there is also a lack of sufficient precedents that could provide an idea of the nature and the extent of "transgenic damages."[36] Consequently, in order to establish a system of liability and compensation for damages derived from the transboundary movement of LMOs, it is necessary to demarcate aspects such as the nature and extent of the uncertain risks observed during an ample period of time in order to arrive at an understanding of damage.

THE CONCEPT OF DAMAGE IN OTHER INTERNATIONAL LAW
PROCESSES

The Intergovernmental Committee for the Cartagena Protocol on Biosafety (ICCP) took on the study of the international norms and procedures in accordance with the mandate contained in Article 27 of the Cartagena Protocol.[37] The study focused on the current multilateral treaties relating to liability and compensation for damages. The texts are very limited in nature and concentrate on damage to health and to property in transboundary contexts. They refer to nuclear damage, hydrocarbon contamination, and the transport of dangerous goods and substances and objects from space.[38] They

---

[35] *Identification of Issues, supra* note 32 at 6, para. 30.

[36] *Ibid.* at 3, para. 14. C. Kummer Peiry, "International Civil Liability for Environmental Damage: Lessons Learned," in C. Kummer Peiry et al., *Liability and Redress and Living Modified Organisms: A Contribution to the Article 27 Process under the Cartagena Protocol on Biosafety* (Brussels: CropLife International, 2004), 11 at 19, <http://www.ecoconsult.ch/uploads/1144-Croplife_Handbook.pdf>.

[37] *Liability and Redress for Damage Resulting from the Transboundary Movements of Living Modified Organisms. Review of Existing Relevant Instruments and Identification of Elements*, Doc. UNEP/CBD/ICCP/2/3 (31 July 2001) at 1 [*Liability and Redress for Damage*]. Kummer Peiry, *supra* note 36 at 11.

[38] *Determination of Damage to the Conservation and Sustainable Use of Biological Diversity, Including Case-Studies*, Doc. UNEP/CBD/BS/WG-L&R/2/INF/3 (1 February 2006), Annex: Definitions of "Damage" or Related Concept from Other International Agreements at 16–20.

take into account indemnification for loss of life or personal injury, damage to property, and damage or harm to the environment. In this last case, liability for transboundary environmental damage has also been considered and has been introduced by amendments into the original texts.[39]

While the texts dealing with nuclear damage and with damages resulting from hydrocarbon contamination have been very effective since the 1960s and 1970s, none of the texts dealing with other dangerous substances have entered into effect as they have not received the necessary number of ratifications and have, as such, been considered "dead letters."[40]

With respect to the first group mentioned earlier — nuclear damage — the Protocol to Amend the Vienna Convention on Civil Liability for Nuclear Damage should be mentioned.[41] It expanded the concept of "nuclear damage" contained in Article 2 of the 1963 Vienna Convention on Civil Liability for Nuclear Damage to cover environmental damage and economic loss caused by nuclear damage, which includes the following: economic loss related to personal damages or damage to property; the cost of restoring a damaged area of the environment; the loss of income due to an economic interest in any use of the environment resulting from significant damage to the environment; and the cost of preventative measures.[42] With respect to liability and redress for hydrocarbon contamination, the Protocol to Amend the International Convention on Civil Liability for Oil Pollution Damage incorporates into the 1969 International Convention on Civil Liability for Oil Pollution Damage damage to the environment and loss of profit stemming from damages but limited "to costs of reasonable measures of reinstatement actually undertaken or to be undertaken."[43]

---

[39] *Liability and Redress for Damages, supra* note 37 at 4, para. 12.

[40] Kummer Peiry et al., *supra* note 36 at 11.

[41] Protocol to Amend the Vienna Convention on Civil Liability for Nuclear Damage, Vienna, 12 September 1997, 36 I.L.M. 1462 (1997). The protocol to amend the Vienna Convention was signed by fifteen states and was ratified by five of these states, thereby reaching the minimum number required by Article 21 in order to come into force. This occurred on 4 October 2003. To consult the ratification process, see <http://www.iaea.org/Publications/Documents/Conventions/protamend_status.pdf>.

[42] Vienna Convention on Civil Liability for Nuclear Damage, 2 I.L.M. 727 (1963).

[43] Protocol to Amend the International Convention on Civil Liability for Oil Pollution Damage, London, 27 November 1992, UN Doc. LEG/CONF.9/15 (2 December 1992). The protocol has been in force since 30 May 1996 and has

The new generation of rules relating to liability for the environment emerged at the end of the 1980s and during the 1990s. These agreements were the subject of complex negotiations before finally being accepted, and none have yet to come into force.[44] In regard to the relative liability for the transport of dangerous goods and substances, the Convention on Civil Liability for Damage Caused during the Carriage of Dangerous Goods by Road, Rail and Inland Navigation Vessels includes among "damages" the following in Article 1.10: loss of human life or injury; the loss of, or damage to, property; damage to the environment through contamination; and the cost of preventative measures. The redress for the damages caused to the environment is limited "to costs of reasonable measures of reinstatement actually undertaken or to be undertaken."[45]

The Convention on Civil Liability for Damage Resulting from Activities Dangerous to the Environment is the treaty that provides the most developed and complete coverage in regard to liability and redress for damage to the environment.[46] In Article 2.7, damage is defined as that which is done to people and property, losses or damages due to harm done to the environment, and the cost of preventative measures. Elsewhere, the understanding of the term "environment" is now extended to include "natural resources both abiotic and biotic, such as air, water, soil, fauna and flora and the interaction between the same factors; property which forms part of the cultural heritage; and the characteristic aspects of the landscape."[47]

---

been signed up to a significant number of states. See the list of parties at <http://www.imo.org/Conventions/mainframe.asp?topic_id=256&doc_id=660>. International Convention on Civil Liability for Oil Pollution Damage, 29 November 1969, 9 I.L.M. 46 (1970).

[44] Kummer Peiry et al., *supra* note 36 at 15.

[45] Convention on Civil Liability for Damage Caused during the Carriage of Dangerous Goods by Road, Rail and Inland Navigation Vessels, Geneva, 10 October 1989, <http://www.unece.org/trans/danger/publi/crtd/crtd_e.html> at Article 1.10.c. This convention has only been signed by two states: Germany and Morocco, and has only been ratified by one non-signatory state: Liberia. Since the minimum required by Article 23 was not reached, it is not yet in force.

[46] Convention on Civil Liability for Damage Resulting from Activities Dangerous to the Environment, Lugano, 21 June 1993, 32 I.L.M. 1228 (1993) [Lugano Convention]. Currently, this convention is signed by only nine states: Cyprus, Finland, Greece, Iceland, Italy, Liechtenstein, Luxembourg, Netherlands, and Portugal, and it has only been ratified by Portugal. It is currently not in force.

[47] Lugano Convention, *supra* note 46, Article 2.10.

The International Convention on Liability and Compensation for Damage in Connection with the Carriage of Hazardous and Noxious Substances by Sea states in Article 1.6 that damages are the loss of life or personal injury, the loss of property or damage to it, and losses or damages due to contamination of the environment and costs of preventative measures.[48] Compensation is said to be limited "to costs of reasonable measures of reinstatement actually undertaken or to be undertaken."

As for the Basel Protocol on Liability and Compensation for Damage Resulting from Transboundary Movements of Hazardous Wastes and Their Disposal (Basel Protocol), this text defines "damage" in its second article as: the loss of life or personal injury; the loss of, or damage to, property; the loss of income directly as a result from an economic interest in any use of the environment; the costs of repairing damage to the environment — these being limited to the costs of the measures that were actually used — and, finally, the cost of preventative measures.[49] The measures of reinstatement of an impaired environment are defined as the reasonable measures to assess, reinstate, or restore damaged or destroyed components of the environment. However, the Basel Protocol goes further and, in Article 3, extends the application of the term "to damage due to an incident occurring during a transboundary movement of hazardous wastes and other wastes and their disposal, including illegal traffic, from the point where the wastes are loaded on the means of transport in an area under the national jurisdiction of a State of export." The Basel Protocol was adopted after ten years of negotiations and has many similarities to the Cartagena Protocol since it was not possible to include rules of liability in the Basel Protocol, and the parties were requested to consider this question at a later date.[50]

---

48 International Convention on Liability and Compensation for Damage in Connection with the Carriage of Hazardous and Noxious Substances by Sea, London, 3 May 1996, 35 I.L.M. 1406 (1996).

49 Basel Protocol on Liability and Compensation for Damage Resulting from Transboundary Movements of Hazardous Wastes and Their Disposal, Basel, 10 December 1999, <http://www.basel.int/meetings/cop/cop5/docs/prot-e.pdf>. The Basel Protocol was signed up to by thirteen states and was ratified by nine states, thereby reaching the minimum number of twenty required by Article 29.1 in order to come into force. See the status of ratifications at <http://www.basel.int/ratif/protocol.htm>.

50 P. Lawrence, "Negotiation of a Protocol on Liability and Compensation for Damage Resulting from Transboundary Movements of Hazardous Wastes and Their Disposal" (1998) 7(3) R.E.C.I.E.L. 249 at 249.

Finally, in the context of liability for space objects, the Convention on Liability for Damage Caused by Space Objects only considers liability for damages caused by space objects and does not include damage to the environment in accordance with the definition of damage in its Article 1 (a).[51]

THE IDEA OF DAMAGE TO BIODIVERSITY

Considering the remit of the Cartagena Protocol and in accordance with Article 27, it is now useful to focus on the risks of causing damage to biological diversity.[52] The environmental impact of GMOs can be studied using a framework based on the causes of change in ecosystems and in biodiversity — taking into account that GMOs constitute one of the main causes of the extinction of organisms.[53] These causes are applicable to GMOs in accordance with the idea of loss of biodiversity contained in Decision no. VII/30 of the COP to the CDB. These include habitat change caused by variation in the use of the terrain, in the use of rivers or water extracted from rivers, or contamination and the introduction of invasive alien species.[54]

Along with the changes of habitats, contamination has been highlighted as one of the main causes for the loss of biological diversity. This is due to the use of herbicides, pesticides, and fertilizers that have caused great harm in many parts of the world.[55] One of

---

[51] Convention on International Liability for Damage Caused by Space Objects, London, Moscow, Washington, 29 March 1972, (1972) 66 A.J.I.L. 702. This convention was ratified by ninety signatory states and was also signed by another twenty-three states that have not yet ratified. However, this convention is the most accepted instrument in the field of responsibility.

[52] Cartagena Protocol, *supra* note 2, Article 6.1 excludes from the application of procedures of the advance informed agreement for "the transboundary movement of living modified organisms destined for contained use undertaken in accordance with the standards of the Party of import."

[53] P. Raven, "The Epic of Evolution and the Problem of Biodiversity Loss," in Ch. McManis, ed., *Biodiversity and the Law: Intellectual Property, Biotechnology and Traditional Knowledge* (London: Earthscan, 2007), 27 at 30.

[54] Decision no. VII/30 on a Strategic Plan: Future Evaluation of Progress, *Report of the Seventh Meeting of the Conference of the Parties to the Convention on Biological Diversity*, Doc. UNEP/CBD/COP/7/21 (13 April 2004) at 379. Millennium Ecosystem Assessment, *Ecosystems and Human Well-Being: Biodiversity Synthesis* (Washington, DC: World Resources Institute, 2005) at 8, <http://www.millenniumassessment.org/en/Synthesis.aspx>. J. Chen, "Across the Apocalypse on Horseback: Biodiversity Loss and the Law," in McManis *supra* note 53, 42 at 43.

[55] Millennium Ecosystem Assessment, *supra* note 54 at 8.

the great indirect benefits of GMOs is the reduction of pesticides. These results, however, have not been the same for all of the GMO crops due to the fact that some require additional pesticides as they are not resistant to all species of weeds. Furthermore, some species have developed particularly strong resistance and have turned into literal "superweeds," which has led to the necessity of applying additional herbicides and pesticides.[56] Nevertheless, it is important to point out that this applies to both traditional and GMO crops.

Finally, one of the biggest risks facing biodiversity is "invasive alien species." These are considered to be one of the greatest dangers for the extinction of species and for biodiversity.[57] These effects would also lead to changes in the environment caused when a new organism replaces another species in the area.[58] GMOs should not be considered "invasive," yet changes can occur in the network of ecological relationships that can cause an organism to become invasive and then to damage the plants in the area of analysis.[59]

Various criteria have been proposed for measuring the invasiveness of GMOs, including the changes in the adaptation characteristics, the adverse effects of the flow or transfer of genes, the adverse effects for non-objective organisms, genotypic or phenotypic instability, and, finally, their capacity to combine with viruses.[60] Various studies, however, have shown that GMO crops do not have the capacity to invade habitats that are superior to that which has the non-modified version of these crops.[61] This research indicates that the agricultural crops do not survive for much time outside of their cultivation. To conclude, it is necessary to be mindful that the

---

56 International Union for the Conservation of Nature (IUCN), *Current Knowledge of the Impacts of Genetically Modified Organisms on Biodiversity and Human Health: An Information Paper* (Gland, Switzerland: IUCN, August 2007) at 26, <http://cmsdata.iucn.org/downloads/ip_gmo_09_2007_1_.pdf>.

57 Chen, *supra* note 54 at 45. IUCN, *Guidelines for the Prevention of Biodiversity Loss Caused by Alien Invasive Species as Approved by 51st Meeting of Council, February 2000*, Information Paper (May 2000) at 2, <http://www.issg.org/infpaper_invasive.pdf>.

58 This is the concept of damage that was put forward in the submission from the government of Norway. *Liability and Redress (Article 27)*, Doc. UNEP/CBD/BS/COP-MOP/1/INF/5 (8 December 2003) at 21.

59 L.L. Wolfenbarger and P.R. Phifer, "The Ecological Risks and Benefits of Genetically Engineered Plants" (15 December 2000) 290 Science 2088 at 2088.

60 IUCN, *supra* note 56 at 27.

61 *Ibid.* at 27.

potential risks and benefits of GMO plants are inevitably quite uncertain and depend a great deal upon the complexity of the ecological systems that can vary in space and time and according to the modification of the crop.[62] An objective evaluation of the risks is particularly difficult due to the fact that natural and human modified systems are very complex and are destined to remain unclear until extensive tests about their introduction have been carried out.[63]

The WG-L&R examined the question of damage to biological diversity, and a series of conclusions were reached, which can be summarized in the following points:

- that a mere change in the state of biological diversity might not necessarily constitute damage — to constitute damage the change must result in an adverse or negative effect that should be measurable;
- that information on baseline conditions for determining and measuring change is often not available, and, in its absence, other methodologies for measuring change would be needed; and
- that some environmental changes do not manifest themselves immediately so that the issue of linking actors and long-term environmental effects also arises.[64]

Evidently, the risks involved in the introduction of GMOs into a new ecosystem need to be examined in a case-by-case approach, along with appropriate risk management measures such as the implementation of the precautionary approach and of suitable mechanisms such as the pest risk assessment introduced by the International Plant Protection Convention.[65]

---

[62] Wolfenbarger and Phifer, *supra* note 59 at 2090.

[63] IUCN, *supra* note 56 at 31.

[64] *Report of the Group of Legal and Technical Experts on Liability and Redress in the Context of para. 2 of Article 14 of the Convention on Biological Diversity*, Doc. UNEP/CBD/COP/8/27/Add.3 (18 October 2005) at para. 19.

[65] International Plant Protection Convention, Rome, 6 December 1951, <http://www.ippc.int/ippctypo3_test/index.php?id=1110485&L=0>. IUCN, *supra* note 56 at 31. See the criteria outlined in "Pest Risk Analysis for Quarantine Pests Including Analysis of Environmental Risks and Living Modified Organisms: ISPM No. 11," in *International Standards for Phytosanitary Measures 1 to 31* (Rome: Food and Agriculture Organization, 2008), Annex 3: Determining the Potential for a Living Modified Organism to Be a Pest, 137, particularly at 159 and 160,

ELEMENTS FOR A DEFINITION OF DAMAGE RESULTING FROM
TRANSBOUNDARY MOVEMENTS OF LMOs

The different areas of risk that have been referred to earlier, taking
into account the concepts of damage proposed in the international
agreements, have been systemized in a large number of operational
texts based on the definition of damage presented in the headquarters of the WG-L&R. These texts were summarized by the WG-L&R,
listing the following components in the definition of damage:

- damage to conservation and sustainable use of biological diversity or its components;
- damage to the environment;
- damage to human health;
- socio-economic damage, especially in relation to indigenous and
  local communities;
- traditional damage; and
- costs of response measures.[66]

Following this summary in the final report of the WG-L&R, these
categories were grouped into two sections in the proposed operational texts on approaches and identified options. The first of these
was related to the definition of damage in the context of an administrative approach to the liability of states in the context of the
Cartagena Protocol and the second was the concept of damage in
the context of the demand for civil liability under the protection
of national rights.[67]

<https://www.ippc.int/servlet/BinaryDownloaderServlet/34163_ISPM_11_E.
pdf?filename=1146658377367_ISPM11.pdf&refID=34163>. The International
Plant Protection Convention entered into force on 3 April 1952. At a later date,
two texts, revised in 1979 and 1997, were signed. All the authentic texts are
available online at <https://www.ippc.int/servlet/CDSServlet?status=NDoxMzI
5MiY2PWVuJjMzPSommMzc9a29z>.

66 *Synthesis of Proposed Texts and Views on Approaches, Options and Issues Identified Per-
taining to Liability and Redress in the Context of Article 27 of the Biosafety Protoco*, Note
by the Co-Chairs, Doc. UNEP/CBD/BS/WG-L&R/2/2 (19 January 2006) at 14
[*Synthesis of Proposed Texts*]. *Synthesis of Proposed Operational Texts on Approaches,
Options and Issues Identified (Sections I to III) Pertaining to Liability and Redress in the
Context of Article 27 of the Biosafety Protocol*, Doc. UNEP/CBD/BS/WG-L&R/3/2/
Add.1 (20 December 2006) at 14 [*Synthesis of Proposed Operational Texts*]. OEWG
Liability Report, *supra* note 22 at 29.

67 See *Final Report of the Open-Ended Ad Hoc Working Group of Legal and Technical
Experts on Liability and Redress in the Context of the Cartagena Protocol on Biosafety,*

Since they were required to do so by Decision no. BS-IV/12 of the COP-MOP, the distinction has been discussed and developed by the GF-L&R in two draft documents.[68] The first of these documents was the Supplementary Protocol on Damage to the Conservation and Sustainable Use of Biological Diversity Resulting from Transboundary Movements of Living Modified Organisms to the Cartagena Protocol on Biosafety, and the second was entitled Guidelines on Civil Liability and Redress in the Field of Damage Resulting from Transboundary Movements of Living Modified Organisms.[69]

DEFINITION OF DAMAGE FOR AN ADMINISTRATIVE APPROACH:
THE DAMAGE TO CONSERVATION AND SUSTAINABLE USE OF
BIOLOGICAL DIVERSITY

As Argentina, the United States, and the European Union (EU) have clearly stated, since Article 27 of the Cartagena Protocol did not clearly contain a definition of damages, it is necessary to refer to Article 1 (Objective) and Article 4 (Scope) of the protocol, which both refer to "adverse effects on the conservation and sustainable use of biological diversity, taking also into account risks to human health."[70] In this sense, the damage, which is referred to in Article 27, should be understood as damage to the conservation and sustainable use of biological diversity — there being an important distinction between the former and the latter.[71] Indeed, as is already done in some of the operational texts, the definition should be reduced simply to the impact on biological diversity.[72]

Damage to the conservation of biological diversity should be approached by taking into account the following three aspects: first, the definition of biodiversity proposed by the CDB; second, the concept of loss of biodiversity according to the definition stated in

---

Doc. UNEP/CBD/BS/COP-MOP/4/11 (7 April 2008) at 8 [*Final Report of the OEWG*].

[68] *Report of the Fourth Meeting, supra* note 29 at 84.

[69] *Report of the Group of the Friends of the Co-chairs on Liability and Redress in the Context of the Cartagena Protocol on Biosafety on the Work of Its First Meeting*, Doc. UNEP/CBD/BS/GF-L&R/1/4 (27 February 2009) at 5, Annex I and II [*Report of the Group of the Friends*]

[70] *Synthesis of Proposed Operational Texts, supra* note 66 at 15 and 16.

[71] *Ibid.* at 16. UNEP/CBD/BS/WG-L&R/3/2/Add.1, n. 65 above, at 15, Operational text 2; and at 17, Operational text 7.

[72] *Synthesis of Proposed Operational Texts, supra* note 66 at 17, Operational Text no. 8.

Decision no. VII/30,[73] which is "reducing the rate of loss of the components of biodiversity, including: (i) biomes, habitats and ecosystems; (ii) species and populations; and (iii) genetic diversity"; and, third, the idea of the costs of the reinstatement measures.[74]

When considering damage to the sustainable use of biological diversity, it is necessary to estimate that there are many different forms of sustainable use of biological diversity, and, thus, the term needs to cover agriculture, horticulture, silviculture, livestock, hunting, gathering, and recreational exploitation.[75] Considering the proposal made by the United States, it was stated that the damage to biological diversity, in its conservation as well as its sustainable use, should be identified by the change in a variable. That is to say, the change should be measurable or observable, and the change should be negative.[76]

The possible integration of damage to the environment in this concept of damage was taken up in some of the proposals.[77] However, the reference was contested by some governments who understood that there was no reference to this in the Cartagena Protocol. According to Argentina, the protocol made mention of the conservation and sustainable use of biological diversity but did not mention the "environment" in general terms.[78] Similarly, the EU and the Global Industry Coalition suggested that there was a superimposition with the idea of conservation and sustainable use of biological diversity.[79]

Subsequently, the WG-L&R moved to define damage, from an administrative perspective, as "damage to the conservation and the sustainable use of biological diversity, taking also into account risks to human health, resulting from transboundary movement of LMOs."[80] It also proposed that both damage to the conservation and to the sustainable use of biological diversity implies, in terms

---

[73] See note 56 in this article and adjacent text.

[74] *Synthesis of Proposed Operational Texts, supra* note 66 at 16.

[75] *Ibid.* at 16.

[76] *Ibid.* at 17. *Addendum on Operational Texts, supra* note 28 at 4.

[77] *Synthesis of Proposed Operational Texts, supra* note 66 at 15, Operational Text no. 1; and at 18, Operational Text no. 9.

[78] *Synthesis of Proposed Operational Texts, supra* note 66 at 19.

[79] *Ibid.* at 19.

[80] *Final Report of the OEWG, supra* note 67 at 8. *Addendum on Operational Texts, supra* note 28 at 3 and 4.

of the text, an adverse or negative effect on biological diversity. In the case of damage to conservation, it is necessary to verify that it is measurable or otherwise observable, and that it is significant. In the case of damage to sustainable use, it is necessary to verify that there has been a loss of income or that there has been a consequential loss to a state, including loss of income.[81] From this affirmation we can deduce that, according to the WG-L&R, the essential difference between damage to conservation and damage to sustainable use is the verification of indirect damages to a state, including the loss of income.

Ultimately, this interpretation was omitted in Article 2(d) of the Supplementary Protocol on Damage to the Conservation and Sustainable Use of Biological Diversity Resulting from Transboundary Movements of Living Modified Organisms to the Cartagena Protocol on Biosafety, which was proposed by the GF-L&R. It concludes by defining damage in the following terms:

(d) Damage to the conservation and sustainable use of biological diversity [in relation to the administrative approach as contained in Articles xx — xx [sic] means an adverse effect on biological diversity that:

   (i) Is measurable or otherwise observable taking account, wherever available, scientifically established baselines recognized by a competent national authority that takes into account any other human induced variation and natural variation; and

   (ii) Is significant as set out in paragraph 3 below [this definition of damage shall be without prejudice to the domestic law of parties in the field of civil liability].[82]

DEFINITION OF DAMAGE FOR A CIVIL LIABILITY: DAMAGE TO
HUMAN HEALTH, SOCIO-ECONOMIC DAMAGE, AND TRADITIONAL
DAMAGE

In the report of the WG-L&R, various aspects appeared linked to the idea of damage in accordance with the Cartagena Protocol. These aspects included damage to human health, socio-economic damage, traditional damage, and, finally, as we have already mentioned, the cost of the response measures. Damages to human health include aspects such as the loss of life or personal damages, the loss of income, measures of public health, and the deterioration of

---

[81] *Addendum on Operational Texts, supra* note 28 at 3.

[82] *Report of the Group of the Friends, supra* note 69 at 9.

health.[83] Some argued that this provision would be in keeping with Article 4 of the protocol, which perceived the need for "taking also into account risks to human health." For others, this was to be a rule that would come into play when it was necessary to evaluate the risks, keeping in mind this category of damages.[84] Other sectors, such as the EU, understood that this type of damage would overlap with aspects that fell within "traditional damage" and considered that these, or some of them, should be dealt with at a national level.[85]

Similarly, the definition of damage should take into account damages of a socio-economic nature, which would cover the loss of income, the loss of cultural, social, or spiritual values, the loss of safety in foodstuffs, and the loss of competitiveness.[86] There were also many divergent opinions, from Argentina and the Global Industry Coalition, which considered that socio-economic damage *per se* did not come under the jurisdiction of the Cartagena Protocol and that there is only one mention of socio-economic considerations in Article 26, which allows them to be taken into account when it comes to adopting a decision prior to the first transboundary movement.[87] For others, such as Canada and the EU, it was not clear how this definition of damage could be differentiated from the traditional concept of damage and to what extent it would superimpose on other components of damage.[88]

In accordance with the synthesis of proposed texts and views on approaches, options, and issues, the concept of traditional damage included the loss of life or personal damage; the loss of, or damage to, property; and economic loss.[89] In some proposals, it was felt that damage should also reflect the interpretation of the term contained in the *actio legis aquiliae,* which is the *actio ex contractu* arising from

---

[83] *Synthesis of Proposed Texts, supra* note 66 at 20. *Synthesis of Proposed Operational Texts, supra* note 66 at 15, Operational text 1 and Operational text 2; at 18, Operational text 9.

[84] *Synthesis of Proposed Texts, supra* note 66 at 20.

[85] *Ibid.* at 21.

[86] *Ibid.* at 14. *Synthesis of Proposed Operational Texts, supra* note 66 at 15, Operational Text no. 1; and at 18, Operational Text no. 9.

[87] *Synthesis of Proposed Texts, supra* note 66 at 23 and 24.

[88] *Ibid.* at 23 and 24. *Synthesis of Proposed Operational Texts, supra* note 66 at 16, Operational Text no. 3; and at 18, Operational Text no. 9.

[89] *Synthesis of Proposed Operational Texts, supra* note 66 at 14; and at 16, Operational Text no. 3.

the Cartagena Protocol and from the *actio damni injuriae*.[90] However, this appraisal has been equally problematic since, as was pointed out earlier, the EU maintains that some of its components overlap with other components of damage such as damage to the sustainable use of biological diversity and damage to human health.[91] Finally, the definition of damage would include the costs of the response measures. These measures are not in themselves a category of damage but, according to the EU and Norway, they are considered relevant for the rest of the categories and should be covered by the rules and procedures that are referred to in Article 27 of the Cartagena Protocol.[92] Furthermore, from the perspective of Greenpeace International, this was a logical consequence of the application of the "polluter pays principle."[93]

The scope of the response measures is described in some of the operational texts, and it would include any reasonable measures taken by any person, including public authorities, following damage that has occurred, or to prevent, minimize, or mitigate possible loss or damage, or to arrange for environmental clean-up.[94] In light of all of these proposals and arguments, the GF-L&R grouped these categories under the heading "civil liability," which, in broad terms, would be composed of the "damage resulting from the transboundary movement of LMOs to legally protected interests as provided for by domestic law, including damage not redressed through administrative approach (no double recovery)."[95] The Guidelines on Civil Responsibility and Redress propose a description of the norms and procedures related to damage in accordance with national rights in the following terms:

(1) These rules and procedures apply to damage [resulting from the transboundary movement of LMOs] as provided for by domestic law.

(2) For the purposes of these rules and procedures, damage [resulting from the transboundary movement of LMOs] as provided for by domestic law may, *inter alia*, include:

---

[90] *Ibid.* at 15, Operational Text no. 2.

[91] *Ibid.* at 24.

[92] *Ibid.* at 25.

[93] *Ibid.* at 26.

[94] *Ibid.* at 16, Operational Text no. 4.

[95] *Final Report of the OEWG, supra* note 67 at 8.

(a) Damage to the conservation and sustainable use of biological diversity not redressed through the administrative approach;
(b) Damage to human health, including loss of life and personal injury;
(c) Damage to, or impaired use of, or loss of property;
(d) Loss of income and other economic loss [resulting from damage to the conservation or sustainable use of biological diversity];
(e) Loss of, or damage to, cultural, social, and spiritual values, or other loss or damage to indigenous or local communities, or loss of, or reduction of, food security.[96]

CONCLUSION

During the past several years, intensive negotiations have taken place in order to develop a mandate resulting from Article 27 of the Cartagena Protocol, which itself had emerged as a compromise solution. It would appear that, finally, nine years after the protocol was accepted, an agreement has been achieved regarding the scope of the problematic concept of damage in the context of the transboundary movement of LMOs.

Considering the difficulties that have been caused by the uncertainty related to the risks deriving from LMOs and the lack of precedents in this area, it has nevertheless been possible to achieve a very relevant systematization of the complex reality of the diverse damages that could be caused by the transboundary movements of LMOs. In light of the international texts related to the responsibility of states in different areas, a clear distinction has been established between two areas — the first being related to the responsibility of the state from an administrative perspective and the second being the claim for civil responsibility as a channel for redress and restatement to individuals. Another significant step in this area has been the proposal from the Group of the Friends of the Co-Chairs, developed in their Supplementary Protocol on Damage to the Conservation and Sustainable Use of Biological Diversity Resulting from Transboundary Movements of Living Modified Organisms to the Cartagena Protocol on Biosafety and in the Guidelines on Civil Responsibility and Redress.

The more ambitious goal of reaching a more precise definition of damage to the conservation of biological diversity and of damage to the sustainable use of biological diversity remains, for the

96 *Report of the Group of the Friends, supra* note 69 at 19.

moment, on the negotiating table. It is possible that the most effective approach is to leave a large margin for interpretation so that a case-by-case approach can be taken.

Similarly, it would be desirable to incorporate in the concept of damage to the conservation and sustainable use of biological diversity the cost of the measures of reinstatement in the same way that occurs with instruments such as the Basel Protocol on Liability and Compensation. However, perhaps it is preferable to develop an instrument that would have a wide consensus and that would at least achieve the acceptance of the LMO-producing countries. If not, it is likely that the whole process will become bogged down in endless negotiations that will only result in "dead letters."

JUAN-FRANCISCO ESCUDERO ESPINOSA
University of León, León, Spain

Sommaire

La définition de préjudice résultant de mouvements transfrontières d'organismes vivants modifiés à la lumière du Protocole de Cartagena sur la biosécurité

La notion de risque nécessite des mesures préventives ainsi que des mesures de responsabilité et de réparation dans le cas de préjudice. Le Protocole de Cartagena sur la biosécurité se limite, à l'article 27, à l'établissement d'un mandat pour l'élaboration des normes et procédures en matière de responsabilité et de réparation. L'accomplissement de ce mandat exige, d'abord, une définition de la notion de préjudice à la conservation et l'utilisation durable de la diversité biologique; d'autre part, une enquête sur l'étendue du préjudice à la santé; et, troisièmement, un examen d'aspects socio-économiques. Dans ce contexte, cet article analyse la notion de préjudice dans les instruments internationaux qui traitent de cette matière, en tenant compte des niveaux de l'implantation. L'article conclut en présentant une définition de préjudice, pour utilisation dans le cadre de l'élaboration du contenu de l'article 27, en se fondant sur une orientation administrative en ce qui concerne la notion de préjudice tiré de la responsabilité civile en droit interne.

Summary

The Definition of Damage Resulting from Transboundary Movements of Living Modified Organisms in Light of the Cartagena Protocol on Biosafety

The concept of risk requires preventative measures as well as measures of liability and redress in the case that damage is actually caused. The Cartagena Protocol on Biosecurity limits itself in Article 27 to the establishment of a mandate for the elaboration of norms and procedures in regard to liability and redress. The fulfillment of this mandate requires, first, a definition of the concept of damage to the conservation and sustainable use of biological diversity; second, a survey of the extent of damage to health; and, third, the consideration of socio-economic aspects. In this context, this article analyzes the concept of damage in the international instruments that deal with this material, taking into account levels of implantation. The article concludes by presenting a definition of damage for use in the context of the development of the content of Article 27, using an administrative focus in regard to the concept of damage for civil liability in domestic law.

Chronique de Droit international économique en 2008 / Digest of International Economic Law in 2008

I Commerce

RICHARD OUELLET

I INTRODUCTION

L'année commerciale 2008 en aura été une de prises de position et de redynamisation pour le Canada.

Un premier événement a donné le ton en début d'année lorsque, aux États-Unis, les deux principaux candidats à l'élection primaire du Parti démocrate ont estimé que la réouverture de l'ALENA était souhaitable afin d'inclure dans le corps même du traité des clauses favorables à la protection des travailleurs et de l'environnement. Forcé de réagir, le ministre du Commerce international, David Emerson, a dû redire les avantages de l'accord qui lie le Canada, les États-Unis et le Mexique. Il a aussi dû insister sur le fait que l'ALENA constitue un tout et que si l'ALENA devait être rouvert — ce que le Canada ne souhaite pas — d'autres questions, notamment les règles relatives à l'approvisionnement en énergie, devraient forcément faire partie de la renégociation.

L'année 2008 a aussi été l'occasion pour le gouvernement canadien d'appliquer ce qu'il considère être une nouvelle approche en matière de commerce international. La "stratégie commerciale mondiale" a été instituée par le gouvernement Harper en vue de promouvoir la prospérité du pays, de créer de nouveaux débouchés aux entreprises canadiennes et de nouer des partenariats économiques à travers le monde.[1] En s'appuyant sur la productivité et

Richard Ouellet est professeur agrégé à la Faculté de droit de l'Université Laval et directeur des programmes à l'Institut québécois des hautes études internationales. L'auteur tient à remercier M. Hervé Agbodjan Prince pour sa précieuse collaboration dans la préparation et la rédaction de cette chronique. Il remercie également le Centre d'études interaméricaines (CEI) pour son soutien financier.

[1] Affaires étrangères et Commerce international Canada, *La stratégie commerciale mondiale pour assurer la croissance et la prospérité du Canada*, en ligne: Affaires

l'accès aux marchés internationaux des entreprises canadiennes, la stratégie commerciale mondiale implique une redynamisation de la politique canadienne en matière de coopération économique et commerciale.

Si, au niveau hémisphérique, il n'y a pas eu d'avancées substantielles sur le désir partagé d'une intégration régionale renforcée, la diplomatie canadienne a tout de même tenté de renforcer sa position sur l'échiquier hémisphérique. De ce point de vue, il importe de remarquer que la démarche canadienne s'inscrit dans une action concertée. De plus, les actions menées par le trio Canada-États-Unis-Mexique au cours de l'année 2008 dans le cadre du Partenariat pour la sécurité et la prospérité (PSP) sont le signe d'une volonté de renforcement de la coopération aux plans économique, politique et commercial. Pour le Canada, les choix politiques opérés tant aux niveaux régional que multilatéral au cours de l'année 2008 marquent un véritable désir d'adaptation à un monde de plus en plus complexe. La multiplication des accords régionaux avec des pays de l'Amérique latine, des Caraïbes ou du Proche-Orient traduit une réelle volonté de repositionnement de la politique commerciale canadienne. Mais un tel dynamisme dans l'intégration économique va de pair avec des contentieux parfois importants. Le Canada a ainsi été impliqué dans plusieurs différends commerciaux au cours l'année 2008. C'est dans le cadre du mécanisme de règlement des différends de l'Organisation mondiale du commerce (OMC) que l'essentiel de ces différends ont été solutionnés.

Observons donc plus en détail les développements commerciaux de l'année 2008 qui ont touché le Canada en voyant d'abord ce qui s'est opéré aux plans bilatéraux et régionaux pour ensuite nous tourner vers le système commercial multilatéral et l'OMC.

II Le commerce canadien aux plans bilatéraux et régionaux

A   Les négociations commerciales aux plans bilatéraux et régionaux

1   L'intégration nord-américaine

Le Canada entretient depuis toujours de bonnes relations commerciales avec ses partenaires dans le cadre de l'ALENA et surtout avec

---

étrangères et Commerce international Canada, <http://www.international.gc.ca/commerce/assets/pdfs/GCS-fr.pdf>. Cette stratégie était partie intégrante du Discours du budget du gouvernement fédéral de 2007.

les États-Unis. Principale destination des exportations canadiennes,[2] les États-Unis sont le partenaire privilégié du Canada malgré la récurrence de leurs divergences portées devant les instances juridictionnelles internationales.[3] Par exemple, le Canada s'est inquiété des répercussions du *Farm Bill 2007*, loi agricole américaine, et a introduit une requête dans ce sens en vue d'examiner les dispositions de la loi portant notamment sur les subventions à l'agriculture.[4] En 2008, ce sont les répercussions possibles du *Farm Bill 2008* qui ont inquiété le Canada, notamment en ce qui concerne ses dispositions portant sur le sucre, les subventions actionnables et les règles d'origine. Ceci a mené le Canada à engager des consultations avec les États-Unis sur ce dernier dossier. Mais, loin de traduire des relations conflictuelles entre les deux pays, il faut plutôt y voir la volonté partagée de régler par voie juridictionnelle les divergences existantes et laisser à la diplomatie le maintien de relations bilatérales solides et apaisées.

En effet, les différends ci-dessus mentionnés n'ont en rien entaché le désir de coopération au niveau nord-américain. Ainsi, lancées en 2005 à Waco au Texas, les discussions sur le Partenariat pour la sécurité et la prospérité (PSP) entre le Mexique, les États-Unis et le Canada se sont poursuivies en 2008. Les rencontres de 2008 entendent répondre à l'objectif du PSP qui est celui de créer un cadre permanent de discussion au niveau trilatéral. Les enjeux préoccupant les trois dirigeants sont notamment ceux portant sur "la facilitation de la circulation aux frontières, l'environnement, la sécurité des aliments et des produits, et [comportent] diverses mesures destinées à améliorer la compétitivité globale de l'Amérique

---

[2] Les exportations canadiennes de marchandises ont atteint 375,5 milliards de dollars en 2008, soit une augmentation de 5,5 % par rapport à 2007 et les exportations canadiennes de services ont atteint 37,2 milliards de dollars, soit une augmentation de 3,2 % par rapport à 2007. Voir, Affaires étrangères et Commerce international Canada, *Rapport du Canada -2009 en matière d'accès aux marchés internationaux*, en ligne : Affaires étrangères et Commerce international Canada, <http://www.international.gc.ca/trade-agreements-accords-commerciaux/cimar-rcami/2009/05.aspx?lang=fra>.

[3] Voir développements infra sur les différends portés à l'ALENA et à l'OMC par les deux pays en 2008.

[4] OMC, Demande de consultations présentée par le Canada, *États-Unis – subventions et autres mesures de soutien interne pour le maïs et d'autres produits agricoles*, (11 janvier 2007), OMC Doc. WT/DS/357/1, G/L/812, G/SCM/D73/1, G/AG/GEN/74 (11 janvier 2007).

du Nord."[5] C'est pourquoi, lors des rencontres des 21 et 22 avril 2008 tenues à la Nouvelle-Orléans en Louisiane, les échanges ont surtout porté sur la sécurité aux frontières et les mouvements transfrontaliers de marchandises. Les dirigeants des trois pays y ont réitéré leurs engagements vis-à-vis de l'ALENA et initié un plan d'action portant sur les cinq secteurs discutés une année plus tôt à Montebello.[6] Les objectifs poursuivis sont ceux du renforcement de la compétitivité de l'Amérique du Nord, la prise en compte des préoccupations liées à la salubrité et la fiabilité des aliments, la sécurité aux frontières, de l'énergie durable et l'environnement ainsi que de la gestion des situations d'urgence et des capacités d'intervention.[7] Malgré ces actions communes, le gouvernement canadien entretient sur des dossiers particuliers des relations singulières avec chacun de ses deux partenaires hémisphériques.

Ainsi, avec le Mexique, le Canada tente de renforcer ses relations commerciales en se fondant non seulement sur les cadres qu'offrent l'ALENA et le PSP mais aussi en s'appuyant sur le Partenariat bilatéral Canada-Mexique (PCM).

Lancé en octobre 2004, le PCM a pour mission d'œuvrer à l'accroissement de la collaboration entre "les milieux d'affaire et les gouvernements des deux pays, de relever le défi de maintenir la prospérité et de rehausser la compétitivité des économies nord-américaines."[8] Lors de la réunion du PCM qui s'est déroulée à Ottawa les 4 et 5 mars 2008, les deux pays ont une fois de plus insisté sur la nécessité de lever les obstacles au commerce et à l'investissement dans leurs relations mutuelles. C'est dans ce cadre qu'a été mis en place un protocole visant à faciliter l'entrée au Mexique en provenance du Canada d'animaux vivants pour fin de reproduction. Dans cet esprit, la démarche canadienne s'inscrit au cours de

---

5 Partenariat nord-américain pour la sécurité et la prospérité, "Au sujet du PSP," en ligne: Partenariat pour la sécurité et la prospérité, <http://www.spp-psp.gc.ca/eic/site/spp-psp.nsf/fra/h_00003.html.

6 Premier ministre du Canada, *Déclaration conjointe du Président Bush, du Président Calderòn et du Premier ministre Harper à l'occasion du Sommet des leaders nord-américains,* (22 avril 2008), en ligne: Premier ministre du Canada, <http://www.pm.gc.ca/fra/media.asp?category=3&id=2074>.

7 *Ibid.*

8 Partenariat Canada-Mexique, Rapport 2007-2008, en ligne: Partenariat Canada-Mexique, *Rapport 2007-2008*, en ligne: Ministère des Affaires extérieures du Mexique, <http://www.sre.gob.mx/images/info07_08.pdf>.

l'année 2008 dans une approche coordonnée nord-américaine visant la surveillance des aspects réglementaires et commerciaux. Le Canada tente ici de tourner la page des incompréhensions qui étaient nées de l'affaire de l'encéphalopathie spongiforme bovine (ESB). L'idée est de réactiver l'accès aux marchés internationaux du bœuf canadien. Dans le même esprit, s'appuyant sur l'expertise de cinq groupes de travail, deux nouveaux groupes ont été créés par les ministres des affaires étrangères des deux pays afin de couvrir les secteurs de l'environnement et de la foresterie ainsi que celui de la mobilité du travail. De plus, l'ancien groupe portant sur le commerce, l'investissement, la science et la technologie a été remplacé lors de la réunion de mars 2008 par celui du commerce, de l'investissement et de l'innovation afin de mieux prendre en compte les nouveaux enjeux liés à la problématique de l'innovation dans les secteurs du commerce et de l'investissement.

2 Les autres développements aux plans bilatéraux et régionaux

Au regard des nombreux accords régionaux et bilatéraux de libre-échange signés au cours de l'année écoulée, on peut, sans risque de se tromper, considérer que l'année 2008 aura été pour le Canada celle du renforcement de la position de ses entreprises sur l'échiquier mondial. Comme nous l'avions déjà signalé, les tergiversations dans la mise en œuvre d'une zone de libre-échange intercontinentale semblent inciter le gouvernement Harper à opter pour la conclusion d'accords bilatéraux tous azimuts en vue d'offrir de nouveaux marchés aux entreprises canadiennes.[9]

Ainsi, en se tournant vers le marché européen, le Canada a conclu en janvier 2008 un accord de libre-échange avec l'Association européenne de libre-échange (AELE) dont l'entrée en vigueur est prévue pour 2009.[10] Cette Association qui regroupe l'Islande, le Liechtenstein, la Norvège et la Suisse constitue un marché important pour le Canada dont les échanges bilatéraux de marchandises se sont élevés à 13,2 milliards de dollars en 2008. Quant aux échanges

---

[9] Richard Ouellet, "Chronique de Droit international économique en 2007" (2007) XLV A.C.D.I. aux pp. 433–48.

[10] Affaires étrangères et Commerce international Canada, *Accord de libre-échange entre le Canada et les États de l'Association européenne de libre-échange (Islande, Liechtenstein, Norvège et Suisse)*, en ligne: Affaires étrangères et Commerce international Canada, <http://www.international.gc.ca/trade-agreements-accords-commerciaux/agr-acc/efta-agr-acc.aspx?lang=fra&redirect=true>.

de capitaux, la valeur des investissements bilatéraux du Canada avec
simplement la Norvège et la Suisse ont atteint 28,4 milliards de
dollars en 2008.[11] Cet accord signé en même temps que trois autres
accords parallèles sur l'agriculture instaure une zone de libre-
échange et de libre concurrence entre les parties concernées.[12]
L'accord ainsi signé entre le Canada et les pays de l'AELE devra
permettre l'élimination des barrières au commerce et instaurer une
zone de libre concurrence en matière de commerce des marchandises, de service et d'investissement.[13] L'accord prévoit que le
commerce des marchandises entre les signataires sera régi par les
principes fondamentaux de traitement national[14] et l'interdiction
des restrictions sur les importations et les exportations.[15] L'accord
prévoit également le respect des droits et obligations découlant
notamment des accords sur les mesures sanitaires et phytosanitaires[16] et celui portant sur les obstacles techniques au commerce[17]
de l'Organisation mondiale du commerce (OMC). Dans la pratique,
les produits originaires des pays signataires visés par l'accord de
libre-échange seront échangés sur les marchés concernés par l'accord en exonération de droits de douane ou selon un tarif réduit
comparativement au taux de la nation la plus favorisée.[18] De la
même manière, l'accord insiste sur l'importance de l'accroissement
des investissements entre signataires et l'ouverture réciproque
nécessaire du commerce des services notamment à travers la facilitation des conditions de séjour temporaire des investisseurs, ges-
tionnaires ou fournisseurs de services des membres.

---

[11] Affaires étrangères et Commerce international Canada, *Le Canada et l'Association
européenne de libre-échange (AELE)*, en ligne: Affaires étrangères et Commerce international Canada, <http://www.international.gc.ca/trade-agreements-accords-
commerciaux/agr-acc/efta-aele.aspx?lang=fra>.

[12] Affaires étrangères et Commerce international du Canada, *Accord sur l'agriculture entre le Canada et la République d'Islande, Accord sur l'agriculture entre le Canada
et le Royaume de Norvège, Accord sur l'agriculture entre le Canada et la Confédération
Suisse*, en ligne: Affaires étrangères et Commerce international Canada, <http://
www.international.gc.ca/trade-agreements-accords-commerciaux/agr-acc/efta-
agr-acc.aspx?lang=fra&redirect=true>.

[13] *Ibid.*, préambule.

[14] *Ibid.*, art. 4.

[15] *Ibid.*, art. 5.

[16] *Ibid.*, art. 6.

[17] *Ibid.*, art. 7.

[18] *Ibid.*, art. 10 et 11.

Mais la stratégie canadienne visant à élargir son champ d'expansion commerciale ne s'arrête pas aux portes des États membres de l'AELE. Il s'agit pour le Canada d'établir à terme un partenariat élargi avec toute l'Europe. C'est dans cet esprit qu'a été tenu un sommet-conjoint Union européenne-Canada le 27 octobre 2008 afin de "définir le périmètre d'un accord économique approfondi et d'établir les points critiques pour son aboutissement, en particulier l'implication des provinces et territoires canadiens et des États membres de l'Union européenne (UE) sur les sujets relevant de leurs compétences."[19] Deux rencontres ont ensuite été tenues successivement les 20 novembre et 3 décembre par le groupe mixte chargé de définir le périmètre de ce partenariat économique. Il en ressort que le futur accord devra aller au-delà des secteurs couverts par l'OMC. Il intègrera alors les questions liées au commerce des marchandises, c'est-à-dire les mesures sanitaires et phytosanitaires, les marchés publics, les obstacles techniques au commerce, la facilitation des échanges, les procédures douanières, le commerce transfrontières des services, les investissements, la coopération en matière de réglementation, la propriété intellectuelle, y compris les indications géographiques, les mouvements des personnes physiques, la politique de concurrence et autres questions connexes, les dispositions institutionnelles et le règlement des différends, le développement durable et d'autres questions bilatérales.[20] C'est là un projet ambitieux visant à inclure tous les chapitres couverts par les différents accords commerciaux bilatéraux entre les deux partenaires commerciaux.

À l'appui de la démarche, une étude conjointe UE-Canada a été lancée. En effet, l'étude portant sur l' "*Évaluation des coûts et avantages d'un partenariat économique plus étroit entre l'Union européenne et le Canada,*"[21] publiée le 26 octobre 2008, démontre qu'une libéralisation des marchandises et des services entre le Canada et l'Union

---

[19] Affaires étrangères et Commerce international Canada, *Rapport conjoint Canada-Union européenne: vers un accord économique approfondi*, en ligne: Affaires étrangères et Commerce international Canada, <http://www.international.gc.ca/trade-agreements-accords-commerciaux/agr-acc/eu-ue/can-eu-report-can-ue-rapport.aspx?lang=fra>.

[20] *Ibid.*

[21] Commission européenne et gouvernement du Canada, *Évaluation des coûts et avantages d'un partenariat économique plus étroit entre l'Union européenne et le Canada*, en ligne: Affaires étrangères et Commerce international Canada, <http://www.international.gc.ca/trade-agreements-accords-commerciaux/assets/pdfs/EU-CanadaJointStudy-fr.pdf>.

européenne pourrait stimuler de 20 % le commerce bilatéral et entraîner une hausse du produit intérieur brut allant jusqu'à 12 milliards de dollars pour le Canada d'ici 2014.[22] L'ambition ainsi affichée par le gouvernement Harper est d'accroître les débouchés et les facilitations commerciales aux entreprises du pays.

Dans les pays de la zone des Amériques, d'Asie et des Caraïbes, il faut noter la conclusion de deux accords bilatéraux au cours de l'année 2008 avec deux pays d'Amérique latine. Le premier accord a été signé par la Secrétaire d'état Helena Guergis au nom du Canada avec le Pérou le 29 mai 2008. L'accord ambitionne de créer un vaste marché de produits et de services ainsi que de nouvelles possibilités d'emplois sur les territoires des deux pays.[23] Pour la ministre Guergis, l'accord traduit la volonté du gouvernement canadien de générer de nouveaux débouchés pour les exportateurs, les fournisseurs de services et les investisseurs canadiens. Il s'agit donc, affirmait-elle d'un important pas en avant dans les relations entre le Canada et le Pérou non seulement en matière commerciale, mais aussi en matière environnementale et de coopération dans le domaine du travail.[24] Sur le fond, l'accord renvoie au respect des principes fondamentaux du GATT de 1994 que sont notamment l'application du traitement national et l'élimination progressive des droits de douane dans les rapports commerciaux entre les deux pays.[25] Aucun des deux partenaires ne pourra ainsi augmenter un droit de douane existant ni en instituer un nouveau à l'égard d'un

---

[22] Affaires étrangères et Commerce international Canada, *Négociations en vue d'un accord économique et commercial global entre le Canada et l'Union européenne*, en ligne: Affaires étrangères et Commerce international Canada, <http://www.international.gc.ca/trade-agreements-accords-commerciaux/agr-acc/eu-ue/can-eu-report-intro-can-ue-rapport-intro.aspx?lang=fra>.

[23] Commission européenne et gouvernement du Canada, *Évaluation des coûts et avantages d'un partenariat économique plus étroit entre l'Union européenne et le Canada*, en ligne: Affaires étrangères et Commerce international Canada, <http://www.international.gc.ca/trade-agreements-accords-commerciaux/assets/pdfs/EU-CanadaJointStudy-fr.pdf>.

[24] Affaires étrangères et Commerce international Canada, *Le Canada signe un accord de libre-échange et des accords en matière d'environnement et de coopération dans le domaine du travail avec le Pérou*, en ligne: Affaires étrangères et Commerce international Canada, <http://international.gc.ca/media/state_sec_etat/news-communiques/2008/386239.aspx?lang=fra>.

[25] Affaires étrangères et Commerce international Canada, *Accord de libre-échange Canada-Pérou*, en ligne: Affaires étrangères et Commerce international Canada, <http://www.international.gc.ca/trade-agreements-accords-commerciaux/agr-acc/peru-perou/peru-toc-perou-tdm.aspx?lang=fra>.

produit originaire. Et pendant le processus d'élimination des droits de douane, les deux Parties se sont engagées à imposer aux produits originaires, le moins élevé des tarifs douaniers conformément aux engagements pris au titre du présent accord et au titre de l'article II du GATT de 1994. Quant aux mesures non tarifaires, l'accord n'introduit pas de dispositions particulières ni de traitement préférentiel. Au contraire, il renvoie de manière quasi-systématique aux différents accords du GATT de 1994 ou aux négociations en cours au sein de l'Organisation mondiale du commerce.[26] Toutefois, l'accord prévoit une panoplie de régimes spéciaux qui touchent principalement à l'admission temporaire de certains produits, aux produits réadmis après des réparations ou des modifications ou à l'admission d'échantillons commerciaux de valeur négligeable et d'imprimés publicitaires.[27] Il faut noter également que le champ d'application de l'accord est assez large. Ainsi, l'accord bilatéral signé avec le Pérou couvrira, dès son entrée en vigueur, les secteurs de l'agriculture et les mesures sanitaires et phytosanitaires, les investissements, le commerce transfrontalier des services, les télécommunications, les services financiers, l'admission temporaire des hommes et des femmes d'affaires, les marchés publics, le commerce électronique et la coopération liée au commerce, au travail et à l'environnement.

Le deuxième accord de libre-échange a été signé le 21 novembre 2008 avec la Colombie.[28] Paraphé en présence du Premier ministre Harper, celui-ci déclarait: "qu'en élargissant notre relation commerciale avec la Colombie, nous offrons de nouvelles occasions aux entreprises canadiennes sur un marché étranger et nous aidons une des plus anciennes démocraties d'Amérique du Sud à renforcer les droits de la personne et la sécurité dans le pays."[29] L'accord signé avec la Colombie couvre les mêmes secteurs que celui signé par le Canada avec le Pérou et se réfère au respect des principes fondamentaux du GATT de 1994 que sont le traitement national,

---

[26] *Ibid.*, section D.

[27] *Ibid.*, section C.

[28] Affaires étrangères et Commerce international Canada, *Accord de libre-échange Canada-Colombie*, en ligne: Affaires étrangères et Commerce international Canada, <http://www.international.gc.ca/trade-agreements-accords-commerciaux/ agr-acc/colombia-colombie/can-colombia-toc-tdm-can-colombie.aspx?lang=fra>.

[29] Premier ministre du Canada, *Le Canada signe un accord de libre-échange avec la Colombie*, en ligne: Premier ministre du Canada, <http://www.pm.gc.ca/fra/ media.asp?category=1&id=2321>.

l'élimination progressive des droits de douane ou le traitement de la nation la plus favorisée.[30] Il est également frappant de remarquer que les régimes spéciaux prévus dans cet accord sont quasi-identiques à ceux prévus dans l'accord bilatéral signé avec le Pérou, à savoir, l'admission temporaire en franchise de droits et quelles que soit leurs origines, d'une série de produits nécessaires à l'exercice des activités des hommes et des femmes d'affaires, les produits sportifs, les échantillons commerciaux, les films et les autres enregistrements publicitaires.[31] S'agissant de mesures non tarifaires, il est intéressant de noter à l'article 212 de l'accord la mention concernant la reconnaissance par la Colombie du "Whisky canadien" et du "Rye Whisky canadien" comme produits distinctifs du Canada dont la Colombie ne peut autoriser la vente sous ces appellations que lorsque ces produits auront été fabriqués au Canada conformément aux lois et règlements canadiens régissant leur fabrication.

Par cet accord, les deux pays entendent ainsi accroître davantage l'intégration économique au niveau hémisphérique. Lancées en même temps que celles ayant débouché à la signature d'un accord de libre-échange avec le Pérou, les négociations canadiennes avec ces deux pays s'inscrivent dans la volonté du Canada de renforcer sa position commerciale dans les Amériques. Ainsi, en l'espace d'une année, deux accords de libre-échange ont ainsi été signés avec les pays membres de la Communauté andine.

Par ailleurs, des négociations ont également été engagées au cours de la même année avec le Panama en vue d'un accord de libre-échange global et des accords parallèles dans les domaines de l'environnement et du travail. Avec le groupe des quatre (Guatemala, Nicaragua, Honduras et El Salvador) de l'Amérique centrale (CA4), le Canada a tenté de débloquer les négociations en vue de la conclusion d'un accord de libre-échange dans l'impasse depuis 2004. Ainsi, le Canada a tenu avec le CA4 des rencontres au niveau des négociateurs en chef, en 2008, dans le but d'accélérer le processus d'intégration économique.[32]

---

30 Affaires étrangères et Commerce international Canada, *supra* note 28, chapitre deux, sections A et B.

31 *Ibid.*, section C.

32 Affaires étrangères et Commerce international Canada, *Rapport 2009 sur l'accès aux marchés internationaux,* en ligne: Affaires étrangères et Commerce international Canada, <http://www.international.gc.ca/trade-agreements-accords-commerciaux/cimar-rcami/2009/index.aspx?lang=fra>.

Il semble bien que la stratégie visant à procéder à des négociations d'ensemble constitue la nouvelle approche du Canada en matière d'intégration régionale. En effet, avec les pays des Caraïbes, l'approche canadienne a aussi consisté à engager des négociations d'ensemble en vue de parvenir à la signature d'un accord de libre-échange global. Menées avec la *Caribbean Community* (CARICOM), les négociations qui ont débuté en 2007 devraient permettre de parvenir à un accord global et moderne qui instaure un "régime plus transparent, plus stable et plus prévisible pour les entreprises canadiennes."[33] L'accord prendra en compte à la fois les questions relatives au commerce des produits, aux services et à l'investissement. Il intègrera les problématiques spécifiques liées à la vulnérabilité des pays insulaires et à l'écart des niveaux de développement. Par contre, avec la République Dominicaine, le processus de négociations semble plus difficile dans la mesure où ce pays a d'ores et déjà signé un partenariat économique avec l'Union européenne et la CARICOM, à savoir un modèle qu'il veut transposer dans ses relations commerciales bilatérales avec le Canada.[34]

En Asie, même si les négociations engagées en vue de la signature d'un accord de libre-échange avec certains pays asiatiques tels que la Corée du Sud ou le Singapour sont encore en cours, des avancées substantielles ont été faites au cours de l'année 2008.[35] Avec la Corée du Sud, la dernière ronde des treize cycles de négociations a eu lieu à Ottawa en 2008. L'enjeu pour le Canada dans ces négociations est de maintenir pour les entreprises canadiennes un niveau de compétitivité comparable à celle de leurs concurrents étrangers dans la région. Cette préoccupation prend un relief particulier lorsqu'on sait que les États-Unis ont déjà signé avec la Corée du Sud un accord de libre-échange en 2007 et des négociations sont en cours entre la Corée du Sud et l'Union européenne en vue de la signature d'un partenariat économique.[36]

Par ailleurs, faisant suite à une étude conjointe Canada-Japon de 2007,[37] les deux pays ont convenu en janvier 2008 d'instaurer

---

[33] Affaires étrangères et Commerce international Canada, *Rapport 2008 sur l'accès du Canada aux marchés internationaux*, en ligne: Affaires étrangères et Commerce international Canada, <http://www.international.gc.ca/trade-agreements-accords-commerciaux/cimar-rcami/2008_07_08.aspx?lang=fra>.

[34] Affaires étrangères et Commerce international Canada, *supra* note 32.

[35] *Ibid.*

[36] *Ibid.*

[37] *Rapport découlant de l'étude conjointe Canada-Japon sur les avantages et les coûts d'un renforcement de la promotion du commerce et de l'investissement bilatéraux*, (octobre

un dialogue en vue d'une collaboration en matières commerciales et de l'investissement. Les premières discussions tenues en novembre 2008 doivent créer les conditions d'une collaboration économique sous la forme d'un partenariat privilégié ou d'un accord de libre-échange.

Dans le même esprit, une étude a été menée en 2007 sur la possibilité de lancer des négociations en vue de la signature d'un accord de libre-échange avec l'Inde. Les recommandations du rapport découlant de la table ronde Inde-Canada publiée en septembre 2008[38] qui préconisait aux dirigeants des deux pays d'engager de telles négociations, devraient être suivies dans les années à venir.

Au Moyen-Orient, une rencontre entre le Premier ministre Harper et le roi Abdallah II de Jordanie a permis de lancer des négociations en vue de conclure un accord de libre-échange entre les deux pays. Lancées en février 2008, les négociations ont été conclues au mois d'août de la même année pour permettre la conclusion d'un accord. Mais l'accord devrait concerner le seul domaine du commerce des marchandises. À cet accord seront joints deux accords parallèles dans les domaines du travail et de l'environnement.

B   LES DIFFÉRENDS LIÉS À L'ALENA IMPLIQUANT LE CANADA

Avec l'accord global sur le bois d'œuvre de 2006 conclu entre les États-Unis et le Canada et notifié à l'Organe de règlement des différends de l'OMC sous forme de solution mutuellement convenue,[39] les deux pays s'engageaient à clôturer définitivement le contentieux du bois d'œuvre. Ainsi, les affaires DS 236, DS 247, DS 257, DS 264, DS 277 et DS 311 trouvaient définitivement une issue par voix consensuelle entre les parties et ne pouvaient plus faire l'objet de recours devant l'Organe de règlement des différends de l'OMC.

2007), en ligne: Affaires étrangères et Commerce international Canada, <http://www.dfait.gc.ca/economist-economiste/assets/pdfs/research/TPR_2007/Chapter7-Joint_Study-fr.pdf>.

[38] Conseil canadien des chefs d'entreprise et Confederation of Indian Industy, *Inde-Canada, une nouvelle ère de coopération*, (2 septembre 2008), en ligne: Conseil canadien des chefs d'entreprise, <http://www.ceocouncil.ca/publications/pdf/test_98f77c9062a9436f8604186f819aaeea/Rapport_aux_Ministres_Inde_et_Canada_Une_Nouvelle_ere_de_cooperation_le_2_septembre_2008.pdf>.

[39] OMC, *États-Unis – Détermination finale de l'existence d'un dumping concernant le bois d'œuvre résineux en provenance du Canada*, Notification de la solution convenue d'un commun accord, OMC Doc. WT/DS 264/29, G/L/566/Add.1, G/ADP/D42/2 (16 novembre 2006).

Mais en 2008, ce sont les mécanismes de règlement des différends de l'ALENA qui ont été sollicités dans l'affaire du bois d'œuvre. Ainsi, un groupe spécial a été saisi d'une requête en rejet des plaintes déposées par Wynndel Box & Lumber Co. et Gorman Bros. Lumber auprès du département du commerce américain (DOC). En effet, le DOC avait rejeté la demande des deux entreprises au motif que "toutes les questions découlant des ordonnances relatives au bois d'œuvre résineux se sont trouvées réglées ... en application de l'Accord sur le bois d'œuvre résineux conclu en 2006 par les gouvernements des États-Unis et du Canada (ABR de 2006)."[40] Le Groupe spécial binational n'a donc pas daigné entendre les plaignants sur le fond. Il s'est déclaré incompétent confirmant les observations du département américain du commerce qui a considéré que l'affaire n'avait pas de portée pratique compte tenu de la révocation des ordonnances relatives au bois d'œuvre résineux et la restitution de tous les droits antidumping et compensateurs perçus en vertu de ces ordonnances conformément à l'ABR de 2006.[41]

La décision du Groupe spécial met donc en relief l'importance de l'accord global de 2006. Dans cet accord, les gouvernements canado-américains entendent opter pour une solution apaisée du règlement de l'affaire du bois d'œuvre. C'est pourquoi ils réaffirment dans l'ABR de 2006 leur renoncement au recours juridictionnel pour solder cette affaire du bois d'œuvre résineux. En ce sens, le Groupe spécial a ainsi affirmé qu'il ne lui appartient pas de vérifier l'application par le Canada de l'ABR de 2006 ni d'offrir aux entreprises les arguments politiques nécessaires à inciter le gouvernement canadien à modifier l'ABR de 2006.[42] Et même dans le cas où le Groupe spécial se serait prononcé sur le fond, sa décision ne pourrait avoir pour effet d'influer sur le champ d'application de l'ABR de 2006. En d'autres termes, l'accord global sur le bois d'œuvre de 2006 est autosuffisant et aucun tribunal américain ni canadien ne détient en la matière de pouvoir consultatif. Ce cas demeure le seul différend dans lequel le Canada est impliqué dans

---

[40] Groupe spécial, *Certains produits de bois d'œuvre résineux en provenance du Canada: décision définitive sur le champ d'application concernant les importations classées dans la sous-position 4409.10.05 du HTSUS*, Dossier du Secrétariat n°USA-CDA-2006-1904-05 (Rapport du Groupe spécial). En ligne: Secrétariat de l'ALENA, <http://registry.nafta-sec-alena.org/cmdocuments/edd5902f-a557-4c9c-a205-cc34660d712e.pdf>.

[41] *Ibid.* aux pp. 9–11 et 14.

[42] *Ibid.* à la p. 15.

le cadre de l'ALENA au cours de l'année 2008, mis à part bien entendu les différends en matière d'investissement qui sont couverts par une autre partie de cette chronique.

III LE COMMERCE CANADIEN ET L'ORGANISATION MONDIALE DU COMMERCE (OMC)

L'OMC étant au cœur des relations commerciales multilatérales, il nous apparaît logique d'analyser l'action canadienne en matière de commerce international au travers de son implication au sein de cet organisme. Deux niveaux d'analyse doivent ainsi être considérés. D'une part, le cadre général du déroulement des négociations commerciales multilatérales et, d'autre part, l'implication du Canada dans les différends commerciaux portés devant l'Organe de règlement des différends de l'OMC.

A   LES DÉVELOPPEMENTS DANS LE SYSTÈME COMMERCIAL MULTILATÉRAL EN 2008

1   Les négociations commerciales multilatérales

Débutées depuis 2001, les négociations de Doha, dont la fin était initialement prévue pour le 1er janvier 2005, n'ont toujours pas débouché sur un accord global à l'Organisation mondiale du commerce. En 2008, le processus de Doha a suivi son cours et nul ne peut réellement en prédire l'issue ou la fin malgré les nombreuses tentatives des différents groupes de négociation. Le dossier agricole, principale pierre d'achoppement des négociations, avait fait l'objet en 2007 d'un projet révisé de modalités visant à faire converger les divergences des négociateurs et à faciliter la suite du processus.[43] Ce document a permis de relancer les négociations et l'année 2008 s'ouvrait avec l'envoi par le président des négociations sur l'agriculture, M. Crawford Falconer, de huit documents de travail concernant l'accès au marché.[44] L'objectif était de focaliser les discussions et de permettre au Président Falconer de préparer le prochain projet de modalités. Ainsi, dès le 8 février 2008, le Président Falconer et son homologue des négociations sur l'accès

---

[43] OMC, Président des négociations sur l'agriculture, *Projet révisé de modalités concernant l'agriculture*, OMC Doc. TN/AG/W/4 (1er août 2007).

[44] OMC, Documents de travail du Président, novembre 2007 à janvier 2008, en ligne: World Trade Organisation, <http://www.wto.org/french/tratop_f/agric_f/chair_workdoc_nov07_f.htm>.

au marché des produits non agricoles (AMNA), l'Ambassadeur canadien Don Stephenson, ont publié un avant-projet sur un accord final sur l'agriculture et sur les produits non agricoles.[45] S'appuyant sur les différentes propositions des Membres de l'OMC, l'avant-projet présentait les formules afin de réduire les droits de douane et les subventions agricoles ayant des effets de distorsion des échanges et les dispositions connexes.

Les documents présentés par les deux présidents mettent l'accent sur les points d'accord possibles et présentent les opinions exprimées par les gouvernements Membres de l'OMC lors des sept années de négociations commerciales multilatérales. Les gouvernements sont ainsi appelés à s'exprimer sur ces nouvelles propositions afin que de nouvelles révisions puissent être faites en vue de l'élaboration de textes définitifs. L'objectif visé est de parvenir à un "équilibre acceptable entre l'ampleur des abaissements des droits de douane sur les produits agricoles et les subventions à l'agriculture et l'importance des abaissements qu'ils souhaitent dans chaque domaine."[46] Cet avant-projet avait soulevé beaucoup d'espoir et le directeur de l'OMC, M. Pascal Lamy, avait déclaré que ces documents ouvraient la voie au lancement d'une nouvelle phase importante des négociations commerciales multilatérales du cycle de Doha. D'après lui, ces documents reflétaient l'effort commun visant à trouver l'équilibre final pour un cycle ambitieux et axé sur le développement.[47] En mai 2008, deux projets révisés suggérant les "modalités" de négociation ont été présentés par les deux présidents des négociations agricoles et des négociations des produits non agricoles.[48] Compte tenu des avancées significatives que présentaient ces textes, Pascal Lamy avait considéré qu'ils montraient bien où se situent les convergences et où les travaux sont encore

---

[45] OMC, Nouvelles 2008, Négociations sur l'agriculture, *Publication d'avant-projets sur un accord final sur l'agriculture et sur les produits non agricoles*, en ligne: World Trade Organisation, <http://www.wto.org/french/news_f/news08_f/ag_draft_modalities_feb08_f.htm>.

[46] *Ibid.*

[47] OMC, Directeur général, *Communiqué de presse 2008*, OMC Doc. Press/513 (8 février 2008), en ligne: World Trade Organisation, <http://www.wto.org/french/news_f/pres08_f/pr513_f.htm>.

[48] OMC, Nouvelles 2008, *Distribution de projets révisés en vue d'un accord final sur le commerce des produits agricoles et non agricoles*, (19 mai 2008), en ligne: World Trade Organisation, <http://www.wto.org/french/news_f/news08_f/ag_nama_may08_f.htm>.

nécessaires.[49] Au cours des mois qui ont suivi, les négociations se sont poursuivies et les Présidents Falconer et Stephenson ont publié, en juillet 2008, leur dernier projet de "modalités" sur l'agriculture et les produits non agricoles.[50] Établis sur la base des positions exprimées par les différents gouvernements Membres de l'OMC, les documents sont des révisions des projets antérieurement distribués et devront servir de base à un accord ultérieur dans le cadre des négociations qui se sont tenues en juillet 2008. Par contre, après plusieurs jours d'intenses négociations, Pascal Lamy annonce, le 29 juillet 2008, que les négociations ont échoué,[51] les négociateurs n'ayant pas réussi à s'entendre sur la clause de sauvegarde spéciale pour les produits agricoles destinés aux pays en voie de développement. Selon le directeur général de l'OMC, sur une liste de 20 thèmes, il y a eu convergence sur 18 d'entre eux. Les divergences n'ont pas pu être surmontées sur le 19ème thème, à savoir le mécanisme de sauvegarde spéciale. En effet, ce mécanisme devait, de manière temporaire, permettre aux pays en voie de développement d'élever leurs droits de douane pour faire face aux poussées des importations de produits agricoles ou aux baisses des prix. Mais le nœud gordien des négociations se situait au niveau du déclenchement de la mesure de sauvegarde. Depuis lors, des consultations se sont poursuivies avec M. Falconer. Elles se sont déroulées, soit sous forme de consultations privées appelées "promenades en forêts,"[52]

[49] OMC, Directeur général, *Communiqué de presse 2008*, OMC Doc. Press/526 (20 mai 2008), en ligne: World Trade Organisation, <http://www.wto.org/french/news_f/preso8_f/pr526_f.htm>.

[50] OMC, Nouvelles 2008, Négociation sur l'accès au marché pour les produits non agricoles, *Publication de nouveaux projets sur le commerce des produits agricoles et non agricoles en vue de négociations cruciales*, (10 juillet 2008), en ligne: World Trade Organisation, <http://www.wto.org/french/news_f/newso8_f/ag_nama_julyo8_f.htm>.

[51] OMC, Nouvelles 2008, *PDD Le paquet de juillet 2008*, en ligne: World Trade Organisation, <http://www.wto.org/french/news_f/newso8_f/meeto8_summary_29july_f.htm>. Voir également OMC, Comité de l'agriculture, Session extraordinaire, *Rapport du Président de la session extraordinaire du comité de l'agriculture, M. l'Ambassadeur Crawford Falconer, au comité de négociations commerciales*, OMC Doc. JOB(O8)/95 (12 août 2008), en ligne: World Trade Organisation, <http://www.wto.org/french/tratop_f/agric_f/chair_texts_11augo8_f.pdf>.

[52] OMC, Nouvelles 2008, Négociations sur l'agriculture, *Le Président des négociations sur l'agriculture parle d'une "promenade en forêt" et établit un nouveau projet*, en ligne: World Trade Organisation, <http://www.wto.org/french/news_f/newso8_f/agric_7julyo8_f.htm>.

soit en réunion avec quelques délégations, soit élargies à l'ensemble des Membres participant aux négociations.

De son côté, M. l'Ambassadeur Luzius Wasescha, qui a pris la relève de M. l'Ambassadeur Stephenson à la tête de la présidence du groupe de négociation sur l'accès aux marchés des produits non agricoles le 2 octobre 2008, a poursuivi ses consultations sur l'AMNA. Ensemble, les deux présidents ont publié, en décembre 2008, deux projets révisés sur l'agriculture et les produits non agricoles en vue des prochaines négociations.[53] Les deux documents constituent des révisions des projets antérieurement distribués par les deux présidents. Ces projets résultent de l'évaluation de ce qui pourrait être convenu pour les formules d'abaissement des droits de douane et des subventions agricoles ayant des effets de distorsion sur les marchés. Depuis, les négociations sont dans l'impasse.

Parallèlement aux négociations sur l'agriculture et les produits non agricoles, les présidents de divers groupes de négociation ont également poursuivi leurs consultations en vue d'un accord global dans le cadre du programme de Doha pour le développement. Ainsi, le président du groupe de négociation sur les règles a distribué des textes sur l'antidumping et les disciplines relatives aux subventions. Les textes publiés présentent un projet de libellé juridique dans les domaines où il y a convergence. Ainsi, des questions ont été identifiées, accompagnées d'un bref résumé des différents points de vue.[54] Quant au président du groupe de négociation sur le commerce des services, celui-ci a publié, en mai 2008, un rapport[55] basé sur ses consultations et les observations des différentes délégations. Il y propose un libellé susceptible de recueillir le consensus des Membres en vue de l'achèvement des négociations sur les services. Globalement, il appert que l'année 2008 aura été

---

53 OMC, Comité de l'agriculture, session extraordinaire, *Projet révisé de modalités concernant l'agriculture*, OMC Doc.TN/AG/W/4/Rev.4. (6 décembre 2008) et OMC, Groupe de négociation sur l'accès aux marchés, *Quatrième révision du projet de modalités concernant l'accès aux marchés pour les produits non agricoles*, OMC Doc. TN/MA/W/103/Rev.3 (6 décembre 2008).

54 OMC, Groupe de négociation sur les règles, *Nouveaux projets de textes récapitulatifs des accords antidumping et SMC présentés par le Président*, OMC Doc. TN/RL/W/236 (19 décembre 2008), en ligne: World Trade Organisation, <http://www.wto.org/french/tratop_f/rulesneg_f/rules_deco8_f.doc>.

55 OMC, Comité du commerce des services, session extraordinaire, Rapport du Président et Annexe, *Éléments requis pour l'achèvement des négociations sur les services*, OMC Doc. TN/S/33 (26 mai 2008).

riche en négociations. Néanmoins, aucun consensus susceptible de
déboucher sur un accord global en vue de la clôture du cycle de
Doha n'aura été possible. C'est d'ailleurs ce qui motivait le directeur
général de l'OMC, Pascal Lamy, à recommander de ne pas convo-
quer les ministres en vue d'une finalisation des modalités en 2008.

Pour autant, tout ceci n'empêche pas le fonctionnement normal
des institutions de l'OMC. En effet, sous la rubrique institution-
nelle, on peut noter la désignation au sein de l'Organe d'appel de
deux nouveaux membres au cours de l'année 2008.[56] Il s'agit de
M. Shotaro Oshima[57] du Japon et de Mme Yuejiao Zhang[58] de la
Chine. Diplômé en droit à l'Université de Tokyo, M. Oshima a
exercé pendant plus de quatre décennies en tant que diplomate au
service des affaires étrangères du Japon. En tant que représentant
de son pays auprès de l'OMC, il a assumé au cours de la période
2002–05 les fonctions de président du Conseil général et de l'Organe de règlement des différends. C'est donc en fin connaisseur
des rouages institutionnels de l'OMC qu'il intègre l'organe juridictionnel de l'Organisation mondiale du commerce. Quant à Mme
Zhang, elle fut professeure de droit à l'Université de Shanton en
Chine et arbitre à la Commission d'arbitrage commercial et économique international. Avocate de profession, elle était la vice-prési-
dente de la société chinoise du droit économique international.
Désignés par l'Organe de règlement des différends (ORD) sur
recommandation du comité de sélection, les deux nouveaux membres de l'Organe d'appel ont commencé leur mandat le 1er juin
2008.

2   *L'action canadienne à l'OMC en 2008*

Le Canada est l'un des acteurs les plus influents des négociations
commerciales multilatérales, non pas seulement à cause du dynamisme de son économie mais aussi à cause de ses nombreuses
contributions au débat multilatéral. Comme le soulignait le rapport
du Secrétariat de l'OMC sur l'examen des politiques commerciales
du Canada en 2007:

---

[56] *Rapport annuel pour 2007*, OMC Doc. WT/AB/9 du 30 janvier 2008 (Organe
d'appel).

[57] *Ibid.* aux pp. 4–5.

[58] *Ibid.*

le Canada participe activement aux travaux de l'OMC; il considère celle-ci comme le pilier central de sa politique commerciale et comme le meilleur cadre pour une amélioration à grande échelle de l'accès aux marchés dans de nombreux domaines qui présentent pour lui de l'intérêt. Il a fait un grand nombre de propositions dans le cadre du cycle de négociations en cours à l'OMC.[59]

Au titre des contributions canadiennes aux négociations en cours à l'OMC, on peut noter quelques-unes considérées comme des plus importantes pour son économie. En effet, les contributions canadiennes au cours de l'année 2008 ont principalement concerné les négociations en matière de facilitation des échanges, les règles d'origine, la propriété intellectuelle et l'accès aux marchés des produits non agricoles.

En ce qui concerne la facilitation des échanges, le Canada aura introduit au moins quatre contributions soit seul, soit avec d'autres Membres de l'OMC, au cours de l'année 2008. La première contribution canadienne datait de mars 2008. L'initiative canadienne visait alors à faire des propositions concrètes en vue du renforcement de la coopération entre les administrations douanières et d'autres autorités en matière de facilitation des échanges et de respect des procédures douanières.[60] D'autres propositions seront introduites par le Canada dans les débats sur la facilitation des échanges avec d'autres Membres de l'OMC. Ces contributions porteront respectivement sur divers projets de textes relatifs au délai en matière de "décisions anticipées,"[61] de "séparation de la mainlevée de la détermination finale et du paiement des droits de douane, taxes et

---

[59] OMC, Organe d'examen des politiques commerciales, Rapport du Secrétariat, *Examen des politiques commerciales – Canada*, OMC Doc. WT/TPR/S/179 (14 février 2007), au para. 7.

[60] OMC, Groupe de négociation sur la facilitation des échanges, Communication présentée par le Canada, OMC Doc. TN/TF/W/154 (10 mars 2008), en ligne: World Trade Organization, <http://docsonline.wto.org/GEN_viewerwindow. asp?http://docsonline.wto.org:80/DDFDOCUMENTS/U/TN/TF/W154. DOC>.

[61] OMC, Groupe de négociation sur la facilitation des échanges, Communication présentée par l'Australie, le Canada, les États-Unis et la Turquie, *Projet de texte sur les Décisions anticipées*, OMC Doc. TN/TF/W/153 (10 mars 2008), en ligne: World Trade Organization, <http://docsonline.wto.org/GEN_viewerwindow. asp?http://docsonline.wto.org:80/DDFDOCUMENTS/U/TN/TF/W153. DOC>.

redevances,"[62] mais aussi de la coordination entre les organismes à la frontière.[63]

À ces contributions, viennent s'ajouter celles relevant des négociations sur les règles d'origine,[64] celles portant sur l'AMNA[65] et celles portant sur la propriété intellectuelle.[66] Toutes ces contributions canadiennes introduites dans les négociations sous formes de projets de texte ou de projets de modalités traduisent l'implication canadienne et l'importance qu'accorde le Canada aux négociations à l'OMC.

[62] OMC, Groupe de négociation sur la facilitation des échanges, communication présentée par le Canada et la Suisse, *Séparation de la mainlevée de la détermination finale et du paiement des droits de douane, taxes et redevances*, OMC Doc. TN/TF/W/136/Rev.2 (28 novembre 2008), en ligne: World Trade Organization, <http://docsonline.wto.org/GEN_viewerwindow.asp?http://docsonline.wto.org:80/DDFDOCUMENTS/U/TN/TF/W136R2.DOC>.

[63] OMC, Groupe de négociation sur la facilitation des échanges, Communication présentée par le Canada et la Norvège, *Projet de texte concernant la coordination entre les organismes à la frontière*, OMC Doc. TN/TF/W/128/Rev.2 (1er décembre 2008), en ligne: World Trade Organization, <http://docsonline.wto.org/GEN_viewerwindow.asp?http://docsonline.wto.org:80/DDFDOCUMENTS/U/TN/TF/W128R2.DOC>.

[64] WTO, Negotiating Group on Rules, Fisheries subsidies-De minimis Exemptions, Communication from Canada, WTO Doc. TN/RL/GEN/156 (2 may 2008), en ligne: World Trade Organization, <http://docsonline.wto.org/GEN_viewerwindow.asp?http://docsonline.wto.org:80/DDFDOCUMENTS/T/TN/RL/GEN156.DOC>.

[65] OMC, Groupe de négociation sur l'accès aux marchés, *Projet de modalités concernant l'accès aux marchés des produits non agricoles*, OMC Doc. TN/MA/W/103/Rev.1 (20 mai 2008), en ligne: World Trade Organization, <http://docsonline.wto.org/GEN_viewerwindow.asp?http://docsonline.wto.org:80/DDFDOCUMENTS/U/TN/MA/W103R1.DOC>.

[66] OMC, Conseil des aspects des droits de propriété intellectuelle qui touchent au commerce, Session extraordinaire, *Proposition de projet de décision du conseil des ADPIC sur l'établissement d'un système multilatéral de notification et d'enregistrement des indications géographiques pour les vins et les spiritueux*, OMC Doc. TN/IP/W/10/Rev.1 (14 juillet 2008), en ligne: World Trade Organization, <http://docsonline.wto.org/GEN_viewerwindow.asp?http://docsonline.wto.org:80/DDFDOCUMENTS/U/TN/IP/W10R1.DOC>; OMC, Conseil des aspects des droits de propriété intellectuelle qui touchent au commerce, Session extraordinaire, *Proposition de projet de décision du conseil des ADPIC sur l'établissement d'un système multilatéral de notification et d'enregistrement des indications géographiques pour les vins et les spiritueux*, OMC Doc. TN/IP/W/10/Rev.2 (24 juillet 2008), en ligne: World Trade Organization, <http://docsonline.wto.org/GEN_viewerwindow.asp?http://docsonline.wto.org:80/DDFDOCUMENTS/U/TN/IP/W10R2.DOC>.

L'implication canadienne au niveau multilatéral se traduit aussi par l'importance que le Canada attache à la résolution des conflits commerciaux par les instances juridictionnelles de l'OMC.

B   LES DIFFÉRENDS DEVANT L'OMC IMPLIQUANT LE CANADA

Le Canada a été impliqué, soit en tant que plaignant, soit en tant que défendeur, dans plusieurs affaires au cours de l'année 2008.

1   Mesures affectant les services financiers d'informations financières et les fournisseurs étrangers d'informations financières (DS 378)

Dans l'affaire des *Mesures affectant les services d'informations financières et les fournisseurs étrangers d'informations financières,*[67] le Canada remettait en cause la validité de certains instruments juridiques et administratifs chinois régissant les services d'information et la fourniture de services financiers par les étrangers. Principalement, le Canada considérait que les mesures mises en œuvre par la Chine en matière de services d'informations financières constituaient des "restrictions et des prescriptions discriminatoires en matière d'accès aux fournisseurs de services étrangers qui cherchent à fournir des informations financières à des clients en Chine."[68] En effet, selon la réglementation chinoise visée, les fournisseurs étrangers d'informations financières doivent fournir leurs services par l'intermédiaire d'une entité unique désignée par l'agence de presse Xinhua, soit le Service chinois d'informations économiques (CEIS) qui est l'une des entreprises commerciales de Xinhua.[69] Les fournisseurs étrangers d'informations financières ne peuvent solliciter des abonnements pour leurs services que par l'intermédiaire de Xinhua.[70] Quant aux utilisateurs de services d'informations financières, ils ne peuvent pas s'abonner directement aux services fournis par les étrangers. Ce n'est pas tout, le renouvellement des licences des fournisseurs étrangers d'informations financières ne peuvent se faire qu'à la condition qu'ils communiquent au Centre d'administration de l'information étrangère une série d'informations détaillées et confidentielles, incluant une copie de l'accord signé

---

67 OMC, Demande de consultation présentée par le Canada portant sur les "*Mesures affectant les services d'informations financières et les fournisseurs étrangers d'informations financières,*" OMC Doc. WT/DS378/1 et S/L/337 (23 juin 2008).

68 *Ibid.*

69 *Ibid.* à la p. 1.

70 *Ibid.*

avec l'agent désigné.[71] Le Canada considère que l'ensemble de ces mesures empêche les fournisseurs étrangers de services financiers d'établir une présence commerciale en Chine autre que les bureaux de représentation limitée.[72]

Ainsi, selon le Canada, le fait de désigner aux fournisseurs étrangers d'informations financières un agent unique pour fournir leurs services constitue une discrimination envers les fournisseurs étrangers et nationaux. De plus, en empêchant les fournisseurs étrangers d'informations financières d'établir une présence commerciale sur le territoire chinois, la Chine viole ses engagements internationaux[73] vis-à-vis de ses partenaires commerciaux à l'OMC et contrevient aux articles XVI, XVII et XVIII de l'Accord général sur le commerce des services (AGCS).

L'affaire, restée au niveau des consultations, s'est conclue par un Mémorandum d'accord signé entre les parties et notifié à l'Organe de règlement des différends le 9 décembre 2008.[74] Aux termes du Mémorandum d'accord signé entre les deux parties, la Chine s'engage à instituer un nouvel organisme gouvernemental de réglementation des services d'informations financières indépendant ainsi qu'un nouveau régime de licences conforme à ses engagements à l'OMC. Les fournisseurs étrangers de services financiers bénéficieront désormais d'un traitement non moins favorable que celui accordé aux fournisseurs chinois relativement aux services d'informations financières. De plus, aucun cadre législatif et réglementaire ne pourra empêcher les fournisseurs étrangers de services financiers d'exercer leurs activités grâce à une présence commerciale.

2   *Certaines prescriptions en matière d'étiquetage indiquant le pays d'origine (DS 384)*

Dans l'affaire *Certaines prescriptions en matière d'étiquetage indiquant le pays d'origine,*[75] le Canada était opposé aux États-Unis. Dans sa

---

[71] *Ibid.* à la p. 2.

[72] *Ibid.*

[73] Annexe 9 du *Protocole d'accession de la République populaire de Chine,* OMC Doc. WT/L/432 (23 novembre 2001).

[74] *Mémorandum d'accord entre la République populaire de Chine et le Canada au sujet des mesures affectant les services d'informations financières et les fournisseurs étrangers d'informations financières,* OMC Doc.WT/DS378/3; S/L/337/Add.1 (9 décembre 2008).

[75] OMC, Demande de consultation présentée par le Canada portant sur *Certaines prescriptions en matière d'étiquetage indiquant le pays d'origine (EPO),* OMC Doc.

demande de consultations, le Canada contestait la conformité de la Loi sur la commercialisation des produits agricoles de 1946, modifiée par la Loi sur les produits alimentaires, la conservation et l'énergie de 2008. Notamment, les contestations portaient sur les obligations des États-Unis au titre de l'Accord instituant l'OMC, de certaines dispositions du GATT de 1994,[76] de l'Accord OTC,[77] de l'Accord SPS[78] et de celui portant sur les règles d'origine.[79]

L'objectif du Canada, dans cette affaire, était de démontrer que la mise en œuvre de la Loi américaine sur l'agriculture de 2008 aurait pour effet d'annuler ou de compromettre les avantages pour le Canada des Accords de l'OMC mentionnés dans la demande de consultation. Sur le fond, le Canada remettait en cause la compatibilité avec le droit de l'OMC des dispositions impératives de la loi américaine en matière d'étiquetage indiquant le pays d'origine. En effet, aux termes de cette loi, seules seraient considérées comme produits originaires des États-Unis et étiquetées comme telles, les viandes issues d'animaux nés, élevés et abattus exclusivement aux États-Unis. Ce que conteste le gouvernement canadien. L'affaire n'a pas connu de développements substantiels au cours de l'année 2008. Il faut aussi noter que d'autres Membres de l'OMC, le Mexique et le Nicaragua, ont obtenu de l'ORD et des États-Unis le droit de participer aux consultations en tant que tierces parties.

3   Canada – Maintien de la suspension d'obligations dans le différend CE- Hormones (DS 321).

Une décennie après les premiers rapports de l'Organe de règlement des différends (ORD) dans l'affaire Hormones, celle-ci continue de faire couler de l'encre. Ainsi, le 31 mars 2008, le Groupe spécial rendait son rapport[80] dans lequel il devait répondre de la légalité du maintien de la suspension de concessions par le Canada envers certains produits en provenance de la Communauté européenne

---

WT/DS384/1; G/L/874; G/TBT/D/33; G/SPS/GEN/890; G/RO/D/6 (4 décembre 2008).

[76] Notamment les articles III: 4, IX: 2 et 4 et X: 3 du GATT de 1994.

[77] *Ibid.*, art. 2.

[78] *Ibid.*, art. 2, 5 et 7.

[79] *Ibid.*, art. 2.

[80] *Canada – Maintien de la suspension d'obligations dans le différend CE-Hormones* (2008), OMC Doc. WT/DS321/R (Rapport du Groupe spécial).

(CE) dans le cadre de l'OMC, en raison du différend CE-Hormones. En particulier, la CE considérait que la notification à l'ORD de la directive 2003/74/CE du 22 septembre 2003, modifiant la directive 96/22/CE du conseil qui interdisait l'utilisation de certaines substances à effet hormonal ou thyréostatique ainsi que des substances ß-agonistes dans les spéculations animales, constituait une mise en œuvre pleine et entière des recommandations et décisions de l'ORD dans le différend CE-Hormones. Ainsi, pour la Communauté européenne, le maintien par le Canada des suspensions d'avantages constituait une violation des articles 3:7, et 21 à 23 du Mémorandum d'accord portant sur les règles et procédures régissant le règlement des différends [ci-après Mémorandum d'accord].

Dans son rapport, le Groupe spécial constate la violation par le Canada de l'article 23:1 et 23:2 a) du Mémorandum d'accord. Par contre, le Groupe spécial a jugé que le Canada n'avait pas contrevenu à l'article 22:8 et que la CE n'avait pas non plus établi l'existence d'une violation par le Canada des articles 23:1 et 3:7 du Mémorandum d'accord par suite d'une infraction à l'article 22:8.

Pour ce qui est de l'article 22:8, l'Organe d'appel, dans son rapport du 16 octobre 2008,[81] a confirmé la décision du Groupe spécial selon laquelle celui-ci peut examiner la compatibilité de la mesure de mise en œuvre des CE avec l'accord SPS dans le cadre de son examen de l'allégation formulée par les Communautés européennes.[82] De plus, puisque la mesure jugée incompatible avec l'accord SPS dans le différend CE-Hormones n'a pas été éliminée, l'Organe d'appel confirme la décision du Groupe spécial selon laquelle les CE n'ont pas établi l'existence d'une violation par le Canada des articles 23:1 et 3:7 du Mémorandum d'accord par suite de la violation de l'article 22:8 du Mémorandum d'accord.[83]

Par contre, l'Organe d'appel infirme la décision du Groupe spécial selon laquelle le Canada chercherait à obtenir réparation pour une violation au sens de l'article 23:1 du Mémorandum d'accord, en maintenant la suspension de concessions à l'égard des CE, malgré la notification par celles-ci de la directive 2003/74/CE, et que le Canada n'a pas non plus violé les dispositions de l'article 23:2a) du Mémorandum d'accord. L'Organe d'appel note toutefois qu'il n'a pas été en mesure de compléter son analyse sur le point de savoir

---

81 *Canada-Maintien de la suspension d'obligations dans le différend CE-Hormones*, (2008), OMC Doc. WT/DS321/AB/4 (Rapport de l'Organe d'appel).

82 *Ibid.* au para. 736.

83 *Ibid.*

si, avec la directive 2003/74/CE, les CE s'étaient conformées au droit de l'OMC au sens de l'article 22:8 du Mémorandum d'accord. Par conséquent, les recommandations et les décisions de l'ORD dans l'affaire CE-Hormones restent exécutoires en l'espèce. Toutefois, l'Organe d'appel recommande à l'ORD de demander aux parties d'engager une procédure au titre de l'article 21:5 du Mémorandum d'accord pour régler leurs désaccords sur certains points afin de savoir si les CE ont éliminé la mesure jugée incompatible dans l'affaire CE-Hormones, et si l'application de la suspension de concession par le Canada reste juridiquement valable.[84] C'est dire que l'affaire Hormones a probablement encore de beaux jours devant elle et qu'il faudra s'attendre à d'autres recours à moins que les parties finissent par trouver une solution par voie diplomatique.

4 Mesures affectant les importations de pièces automobiles (DS342)

Le 18 juillet 2008, le Groupe spécial rendait sa décision dans l'affaire *Mesures affectant les importations de pièces automobiles,*[85] dans laquelle étaient impliqués le Canada (DS342), les Communautés européennes (DS339) et les États-Unis (DS340). Les mesures contestées par les plaignants visaient une série de dispositions chinoises en matière d'exportation de pièces automobiles en direction de la Chine, qui pourraient être déclarées contraires au droit de l'OMC. Principalement, le Canada visait à ce que le Groupe spécial déclare certaines mesures chinoises comme étant contraires au droit de l'OMC et susceptibles d'annuler ou de compromettre certains avantages résultant des accords de l'OMC. Les mesures contestées par le Canada concernent la politique chinoise en matière de développement de l'industrie automobile, notamment les mesures encadrant l'administration de l'importation de pièces et de composantes automobiles pour véhicules complets, les règles applicables pour déterminer si des pièces et des composantes automobiles importées constituent des véhicules complets ainsi que tous les remplacements, modifications, prolongations, mesures d'application ou autres aspects connexes.

Dans ses allégations, le Canada déclare que ces mesures sont attentatoires à la règle du traitement national, à l'article 2 de l'Accord

---

[84] *Ibid.* au para. 737.

[85] *Mesures affectant les importations de pièces automobiles* (2008), OMC Doc. WT/DS339/R, WT/DS3340/R, WT/DS342/ (Rapport du Groupe spécial).

sur les mesures d'investissement liées au commerce (MIC), à l'article 2 de l'Accord sur les règles d'origine, à l'article 3 de l'Accord sur les subventions et mesures compensatoires (SMC) ainsi qu'au protocole d'accession de la Chine.

Dans son rapport, le Groupe spécial valide les allégations canadiennes.[86] Ce que confirme l'Organe d'appel dans sa décision rendue le 15 décembre 2008.[87] En effet, l'Organe d'appel confirme surtout le caractère discriminatoire des mesures chinoises et les déclare contraires à l'article II:2 et 4 du GATT de 1994. Toutefois, l'Organe d'appel constate qu'il n'est pas nécessaire de se prononcer sur la constatation "subsidiaire" du Groupe spécial selon laquelle les mesures en cause, en ce qui concerne les pièces automobiles importées, étaient incompatibles avec les articles II:1 a) et b) du GATT de 1994. L'Organe d'appel infirme la constatation du Groupe spécial qui déclarait valables les allégations du Canada selon lesquelles la Chine avait violé son engagement figurant au paragraphe 93 du rapport du Groupe de travail sur l'accession de la Chine.

5   Les développements dans les autres affaires touchant le Canada en 2008

Dans deux autres affaires en cours depuis plusieurs années et dans lesquelles le Canada est impliqué, on peut noter, au cours de l'année 2008, quelques éléments factuels nouveaux ou certaines actions juridiques plus ou moins pertinentes.

Dans l'affaire *Communautés européennes – Mesures affectant l'approbation et la commercialisation des produits biotechnologique*,[88] au sein de laquelle les Communautés européennes (CE) avaient été condamnées en 2006, le débat a tourné tout au long de l'année 2008 autour de la question du délai raisonnable de mise en œuvre de la décision de l'ORD. En effet, le rapport du Groupe spécial avait, conformément aux demandes canadiennes, établi que les CE avaient institué un moratoire de facto sur l'approbation des produits technologiques[89]

---

86 *Ibid.*

87 *Chine- Mesures affectant les importations de pièces automobiles* (2008), OMC Doc. WT/DS339/AB/R, WT/DS349/AB/R, WT/DS342/AB/R (Rapport de l'Organe d'appel).

88 *Communautés européennes- Mesures affectant l'approbation et la commercialisation des produits biotechnologiques* (2006), OMC Doc. WT/DS 291/R, WT/DS 292/R, WT/DS 293/R (Rapport du Groupe spécial).

89 *Ibid.* au para. 7.1272

et qu'en appliquant ce moratoire, les CE avaient agi d'une manière incompatible avec leurs obligations au titre de l'Annexe C 1)
a)[90] et de l'article 8 de l'Accord sur les mesures sanitaires et phytosanitaires (SPS).[91] Dans ses constatations, le Groupe spécial avait
fait remarquer que le moratoire européen n'avait pas été adopté
dans le cadre d'un processus communautaire formel d'élaboration
de règles ou de prise de décision. Toutefois, le groupe des cinq ou
la Commission empêchait l'approbation finale des demandes par
leurs actions ou leurs omissions.[92] Au surplus, le Groupe spécial
avait établi la violation par les CE des articles 5:1 et 2:2 de l'accord
SPS en ce qui concerne les mesures de sauvegarde prises par les
États de l'Union européenne.[93]

Enfin, dans l'affaire *Canada – Exonérations et réductions fiscales pour
le vin et la bière*,[94] les Communautés européennes contestaient l'application par le Canada d'exonérations de droits d'accise fédéraux
pour le vin canadien composé entièrement de produits agricoles
ou végétaux produits et cultivés au Canada. Les Communautés
européennes contestaient également la réduction des taux de droits
d'accise appliquée par le Canada pour une certaine quantité de
bière ou de liqueur de malt produite ou emballée annuellement
au Canada. Selon les Communautés européennes, ces mesures
canadiennes violaient l'Accord sur les subventions et mesures compensatoires de l'OMC ainsi que le GATT de 1994. Par contre, en
décembre 2008, les deux parties ont notifié à l'Organe de règlement
des différends qu'elles étaient parvenues à régler le conflit. Dans
l'accord mutuellement convenu par les Parties, le Canada s'est
engagé à réduire, sur la base du principe de la nation la plus favorisée, les droits de douane appliqués à certains produits importés
au Canada.[95]

IV CONCLUSION

Au total, l'année 2008 aura été pour le Canada assez fructueuse
tant dans ses relations bilatérales, régionales que multilatérales. Par

---

[90] *Ibid.* au para. 7.1567.

[91] *Ibid.* aux para. 7.1569-7.1570.

[92] *Ibid.* au para. 7.1272.

[93] *Ibid.* aux para. 4.570-4.571.

[94] Solution mutuellement convenue, *Canada – Exonérations et réductions fiscales pour
le vin et la bière*, OMC Doc. WT/DS 354/2, G/L/806/Add.1, G/SCM/D 72/1/
Add.1 (23 décembre 2008).

[95] *Ibid.* à la p. 2.

son intense activité sur la scène commerciale internationale, le Canada a renforcé la position de ses entreprises sur l'échiquier international. Grâce aux nombreux accords régionaux conclus ou en négociation, ce sont de nouveaux débouchés qui s'offrent aux entreprises canadiennes tant en termes de nouveaux marchés qu'en termes d'emplois.

Malheureusement, au plan multilatéral, l'impasse de Doha retarde la conclusion d'un accord global alors même que la politique commerciale du Canada découle largement des concessions qu'il réussira à obtenir de ses partenaires commerciaux. C'est peut-être ce qui justifie le dynamisme dont il fait preuve dans la conclusion d'accords bilatéraux ou régionaux. Mais il s'agit là en réalité d'une tendance mondiale qui consiste pour les États à chercher dans les accords bilatéraux ou régionaux des concessions ou avantages qu'ils ne peuvent obtenir dans le cadre multilatéral. Il reste à espérer que les accords régionaux qui lient le Canada continuent de lui profiter et que des déclarations comme celles des candidats à l'investiture démocrate aux États-Unis n'aient pas de suite malheureuse pour les relations commerciales canado-américaines.

II Le Canada et le système financier international en 2008

BERNARD COLAS

Affectée par la crise financière et la hausse des prix et des combustibles, la communauté internationale a placé au centre de
ses préoccupations la nécessité d'élaborer un plan de relance de
l'économie à l'échelle mondiale. Pour autant, la communauté a
conservé ses impératifs de lutte contre le blanchiment d'argent et
le financement du terrorisme en tête de liste des priorités. Ces divers
travaux ont été menés de concert par: (1) le Groupe des 20 (G-20),
(2) les institutions financières internationales, (3) les organismes
de contrôle des établissements financiers, (4) le groupe d'action
financière et (5) le Joint Forum. Au sein de ces institutions, le Canada joue un rôle de premier plan.

I LE GROUPE DES 20 (G-20)

La dixième réunion du G-20 s'est déroulée les 14 et 15 novembre
2008 à Washington et a réuni pour la première fois non seulement
les ministres des finances mais également les chefs d'États ou de
gouvernement. Le contexte de récession mondiale, déjà annoncé
en 2007 à travers l'apparition de perturbations sur le marché américain, a été l'évènement qui a amené la communauté internationale à réagir face à la hausse considérable du prix des aliments, des
produits agricoles et du carburant.

Les axes majeurs de ce sommet ont été la réitération des objectifs
prédéfinis en 2007,[1] l'accélération de l'adoption de mesures afin

---

Bernard Colas est avocat associé de l'étude Colas Moreira Kazandjian Zikovsky
(CMKZ) à Montréal et Docteur en droit. L'auteur remercie Xavier Mageau LL.M.
de la même étude ainsi qu'Isabelle Chaumun pour leur importante contribution
à la préparation de cet article.

[1] Bernard Colas, "Le Canada et le système financier international en 2007" (2008)
XLV A.C.D.I. à la p. 450.

de stabiliser les marchés financiers[2] ainsi que la construction d'une nouvelle architecture financière internationale afin de favoriser la croissance économique. Le diagnostic offert par la réunion du G-20 demeure sombre mais appelle à la vigilance et à la réaction des États face à la nécessité de réguler le capitalisme financier afin de relancer l'économie.

Les causes de la crise ont été identifiées par le Groupe des 20 comme provenant d'une absence de vérification diligente caractérisée dans la prise de risques des acteurs des marchés de capitaux. La crise des "*Subprimes*," soit la défiance envers les créances titrisées que les détenteurs ne parvenaient plus à liquider sur le marché interbancaire, a été la source, mais encore l'illustration la plus flagrante de la précarité du système financier international.

Face à cette absence de régulation, l'anticipation a été la principale perspective envisagée par le Groupe des 20 afin de prévenir les crises à venir. Le Groupe a par ailleurs affirmé la nécessité de stabiliser le système financier international en encourageant les États à dynamiser l'économie. L'adoption de mesures destinées à libérer le marché du crédit telles que la fourniture massive de liquidités[3] a été recommandée avec insistance. Ce n'est pas tout, le G-20 a rappelé qu'une telle relance ne saurait être effective qu'avec le concours d'une amélioration des règles techniques monétaires et financières ainsi que de l'émergence d'une coopération macro-économique entre les États.[4] Le FMI s'est montré très enclin à cette perspective. De nombreux plans de relance nationaux ont été proposés par le Fonds dont le montant serait évalué à 2 % du PIB des États participants. Le Groupe a, enfin, réaffirmé le souhait d'une réforme des institutions de Bretton Woods.[5]

II LES INSTITUTIONS FINANCIÈRES INTERNATIONALES

En 2008, la crise a fait émerger, au sein de la communauté internationale, la volonté unanime de reconsidérer la gouvernance des institutions financières internationales. De nombreuses propositions de réformes ont été formulées avec pertinence dans lesquelles le Canada a occupé une place de premier plan.

---

2 É.-U., Office of the Press Secretary, *Declaration Summit on Financial Markets and the World Economy*, Washington, 15 novembre 2008 à la p. 1.

3 *Ibid.*

4 *Ibid.* à la p. 2.

5 *Ibid.* à la p. 3.

A LE FONDS MONÉTAIRE INTERNATIONAL (FMI)

Face à la crise financière, le Fonds monétaire international (FMI) ne pouvait que faire de la reprise durable et de la restauration de la stabilité financière deux priorités à réaliser. En 2008, la contribution des 186 membres du FMI s'est évaluée à 217,4 milliards de DTS.[6] Devant l'afflux massif des demandes de prêts totalisant une année record pour le FMI,[7] le contexte de récession a appelé la contribution des États afin que le Fonds constitue des réserves de liquidités plus solides. Le Canada totalise un montant maximal de 6,37 milliards de DTS,[8] soit une somme que le FMI serait en mesure de solliciter pour compléter ses réserves, ce qui représente 2,93 % de l'ensemble de ses quotes-parts.

Pour l'ensemble de l'économie mondiale, le FMI demeure optimiste. A l'instar de l'année 2007, où la croissance se situait à 4,9 %, une croissance de 3,7 % a été enregistrée en 2008. Les ralentissements dus à la crise financière ne pourront être évités par les pays industrialisés ainsi que par les pays émergents. Pourtant, ces derniers peuvent espérer conserver un rythme de croissance supérieur aux prévisions du FMI. Le Canada ne peut échapper entièrement aux conséquences de la crise financière mondiale comme en témoigne le taux de croissance évalué à 1,3 % cette année. Néanmoins, sa position stratégique lui permet de faire face aux fluctuations du marché économique mondial.[9]

L'efficacité du mandat de surveillance de l'économie mondiale du FMI révèle un bilan ombrageux. Malgré l'identification des risques et l'émission de nombreux avertissements par le FMI, le Fonds n'a pas su anticiper la situation de récession financière. Le dernier rapport du Bureau indépendant d'évaluation (BIE) du FMI fait état de lacunes d'ordre structurel au sein de l'organisation du

---

6 Direction des finances et des échanges internationaux, *Rapport sur les opérations effectuées en vertu de la Loi sur les accords de Bretton Woods et des accords connexes 2008* à la p. 19 [*Rapport Bretton Woods*].

7 *Ibid.* à la p. 22. L'Ukraine et la Hongrie ont totalisé un prêt de plus de 20 milliards de DTS.

8 *Ibid.* à la p. 19.

9 Ministère des finances Canada, Communiqué 2008–020, "Un rapport du FMI indique que le Canada jouit d'une position enviable pour surmonter les défis économiques" (23 février 2008) en ligne: Ministère des Finances Canada, <http://www.fin.gc.ca/n08/08-020-fra.asp>.

Fonds. Selon le BIE, l'action du FMI nécessiterait d'instaurer un climat de transparence au sein de ses organes de gouvernance.[10] Le FMI a fait preuve de réactivité en ciblant son action sur l'urgence d'envisager la relance. De nombreux financements ont été accordés grâce à la flexibilisation des conditions d'octroi de prêt. Le FMI a manifesté le souci de limiter les effets de la crise dans les pays à faible revenu par l'octroi d'aides financières additionnelles. De plus, une réforme en matière de facilités de prêts a été adoptée au cours du mois d'octobre 2008, créant ainsi la facilité de liquidité à court terme (FLC).[11] Cette facilité est destinée à soutenir les pays dont la viabilité financière s'est retrouvée affectée par les turbulences des marchés extérieurs. Le Canada a activement participé à l'élaboration d'un tel programme par la promotion de standards de transparence appliqués aux autres facilités du FMI afin de protéger les liquidités du Fonds. Une réforme de la surveillance a également été envisagée avec pertinence par la mise en place d'un nouvel examen de taux de change et du Programme d'évaluation du secteur financier (PESF) afin d'anticiper les situations à risques.

Alors que l'année 2007 avait constaté le déficit budgétaire du FMI, l'année 2008 a été consacrée à la relève. Deux mesures ont été adoptées afin de cristalliser la dépendance du Fonds vis-à-vis des revenus générés par les intérêts sur les prêts consentis et de développer de nouvelles sources de revenus pour le Fonds. En 2008, le bilan des actions du Canada au sein du FMI fait preuve de solidarité. L'implication du gouvernement canadien s'est manifestée à travers de nombreuses recommandations auprès du FMI dans le but de développer un plan d'action. Le contrôle des dépenses prévisionnelles, la transparence et la définition des rôles et des responsabilités des organes de direction demeurent les principales observations identifiées par le Canada, lesquelles permettraient de renforcer l'efficacité du mandat de surveillance de l'économie financière du FMI. En 2008, le gouvernement du Canada, par exemple, n'a pas voté en faveur de l'allègement de la dette de la Guinée-Bissau en raison d'une absence de preuve d'un engagement significatif de saine gouvernance.

Le Canada a également participé à la promotion d'une coopération internationale dans le but de pallier la situation de récession

10 *Rapport Bretton Woods, supra* note 6.

11 "Le FMI crée une facilité de prêt à court terme" *Bulletin du FMI,* 37:11 (novembre 2008), en ligne: FMI, <http://www.imf.org/external/pubs/ft/survey/fre/2008/113008f.pdf>.

et a fermement encouragé l'octroi de prêts à certains pays touchés par la crise. La collaboration du FMI avec le Forum de stabilité financière (FSF) était par ailleurs à l'ordre du jour des recommandations émises par le gouvernement canadien dans le but de renforcer l'analyse des risques et d'anticiper toute situation susceptible d'affecter la stabilité du marché monétaire et financier afin de rénover le FMI en "un centre d'excellence de la surveillance macrofinancière."[12]

En ce qui concerne les quotes-parts,[13] une nouvelle formule de calcul a été élaborée dans le but de refléter les réalités du marché économique et notamment d'assurer une plus grande représentativité des marchés émergents. Le Canada est le premier pays à subir les conséquences de cette mesure par une réduction de 0,4 % de ses droits de vote mais le gouvernement demeure convaincu que cette mesure aura pour effet de renforcer la crédibilité du FMI. Cette réforme devrait entrer en vigueur dès que 85 % des membres du FMI ont ratifié cette disposition dans leur ordre interne. Le Canada prévoit de prendre les mesures nécessaires en vue d'une ratification dès 2009 et d'inciter les autres membres du Fonds à contribuer à l'application de cette nouvelle réforme de gouvernance assurant une représentativité plus juste.

B   LA BANQUE MONDIALE

La crise financière s'est traduite par un ralentissement de la croissance. Le faible taux de PIB a eu pour conséquence de réviser les prévisions de la Banque mondiale à la baisse. La Banque mondiale a joué un rôle crucial dans l'élaboration de nouvelles solutions palliatives afin d'amoindrir les conséquences de la récession et de mettre en place un plan de relance mondial. Son action a bénéficié du concours du gouvernement canadien dans l'élaboration de plusieurs mesures. Celles-ci concernent de prime abord la réduction du prix des aliments et des combustibles pour laquelle la Banque a agi de manière pragmatique en apportant son soutien technique ainsi que de nombreux financements pour aider les pays les plus touchés par la crise alimentaire.

---

[12] *Rapport Bretton Woods, supra* note 6.

[13] Fonds monétaire international, "Reform of IMF Quotas and Voice: Responding to Changes in the Global Economy" *Issues Briefs* 01:08 (April 2008), en ligne: FMI, <http://www.imf.org/external/np/exr/ib/2008/pdf/040108.pdf>.

Une place centrale a été accordée aux pays en développement emprunteurs par les institutions de la Banque mondiale, notamment l'Association internationale de développement (IDA).[14] À cet effet, les objectifs du millénaire pour le développement ont été réitérés pour l'année 2008[15] et des mesures réglementaires ont été prises afin d'en assurer l'efficacité.[16] De plus, la Banque mondiale a révisé à la hausse le montant des prêts à consentir pour les pays en développement, ce dernier étant évalué à trois fois le montant répertorié l'année précédente. De nouvelles facilités ont été mises en place afin de mettre à disposition des fonds plus rapidement pour les dépenses liées aux filets de sécurité, aux infrastructures, à l'éducation et aux services de santé.[17]

La Banque mondiale a par ailleurs conservé le même objectif que le FMI, soit d'assurer la représentativité des pays les moins développés. Cette perspective révèle le débat sur une potentielle réforme de la gouvernance de la Banque mondiale, laquelle a suscité l'intérêt du Groupe des 20. Le contexte de récession a impulsé, au cours de l'année 2008, la création par le Groupe des 20 d'un groupe de travail sur la Banque mondiale auquel participe le Canada,[18] placé sous l'angle du renouveau de l'institution et de la modernisation de ses organes de gouvernance. Le gouvernement du Canada déplore en effet des lacunes dans la surveillance des fonds fiduciaires, laquelle nécessiterait des impératifs de transparence renforcée et stratégique, une défaillance dans l'évaluation des résultats, et une meilleure répartition des dépenses.

En 2008, le Canada a apporté une contribution de 384M $ afin de corroborer le cadre de la quinzième reconstitution de l'IDA (IDA15).[19] Son activité s'est, de plus, illustrée par l'adoption de la Loi de mise en œuvre de la convention pour le règlement des différends relatifs aux investissements entre États et ressortissants

---

[14] *Rapport Bretton Woods, supra* note 6 à la p. 39. L'IDA a concentré plus de la moitié de ses ressources au développement des infrastructures en Afrique et en Asie du Sud pour un montant approximatif de 8,5 G $ US.

[15] *Ibid.* à la p. 29.

[16] *Ibid.* à la p. 45. Le Canada a adopté la Loi sur la responsabilité en matière d'aide au développement officielle. Entrée en vigueur le 28 juin 2008, celle-ci définit les conditions de recevabilité de l'aide internationale afin qu'elle soit reconnue comme aide officielle.

[17] *Ibid.* à la p. 28.

[18] *Ibid.* à la p. 64.

[19] *Ibid.* à la p. 44.

(projet de loi C-9) et par un soutien formel à la mise en place, par la Banque mondiale, d'un fonds d'investissement climatiques (FIC)[20] destiné à cristalliser un plan de relance mondial et à faciliter la recherche de nouvelles sources de financements rentables. Le Canada s'est prononcé favorablement sur cette dernière mesure, laquelle est l'occasion de raviver le débat sur les changements climatiques et les réformes à envisager à cet effet.

III LES ORGANISMES DE CONTRÔLE DES ÉTABLISSEMENTS FINANCIERS

A LE COMITÉ DE BÂLE SUR LE CONTRÔLE BANCAIRE

Le Comité de Bâle sur le contrôle bancaire (CBCB) a pour objectif de concentrer ses efforts sur la promotion d'un marché monétaire stable et l'harmonisation de la réglementation financière internationale.[21] En 2008, l'action du Comité a concentré ses efforts sur l'élaboration d'un plan d'action pour limiter les effets de la crise.

Depuis le remplacement de l'accord de Bâle I par l'accord de Bâle II en 2006,[22] de nouvelles préoccupations sont apparues avec la crise financière, notamment celles concernant les agences de notation. La Commission fédérale suisse des banques, dénonçant les lacunes de la mondialisation de la bulle du crédit,[23] a souligné la nécessité de renforcer l'application des accords de Bâle II pour un meilleur contrôle des agences de notation.

Le CBCB a manifesté un intérêt particulier pour les risques de liquidités à travers un rapport publié le 21 février 2008 dans lequel le Comité recense les lacunes dans la gestion de ces risques. Le Bureau du surintendant des institutions financières (BSIF) a apporté son concours à de nombreux travaux menés par le CBCB afin de combler les défaillances du système par l'élaboration de nouvelles règles de saine gouvernance et de saine gestion des risques. La

---

[20] Banque mondiale, Communiqué 2009/092/SDN, "Plus de 6,1 milliards de dollars pour les fonds d'investissement climatiques" (26 septembre 2008), en ligne: Banque mondiale, <http://go.worldbank.org/IQVoYECUNo>.

[21] Marion Navarro, "Les accords de Bâle" (2008) 1(3) Regards croisés sur l'économie 243.

[22] Colas, *supra* note 1 à la p. 454.

[23] Daniel Zuberbühler, Directeur de la Commission fédérale suisse des banques, Conférence de presse annuelle du 1er avril 2008, "*Crise mondiale du crédit — conséquences pour la surveillance des banques,*" en ligne: Autorité fédérale de surveillance des marchés financiers, <http://www.finma.ch/archiv/ebk/f/medien/medienkonferenz/referat-mko8-zuberbuehler-f.pdf>.

crise financière a dynamisé l'action du Comité, lequel a publié une version révisée, en septembre 2008, du document relatif aux saines pratiques de gestion des risques de liquidités dans les banques (*Sound Practices for Managing Liquidity Risk in Banking Organisations*).[24] Ce document précise la nécessité d'élaborer des stratégies de gestion efficaces mesurant les risques de liquidités par la mise en place de simulations de crise. Cette mesure a entraîné la révision de la directive B-6 *Liquidités* par le BSIF afin de se conformer aux nouvelles dispositions introduites par le CBCB.[25]

Le BSIF entend accélérer l'application des accords de Bâle II en incitant les banques canadiennes à moderniser leurs règles prudentielles en matière de crédit et d'investissement par la construction d'un dispositif plus sévère d'évaluation des risques afin de concourir à la rénovation du système de surveillance des banques au niveau mondial.[26] Il a par ailleurs apporté son concours ainsi que son soutien à la création de nouveaux mandats d'évaluation du bouleversement des marchés financiers en 2008 à travers l'élaboration des documents intitulés *Principles for home-host supervisory cooperation and allocation mechanisms in the context of Advanced measurement approaches* (AMA) et *Guidelines for Computing Capital for Incremental Default Risk in the Trading Book*. Le BSIF a également définit de nouveaux défis en matière de liquidité à travers le *Liquidity Risk: Management and Supervisory Challenges*. Enfin, lors de l'élaboration de ses travaux avec le CBCB et les banques canadiennes, le BSIF a soulevé avec pertinence l'importance des initiatives de normalisation comptable et a observé avec insistance que les principes de saine gouvernance ne visent pas seulement les institutions bancaires mais s'appliquent également, dans une perspective globalisante, aux sociétés d'assurance-vie.[27]

---

[24] Banque des règlements internationaux, Comité de Bâle sur le contrôle bancaire, *Principles for Sound Liquidity Risk Management and Supervision*, (septembre 2008), en ligne: Banque des règlements internationaux, <http://www.bis.org/publ/bcbs144.htm>.

[25] Bureau du surintendant des institutions financières Canada, Communiqué du 23 janvier 2009, en ligne: Bureau du surintendant des institutions financières Canada, <http://www.osfi-bsif.gc.ca/app/DocRepository/1/fra/directrices/prudentielles/preavis/b6_adv_f.pdf>.

[26] Bureau du surintendant des institutions financières Canada, *La réglementation prudentielle en période de défis. Rapport annuel 2008-2009 du BSIF*, en ligne: Bureau du surintendant des institutions financières Canada, <http://www.osfi-bsif.gc.ca/app/DocRepository/1/fra/rapports/bsif/aro809_f.pdf>.

[27] *Ibid.* à la p. 19.

B L'ORGANISATION INTERNATIONALE DES COMMISSIONS DES VALEURS (OICV)

La 33ème conférence annuelle de l'OICV s'est tenue en mai 2008 à Paris sur invitation de l'Autorité française des marchés financiers. Créée en 1983, l'organisation compte à présent 190 membres. Ayant décidé que tous les membres (annexe A) devaient être signataires ou avoir mis en œuvre tous les moyens nécessaires (annexe B) du MMoU, l'organisation a exprimé, lors de la conférence, être satisfaite des mesures qui avaient été prises par certains États afin d'honorer l'axe de coopération multilatéral (*MMoU-Multilateral Memorandum of Understanding*) signé en 2002. L'objet de la conférence a mis en exergue la nécessité de développer un dialogue avec la Commission des services financiers (*FSC-Financial Services Commission*) afin d'élaborer de nouvelles stratégies réglementaires tournées vers les marchés de capitaux et les risques qu'ils comportent.

En 2008, l'OICV a concentré ses efforts sur l'adoption de mesures et de propositions pour pallier la situation de récession mondiale.[28] L'organisation a fait preuve de modernité en inscrivant à l'ordre du jour de la conférence les questions d'audit, l'élaboration d'un code de conduite sur les agences d'évaluation de crédit et l'étude des travaux menés par le Groupe de travail sur les agences de notations *(Task Force on Credit Rating Agencies)*, le Groupe de travail sur la crise des *subprimes (Task Force on Subprimes Crisis)* ainsi que le Comité technique présidé par Christopher Cox. Les *Task Forces* ont, à cette occasion, rappelé la nécessité de faire de la transparence et de la vérification diligente au cœur des marchés financiers des priorités ainsi que de dynamiser les règles prudentielles et la gestion de l'évaluation et des risques. Le défi de l'OICV a été de faire face et de réguler les encours de crédit ainsi que de recommander aux autorités régulatrices de demeurer alertes à la fluctuation imprévisible des marchés afin qu'elles continuent de promouvoir la transparence, la protection des investisseurs par la communication d'informations comptables précises, et l'efficience à travers les frontières mais également au-delà du cadre strict de la réglementation. L'OICV envisage d'encadrer les produits dérivés dans le but d'opérer une meilleure gestion globale des risques liés

---

[28] Organisation internationale des commissions de valeurs, Communiqué IOSCO/MR/002/2008, "IOSCO addresses Subprime Crisis" (6 février 2008), en ligne: International Accounting Standards, <http://www.iasplus.com/iosco/0802 subprime.pdf>.

à la titrisation et aux marchés des swaps sur défaillance de crédit. Cette initiative permettrait d'appliquer les recommandations du Groupe des 20 afin de limiter les effets de la crise et de dynamiser la relance.

Par ailleurs, l'OICV a introduit deux nouveaux groupes de travail, l'un axé sur l'étude du marché des marchandises, l'autre mis en place par le Comité des marchés émergents (CME) de l'OICV, dont le but est d'effectuer une étude des impacts de la crise financière sur les marchés émergents.

Les Autorités canadiennes en valeurs mobilières ont appliqué des mesures consacrées à l'élaboration de principes généraux pour les *Hedge funds* et aux informations à communiquer aux clients non professionnels avant ou lors de la vente d'Organismes de Placement Collectif en Valeurs Mobilières (OPCVM) ou de produits similaires en 2007. Ainsi, les Autorités canadiennes ont adopté un règlement 81–101[29] destiné à améliorer l'information communiquée aux investisseurs de placement collectif.

IV LE GROUPE D'ACTION FINANCIÈRE (GAFI)

L'année 2008 a été, pour le Groupe d'action financière (GAFI), riche en actions menées par les États, notamment le Canada, dans la lutte mondiale contre le blanchiment d'argent et le financement du terrorisme. La présidence du Canada en 2007 a profondément instigué le renforcement de la communication avec le public. Cet objectif a été conservé par la présidence britannique en 2008.

Parallèlement à la réglementation en vigueur au mois de juin 2008, à la mise en conformité avec les standards et à la cinquième recommandation du GAFI,[30] l'essentiel des mesures prises par le Canada a consisté à incriminer le blanchiment d'argent et le financement des activités terroristes, à définir les confiscations et le gel, à inciter les institutions financières à adopter des mesures préventives, à structurer le contrôle des risques, à renforcer la coopération nationale et internationale et également, depuis le 30 décembre

---

29 *Règlement 81–101 sur le régime de prospectus des organismes de placement collectif,* en ligne: Autorité des marchés financiers, <http://www.lautorite.qc.ca/userfiles/File/reglementation/valeurs-mobilieres/autres-reglements-texte-vigueur/opc/81-101fr.pdf>.

30 Groupe d'action financière, *Recommandation spéciale V du GAFI: Coopération internationale,* en ligne: Groupe d'action financière, <http://www.fatf-gafi.org/document/16/0,3343,fr_32250379_32236920_44259472_1_1_1_1,00.html>.

2008, à permettre au Centre d'analyse des opérations et déclarations financières du Canada (CANAFE) de rendre effectives des pénalités administratives pécuniaires en cas de non-conformité à la Loi sur le recyclage des produits de la criminalité et le financement des activités terroristes (LRPCFAT).[31]

Les turbulences issues de la crise ont fait apparaître la nécessité pour le GAFI de réitérer la définition des normes internationales de lutte contre le blanchiment de capitaux[32] et d'inscrire la prévention des risques et la vigilance dans la procédure de surveillance des juridictions ayant des difficultés à mettre en place un système fiable. À cet effet, le cas de l'Iran réapparaît au cœur des discussions sur la scène internationale. Le GAFI a recensé dans un rapport du 16 octobre 2008[33] les défaillances du système mis en place par l'Iran de lutte contre le recyclage des produits de la criminalité et le financement des activités terroristes. Depuis l'adoption de mesures de vigilance par la résolution 1803 du Conseil de Sécurité des Nations Unies,[34] le BSIF a contribué au développement de l'action du GAFI par la diffusion d'un avis auprès des institutions financières qui interagiraient avec l'Iran et l'Ouzbékistan[35] ainsi que d'une ligne directrice révisée afin de décourager le recyclage de produits de la criminalité des activités terroristes.[36]

---

[31] *Règlement modifiant le Règlement sur les pénalités administratives – recyclage des produits de la criminalité et financement des activités terroristes*, au para. 28, en ligne: <http://www.gazette.gc.ca/rp-pr/p2/2008/2008-06-25/html/sor-dors194-fra.html>. Voir également Bureau du surintendant des institutions financières Canada, *Mécanisme de dissuasion et de détection du recyclage des produits de la criminalité et du financement des activités terroristes*, (décembre 2008), en ligne: Bureau du surintendant des institutions financières Canada <http://www.osfi bsif.gc.ca/app/DocRepository/1/fra/directrices/saines/directrices/B8_GIAS_f.pdf>.

[32] Groupe d'action financière, *Rapport annuel 2008-2009*, en ligne: Groupe d'action financière, <http://www.fatf-gafi.org/dataoecd/55/62/44086975.pdf>.

[33] Groupe d'action financière, Déclaration du GAFI, 16 octobre 2008, en ligne: Groupe d'action financière, <http://www.fatf-gafi.org/dataoecd/25/16/41509221.pdf>.

[34] Conseil de sécurité des Nations Unies, Résolution 1803, en ligne: Nations Unies <http://www.un.org/News/Press/docs/2008/sc9268.doc.htm>.

[35] Bureau du surintendant des institutions financières Canada, Avis du 16 octobre 2008 sur les Opérations financières liées à l'Iran et à l'Ouzbékistan, en ligne: Bureau du surintendant des institutions financières Canada, <http://www.osfi-bsif.gc.ca/app/DocRepository/1/fra/gafi/2008_10_16_f.pdf>.

[36] Groupe d'action financière, *supra* note 32.

Par ailleurs, le GAFI a procédé à une évaluation de la santé financière du Canada à travers un rapport d'évaluation mutuelle,[37] lequel a révélé que son système de surveillance était satisfaisant. Une réponse à ce rapport a été formulée par le Canada, laquelle devrait être étudiée par le GAFI en février 2009. Cette réponse comporte des mesures tendant à dynamiser les dispositions de la LRPCFAT dans le but de les rendre plus effectives.[38]

V LE JOINT FORUM

Créé en 1996, le Joint Forum est un organisme de concertation sur les thèmes prudentiels transectoriels en vue de l'élaboration de normes de contrôle des conglomérats financiers.

En 2008, la récession a atteint son paroxysme. Les travaux menés par le Joint Forum ne pouvaient que s'intéresser de près aux transferts de risques de crédit entre banques et institutions financières. Un rapport a été publié le 31 juillet 2008,[39] lequel suggérait la réforme d'un système bancaire où la gestion des liquidités serait renforcée afin d'anticiper les lacunes structurelles des institutions bancaires et d'instaurer un climat de transparence financière.

L'action du BSIF a placé le Canada au centre d'une coopération internationale par la conclusion de plus de vingt-cinq accords internationaux avec divers organismes de surveillance financière internationale.[40] Les institutions financières canadiennes se sont montrées très réceptives aux impératifs de transparence avancés par le Joint Forum. Un projet cadre relatif à l'information au moment de la souscription des organismes de placement collectif et des fonds distincts a vu le jour le 24 octobre 2008.[41] La Commission

---

37 Groupe d'action financière, *Third Mutual Evaluation on Anti-Money Laundering and Combating the Financing of Terrorism,* en ligne: Groupe d'action financière, <http://www.fatf-gafi.org/dataoecd/5/3/40323928.pdf>.

38 Bureau du surintendant des institutions financières Canada, *supra* note 31.

39 Banque des règlements internationaux, Communiqué "Joint Forum final release of "Credit risk transfer" paper" (30 juillet 2008), en ligne: Banque des règlements internationaux, <http://www.bis.org/press/p080731.htm>.

40 Bureau du surintendant des institutions financières Canada, *Rapport annuel 2008-2009,* en ligne: Bureau du surintendant des institutions financières Canada, <http://www.osfi-bsif.gc.ca/app/DocRepository/1/fra/rapports/bsif/ar0809_f.pdf>.

41 *Projet-cadre repris par le règlement modifiant le Règlement sur les renseignements à fournir au consommateur* (entrée en vigueur: 4 septembre 2009), en ligne: Autorité des

des valeurs mobilières de l'Ontario (CVMO) a, quant à elle, orienté son action sur la gestion des risques par la publication de l'Avis 81–709 sur le rapport de l'examen de l'information continue des fonds d'investissement par le personnel.[42] Dans cet avis, la Commission recense les défaillances que peuvent accompagner les rapports de gestion ainsi que les solutions à envisager pour la construction d'une saine gouvernance des états financiers. En 2008, le contexte de crise a fait émerger la nécessité de réformer les organes de gouvernance des institutions financières internationales afin de construire un système financier international plus performant, en mesure de répondre aux impératifs de croissance et de relance économique, mais également capable de jouer un rôle de premier plan dans la gestion des risques. Le Canada et les forums dans lesquels il intervient ont réitéré les objectifs de surveillance, de saine transparence ainsi que de réforme.

---

marchés financiers, <http://www.lautorite.qc.ca/userfiles/File/Consultations/090904_Reg13_cons_publ_fr.pdf>.

[42] Commission des valeurs mobilières de l'Ontario, *Rapport Annuel 2008*, à la p.15, en ligne: Commission des valeurs mobilières de l'Ontario, <http://www.osc.gov.on.ca/documents/fr/About/rpt_2008-osc-fr.pdf>.

III Investissement

CÉLINE LÉVESQUE

I Introduction

L a chronique de l'année 2008 est principalement consacrée à
l'étude comparative de deux sentences rendues dans les affaires
mexicaines concernant les édulcorants[1] sous le régime du chapitre
11 (Investissement) de l'Accord de libre-échange nord-américain
(ALENA).[2] Dans ces affaires, des investisseurs américains se sont
plaints de l'imposition par le Mexique d'une taxe de 20 % sur les
boissons gazeuses qui utilisaient un édulcorant autre que le sucre
de canne. Dans les deux sentences, les tribunaux ont conclu que la
mesure était discriminatoire, car elle visait à protéger l'industrie
mexicaine du sucre aux dépens des producteurs étrangers de sirop

Céline Lévesque est professeure agrégée, Faculté de droit, Section de droit civil,
Université d'Ottawa. En 2008–09, la professeure Lévesque occupait le poste d'uni-
versitaire en résidence à la Direction générale du droit commercial international,
Ministère des Affaires étrangères et du Commerce international. Les opinions
exprimées dans cette chronique sont celles de l'auteure et ne reflètent pas nécessairement celles du gouvernement du Canada. L'auteure remercie Stanko Krstic
pour son assistance de recherche et le Conseil de recherche en sciences humaines
du Canada pour son soutien financier.

1 *Corn Products International, Inc. c. Mexico,* Decision on Responsibility, ICSID Case
no. ARB(AF)/04/01 (15 janvier 2008) [*CPI*]; *Archer Daniels Midland Company
and Tate & Lyle Ingredients Americas, Inc. c. Mexico,* Award, ICSID Case no.
ARB(AF)/04/05 (21 novembre 2007) [*ADM*]. Voir aussi *Archer Daniels Midland
Company et al. c. Mexico,* Decision on the Requests for Correction, Supplementary Decision and Interpretation, ICSID Case no. ARB(AF)/04/05 (10 juillet
2008).

2 *Accord de libre-échange nord-américain entre le gouvernement du Canada, le
gouvernement des États-Unis d'Amérique et le gouvernement du Mexique,* 17
décembre 1992, R.T. Can. 1994 no. 2, 32(3) I.L.M. 605 (entrée en vigueur: 1er
janvier 2004) [ALENA].

de maïs à haute teneur en fructose.[3] Cette conclusion commune, toutefois, ne doit pas cacher les nombreux désaccords entre les tribunaux, certains ayant une importance majeure en droit international des investissements. Aussi l'intérêt de ces sentences dépasse-t-il largement celui porté à l'interprétation de l'une ou l'autre obligation du chapitre 11 de l'ALENA. Ces affaires posent le problème du risque d'incohérence inhérent au droit international des investissements et se situent dans le débat plus large de l'unité de l'ordre juridique international.

D'autres développements de l'année 2008 concernant le Canada méritent toutefois d'être soulignés. Le 28 janvier 2008, le Tribunal a rendu sa décision dans l'affaire *Canadian Cattlemen for Fair Trade c. Unites States.*[4] Dans cette affaire, plus de cent demandeurs canadiens ont porté plainte contre les États-Unis en vertu du chapitre 11 de l'ALENA. La plainte concernait notamment la fermeture de la frontière américaine à l'exportation de bovins canadiens suite à la découverte d'un cas de maladie dite de la vache folle en Alberta.[5] Le Tribunal dans cette affaire a décliné l'exercice de sa compétence. Suite à un accord entre les parties, une seule question avait été soumise au Tribunal. En bref, le Tribunal devait décider si des investisseurs canadiens, qui n'ont pas d'investissements aux États-Unis mais qui opèrent dans un marché nord-américain intégré, peuvent se prévaloir du chapitre 11 de l'ALENA pour faire valoir des allégations de discrimination.[6] Le Tribunal a confirmé que le chapitre 11 visait la protection des investissements *étrangers* et que les investisseurs ne pouvaient pas être séparés de leurs investissements.[7]

La sentence dans l'affaire *Bayview Irrigation c. Mexico,*[8] qui portait aussi sur des questions de territorialité, a fait l'objet d'une demande

---

3   Dans l'affaire *ADM, supra* note 1, le Mexique a été condamné à payer un montant de 33 millions de dollars américains à titre de dommages tandis que dans l'affaire *CPI, supra* note 1, le Mexique a été condamné à payer 58 millions de dollars. Il est à noter que la sentence dans l'affaire *CPI* ne contient pas l'évaluation des dommages. Le montant a été rendu public en 2009 bien que le texte de la décision ne soit toujours pas disponible.

4   *Canadian Cattlemen for Fair Trade c. United States,* Award on Jurisdiction, UNCITRAL (28 janvier 2008) [*CCFT*].

5   Voir *ibid.* au para. 2.

6   *Ibid.* au para. 31.

7   *Ibid.* aux para. 112, 118–23 et 127.

8   *Bayview Irrigation District et al. c. Mexico,* ICSID Case no. ARB(AF)/05/01 (19 juin 2007).

d'annulation de la part des demandeurs américains.[9] Cette demande a été rejetée sans peine par la Cour supérieure de l'Ontario en janvier 2008.[10]

Par ailleurs, il faut souligner la signature en 2008 des Accords de libre-échange entre le Canada et le Pérou,[11] et entre le Canada et la Colombie[12] qui contiennent tous deux un chapitre portant sur l'investissement. On se rappelle que le Canada et le Pérou avait signé en 2006 un accord de promotion et de protection des investissements (APIE Canada-Pérou).[13] L'accord de libre-échange signé entre ces pays prévoit que l'APIE est suspendu à partir de l'entrée en vigueur de l'accord de libre-échange.[14] Hormis les différences auxquelles on s'attend entre un accord de libre-échange et un APIE (par exemple, l'emplacement dans différents chapitres d'obligations communes et l'ajout de dispositions visant l'interaction entre les chapitres), les dispositions de ces deux accords sont très similaires. Les innovations dans l'APIE (le plus souvent fondées sur le modèle de 2004) se retrouvent dans le nouvel accord.[15] La disposition qui retient le plus l'attention est celle portant sur la responsabilité sociale des entreprises.[16] En effet, il semble qu'il s'agisse de

[9] C. Lévesque, "Chronique de Droit international économique en 2007: Investissement," (2008) XLVI A.C.D.I. aux pp. 478–85.

[10] *Bayview Irrigation District no. 11 et al. c. Mexico*, Reasons for Judgment, Court file no. 07-CV-340139-PD2 (5 mai 2008) (Ont. Sup. Ct. J.), Allen J.

[11] Accord de libre-échange Canada-Pérou, 29 mai 2008 (entrée en vigueur: 1er août 2009), en ligne: Affaires étrangères et Commerce international Canada <http://www.international.gc.ca/trade-agreements-accords-commerciaux/agr-acc/peru-perou/peru-toc-perou-tdm.aspx?lang=fra> [ALE Canada-Pérou].

[12] Accord de libre-échange Canada-Colombie, 21 novembre 2008, en ligne: Affaires étrangères et Commerce international Canada <http://www.international.gc.ca/trade-agreements-accords-commerciaux/agr-acc/colombia-colombie/can-colombia-toc-tdm-can-colombie.aspx?lang=fra> [ALE Canada-Colombie].

[13] C. Lévesque, "Chronique de Droit international économique en 2006: Investissement," (2007) XLV A.C.D.I. aux pp. 377–80.

[14] ALE Canada-Pérou, *supra* note 11, art. 845.

[15] Voir Lévesque, *supra* note 13.

[16] Voir ALE Canada-Pérou, *supra* note 11, art. 810: "Chaque Partie devrait encourager les entreprises exerçant leurs activités sur son territoire ou relevant de sa juridiction à intégrer volontairement des normes de responsabilité sociale des entreprises internationalement reconnue dans leurs politiques internes, telles que des déclarations de principe qui ont été approuvées ou qui sont appuyées par les Parties. Ces principes portent sur des questions telles que le travail,

la première fois qu'un accord de libre-échange inclu une telle disposition. Son effet utile reste, bien sûr, à voir.

Le chapitre sur l'investissement de l'ALE Canada-Colombie ressemble en grande partie à l'ALE Canada-Pérou. Il contient notamment le même article sur la responsabilité sociale des entreprises.[17] On note toutefois des différences, par exemple, quant à la norme minimale de traitement (notamment, l'ajout d'une définition de l'expression "droit international coutumier" et d'une référence spécifique au déni de justice)[18] et quant au droit applicable (en référence à la pertinence du droit interne d'une Partie).[19]

II   LES AFFAIRES MEXICAINES CONCERNANT LES ÉDULCORANTS ET LES DÉFIS DU DROIT INTERNATIONAL DES INVESTISSEMENTS

La comparaison des sentences dans les affaires *ADM* et *CPI* est fascinante, car elle illustre le risque d'incohérence inhérent au droit international des investissements. L'exemple est d'autant plus frappant que ces affaires sont presque identiques. Les plaintes ont été portées en vertu du même traité, contre la même partie défenderesse, par des investisseurs qui sont producteurs et distributeurs d'un même produit, et qui se plaignent de la même mesure gouvernementale. Malgré cela, les tribunaux sont arrivés à des conclusions divergentes sur plusieurs points. Une jonction (ou *"consolidation"*) de ces affaires aurait pu permettre d'éviter ce résultat.[20] Toutefois,

---

l'environnement, les droits de l'homme, les relations avec la collectivité et la lutte contre la corruption. Les Parties rappellent à ces entreprises l'importance d'intégrer ces normes de responsabilité sociale des entreprises dans leurs politiques internes." Voir aussi les art. 801(1)(c) et 817.

17 ALE Canada-Colombie, *supra* note 12, art. 816.

18 *Ibid.*

19 *Ibid.*, art. 832, note 10 qui prévoit que: "Conformément au droit international, et dans les cas où cela est pertinent et approprié, le tribunal peut prendre en considération le droit de la Partie contestante. Toutefois, le tribunal n'a pas compétence pour se prononcer sur la légalité de la mesure dont on allègue qu'elle constitue un manquement au présent accord en vertu de la législation interne de la Partie contestante."

20 Voir ALENA, *supra* note 2, art. 1126 (Jonction) qui prévoit que: "Un tribunal établi aux termes du présent article qui est convaincu que les plaintes soumises à l'arbitrage en vertu de l'article 1120 portent sur un même point de droit ou de fait pourra, dans l'intérêt d'un règlement juste et efficace des plaintes, et après audition des parties contestantes, par ordonnance: a) se saisir de ces plaintes et en connaître ensemble, en totalité ou en partie; ou b) se saisir de

on se rappelle que la demande de jonction faite par le Mexique en 2004 avait été rejetée par un tribunal constitué pour en décider.[21]

Un aspect de ces sentences qui retient l'attention est celui de l'interaction du droit international des investissements avec le droit international du commerce, d'une part, et avec le droit international général, d'autre part. En effet, les tribunaux ont notamment eu à se demander quelle valeur ils devaient accorder à des décisions rendues par les organes juridictionnels de l'Organisation mondiale du commerce (OMC), dans un différend opposant les États-Unis et le Mexique, concernant la même mesure et des allégations similaires de discrimination. Ils ont également eu à se prononcer sur l'application, sous le régime du chapitre 11 de l'ALENA, de la défense de contre-mesures présentée par le Mexique; la contre-mesure tirant ici sa source dans le droit international général. Dans les deux cas, les tribunaux ont appréhendé ces questions relationnelles de façon différentes.

A FAITS ET CONTEXTE JURIDIQUE

Archer Daniels Midland Company et Tate & Lyle Ingredients Americas, Inc. (ci-après collectivement, ADM) et Corn Products International, Inc. (CPI) sont des compagnies américaines qui produisent et distribuent du sirop de maïs à haute teneur en fructose (SHTF).[22] Le SHTF est utilisé pour l'édulcoration des boissons gazeuses et des produits alimentaires. Aux États-Unis, il a graduellement remplacé le sucre comme édulcorant, mais ce n'est pas avant le milieu des années 1980 qu'il est devenu le produit de choix pour sucrer les aliments, et particulièrement les boissons gazeuses. Le SHTF est en effet moins coûteux et plus facile à utiliser que le sucre parce qu'il est sous forme liquide. Au Mexique, pendant ce temps, le sucre était exclusivement utilisé pour dulcifier les boissons gazeuses

---

l'une ou de plusieurs des plaintes dont le règlement, selon le tribunal, faciliterait le règlement des autres, et en connaître."

21 *Corn Products International, Inc. c. Mexico* and *Archer Daniels Midland Company and Tate & Lyle Ingredients Americas, Inc. c. Mexico*, Order of the Consolidation Tribunal, ICSID Case no. ARB(AF)/04/01 (20 mai 2005) [*Consolidation Decision*]. Le Tribunal avait conclu que l'efficacité des procédures serait compromise. Il a jugé que la relation de concurrence existant entre les demandeurs aurait exigé la mise en place d'arrangements complexes afin de protéger l'information confidentielle, ce qui aurait aussi causé des délais. Voir *Consolidation Decision*, aux para. 8–14 et 18–19. Voir aussi plus bas à la Partie II. D.

22 *ADM, supra* note 1 au para. 39; *CPI, supra* note 1 au para. 27.

jusqu'au début des années 1990, lorsque les compagnies américaines ont commencé à pénétrer ce marché.[23] ADM et CPI ont toutes deux choisi d'investir dans la production locale de SHTF au Mexique, important à cette fin le maïs jaune des États-Unis. Elles ont aussi exporté le SHTF vers le Mexique à partir de leurs usines de production aux États-Unis.[24]

Le commerce du sucre et des sirops avait été l'objet d'une attention particulière dans le cadre des négociations de l'ALENA. Une annexe concernant l'accès aux marchés prévoyait une période de transition de quinze ans vers une libéralisation dans le secteur entre le Mexique et les États-Unis. L'atteinte du statut de "producteur excédentaire net" de sucre par une des Parties avait pour conséquence un accès accru en franchise au marché de l'autre. L'excédent net de production était calculé en rapport avec la consommation de sucre sur le territoire d'une Partie.[25] Le manque de clarté de cette annexe est rapidement devenu un problème.

En 1993, après la signature de l'ALENA, mais avant son entrée en vigueur, les États-Unis ont informé le Mexique de certaines ambiguïtés en ce qui a trait aux articles portant sur le sucre et les sirops. Malgré un échange de lettres pour régler le problème, des désaccords persistaient quant à la teneur de l'accord. Les Parties ne s'entendaient pas sur le traitement du SHTF dans le calcul de l'excédent net de production d'une Partie.[26] Cette mésentente a pris une signification particulière en 1995, lorsque le Mexique est devenu un producteur excédentaire, mais les Parties ne pouvaient pas s'entendre sur l'ampleur de ce surplus.[27]

Un déséquilibre important s'en est suivi. Les producteurs mexicains ne pouvaient pas exporter leur surplus de sucre sans droits de douane aux États-Unis (selon leur point de vue, contrairement aux dispositions de l'ALENA), tandis que plus de SHTF était exporté et produit au Mexique, accentuant le surplus de sucre.[28] Le Mexique a porté plainte au plus haut niveau du gouvernement américain sans résultat. Suite à des démarches de consultations

---

23 *ADM, supra* note 1 aux para. 39–40 et 55; *CPI, supra* note 1 aux para. 26–27.

24 *ADM, supra* note 1 aux para. 42–43; *CPI, supra* note 1 aux para. 27–30.

25 *ADM, supra* note 1 au para. 59; *CPI, supra* note 1 aux para. 6 et 33. Voir également ALENA, *supra* note 2 à l'Annexe 703.2.

26 *ADM, supra* note 1 aux para. 57–68; *CPI, supra* note 1 au para. 34.

27 *ADM, supra* note 1 au para. 69; *CPI, supra* note 1 aux para. 82–83.

28 *ADM, supra* note 1 au para. 71; *CPI, supra* note 1 au para. 35.

infructueuses, le Mexique a finalement demandé la constitution d'un groupe spécial en vertu du chapitre 20 (règlement des différends entre États) de l'ALENA. Cependant, le groupe spécial n'a jamais été constitué. Le Mexique a accusé les États-Unis de faire obstacle à la constitution du groupe, alors que les États-Unis ont nié avoir agi à l'encontre de leurs obligations en vertu de l'ALENA.[29]

Devant cette impasse et la crise dans l'industrie sucrière, le Mexique a adopté une série de mesures visant à protéger l'industrie mexicaine du sucre. Ces mesures ont affecté négativement l'industrie du SHTF, une industrie américaine comptant les producteurs ADM et CPI. Ces différentes mesures ont aussi donné lieu à des recours multiples en vertu de l'ALENA, mais aussi à l'OMC.

En juin 1997, le Mexique a imposé des droits antidumping sur le SHTF importé. Ces droits ont été contestés par les États-Unis devant l'OMC et un Groupe spécial a conclu en 2000 que ces mesures étaient incompatibles avec les obligations du Mexique en vertu de l'accord antidumping. Les États-Unis sont retournés devant l'OMC en 2001, qui a statué une fois de plus que le Mexique ne respectait pas ses obligations.[30] Parallèlement, certains fournisseurs de SHTF ont entamé des procédures en vertu du chapitre 19 (Examen et règlement des différends en matière de droits antidumping et compensateurs) de l'ALENA.[31] Dans des décisions rendues en 2001 et 2002, le Groupe spécial a demandé au Mexique de révoquer ses droits antidumping et de rembourser les sommes versées par les demandeurs.[32]

À l'automne 2001, essayant d'atténuer les impacts sur son industrie du sucre, le Mexique a procédé à l'expropriation d'un certain nombre de raffineries de sucre qui traversaient une période financière difficile. Ces mesures ont mené à une plainte en vertu du chapitre 11 de l'ALENA par les investisseurs minoritaires américains d'une des compagnies dont la raffinerie a été expropriée. Le Mexique a eu gain de cause dans cette affaire.[33]

---

[29] *ADM, supra* note 1 aux para. 71 et 77–79; *CPI, supra* note 1 aux para. 37–39.

[30] *ADM, supra* note 1 aux para. 72–74.

[31] Le chapitre 19 de l'ALENA prévoit la possibilité d'un examen des déterminations finales d'une Partie en matière de droits antidumping et compensateurs par un groupe spécial. Voir ALENA, *supra* note 2.

[32] *ADM, supra* note 1 au para. 75.

[33] *CPI, supra* note 1 au para. 36 en référence à l'affaire *GAMI Investments, Inc. c. Mexico,* Final Award, UNCITRAL (15 novembre 2004) [*GAMI*].

Le 31 décembre 2001, le Mexique a modifié une loi qui imposait une taxe d'accise sur certains biens et services. La modification, qui prenait effet le lendemain, imposait une taxe de 20 % notamment sur les boissons gazeuses qui utilisaient un édulcorant autre que le sucre de canne (la taxe IEPS).[34] L'impact sur l'industrie du SHTF a été immédiat: plusieurs producteurs de boissons gazeuses ont recommencé à utiliser du sucre et les producteurs et fournisseurs de SHTF ont en conséquence encaissé des pertes importantes.[35] La taxe IEPS est la mesure au cœur des affaires *ADM* et *CPI*.[36]

C'est en 2003–04 que la contestation de la taxe IEPS par les investisseurs américains et par l'État américain a pris son envol. Un an après l'entrée en vigueur de la taxe, CPI a présenté au Mexique une notification de son intention de soumettre une plainte en vertu du chapitre 11 de l'ALENA. ADM a fait la même chose en octobre 2003, mois au cours duquel CPI a soumis sa plainte à l'arbitrage. La plainte d'ADM a suivi en août 2004.[37] Le Mexique a présenté sa demande pour la jonction de ces deux affaires en septembre 2004, requête qui a été rejetée par le tribunal en mai 2005.[38] Pendant ce temps, un autre investisseur américain, Cargill Incorporated, a signifié au Mexique en septembre son intention de soumettre une plainte à l'arbitrage et soumis sa plainte en décembre 2004.[39]

Alors que les plaintes des investisseurs se multipliaient, les États-Unis ont, en juin 2004, contesté la taxe IEPS devant l'OMC. En octobre 2005, un Groupe spécial a jugé que le Mexique n'avait pas respecté ses obligations en vertu de l'article III du GATT.[40] Avant

---

34 *ADM, supra* note 1 aux para. 81–82; *CPI, supra* note 1 au para. 40.

35 *ADM, supra* note 1 au para. 49; *CPI, supra* note 1 au para. 44.

36 Dans les années qui ont suivi, quelques embouteilleurs de boissons gazeuses ont gagné leurs recours *en amparo* contre la taxe IEPS et l'obligation d'obtenir une licence d'importation (adoptée à la même date que la taxe). Cette exonération, cependant, n'était accordée que sur une base individuelle et, de façon plus générale, n'a pas résolu les problèmes des demandeurs ADM et CPI. Voir *ADM, supra* note 1 au para. 7; *CPI, supra* note 1 au para. 45.

37 *ADM, supra* note 1 aux para. 13–15; *CPI, supra* note 1 au para. 15.

38 *ADM, supra* note 1 aux para. 16–22; *CPI, supra* note 1 aux para. 18–21. Voir également *Consolidation Decision, supra* note 21.

39 *Cargill, Incorporated c. Mexico*, Notice of Intent (30 septembre 2004) et *Cargill, Incorporated c. Mexico*, Request for Institution of Arbitration Proceedings (29 décembre 2004).

40 *ADM, supra* note 1 aux para. 87–96; *CPI, supra* note 1 au para. 47. Voir également *Mexique – Mesures fiscales concernant les boissons sans alcool et autres boissons* (2005)

d'arriver à cette conclusion, toutefois, le Groupe spécial a dû répondre aux arguments du Mexique qui tentait de le convaincre de ne pas exercer sa compétence et de renvoyer les Parties aux procédures de règlement des différends prévus au chapitre 20 de l'ALENA.[41] Subsidiairement, le Mexique a tenté de justifier la taxe en vertu de l'Article XX (Exceptions générales) du GATT. Ces deux tentatives ont été rejetées par le Groupe spécial et ensuite par l'Organe d'appel de l'OMC.[42]

Au sujet du manquement à l'obligation de traitement national, le Groupe spécial a conclu "qu'en tant qu'édulcorants pour les boissons sans alcool et sirops, le sucre de canne et le SHTF sont des produits entre lesquels un étroit rapport de concurrence existe et qu'ils peuvent sans aucun doute être considérés comme des 'produits similaires' au regard de l'article III:4."[43] Pour le Groupe spécial, il ne fait aucun doute que les boissons et sirops édulcorés avec du SHTF sont moins favorablement traités que ceux qui le sont avec du sucre de canne.[44] Il a estimé que "bien que les mesures, à première vue, n'établissent pas de distinction entre les édulcorants importés et les édulcorants nationaux, la distinction qu'elles font entre l'utilisation du sucre de canne et celle des édulcorants autres

---

OMC Doc. WT/DS308/R (Rapport du Groupe spécial) [*Mexique – Mesures fiscales concernant les boissons*].

[41] *Mexique – Mesures fiscales concernant les boissons, supra* note 40 aux para. 7.1–7.18. Le rapport du Groupe spécial rappelle que: "Le 18 janvier 2005, le Groupe spécial a rendu une décision préliminaire, rejetant la demande du Mexique visant à ce qu'il décline l'exercice de sa compétence dans l'affaire en faveur d'un groupe spécial arbitral établi au titre du chapitre 20 de l'Accord de libre-échange nord-américain (ALENA). Le Groupe spécial a conclu que, conformément au Mémorandum d'accord, il n'avait pas le pouvoir discrétionnaire de décider d'exercer ou non sa compétence dans une affaire qui lui était soumise à bon droit. En outre, même s'il avait eu ce pouvoir discrétionnaire, le Groupe spécial ne considérait pas qu'il y avait dans le dossier des faits qui auraient justifié qu'il décline l'exercice de sa compétence en l'espèce." (*ibid.* au para. 7.1) Dans son raisonnement, il a souligné que ces différends n'étaient pas en toute hypothèse identiques. (*ibid.* au para. 7.14).

[42] *ADM, supra* note 1 au para. 95; *CPI, supra* note 1 au para. 47. Voir également *Mexique – Mesures fiscales concernant les boissons sans alcool et autres boissons*, OMC Doc. AB-2005–10 (2006) (Rapport de l'organe d'appel).

[43] *Mexique – Mesures fiscales concernant les boissons, supra* note 40 au para. 8.106. Voir aussi le résumé des constatations dans *ADM, supra* note 1 aux para. 91–92; et dans *CPI, supra* note 1 au para. 47.

[44] *Mexique – Mesures fiscales concertant les boissons, supra* note 40 au para. 8.118.

que le sucre de canne est en fait une distinction entre les édulcorants importés et les édulcorants nationaux."[45]

Le Groupe spécial a ensuite rejeté le moyen de défense du Mexique selon lequel les mesures étaient justifiables en vertu de l'article XX d) du GATT, même si le Groupe spécial jugeait que la taxe IEPS violait l'article III.[46] Le Mexique avait notamment allégué que la taxe était une mesure "nécessaire pour assurer le respect" par les États-Unis de leurs obligations en vertu de l'ALENA et que de telles obligations étaient couvertes par les termes "lois et règlements." Le Mexique ayant qualifié ce moyen de défense de "contre-mesures," le Groupe spécial a discuté du rôle des contre-mesures dans le contexte de l'article XX d) et en particulier de la question de savoir si des contre-mesures étaient capables "d'assurer le respect" de lois et règlements. Il a conclu par la négative. Qui plus est, selon lui, les "lois et règlements" renvoyaient à des mesures intérieures, et ne comprenaient pas un accord international.[47]

En définitive, le Mexique a abrogé sa taxe IEPS, le 1er janvier 2007, cinq ans après son entrée en vigueur.[48] Cette abrogation faisait partie d'un accord conclu entre les deux pays en juillet 2006 pour mettre fin au litige sur les édulcorants.[49] Cependant, en date de 2007, le Mexique faisait apparemment toujours pression sur les États-Unis pour la constitution d'un groupe spécial en vertu du chapitre 20 de l'ALENA.

B QUESTIONS EN LITIGE ET CONCLUSIONS DES TRIBUNAUX

Dans les deux affaires, les demandeurs ont allégué la violation par le Mexique des obligations du chapitre 11 de l'ALENA prévues aux

---

[45] *Ibid.* au para. 8.119.

[46] *Ibid.* aux para. 8.162–8.203. Voir aussi *ADM, supra* note 1 aux para. 93–95; *CPI, supra* note 1 aux para 47 et 154–56. L'article XX du GATT prévoit que: "Sous réserve que ces mesures ne soient pas appliquées de façon à constituer soit un moyen de discrimination … rien dans le présent Accord ne sera interprété comme empêchant l'adoption ou l'application par toute partie contractante des mesures … d) nécessaires pour assurer le respect des lois et règlements qui ne sont pas incompatibles avec les dispositions du présent Accord."

[47] *Mexique – Mesures fiscales concernant les boissons, supra* note 47 aux para. 8.178–8.179. L'Organe d'appel a confirmé les conclusions du Groupe spécial même si certains des motifs étaient différents.

[48] *ADM, supra* note 1 aux para. 97–99; *CPI, supra* note 40 aux para. 43 et 48. Il est à noter que la taxe avait été suspendue pour une durée de quelques mois et rétablie par la suite.

[49] *ADM, supra* note 1 aux para. 13–15; *CPI, supra* note 1 au para. 48.

articles 1102 (Traitement national), 1106 (Prescriptions de résultats) et 1110 (Expropriation et indemnisation). Dans les deux cas, le Mexique a présenté une défense de contre-mesures. Les deux tribunaux ont conclu à la violation de l'article 1102 et ont rejeté les allégations de manquement à l'article 1110. Ils sont toutefois arrivés à des conclusions opposées sur la violation de l'article 1106: seul le Tribunal dans l'affaire *ADM* a conclu à un manquement de la part du Mexique. Tous deux ont rejeté la défense de contre-mesures offerte par la Mexique, mais pour des motifs diamétralement opposés.

C   RAISONNEMENT DES TRIBUNAUX ET ANALYSE COMPARATIVE

1   Traitement national: Article 1102

L'argument de discrimination était au cœur des plaintes portées par ADM et CPI en vertu de l'ALENA. L'article 1102(1) de cet accord prévoit que:

Chacune des Parties accordera aux investisseurs d'une autre Partie un traitement non moins favorable que celui qu'elle accorde, dans des circonstances similaires, à ses propres investisseurs, en ce qui concerne l'établissement, l'acquisition, l'expansion, la gestion, la direction, l'exploitation et la vente ou autre aliénation d'investissements.[50]

Dans les circonstances de ces affaires, les deux tribunaux n'ont eu aucune peine à conclure à la violation de l'obligation de traitement national. L'intention et l'effet de la taxe IEPS étaient de protéger l'industrie sucrière mexicaine et de désavantager l'industrie du SHTF sous contrôle étranger.[51] Le raisonnement des tribunaux démontre un accord sur plusieurs principes fondamentaux de l'obligation de traitement national mais aussi certaines divergences notamment quant à l'interaction du droit des investissements et du droit du commerce de l'OMC.

Les deux tribunaux s'entendent pour dire que l'objet de l'article 1102 est de s'assurer qu'une mesure étatique ne vienne pas altérer la relation de concurrence qui existe entre les investisseurs nationaux et étrangers, ou entre leurs investissements.[52] Selon eux, l'article

---

[50] ALENA, *supra* note 2, art. 1102(1). L'article 1102(2) impose la même obligation aux Parties, cette fois vis-à-vis des "investissements."

[51] *ADM, supra* note 1 aux para. 212–13; *CPI, supra* note 1 aux para. 137–38.

[52] *ADM, supra* note 1 au para. 199; *CPI, supra* note 1 aux para. 111 et 120.

prohibe la discrimination sur la base de la nationalité, qu'elle soit *de jure* ou *de facto*.[53] Ils établissent tous les deux un "test" comptant trois éléments, dont les deux éléments principaux sont communs. Il s'agit de l'identification des termes de comparaison, c'est-à-dire quels investisseurs ou investissements doivent être comparés, afin de déterminer ceux qui sont "dans des circonstances similaires" et, ensuite, de la comparaison du traitement reçu afin de déterminer si le traitement des investisseurs ou des investissements étrangers est "moins favorable."[54] Le Tribunal dans l'affaire *CPI* inclut un premier élément qui est de savoir si la mesure (ici, la taxe) constitue un "traitement" de l'investisseur ou de l'investissement. Cette étape de l'analyse semble sous-entendue dans le raisonnement du Tribunal dans l'affaire *ADM*. Par contre, ce dernier inclut dans son test un troisième élément qui permet au Tribunal de considérer des facteurs pouvant justifier la différence de traitement. Dans son raisonnement, toutefois, le Tribunal n'atteint pas cette étape de l'analyse et le Tribunal dans l'affaire *CPI* n'en traite pas directement.[55]

Quant aux "circonstances similaires," les deux tribunaux confirment que la première étape est d'évaluer si les investisseurs ou les investissements sont dans le même secteur des affaires ou secteur économique. L'existence d'une relation de concurrence entre les investisseurs ou les investissements joue un rôle clé dans la détermination des termes de comparaison et, dans les faits, les tribunaux n'ont eu aucune peine à établir cette relation entre les producteurs et distributeurs de SHTF et de sucre de canne.[56] Néanmoins, les tribunaux n'ont pas donné le même poids aux conclusions des organes juridictionnels de l'OMC quant à savoir si le SHTF et le sucre de canne étaient des "produits similaires." Le Tribunal dans l'affaire *CPI* leur a donné une signification beaucoup plus importante que le Tribunal dans l'affaire *ADM*.

---

53 *ADM*, *supra* note 1 au para. 193; *CPI*, *supra* note 1 aux para. 115 et 138.

54 *ADM*, *supra* note 1 au para. 196; *CPI*, *supra* note 1 aux para. 116–17.

55 Une analyse de justification, à une étape ou une autre du "test," se retrouve dans la majorité des sentences de l'ALENA portant sur l'article 1102. Voir, par exemple, *Pope & Talbot, Inc. c. Canada*, Award on the Merits of Phase 2, UNCITRAL (10 avril 2001) [*Pope & Talbot, phase 2*]; *S.D. Myers Inc. c. Government of Canada*, Partial Award, UNCITRAL (13 novembre 2000) [*S.D. Myers*]; *Marvin Roy Feldman Karpa c. Mexico*, ICSID Case No. ARB(AF)/99/1 (16 décembre 2002) [*Feldman*]; et *GAMI*, *supra* note 33.

56 *ADM*, *supra* note 1 au para. 201; *CPI*, *supra* note 1 au para. 120.

Dans l'affaire *CPI*, le Tribunal note d'abord la mise en garde, faite par le Tribunal dans l'affaire *Methanex*, selon laquelle les termes de l'article III du GATT, en ce qui concerne la similarité des produits, ne se retrouvent pas au chapitre 11 mais bien au chapitre 3 de l'ALENA. Il se dit aussi conscient que sa compétence est limitée au chapitre 11. Qui plus est, il dit accepter que CPI ne peut faire la preuve d'un manquement à l'article 1102 simplement en démontrant que le SHTF et le sucre sont des "produits similaires" en vertu de l'article III du GATT. Il affirme donc que le test selon l'article 1102 est "séparé et distinct" du test selon l'article III du GATT.[57]

Après avoir pris toutes ces précautions, le Tribunal affirme que le fait que le SHTF et le sucre soient des "produits similaires" pour les fins du GATT est "hautement pertinent" pour l'application de l'article 1102 de l'ALENA. Il précise que:

> *While the Tribunal would not suggest that the fact that a foreign investor and a domestic investor are producing like products will necessarily mean that they are to be considered as being in like circumstances for the purposes of Article 1102, or that differential treatment will necessarily entail a violation of that provision, where the measure said to constitute the violation of Article 1102 is directly concerned with the products and designed to discriminate in favour of one and against the other, then that is a very strong indication that there has been a breach of Article 1102.*[58]

Le Tribunal dans l'affaire *ADM* n'analyse pas cette question en tant que telle. Dans le contexte de son analyse des "circonstances similaires," il note que les autorités mexicaines ont confirmé, dans le cadre des procédures anti-dumping et en droit de la concurrence, l'existence d'une relation de concurrence entre le SHTF et le sucre.[59] À la fin de son analyse sur le traitement discriminatoire, il conclut que la preuve au dossier démontre que la taxe IEPS discriminait le sucre et le SHTF et que cette taxe était conçue afin de

---

[57] *CPI, supra* note 1 au para. 121.

[58] *CPI, ibid.* au para. 122 [nous soulignons]. Voir aussi au para. 126: "We conclude that where the products at issue are interchangeable and indistinguishable from the point of view of the end-users (i.e. the purchaser of soft drinks), the products, and therefore the respective investments, are in like circumstances. Any other interpretation would negate the effect of the non-discrimination clauses, because it would always be possible to find differences between the way competing products are owned, managed, regulated, or priced."

[59] *ADM, supra* note 1 au para. 201.

protéger l'industrie mexicaine du sucre de canne. Il cite alors les conclusions dans le même sens du Groupe spécial et de l'Organe d'appel de l'OMC, mais sans plus d'analyse.

La question de savoir si un autre terme de comparaison était plus approprié n'a pas réellement préoccupé ces tribunaux. En l'absence d'une industrie nationale de SHTF et compte tenu de la relation de concurrence entre le SHTF et le sucre dans l'édulcoration des boissons gazeuses, aucune "circonstance" n'était davantage "similaire."[60] Le Tribunal dans l'affaire *CPI* a toutefois fait une remarque qui pourrait s'avérer influente dans d'autres circonstances. En réponse aux arguments du Mexique que l'affaire *GAMI*[61] offrait un précédent valable permettant d'établir que les producteurs de sucre et de SHTF n'étaient pas dans "des circonstances similaires" (car les premiers n'avaient pas accès au marché américain tandis que les seconds avaient accès aux marchés mexicain et américain), le Tribunal a noté ce qui suit:

> *The present case might be analogous to GAMI if HFCS had been produced in equal (or nearly equal) volume by Mexican-owned and US-owned firms. In that circumstance, a measure designed adversely to affect the market for HFCS in order to protect the position of the sugar industry could not have been held to violate the requirement of national treatment.*[62]

Cette approche semble conforme à celle de l'"avantage disproportionné" retenue à l'OMC pour l'interprétation de l'obligation de traitement national.[63] En vertu de cette approche, les *groupes* de produits sont comparés et non seulement les produits *individuels* (c.-à-d. un produit national avantagé par rapport à un produit importé).[64]

Le Tribunal dans l'affaire *ADM* ne se prononce pas sur cette hypothèse de l'égalité ou presque dans la production. Il formule cependant de la façon suivante l'obligation imposée par l'article 1102:

> *Nationality discrimination is established by showing that a foreign investor has unreasonably been treated less favorably than domestic investors in like circumstances.*

---

[60] *ADM*, *supra* note 1 aux para. 202–4; *CPI*, *supra* note 1 au para. 132.

[61] *GAMI*, *supra* note 33.

[62] *CPI*, *supra* note 1 au para. 132 [nous soulignons].

[63] Voir *Communautés européennes – Mesures affectant l'amiante et les produits en contenant*, Doc. WT/DS135/AB/R (2001) (Rapport de l'Organe d'appel) [*Asbestos*].

[64] Voir *ibid.* au para. 100.

Accordingly, Claimants and their investment are entitled to the best of treatment available to any other domestic investor or investment operating in like circumstances, including the domestic cane sugar producers.[65]

Le concept du "meilleur traitement" se retrouve dans d'autres décisions rendues en vertu du chapitre 11 de l'ALENA.[66] L'une d'elles, contenant une étude détaillée de la question, a rejeté la pertinence, dans l'interprétation de l'article 1102, du concept de l'"avantage disproportionné" utilisé à l'OMC.[67]

En somme, bien qu'aucune contradiction ne se soit avérée en l'espèce (car dans les faits tous les producteurs de SHTF étaient étrangers), ces sentences montrent les tensions qui existent quant à l'interprétation de l'obligation de traitement national à l'article 1102, et en particulier quant à l'influence de l'analyse qui a cours à l'OMC.[68]

2   *Prescriptions de résultats: Article 1106*

Les deux tribunaux ont traité de l'obligation de l'article 1106 de façon diamétralement opposée. L'article 1106 de l'ALENA prévoit que:

(1) Aucune des Parties ne pourra imposer ou appliquer l'une des prescriptions suivantes ou faire exécuter un engagement s'y rapportant, en ce qui concerne l'établissement, l'acquisition, l'expansion, la gestion, la direction ou l'exploitation d'un investissement d'un investisseur d'une autre Partie ou d'un pays tiers sur son territoire:

  (a) exporter une quantité ou un pourcentage donné de produits ou de services;

  (b) atteindre un niveau ou un pourcentage donné de contenu national;

  (c) acheter, utiliser ou privilégier les produits ou les services produits ou fournis sur son territoire, ou acheter des produits ou services de personnes situées sur son territoire ...

---

[65] *ADM, supra* note 1 au para. 205 [nous soulignons].

[66] Voir, par exemple, *Pope & Talbot, phase 2, supra* note 55 au para. 42; et *United Postal Services of America Inc. c. Canada*, Separate Opinion of Dean Ronald A. Cass, UNCITRAL (14 mai 2007), aux para. 59–63.

[67] Voir *Pope and Talbot, phase 2, supra* note 55 aux para. 43–72.

[68] Voir N. DiMascio et J. Pauwelyn, "Nondiscrimination in Trade and Investment Treaties: Worlds Apart or Two Sides of the Same Coin?" (2008) 102 A.J.I.L. 48. Voir aussi J. Kurtz, "The Use and Abuse of WTO Law in Investor-State Arbitration: Competition and its Discontents" (2009) 20 E.J.I.L. 749.

(3) Aucune des Parties ne pourra subordonner l'octroi ou le maintien de l'octroi d'un avantage, en ce qui concerne un investissement d'un investisseur d'une autre Partie ou d'un pays tiers sur son territoire, à l'observation de l'une quelconque des prescriptions suivantes:
(a) atteindre un niveau ou un pourcentage donné de contenu national;
(b) acheter, utiliser ou privilégier les produits produits sur son territoire, ou acheter des produits de producteurs situés sur son territoire.[69]

Dans l'affaire *ADM,* le Tribunal a interprété le paragraphe 3 de l'article 1106 et a jugé que l'exemption de la taxe — opérant lorsque le sucre de canne était utilisé, plutôt que le SHTF — constituait un *avantage* pour l'industrie du sucre et plaçait l'industrie du SHTF dans une position de désavantage concurrentiel.[70] Afin d'arriver à cette conclusion, le Tribunal a mis l'accent sur le fait que le paragraphe 1(c) de l'article 1101 prévoit que l'obligation de l'article 1106 s'applique à tous les investissements effectués sur le territoire d'une Partie (et non pas uniquement aux investissements étrangers).[71] Ainsi, le Tribunal a conclu que: "[t]he performance requirement in the present case consists of the requirement to use cane sugar instead of the Claimants' HFCS in order to benefit from the tax exemption."[72] Cet avantage était offert, selon l'article 1106, "en ce qui concerne un investissement d'un investisseur," car l'exemption de la taxe avait un effet négatif sur la profitabilité de l'investissement d'ADM.[73] Le Tribunal a donc conclu à la violation de l'article 1106.

Le Tribunal dans l'affaire *CPI* a rejeté sommairement cette allégation, dans un unique paragraphe qui suit:

CPI freely admits that its claim is without precedent. Counsel for Mexico described it as 'fanciful.' The Tribunal would not go that far but it is clear that CPI has not made out its case under this provision. No requirement was imposed on CPI by the tax enacted by the Mexican Congress on soft drinks using HFCS as a sweetener.

---

[69] ALENA, *supra* note 2, art. 1106.

[70] *ADM, supra* note 1 au para. 222.

[71] *Ibid.* Voir ALENA, *supra* note 1, art. 1101. L'article 1101(1) prévoit que: "Le présent chapitre s'applique aux mesures adoptées ou maintenues par une Partie concernant: ... c) pour ce qui est des articles 1106 et 1114, tous les investissements effectués sur son territoire."

[72] *ADM, supra* note 1 au para. 223.

[73] *Ibid.* au para. 227.

Mexico made no demand on CPI for increased investment, increased local procurement or a greater level of local employees. Nor did the tax or any other regulation cited by CPI purport to prescribe the level of its domestic sales, imports, exports, or foreign exchange earnings. While the tax here challenged was adopted with the intent and effect of reducing the use by CPI's customers of CPI's product, the performance requirement, if any, was placed on the soft drink manufacturers, and even that was not mandatory. The claim under Article 1106 fails.[74]

Bien que la sentence ne permette pas de savoir si CPI avait présenté des arguments similaires à ceux d'ADM — surtout concernant le paragraphe 3 et la notion d'"avantage" — il appert que ces tribunaux sont en désaccord quant à savoir si une prescription de résultats doit être imposée directement à un investissement ou non. Ils sont également en désaccord quant au caractère obligatoire des prescriptions de résultats. Autrement dit, ils ne s'entendent pas sur la question de savoir si l'article 1106 couvre les prescriptions *de facto*.

3 Expropriation: Article 1110

Les tribunaux ont tous deux rejeté, sans difficulté, les allégations de manquement à l'article 1110. Cet article prévoit que:

Aucune des Parties ne pourra, directement ou indirectement, nationaliser ou exproprier un investissement d'un investisseur d'une autre Partie sur son territoire, ni prendre une mesure équivalant à la nationalisation ou à l'expropriation d'un tel investissement ("expropriation"), si ce n'est:
a)   pour une raison d'intérêt public;
b)   sur une base non discriminatoire;
c)   en conformité avec l'application régulière de la loi et le paragraphe 1105(1); et
d)   moyennant le versement d'une indemnité conformément aux paragraphes 2 à 6.[75]

L'analyse des tribunaux ne surprend pas, car elle est conforme à celle contenue dans la majorité des sentences du chapitre 11 portant sur l'expropriation, où une norme assez stricte a été appliquée. Il faut toutefois mentionner que la sentence dans l'affaire *CPI* est plus catégorique et laisse moins de place à interprétation (voire même confusion) que la sentence dans l'affaire *ADM*.

---

[74] *CPI, supra* note 1 au para. 80.
[75] ALENA, *supra* note 2, art. 1110(1).

Afin de déterminer si les demandeurs avaient été l'objet d'une expropriation, les deux tribunaux ont mis l'accent sur le degré d'ingérence dans l'investissement qui doit être important ou "*substantial*."[76] Dans les faits, aucun bien n'avait été enlevé aux entreprises, aucun droit fondamental de propriété n'avait été enlevé, il n'y avait eu aucune perte de contrôle sur la gestion ou les opérations des entreprises. Durant toute la période où la taxe était en place, les entreprises avaient continué à opérer et à vendre leurs produits.[77] À aucun moment, les entreprises n'avaient été "stérilisées" ou leurs affaires "anéanties" à cause de l'imposition de la taxe IEPS.[78]

Le Tribunal dans l'affaire *ADM* a analysé un autre critère possible en matière d'ingérence qui consiste à se demander: "*whether the host State measure affects most of the investment's economic value or renders useless the most economically optimal use of it.*"[79] Dans ce contexte, il a traité plus spécialement de la question de savoir si une diminution de profits pouvait constituer une expropriation, comme l'investisseur l'alléguait. Il a jugé qu'une perte de profits n'était pas nécessairement suffisante à elle seule pour constituer une expropriation et qu'en l'espèce, elle était insuffisante.[80]

Les demandeurs dans les deux affaires avaient mis l'accent sur la nature discriminatoire de la taxe dans leurs soumissions en matière d'expropriation. Le Tribunal dans l'affaire *CPI* a rejeté la pertinence de ce fait en l'espèce, tandis que le Tribunal dans l'affaire *ADM* a donné une réponse plus confuse.

Dans l'affaire *CPI*, le Tribunal a précisé l'importance de ne pas confondre la question de savoir si une mesure constituait une expropriation et celle de savoir si cette expropriation répondait aux critères prévus aux paragraphes (a) à (d) de l'article 1110(1) — dont la non-discrimination. Autrement dit, ce n'est pas parce qu'une mesure est discriminatoire qu'elle constitue pour autant une expropriation.[81]

Dans l'affaire *ADM*, le Tribunal mêle les cartes lorsqu'il note que d'autres facteurs, en plus de ceux concernant l'effet de la mesure, peuvent être pris en compte par un tribunal, y compris "*whether the*

---

76 *ADM, supra* note 1 aux para. 240–45; *CPI, supra* note 1 aux para. 91–92.

77 *ADM, supra* note 1 aux para. 245–51; *CPI, supra* note 1 aux para. 82 et 92.

78 *ADM, supra* note 1 au para. 247; *CPI, supra* note 1 aux para. 92–93.

79 *ADM, supra* note 1 au para. 246.

80 *Ibid.* aux para. 246 et 248.

81 *CPI, supra* note 1 aux para. 89–90.

measure was proportionate or necessary for a legitimate purpose; whether it discriminated in law or in practice; whether it was not adopted in accordance with due process of law; or whether it interfered with the investor's legitimate expectations when the investment was made."[82]

4   Défense de contre-mesures

En défense aux allégations des investisseurs, le Mexique a plaidé l'existence d'une circonstance excluant l'illicéité de son comportement en vertu du droit international coutumier: la contremesure. Afin d'encadrer la discussion de cette défense inédite dans un arbitrage entre un investisseur et un État fondé sur un traité d'investissement, les deux tribunaux ont fait référence au Projet d'articles sur la responsabilité de l'État pour fait internationalement illicite et aux commentaires relatifs, adopté par la Commission du droit international en 2001.[83] Les deux tribunaux ont souligné que les contre-mesures ne pouvaient être prises qu'à l'encontre d'un autre État.[84] Par ailleurs, ils ont reconnu que les États pouvaient créer certains droits au profit de personnes ou entités autres que des États.[85] Ils ont tous les deux cité l'article 49 qui prévoit que: "L'État lésé ne peut prendre de contre-mesures à l'encontre de l'État responsable du fait internationalement illicite que pour amener cet État à s'acquitter des obligations qui lui incombent en vertu de la deuxième partie [Contenu de la responsabilité internationale de l'État]."[86]

En fin de compte, le Tribunal dans l'affaire *ADM* a jugé que les contre-mesures pouvaient être invoquées dans le cadre d'un différend en vertu du chapitre 11 de l'ALENA; tandis que le Tribunal dans l'affaire *CPI* a jugé que cette défense était inadmissible. Les

---

[82] *ADM, supra* note 5 au para. 250.

[83] Voir le "Projet d'article sur la responsabilité de l'État pour fait internationalement illicite et commentaires relatifs" dans *Rapport de la commission du droit international,* Doc. Off. AG NU , 53ᵉ sess., supp. nᵒ 10, Doc. NU A/56/10 (2001) ["Projet d'articles sur la responsabilité de l'État"].

[84] Voir l'art. 22 du "Projet d'articles sur la responsabilité de l'État," cité dans l'affaire *ADM, supra* note 1 aux para. 121 et 125.

[85] Voir l'art. 33 du "Projet d'articles sur la responsabilité de l'État," cité dans l'affaire *ADM, supra* note 1 au para. 118. Sur le même point, voir l'affaire *CPI, supra* note 1 au para. 168.

[86] "Projet d'articles sur la responsabilité de l'État,"*supra* note 83, art. 49, cité dans l'affaire *ADM, supra* note 1 au para. 125 et dans l'affaire *CPI, supra* note 1 aux para. 146, 163 et 186–87.

tribunaux sont arrivés à ces conclusions opposées par le biais d'une analyse de la nature des droits détenus par les investisseurs. Et bien qu'ils aient tous deux reconnu que les investisseurs étaient détenteurs de droits en vertu du chapitre 11, ils sont en désaccord sur la nature de ces droits. Le Tribunal dans l'affaire *ADM* a conclu que les investisseurs avaient le droit de saisir une instance arbitrale sur le fondement de la Section B du Chapitre 11; ils bénéficiaient ainsi d'un droit de nature "procédurale." Toutefois, ils n'étaient pas titulaires de droits individuels ou de droits indépendants de ceux des États membres et donc la défense de contre-mesures était en principe admissible.[87] Le Tribunal dans l'affaire *CPI* a estimé pour sa part que les investisseurs avaient des droits individuels, distincts de ceux de l'État et, en conséquence, la défense de contremesures n'était pas admissible.[88] L'étude du raisonnement des tribunaux est utile afin de juger de l'étendue du désaccord.

Dans l'affaire *ADM*, la majorité des membres du Tribunal a estimé que puisque le chapitre 11 de l'ALENA ne faisait pas référence aux contre-mesures, le droit international coutumier en la matière s'appliquait à titre subsidiaire.[89] Le Tribunal a énoncé le principe suivant: "*Countermeasures may constitute a valid defence against a breach of Chapter Eleven insofar as the Respondent State proves that the measure in question meets each of the conditions required by customary international law, as applied to the facts of the case.*"[90] Il a alors établi quatre conditions cumulatives que devait remplir le Mexique et les a analysées une par une.

En ce qui a trait à la première condition, le Tribunal a estimé qu'il n'avait pas compétence pour juger si les États-Unis avaient violé leurs obligations en vertu de l'ALENA (sur la question de l'accès au marché ou sur le règlement des différends).[91] Il a tout de même poursuivi son analyse et, quant à la seconde condition, a jugé que la taxe n'avait pas été édictée en réponse aux violations américaines alléguées et n'avait pas pour but d'obliger les États-Unis à s'y conformer. La taxe avait plutôt été adoptée pour protéger l'industrie nationale du sucre de canne.[92] Quant à la troisième

---

87 *ADM, supra* note 1 aux para. 121 et 173.

88 *CPI, supra* note 1 aux para. 161 et 167.

89 *ADM, supra* note 1 aux para. 120–22.

90 *Ibid.* au para. 121.

91 *Ibid.* aux para. 128–32.

92 *Ibid.* aux para. 144–51.

condition, le Tribunal a estimé que la taxe ne répondait pas à l'exigence de proportionnalité du droit international coutumier. D'autres mesures ne portant pas atteinte à la protection des investissements auraient pu être adoptées par le Mexique.[93] Pour ce qui est de la quatrième condition, il s'est demandé si la taxe mettait en péril les droits individuels des demandeurs. Il a répondu par la négative, mais pas avant d'avoir procédé à une analyse détaillée portant sur la question de savoir si les investisseurs étaient détenteurs de droits individuels ou indépendants de ceux des États (*"individual substantive rights"*).[94]

La majorité dans l'affaire *ADM* a adopté la "théorie intermédiaire" des droits des investisseurs, selon laquelle l'investisseur détient des droits procéduraux alors que les droits "substantiels" n'appartiennent qu'aux États.[95] Cette théorie se trouve entre la théorie traditionnelle des droits dérivés (selon laquelle l'investisseur se met à la place de l'État lorsqu'il porte plainte et fait valoir les droits de l'État) et la théorie des droits directs des investisseurs (en vertu de laquelle une relation juridique distincte existe entre l'investisseur et l'État).[96]

La reconnaissance que le droit international peut conférer des droits directs aux individus (par exemple en matière de protection des investissements étrangers, des droits de la personne ou de l'environnement) a en toute apparence mené le Tribunal a rejeté la théorie dérivée des droits. Cependant, il a fait une distinction entre les droits issus de traités d'investissement et les droits de la personne qui peuvent avoir en commun un aspect procédural mais qui demeurent fondamentalement différents en substance. Le Tribunal a expliqué ainsi la difference: "*Chapter 11 does not provide individual substantive rights for investors, but rather complements the promotion and protection standards of the rules regarding the protection of aliens under customary international law.*"[97] Pour ce motif, il rejette également la théorie des droits directs.

---

[93] *Ibid.* aux para. 153–60.

[94] *Ibid.* aux para. 168–80.

[95] *Ibid.* au para. 163.

[96] *Ibid.* aux para. 161–63 et 169. Sur ces théories, voir Z. Douglas, "The Hybrid Foundations of Investment Treaty Arbitration" (2003) Brit. Y.B. Int'l L.; Z. Douglas, "Nothing If Not Critical for Investment Treaty Arbitration: *Occidental, Eureko* and *Methanex*" (2006) Arb. Int'l 27.

[97] *CPI, supra* note 1 au para. 171.

Pour le Tribunal, le chapitre 11 prévoit deux types séparés d'obligations: les obligations de traitement et autres de la Section A qui s'appliquent entre les États, et les obligations procédurales de la Section B auxquelles l'État s'est engagé au profit des investisseurs (à titre de détenteurs de droits secondaires). Ainsi, l'investisseur pourrait renoncer à ses droits procéduraux, mais ne pourrait pas renoncer aux droits prévus dans la Section A, car ils ne lui appartiennent pas.[98]

Un des arbitres, Arthur W. Rovine, s'est dissocié de la majorité sur ce point et a écrit une opinion concordante de 42 pages en ce qui a trait à la nature des droits des investisseurs et aux contre-mesures.[99] Il estime que les droits des investisseurs aux recours prévus au chapitre 11 de l'ALENA appartiennent à l'investisseur et non pas à l'État, de sorte qu'ils ne peuvent être suspendus ou éliminés par des contre-mesures prises à l'encontre de l'État de l'investisseur. Selon lui, il importe peu que ces droits soient qualifiés de "directs et substantiels" ou "dérivés et procéduraux"—bien qu'il soit d'avis qu'ils sont "substantiels."[100]

Dans l'affaire *CPI*, le tribunal a conclu que la doctrine de contre-mesures ne s'appliquait pas au chapitre 11 de l'ALENA. La majorité a statué que:

> *A central purpose of Chapter XI of the NAFTA was to remove such claims from the inter-State plane and to ensure that investors could assert rights directly against a host State. The Tribunal considers that, in the context of such a claim, there is no room for a defence based upon the alleged wrongdoing not of the claimant but of its State of nationality, which is not a party to the proceedings.*[101]

Comme dans l'affaire *ADM*, le Tribunal est arrivé à cette conclusion après avoir jugé de la nature des droits détenus par les investisseurs et des obligations du chapitre 11. L'analyse de la majorité[102] était divisée en trois parties. Premièrement, le Tribunal a estimé que le rejet de la défense de contre-mesures au titre de l'article XX

---

[98] *Ibid.* aux para. 172–74 et 177.

[99] *Ibid. Concurring Opinion of Arthur W. Rovine, Issues of Independent Investor Rights, Diplomatic Protection and Countermeasures*, 20 septembre 2007 [*Opinion of Rovine*].

[100] *Opinion of Rovine, supra* note 99 à la p. 1.

[101] *CPI, supra* note 1 au para. 161.

[102] Un des arbitres, Andreas F. Lowenfeld, a convenu que les contre-mesures ne s'appliquaient pas, mais il n'était pas satisfait du traitement réservé à cette question par la majorité. Voir *ibid., Separate Opinion of Andreas F Lowenfeld.*

du GATT dans le cadre des procédures à l'OMC n'empêchait pas le Mexique de soulever une défense de contre-mesures dans le cadre de l'ALENA.[103]

Deuxièmement, le Tribunal a analysé la nature des droits des investisseurs et a conclu que l'ALENA *"confers upon investors substantive rights separate and distinct from those of the State of which they are nationals."*[104] Le Tribunal a cité l'article 49 du Projet d'articles sur la Responsabilité des États et son commentaire, et mis l'accent sur la distinction entre les "droits" des tiers et les "intérêts" des tiers.[105] Si, comme il le croyait, les investisseurs avaient de tels "droits," alors la défense de contre-mesures ne pouvait pas s'appliquer contre eux. Le Tribunal a estimé que le texte du traité révélait clairement l'intention des parties à l'ALENA:

> *In the case of Chapter XI of the NAFTA, the Tribunal considers that the intention of the Parties was to confer substantive rights directly upon investors. That follows from the language used and is confirmed by the fact that Chapter XI confers procedural rights upon them. The notion that Chapter XI conferred upon investors a right, in their own name and for their own benefit, to institute proceedings to enforce rights which were not theirs but were solely the property of the State of their nationality is counterintuitive.*[106]

Troisièmement, le Tribunal a décidé qu'il n'était pas nécessaire et qu'il était même inapproprié de déterminer si les exigences pour l'application d'une contre-mesure étaient remplies.[107] Cependant, le Tribunal n'a pu résister à la tentation de se prononcer sur les limites à la compétence du tribunal lorsqu'il considère une défense

---

[103] *Ibid.* aux para. 154–60.

[104] *Ibid.* au para. 167.

[105] Voir "Projet d'articles sur la responsabilité de l'État," *supra* note 83, commentaire à l'art. 49 qui précise que: "Les contre-mesures ne peuvent être dirigées contre des États autres que l'État responsable. Dans le cas où un État tiers est le bénéficiaire d'une obligation internationale incombant à l'État qui prend des contre-mesures et que cette obligation est violée par les contre-mesures, l'illicéité de la mesure n'est pas exclue à l'égard de l'État tiers. En ce sens, l'exclusion de l'illicéité des contre-mesures a un effet relatif, et ne concerne que les relations juridiques entre l'État lésé et l'État responsable. Cela ne signifie pas que les contre-mesures ne peuvent pas avoir, incidemment, des effets sur la situation d'États tiers ou *même d'autres tierces parties* … S'ils n'ont aucun *droit individuel* à cet égard, ils ne peuvent protester … De tels effets indirects ou collatéraux ne peuvent être totalement évités" [nous soulignons].

[106] *CPI, supra* note 1 au para. 169.

[107] *Ibid.* au para. 180.

de contre-mesures. Le Tribunal a estimé que l'exigence d'une violation préalable du droit international était une pré-condition absolue du droit de prendre des contre-mesures, et puisqu'un tribunal constitué en vertu du chapitre 11 n'a pas compétence pour juger de la violation alléguée de l'ALENA par les États-Unis, cela portait un coup fatal à cette défense.[108] Une suspension des procédures ne serait pas une option pratique dans de tels cas.[109]

D   OBSERVATIONS

Les sentences dans les affaires *ADM* et *CPI* offrent un exemple du risque d'incohérence inhérent au droit international des investissements. Ce risque est inhérent, car il découle de la nature *ad hoc* de l'arbitrage international entre investisseurs et États en vertu des accords portant sur l'investissement et de l'absence, dans ce régime, d'une règle de précédent. Cet exemple est éloquent, car ces affaires étaient presque identiques.

Comme on l'a vu plus haut, le Mexique avait demandé la jonction de ces affaires, une demande qui fut rejetée. Notamment, le Tribunal n'a pas été convaincu par les arguments du Mexique quant au risque de sentences contradictoires. Il a estimé que ce risque n'était pas important dans ces affaires, car les plaintes lui paraissaient suffisamment différentes quant à la responsabilité étatique (par exemple, une expropriation pourrait exister dans un cas et pas dans l'autre) et au montant des dommages. Le Tribunal a décidé que, de toute façon, le risque que des décisions contradictoires soient injustes pour le Mexique ne l'emportait pas sur le risque d'injustice couru par les demandeurs découlant de l'inefficacité des procédures.[110]

À certains égards, évidemment, ces décisions ne sont pas contradictoires ou incohérentes. Les deux tribunaux sont arrivés à une même conclusion: la mesure mexicaine visée était discriminatoire. Et les deux tribunaux ont en conséquence condamné le Mexique à payer des dommages substantiels. Ils ont tous les deux conclu à l'absence d'une expropriation. Où donc, se demanderont certains, se situe le problème?

L'incohérence, dans l'interprétation de l'une ou l'autre obligation d'un traité d'investissement, est une réalité de tous les jours pour

---

108 *Ibid.* aux para. 181–89.

109 *Ibid.* au para. 191.

110 *Consolidation Decision, supra* note 21 aux para. 15–17.

les praticiens et les observateurs du droit international des investissements. Les obligations des États sont souvent formulées de manière générale dans les traités et font l'objet d'interprétations
diverses, voire contradictoires, même en vertu d'un seul accord.
L'interprétation de l'article 1106 par les tribunaux dans les affaires
ADM et *CPI* en fournit un bon exemple (malgré un degré de pré-
cision peu ordinaire). À la lecture de ces décisions, ni les États
membres ni les investisseurs ne sont en mesure de savoir, avec un
quelconque degré de certitude, si l'article 1106 prohibe uniquement les prescriptions de résultats imposées directement à l'investisseur. Deux tribunaux ont donné deux réponses différentes à
cette question.

Cela étant, il existe des défis encore plus importants. Que dire
des constatations contradictoires des tribunaux sur la nature des
droits des investisseurs? Que penser du désaccord sur l'application
de la défense de contre-mesures? Ces questions ne sont pas banales;
elles mettent en jeux la relation entre le droit international général
et le régime spécialisé du droit des investissements. Elles ont un
impact systémique: est-ce que les droits accordés aux investisseurs
viennent *compléter* ou *remplacer* les normes sur la protection des
étrangers existant en droit international coutumier?

Les tribunaux dans les affaires *ADM* et *CPI* ont également appréhendé la relation entre le droit du commerce et le droit des investissements de façon quelque peu différente. Bien que le résultat ait
été le même — la conclusion de violation à l'obligation de traitement national — le raisonnement des tribunaux n'a pas été influencé au même degré ou de la même manière par le droit de
l'OMC. En toute apparence, le Tribunal dans l'affaire *CPI* a donné
plus de poids aux conclusions des organes juridictionnels de l'OMC
que le Tribunal dans l'affaire *ADM*. Aussi, l'approche décrite dans
l'affaire *CPI* quant à la question du traitement "le plus favorable"
semble plus influencée par le droit de l'OMC que celle de l'affaire
ADM. Malgré le fait que ces différences soient plus nuancées, elles
représentent tout de même des défis importants pour le droit des
investissements.

La problématique découlant de la spécialisation normative et de
la multiplication des recours en droit international est bien connue.
Les thèmes de la "fragmentation" ou de "l'unité de l'ordre juridique
international" ont fait couler beaucoup d'encre.[111] Ces thèmes

---

[111] Voir, par exemple, Commission du droit international, *Fragmentation du droit
international: difficultés découlant de la diversification et de l'expansion du droit*

couvrent aussi bien la relation entre le droit international général et le droit des investissements (*lex generalis* / *lex specialis*) que la relation entre le droit international du commerce et le droit des investissements (relation entre régimes spécialisés).[112] Les nombreuses affaires ayant découlé du différend entre le Mexique et les États-Unis concernant le sucre et les édulcorants témoignent de façon éloquente de cette problématique. Tel que décrit plus haut, les différentes mesures mexicaines ont donné lieu à des décisions en vertu du chapitre 11 et 19 de l'ALENA et à plusieurs décisions à l'OMC.[113]

En conclusion, les sentences examinées dans cette chronique soulèvent des interrogations importantes concernant le risque d'incohérence entre les sentences arbitrales mais aussi par rapport à l'unité du droit international. Comme le remarquait Pierre-Marie Dupuy, "[1]e fond du problème est alors de réussir à sauvegarder l'unité d'interprétation du droit international, condition de son application cohérente."[114] À tout le moins, il est à espérer qu'un tribunal à qui une demande de jonction est faite à l'avenir prendra en compte les défis posés par l'incohérence entre les sentences arbitrales. Les conséquences *pratiques* dans les affaires mexicaines sur les édulcorants ont été, somme toute, mineures, mais il pourrait en être tout autrement dans d'autres circonstances.[115]

---

international, Rapport du Groupe d'étude de la Commission du droit international, Doc. off. AG NU, 58 ᵉ sess., Doc. NU A/CN.4/L.682 (2006); B. Simma et D. Pulkowski, "Of Planets and the Universe: Self-contained Regimes in International Law" (2006) 17(3) E.J.I.L.; P-M. Dupuy, "Un Débat Doctrinal à l'Ere de la Globalisation: Sur la Fragmentation du Droit International" (2007) 1 Eur. J. Legal Stud. et P-M. Dupuy, "L'unité de l'ordre juridique international" (2002) 297 Rec. des Cours.

112 Voir Commission du droit international, *supra* note 111.

113 J. Pauwelyn, "Adding Sweeteners to Softwood Lumber: the WTO-NAFTA 'Spaghetti Bowl' is Cooking" (2006) 9 J. Int'l Econ. L.1. Voir aussi A. K. Bjorklund, "Private Rights and Public International Law: Why Competition Among International Economic Law Tribunals Is Not Working" (2007) U.C. Davis Legal Studies Research Paper Series, Research Paper no. 124.

114 Dupuy, "Fragmentation," *supra* note 111 à la p. 15.

115 Sur l'incohérence et les problèmes de légitimité qui en découlent, voir notamment Susan D. Frank, "The Legitimacy Crisis in Investment Treaty Arbitration: Privatizing Public International Law Through Inconsistent Decisions" (2005) 73 Fordham L. Rev.

Canadian Practice in International Law / Pratique canadienne en matière de droit international

At the Department of Foreign Affairs and International Trade in 2008–9 / Au ministère des Affaires étrangères et du Commerce international en 2008–9

compiled by / préparé par
ALAN KESSEL

INTERNATIONAL HUMAN RIGHTS AND INTERNATIONAL
HUMANITARIAN LAW

Exercising the Right to Self-Defence: Protection of Nationals Abroad

In May 2009, in preparation for informal discussions with government lawyers from like-minded states, the Department of Foreign Affairs and International Trade (DFAIT) provided the following views relating to the Charter of the United Nations and the use of force in the context of the protection of nationals abroad:

A series of UN Security Council resolutions, in particularly SC Res 1373 (2001), confirm the right to self-defence in the context of terrorist attacks, as well as the obligation of states to cooperate in the fight against terrorism, and to refrain from granting safe haven or acquiescing to terrorist activities in their territory. Failure to comply with these obligations engages state

Alan Kessel is the Legal Adviser in the Department of Foreign Affairs and International Trade, Ottawa. The extracts from official correspondence contained in this survey have been made available by courtesy of the Department of Foreign Affairs and International Trade. Some of the correspondence from which extracts are given was provided for the general guidance of the enquirer in relation to specific facts that are often not described in full in the extracts within this compilation. The statements of law and practice should not necessarily be regarded as definitive.

responsibility, and it is accepted, for example, that Operation Enduring Freedom in Afghanistan was a lawful and appropriate exercise of the right to self-defence following the events of September 11, 2001.

While the resolutions do not provide an express legal basis for the exercise of the right to self-defence in the protection of nationals, they serve as a useful context for the relevance of a state's willingness and ability to undertake the necessary action to suppress the attack against foreign nationals by non-state actors (NSAs) in their territory.

The right of states to use force in the protection of nationals abroad flows from the universally accepted principle of international law that injury to a state's national may be considered injury to the State itself; as such, it is properly accommodated within the inherent right to self-defence, including as exercised against non-state actors. The right arises in situations where nationals are at risk of death or grave injury, and the "host" (territorial) state is unwilling or unable to secure their safety, or otherwise take necessary action in compliance with its obligations under international law, including SC Res 1373 (et al.) and relevant counter-terrorism treaties.

The host state in such a situation is not the *prima facie* target of military action, but as force is exercised within its territory, would be considered the victim of a breach of Art. 2(4) of the *Charter* but for the lawful exercise of the right to self-defence.

Considerable thought has been devoted to this issue, borne out of the exercise of the right to protect nationals abroad as a matter of infrequent, but regular, state practice. "The right of the State to intervene by the use or threat of force for the protection of its nationals suffering injuries within the territory of another State is generally admitted, both in the writings of jurists and in the practice of States" [citation omitted]. Historically, the exercise by states of the right of self-defence in the context of protection of nationals has attracted debate among those concerned with a *prima facie* breach of Art 2(4) of the *UN Charter,* especially in the context of large-scale, longer-term sustained military intervention where arguably other interests were at play (Belgium/Congo in 1960 and 1964; Turkey/Cyprus in 1964; US/Grenada in 1983; Russia/Georgia in 2008).

In the Grenada case, the US intervention — in the absence of SC authorization — was considered incompatible with Article 2(4) by a large number of states, but it should be noted that the tenor of the intervention suggests that any condemnation was linked more to the facts, namely the US' failure to demonstrate a substantial and credible threat to its nationals, rather than a rejection of the legal proposition that protection of nationals can give rise to the right of self-defence. [See statements delivered during Security Council Debate, S.C.O.R. (XXXVIII), 26–27 October 1983.

For useful summary of this and other historical debates on the issue, see also Thomas M. Franck, *Recourse to Force: State Action against Threats and Armed Attack* (2002), Chapter 6].

A similarly non-conclusive debate — long on expressions of concern, but short on outright questioning of the right of states to protect citizens abroad, including through use of force — took place in the context of Israel's raid on Entebbe following the hijacking of an Air France plane en route from Israel to Paris in 1976. [In the context of this debate the US and UK introduced a resolution calling on nations to "prevent and punish terrorist acts," which was defeated by a vote of 6–0-2 (no. P-5), because a number of SC members (including the USSR and China) were absent when the vote was called.]

The facts in that case more closely reflect the particular circumstances in which the exercise of the right to self-defence in the protection of nationals abroad could be considered appropriate, based on a number of criteria, namely:

- the precedent act by state actors or NSAs that results in the danger to nationals is in violation of international law (e.g. it constitutes an offence under one or more of the counter-terrorism conventions such as those on hostage-taking or hijacking);
- the act results in imminent and credible threat to the life or physical integrity of nationals;
- the act triggers host state obligations to act;
- the host state is complicit, or unable or unwilling to act;
- the intervention is limited to the protection/rescue objective;
- the intervention is limited by the principles of necessity and proportionality.

Additional measures a State should consider, in order to support the lawfulness of an exercise of the right to self-defence in the protection of nationals, include the following:

- host state consent (including *ex post facto* if operational security considerations prevent prior consent from being obtained);
- requirement for notification of the Security Council pursuant to Art. 51 of the Charter.

Use of Restraints on Detained Persons

In April 2009, the Legal Bureau commented on legal standards relating to the use of physical restraints, particularly leg shackles:

Legal Analysis

Instruments of restraint, such as handcuffs or leg shackles, are not prohibited by international law provided that their use can be justified in the circumstances. Restraints must not cause unnecessary pain or humiliation, their use must be recorded, and they must be used under the supervision of medical personnel.

The definitive authority on their use is contained in the *Standard Minimum Rules for the Treatment of Prisoners,* rule 33. While restraints cannot be used as a method of punishment, instruments of restraint may be used in the following situations:

- As a precaution against escape during a transfer, provided that they shall be removed when the prisoner appears before a judicial or administrative authority;
- On medical grounds by direction of the medical officer;
- By order of the director, if other methods of control fail, in order to prevent a prisoner from injuring himself or others or from damaging property; in such instances the director shall at once consult the medical officer and report to the higher administrative authority.

The patterns and manner of use of instruments of restraint shall be decided by the central prison administration. Such instruments must not be applied for any longer time than is strictly necessary (Treatment of Prisoners rule 34). In the context of armed conflict, an important consideration is that detainees or prisoners must always be humanely treated (Third Geneva Convention, Article 13, considered customary international law; also Common Article 3). Any use of restraints to humiliate, debase, intimidate, or otherwise inhumanely treat a prisoner will be a violation. The supervision of medical personnel is also necessary. Any use of restraints that seriously endangers the health of a prisoner of war is prohibited. The prisoner concerned should be kept under constant and adequate supervision. Further, instruments of restraint should be removed at the earliest possible opportunity (European Committee for the Prevention of Torture's 2nd General Report). The state must keep under constant review the use of instruments of restraint that may cause unnecessary pain and humiliation, and ensure that their use is appropriately recorded (A/56/44, report of the UN Committee against Torture).

Extraterritorial Application of the Canadian Charter of Rights and Freedoms

In March 2009, the Legal Bureau, in conjunction with the Office of the Judge Advocate General, provided the following input regarding the extraterritorial application of the Charter in the government of Canada's pleadings in: *Amnesty International Canada and British Columbia Civil Liberties Association* (Applicants) *v. Chief of the Defence Staff for the Canadian Forces, Minister of National Defence and Attorney General of Canada* (Respondents) before the Supreme Court of Canada:

Overview

The substantive legal issue in this case is whether the *Canadian Charter of Rights and Freedoms* applies to non-Canadians detained and transferred by the Canadian Forces in the course of the armed conflict in the sovereign state of Afghanistan. The legal principles governing the extra-territorial application of the *Charter* have been settled by recent decisions of this Court and correctly applied by the Federal Court and the Federal Court of Appeal. No reconsideration of the relevant principles or their application in this case is required.

The Respondents do not argue that the *Charter* should be sidelined in times of war. Rather, their position is that its scope must at all times be determined in accordance with the principles governing extra-territorial application of the *Charter* articulated by this Court in *R. v. Hape*. Those principles were not altered by the subsequent decision of this Court in *Canada (Justice) v. Khadr*. The Federal Court of Appeal correctly interpreted and applied those principles in confirming that the *Charter* does not apply in this case.

The Federal Court of Appeal also confirmed that there is no legal vacuum in respect of the protection of the fundamental human rights of individuals detained by the Canadian Forces in Afghanistan. Those individuals are protected by norms of customary international law, by Afghan law, and by the international human rights obligations by which Afghanistan is bound. In addition, the norms of customary international law and, in particular, international humanitarian law (IHL), govern the actions of the Canadian Forces in Afghanistan. These norms are embodied in and enforced through Canadian law. They include the prohibition against torture, which is *jus cogens* — a peremptory and non-derogable norm of international law, and the customary IHL prohibition against transferring a detainee to a real risk of inhumane treatment or torture.

These legal protections of detainees exist independently of the *Charter* and do not require the application of the *Charter* for their recognition and enforcement.

The principles recently articulated by this Court governing the application of the *Charter* outside Canadian territory have not been obscured by decisions of other Canadian appellate courts. Moreover, these principles are consistent with the general international law principles governing the sovereignty and jurisdiction of states, principles which have been recognized and applied in decisions of the Supreme Court of the United States, the House of Lords and the European Court of Human Rights. This Court's jurisprudence on the application of the *Charter* and the reasoning of the Federal Court and Federal Court of Appeal in this case are consistent with the jurisprudence of other national and international courts. There is no controversy that requires this Court to reconsider those principles.

Canadian Law Is Consistent with International Decisions

Canada's jurisprudence is consistent with the decisions of the United States Supreme Court, the House of Lords, and the European Court of Human Rights respecting the fundamental principles of jurisdiction, comity, and extra-territoriality.

The jurisprudence of these courts was reviewed by the motions judge and her reasoning was approved by the Federal Court of Appeal.

As this Court did in *Hape*, the United States Supreme Court, the House of Lords, and the European Court of Human Rights have all held, in determining the extraterritorial application of different human rights instruments, that a state exercises jurisdiction outside its own territory only under very limited, exceptional circumstances recognized at international law. The European Court of Human Rights has indicated that those exceptional circumstances are:

- consent: the government of the state with *de jure* sovereignty over the territory consents to the application of the laws of a foreign state;
- effective control of territory: a state occupies territory of another state, exercising all or some of the public powers normally exercised by the government; or
- specific situations where customary international law and treaty provisions have recognized the extraterritorial exercise of jurisdiction, such as within embassies or on board aircraft and vessels registered in or flying the flag of that state.

In the case at bar, the courts below found that:

- Afghanistan has not consented to the extension of *Charter* rights to non-Canadians detained by Canadian Forces in the course of armed conflict on Afghan territory;
- Canada does not exercise effective control over any territory in Afghanistan. It is not an occupying power. It exercises none of the powers of government there. Those powers are exercised by the democratically elected government of Afghanistan; and

- No other specific exception applies.

The Applicants argue that there is support in international legal jurisprudence for a new exception to territorial jurisdiction based on effective military control over individuals as distinct from the exception based on effective control of territory. However, the jurisprudence does not go so far, as the following passage from the unanimous decision of the Grand Chamber of the European Court of Human Rights in *Bankovic* demonstrates:

> the case-law of the Court demonstrates that its recognition of the exercise of extra-territorial jurisdiction by a Contracting State is exceptional: it has done so when the respondent State, *through effective control of the relevant territory and its inhabitants abroad, as a consequence of military occupation or through the consent, invitation or acquiescence of the Government of that territory* exercises all or some of the public powers normally to be exercised by the Government. [emphasis added]

Bankovic provides no support for the proposition that military detention of an individual on foreign territory constitutes effective control to a sufficient degree to attract jurisdiction. The facts of the case do not relate to detention, military or otherwise, of any person.

The Applicants rely on the England and Wales Court of Appeal decision in *Al-Skeini v. Secretary of State* as authority for an "effective control of the person" test. In doing so, they fail to recognize that that case arose in the context of the United Kingdom's effective control (through military occupation) of the province of Basra in southern Iraq. Moreover, the test they assert was explicitly rejected on appeal to the House of Lords:

> [S]uch wider view of jurisdiction would clearly be inconsistent both with the reasoning in *Bankovic* and, indeed, with its result ... [I]t would stretch to breaking point the concept of jurisdiction extending extra-territorially to those subject to a state's "authority and control." It is one thing to recognise as exceptional the specific narrow categories of cases I have sought to summarize above; it would be quite another to accept that whenever a contracting state acts (militarily or otherwise) through its agents abroad, those affected by such activities fall within its article 1 jurisdiction. Such a contention would prove altogether too much ... It would, indeed, make redundant the principle of effective control of an area: what need for that if jurisdiction arises in any event under a general principle of "authority and control" irrespective of whether the area is ... effectively controlled?

The Applicants point to the House of Lords' purported "unreserved" conclusion that one of the Iraqi civilians at issue in that case — Mr. Mousa — was within the jurisdiction of the United Kingdom for the purposes of the European Convention of Human Rights. However, the UK government chose not to dispute this point. Accordingly, it was not argued before or decided by the House of Lords.

In *Al-Skeini,* the House of Lords clearly understood the problems associated with extra-territorial enforcement:

> My point is this: except where a state really does have effective control of territory, it cannot hope to secure Convention rights within that territory and ... it is unlikely in any event to find certain of the Convention rights it is bound to secure reconcilable with the customs of the resident population ... Often (for example where Sharia law is in force) Convention rights would clearly be incompatible with the laws of the territory.

Precisely the same point was made by this Court in *Hape:*

> Were *Charter* standards to be applied in another state's territory without its consent, there would by that very fact always be interference with the other state's sovereignty ... Canadian law cannot be enforced in another state's territory without that state's consent. Since extra-territorial enforcement is not possible, and enforcement is necessary for the *Charter* to apply, extraterritorial application of the *Charter* is impossible.

The motions judge in this case relied on *Hape* for the proposition that mere control over the person or activity is an insufficient basis for extra-territorial jurisdiction, whether in the context of police searches or military detentions. Such conduct involves the invasion of "the private sphere of persons," which invasion is paradigmatic of state sovereignty. The motions judge thoroughly reviewed and analyzed all of the relevant international and foreign decisions before observing that "military control over the person" would create an unworkable patchwork of different legal norms applying to detainees in Afghanistan, a "most unsatisfactory result in the context of a United Nations-sanctioned multinational military effort." The Court of Appeal found no error in this reasoning.

These principles of sovereign equality, territorial integrity and non-interference in the internal affairs of a state were also recently affirmed by the Supreme Court of the United States in *Munaf v. Geren,* a *habeas corpus* case arising from the detention of American dual citizens in Iraq. That Court noted that the petitioners' requests would "interfere with Iraq's sovereign right to 'punish offences against its laws committed within its borders,'" and that this was contrary to the principle that "[t]he jurisdiction of the nation within its own territory is necessarily exclusive and absolute," that "a nation state reigns sovereign within its own territory":

[T]o permit the validity of the acts of one sovereign state to be re-examined and perhaps condemned by the courts of another would very certainly "imperil the amicable relations between governments and vex the peace of nations."

The Applicants misstate the ratio of the Supreme Court of the United States in *Boumediene v. Bush,* a decision released the same date as *Munaf.* At issue was whether "enemy combatants" detained at the United States military base at Guantanamo Bay, Cuba had the constitutional privilege of *habeas corpus.* The Court found that under the terms of the indeterminate lease entered into between Cuba and the United States, Cuba retains "ultimate sovereignty" over the territory but has no rights as a sovereign while the United States exercises "complete jurisdiction and control." By virtue of its "complete jurisdiction and control over the base," the United States maintains *de facto* sovereignty over the territory. This was the basis for the decision that the petitioners could invoke *habeas corpus.*

The *Munaf* and *Boumediene* decisions, like those in *Bankovic* and *Al Skeini,* are consistent with this Court's decision in *Hape:* a state may apply and enforce its laws only where there is consent, where it has effective control of territory, or where some other exceptional basis recognized at international law exists. In particular, the *Boumediene* decision does not, as the Applicants assert, stand for the broad proposition that "individuals detained in military custody on foreign soil ... cannot be denied the fundamental protections of the U.S. constitution." [Similarly, the International Court of Justice, in *Legal Consequences of the Construction of a Wall in the Occupied Palestinian Territory, Advisory Opinion,* I.C.J. Reports 2004, did not — as the applicants assert — "unreservedly" conclude anything. Its conclusions were made in a factual context that does not exist in the present case — Israel's military occupation of the occupied territories.]

The jurisprudence of these courts does not support the Applicants' assertion that a state may apply and enforce its laws in the territory of another state (absent consent) where the first state merely exercises military control over individuals. That proposition clearly offends the principles of territoriality and sovereignty set out in *Hape.* The motions judge and the Court of Appeal so held and it is not necessary for this Court to repeat that message.

The jurisprudence, both in Canada and in the highest courts of the United States, the United Kingdom, and Europe, was accurately summarized by this Court in *Hape:*

It is a well-established principle that a state cannot act to enforce its laws within the territory of another state absent either the consent of the other state or, in exceptional cases, some other basis under international law.

INTERNATIONAL ENVIRONMENTAL LAW

Amicus Curiae Appearance in the Northwest Area Water Supply (NAWS) Case

In a communication dated 4 March 2009, the Legal Bureau wrote:

This case, *The Government of the Province of Manitoba v. Ken Salazar et al and State of North Dakota* was the subject to litigation in 2005 in the US Federal Court for the District of Columbia. That court issued an injunction preventing construction of certain aspects of the NAWS project. According to an agreed "Joint Proposed Case Management and Briefing Schedule," the Defendants intend to move for lifting the injunction on or before March 10 while the Province of Manitoba shall file its brief, opposing lifting of the injunction and supplementing its original complaint on or before April 10, 2009. *Amici* appearing in support of the province must file a brief at the same time as Manitoba, i.e. April 10, 2009.

The NAWS project is a municipal water project where water from the Missouri River basin is partially treated and transferred by closed pipeline across the Continental Divide to the town of Minot, within the Hudson Bay basin, and then fully treated and piped to various municipalities in northern North Dakota.

Both the Canadian Government and the Government of the Province of Manitoba have concerns that any failure in the system prior to full treatment may result in Missouri River water entering the Hudson Bay system, and introducing foreign biota and/or invasive species that will result in irretrievable injury to the water quality and species native to the Hudson Bay system.

Additionally, we are concerned and object to conclusions reached by the Bureau of Reclamation in its Record of Decision (ROD) on the NAWS Project, issued on January 15, 2009 (merely five days before the inauguration of the new US Administration). In the section of the ROD entitled "Consequences to Canada," the Bureau affirms (page 8):

analyzing the potential consequences to the environment of the Hudson Bay basin within Canada is outside the scope of the EIS. The statutory provisions of NEPA (and the Council of environmental Quality's regulations implementing NEPA) do not require assessment of environmental impacts within the territory of a foreign country.

It is our view that international law and a proper interpretation of US domestic law based on principles of international law require a state to take into consideration the potential of environmental harm to another state arising from actions within its territory. The basic principle, well established in international law and recognized as such by the United States, is that of *sic utere tuo ut alienum non laedas* (use your own property so as not to injure the property of another). This principle was accepted by both Canada and the United States as the basis for the decision in the *Trail Smelter Case* (1941), 3 R.I.A.A. 1905.

Para. 601 of the *Third Restatement of the Foreign Relations Law of the United States* is grounded on and further extends the *sic utere* principle:

(1) A State is obligated to take such measures as may be necessary, to the extent practicable under the circumstances, to ensure that activities within its jurisdiction or control (a) conform to generally accepted international rules and standards for the prevention, reduction, and control of injury to the environment of another state or of areas beyond the limits of national jurisdiction; and (b) are conducted so as not to cause significant injury to the environment of another state or of areas beyond the limits of national jurisdiction.

It is not possible for the United States to carry out its international law obligations without assessing the potential for transboundary environmental harm. In our view, this failure should form the central argument in our proposed *amicus curiae* brief, as it did in the Canadian government's original brief in the 2005 litigation.

OCEANS LAW

Canadian Arctic Sovereignty

In a presentation dated 14 June 2009, the Legal Bureau stated:

Canadian Arctic Sovereignty: Myths and Realities

The Arctic is increasingly the focus of international interest and attention. Current climate change challenges can lead to a misperception that there are threats to Canadian sovereignty in the Arctic. An understanding of the legal context will show there are, in reality, few geopolitical tensions in this region.

Managing the Disputes

Canada's Arctic sovereignty is longstanding, well established and based on historic title. No country questions this. However, there are three discrete areas on the outer edges of the Canadian Arctic where we have well-managed disputes with our neighbours. These will be resolved in due course in accordance with international law.

In the *Beaufort Sea,* Canada and the United States dispute the maritime boundary north of Yukon Territory and Alaska. An 1825 treaty sets the boundary as 1410 west longitude. Canada relies on this treaty for both the land and maritime boundary, but the US argues that the equidistance principle should apply in the waters. The United States and Canada have both offered oil and gas exploration licenses and leases in this 6,250 square nautical mile disputed zone. Neither country has allowed exploration or development in the area pending resolution of the dispute.

Hans Island is the only land under dispute in the Canadian Arctic. This 1.3 km² island is claimed by Denmark. The maritime boundary between Canada and Denmark was settled by a 1973 treaty, so the dispute is only about the island, not the surrounding waters or seabed. Since 2005, Canada and Denmark have met yearly to discuss the island, and there is a joint scientific project between a Canadian and a Danish university on the island.

Canada and Denmark also dispute two small zones in the *Lincoln Sea* north of Ellesmere Island and Greenland. This arises from differing views over the factors to use to define the exact boundary line.

The "Northwest Passage"

No one disputes that the various waterways known as the "Northwest Passage" are Canadian. The issue is the legal status of these waters — control over foreign navigation. These waters are internal waters of Canada, which means Canada has an unfettered right to regulate as it would in land territory. The United States agrees the waters are Canadian, but contends that a "strait used for international navigation" runs through them, giving foreign vessels a right of transit. Through the 1988 *Arctic Cooperation Agreement* Canada and the US have agreed to disagree without prejudice to either position. The US asks for permission for its icebreakers to enter these waters, and Canada grants this permission.

Canada permits navigation in its internal waters, including the "Northwest Passage," providing ships respect Canadian conditions and controls related to safety, security, the environment, and Inuit interests. Ice conditions remain extremely variable and the "Northwest Passage" is unlikely to attract routine transits in the short to medium term.

Shipping Controls in the Canadian Arctic

On June 11, 2009 Bill C-3 (An Act to Amend the *Arctic Waters Pollution Prevention Act)* amending the definition "arctic waters" — to extend the geographic application of the AWPPA to the outer limit of Canada's EEZ north of 60 — received Royal Assent. The right to exercise strict pollution prevention measures in ice-covered waters out to a maximum of 200 nautical miles is codified in Article 234 of the *United Nations Convention on the Law of the Sea* (UNCLOS).

Canada is currently in the process of developing the necessary regulations to formally establish the Northern Canada Vessel Traffic Services (NORDREG) zone with mandatory ship reporting requirements. The proposed regulations, expected to be in place for the 2010 shipping season, will replace the current voluntary system, which enjoys a high degree of compliance. These regulations are expected to be in place for the 2010 shipping season. Mandatory reporting to NORDREG will enhance the safety and security of vessels navigating in Arctic waters, and will provide better tools for pollution prevention in these waters.

Extended Continental Shelf

Having ratified UNCLOS in 2003, Canada has until 2013 to make a submission to the UN regarding the outer limits of our continental shelf beyond 200 nautical miles. Scientific work is taking place in both the Atlantic and Arctic Oceans for Canada to establish the maximum extent of its continental shelf.

The delineation process is not a land or resource "grab." Canada's sovereign rights to explore, conserve and exploit resources in and on the seabed already exist, but the process will help determine the extent of the area over which we can exercise these rights. The Commission on the Limits of the Continental Shelf does not resolve disputes or overlapping submissions. If overlaps between the submissions of circumpolar neighbours become apparent, they will be resolved in accordance with international law.

The Ilulissat Declaration

In May 2008, Canada and the other four Arctic Ocean coastal states met at the political level in Ilulissat, Greenland. They recalled that:

> an extensive international legal framework applies to the Arctic Ocean ... Notably, the law of the sea provides for important rights and obligations concerning the delineation of the outer limits of the continental shelf, the protection of the marine environment, including ice-covered areas, freedom of navigation, marine scientific research and other uses of the sea. We remain committed to this legal framework and to the orderly settlement of any possible overlapping claims.

This framework provides a solid foundation for responsible management by the five coastal States and other users of this Ocean ... We therefore see no need to develop a new comprehensive legal regime to govern the Arctic.

The complete text of the Ilulissat Declaration can be found at the following Internet address: http://www.oceanlaw.org/downloads/arctic/Ilulissat_Declaration.pdf.

Does Article 14.4 of the Convention on International Trade in Endangered Species (CITES) Exempt Parties to the International Commission for the Conservation of Atlantic Tuna from the Provisions under CITES for a Marine Species Listed in Appendix II?

In a memorandum dated 1 June 2009, the Legal Bureau wrote:

Article 14 of CITES is entitled: Effect on Domestic Legislation and International Conventions. Article 14.4 states:

> A State party to the present Convention, which is also a party to any other treaty, convention or international agreement which is in force at the time of the coming into force of the present Convention and under the provisions of which protection is afforded to marine species included in Appendix II, shall be relieved of the obligation imposed on it under the provisions of the present Convention with respect to trade in specimens of species included in Appendix II that are taken by ships registered in that State and in accordance with the provisions of such other treaty, convention or international agreement.

According to this Article, in order for a Party to be relieved of obligations imposed under CITES with respect to trade in an Appendix II marine species, the following is required:

a. the Party must be a Party to a treaty, convention or international agreement which was in force at the coming into force of CITES, which occurred on 1 July, 1975;
b. the provisions of the other treaty, convention or international agreement afford protection to the particular marine species in question in Appendix II;
c. the marine species in question taken by ships registered in that Party are taken in accordance with the provisions of such other treaty, convention or international agreement.

Criterion A

The International Convention for the Conservation of Atlantic Tunas (ICCAT) came into force in 1969, which predates the coming into force of CITES by six years, so Criterion A is met.

Criterion B

Criterion B would require that ICCAT's provisions afford protection to the particular marine species in question in Appendix II, in this case Atlantic Tuna.

ICCAT

ICCAT creates a Commission to carry out its objectives. According to Article 8.1: "The Commission may, on the basis of scientific evidence, make recommendations designed to maintain the populations of tuna and tuna-like fishes that may be taken in the Convention area at levels which will permit the maximum sustainable catch."

Further, under Article 8.2: "Each recommendation made under paragraph 1 of this Article shall become effective for all Contracting Parties six months after the date of the notification from the Commission transmitting the recommendation to the Contracting Parties, except as provided in paragraph 3 of this Article." Article 8.3 deals with objections of Parties to recommendations.

The Commission sets annual quotas for sustainable tuna harvests, which become binding on the Parties to ICCAT. These quotas are designed to "maintain the populations of tuna and tuna-like fishes that may be taken in the Convention area at levels which will permit the maximum sustainable catch" (ICCAT Art. 8.1 (a)).

"Protection is afforded"

Neither CITES, nor any subsequent resolution adopted at a Conference of the Parties to CITES, considers whether the Article XIV (4) term "under the provisions of which protection is afforded to marine species" requires only the inclusion of protection provisions, or whether the provision needs to provide effective protection to the marine species. However, the formulation used in Article XIV (4) and the centrality of "protection is afforded" introduced by "under the provisions of which" points to an effect or a result rather than to the provisions of the convention themselves.

The Oxford Dictionary of Modern Legal usage defines "afford" as: "to furnish (something) as an essential concomitant." The Cage Canadian dictionary defines "afford" as: "yield or give as an effect or as a result; provide."

A useful analogy can be found in Resolution Conf. 9.24 (Rev. CoP 14) in its Annex 6 on the format for proposals to amend the Appendices, which provides specific instructions for other international legal instruments:

7.2 International

Provide details of international instruments relating to the species in question, including the nature of the protection afforded by such instruments. Provide an assessment of the effectiveness of these instruments in ensuring the conservation and/or management of the species.

Provide similar information on international instruments relating to the management of trade in the species in question. Provide an assessment of the effectiveness of these instruments in controlling illegal trade in the species.

Therefore, in order to meet the requirement of Criterion B it seems necessary to consider the effectiveness of the ICCAT in ensuring the conservation of the species in question as well as the nature of the protection afforded.

Criterion C

If ICCAT Parties were able to satisfy criteria a. and b., they would still only be exempt from the application of CITES as long as their Atlantic Tuna catches are taken "in accordance with the provisions" of the ICCAT.

If the reference to "the provisions" refers specifically to the protection provisions of the ICCAT, which would centre on the catch quota recommendations of the Commission, in order to meet Criterion C, Parties would have to respect the recommendations of the Commission. In this case, if an ICCAT Party objects to a recommendation, such as the annual quota, or refuses to adhere to the annual quota, Criterion C would not be met. Therefore CITES provisions would apply to contracting parties which do not comply with the ICCAT Commission's recommendations.

Summary

In summary, ICCAT predates the coming into force of CITES. However, CITES' requirements for the provisions of the pre-dating Convention to "afford protection" to marine species included in Appendix II would also have to be met by ICCAT. Further, even if ICCAT does afford protection, a Party would only be relieved of CITES obligations if it adhered to the protection provisions. If adherence to ICCAT provisions refers specifically to its protection provisions, this would include adherence to the catch quota recommendations of the ICCAT Commission.

Therefore, Parties to ICCAT would not automatically be exempt from CITES Appendix II obligations for marine species.

TREATY LAW

Basic Principles Regarding the Capacity to Conclude Treaties

In a legal opinion from May 2009, the Legal Bureau wrote:

What Are Treaties?

Treaties are binding legal instruments under international law. Treaties can be contrasted with non-legally binding instruments, usually titled by Canada and a number of countries Memorandums of Understanding (MOUs) or 'Arrangements.' MOUs only create so called moral obligations, and in contrast with Treaties, are not justiciable under international law.

Who Can Enter into Treaties?

Every state possesses the capacity to conclude treaties (Art 6, *Vienna Convention on the Law of Treaties* (VCLT)). State refers to a sovereign independent state (Aust, Anthony: *Modern Treaty Law and Practice*, 2000 at 47). Certain international organizations also possess the treaty making power: discussion of this specific area of the treaty making power is beyond the scope of this examination.

The capacity to conclude treaties can be contrasted with the capacity to conclude MOUs. MOUs can, and are, routinely undertaken by 'sub-state' entities. For example, an MOU can be negotiated between departments in two different countries, between an overseas territory and another state, or of greater interest for our purposes, between a dependant territory and the state to which it belongs.

So-called "dependant territories" (which include crown dependencies), do not have the power to enter into treaties independently. However, they may be authorized by the state to which they belong to enter into a treaty. In such a case, the state to which they belong remains ultimately responsible for the performance of any treaties they enter into.

Use of Commentaries and Interpretive Guidance and the OECD Convention on Combating Bribery of Foreign Public Officials in International Business Transactions

In March 2009, the Legal Bureau submitted the following views to a meeting of the Organization for Economic Co-operation and Development (OECD) Working Group on Bribery Review of the Instruments:

The OECD is a like-minded-forum, and as such it possesses a greater scope for "progressive development" of persuasive or binding practice, interpretations and obligations than most multilateral fora. Canada considers that this is largely beneficial as it enables OECD countries and other like-mindeds to continually develop and advance issues of mutual concern where consensus exists to do so.

However, Canada's longstanding position remains that the Commentaries — evolving practice or country recommendations — provide useful interpretive guidance but are not themselves binding.

Canada supports a high degree of transparency in any process of clarifying obligations through the issuance of interpretations or in modifying legal obligations through formal amendment. The Working Group on Bribery Review of the Instruments is such a transparent process in that it seeks to ascertain whether States Parties are prepared to agree by consensus on interpretations or amendments. This takes us to the question of the manner in which interpretations or new commitments can be expressly consented to by States Parties of the Bribery Convention ...

Canada agrees with the Secretariat's view that States Parties may adopt "interpretive declarations," or "authentic interpretations." This would be a way of clarifying pre-existing legal obligations under the Convention. Canada would not support either the creation of new legal obligations or any interpretations that would depart from the ordinary meaning of the text, through the process of issuing interpretative declarations. In Canadian practice, new international legal obligations undertaken must first be ratified by our Cabinet and placed before Parliament. Thus, in our view, new obligations or departures from the ordinary meaning of the text must always be assumed by way of Amendment to the Convention rather than interpretive declarations.

The Secretariat notes that interpretative declarations may take a number of forms, including a *decision* or *resolution* of a body in which all parties to the treaty are represented. Canada notes that OECD Council "decisions" are *binding* on Member States pursuant to the OECD Convention, article 5(a). In our view, interpretative declarations cannot be binding on States Parties.

Canada agrees ... that the Working Group on Bribery *per se* may not possess the international legal competence to issue interpretative declarations. Although Member States of the Convention could agree by consensus to designate the Working Group on Bribery as the Conference of the Parties to the Convention, this is a decision that would have to be taken by a formal meeting of States Parties convened for the purpose.

Canada agrees ... that the decision on which procedure should be followed in formally interpreting or amending the Convention should be taken after the substance of the changes is determined, depending on the nature of the change.

INTERNATIONAL ECOMOMIC LAW AND SANCTIONS

Implementation of UN Security Council Sanctions

On 17 April 2009, the Legal Bureau wrote:

As a member of the UN, Canada has the international legal obligation to implement into domestic law the binding provisions of United Nations Security Council Resolutions. In some cases, no action is required as the substance of the binding provision has already been implemented into Canadian law (i.e. in *Export and Import Permits Act* ("*EIPA*"), *Criminal Code, Immigration and Refugee Protection Act* ("*IRPA*") etc.). For example, Canada need not take further steps to implement the travel bans required by certain UNSCRs as they are already assured by provisions of the *IRPA*. However, if the terms of the UNSCR create a binding obligation upon Canada that is not already implemented in Canadian domestic law, it has an international obligation to act. It is in these cases it turns to the *UN Act*.

Article 2 of the *UN Act* states:

When, in pursuance of Article 41 of the Charter of the United Nations, set out in the schedule, the Security Council of the United Nations decides on a measure to be employed to give effect to any of its decisions and calls on Canada to apply the measure, the Governor in Council may make such orders and regulations as appear to him to be necessary or expedient for enabling the measures to be effectively applied.

...

The *UN Act* is limited to these circumstances and cannot be used to implement controls in excess of what the UNSC has mandated.

As there is no clear external authority to interpret the UNSC resolutions, Member States must determine themselves whether the provisions are "binding" and thus require domestic implementation. This is generally done by analyzing the language of the provision itself:

The question as to whether the Council has imposed an obligation binding under articles 24 and 25 should be determined from the Council's actual language in any given situation [and] ... in most cases, the Council does use relatively clear language in its operative paragraphs. For example, it can be clearly established that by using "urges" and "invites," as opposed to "decides," the paragraph is intended to be exhortatory and not binding. [*Security Council Action under Chapter VII*, Security Council Report — Special Research Report, 2008 No. 1, 23 June 2008, at p. 12.]

The language "decides" clearly indicates that the UNSC deemed this provision to be binding.

Sanctions under the Special Economic Measures Act (SEMA)

On 8 December 2008, the Legal Bureau wrote:

There are two mechanisms by which the Canadian government may impose economic sanctions: the *United Nations Act* ("UN Act") and the *Special Economic Measures Act* ("SEMA"). In the absence of a United Nations Security Council decision that requires all Member States to impose sanctions, Canada may unilaterally impose sanctions under the SEMA. The SEMA provides the Government of Canada the discretionary authority to impose sanctions against a foreign nation if the triggers it sets out in section 4(1) have been met. Section 4(1) states:

The Governor in Council may, for the purpose of implementing a decision, resolution or recommendation of an international organization of states or association of states, of which Canada is a member, that calls on its members to take economic measures against a foreign state, or where the Governor in Council is of the opinion that a grave breach of international peace and security has occurred that has resulted or is likely to result in a serious international crisis.

The first trigger enables Canada to impose sanctions in response to a call of an international organization or association of states of which Canada is a member. Were Canada in its consultations with various international fora to receive a call for additional sanctions from an appropriate international body then this trigger would be satisfied.

Under SEMA's second trigger, sanctions can be imposed outside of a multilateral scheme when a "grave breach of international peace and security has occurred that has resulted or is likely to result in a serious international crisis." This may be a more legally onerous standard than that which appears in the UN Charter for Security Council action. Article 39 of the Charter of the United Nations enables sanctions action in situations of threats to the peace only. The Security Council has found actual breaches (as opposed to threats) in few instances (breaches were only declared in 1950 following North Korea's invasion of South Korea, in 1982 following Argentina's invasion of the Falkland Islands, in 1987 regarding the Iran-Iraq conflict, and upon the Iraq invasion of Kuwait in 1990). In addition, the second trigger of the SEMA must not only constitute a grave breach but that breach must have "resulted or is likely to result in a serious international crisis."

Canada has invoked sanctions under the SEMA four times. Sanctions have been imposed under the call from an international body in the cases of Haiti (a call from the OAS) and the Former Republic of Yugoslavia (a call from the G8). The second trigger was used for the first time with the sanctions imposed against Burma in December 2007, and was used again with sanctions imposed against Zimbabwe in September 2008.

The SEMA allows Canada to impose various measures against a foreign State, including:

- A prohibition to import all or specified goods from that foreign State;
- A prohibition to export all or specified goods to that foreign State or any person in that foreign State;
- An assets freeze against designated individuals and/or entities;
- A prohibition on the transfer of technical data to that foreign State or any person in that foreign State;
- A prohibition on the provision or acquisition of financial services or other services to, from or for the benefit of, or on the direction or order of that foreign State or any person in that foreign State;
- A prohibition on Canadian-registered ships or aircraft from docking/ landing in a foreign State; and
- A prohibition on foreign State-registered ships or aircraft from docking/ landing in Canada.

INTERNATIONAL CRIMINAL LAW

Criminal Jurisdiction over International Civil Servants

On 20 October 2008, the Legal Bureau wrote:

It is UN policy that its officials be held accountable whenever they commit criminal acts due to the harm inflicted on both the victims and the work and image of the UN, [but] criminal prosecution is still generally referred to the State Parties following an internal consideration of the allegation and the waiving of immunity by the UN. [See UNGA Resolution 62/63: *Criminal Accountability of United Nations Officials and Experts on Mission,* Doc. A/RES/62/63 and *Criminal Accountability of United Nations Officials and Experts on Mission,* Report of the Secretary General, Doc. A/63/260] Notwithstanding that is not bestowed with criminal authority over its officials (as a State Party is for its nationals and or territory), it is unlikely that State Parties would be willing to recognize such independence given past practice and the current legal framework.

In this respect, it should be noted that a majority of expert delegates to the 2008 Conference of States Parties to the United Nations Convention Against Corruption resisted the suggestion that an independent international mechanism be created to decide requests for waivers of immunity from offences under article 16, paragraph 2:

68. In discussing best ways to implement effectively at the national level article 16, paragraph 2, of the Convention (on the passive bribery of foreign public officials and officials of public international organizations), one speaker expressed the view that an independent mechanism should be established to handle requests for a waiver of immunities for such perpetrators. The same speaker stated that, for purposes of transparency, integrity and impartiality, such a mechanism could bring together representatives from the organization concerned, the national prosecution authorities of the host country and the United Nations Office on Drugs and Crime, which would function as an advisory body to deliver opinions on issues related to the immunities of officials of public international organizations.

69. While two speakers argued in support of the aforementioned proposals, many speakers, including the observer for the International Association of Prosecutors, were opposed to the establishment of such a mechanism for a number of reasons. Firstly, it was stressed that the necessary condition for the implementation of article 16, paragraph 2, of the Convention was, in the first instance, the criminalization of the conduct described therein per se and that issues related to immunities were associated with the assessment of whether or not prosecution was feasible in a given case. Secondly, it was argued that, as privileges and immunities were granted to organizations and not to individuals, only international organizations were empowered to waive such immunities when they were of the opinion that doing so would be in their interest and would not impair the independence of their functions. Thirdly, it was stressed that there was no legal basis for adopting a uniform procedure for the waiver of immunities and that the Convention on the Privileges and Immunities of the United Nations (General Assembly resolution 22 A (I)) and the Convention on the Privileges and Immunities of the Specialized Agencies (Assembly resolution 179 (II)) provided the legal framework for dealing with such issues. In addition, it was stated that no mandate had been provided to the Conference to adopt rules regulating waivers for immunities in the context of practical application of article 16, paragraph 2, of the Convention. In any case, one speaker proposed that more working group meetings, involving representatives from internation-

al organizations and judicial and prosecutorial authorities of Member States, should be conducted in future to further discuss the issue. It was noted that an open-ended dialogue among States and intergovernmental organizations on the criminalization of bribery of officials of public international organizations, taking into account related privileges and immunities, was conducted in September 2007 at the initiative of the secretariat.

[Although] the question of the UN exercising some jurisdiction over its officials remains open for discussion, there is little to indicate that participants in this dialogue are actively advancing the idea of expanding UN powers into a pseudo criminal law enforcement capacity pursuant to UNCAC. Rather, State Parties are focussing on criminalizing UNCAC offences nationally, extending nationality to ensure its nationals remain accountable when working for an international institution outside of their country and by encouraging public international organizations to waive immunity for some offences.

INTERNATIONAL TRADE AND INVESTMENT LAW

Cure of the Breach in the Adjustment Factor Arbitration under the Softwood Lumber Agreement (SLA) — London Court of International Arbitration — Canada (Claimant) v. United States of America (Respondent)

In its submission of 12 May 2009, Canada wrote:

This arbitration arises under Article XIV(29)(c) of the Softwood Lumber Agreement Between Canada and the United States ("SLA"). Pursuant to that paragraph, Canada requests the Tribunal to determine that a cash payment of USD$34 million, plus simple interest at 4 percent, which Canada has tendered, fully cures the breach found in LCIA Case No. 7941 ("LCIA 7941"). The United States to date has refused Canada's tender of payment on grounds that the United States does not consider such payment to cure the breach, in whole or in part. The United States has thus imposed import duties pursuant to Article XIV(27). In these circumstances, Article XIV(29)(c) of the SLA provides for the Tribunal to determine whether the cash payment which Canada has tendered cures the breach, in whole or in part, and if so to require that the United States cease or modify its imposition of import measures and refund in whole or in part duties already collected.

In LCIA 7941, the Tribunal rightly found that its mandate was limited to determining compensatory adjustments, which, under the SLA, must take the form of adjustments to Export Measures. Acknowledging that this limitation posed difficulties for its objectives, the Tribunal nevertheless chose what it considered the appropriate remedy among those proposed by the United States, to be applied if Canada did not cure the breach within the reasonable period of time determined by the Tribunal.

Canada comes before this Tribunal because Canada considers that a cash payment of USD $34 million cures the breach. Such a lump-sum payment provides the United States with full reparation for the only harm that the United States attempted to demonstrate in LCIA 7941 — harm to U.S. producers during the period of Canada's breach. Such a payment meets the objective of a cure identified by the Tribunal — wiping out the consequences of the breach in the sense of customary international law and the ILC Articles — and with much greater certainty and fewer collateral distortions than any remedy the LCIA 7941 Tribunal could determine within the SLA's constraints with respect to compensatory adjustments.

Canada's position in this proceeding can be summarized succinctly. First, a cure of the breach can take the form of cash compensation, which is also the best means in this case to provide full reparation for any harm suffered by U.S. producers. Article XIV restricts the form that the compensatory adjustments may take, but does not restrict the form that a "cure" may take, as the United States conceded in the LCIA 7941 proceedings. Second, USD $34 million provides full reparation to the United States for any injury to its softwood lumber producers. That sum represents the amount of lost producer surplus to U.S. producers, as calculated using the methodology and assumptions made by Dr. Neuberger, who testified in the LCIA 7941 remedy proceeding, and whose testimony and reports were endorsed by the United States in that proceeding. As testified by Dr. Joseph Kalt in a report appended to this Statement of Case (the "Kalt Report"), producer surplus is the standard measure of economic effects on a market's producers of an event or government program that changes supply and demand in the market and the sum of USD $34 million equals the amount of lost producer surplus. A cash payment of USD $34 million corresponds to the United States' own calculations as to the harm suffered by its producers. The United States is not entitled to anything more under the SLA or customary international law than full reparation for the harm to its producers.

Accordingly, the compensatory measures imposed by the United States should be terminated because a cash payment of USD $34 million constitutes a cure of the breach found by the Tribunal in LCIA 7941. Furthermore, all customs duties collected by the United States should be refunded retroactively to the date the compensatory measures were imposed.

As Canada will show, supported by the Kalt Report, the cash payment is sufficient to compensate the United States for the only harm it alleged in the LCIA 7941 proceeding — the harm to U.S. softwood lumber producers. Neither the SLA nor customary international law requires more.

Provincial Programs Arbitration under the Softwood Lumber Agreement (SLA) — London Court of International Arbitration — United States of America (Claimant) v. Canada (Respondent)

In its Statement of Defence dated 27 February 2009, Canada wrote:

A full reading of Article XVII shows that only paragraph 1 of Article XVII establishes an obligation on the Parties not to take action to circumvent the obligations under the Agreement, including any actions having the effect of reducing or offsetting Export Measures. The obligation is not "free-standing" but rather is an obligation not to take any action to circumvent other obligations of the Agreement.

Paragraph 2 of Article XVII establishes no obligations — there is no provision of paragraph 2 that requires a Party to do, or not do, anything. Rather, paragraph 2 adds some clarifications of what does and what does not constitute a measure that may violate the anti-circumvention obligations of paragraph 1. The first sentence of paragraph 2 states that government grants or other benefits "shall be considered to reduce or offset the Export Measures if they are provided on a de jure or de facto basis to producers or exporters of Canadian Softwood Lumber Products." The second sentence of paragraph 2 modifies the first sentence and the obligations of paragraph 1 by providing that, "notwithstanding the foregoing," measures that "shall not be considered" to reduce or offset Export Measures "include, without limitation" the five categories set out in (a)–(e) of Article XVII(2).

The introductory phrase "notwithstanding the foregoing" at the beginning of the second sentence of paragraph 2 means that the second sentence is intended to override the first sentence of paragraph 2. In other words, there are benefits that meet all of the terms of the first sentence that nevertheless "shall not be considered" to reduce or offset Export Measures. The absence of a similar "notwithstanding" clause in the first sentence of paragraph 2 indicates that the first sentence of paragraph 2 is not intended to override the requirements of paragraph 1 of Article XVII.

If, as argued by the United States, the drafters had intended to establish a flat prohibition of benefits (with limited exceptions), they could have drafted the first sentence of paragraph 2 as such an obligation. They did not do so. The sentence makes clear that grants or other benefits meeting its criteria "shall be considered to offset or reduce Export Measures." By itself, the first sentence does not prohibit grants or other benefits.

If the first sentence were the only provision of paragraph 2, it would create at least a strong presumption that a grant or benefit described in that sentence would infringe the anti-circumvention obligation of paragraph 1 by reducing or offsetting the Export Measures. However, the first sentence does not stand alone and must be read in context.

The second sentence of paragraph 2 is clear on its face that items (a)–(e) are not an exclusive list. The chapeau to items (a)–(e) provides: "measures that shall not be considered to reduce or offset the Export Measures in the SLA 2006 include without limitation" [emphasis added] items (a)–(e). This can only mean that there are grants or other benefits provided on a de facto or de jure basis to softwood lumber producers, in addition to measures falling within items (a)–(e), that shall not be considered to reduce or offset Export Measures notwithstanding the first sentence of paragraph 2.

One of the corollaries of the general rule of interpretation of Article 31 of the VCLT is that the interpretation of a treaty must give meaning and effect to all terms of the treaty. The first sentence of paragraph 2 thus must be read in the context of paragraph 1, which it does not expand, and subject to the second sentence, which, contrary to the U.S. contention, contains a plainly non-exclusive list of measures that must not be considered to reduce or offset Export Measures, even if they would otherwise fall within paragraph 1 and the first sentence of paragraph 2.

World Trade Organization (WTO) — Ordinary Customs Duties — China — Measures Affecting Import of Auto Parts

In a Written Submission to the WTO Appellate Body dated 10 October 2008, Canada wrote:

The Panel correctly applied the *Vienna Convention* to determine the meaning of "ordinary customs duties" in [GATT] Article II:1 (b), first sentence. The Panel was correct to find that the relevant context for this interpretation is the provisions of the GATT 1994 and WTO Member practice, and was correct to reject China's argument that the Harmonized System is determinative context with respect to the threshold issue.

Canada will begin by showing that the Panel interpreted "ordinary customs duties" properly by addressing its ordinary meaning in the context of other GATT provisions. The Panel correctly found that the *key* interpretative issue before it with respect to determining the meaning of "ordinary customs duties" was the phrase "on their importation" in Article II:1 (b), first sentence. Article II:1 (b), first sentence provides:

The products described in Part I of the Schedule relating to any contracting party, which are the products of territories of other contracting parties, shall, *on their importation* into the territory to which the Schedule relates, and subject to the terms, conditions or qualifications set forth in that Schedule, be exempt from *ordinary customs duties* in excess of those set forth and provided therein [emphasis added].

The complainants argued that this meant customs duties could apply based only on the state of the product at the border, and thus that "on their importation" had a strict and precise temporal limit. In contrast, China argued for a much broader interpretation of "ordinary customs duties" by claiming that "on their importation" did not limit the ability to assess an ordinary customs duty to the "state" or "condition" of the product at the border, but rather it could apply so long as a duty liability *attached* as a "condition of" or "by reason of" importation of that product.

The Panel started with Article II:1 (b), first sentence, and then correctly found that the relevant context for interpreting "on their importation" as it relates to the meaning of "ordinary customs duties" is other GATT provisions, and particularly Article II:1 (b), second sentence. The Panel appropriately considered the context provided by the similar but slightly different wording contained in Article II:1 (b), second sentence, Article I, and Article XI of the GATT, and took into account the basis upon which other WTO Members apply ordinary customs duties as subsequent practice.

The Panel concluded that "on their importation," when considered in context and in the light of the object and purpose of the GATT, establishes a strict and precise temporal element, such that to be an "ordinary customs duty" a charge must be based on the physical state or condition of the product at the border and not after this specific point in time.

In reaching its conclusions, the Panel recognized the absurdity of China's interpretation of "ordinary customs duties" when it stated:

[T]he "security and predictability of the reciprocal and mutually advantageous arrangements directed to the substantial reduction of tariff and other barriers to trade," which is a recognized object and purpose of the WTO Agreement, would be undermined if a charge were to be considered as an ordinary customs duty even when the obligation to pay the charge accrues after goods have already entered into the customs territory of China and been assembled into complete goods of the corresponding kind. We therefore share the systemic concerns expressed by the complainants that if the assembly of the products after their importation into the customs territory of a Member could provide a basis for tariff classification, the tariff classification system would undermine the national treatment obligations under

Article III of the GATT 1994, which is one of the core principles of the WTO Agreements. Such an interpretation would blur the fundamental distinction between Measures falling within the scope of Article III:2 and those falling within the scope of Article II:1 (b), first sentence, of the GATT 1994.

Having recognized the GATT provisions that are relevant context, the Panel first, and correctly, looked to the immediate context provided by Article II:1 (b), second sentence, which provides in relevant part:

> Such products shall also be exempt from all *other duties or charges* of any kind *imposed on or in connection with* the importation in excess of those imposed on the date of this Agreement or those directly and mandatorily required to be imposed thereafter by legislation in force in the importing territory on that date [emphasis added].

Unlike the first sentence of Article II:1 (b), which uses "on their importation" with respect to "ordinary customs duties," the second sentence refers to "on or in connection with" importation in respect of "other duties and charges" in a Member's Schedule. The Panel correctly found that the difference between "on or in connection with" and "on their interpretation" must mean that the drafters intended "other duties and charges" to have a broader scope than "ordinary customs duties" as "any interpretation giving these two expressions the *same meaning* would risk reducing the intention of the drafters of the GATT 1994 to regulate 'ordinary customs duties' and 'all other duties and charges of any kind' differently."

The Panel then confirmed its view of the ordinary meaning of "on" in Article II:1 (b), first sentence, by reference to relevant contextual language in Articles I and XI. Taking all relevant contextual language in the GATT into account, the Panel concluded that:

> [I]nterpreting "on" as also meaning "in connection with" (or any similar meaning) would eviscerate such difference. We are however bound by the general rules of interpretation of the *Vienna Convention* to "give meaning and effect to all terms of the treaty" and we therefore are not "free to adopt a reading that would result in reducing whole clauses or paragraphs of a treaty to redundancy or inutility." Hence, this contextual analysis confirms our conclusion above at paragraph 7.165 that the ordinary meaning of "on" in the first sentence of Article II:1 (b) of the GATT 1994 contains a *strict temporal* connotation.

Last, in accordance with Article 31 (3) (b) of the *Vienna Convention*, the Panel appropriately considered subsequent practice to see if other WTO

Members apply ordinary customs duties based on the state of the product at the border or "conditionally upon" or "by reason of" importation of the product as China argued. This again was particularly relevant to addressing the Parties' competing views on "on their importation." The Panel concluded that:

> We have reviewed the examples of customs practices from the complainants and other Members submitted by China on this issue and consider, as the United States and Canada correctly argue, that these practices, in fact, reinforce the evidence that WTO Members impose ordinary customs duties based on the state of the product as they are presented at the border ... This supports our conclusion above that the ordinary meaning of "on their importation" in the first sentence of Article II:1 (b) of the GATT 1994 indicates a *strict temporal element*.

Appropriately, having considered the WTO text and WTO Member practice first, the Panel then assessed whether the Harmonized System has any relevance to the threshold issue.

North American Free Trade Agreement (NAFTA) — *Chemtura v. Canada*

In its Counter-Memorial, dated 20 October 2008, Canada wrote:

Expropriation — What Constitutes an Investment

When addressing whether the Claimant's investment has been expropriated, the Tribunal must consider Chemtura Canada as a whole enterprise; the Claimant cannot artificially isolate aspects of its business and claim that these pieces constitute a standalone investment under Article 1139.

The proposition that an investment must be considered as a whole is supported by both NAFTA and non-NAFTA investment awards. Those awards have consistently held that, while subsidiary elements of an investment are relevant to a determination of its value, they are not, in themselves, investments ...

In its Memorial, the Claimant appears to allege that customers, goodwill, and market constitute its investment under the NAFTA. It is unclear whether the Claimant is arguing that these elements are investments in and of themselves, or that they are merely parts of the value of Chemtura's "Canadian investment," which it has defined as its wholly-owned subsidiary. If the Claimant is arguing that these elements are standalone investments, Canada submits that that argument must fail because such interests do not fit within the definition of investment in Article 1139.

The terms included in Article 1139's definition of investment provide clear indicia of what this Tribunal may consider as an "investment": these include an enterprise, an equity security, a debt security, a loan, or an interest entitling its owner to share in income, profits, or assets upon dissolution. These items share attributes in that they are concrete, definite interests that are liable to be bought, sold, traded, or borrowed against. The NAFTA Parties have assigned a core meaning to what comprises an investment under Article 1139, which does not include customers, goodwill, or market share.

The Claimant has not indicated in its Memorial which paragraph of Article 1139 includes customers, goodwill, or market share as investments. On a plain reading of Article 1139, it is obvious that these concepts are not investments under paragraphs (a) to (f) of that Article. As such, Canada assumes that the Claimant is relying on Article 1139 (g) and (h), and will therefore analyze those alleged "investments" under those headings. Even under those broad categories, however, the Claimant's characterization of customers, market share, and goodwill as NAFTA investments still fails. NAFTA Articles 1139(g) and (h) define investment as:

(g) real estate or other property, tangible or intangible, acquired in the expectation or used for the purpose of economic benefit or other business purposes; and

(h) interests arising from the commitment of capital or other resources in the territory of a Party to economic activity in such territory, such as under

(i) contracts involving the presence of an investor's property in the territory of the Party, including turnkey or construction contracts, or concessions, or

(j) contracts where remuneration depends substantially on the production, revenues or profits of an enterprise.

NAFTA Article 1139(g) lists real estate and tangible or intangible property as covered investments. The ordinary meaning of "property" is a thing or possession that a person or entity owns. At international law, "property" consists of a bundle of rights including the right to use, the right to enjoy and the right to destroy or dispose of the property (*i.e., usus, fructus, abusus*). In a similar manner, the *Shorter Oxford Dictionary* defines "property" as "that which one owns; a thing or things belonging to a person or persons" and "the condition or fact of owning or being owned; the (exclusive) right to the possession, use or disposal of a thing, ownership." Generally, property can be acquired, owned, and alienated by its owner.

Customers, goodwill, and market share are not within the ordinary meaning of tangible or intangible property. No one, including the Claimant, can own, acquire, possess, use, rent, mortgage, dispose of or otherwise alienate customers, goodwill, or market share. Nor does the Claimant manage or control these so-called investments. They are elements of a business, and could even be considered benefits that flow from its success, but they are not interests that constitute stand-alone investments and they do not attract protection under NAFTA Chapter 11.

Similarly, the ordinary meaning of the terms used in Article 1139(h) would not include the interests alleged by the Claimant. The *Shorter Oxford Dictionary* defines "interest" as a "right or a title, esp. to a share in property." The things described as investments by the Claimant are clearly not legal concerns, rights or titles. In the same vein, "commitment" denotes an obligation that restricts freedom of action, while the verb "commit" refers to conduct in the nature of a pledge, undertaking, or guarantee. Again, the alleged investments are not of the same nature as an obligation, pledge, undertaking, or guarantee.

Articles 1139(h)(i) and (ii) provide relevant context for the interpretation of "interests arising from the commitment of capital." Articles 1139(h) (i) and (ii) narrow the potential scope of "interests arising from the commitment of capital" by limiting them to interests "such as" contracts and concessions. The *ejusdem generis* rule of interpretation would restrict the scope of the word "interests" to things like "contracts" and "concessions." Customers, goodwill or market share are not remotely like interests that arise from contracts or concessions.

Nothing in the object and purpose of the NAFTA justifies expanding the definition of investment to include the interests alleged by the Claimant. In particular, the NAFTA's objective to "increase substantially investment opportunities in the territories of the Parties" is not a licence to transform benefits flowing from a successful investment into a stand-alone investment for the purposes of investor promotion and protection ...

Customers, goodwill, and market share are also "transient circumstances" that are subject to change. They are not stand-alone investments for the purposes of NAFTA Article 1139. They are merely benefits that add value to the enterprise but do not constitute investments in and of themselves. As a result, the Tribunal should dismiss the claims for breach of Chapter 11 based on these alleged rights without further consideration of their merits.

Customary International Law Minimum Standard of Treatment — Proving Alleged Expansion of the Standard

It is fundamental that a customary international law standard is proved by evidence of (1) State practice, coupled with (2) *opinio juris*.

This is confirmed by Article 38 of the Statute of the International Court of Justice which establishes among the sources of international law, "international custom, as evidence of *a general practice accepted as law.*" The definition reflects the classic two-part test (consistent State practice and *opinio juris*) that has been repeatedly confirmed by the ICJ itself. In the context of the NAFTA, the *UPS* Tribunal has acknowledged that "to establish a rule of customary international law two requirements must be met: consistent state practice and an understanding that that practice is required by law."

Arbitral awards do not constitute a formal source of State practice. As explained by Lauterpacht, "[d]ecisions of international courts are not a source of international law ... [t]hey are not direct evidence of the practice of States or of what States conceive to be the law." Arbitral decisions are relevant only to the extent that they contain valuable analysis of State practice. They may provide a useful tool for determining the content of customary international law in this way. They do not in themselves constitute the practice of States.

The Claimant comments that "the task of identifying particular conduct which is unfair or inequitable thereby giving rise to a breach of minimum standard has ... been left to arbitral tribunals." This analysis is incorrect. It wrongly suggests that NAFTA Chapter 11 Tribunals are mandated to assess the conduct of State Parties based on their own subjective sense of what might constitute a "minimum standard" and divorced from an objective and uniformly shared legal definition. As noted above, the minimum standard is an objective standard whose content is defined by customary international law ...

The Claimant cites the comments of some recent arbitral decisions, referring to the entry into force of various BITs over the past few decades, as evidence of the increased scope of international customary protection of investments. The Claimant argues that the comments of various NAFTA tribunals "establish the principle" that "the content of the customary international law minimum standard is shaped by the more than 2000 BITs which, for the most part, provide for fair and equitable treatment."

NAFTA decisions do not support the notion that customary international law has expanded to the extent suggested by the Claimant. The Claimant notably fails to cite the decision of the *ADF* Tribunal on this point:

> We are not convinced that the Investor has shown the existence, in current customary international law, of a general and autonomous requirement (autonomous, that is, from specific rules addressing particular, limited, context) to accord fair and equitable treatment and full protection and security to foreign investments. The Investor, for instance, has not shown that such a requirement has been brought

into the corpus of present day customary international law by the many hundreds of bilateral investment treaties now extant. It may be that, in their current state, neither concordant state practice nor judicial or arbitral case law provides convincing substantiation (or, for that matter, refutation) of the Investor's position. It may also be observed in this connection that the Tribunal in *Mondev* did not reach the position of the Investor, while implying that the process of change is in motion.

In any event, Canada rejects the notion that the signature of BITs containing reference to "fair and equitable treatment" has altered the minimum customary standard of treatment at international law.

Article 38 of the *ICJ Statute* distinguishes "treaties" from customary international law. It cannot be assumed that the State Parties are codifying a customary international obligation every time they set out a specific commitment in a treaty. The *Mondev* Tribunal acknowledged that "[i]t is often difficult in international practice to establish at what point obligations accepted in treaties, multilateral or bilateral, come to condition the content of a rule of customary international law binding on States not party to those treaties." As the *UPS* Tribunal noted, "in terms of *opinio juris* there is no indication that [the BITs] reflect a general sense of obligation."

Moreover, the creation of custom is not a mere mechanical exercise of counting treaties. The simple existence of treaties on a subject-matter cannot lead to any definitive conclusions regarding the existence of a customary rule. As the International Law Association (ILA) recently noted, "[t]here is no *presumption* that a succession of similar treaty provisions gives rise to a new customary rule with the same content."

The requirement of proving consistent State practice is particularly apposite where, as in the case of BITs, the alleged customary rule is thought to have emerged recently, and quickly. As the ICJ noted in the *North Sea Continental Shelf Case*, State practice must be "both extensive and virtually uniform" where it is asserted that a rule of customary international law has emerged in a short period of time. Yet the diversity of scope and content in BITs has been noted by many authors.

As for *opinio juris*, the requirement for this element has been repeatedly noted by tribunals in the context of investor-State disputes. In the NAFTA context, all three NAFTA Parties rejected the *Pope* Tribunal's equation of customary international law with BITs, which failed to mention the *opinio juris* requirement. The *Mondev* tribunal reviewed this:

> In their post-hearing submissions, all three NAFTA Parties challenged holdings of the Tribunal in *Pope & Talbot* which find that the content

of contemporary international law reflects the concordant provisions of many hundreds of bilateral investment treaties. In particular, attention was drawn to what those three States saw as a failure of the *Pope & Talbot* Tribunal to consider a necessary element of the establishment of a rule of customary international law, namely *opinio juris*. These States appear to question whether the parties to the very large numbers of bilateral investment treaties have acted out of a sense of legal obligation when they include provisions in those treaties such as that for "fair and equitable" treatment of foreign investment.

Canada, the United States and Mexico have consistently rejected the notion that BITs establish customary international law. For instance, in the context of the *Loewen* case, Mexico made the following submission pursuant to Article 1128:

> Mexico is particularly concerned about the suggestion that the fact that the mere existence of some 1800 BITs in the world means that somehow that the corpus of these treaties creates customary international law obligations. The fact that States may agree to the same or similar obligations through different treaties involving different parties, or even the same obligations through multilateral treaties is not sufficient on its own to build customary international law.

It is impossible to infer from the existence of a large number of BITs alone that any particular provision therein represents a rule of customary international law merely by reason of its commonality.

The same position was adopted by the United States and Canada in the *Loewen* case as well as by the United States in the *Glamis* case.

Awards under different treaties are only relevant if they apply the customary international law minimum standard of treatment.

As a general matter, tribunals' articulations of customary international law are only valid to the extent they are firmly grounded in State practice, and *opinio juris*.

Non-NAFTA cases interpreting minimum treatment provisions that are not based on the customary international law minimum standard of treatment are of little or no guidance in interpreting NAFTA Article 1105.

Further, non-NAFTA decisions relied upon by the Claimant are striking in their absence of any analysis or evidence justifying the content that they ascribe to their standard of treatment. The comments of these Tribunals do not define the international minimum standard of treatment under Article 1105 and ignore the rigorous standard required to prove customary international law.

Minimum Standard of Treatment — No Requirement to Maintain the
Legal and Regulatory Environment in Place at the Time the Investment
Was Made

Having failed to prove an expanded minimum treatment obligation in
customary international law, the Claimant asserts a "standstill" obligation:
that Article 1105 prevents a State from changing its laws or regulatory
regime as of the time an investment is made. This, of course, is contrary
to the longstanding principle of public international law that a foreign
investor assumes the risk of investing in a foreign country, including that
the legal regime in place in that country may change:

> In application of a generally accepted principle, any person taking up
> residence or investing capital in a foreign country must assume the
> concomitant risks and must submit, under reservation of any measures
> of discrimination against him as a foreigner, to all the laws of that
> country. [Cheng, Bin, *General Principles of Law as Applied by Internation-
> al Courts and Tribunals* (Cambridge: Grotius Publications, 1987) at
> 36–37, quoting *Standard Oil v. Germany* (1926) 7 R.I.A.A. 301.]

The applicability of a "standstill" principle has been particularly challenged
in the regulatory context, where investors should expect that the situation
will change and evolve. As Professor Schreuer writes:

> It is clear that a reasonable evolution of the host State's law is part of
> the environment with which investors must contend. For instance, an
> adjustment of environmental regulations to internationally accepted
> standards or general improvements in labour law for the benefit of
> the host State's workforce would not lead to a violation of the fair and
> equitable treatment standard if applied in good faith and without
> discrimination.

The Investor invokes the concept of "legitimate expectations" to effect a
"standstill" obligation through Article 1105. However, customary international law does not recognize "legitimate expectations" as the source of
State obligations. Two recent decisions of ICSID Annulment Committees
support this proposition.

In February 2007, the MTD Annulment Committee noted:

For example the *TECMED* Tribunal's apparent reliance on the foreign
investor's expectations as the source of the host State's obligations (such
as the obligation to compensate for expropriation) is questionable. The

obligations of the host State towards foreign investors derive from the terms of the applicable investment treaty and not from any set of expectations investors may have or claim to have. A tribunal which sought to generate from such expectations a set of rights different from those contained in or enforceable under the BIT might well exceed its powers, and if the difference were material might do so manifestly.

In August 2007, the *CMS* Annulment Committee noted: "[a]lthough legitimate expectations might arise by reason of a course of dealing between the investor and the host State, these are not, as such, legal obligations." These recent decisions undermine the *Tecmed* award, which had became for some the high water mark for its alleged interpretation of the concept of "legitimate expectations." The Claimant relies heavily on *Tecmed* as well as on other awards, including *Occidental, LG & E* and *Sempra,* all of which cite *Tecmed.* Unfortunately, none of these awards justifies their interpretation beyond general references to good faith or to preambular language referring to the stability of the legal framework.

The concept of "legitimate expectations" has not figured prominently in Chapter 11 cases. The Tribunal in *Thunderbird* went the furthest when it stated:

> Having considered recent investment case law and the good faith principle of international customary law, the concept of "legitimate expectations" relates, within the context of the NAFTA framework, to a situation where a Contracting Party's conduct creates reasonable and justifiable expectations on the part of an investor (or investment) to act in reliance on said conduct, such that a failure by the NAFTA Party to honour those expectations could cause the investor (or investment) to suffer damages.

The *Waste Management II* Tribunal, noted that "[i]n applying this standard it is relevant that the treatment is in breach of representations made by the host State which were reasonably relied on by the claimant."

In *Methanex,* while in the different context of expropriation, the Tribunal also noted that:

> But as a matter of general international law, a non-discriminatory regulation for a public purpose, which is enacted in accordance with due process and, which affects, inter alios, a foreign investor or investment is not deemed expropriatory and compensable *unless specific commitments had been given by the regulating government to the then putative foreign investor contemplating investment that the government would refrain from such regulation* [emphasis added].

The NAFTA cases cited above when addressing legitimate expectations do so only in the context of there being specific *representations* or *commitments* by the State. In other words, the concept of "legitimate expectations" must be based on objective rather than subjective expectations.

Further, in the cases that have applied this concept, even broadly, outside the NAFTA context, it has been with regard to undertakings that induced an investor to make its investment in the first place. As the *Enron* Tribunal noted:

> What seems to be essential, however, is that these expectations derived from the *conditions* that were *offered* by the State to the investor *at the time of the investment* and that such conditions were *relied upon* by the investor *when deciding to invest.*

As the Tribunal in *Sempra* noted:

> The measures in question in this case have beyond any doubt substantially changed the legal landscape and business framework *under which the investment was decided and implemented.*
>
> Even the *Tecmed* Tribunal comments were with reference to "international investments treatment that does not affect the basic expectations that were taken into account by the foreign investor *to make the investment.*"

Parliamentary Declarations in 2008–9 / Déclarations parlementaires en 2008–9

compiled by / préparé par
ALEXANDRA LOGVIN

A STATEMENTS MADE ON THE INTRODUCTION OF LEGISLATION /
DÉCLARATIONS SUR L'INTRODUCTION DE LA LÉGISLATION

Alexandra Logvin is a graduate of the University of Ottawa LL.M. (2003) and LL.B. (2009) programs. She is a lawyer with Heenan Blaikie LLP in Ottawa.

C-57 (Canada-Jordan Free Trade / Libre-échange entre le
        Canada et la Jordanie)

B   STATEMENTS IN RESPONSE TO QUESTIONS / DÉCLARATIONS EN
      RÉPONSE AUX QUESTIONS

1   Environment / L'environnement

The Arctic / Arctique
Clean Energy / Énergie propre
Climate Change / Changements climatiques
Corporate Social Responsibility / Responsabilité sociale des
    entreprises
Nuclear Energy / Énergie nucléaire
Seal Hunt / Chasse au loup-marin

2   Foreign Affairs / Affaires étrangères

China / Chine
Cuba
G-20 / G20
Honduras / Honduras
India / Inde
Iran / Iran
Mexico / Mexique
Russia / Russie
Ukraine / Ukraine
United States / États-Unis

3   Health / Santé

4   Human Rights / Droits de la personne

China and Tibet / Chine et le Tibet
Durban Conference on racism / Conférence de Durban sur
    le racisme
Housing / Logement
Immigration / Immigration
Iran / Iran
Israel / Israël
Poverty / Pauvreté
Protecting Canadians Abroad / Protection des Canadiens à
    l'étranger
Rights of Disabled / Droits des personnes handicapées
Rights of Women / Droits des femmes

Dispute Settlement / Règlement des différends
Dumping
Executive Pay / Rémunération accordée aux dirigeants de
    compagnies
Global Recession and Canada's budget / Récession mondiale
    et le budget du Canada
Investments / Investissement
Labelling / Étiquetage
Manufacturing Industry / Secteur manufacturier
Procurement / Marchés publics
Science and Technology / Sciences et la technologie
Securities / Valeurs mobilières
Softwood Lumber and Forestry Industry / Bois d'œuvre et
    l'industrie forestière
Taxation / Fiscalité
Trade- and Trade-Related Agreements / Accords
    commerciaux et liés au commerce
Trade in medicines / Commerce des médicaments
Trade and Human Rights / Commerce et les droits du
    personne
World Trade Organization / Organisation mondiale de
    commerce

8   *Law of the Sea / Droit de la mer*

Fisheries / Pêches

9   *Sports*

C   STATEMENTS MADE ON THE INTRODUCTION OF LEGISLATION /
     DÉCLARATIONS SUR L'INTRODUCTION DE LA LÉGISLATION

1   Bill S-2: Customs Act / Loi S-2: Loi sur les douanes[1]

Mr. Dave MacKenzie (Parliamentary Secretary to the Minister of
Public Safety):

The Canada Border Service Agency operates at 1,200 service points across
Canada and nearly 40 locations abroad and employs over 14,000 public
servants. Since its inception, [it] has been working to integrate and build

---

[1] Editor's note: An Act to Amend the Customs Act / Loi modifiant la Loi sur les
douanes, S.C. 2009, c. 10, was introduced in Senate by Hon. Marjory LeBreton
(Leader of the Government in the Senate) on 29 January 2009 and in the House
of Commons on 27 April 2009. The bill received Royal Assent on 11 June 2009.

on the many risk management strategies and processes adopted by their legacy organizations, the Canada Revenue Agency, Citizenship and Immigration Canada and the Canadian Food Inspection Agency.

The proposed legislation will enhance our ability to manage risk and improve border operations by strengthening the systems for obtaining advance data on goods and people arriving in Canada and by better managing the risks existing at air and sea ports. Indeed, the provisions of the legislation help us to address some of the concerns of the Auditor General of Canada, identified in her November 2007 report entitled, "Keeping the Border Open and Secure."

It is clear that free nations, including Canada, cannot guarantee absolute safety against border threats. For example, Canada welcomes more than 95 million travellers to Canada every year and approves the entry of over $400 billion in imported goods annually. Therefore, our focus must be on risk management.

CBSA's risk management is multi-layered. Operations are based on three fundamental strategies: pre-approval programs to facilitate low-risk people and goods; advance information on what and who is coming to the border; and intelligence using partnership networks, sophisticated science and technology.

The development and deployment of science and technology is crucial in supporting these strategies: electronic commerce systems to receive advanced trade data; biometrics for identifying trusted travellers; and sophisticated technologies to detect radiation, drugs, guns and other contraband and potentially dangerous goods.

During the past five years, the Canada Border Service Agency has developed a robust and sophisticated border management regime with a scientific approach to risk assessment and detection, and the results are impressive. Consider that over 10,800 drug seizures were made in the 2007–08 fiscal year, 5,700 weapons were seized, including 671 firearms prevented from entering Canadian communities. Over 7,000 items of child pornography, hate propaganda and obscenities were stopped at the border. In 2007–08 the Canada Border Service Agency removed 12,349 individuals who were inadmissible to Canada, including 1,664 criminals who posed a high risk to our country. That is a 40% increase from 2002–03.

The CBSA is now engaged in important initiatives that will further transform and modernize border management, including arming border guards and eliminating situations where they are working alone, implementing a new manifest system, which will provide advance electronic reporting for goods at the land border, and working with our U.S. counterparts to ensure that the western hemisphere travel initiative is implemented as smoothly as possible and does not impede travel and cross-border trade.

While the Canada Border Service Agency has increased its ability to detect and respond to security threats, the *Customs Act* has not changed substantially since 2001. The proposed changes will ensure that the CBSA continues to evolve, while strengthening its officers' abilities to combat internal conspiracies and organized crime at ports of entry ...

The current legislation gives Canada Border Service Agency officers the authority to examine goods and question and search people only as they exit the customs controlled area, including persons working inside the area who would otherwise not have to present themselves to the CBSA. The proposed amendments will provide border service officers with greater flexibility to patrol and monitor these controlled areas. In particular, they will have the authority to question and search people, as well as examine their goods both within customs controlled areas and when they exit these designated areas. This initiative will improve the security of Canadians as it will act as a deterrent to internal conspiracies at points of entry and decrease the risks posed by organized crime and national security threats.

The proposed changes to the Customs Act will also enable the CBSA to implement its eManifest initiative. The eManifest initiative is the next planned phase of the advanced commercial information initiative, which currently provides border services officers with electronic air and marine cargo information in advance so they are equipped with the right information at the right time to identify health, safety and security threats before goods arrive in Canada ... As a result of this legislation, the Canada Border Services Agency will be better able to make informed decisions about the admissibility of goods, including identifying unknown and high-risk threats before the shipments arrive. The Canada Border Services Agency will be able to focus its resources on those goods that pose the greatest risk to Canada's security and prosperity. As well, low-risk shipments will be processed in a timely and efficient manner, which is vital to Canada's prosperity and economic competitiveness.

There are some additional elements within the proposed legislation that will further strengthen border security ... [such as t]he advance passenger information/passenger name record program ... incorporation by reference, [and a number of] housekeeping amendments that will align the act with Canada's obligation as a signatory to the 1994 agreement on the implementation of article 7 of the General Agreement on Tariffs and Trade.

(House of Commons Debates, 4 May 2009, pp. 3017–19)
(Débats de la Chambre des communes, le 4 mai 2009, pp. 3017–19)

2   *Bill C-2: Canada–EFTA Free Trade Agreement Implementation
Act / Loi C-2: Loi de mise en oeuvre de l'Accord de libre-échange
Canada–AELE*[2]

Hon. Stockwell Day (Minister of International Trade and Minister
for the Asia-Pacific Gateway):

[I]t is very timely that our colleagues on all sides of the House are giving
consideration to this important legislation ... The timing of this is really
fortuitous because we are engaged right now, whether we like it or not, in
a synchronized global downturn of economies and the world is gripped
by this. We are looking for ways in which trade and commerce can move
and sending signals that the opportunities for workers, producers and
manufacturers are there ...

As Canadians, as a country, we are as prosperous as we are because we
are free traders. We believe in the importance and the power of doing that.
As a nation, we cannot in and of ourselves consume everything we can
produce. We must have ways to sell and to market not only our products
but our services if we are to continue to be prosperous.

The backdrop to our discussion today is the fact that there are clouds on
the horizon related to the whole issue of protectionism. Some countries
possibly are reflecting that the best thing they can do is build protectionist
trade walls. We know this would be a negative thing to see happen. We know
history is very clear. When we look at the conglomeration of nations and
how nations encourage and move along in terms of prosperity, we only have
to look back to the horrific economic ramifications of the Great Depression.

In 1930, when that global economic downturn took place, some economic specialists speculated that they were facing probably a one or two
year recession at the time. The United States came out famously with the
Smoot-Hawley legislation that started to build a protectionist barrier. Other

___

[2] Editor's note: An Act to Implement the Free Trade Agreement Between Canada
and the States of the European Free Trade Association (Iceland, Liechtenstein,
Norway, Switzerland), the Agreement on Agriculture between Canada and the
Republic of Iceland, the Agreement on Agriculture between Canada and the
Kingdom of Norway and the Agreement on Agriculture between Canada and
the Swiss Confederation / Loi portant mise en œuvre de l'Accord de libre-
échange entre le Canada et les états de l'Association européenne de libre-
échange (Islande, Liechtenstein, Norvège Et Suisse), de l'Accord sur
l'agriculture entre le Canada et la République d'Islande, de l'Accord sur l'agriculture entre le Canada et le Royaume de Norvège et de l'Accord sur l'agriculture entre le Canada et la Confédération suisse, S.C. 2009, c. 6, introduced in
the House of Commons by Hon. Stockwell Day (Minister of International Trade
and Minister for the Asia-Pacific Gateway) on 28 January 2009. The bill received
Royal Assent on 29 April 2009.

countries responded in kind and pretty soon around the world we had situations where countries could not sell or export the very things that were needed and that would have led to prosperity. In fact, the recession was deepened, leading to the Great Depression ...

Our competitors are many and are friendly allies, whether it is the United States, or Australia, or the U.K. or the EU. We are friendly nations, but we compete and do have things that we can sell back and forth and encourage our mutual prosperity.

We should be aware that in the pursuit of free trade agreements our competitors have been very busy and active. The United States just over the last short period of time has concluded some 17 free trade agreements. It is in the process of pursuing another eight. Mexico, our other partner in NAFTA, has concluded 12 free trade agreements. If we go further south in the Americas, Chile has concluded 13 free trade agreements with other countries. In fact, its 13 agreements cover 43 separate countries.

Therefore, if we look at a situation where we want to deal with a country that has a free trade agreement with somebody else, its goods and services will get into those countries tariff and barrier free. That puts our manufacturers at a serious disadvantage. We need to look at reducing those obstacles and increasing and expanding our doors of opportunity.

At what is now referred to as the Washington conference last fall, the G20 leaders made a declaration that countries should not fall back into or delve into areas of protectionism. It is called a stand still on any protectionist activity. I would suggest that a stand still is necessary, and that was endorsed by trade ministers around the world at the following discussions that took place in Peru at the Asia Pacific economic meetings. From our perspective, we are going even further than that. We are not saying stand still, we are saying move ahead and overcome the inertia that is gripping the world in terms of trade right now.

Therefore, we have before us the European free trade area agreement. When we talk about what those letters stand for, some people might think this is a deal that engages all the European community. In fact, it does not. We are talking about four very sophisticated entities: Iceland, Norway, Switzerland and tied in with that, Liechtenstein. These are modern, sophisticated entities. They say that they want to engage with us and we want to engage with them to reduce and eliminate trade barriers.

The numbers coming in at the end of 2007 for two-way trade and investment with Norway were $4.7 billion. In the summer of 2008, Norway added to that investment another $3 billion just in the areas of oil, gas and agriculture.

There is a broader platform and picture that needs to be taken into account, because we are talking about engaging these four entities. However, for us, this is an entry and lever into the broader EU community for an eventual and much hoped for Canada-EU free trade agreement. This is something we are zeroing in on, something we have been discussing for some time. The Czech Republic has the presidency of the EU for the next six months. I was in Prague last month and I talked to officials there. I made it clear that we were ambitious on that score. We made that point with the European Commission as well. On another free trade area, being the EU area, we are very ambitious and are working toward the conclusion of discussions to get a formal framework in place to start that process.

In and of itself, the so-called EFTA agreement before us today is important for the prosperity of our citizens and the four entities named. However, there is the broader context which is important to keep in mind. Clearly, consultation between us and the provinces is very important when we look at these types of agreements. The consultation process involved in the EFTA agreement was extensive, and will continue to be. We want provinces to come forward with their areas of concern and sensitivity. That has been done in this process and those have been thoroughly fleshed out and addressed to the point where we could sign the agreement.

As an example, we had concerns from the shipbuilding industry in Canada. What happens when we take away the tariffs related to shipbuilding, we open ourselves up to global competition. We believe we can rise to that competition and meet any of the challenges the world has to offer, but we looked at those sensitivities, particularly those in Quebec and other provinces with shipbuilding industries. In a spirit of co-operation and understanding, as we discussed this with our four partners on the other side of the EFTA agreement, we agreed we need to look at the removal of those tariff barriers, but do it over an extended period of time, 15 years in this case related to the shipbuilding industry. Therefore, the sensitivities we hear from around our country and from various industries are taken into account as we move along this road.

It also fits with our government's global commerce strategy, as we have talked about in our comprehensive action plan in which $60 million has been committed just to the area of doing what we can in terms of our global strategy to assist manufacturers, exporters, entrepreneurs and innovators to get not just the message but the products out there in a way that gets worldwide attention and shows that Canada has something to offer, which then increases our ability to manufacture, export and to be prosperous.

We are not stopping with this agreement. We have been very clear that we have agreements now concluded with Peru and Colombia. These will eventually come to the House. We had an earlier agreement with Jordan, and there are others in process. Our officials are in discussion with South Korea, Panama, the Dominican Republic, the CARICOM nations in the

Caribbean, Singapore and the group of nations called the Central American Four, being Guatemala, Honduras, Nicaragua and El Salvador. We are actively engaged to ensure we do everything globally in our commerce strategy to keep the doors open and the opportunities very much alive for Canadians.

It is not strictly on a trade side. There are other areas that have to be pursued, and we do that in concert with the trade discussions. For instance, if we are going to invest in another country, our investors and business people have to be assured that there is a platform, a framework, that offers the benefits of rule of law, respect for contract law and other similar areas. We call these our foreign investment protection agreements. It is necessary to strike these with other countries. We will never guarantee that somebody's product will sell, but we can work with another country to ensure that the investment itself is subject to certain standardized rules and certain rules of contract law and investment law, banking law and credit, so at least our investors and business people know they have a level playing field and a platform when they go into those countries.

Along with that are science and technology agreements. We have put in place these very important initiatives with a number of countries, and I signed one not long ago with Brazil, where industry and the academic communities will know we have science and technology agreements, where both governments would pool an agreed upon amount of funds and then send out a message inviting the universities or scientific communities to bid for procurement of those funds to mutually pursue areas of science and technology.

Along with those, we look at a variety of other agreements that affect our economies. Air service agreements are very important when we are talking about giving choice to consumers, but also keeping costs down in terms of transporting and shipping product.

I might add we have in our budget considerable funds, into the billions of dollars, for our great gateways in our nation for shipping, such as the Asia-Pacific gateway. We have a gateway proposal and the funds to back it up for the Atlantic region.

We are doing everything we can, on a variety of levels, to build the platforms and construct the frameworks for Canadian entrepreneurs, innovators, manufacturers and exporters in virtually any area of endeavour who feel they have something worth selling. We will never guarantee they will be able to sell that, but we can guarantee we will smooth the way as evenly as possible within the context of the various trade agreements that are signed onto globally so their products can be established and Canada can continue to be prosperous.

I arrived in Switzerland for meetings on Friday and met with the vice-president. Literally moments before my arrival the upper house had in fact passed its portion of the agreement before us today. I am certainly not saying it was my arrival that moved that along. I would not even suggest that. However, it gave me great encouragement that the Switzerland legislators were dealing with it, that they saw this as positive and that they were moving it along. I assured them that we would be going through a similar process here and that, respectfully, with the input of colleagues here, we hoped for a successful conclusion of the discussions, the ratification of the agreement in our Parliament and the ongoing prosperity of Canadians, especially in this era of global concern.

(*House of Commons Debates*, 2 February 2009, *pp. 191–93*)
(*Débats de la Chambre des communes, le 2 février 2009, pp. 191–93*)

3   Bill C-3: *Arctic Waters Pollution Prevention Act / Loi C-3: La Loi sur la prévention de la pollution des eaux arctiques*[3]

Hon. John Baird (Minister of Transport, Infrastructure and Communities):

The *Arctic Waters Pollution Prevention Act* is a small but important symbolic piece of legislation. Our vast Arctic region remains a Canadian icon known the world over. This government has taken unprecedented and historic steps toward keeping Canada's north safe. Bill C-3 is another example of this action.

Protecting Canada's Arctic waters from pollution is one of our government's key priorities. Our proposed amendment would double the geographic application of the Arctic Waters Pollution Prevention Act from 100 to 200 nautical miles midway between Greenland and the islands in the Canadian Arctic. Presently, the discharge of waste is permitted at internationally agreed levels in the area between 100 and 200 nautical miles. Our proposed changes would disallow this practice and further strengthen the pollution protection regime in our Arctic region ... This increased range would allow Canadian environmental laws and shipping regulations to be enforced to the fullest extent and give us greater control over the movement of ships through the Northwest Passage ...

---

[3] Editor's note: An Act to Amend the Arctic Waters Pollution Prevention Act / Loi modifiant la Loi sur la prévention de la pollution des eaux arctiques, S.C. 200, c. 11, introduced in the House of Commons by Hon. John Baird (Minister of Transport, Infrastructure and Communities) on 28 January 2009. The bill received Royal Assent on 11 June 2009.

The baselines around Canada's Arctic Archipelago were formalized in 1986 and are consistent with the 1982 *United Nations Convention on the Law of the Sea* and with the 1996 *Oceans Act,* which established an exclusive economic zone of up to 200 nautical miles off Canada's coasts, including around the Arctic Archipelago. Canada has jurisdiction regarding the protection and preservation of the marine environment, which is an incredible sensitive ecosystem, including the ice covered waters within the exclusive economic zone.

In 2003, Canada became a party to the *United Nations Convention on the Law of the Sea.* Article 234 of the convention enables a coastal state to put in place special requirements for pollution protection in ice covered areas within its exclusive economic zone. Extending the pollution protection from 100 to 200 nautical miles would enable Canada to exercise enhanced jurisdiction with regard to pollution control north of the 60th parallel.

In addition, this government will act to ensure that new regulations under the *Canada Shipping Act* are in place for the 2010 season. These regulations will require the mandatory registration of vessels entering this expanded zone. There is nothing more fundamental than the protection of our nation's sovereignty and security and our government will continue to rigorously defend Canada's place in the world and our rightful territories, and the Arctic is no exception ...

To this end, our government has established a northern strategy that rests on four key pillars: northern economic development, protecting our fragile northern environment, asserting Canada's sovereignty in the Arctic and providing northerners with more control over their own destiny. The expansion of coverage of the Arctic shipping legislation is directly linked to this strategy which commits our government to ensuring a sustainable and comprehensive approach to Arctic shipping ...

[As for the first pillar,] [s]trong worldwide demand for our natural resources increases the viability of resource exploration and extraction in Canada's Arctic. It is estimated that Canada's north possesses 33% of our remaining conventionally recoverable sources of natural gas and 25% of the remaining recoverable light crude oil. The discovered resource of the Arctic basin approaches 31 trillion cubic feet of gas and 1.6 billion barrels of oil. The potential for resource extraction in the area is thought to be approximately 14.7 billion barrels of oil and approximately 433 trillion cubic feet of gas.

The second pillar, environmental protection, aims to protect the unique and fragile Arctic ecosystem for future generations ...

The third pillar, sovereignty, asserts and defends Canada's sovereignty and security in the Arctic. Our government recognizes the challenges Canada's sovereignty in the Arctic could face in the future. In the coming years, sovereignty and security challenges will become more pressing as the impact of climate change leads to increased activity throughout this ecologically sensitive region ...

The waters of the Arctic Archipelago are internal waters of Canada by virtue of historic title. This means that Canada has sovereignty over these waters. Canada must therefore move quickly to affirm and protect its sovereignty over this archipelago, including the navigable waters in it. We are working to strengthen our Arctic maritime security in the future. After all, maritime activity is critical to our Arctic communities. Getting fuel, food, medical and other supplies all depends on reliable and effective maritime shipping.

Arctic security is also key to Canada's security as a whole. All of these will assist in detecting and preventing criminal and terrorist activities that may pose a serious threat to national and international security. It also allows us to find those who pollute our waters and harm our northern environment. To that extent, our government has introduced new Arctic patrol ships and expanded aerial surveillance that will guard Canada's far north and the Northwest Passage. Funding has also been committed for a new polar class icebreaker for the Canadian Coast Guard ...

[Finally,] [w]ith this amendment our government will help address concerns from Inuit communities regarding pollution in waters surrounding their homes and workplaces. Expanding the application of the Arctic Waters Pollution Prevention Act to 200 miles improves Canada's ability to prevent ship source pollution from happening, helping to keep the Arctic waters clean. Northern communities support clean and sustainable economic development in the north, as do all Canadians who want to protect the integrity of Canada's Arctic waters.

(*House of Commons Debates, February 23, 2009, pp. 855–57*)
(*Débats de la Chambre des communes, le 23 février 2009, pp. 855–57*)

4   *Bill C-7: Marine Liability Act / Loi C-7: La Loi sur la responsabilité en matière maritime* [4]

Mr. Brian Jean (Parliamentary Secretary to the Minister of Transport, Infrastructure and Communities):

---

[4] Editor's note: An Act to Amend the Marine Liability Act and the Federal Courts Act and to Make Consequential Amendments to Other Acts / Loi modifiant la Loi sur la responsabilité en matière maritime, la Loi sur les Cours fédérales et d'autres lois en conséquence, S.C. 2009, c. 21; introduced in the House of Commons by Hon. John Baird (Minister of Transport, Infrastructure and Communities) on 29 January 2009. The bill received Royal Assent on 23 June 2009.

[The purpose of the amendments is] to protect our environment from the effects of marine pollution from ships[.] If the government's proposed amendments to the Marine Liability Act, as outlined in Bill C-7, are passed into law, they would have important environmental and economic impacts for all Canadians ...

The act as it stands now is very ill-equipped to tackle the realities of marine transport today and inadequate to realize our 21st century ambitions ...

As a trading nation, Canada relies on shipping to provide Canadians with one of the world's highest standards of living. In 2007, for instance, ships carried more than 365 million tonnes of international cargo. This represents some $160 billion worth of international trade and includes more than $81 billion in exports. That $160 billion is a staggering sum to say the least. Seventy million tonnes of cargo are transported domestically each year by ships operating between Canadian ports on the Pacific, Atlantic and Arctic coasts; along the St. Lawrence Seaway; and throughout the Great Lakes system. Canadian ferries actually carry some 40 million passengers and 16 million automobiles each and every year. They are also part of daily commuting for many Canadians in cities such as Halifax and Vancouver. Almost 1.5 million people, Canadians and foreign visitors alike, enjoy scenic cruises on Canadian waters each and every year.

Shipping is among the most efficient modes of transport and among the most effective in reducing road congestion, which helps reduce greenhouse gas emissions, and that is important to our future. Transport Canada is collaborating as I speak with Canadian industry and the governments of the United States and Mexico to promote a more ecological use of North American shipping routes. We are encouraging increased shipping of people and goods along our coasts and using internal waterways ...

Marine transport is absolutely essential to Canada's economic viability in the future. We see it as a real growth industry for Canada. It can also, however, constitute a potential risk to people, to goods and to the environment. Hence, the reason for the bill. Most of these risks actually stem from the potential for mishaps inherent in most forms of industrial activity and all modes of transport. Most notable in shipping is the risk of collisions or grounding during which passengers and crew members can be injured, not to mention the risk of oil spills and other similar situations that arise as a result of these incidents. These amendments would build upon initiatives that this government has already taken while fostering marine transportation activity to improve Canada's economy.

Shipping is a global activity and, therefore, it needs globally harmonized rules. Canada is a founding member of the International Maritime

Organization and has worked diligently toward multilateral solutions for issues facing marine transportation. Achieving global consistency in these rules would benefit the marine industry and Canada's trade with other nations and, ultimately, all Canadians.

These amendments would demand that commercial ships which carry Canadians have proper insurance. This covers all ships including commuter ferries and tour boats, and it simply makes sense for today's environment ...

Tourism is also a very important sector of the economy and is actually in a state of growth. Thousands upon thousands of Canadian jobs depend on tourism. These amendments would ensure that Canadians are protected while meeting the unique needs of marine adventure tourism. Most importantly, from an environmental perspective, these amendments to the *Marine Liability Act* would enhance the liability and compensation regimes that Canada has in place to respond to oil pollution from ships.

Canada has one of the longest coastlines in the world. We are bordered by three oceans and we use ships to carry a very significant portion of our trade each year. Large volumes of oil and other petroleum products pass through our ports every year, some 70 million tonnes annually. Much of that is on tankers with far bigger capacities than for instance, the *Exxon Valdez*, and most of us remember what happened in Alaska in 1989 in relation to that disastrous spill. With the limitations of our current legislation Canada simply would not be able to cope with a spill of that magnitude if one were to happen tomorrow in our waters ...

These amendments would actually do something very significant. They would actually triple the level of compensation available to victims of oil spills from the maximum of $500 million, which seems like a great sum but it is not in these kinds of situations, to $1.5 billion, a tremendous sum. That is $1.5 billion for each and every incident. These massive increases in compensation would ensure strong protection for Canadians and the environment while maintaining a balance between associated interests, namely the ship owners and the oil companies that pay contributions into the fund's system. Taxpayers should not be on the hook for these costs ...

The bill also introduces an enhanced regime for shipowner liability for spills of bunker oil used to propel ships ... Like the requirement already in place for tankers, this bunker oil liability regime would include a compulsory insurance provision which is a good thing ... [T]hese enhancements would enable Canada to also ratify two international maritime organization conventions that are based on the polluter pays principle [... and] actually establish a mandatory insurance requirement for passenger ships as well. Canadian businesses would benefit also and these amendments would put Canadian companies supplying foreign ships docked in our ports on equal footing with their American counterparts.

(*House of Commons Debates, February 25, 2009, pp. 974–77*)
(*Débats de la Chambre des communes, le 25 février 2009, pp. 974–77*)

5   Bill C-9: *Transportation of Dangerous Goods Act, 1992 / Loi C-9:
    La Loi de 1992 sur le transport des marchandises dangereuses*[5]

Mr. Brian Jean (Parliamentary Secretary to the Minister of Transport, Infrastructure and Communities):

Some of my Ontario colleagues might remember what happened on Saturday, November 10, 1979 in Mississauga, Ontario. A few minutes before midnight, CP train No. 54 derailed while carrying a shipment of chlorine and 250,000 people had to be evacuated from that area. Indeed, this particular incident stands as the second largest peacetime evacuation in North America, surpassed only by the evacuation of New Orleans during hurricane Katrina in 2005. Very fortunately, no one was injured in that incident, but the risk was indeed extreme. As is the case whenever we are dealing with transportation of dangerous goods, no chances should be taken. We can never predict when incidents like that may happen, whether accidentally or on purpose. That is why this government has the Transportation of Dangerous Goods Act in place. Originally introduced in 1980 and updated in 1982, it provides the federal government with the authority to develop policy, to verify compliance, to conduct research, to guide emergency response, and develop regulations and standards to manage risk and promote public safety during the transportation of dangerous goods.

In the bill before the House today, our government is proposing amendments to ... protect and improve Canadians' way of life and public safety in Canada.

Today there are more than 26 million commercially available chemicals sold around the world, and more than 46 million organic and inorganic substances registered with the Chemical Abstract Society. Indeed, more than 30 million shipments of dangerous goods are transported every year in Canada alone. That is right, over 30 million shipments of dangerous goods in Canada alone.

---

[5]   Editor's note: An Act to Amend the Transportation of Dangerous Goods Act, 1992 / Loi modifiant la Loi de 1992 sur le transport des marchandises dangereuses, S.C. 2009, c. 9; introduced in the House of Commons by Hon. John Baird (Minister of Transport, Infrastructure and Communities) on 2 February 2009. The bill received Royal Assent on 14 May 2009.

Trade, whether between the provinces or across the border with the United States, continues to grow steadily. Dangerous goods are likewise being transported across national and provincial boundaries more often than ever before ...

Between Canada and the United States, agreements ensure ease of trade while maintaining safety. In most cases, this permits a shipment of dangerous goods originating in one country to be transported to its final destination in another country without interference, provided, of course, that the shipment is in compliance with the rules of the originating country ...

Our program is actually harmonized and aligned, as appropriate, to international, United Nations and United States conventions. This new bill will be no different. In fact the Transportation of Dangerous Goods Act, 1992 is under criminal law and applies to all matters relating to the importation, transportation and handling of dangerous goods ...

The current act is based primarily on prevention of disasters during the transportation of ... dangerous substances and right now focuses less on the safety and the response capabilities of the government. This government's proposed amendments in this bill ... would significantly expand the measures used by the federal government in cases involving dangerous goods ...

Under this revised legislation, shippers of dangerous goods would be required to submit an emergency response assistance plan, an ERAP, to the federal government prior to shipping dangerous substances. These plans outline detailed actions that would be taken by the shipper in case of an accident, including a list of specialized equipment needed to clean up the area. Preparation is the key to this. The plans also provide on-site assistance to local authorities. In the event an incident did occur, this new legislation would allow the federal government to use the measures and resources outlined in the corresponding ERAP to respond to the situation accordingly.

The proposed changes would also allow the federal government to use resources from the private companies that transport the substances in question to respond to the emergency itself, with the understanding, of course, that they would be properly compensated for whatever they were out.

On the security and prevention side, the bill would provide the authority to establish performance regulations for security plans and for training. These would be based on international and United Nations recommendations and in line, quite frankly, with existing U.S. regulations.

(*House of Commons Debates, 12 February 2009, pp. 775–77*)
(*Débats de la Chambre des communes, le 12 février 2009, pp. 775–77*)

6   Bill C-11: Human Pathogens and Toxins Act / Loi C-11: La Loi sur les agents pathogènes humains et les toxines[6]

Mr. Colin Carrie (Parliamentary Secretary to the Minister of Health):

The important issues of the safety and security of human pathogens and toxins ... is a primary reason behind Bill C-11 ...

A human pathogen is a micro-organism capable of causing disease or death in humans. Examples include: salmonella bacteria, the agent of anthrax, listeria bacteria and the Ebola virus. The need to enhance biosafety in Canada's laboratories and prevent an inadvertent release of these agents is one of the two primary focuses of Bill C-11.

The need to safeguard Canadians from the risk of an intentional release of these dangerous agents constitutes the second primary focus of the proposed human pathogens and toxins act ... The cost of a bioterror attack is high, both in terms of lives lost, lives affected and economic consequences. It is the responsibility of government, of this Parliament, to put in place the necessary measures to minimize the likelihood of such an event.

There are approximately 3,500 laboratories that import human pathogens into Canada. These laboratories are regulated under the existing human pathogens importation regulations which have been in force since 1994. They must also comply with our laboratory biosafety guidelines which are widely accepted as Canada's national biosafety standard.

Unfortunately, these regulations and associated laboratory biosafety guidelines are only mandatory for facilities that import human pathogens. They are not mandatory for the additional 4,000 laboratories that do not import, but which acquire human pathogens within Canada.

While labs working with these pathogens do so in a safe manner and widely apply these guidelines on a voluntary basis, we need legislation and regulations in place to reinforce these safe practices, and establish consistency by ensuring all labs in Canada, whether federal, provincial or private, are adhering to these guidelines.

Canada faces some serious risks as a result of this legislative and regulatory gap. These include risks to the safety of persons working in and around laboratories and risks to our national security. There is always the potential for accidental release of human pathogens or toxins ...

---

6   Editor's note: An Act to Promote Safety and Security with Respect to Human Pathogens and Toxins / Loi visant à promouvoir la sûreté des agents pathogènes humains et des toxines, S.C. 2009, c. 24; introduced in the House of Commons by Hon. Leona Aglukkaq (Minister of Health) on 9 February 2009. The bill received Royal Assent on 23 June 2009.

It is time to level the playing field in Canada so that all persons working with these agents, and especially all laboratories, are required to operate under the same rules and to comply with the same national biosafety guidelines. To this end the new human pathogens and toxins act is designed to ensure that unless exempted, no person may carry on activities with these dangerous substances without a licence and without complying with the laboratory biosafety guidelines.

Beyond accidental release, Canada also faces the risk of a deliberate release of a human pathogen or toxin. This is not a pleasant scenario but one which we must consider fully in order to protect Canadians. To address this risk the new legislation includes a provision for a new national system of security screening for persons handling the most dangerous of these agents. Other than for individuals working in federal government laboratories, there is no such system in place in Canada at this moment ...

The new legislation will address both biosafety and biosecurity risks through a range of mechanisms including: new criminal prohibitions, offences, and penalties; expanded inspection and enforcement; a new authority to make regulations; and new security screening requirements for persons having access to the most dangerous human pathogens and toxins.

This proposal would render Canada more consistent with its international partners and allies, including the United States, the United Kingdom and Australia, which have all passed new security legislation. It is time that Canada joined them.

(*House of Commons Debates, 23 February 2009, pp. 821–22*)
(*Débats de la Chambre des communes, le 23 février 2009, pp. 821–22*)

7   *Bill C-16: Environmental Enforcement Act / Loi C-16: Loi sur le contrôle d'application de lois environnementales*[7]

Mr. Mark Warawa (Parliamentary Secretary to the Minister of the Environment):

Bill C-16 ... proposes to introduce sweeping changes to the offence, penalty and enforcement provisions of nine environmental protection and wildlife conservation statutes to ensure they achieve all of these goals ...

---

[7] Editor's note: Act to Amend Certain Acts That Relate to the Environment and to Enact Provisions Respecting the Enforcement of Certain Acts That Relate to the Environment / Loi modifiant certaines lois environnementales et édictant des dispositions ayant trait au contrôle d'application de lois environnementales, S.C. 2009, c. 14; introduced in the House of Commons by Hon. Jim Prentice (Minister of the Environment) on 4 March 2009. The bill received Royal Assent on 18 June 2009.

These include:

- CEPA, 1999, the Canadian Environmental Protection Act, one of Canada's most important environmental protection laws, [that] addresses the prevention and management of risks posed by toxic and other harmful substances and the environmental and human health impacts related to biotechnology, marine pollution, disposal at sea, vehicle, engine and equipment emissions, fuels, hazardous wastes and environmental emergencies;
- the Migratory Birds Convention Act of 1994, a key tool for protecting migratory birds in Canada;
- [the] Trade and Endangered Species legislation, which forbids the unlawful import, export and interprovincial transport of species on the Convention on International Trade in Endangered Species of Wild Fauna and Flora control list and of foreign species whose capture, possession and export are prohibited or regulated by the laws of another country;
- the Antarctic Environmental Protection Act, which implements a protocol to the Antarctic treaty and the Canada Wildlife Act under which national wildlife areas are established and maintained for wildlife conservation and research activities;
- the International River Improvements Act, a statute that governs the construction, operation and maintenance of large projects such as dams on rivers flowing from Canada into the United States;
- the Canada National Parks Act, under which our national parks and reserves are created and managed;
- the Canada National Marine Conservation Areas Act, which authorizes the creation and management of marine conservation areas that are representative of the Atlantic, Arctic and Pacific Oceans, and the Great Lakes; [and]
- the Saguenay-St. Lawrence Marine Park Act which protects the Saguenay-St. Lawrence Marine Park for the benefit of this generation and generations to come ...

The need for the amendments proposed in the environmental enforcement act are clear. At the Global Judges Symposium held in Johannesburg, South Africa in 2002, where Canada's Supreme Court was represented, the Johannesburg Principles on the Role of Law and Sustainable Development were adopted. The principles include the following statement:

> We are strongly of the view that there is an urgent need to strengthen the capacity of judges, prosecutors, legislators and all persons who play a critical role ... in the process of implementation, development

and enforcement of environmental law ... especially through the judicial process.

Current fines are too low to be effective deterrents ... Finally, when fines are collected, they are currently most often directed toward the consolidated revenue fund. Our government has proposed amendments in Bill C-16 that would see those fines made available for remediation of the harm caused by that environmental offence ...

If the environmental enforcement act becomes law, fines for individuals who commit the most serious offences will range from a minimum of $5,000 to a maximum of $1 million per day. Large corporations that commit the most serious offences will be liable to fines ranging from $100,000 to $6 million per day of an offence.

Beyond increasing fines, the bill would also improve sentencing guidance by introducing purpose and principle clauses that recognize the sentencing objectives of deterrence, denunciation and restoration and the importance of taking into account the aggravating factors. It would also ensure courts have access to a full suite of powers to order offenders to undertake certain activities, including remediating harm caused by their offences, compensating those who take remedial action or who lose property as a result of the offences, and contributing to communities harmed by the environmental offences ...

The new act would authorize the Governor in Council to make regulations needed to implement the administrative monetary penalty scheme, including regulations identifying for what offences administrative monetary penalties may be used and a method for calculating the fine amount. The new act would restrict the amount of these monetary penalties to $5,000 for an individual and $25,000 for any person or ship, creating a continuum of enforcement responses from warnings to compliance orders to administrative monetary penalties to charges.

Persons issued an administrative monetary penalty may have them reviewed by an administrative tribunal to ensure fairness that may determine whether the person committed the violation and, if the tribunal determines the penalty for the violation is not determined in accordance with regulations, it may correct the amount of the penalty.

(*House of Commons Debates, 23 March 2009, pp. 1822–24*)
(*Débats de la Chambre des communes, le 23 mars 2009, pp. 1822–24*)

*8   Bill C-23: Canada–Colombia Free Trade Agreement Implementation
     Act / Loi C-23: Loi de mise en oeuvre de l'Accord de libre-échange
     Canada–Colombie* [8]

Hon. Stockwell Day (Minister of International Trade and Minister
for the Asia-Pacific Gateway):

[W]hen we look at free trade, especially in a time of economic downturn[,]
this is a time when we need to open doors of opportunity for investors,
producers, innovators, and Canadian workers. Not only do we have to
maintain an open door policy, but we have to pursue more open doors
around the world.

Canada is a member of the World Trade Organization and that entire
process. Many countries are involved in this organization as well. The Doha
round is somewhat stalled. Our Prime Minister and other world leaders
have said the Doha round has to get moving and brought to a conclusion.
That is our goal.

As we go through that somewhat difficult and prolonged process, we
cannot have everything remain static. We cannot wait for the World Trade
Organization process to be completed. It is a good process and a process
that will lower tariffs and lower barriers for many countries around the
world, but we cannot wait. We want to see the Doha round conclude, but
at the same time we are pursuing free trade agreements with other countries.

Right here in this House of Commons, we are debating a free trade
agreement with Peru, looking at it and hopefully moving it along ... We
were also engaged just recently in bringing to a conclusion an agreement
that we called the EFTA, a European free trade agreement with four countries: Norway, Iceland, Switzerland and Liechtenstein. In this agreement
we saw the removal or the significant reduction of tariffs right across the
board, allowing many Canadian products to go into those countries without the producers being hit with big tariff penalties. In other words, those
Canadian products can move into those countries and Canadian producers

---

[8] Editor's note: An Act to Implement the Free Trade Agreement Between Canada
and the Republic of Colombia, the Agreement on the Environment Between
Canada and the Republic of Colombia and the Agreement on Labour Cooperation Between Canada and the Republic of Colombia / Loi portant mise en
oeuvre de l'Accord de libre-échange entre le Canada et la République de Colombie, de l'Accord sur l'environnement entre le Canada et la République de
Colombie et de l'Accord de coopération dans le domaine du travail entre le
Canada et la République de Colombie; introduced in the House of Commons
by Hon. Stockwell Day (Minister of International Trade and Minister for the
Asia-Pacific Gateway) on 26 March 2009.

will not have to face a competitive disadvantage of having a tariff laid on top of those Canadian products.

We know that we will see increased production. We will see more product going from Canadian producers to those particular countries because we will be more competitive in pricing ... We apply the same principle to what is happening in Colombia. Colombia is pursuing free trade agreements with other countries and it is bringing them to a conclusion. That means producers and the providers of a variety of services in other countries are going to have a competitive advantage over Canadian producers as they market their goods and services into Colombia because tariffs on a wide range of products are going to be reduced. That means Canadian producers and Canadian workers are going to be at a disadvantage if we do not move on and complete this free trade deal.

It is worthy to note, and I brought this out to people with whom I met at Amnesty International and other groups who have raised issues about human rights and the past record of Colombia, that the past record of Colombia has not been an enviable one, to say the least, when it comes to human rights issues. However, its present administration has made great gains and shown great commitment to principles that are related to democracy, human rights and protections that we have come to expect, that is part of our own history, and that we have advanced around the world.

It is interesting that concerns have been raised about the free trade deal between Canada and Colombia, for instance on the labour side, yet we have signed a labour accord with Colombia that insists on both countries following the ILO, the International Labour Organization, rules, regulations and obligations related to trade and labour, which of course Canada already does. That covers everything from child labour to hours worked, to a full array of occupational health and safety issues that we would expect workers to have made available to them.

What is interesting here is that Colombia has signed agreements with European countries that have not even required those same labour agreements that we have. We have certain groups raising issues about Canada's agreement with Colombia but they never raised the issues with the European countries that have signed these agreements.

We feel it is very important that when a country is making progress, as Colombia is, that has to be acknowledged. The way we make sure progress continues is to get those countries to actually sign on the dotted line to certain levels of human rights and rights of workers and others. These signatures between Canada and Colombia require that independent organizations do the evaluation. There are sanctions attached to each country. Obviously, we do not think Canada will run afoul of these principles because we have embraced them for decades, but there are sanctions should the countries fall short of following through on their commitments.

There are 46 million people in Colombia who are gradually experiencing a raise in their standard of living ... Two-way trade in 2008 was something like $1.35 billion between Canada and Colombia. There is always a good platform of trade. About 80% of that trade has to do with agriculture. Tariffs have been applied to Canadian industry; just in that one trading year, 2008, Canadian companies, and really, Canadian workers, paid about $25 million worth of tariffs on products that they were selling into Colombia. There is a range of tariffs that we would hope to see reduced in this agreement. Some products are being taxed with a tariff, Canadian products going into Colombia and Colombian products coming into Canada, as low as 17%. Some of the tariff lines go as high as over 80%. This is being tacked on to a product either going into Colombia or coming into Canada. It is time to reduce them. We should eliminate as many of them as possible and open up the doors of opportunity for people in Colombia as well as for people in Canada. That is why these deals are two-way streets.

(*House of Commons Debates, 25 May 2009, pp. 3639–41*)
(*Débats de la Chambre des communes, le 25 mai 2009, pp. 3639–41*)

9   *Bill C-24: Canada-Peru Free Trade Agreement Implementation Act /*
    Loi C-24: Loi de mise en oeuvre de l'Accord de libre-échange
    Canada-Pérou[9]

Mr. Gerald Keddy (Parliamentary Secretary to the Minister of International Trade):

Bill C-24 [is] a bill dealing with trade liberalization and market access ... The government's policy of re-engagement with the Americas has made a lot of economic sense. It is only reasonable, practical and intelligent foreign policy and trade policy on Canada's behalf that we have become more active in the Americas at our very own doorstep.

---

[9] Editor's note: An Act to Implement the Free Trade Agreement Between Canada and the Republic of Peru, the Agreement on the Environment Between Canada and the Republic of Peru and the Agreement on Labour Cooperation Between Canada and the Republic of Peru / Loi portant mise en œuvre de l'Accord de libre-échange entre le Canada et la République du Pérou, de l'Accord sur l'environnement entre le Canada et la République du Pérou et de l'Accord de coopération dans le domaine du travail entre le Canada et la République du Pérou, S.C. 2009, c. 16; introduced in the House of Commons by Hon. Stockwell Day (Minister of International Trade and Minister for the Asia-Pacific Gateway) on 26 March 2009. The bill received Royal Assent on 18 June 2009.

In Latin America, Peru is a leader, a lynchpin in the political and economic stability of the region. It has been an economic engine with a gross domestic product growth rate of 9.1% in 2008, near the top of the Latin American countries. Peru also has a solid outward orientation. A leader in trade liberalization, Peru is currently pursuing trade negotiations with a number of countries. We need partners like Peru, especially as we move forward on engaging with like-minded countries throughout the Americas. Canadians will benefit. Peru is already an established and growing market for our businesses. Exports like wheat, pulses and mining equipment are just part of that picture.

Canadians also offer services in the financial and engineering fields and this activity is driving strong, two-way commerce between our businesses. In 2008. two-way merchandise trade between our countries totalled $2.8 billion ...

Peru is an important supplier to Canada of gold, zinc, copper and petroleum. Canadian investors, too, have a significant presence in the Peruvian market. In fact, Canada is one of Peru's largest overall foreign investors with an estimated $1.8 billion worth of investment stock in Peru in 2007 led by the mining and financial services sectors ...

We have negotiated a high quality and comprehensive free trade agreement covering everything from market access for goods to cross-border trade and services to investment and government procurement. Canadian exporters will certainly benefit. The agreement would create new opportunities for Canadian businesses and producers in the Peruvian market. Under the agreement, Peru will immediately eliminate its tariffs on nearly all current Canadian imports with remaining tariffs to be gradually eliminated over the next five to ten years.

Canadian producers will enjoy immediate duty-free access to Peru products like wheat, barely, lentils and peas. A variety of paper products, machinery and equipment will also enjoy the same benefit.

However, an effective free trade agreement should do more than eliminate tariffs. It should also tackle the non-tariff barriers that keep a trade relationship from reaching its full potential. We have done that by including new measures to ensure greater transparency, including better predictability for incoming regulations and the right by industry to be consulted at an early stage in the development of regulations, promoting the use of international standards and creating a mechanism to promptly address problems ...

[T]his agreement ... also includes important side agreements that demonstrate our joint commitment to corporate social responsibility, the rights of workers and preserving the natural environment. Our nations recognize that prosperity must not come at the expense of the environment and workers' rights.

This agreement paves the way for significant dialogue on other areas of mutual interest, including poverty reduction and trade related cooperation. In fact, this approach builds on our successful experience with free trade partners such as the U.S., Mexico, Chile and Costa Rica.

(*House of Commons Debates, 20 April 2009, pp. 2450–52*)
(*Débats de la Chambre des communes, le 20 avril 2009, pp. 2450–52*)

10   Bill C-27: Electronic Commerce Protection Act / Loi C-27: Loi sur la protection du commerce électronique[10]

Mr. Mike Lake (Parliamentary Secretary to the Minister of Industry):

This is a bill to protect and promote the Canadian economy to allow electronic commerce to reach its full potential and to increase confidence in the e-economy. We need to take strong steps to protect the integrity of the electronic marketplace by reducing the harmful effects of threats to the online economy ...

In the past decade, online commerce and e-business has continued its rapid growth in Canada and around the world. In fact, Canada has become one of the most connected countries in the world and Canadians are avid users of the Internet, but there are some areas of Internet use where we should not be proud of our distinction. When measured by the percentage of spam that originates in a particular country, Canada stands in fourth place worldwide, behind Russia and just ahead of Brazil. Some 4.7% of the world's spam originates in Canada ...

Malware is becoming increasingly sophisticated. Sometimes it connects infected computers so that they become part of a botnet and their processing power and bandwidth are made available to others. Botnets are often used to send out massive amounts of spam ...

---

[10] Editor's note: An Act to Promote the Efficiency and Adaptability of the Canadian Economy by Regulating Certain Activities That Discourage Reliance on Electronic Means of Carrying Out Commercial Activities, and to Amend the Canadian Radio-Television and Telecommunications Commission Act, the Competition Act, the Personal Information Protection and Electronic Documents Act and the Telecommunications Act / Loi visant à promouvoir l'efficacité et la capacité d'adaptation de l'économie canadienne par la réglementation de certaines pratiques qui découragent l'exercice des activités commerciales par voie électronique et modifiant la Loi sur le Conseil de la radiodiffusion et des télécommunications canadiennes, la Loi sur la concurrence, la Loi sur la protection des renseignements personnels et les documents électroniques et la Loi sur les télécommunications; introduced in the House of Commons by Hon. Tony Clement (Minister of Industry) on 24 April 2009.

Spam represents about 87% of email traffic around the world. It is estimated that last year a total of 62 trillion spam emails were sent. In June 2007, Ipsos Reid found that Canadians received an average of 130 spam messages each week. This is up 51% from the previous year. In April 2008 an EKOS survey showed 72% of Canadians considered spam a major problem. In spring 2008 Phoenix surveyed Canadian CEOs and senior executives, and found that 80% considered spam to be a problem for their company; 21% considered it to be a big problem. Their greatest concern was wasted time and reduced productivity. More than two-thirds believed that the Government of Canada should bring in anti-spam legislation ...

[O]ne of the most effective ways to combat spam is through effective anti-spam legislation. Take the example of Australia. A few years ago, like Canada, it was on the top 10 list of countries where spam originated. After introducing anti-spam legislation in 2003, and with the help of a carefully crafted public awareness campaign, Australia dropped off the top 10 list by 2005. Anti-spam legislation works.

Canada represents the only G8 country and one of only four OECD countries without anti-spam legislation. It is time that we joined with our key global partners, including the U.S., the U.K. and Australia in passing strong domestic laws to combat spam and related threats.

The bill before us will reduce the burden of spam on Canadian businesses and the risks to individual Canadians. Our goal is to ensure continued confidence in electronic commerce by addressing the personal privacy and security concerns that surround Internet spam and related threats.

The bill proposes an opt-in approach for all forms of unsolicited commercial electronic messages without a pre-existing business relationship or consent. It would introduce a regime that would follow the money. This would ensure that anyone who benefits commercially from the spam would be held as equally responsible as the person who sent the spam ...

The regime would allow for email marketing based on a consumer opt-in approach long practised by the Canadian Marketing Association and reflected in its code of conduct. Businesses will need to get consent prior to sending commercial emails or have a pre-existing business relationship with the customer.

The bill before us provides two different kinds of remedy to eliminate spam and related online threats. One is a regulatory approach. The other involves actions that can be taken by individuals and businesses.

[Under t]he regulatory approach, the CRTC, the Competition Bureau and the Privacy Commissioner would be able to investigate and take action against the sending of unsolicited commercial electronic messages,

installation of computer programs, and the altering of Internet addresses without consent. The CRTC would be able to take action on these
matters in a manner that will be technology neutral ... The Competition
Bureau would be responsible for those aspects of spam that relate to
unfair and deceptive marketing practices, including false headers and
website content.

[B]oth the CRTC and the Competition Bureau would be able to impose
administrative monetary penalties, or AMPs, to those who violate the act
... The amounts of the penalties would not exceed $1 million for individuals
and $10 million in all other cases ...

[T]he Office of the Privacy Commissioner would address the misuse of
personal information. This would include specific provisions added by
amendments to the Personal Information Protection and Electronic Documents Act. This would deal with the electronic compiling or supplying of
lists of personal electronic addresses without consent ...

Consistent with this bill, we would establish a spam reporting centre
which would monitor the legislation's effectiveness through trend analysis
and metrics. It would also manage the public awareness campaign that
would build awareness of the new act and ensure its success ...

The second remedy involves the power of each of us as citizens, consumers and businesses to pursue remedies against spammers. The bill before
us would provide a private right of action that would allow consumers and
businesses to take civil action against anyone who violates the act. This
remedy has been very effective in the United States and it is one example
of how we have taken best practices from around the world and incorporated them into this bill.

(*House of Commons Debates, 7 May 2009, pp. 3233–34*)
(*Débats de la Chambre des communes, le 7 mai 2009, pp. 3233–34*)

*11 Bill C-35: Justice for Victims of Terrorism Act / Loi C-35: Loi sur la
justice pour les victimes d'actes de terrorisme*[11]

Hon. Peter Kent (for the Minister of Public Safety):

Bill C-35 is a result of victims' initiatives championed by an organization
called the Canadian Coalition Against Terror, known by its acronym C-CAT,

---

[11] Editor's note: An Act to Deter Terrorism, and to Amend the State Immunity
Act / Loi visant à décourager le terrorisme et modifiant la Loi sur l'immunité
des États; introduced in the House of Commons by Hon. Peter Van Loan (Minister of Public Safety) on 2 June 2009.

which represents Canadian terror victims. C-CAT has played a critical role in driving this bill forward ... The legislation before us today would provide the Government of Canada with another important tool to protect Canadians from acts of terrorism while ensuring that victims of these heinous acts have the chance to seek justice ...

Canada has been designated as a potential target for terrorist attacks by organizations like al-Qaeda ... We need to take steps to prevent these acts from occurring in the first place, and when they do occur we need to ensure that victims' voices are heard. That is what Bill C-35 is all about.

Bill C-35 ... would create a course of action to allow victims of terrorism to sue perpetrators and supporters of terrorism. It would modify the State Immunity Act to allow the Government of Canada to lift the immunity of states that are deemed to support terrorism. The bill demonstrates Canada's leadership in combatting terrorism and terrorist supporters.

Providing victims with an opportunity to seek justice for violent acts committed against them is a fundamental tenet of our legal system and a cornerstone of Canadian society. Criminals, including terrorists, need to be held to account. They need to know there are consequences to their actions. Victims too need to know that their interests are paramount and that they can move on with their lives to every extent possible.

Canada applies these principles domestically. The bill before us today would further extend them to some of the most callous acts of violence imaginable, regardless of whether they are committed here in Canada or overseas.

Bill C-35 would allow victims to use courts to seek redress provided they can show a real and substantial connection between their action and Canada. The burden of proof is smaller in civil cases. Civil suits would deter future acts of violence by bankrupting or financially impairing the terrorist infrastructure through successful judgments and/or by causing terrorist sponsors to refrain from future sponsorship out of fear of the publicity and exposure that would result from a civil suit. Bill C-35 proposes to allow victims to seek redress not just from the perpetrators of terrorist acts but also from their supporters ...

Bill C-35 proposes to ... lift[] state immunity for states known to support terrorism. The decision to list such countries will be made by the Minister of Foreign Affairs in consultation with the Minister of Public Safety and will be subject to review every two years. Listed countries will also be able to make a written application for delisting.

(*House of Commons Debates, 30 October 2009, pp. 6385–87*)
(*Débats de la Chambre des communes, le 30 octobre 2009, pp. 6385–87*)

12   Bill C-44: Canada Post Corporation Act / Loi C-44: La Loi sur la Société canadienne des postes [12]

Hon. Rob Merrifield (for the Minister of Transport, Infrastructure and Communities):

[T]he Canada Post Corporation Act ... has gone to court. The courts did not rule on whether they agree with outboard or international mailing. What they did was interpret the act as saying that Canada Post had the exclusive right to outboard and international mailing. The legislation would make outboard international remailing legal, which in the law today is the exclusive privilege of Canada Post ...

Things have changed over a number of years. I would like to explain why it is not needed at this time. This is not unique to Canada. It has changed in Europe. Most of Europe's international remailers have the opportunity to exercise international remailing. It has also changed in the United States. When one sees exactly what has happened internationally, we are just trying to catch up with other countries.

There are two kinds of outboard international remails ... First, a piece of mail going to another country can go to a country with a lower regime cost. Bulk pieces of mail will go to foreign developing countries, such as Jamaica, that have a cheaper rate because of their costs of doing business in those areas. Then the mail moves on to a third country where the mail is actually distributed. It is not exercised that way as often, but that is one way that it can and would be allowed. This actually goes back to the ratification of the 1999 Beijing congress on the Universal Postal Union. That is one way that it can be done.

The other way, which is the way more commonly done in Canada, is when an outboard international remail occurs with remailers that collect the outboard international mail from their consumers. Usually it is sorted and bagged by a country of destination and then directly deposited in that foreign country.

That is most likely what would happen. It is most common with us because of our proximity to the United States. These bags are taken to the United States and distributed domestically. Domestic rates are always much cheaper than international rates and that is the reality of the situation. With the way the act is written and the way that the monopoly is given to Canada Post, that is illegal in the country ...

---

[12] Editor's note: An Act to Amend the Canada Post Corporation Act / Loi modifiant la Loi sur la Société canadienne des postes; introduced in the House of Commons by Hon. John Baird (Minister of Transport, Infrastructure and Communities) on 17 June 2009.

The world is changing. Eighty-five per cent of our exports used to go to the United States. That figure went down to about 75% and then 70%. Last year it was 66%. We are seeing a trend where our exports are not going directly to the United States and that is because we are capitalizing on international markets.

That is why this legislation is so important. It would allow us to have a competitive edge internationally ... CUPW, the Canada Post union, does not really like this, but it is actually going to be good for them. It allows them to actually compete. It allows them to be able to test themselves, as to whether they actually can be competitive as they move forward with regard to this.

We are not compromising Canada Post's universality in Canada. We want Canada Post. We demand Canada Post. In fact we have a charter and will have a contractual arrangement between the people of Canada and Canada Post that will insist they deliver mail in an appropriate time period from one side of this country to another ... No one needs to worry that Canada Post is going anywhere on their mandate or that we are going to compromise in any way the Canada Post Corporation Act.

(*House of Commons Debates, 7 October 2009, pp. 5704–06*)
(*Débats de la Chambre des communes, le 7 octobre 2009, pp. 5704–06*)

13 Bill C-47: Technical Assistance for Law Enforcement in the Twenty-First Century Act / Loi C-47: Loi sur l'assistance au contrôle d'application des lois au XXIe siècle[13]

Mrs. Shelly Glover (Parliamentary Secretary for Official Languages):

This bill ... will enable the law enforcement community and our justice partners to investigate and prosecute crime in a rapidly evolving communications environment. The bill, in a nutshell, will give them the same capability to access Internet and cellphone messages with warrants as they currently have to access wiretap telephone calls. Equally important, it will give national security agencies new intercept capabilities to combat terrorism and to work more effectively with their global counterparts.

Many of our closest allies have had similar legislation in place for quite some time now. In fact, last year the G8 called on members to beef up their intercept capability to fight international crime. That is precisely what this legislation will do.

---

[13] Editor's note: An Act Regulating Telecommunications Facilities to Support Investigations / Loi régissant les installations de télécommunication aux fins de soutien aux enquêtes; introduced in the House of Commons by Hon. Peter Van Loan (Minister of Public Safety) on 18 June 2009.

Bill C-47 will remove the competitive advantage which technology has given to criminals and to terrorists for far too long. As it now stands, when Canadian police officers and national security officials try to intercept messages being sent by criminals or terrorists using the latest technologies, they are hamstrung by legislation dating back decades. Canada's intercept laws are 35 years old ...

The previous government introduced lawful access legislation recognizing the need to give public safety officials the tools they require to do their jobs. While it was a good start, Bill C-47 builds on that effort and strengthens it further. Specifically, the bill before us today will ensure that when law enforcement and security officials have a warrant to intercept messages by criminals or terrorists, they are not prevented from doing so due to a lack of technical ability ...

In modernizing Canada's lawful access laws, we are not providing new powers or expanding on existing interception authorities that have been in place since 1974, nor are we compromising individuals' personal information, or putting an undue burden on business. We are simply bringing our country's legislation out of the cold war era and into the 21st century ... Our government's proposed changes will be introduced gradually to allow businesses to adjust to these new obligations.

Bill C-47 provides an initial transition period of 18 months to allow service providers time to integrate lawful interception requirements into new equipment and services. It includes the possibility of a two-year exemption to respond to new technologies. This will serve to protect innovation and competitiveness. The legislation is also flexible enough to respond to a company's particular circumstances. The specific needs of smaller firms have in fact been taken into account. The bill contains a three-year exemption for service providers with less than 100,000 subscribers from certain requirements that are too costly for them at this time. Certain organizations, such as schools, libraries and charities, are also exempt entirely ...

[A] major component of the government's proposed legislation is the requirement for service providers to make basic subscriber information available on request to designated members of the law enforcement community and CSIS. Timely access to this information is essential in the fight against crime, especially crimes committed over the Internet such as online fraud, identity theft and child sexual exploitation.

At the moment, there is no federal legislation specifically designed to allow for obtaining basic subscriber information, identifiers that are often crucial in the early stages of an investigation. As a result, when this information is required, the police face a patchwork of responses from service providers across the country. Some companies release this information readily while others demand a warrant.

Without Bill C-47, unscrupulous con artists can continue to defraud unsuspecting Internet users responding to email scams. Child abusers and pornographers will anonymously exploit Internet chat rooms, luring young victims away from their homes and into harm's way ... This is a crucial piece of legislation required to make our families, homes and communities safer.

(*House of Commons Debates,* 27 *October* 2009, *pp.* 6224–26)
(*Débats de la Chambre des communes, le* 27 *octobre* 2009, *pp.* 6224–26)

14 Bill C-57: Canada-Jordan Free Trade Act / Loi C-57: Loi sur le libre-échange entre le Canada et la Jordanie[14]

Mr. Gerald Keddy (Parliamentary Secretary to the Minister of International Trade):

This agreement with Jordan will directly benefit a number of sectors of the Canadian economy at precisely the time when Canadians need competitive access to global markets. In these challenging economic times, we need to do everything we can to help Canadians and Canadian businesses build links to the global economy. Protectionism is not the answer; partnerships are ...

Over the years, Canada and Jordan have built a strong mutually beneficial relationship. It is a relationship grounded in common aspirations such as peace, stability and prosperity for our citizens. [I]t is a relationship with deep commercial roots as well. Many Canadian companies already have a solid presence in the Jordanian marketplace. The Potash Corporation of Saskatchewan, for instance, is one of Jordan's top foreign investors. It is joined by companies like Research In Motion, Bombardier, SNC-Lavalin, Four Seasons Hotels, Second Cup coffee shops and many others which are also active in Jordan.

Our two-way trade is very diverse, covering everything from forestry to agriculture, from food to machinery, as well as communications, technologies and apparel. Canada's expertise in nuclear power is another

---

[14] Editor's note: An Act to Implement the Free Trade Agreement Between Canada and the Hashemite Kingdom of Jordan, the Agreement on the Environment Between Canada and the Hashemite Kingdom of Jordan and the Agreement on Labour Cooperation Between Canada and the Hashemite Kingdom of Jordan / Loi portant mise en oeuvre de l'Accord de libre-échange entre le Canada et le Royaume hachémite de Jordanie, de l'Accord sur l'environnement entre le Canada et le Royaume hachémite de Jordanie et de l'Accord de coopération dans le domaine du travail entre le Canada et le Royaume hachémite de Jordanie; introduced in the House of Commons by Hon. Stockwell Day (Minister of International Trade and Minister for the Asia-Pacific Gateway) on 17 November 2009.

sector of great interest to Jordan, especially as it embarks on a nuclear energy program to meet its energy needs in the years ahead. Canada's nuclear industry has a lot to offer the government and the private sector in Jordan, especially following the signing of our bilateral nuclear cooperation agreement earlier this year. It is yet another example of how sophisticated our relationship is becoming on several fronts.

In 2008, our two-way merchandise trade reached over $90 million. Canada is the supplier to Jordan of a range of goods including paper, copper, vegetables, machinery and wood. In fact Canadian exporters enjoyed a 21% rise in exports over the previous year, making Jordan a growing market in the Middle East for Canada ...

The free trade agreement ... will benefit Canadians and Jordanians alike. It will give Canadian and Jordanian exporters unprecedented access to our respective markets, eliminating tariffs on a number of key products. World-leading Canadian sectors such as forestry, manufacturing and agriculture and agri-food will benefit.

Our beef producers too stand to benefit from the agreement. Not only did Jordan fully reopen its market to Canadian beef and cattle in February, but through this FTA, Canadian beef producers will enjoy competitive advantages in a market that the Canada Beef Export Federation estimates to be worth approximately $1 million per Canadian exporter.

In addition to providing these great benefits, this agreement also sharpens our competitive edge. After all, Jordan has free trade agreements with some of our key competitors such as the United States and the European Union. This FTA will help ensure a level playing field for Canadians in the Jordanian market. In fact 67% of Jordan's tariff lines, covering over 99% of Canadian exports, will be eliminated when the agreement is first implemented, and the remaining tariff reductions will take place within three to five years.

An FTA with Jordan also demonstrates Canada's support for an Arab state that supports peace and security in the Middle East, but as I have said before, the FTA was just one agreement we signed with Jordan this year. We also signed parallel labour cooperation and environmental agreements that will help ensure progress on labour rights and environmental protection. Our government firmly believes that increased commerce can play a positive role in society, and these agreements prove our commitment.

We also signed a bilateral foreign investment protection and promotion agreement, or FIPA, that establishes clear rules for investment between our countries. It provides Canadian and Jordanian investors alike with the predictability and certainty they need when investing in each other's markets.

Canadian investors are particularly excited about opportunities in Jordan's resource extraction, nuclear energy, telecommunications, transportation and infrastructure sectors, and Jordan has been very receptive to Canada's many investment advantages, such as our sound, stable economy; our globally recognized banking system; our competitive business taxes; our ongoing investments in infrastructure, science and education; our unmatched position in the North American market; and the skills, ingenuity and innovation of the Canadian people.

This agreement will help us promote investment between our nations and create new opportunities for our citizens. Canada believes that our ability to weather the current economic storm depends in great part on the global partnerships we pursue. That is why this Conservative government is moving so aggressively on trade negotiations with our global partners.

(*House of Commons Debates, 19 November 2009, pp. 6959–61*)
(*Débats de la Chambre des communes, le 19 novembre 2009, pp. 6959–61*)

D   STATEMENTS IN RESPONSE TO QUESTIONS / DÉCLARATIONS
     EN REPONSE AUX QUESTIONS

1   Environment / L'environnement

(a) Arctic / Arctique

Mr. Ron Cannan (Kelowna — Lake Country):

[What] efforts ha[s] [the government] taken and will take to preserve our Arctic sovereignty?

Hon. John Baird (Minister of Transport, Infrastructure and Communities):

The Prime Minister announced this past August that we will extend our jurisdiction of enforcing Canada's top environmental enforcement laws to a full 200 nautical miles off our coast. We will get tough with Arctic polluters and we will ensure that our Arctic waters are kept clean.

(*House of Commons Debates, 24 November 2008, p. 177*)
(*Débats de la Chambre des communes, le 24 novembre 2008, p. 177*)

Hon. Larry Bagnell (Yukon):

[W]hat can the minister possibly tell the Arctic Council countries at their upcoming meeting to credibly assert our sovereignty?

Hon. Chuck Strahl (Minister of Indian Affairs and Northern Development and Federal Interlocutor for Métis and Non-Status Indians):

[There are] many things in [the budget] for the north: $80-some million for improving research facilities; a further study on the permanent research facilities that will be there; increased funding for the military in the north; more money for health care in the north; and money is being set aside for housing in the north ... We are continuing with increased regulation of transportation for boats travelling through the Arctic to ensure they meet our environmental standards. We are continuing with an election promise to develop a northern development agency. We are renewing the SINED program. We are continuing with devolution talks with Nunavut and working with the Northwest Territories. We have $36 million to improve the regulatory process on the Mackenzie Valley pipeline.

(*House of Commons Debates, 3 February 2009, p. 298*)
(*Débats de la Chambre des communes, le 3 février 2009, p. 298*)

(b) Clean Energy / Énergie propre

Mr. Ron Cannan (Kelowna — Lake Country):

[O]n February 19, the Prime Minister and President Obama ... agreed in a U.S.-Canada clean energy dialogue that would co-operate on several critical energy science and technology issues in pursuit of a clean environment ... What measures have been] taken since this ... meeting?

Le très hon. Stephen Harper (premier ministre):

Le ministre de l'Environnement est à Washington aujourd'hui afin de poursuivre le dialogue sur l'énergie propre conclu entre nos gouvernements quand le président Obama était à Ottawa. While in Washington, with regard to the clean energy dialogue, the Minister of the Environment will talk to the American administration about the expansion of clean energy research, the development and deployment of clean energy technology, the promotion of clean and renewable energy sources like hydroelectricity.

(*House of Commons Debates, 2 March 2009, p. 1150*)
(*Débats de la Chambre des communes, le 2 mars 2009, p. 1150*)

Hon. Jim Prentice (Minister of the Environment):

[T]his government and the Obama administration share the same vision and the same principles with respect to reducing greenhouse gases. Our two countries believe in particular in expanding clean energy research as well as developing and deploying clean energy technology. Our two countries will continue to lead green energy developments, including renewables and hydro, as well as carbon capture and storage to clean their coal and our oil.

(*House of Commons Debates, 4 March 2009, p. 1282*)
(*Débats de la Chambre des communes, le 4 mars 2009, p. 1282*)

(c) Climate Change / Changements climatiques

M. Gilles Duceppe (Laurier — Sainte-Marie):

À la veille de la Conférence des Nations Unies sur les changements climatiques, le ministre de l'Environnement laisse entendre que l'alentissement économique, celui qu'il niait il y a quelques semaines, pourrait avoir priorité sur la lutte contre les changements climatiques. Le premier ministre ne devrait-il pas plutôt écouter le secrétaire général des Nations Unies qui a déclaré que la crise économique ne devrait pas servir d'excuse à l'inaction dans la lutte contre les changements climatiques?

L'hon. Jim Prentice (ministre de l'Environnement):

Je vais participer à la rencontre de Poznan. À cette rencontre, le Canada défendra le développement d'une nouvelle entente sous l'égide de la CCNUCC, comme les autres tables de négociations de Copenhague et de Poznan.

M. Gille Duceppe:

Le premier ministre va-t-il profiter de son énoncé économique pour proposer des mesures qui encouragent le développement durable?

Hon. Jim Prentice:

[W]e are committed to reducing Canada's greenhouse gases, and in particular, in the context of renewable energies, achieving by 2020 perhaps as much as 90% of Canada's electricity from non-emitting sources. This will clearly require investments in renewable energy, whether we speak of geothermal energy, solar energy, the bringing on of new hydroelectricity. These are all issues with which the government will deal in the days ahead.

M. Bernard Bigras (Rosemont — La Petite-Patrie):

Il n'y a pas d'opposition entre le développement économique et l'environnement. Les papetières et les forestières l'ont compris et ont fait des efforts importants pour réduire leurs émissions de gaz à effet de serre. Ce qu'elles veulent maintenant, ce sont des cibles absolues et l'adoption de 1990 pour année de référence afin d'avoir une véritable bourse du carbone. Les grandes entreprises voient l'intérêt de Kyoto. Pourquoi le gouvernement ne pourrait-il pas en faire autant?

L'hon. Jim Prentice:

Ce sont des questions qui seront soulevées à Poznan. Les changements climatiques continuent d'être une grande priorité pour les Canadiens et les Canadiennes ... [J]e vais participer aux rencontres à Poznan. J'y approcherai les principaux joueurs au cours des négociations lors de ce congrès. C'est clair, nous avons certains principes, et je veux établir une compréhension de la position du Canada à ce congrès.

(*House of Commons Debates, 26 November 2008, p. 282*)
(*Débats de la Chambre des communes, le 26 novembre 2008, p. 282*)

M. Pierre Paquette (Joliette):

Le premier ministre comprend-il que le laxisme de son gouvernement est scandaleux et qu'il n'y a plus aucune crédibilité, ici et dans le monde, dans la lutte contre les changements climatiques par les conservateurs?

Mr. Mark Warawa (Parliamentary Secretary to the Minister of the Environment):

[W]e are working with President Obama. We are working with the provinces and the territories, and all our international partners to tackle climate change. Our targets in Canada, 20% absolute reductions by 2020, are some of the toughest in the world ... Our commitment to cleaning up the environment has never been stronger. In our budget we have $1 billion for green infrastructure, $300 million for eco-energy retrofits, and $1 billion for clean energy projects like carbon capture and storage. These investments in green technologies of tomorrow will help us combat climate change. It will clean up the air. It will provide good clean jobs.

(*House of Commons Debates, 13 February 2009, p. 800*)
(*Débats de la Chambre des communes, le 13 février 2009, p. 800*)

L'hon. Jack Layton (Toronto — Danforth):

La conférence de Copenhague sur les changements climatiques est très importante pour l'avenir de notre planète. Le président américain

Barack Obama y sera. La chancelière allemande, les premiers ministres britannique et australien y seront, de même que les présidents brésilien et français ... Le premier ministre va-t-il confirmer qu'il sera à Copenhague pour discuter de ce problème très important pour nous et pour l'avenir?

Hon. John Baird (Minister of Transport, Infrastructure and Communities):

Canada is committed to a successful climate change outcome. The Prime Minister ... will be in Copenhagen ... Many government officials, the Minister of the Environment ... will be there to forcefully argue for a strong agreement. We believe that an agreement must be effective. We believe that an agreement must be ambitious and must include all emitters.

(House of Commons Debates, 26 November 2009, p. 7269)
(Débats de la Chambre des communes, le 26 novembre 2009, p.7269)

(d) Corporate social responsibility / Responsabilité sociale des entreprises

Mme Ève-Mary Thaï Thi Lac (Saint-Hyacinthe — Bagot):

La Norvège vient de mettre sur la liste noire de son fonds d'investissement d'État la minière canadienne Barrick Gold pour ses agissements risqués en matière d'environnement. Cette décision ne devrait-elle pas amener le gouvernement à donner rapidement suite au rapport du Groupe consultatif pour les discussions des Tables rondes nationales sur la responsabilité sociale et l'industrie de l'extraction minière dans les pays en développement?

Mr. Gerald Keddy (Parliamentary Secretary to the Minister of International Trade):

Our social responsibility for our international extractive sector is the highest in the world. Our companies are the best in the world and they continue to be that. We work closely with them and we will continue to work closely with them. Corporate social responsibility is alive and well in the extractive sector in Canada and overseas.

(House of Commons Debates, 5 February 2009, p. 450)
(Débats de la Chambre des communes, le 5 février 2009, p. 450)

(e) Nuclear energy / Énergie nucléaire

L'hon. Geoff Regan (Halifax-Ouest):

En décembre, il y a eu un déversement radioactif à la centrale nucléaire. Quelle est la cause de cet accident? Quelles évaluations ont été faites de l'impact sur la santé humaine et sur l'environnement et pourquoi le public n'a-t-il pas été informé?

Hon. Lisa Raitt (Minister of Natural Resources):

The health and safety of Canadians is always our foremost concern. In fact, the Canadian Nuclear Safety Commission and AECL, the operator, were on the ground working together during the stoppage of the NRU and, as well, they were working together during this incident at Chalk River. I have been informed that Chalk River has had no adverse effects on human health or the environment during this period of time ... [The] CNSC was on site, and the communications were in place between AECL and CNSC. Regardless, I have asked for a written report on the incident and CNSC officials continue to work with AECL in these matters ... The reactor at Chalk River continues to operate consistently and meets all safety regulations and security regulations. We continue to work with CNSC to ensure safety requirements at Chalk River labs continue today.

(*House of Commons Debates*, 27 January 2009, p. 17)
(*Débats de la Chambre des communes, le 27 janvier 2009, p. 17*)

(f) Seal hunt / Chasse au loup-marin

M. Raynald Blais (Gaspésie — Îles-de-la-Madeleine):

La Commission européenne du marché intérieur a récemment appuyé un règlement visant à imposer un embargo partiel sur les produits du loup-marin. Cet embargo aurait de graves conséquences pour plusieurs chasseurs qui vivent de cette chasse traditionnelle et honorable. Les décideurs européens voteront très bientôt sur le projet de loi final. Qu'est-ce que le gouvernement entend faire pour contrer cette nouvelle attaque contre la chasse au loup-marin? ... Qu'est-ce que le gouvernement attend pour présenter une campagne d'information à l'échelle internationale pour favoriser l'expansion des marchés des produits du loup-marin et assurer la viabilité de cette industrie, notamment en augmentant le nombre de prises?

Hon. Gail Shea (Minister of Fisheries and Oceans):

[This] government will continue to defend the rights of Canadian sealers to provide a livelihood for their families through a lawful, sustainable and humane hunt. We will continue to inform international discussions with factual material ... The hunt came under attack in Europe and now it is under attack right here in Canada.

(*House of Commons Debates, 3 March 2009, p. 1228*)
(*Débats de la Chambre des communes, le 3 mars 2009, p. 1228*)

2   Foreign Affairs / Affaires étrangères

(a) China / Chine

Hon. Bob Rae (Toronto Centre):

Just last week David Emerson ... was enormously critical of the government for its failure to engage on China, for its failure to pay attention to the importance of this relationship, and for allowing a few ideological enthusiasts to take over Canada's China policy. Why has the minister allowed this to happen on his watch?

Hon. Lawrence Cannon (Minister of Foreign Affairs):

[W]e have been extremely active on that file. I personally had the opportunity of meeting with the foreign affairs minister. Colleagues of mine have travelled to China. The Minister of International Trade intends to go there very shortly. Not only will we be increasing our presence in China, but we also will be increasing our presence in Asia. [We] will be able to open up six new trade offices in China very shortly.

(*House of Commons Debates, 23 February 2009, p. 850*)
(*Débats de la Chambre des communes, le 23 février 2009, p. 850*)

Hon. Scott Brison (Kings — Hants):

Do[es] the [government] not realize that their failure to effectively engage China is hurting Canadian industries, like agriculture, and that their failure to promote Canada's clean energy is killing Canada's capacity to grow in the future?

Hon. Peter Kent (Minister of State of Foreign Affairs (Americas)):

Between 2006 and 2008 Canada's exports to China grew by over 33%. We have announced the Asia-Pacific Gateway and the corridor initiative infrastructure projects worth almost $2.5 billion, including federal contributions of over $900 million to ensure that new doors to China are opened.

(*House of Commons Debates, 19 November 2009, p. 6973*)
(*Débats de la Chambre des communes, le 19 novembre 2009, p. 6973*)

(b) Cuba

Mr. Phil McColeman (Brant):

What kind of ties [does] Canada [have] with Cuba?

Hon. Stockwell Day (Minister of International Trade and Minister for the Asia-Pacific Gateway):

In a recent meeting that I had with my counterpart from Cuba, we reflected on the fact that last year Canadians exported almost three-quarters of a billion dollars worth of goods to Cuba. Two-way trade was $1.6 billion, that is a 36% increase over 2007. Last year, 820,000 Canadians visited Cuba. It is our fifth most popular destination. We have had diplomatic relations with Cuba since 1945. That is 64 years.

(*House of Commons Debates, 14 May 2009, p. 3525*)
(*Débats de la Chambre des communes, le 14 mai 2009, p. 3525*)

(c) G-20 / G20

L'hon. John McCallum (Markham — Unionville):

Il y a 10 ans, Paul Martin, le père du G20, a milité pour la création d'un système de surveillance internationale des banques. C'est ce dont le G20 discute cette semaine. Or, avant que George Bush ne convoque le G20, ce premier ministre n'avait pas de temps pour ce groupe, disant que le G20 avait pour but "de tenir en échec les États-Unis." Le premier ministre admet-il que dès le début, il avait tort et que Paul Martin avait raison?

Mr. Ted Menzies (Parliamentary Secretary to the Minister of Finance):

Our Prime Minister and our finance minister are participating in the G20 meetings. We have other ministers at G8 meetings simultaneously ... In fact, we co-chair with India the most important committee in the G20. We are leading all around the world.

(*House of Commons Debates, 1 April 2009, p. 2259*)
(*Débats de la Chambre des communes, le 1er avril 2009, p. 2259*)

(d) Honduras

Mr. Ed Holder (London West):

During the serious crisis in Honduras ... how Canada is working to assist in resolving this crisis?

Hon. Lawrence Cannon (Minister of Foreign Affairs):

At the outset of this crisis, the Minister of State of Foreign Affairs for the Americas has taken a lead role in discussions through the OAS, the Organization of American States, to initiate a national dialogue between the parties. The government supports the plan put forward by Costa Rican President Arias as a means to come to a peaceful and negotiated settlement. The minister is currently, as a key member, participating in a mission to bring long-lasting peace to Honduras and to bring back a legitimate democracy.

(House of Commons Debates, 7 October 2009, pp. 5683–84)
(Débats de la Chambre des communes, le 7 octobre 2009, pp. 5683–84)

(e) India / Inde

Mr. Kevin Sorenson (Crowfoot):

[What is] Canada's position on ... the disputed Kashmir region?

Hon. Lawrence Cannon (Minister of Foreign Affairs):

Canada has not deviated from its approach that supports efforts by both India and Pakistan to resolve Kashmir and other issues through the composite dialogue process. We want to see the Kashmir issue resolved through peaceful means. I was able today to reiterate that to the High Commissioner of India to Canada.

(House of Commons Debates, 24 March 2009, p. 1877)
(Débats de la Chambre des communes, le 24 mars 2009, p. 1877)

(f) Iran

Mr. John Weston (West Vancouver — Sunshine Coast — Sea to Sky Country):

[W]hat [is] the government's position on Iran's presidential election?

Hon. Lawrence Cannon (Minister of Foreign Affairs):

We are extremely troubled by the current situation in Iran. We have called for a full and transparent investigation into electoral fraud and discrepancies. The security force's brutal treatment of peaceful demonstrators is unacceptable. We are also investigating allegations of mistreatment of a *Globe and Mail* reporter. I have directed my officials to call in Iran's top diplomat here in Ottawa so that we can have an explanation.

(*House of Commons Debates, 15 June 2009, p. 4603*)
(*Débats de la Chambre des communes, le 15 juin 2009, p. 4603*)

(g) Mexico / Mexique

Mme Ève-Mary Thaï Thi Lac (Saint-Hyacinthe — Bagot):

Des organismes canadiens et mexicains de défense des droits désapprouvent l'arrivée du nouvel ambassadeur mexicain au Canada qui a affiché une désinvolture et une indifférence inqualifiables devant les meurtres et les viols de plusieurs femmes, alors qu'il était gouverneur de l'État mexicain de Chihuahua. Comment le ministre des Affaires étrangères a-t-il pu reconnaître les lettres de créance de Barrio Terrazas, alors qu'il arrive au Canada avec un passé qui le rend indigne d'occuper ce poste?

Hon. Peter Kent (Minister of State of Foreign Affairs (Americas)):

Mr. Barrio Terrazas' nomination by President Calderón and his confirmation by the Mexican Congress was accepted by Canada. The Prime Minister has built a strong relationship with President Calderón over the years. President Calderón is championing deep reforms of the judicial sector and human rights institutions in his country.

(*House of Commons Debates, 5 March 2009, p. 1358*)
(*Débats de la Chambre des communes, le 5 mars 2009, p. 1358*)

(h) Russia / Russie

Mr. Rick Norlock (Northumberland — Quinte West):

Today we learned that Russian aircraft attempted to fly over Canadian airspace on the eve of President Obama's visit. [W]hat is Canada doing to ensure our sovereignty is protected?

Mr. Laurie Hawn (Parliamentary Secretary to the Minister of National Defence):

Canada will continue to defend its sovereignty on land, on the sea and in the air. The Russians never entered Canadian airspace. Our fighter pilots met them and turned them around. As a proud partner in Norad, we have stood up to Russians and others in the defence of North America with our allies, the United States, for over 50 years.

(*House of Commons Debates, 27 February 2009, p. 1096*)
(*Débats de la Chambre des communes, le 27 février 2009, p. 1096*)

(i) Ukraine

Mr. Borys Wrzesnewskyj (Etobicoke Centre):

When will the minister increase [immigration file] staffing in Kyiv?

Hon. Jason Kenney (Minister of Citizenship, Immigration and Multiculturalism):

With respect to immigration, we have a large and robust immigration program in Ukraine. I visited Kyiv in November and I am pleased to say that we are seeing a significant number of immigrants from Ukraine choosing to come to Canada, and a growing number through the provincial nominee program. In fact, when I was there, I saw over 20 employers from Saskatchewan working with our officials to identify Ukrainian workers to come and help build Canada, and we are proud of that.

(*House of Commons Debates, 4 March 2009, p. 1281*)
(*Débats de la Chambre des communes, le 4 mars 2009, p. 1281*)

Hon. Ralph Goodale (Wascana):

More Canadian observers are needed to help monitor the presidential election in Ukraine in January. The leading expert on this issue, Mr. Davidovich, says Canada should match what we did so well in 2004. In that election, beyond the Organization for Security and Co-operation in Europe, Canada sent 500 additional observers. Now they are needed again ... Why has the government slashed Canada's support by nearly 90%?

Mr. Deepak Obhrai (Parliamentary Secretary to the Minister of Foreign Affairs):

The Government of Canada is supporting free and fair elections in Ukraine by deploying Canadian election observers through the Organization for Security and Co-operation in Europe. Because of our strong commitment to Ukraine, Canada will be sending the maximum number of observers requested by the OSCE. The OSCE has a respected track record and has observed elections in Ukraine since 1998. Supporting the OSCE mission improves voter coordination and ensures effectiveness.

(*House of Commons Debates, 4 December 2009, pp. 7623–24*)
(*Débats de la Chambre des communes, le 4 décembre 2009, pp. 7623–24*)

(j) United States / États-Unis

Mr. Ron Cannan (Kelowna — Lake Country):

[What are] recent developments regarding the planned visit of President Obama to Canada?

Le très hon. Stephen Harper (premier ministre):

Je suis ravi d'informer la Chambre que le président Obama visitera Ottawa le jeudi 19 février. This will be ... his first foreign visit as President of the United States. This is a testament not just to the size of our trading relationship and the closeness of our alliance, but also to the strength of our friendship. I look forward to an important and productive working visit.

(*House of Commons Debates, January 28, 2009, p. 47*)
(*Débats de la Chambre des communes, le 28 janvier 2009, p. 47*)

Mr. Michael Ignatieff (Leader of the Opposition):

The tourist industry, the auto sector and communities next door to the American border have all suffered from the U.S. tightening of the border. What specific measures will the Prime Minister propose to the president to loosen that chain?

Right Hon. Stephen Harper (Prime Minister):

We always indicate to our American friends that this government views the United States as our closest ally and partner, that we share not only a vibrant commercial relationship with it but also its security concerns, and that we are always willing to work as a partner.

(*House of Commons Debates, 12 February 2009, p. 747*)
(*Débats de la Chambre des communes, le 12 février 2009, p. 747*)

3   Health / Santé[15]

M. Michael Ignatieff (chef de l'opposition):

Quelles mesures le gouvernement propose-t-il face à [la grippe porcine]?

Hon. Leona Aglukkaq (Minister of Health):

Canada is well positioned to deal with this issue. We have a national plan for disease outbreaks and we are following it. I am having regular discussions with our international partners, including Margaret Chan, who is the

---

[15] See also the section on agriculture in the Trade and Economy section later in this chapter.

director-general of the World Health Organization; the U.S. Secretary of Health, Charles Johnson; and Jose Cordova, the Mexican health minister. I have also spoken with my provincial and territorial colleagues over the weekend, our counterparts across Canada, and provided them with updates on the situation. Our departments are working very closely together ... [W]e are engaged with the Departments of Foreign Affairs, Public Safety, Citizenship and Immigration, and Transport to ensure a coordinated response on this. In Canada, we have issued a notice to all travellers. That notice is for individuals travelling to Mexico, and from Mexico to Canada, to be aware of the situation, to be aware of the symptoms, to wash their hands continuously and to cover their mouth when they cough. That is what is in place at the moment. We are working together to address the situation and are monitoring the situation very closely with our international partners.

M. Michael Ignatieff:

Le secteur agricole au Canada, mais surtout au Québec, dépend chaque année de la contribution de milliers de travailleurs saisonniers d'origine mexicaine. Qu'est-ce que le gouvernement entend faire pour s'assurer que ces travailleurs puissent continuer à contribuer à l'agriculture canadienne, sans poser aucun risque?

L'hon. Jason Kenney (ministre de la Citoyenneté, de l'Immigration et du Multiculturalisme):

Nous avons pris des mesures supplémentaires pour nous assurer de la santé des Canadiens en ce qui concerne les travailleurs et les visiteurs du Mexique. En réponse à la situation, tous les travailleurs étrangers et temporaires du Mexique sont désormais tenus de se soumettre à un examen de santé avant le départ. Cela comprend un questionnaire, un examen physique et la mesure de la fièvre par deux médecins. Cet examen sera effectué avant le départ.

(*House of Commons Debates, 27 April 2009, pp. 2740–41*)
(*Débats de la Chambre des communes, le 27 avril 2009, pp. 2740–41*)

L'hon. Bob Rae (Toronto-Centre):

[U]ne question pour le ministre des Affaires étrangères au sujet des 25 Canadiens gardés en quarantaine en Chine. Il semble qu'il n'y ait pas de justification de santé publique pour cette décision de la part du gouvernement chinois. Que fera le ministre pour ces Canadiens à ce moment-ci?

L'hon. Lawrence Cannon (ministre des Affaires étrangères):

J'ai demandé aux autorités et à nos forces consulaires en Chine de se dé-
placer et de rencontrer ces gens afin de s'assurer, d'abord, que tous les
services sont donnés, mais aussi que tout est conforme sur le plan de la
santé. Je leur ai ensuite demandé de faire les démarches nécessaires auprès
des autorités chinoises de façon à clarifier la situation.

(*House of Commons Debates, 4 May 2009, p. 2999*)
(*Débats de la Chambre des communes, le 4 mai 2009, p. 2999*)

Hon. Ralph Goodale (Wascana):

Could the government explain the logic of any plan that ... puts Canada
behind the rest of the world in protecting citizens against H1N1?

Right Hon. Stephen Harper (Prime Minister):

The government bases its flu planning on the best advice of medical experts, including the chief medical officer. The immediate priority is sea-
sonal flu vaccination. Canada will ensure that there is enough vaccine for
every member of our population. That vaccine will be widely available the
first week of November, as the government has said all along.

(*House of Commons Debates, October 8, 2009, p. 5751*)
(*Débats de la Chambre des communes, le 8 octobre 2009, p. 5751*)

4   Human Rights / Droits de la personne

(a) China and Tibet / Chine et le Tibet

Mr. Gerard Kennedy (Parkdale — High Park):

Dhondup Wangchen, a Tibetan filmmaker, has been imprisoned since
March for making a documentary about the treatment of Tibetans and
their views. Mr. Wangchen has contracted hepatitis B during his incar-
ceration and there is a question as to whether he is receiving any medical
treatment for his condition. Thirty prominent Canadian filmmakers have
signed a statement calling for his immediate release in recognition of the
right to free speech. During his current trip to China, will the Prime Minister specifically raise this issue with the Chinese government and call for
Mr. Wangchen's release?

Hon. Jason Kenney (Minister of Citizenship, Immigration and
Multiculturalism):

The Prime Minister was proud to meet here in his own office with His
Holiness the Dalai Lama during his visit to Canada. This government was

proud to sponsor the motion to recognize the Dalai Lama as an honorary Canadian citizen. We condemned the abuse of state and police power against protests in the Tibetan region last year. We called for negotiations between China and the representatives of the Dalai Lama. I know the Prime Minister did raise issues related to human rights in China today. Our government will continue to do so proudly.

(*House of Commons Debates, December 3, 2009, pp. 7574–75*)
(*Débats de la Chambre des communes, le 3 décembre 2009, pp. 7574–75*)

(b) Durban Conference on Racism / Conférence de Durban sur le racisme

Mr. Scott Reid (Lanark — Frontenac — Lennox and Addington):

In January 2008, the Minister of Immigration announced that Canada would be the first country in the world to withdraw from the Durban review process. Since then, much of the world has followed Canada's lead, including Italy, Australia, New Zealand, the Obama administration in the United States and Israel ... Will the Minister of Immigration describe the government's policy on the Durban process?

Hon. Jason Kenney (Minister of Citizenship, Immigration and Multiculturalism):

Canada was the first country in the world to withdraw from the Durban process. We did so last January because of our concerns that it would be a repeat of the fiasco of Durban I. Yesterday's speech by Mahmoud Ahmadinejad and his odious remarks vindicate our decision, which has been followed by a number of other countries. He made those remarks on the eve of Holocaust commemoration day. Bizarrely, a UN spokesman actually said that at least he did not deliver all of his lines about Holocaust denial. Canada was right to lead the world in removing itself from this incredibly inappropriate process that is promoting and not combating racism. We are leading the world and not following.

House of Commons Debates, 21 April 2009, p. 2518)
(*Débats de la Chambre des communes, le 21 avril 2009, p. 2518*)

(c) Housing / Logement

Ms. Libby Davies (Vancouver East):

A report to be tabled at the UN Monday ... spells out that Canada urgently needs a comprehensive and coordinated national policy [on housing].

Will the minister implement the recommendations in the UN report and commit to a national housing strategy?

Mr. Ed Komarnicki (Parliamentary Secretary to the Minister of Human Resources and Skills Development and to the Minister of Labour):

We have committed a number of dollars with respect to housing: $1 billion to support much-needed repairs to social housing, $600 million for new housing and repairs to existing housing on reserve, $400 million for on reserve, $200 million for the North, $400 million to build more seniors housing, and $75 million for new housing for people with disabilities. We are addressing that issue in a significant and substantial way ... With respect to homelessness, we have committed $1.9 billion over the next five years to improve and build new affordable housing and to help the homeless.

(House of Commons Debates, 6 March 2009, p. 1406)
(Débats de la Chambre des communes, le 6 mars 2009, p. 1406)

(d) Immigration

Mrs. Nina Grewal (Fleetwood — Port Kells):

Many newcomers to our great country continue to have difficulty finding the job that best suits their education and qualifications because their credentials are not fully recognized here in Canada. Our Conservative government is committed to working with the provinces to make the recognition of foreign credentials a priority ... [H]ow [does] budget 2009 build on this commitment?

Hon. Jason Kenney (Minister of Citizenship, Immigration and Multiculturalism):

This is a very important issue for new Canadians and our entire economy. That is why our government created the foreign credentials referral office and the Canadian immigration integration project overseas which, for the first time ever, is providing a head start for newcomers in the process of credential recognition before they even arrive in Canada. It is why the Prime Minister met his platform commitment to raise this issue with the first ministers, recently developing a national action plan for credential recognition. It is also why we introduced $50 million in additional investments to accelerate credential recognition, working with the provinces and the professional agencies. We are delivering for new Canadians.

(House of Commons Debates, 30 January 2009, p. 169)
(Débats de la Chambre des communes, le 30 janvier 2009, p. 169)

Hon. Maurizio Bevilacqua (Vaughan):

Yesterday in committee the Minister of Citizenship, Immigration and Multiculturalism claimed that Canada would stand alone in maintaining its current immigration levels, but moments later he told reporters that might change ... What is the real story?

Hon. Jason Kenney (Minister of Citizenship, Immigration and Multiculturalism):

What there is is a remarkable record of bringing new Canadians to this country and successfully integrating them. Last year we welcomed the largest number of newcomers ever to our shores: half a million newcomers and 250,000 permanent residents. We have announced for 2009 a planning level of 245,000 to 260,000, the only developed country in the world to be maintaining immigration levels. We intend to keep that and we are proud of our record.

(*House of Commons Debates, 11 February 2009, p. 674*)
(*Débats de la Chambre des communes, le 11 février 2009, p. 674*)

(e) Iran

Hon. Irwin Cotler (Mount Royal): What action will the government take to protect [the] persecuted Baha'i minority and the persecuted prisoners in Iran?

Hon. Lawrence Cannon (Minister of Foreign Affairs):

The Government of Canada has been extremely active in terms of human rights in Iran. One can refer back to the condemnation. Canada led a multinational initiative at the United Nations where we condemned Iran for its human rights behaviour. [W]e will continue exactly in that direction.

(*House of Commons Debates, 13 February 2009, p. 806*)
(*Débats de la Chambre des communes, le 13 février 2009, p. 806*)

Hon. Irwin Cotler (Mount Royal):

Will Canada seek sanctions in support of our United Nations resolution, including sanctioning the Iranian revolutionary guards? Will Canada, as a state party to the genocide convention, implement our legal obligations to combat state-sanctioned incitement to genocide? Will Canada support the Interpol arrest warrant against Iran's defence minister for the 1994 terrorist bombing in Argentina?

Hon. Lawrence Cannon (Minister of Foreign Affairs):

Canada is leading the way in the world to make clear that we stand up at the United Nations, that we table and co-sponsor a resolution against Iran's outrageous handling of human rights.

(*House of Commons Debates, 28 October 2009, p. 6282*)
(*Débats de la Chambre des communes, le 28 octobre 2009, p. 6282*)

(f) Israel / Israël

Mr. David Tilson (Dufferin — Caledon):

Ontario's largest public sector union recently passed a motion calling for a boycott of all Israeli academics. The Canadian Union of Public Employees' deliberate targeting of the Jewish people is not new. In fact, CUPE's president, Sid Ryan, recently compared the Israeli government with the Nazis. [What is] the government's reaction to the motion by CUPE?

Hon. Jason Kenney (Minister of Citizenship, Immigration and Multiculturalism):

All Canadians should be concerned about the growing wave on Canadian campuses by organizations such as CUPE that are singling out and targeting the Jewish democratic state of Israel for opprobrium in the most vile language possible. Last week Jewish students at the Hillel Club at one of our universities faced an angry mob shouting anti-Jewish slogans. The resolution passed by CUPE is in the same spirit. All these people are rejecting the right alone of the Jewish people to a homeland. On behalf of all Canadians, we denounce this kind of intolerance and extremism that is totally unacceptable.

(*House of Commons Debates, 23 February 2009, p. 850*)
(*Débats de la Chambre des communes, le 23 février 2009, p. 850*)

Mr. Paul Calandra (Oak Ridges — Markham):

Jewish students across the country are under siege as anti-Semites unveil their plans for Israel Apartheid Week ... W]hy [does] the government believe that Israel Apartheid Week is anti-Semitic?

Hon. Jason Kenney (Minister of Citizenship, Immigration and Multiculturalism):

Canadians are free to express different views about the policies of foreign government but Israel Apartheid Week is not about that. It is about a systematic effort to delegitimize the democratic homeland of the Jewish people, a country born out of the Holocaust. We find very troubling this resurgence of the old slander that Zionism is racism. That is the notion that lies at the heart of Israel Apartheid Week. Jewish students at campuses across the country are subsequently feeling increasingly vulnerable. We condemn these efforts to single out and attack the Jewish people and their homeland in this terrible way.

(*House of Commons Debates, 3 March 2009, p. 1227*)
(*Débats de la Chambre des communes, le 3 mars 2009, p. 1227*)

Mr. James Lunney (Nanaimo — Alberni):

This week the UN Human Rights Council released its latest anti-Israel missive ... The report accuses Israel of war crimes in the recent Gaza conflict ... W]hat [is] the government's response to this report?

Hon. Peter Kent (Minister of State of Foreign Affairs (Americas)):

The so-called fact-finding commission was the creation of one of the United Nations' most flawed bodies, the Human Rights Council, which includes some of the UN's least democratic states. In commissioning this study, the Human Rights Council pre-emptively assumed Israel's culpability. This government has never equated Israel, a democratic state, with terrorist groups that seek to destroy both it and its people.

(*House of Commons Debates, 17 September 2009, p. 5146*)
(*Débats de la Chambre des communes, le 17 septembre 2009, p. 5146*)

Ms. Lois Brown (Newmarket — Aurora):

[What has been] the government's leadership to ensure the security and dignity of the people of Israel in the face of terror and anti-Semitism?

Hon. Peter Kent (Minister of State of Foreign Affairs (Americas)):

Canada was the first country to refuse to attend Durban II, a forum for hate. When Hamas formed the government of the Palestinian Authority, Canada was the first country to suspend aid. When Iran's Ahmadinejad addressed the UN with repugnant anti-Israel and anti-Jewish declarations, Canada was the first to stand and walk out. Our government has been a strong, consistent and unequivocal supporter of Israel, and that will continue.

(*House of Commons Debates, 19 November 2009, p. 6976*)
(*Débats de la Chambre des communes, le 19 novembre 2009, p. 6976*)

(g) Poverty / Pauvreté

L'hon. Jack Layton (Toronto — Danforth):

Le premier ministre rencontrait ce matin le Secrétaire général des Nations Unies. L'ONU multiplie ses rapports qui indiquent un recul au Canada par rapport à la pauvreté, surtout chez les enfants, les femmes et particulièrement les Autochtones ... Quel rapport le premier ministre a fait sur ces problèmes ce matin, à l'ONU?

Hon. Chuck Strahl (Minister of Indian Affairs and Northern Development and Federal Interlocutor for Métis and Non-Status Indians):

[In] our presentation before the United Nations, [w]e dealt candidly and openly with every kind of issue, from aboriginal issues to housing issues and so on. It was a pleasure to talk not only about what we have done, in our case, for aboriginal people, with inclusion under the Canadian Human Rights Act for aboriginals living on reserve, for example, but also to talk about some of the new initiatives. In my ministry, there is $1.4 billion in aboriginal-related funding, because we realize there has been a gap which needs to be addressed ... I can talk specifically about some progress on specific claims settlements in British Columbia ... where last year we settled 31 land claims. We also urge the [House] to help us pass the matrimonial real property rights bill, which would finally give aboriginal women and children the property rights they deserve and which every other Canadian takes for granted.

(House of Commons Debates, 23 February 2009, p. 847)
(Débats de la Chambre des communes, le 23 février 2009, p. 847)

Ms. Jean Crowder (Nanaimo — Cowichan):

On March 11, this House unanimously mandated the government to make poverty reduction a top priority at upcoming G8 and G20 meetings. [However, the government] [has] relegated this issue to a secondary concern at the G8 social summit ... Why is [the government] ignoring the will of the House?

Mr. Deepak Obhrai (Parliamentary Secretary to the Minister of Foreign Affairs):

The Prime Minister will be attending the G20 conference in London next week and he will be working with the world leaders to fight on many issues that the Prime Minister has said are important for everyone. It is important to recognize that this is a collective effort with all G20 countries and those that are coming to London to fight against poverty and stimulate the economy. We are looking forward to some positive results out of that conference.

(House of Commons Debates, 30 March 2009, pp. 2130–31)
(Débats de la Chambre des communes, le 30 mars 2009, pp.2130–31)

(h) Protecting Canadians Abroad / La protection des Canadiens à l'étranger[16]

M. Serge Ménard (Marc-Aurèle-Fortin):

[L]e ministre des Affaires étrangères a déclaré qu'il n'avait nullement l'intention de demander le rapatriement d'Omar Khadr, ce jeune Canadien détenu à Guantanamo …Qui plus est, le jeune est un enfant soldat torturé et maltraité. Alors que l'on sait que le nouveau président des États-Unis a l'intention de fermer Guantanamo, le gouvernement va-t-il enfin demander le rapatriement du jeune Khadr au lieu de nous servir toujours la même cassette?

Mr. Deepak Obhrai (Parliamentary Secretary to the Minister of Foreign Affairs):

[O]ur position remains unchanged. Unlike many prisoners held in Guantanamo Bay, Omar Khadr has actually been charged with serious crimes and is in a judicial legal process to determine his guilt or innocence. We support this process.

(House of Commons Debates, 21 November 2008, p. 115)
(Débats de la Chambre des communes, le 21 novembre 2008, p. 115)

M. Jean Dorion (Longueuil — Pierre-Boucher):

En Thaïlande, la situation est tellement grave que des pays comme la France, l'Australie, la Chine, la Suisse et l'Espagne ont pris les mesures nécessaires pour rapatrier leurs ressortissants. Pendant ce temps, les Québécois et les Canadiens sur place sont toujours sans nouvelles de leur gouvernement. Qu'attend le ministre des Affaires étrangères pour reconnaître qu'il y a urgence d'agir et mettre en place un plan de rapatriement?

---

[16] See also the section on extradition and the death penalty / L'extradition et la peine de mort in the International Criminal Law section later in this chapter.

L'hon. Lawrence Cannon (ministre des Affaires étrangères):

L'ambassade continue de travailler 24 heures par jour pour aider les Canadiens qui sont pris à Bangkok. Nous examinons toutes les options, ce qui inclut de noliser des avions pour aider les Canadiens à se rendre à Hong-Kong à partir de la Thaïlande. J'ai également parlé cet après-midi avec le président d'Air Canada pour solliciter son appui en vue, justement, d'aider les agents consulaires à organiser le déplacement et le retour de ces Canadiens.

(*House of Commons Debates, 1 December 2008, p. 463*)
(*Débats de la Chambre des communes, le 1er décembre 2008, p. 463*)

L'hon. Lawrence Cannon (ministre des Affaires étrangères):

The first planeload of 34 Canadians landed this morning in Hong Kong. The embassy continues to work around the clock to address this. Flights are leaving; people are departing Thailand. The embassy has secured blocks of seats, an additional 70 today and 100 tomorrow, on Bangkok Airways flights to Hong Kong and has contacted all tour groups to make sure that there is available space.

(*House of Commons Debates, 2 December 2008, p. 534*)
(*Débats de la Chambre des communes, le 2 décembre 2008, p. 534*)

Mme Nicole Demers (Laval):

Depuis mars 2005, Natalie Morin et ses trois enfants sont retenus en Arabie Saoudite. Elle désire quitter ce pays avec ses enfants, mais elle ne peut le faire sans l'autorisation de son mari, Saeed Al-Sahrami. Le secrétaire parlementaire du ministre des Affaires étrangères a rendu visite à Mme Natalie Morin le 22 décembre dernier ... Le ministre a-t-il entrepris de nouvelles démarches pour rapatrier Natalie Morin le plus rapidement possible?

Mr. Deepak Obhrai (Parliamentary Secretary to the Minister of Foreign Affairs):

This is a very complex family dispute with no easy solution ... I just visited Saudi Arabia in December and I met with the Saudi authorities and visited Ms. Morin and her family. We are bound, however, by both Saudi law and our own adherence to the 1980 Hague *Convention on the Civil Aspects of International Child Abduction*, under which children cannot leave without the father's permission. With the assistance of Saudi officials, we are working to facilitate an agreement between Ms. Morin and her husband for a positive resolution to the case.

(*House of Commons Debates, 30 January 2009, p. 167*)
(*Débats de la Chambre des communes, le 30 janvier 2009, p. 167*)

Mr. Paul Dewar (Ottawa Centre):

Canadian citizen Bashir Makhtal continues to face harsh prison conditions in Ethiopia, unclear charges, and lack of access to legal representation ... [Is it] time for Canada to request Ethiopia to drop all charges and to bring Mr. Makhtal home now[?]

Mr. Deepak Obhrai (Parliamentary Secretary to the Minister of Foreign Affairs):

Mr. Makhtal's trial has already started and he has received access to legal counsel. We have received assurances that Mr. Makhtal will be granted due process under Ethiopian law. Canada has repeatedly made its concerns regarding Mr. Makhtal's case clear to the Government of Ethiopia. I myself have made two visits to Ethiopia to make representation on this file.

(*House of Commons Debates, 27 February 2009, p. 1096*)
(*Débats de la Chambre des communes, le 27 février 2009, p. 1096*)

Mr. Paul Dewar (Ottawa Centre):

Could the government confirm if rendition of a Canadian citizen to Sudan is consistent with Canadian law?

Mr. Deepak Obhrai (Parliamentary Secretary to the Minister of Foreign Affairs):

We continue to provide Mr. Abdelrazik with counsel assistance. However, Mr. Abdelrazik is on the UN [Security Council 1267] international no-fly list ... and is, therefore, subject to a travel ban and assets freeze. [T]his matter is currently under litigation.

(*House of Commons Debates, 6 March 2009, p.1412; 27 March 2009, p. 2074*)
(*Débats de la Chambre des communes, le 6 mars 2009, p.1412; le 27 mars 2009, p. 2074*)

Hon. Ujjal Dosanjh (Vancouver South):

Pavel Kulisek has spent 13 months in a Mexican prison. He was publicly declared a criminal before the sole witness against him even made a statement ... When will the government [act]?

Hon. Peter Kent (Minister of State of Foreign Affairs (Americas)):

Our ambassador and ... the ambassador of Mexico [have] assured that the Canadian now held in prison is receiving due process of law, and the case is proceeding. The case has been slowed because of the lawyer involved who has been appealing at every corner and delaying the process.

(*House of Commons Debates, 28 April 2009, p. 2823*)
(*Débats de la Chambre des communes, le 28 avril 2009, p. 2823*)

Hon. Jack Layton (Toronto — Danforth):

Nobel Prize winner, democracy activist and Canadian citizen Aung San Suu Kyi is facing five years in prison after an American swam to her house, violating her house arrest conditions ... [W]hat representations, if any, has [the government] made to the Burmese junta to insist upon her immediate release?

Hon. Peter Kent (Minister of State of Foreign Affairs (Americas)):

Our government is alarmed by the new charges laid against Nobel Laureate Aung San Suu Kyi. We have called for her immediate release, along with all political prisoners in Burma. We strongly urge the Burmese authorities to provide appropriate medical care for Aung San Suu Kyi and for all inmates held unjustly in Burma's prisons.

(*House of Commons Debates, 14 May 2009, p. 3522*)
(*Débats de la Chambre des communes, le 14 mai 2009, p. 3522*)

Mr. Wayne Marston (Hamilton East — Stoney Creek):

Canadian citizen Huseyin Celil has been imprisoned in China on trumped up charges since 2006 ... Will the Prime Minister ... ask for the release of Mr. Celil?

Mr. Deepak Obhrai (Parliamentary Secretary to the Minister of Foreign Affairs):

Mr. Celil's case remains a top priority for this government. We are deeply concerned at China's refusal to recognize his Canadian citizenship and permit Canadian consular access to visit him. We continue to raise Mr. Celil's case with senior Chinese officials, in particular the issues of respect for human rights, consular access and due process. We will continue to be in contact with Mr. Celil's family and provide them with all consular access.

(*House of Commons Debates, 26 November 2009, p. 7274*)
(*Débats de la Chambre des communes, le 26 novembre 2009, p. 7274*)

(i) Rights of Disabled / Droits des personnes handicapées

Ms. Judy Wasylycia-Leis (Winnipeg North):

Today marks the second anniversary of the signing of the UN *Convention on the Rights of Persons with Disabilities,* yet the government refuses to ratify this convention despite the support of Canadians and a unanimous motion passed by the House ... Will the government support people with disabilities and ratify the convention now?

Mr. Deepak Obhrai (Parliamentary Secretary to the Minister of Foreign Affairs):

This government stands for human rights. This is one of its key foreign affairs policies ... We are working with the provinces to address [this] issue.

(*House of Commons Debates, 30 March 2009, pp. 2129–30*)
(*Débats de la Chambre des communes, le 30 mars 2009, pp. 2129–30*)

(j) Rights of Women / Droits des femmes

(*i*) *Afghanistan / L'Afghanistan*

Ms. Dawn Black (New Westminster — Coquitlam):

There is disturbing news from Afghanistan today that laws passed by the Karzai government will make women even more vulnerable. Afghan women's groups and the UN say these new laws restrict a woman's right to leave her home, permit child marriage and, most disturbingly, legalize rape ... Will the government ... let President Karzai know that this is totally unacceptable?

Hon. Stockwell Day (Minister of International Trade and Minister for the Asia-Pacific Gateway):

If these reports are true, this will create serious problems for Canada. The onus is on the government of Afghanistan to live up to its responsibilities for human rights, absolutely including rights of women. If there is any wavering on this point from the government of Afghanistan, this will create serious problems and be a serious disappointment for us.

(*House of Commons Debates, 31 March 2009, p. 2220*)
(*Débats de la Chambre des communes, le 31 mars 2009, p. 2220*)

(ii) Violence against Women / Violence à l'égard des femmes

Mr. Todd Russell (Labrador):

Canada's record on dealing with violence against women has been harshly criticized by the United Nations. Shockingly, a recent UN report cites the tragic cases of more than 500 missing or murdered first nations, Métis and Inuit women. Wh[at] [is] the [government] doing ... about this disgraceful and shameful stain on our national and international reputation?

Hon. Helena Guergis (Minister of State (Status of Women)):

Ending violence against women is a priority for the government. We have worked very closely with the Sisters in Spirit program, which is a program that is funded by Status of Women Canada, and we have worked closely with the aboriginal community to identify violence against women issues. In fact, the number of women who have now been identified is as a result of the good work of the Sisters in Spirit program. I note that in budget 2008 we announced the development of an action plan and it will include further work on violence against women, especially in the aboriginal communities.

(*House of Commons Debates, 25 November 2008, p. 249*)
(*Débats de la Chambre des communes, le 25 novembre 2008, p. 249*)

Mme Alexandra Mendes (Brossard — La Prairie):

Aujourd'hui est la Journée internationale pour l'élimination de la violence à l'égard des femmes, et nous soulignons le début d'une campagne visant à mettre un terme à la violence basée sur le sexe. L'ONU a demandé au Canada de prendre plus de mesures pour stopper la violence faite aux femmes et a critiqué les coupes sombres qui ont touché le Programme de contestation judiciaire. Quand le[] [gouvernement] réaliser[a-t]-il[] que pour mettre fin à la violence faite aux femmes, ils devront prendre au sérieux la question de l'égalité des femmes?

Hon. Helena Guergis (Minister of State (Status of Women)):

Canada just signed on to the UNIFEM campaign to say no to violence against women ... [O]ur action plan . . . [will] not only ... talk about economic security for women, but there will be a huge component on violence against women and on women in more leadership roles across Canada.

(*House of Commons Debates, 25 November 2008, p. 250*)
(*Débats de la Chambre des communes, le 25 novembre 2008, p. 250*)

(k) Self-Determination / Autodétermination

M. Steven Blaney (Lévis — Bellechasse):

[Quelles sont les] des gestes concrets que notre gouvernement conserva-teur a posés pour le Québec et pour le Canada, afin qu'on ait un Québec fort dans un Canada uni [?]

L'hon. Josée Verner (ministre des Affaires intergouvernementales, présidente du Conseil privé de la Reine pour le Canada et ministre de la Francophonie):

Tout d'abord, ... notre gouvernement est décentralisateur et respecte les provinces et le Québec. Nous avons augmenté considérablement les transferts au Québec depuis 2006 et nous avons reconnu la nation qué-bécoise ... Le Québec est d'ailleurs bien représenté ici, à la Chambre des communes ... Nous croyons qu'un Québec doit être fort à l'intérieur du Canada.

(*House of Commons Debates, 23 March 2009, p. 1798*)
(*Débats de la Chambre des communes, le 23 mars 2009, p. 1798*)

(l) Sustainable development / Développement durable[17]

(i) Labour rights / Droits des travailleurs

Mme Josée Beaudin (Saint-Lambert):

L'OCDE dit que le Canada n'en fait pas assez. Selon l'organisme, le chô-mage augmentera de façon dramatique entre 2010 et 2011. En consé-quence, le filet social doit être amélioré et renforcé. Le gouvernement ne pense-t-il pas que l'élimination du délai de carence pourrait être un bon moyen pour venir en aide aux chômeurs, mais aussi pour relancer l'éco-nomie?

L'hon. Jean-Pierre Blackburn (ministre du Revenu national et ministre d'État (Agriculture)):

Nous investirons 12 milliards de dollars dans le programme Chantiers Canada afin de créer un vaste chantier de travail au Canada et au Québec. De plus, on permet aux gens qui veulent rénover leur maison d'avoir un crédit d'impôt de 1 350 $. Cela permettra aux entreprises qui fabriquent les produits d'avoir des occasions d'emploi à offrir à leurs travailleurs,

---

[17] See also the section on trade and human rights / Le commerce et les droits de la personne in the Trade and Economy section later in this chapter.

ainsi que de stimuler l'activité économique dans leur entreprise. Il s'agit de deux mesures que l'on instaure pour soutenir l'activité économique au Canada.

(*House of Commons Debates, 31 March 2009, p. 2217*)
(*Débats de la Chambre des communes, le 31 mars 2009, p. 2217*)

(ii) Uganda

Mr. Bill Siksay (Burnaby — Douglas):

Uganda's anti-homosexuality bill is reprehensible ... It violates human rights by imposing life in prison on gays and lesbians and a death sentence for those who are gay and have AIDS. At the Commonwealth meeting, will the Prime Minister meet face to face with Uganda's prime minister to help stop this bill, and will he make gay, lesbian and trans rights essential to development and educational work supported by Canadian foreign aid in Uganda and elsewhere?

Hon. John Baird (Minister of Transport, Infrastructure and Communities):

The current legislation before Uganda's parliament is vile, abhorrent, offensive and it offends Canadian values and decency. We strongly condemn that and the Prime Minister will make that strong condemnation as well.

(*House of Commons Debates, 26 November 2009, p. 7274*)
(*Débats de la Chambre des communes, le 26 novembre 2009, p. 7274*)

(iii) Ukraine

Mr. Leon Benoit (Vegreville — Wainwright):

Our ... government recently co-sponsored a motion at UNESCO to honour the millions who were murdered during the Ukrainian famine genocide, the Holodomor. Our government also supported Bill C-459 ... which established the Ukrainian Famine and Genocide Memorial Day ... [W]hat [has] the government done to commemorate this historic crime against humanity[?]

Hon. Jason Kenney (Minister of Citizenship, Immigration and Multiculturalism):

I was honoured, together with Senator Andreychuk of the other place, to represent Canada at the 75th anniversary commemorations of Holodomor in Kiev this past weekend to extend to President Yushchenko and the

Ukrainian people the solidarity of Canadians who recall that terrible crime against humanity which occurred under the Communist dictatorship of Joseph Stalin in 1932–33 that left millions of Ukrainians and others the victims of that totalitarian regime. This Parliament led the way as the first and only G8 country to recognize its genocidal nature.

(*House of Commons Debates, 25 November 2008, p. 250*)
(*Débats de la Chambre des communes, le 25 novembre 2008, p. 250*)

5   *International Criminal Law / Le droit pénal international*

(a) Extradition and death penalty / L'extradition et la peine de mort[18]

Hon. Dan McTeague (Pickering — Scarborough East):

Despite the concerns raised by several senior courts, including the Saudi King's own supreme council, that the case of Mohamed Kohail must be seen as a matter of self defence and not murder, a lower court has once again reaffirmed its sentence of death on Mr. Kohail, which may also imperil the life of his brother Sultan. The Prime Minister is with the King of Saudi Arabia in London today. Will he finally act directly and raise this serious miscarriage of justice with King Abdullah?

Mr. Deepak Obhrai (Parliamentary Secretary to the Minister of Foreign Affairs):

We are deeply disappointed at the reports that a Saudi court has upheld its decision to sentence Mohamed Kohail to death. The Minister of Foreign Affairs has requested an official review of the Saudi court decision when it is issued. Canada continues to express its concern for a fair and transparent review of the wording and the sentence. Since 2007, we have remained in regular contact with the Kohail family, including their lawyer.

(*House of Commons Debates, 2 April 2009, p. 2336*)
(*Débats de la Chambre des communes, le 2 avril 2009, p. 2336*)

Mme Ève-Mary Thaï Thi Lac (Saint-Hyacinthe — Bagot):

A l'initiative du Danemark et des Pays-Bas, l'ONU demande au Canada de mettre fin à sa politique qui consiste à ne plus solliciter la clémence des Canadiens condamnés à la peine de mort à l'étranger. Le ministre des

---

[18] See also the section on protecting Canadians abroad in the Human Rights section later in this chapter.

Affaires étrangères entend-il donner suite aux recommandations de l'ONU et ainsi décider de ne pas abandonner ... Ronald Smith, un Canadien qui attend son exécution depuis plus de 25 ans au Montana?

L'hon. Lawrence Cannon (ministre des Affaires étrangères):

Dans le cas de M. Smith ... le gouvernement sera assujetti à la décision des tribunaux, mais dans tous les autres cas ... la clémence n'est pas une obligation. La clémence doit nécessairement se mériter. Dans chaque cas, nous étudierons les demandes de clémence.

(*House of Commons Debates, 15 June 2009, p. 4603*)
(*Débats de la Chambre des communes, le 15 juin 2009, p. 4603*)

Mme Francine Lalonde (La Pointe-de-l'Île, PQ):

Le ministre des Affaires étrangères a confirmé cette semaine que pour son parti, la peine de mort est acceptable. Toutefois le ministre a dit vouloir l'accepter au cas par cas. Mis à mort par injection aux États-Unis, fusillé en Chine ou décapité en Arabie saoudite, quelle est la différence?

L'hon. Lawrence Cannon (ministre des Affaires étrangères):

Une personne jugée dans une démocratie qui souscrit à la primauté du droit ne doit pas s'attendre à ce que le gouvernement canadien intercède nécessairement en sa faveur, en particulier lorsqu'elle s'est rendue coupable de crimes graves ou violents. Les mesures fortes prises par le gouvernement pour combattre le crime violent au Canada se fondent, elles aussi, sur ces valeurs canadiennes: le respect de la liberté, la démocratie, les droits de la personne.

(*House of Commons Debates, 19 June 2009, pp. 4853–54*)
(*Débats de la Chambre des communes, le 19 juin 2009, pp. 4853–54*)

(b) Smuggling / Contrebande

Hon. Carolyn Bennett (St. Paul's):

This week, the 52nd session of the committee on narcotic drugs convenes in Vienna. Will the minister reassure this House that Canada will not be embarrassed, and bring back a drug policy that is evidence based and in step with our international partners who support the four pillars of prevention, treatment, enforcement and harm reduction?

Hon. Rob Nicholson (Minister of Justice and Attorney General of Canada):

Our approach is a complete, comprehensive approach. I would refer ... to the national anti-drug strategy and all the different initiatives this government has taken to assist individuals who have become addicted. At the same time, we are sending out a very clear message to those individuals who think it is a good idea to get into the grow-op business or who want to get into the import or export of illegal drugs into this country. The message is that they will go to jail.

(*House of Commons Debates, 12 March 2009, p. 1681*)
(*Débats de la Chambre des communes, le 12 mars 2009, p. 1681*)

Ms. Yasmin Ratansi (Don Valley East):

Criminal gangs are raking in huge profits in the illegal trade of tobacco products which flow freely across the Canada-U.S. border ... While the RCMP is trying to stop this criminal activity, the CRA is giving licences to operators linked to organized crime. Will the Minister of Public Safety talk to the Minister of National Revenue and stop this farce?

L'hon. Jean-Pierre Blackburn (ministre du Revenu national et ministre d'État (Agriculture)):

Lorsqu'un promoteur nous demande une licence afin de produire du tabac, un processus très rigoureux est mis en place. D'abord, nous vérifions auprès de la GRC si ladite personne a des antécédents judiciaires au criminel. Si tel est le cas, il est certain qu'aucune licence n'est émise. Ensuite, une licence est accordée après que le processus a été effectué et qu'il a été démontré que la personne est correcte. Mais si le statut de cette personne change en cours de route et que des aspects criminels s'ajoutent, la licence sera révoquée. Chaque fois que l'on accorde une licence, on demande à la GRC de vérifier.

(*House of Commons Debates, 2 April 2009, p. 2343*)
(*Débats de la Chambre des communes, le 2 avril 2009, p. 2343*)

Mr. Scott Reid (Lanark — Frontenac — Lennox and Addington):

What [is] Canada doing to stop arms smuggling into Gaza?

Hon. Lawrence Cannon (Minister of Foreign Affairs):

Our government firmly believes that the continued threat of terrorism and arms smuggling as well as Hamas' continued rocket attacks against Israel's citizens are major obstacles to a lasting peace in the Middle East. The government is leading international efforts to ensure action is taken to stop the flow of arms into the Gaza Strip. This week, Canada hosted an expert level panel meeting on the Gaza counter-arms smuggling initiative.

(*House of Commons Debates, 12 June 2009, p. 4554*)
(*Débats de la Chambre des communes, le 12 juin 2009, p. 4554*)

Mme France Bonsant (Compton — Stanstead):

Ce gouvernement réalise-t-il que sa stratégie de lutte contre la contre-bande est un échec?

Hon. Peter Van Loan (Minister of Public Safety):

We actually have a very robust anti-contraband tobacco strategy that is being implemented ... very successfully. Seizures of contraband tobacco and charges this year are up significantly as a result of the excellent work of our police forces in implementing the strategy. We will continue to do that. I recently implemented and made permanent the shiprider arrangement whereby we can, together with the Americans, police our joint maritime borders where a lot of this kind of trafficking has happened in the past. We think it is a serious problem. We are serious about tackling crime and we will continue to do so.

(*House of Commons Debates, 20 November 2009, p. 7025*)
(*Débats de la Chambre des communes, le 20 novembre 2009, p. 7025*)

(c) Terrorism / Terrorisme

Hon. Stéphane Dion (Leader of the Opposition):

[What is . . .] the status of Canadians at risk in the Mumbai situation[?]

Le très hon. Stephen Harper (premier ministre):

J'ai téléphoné au commissaire de l'Inde aujourd'hui et le ministre des Affaires étrangères a fait la même chose avec son homologue, afin d'exprimer nos sympathies et notre solidarité envers leur pays contre les attaques terroristes à Mumbai. We would obviously like to extend all our sympathies to anyone from any country and their families who have been affected by loss of life or injury in this terrible tragedy. The ministry of foreign affairs is doing all it can to contact and help Canadian citizens who are affected by this. Let me be very clear. We join with the entire world in expressing our outrage against this kind of unforgivable hatred, brutality and violence, and we will always stand with our friends in the democratic world against this.

(*House of Commons Debates, 27 November 2008, p. 236*)
(*Débats de la Chambre des communes, le 27 novembre 2008, p. 236*)

Mr. Royal Galipeau (Ottawa — Orléans):

This week Canadians have watched with horror the terrible events unfolding in Mumbai, India. These appalling terrorist attacks have killed well over 100 people, with hundreds more injured. [W]hat [is] the government ... doing to assist during this extremely difficult period?

Hon. Lawrence Cannon (Minister of Foreign Affairs):

[T]he Government of Canada continues to deploy every effort to assist Canadians in Mumbai, including assistance in travel documents, replacing documents that might have been taken away, facilitating the departure of those wishing to leave through commercial means and, of course, providing financial assistance to those in need.

(*House of Commons Debates, 28 November 2008, p. 405*)
(*Débats de la Chambre des communes, le 28 novembre 2008, p. 405*)

Mr. James Rajotte (Edmonton — Leduc):

What is our government prepared to do to ensure that victims of terror are able to seek justice and redress from those organizations and states that use terrorism as a weapon in the war against democracy and freedom?

Hon. Peter Van Loan (Minister of Public Safety):

Today the government is taking action to provide victims the right to sue terrorists.[19] Individual terrorist organizations and foreign states that support and sponsor terrorism will now be subject to another way that they can be brought to justice. Our government will hold sponsors and perpetrators accountable for their crimes. I want to thank the Canadian Coalition Against Terror for its work on this. It has been a voice for victims of terror, it has stood up for them and it has been a driving force behind our government's action.

(*House of Commons Debates, 2 June 2009, p. 4073*)
(*Débats de la Chambre des communes, le 2 juin 2009, p. 4073*)

---

19 See Bill C-35 earlier in this chapter.

6   *International Humanitarian Law / Droit international humanitaire*

(a) Humanitarian Intervention and Aid / Aide et l'intervention humanitaire

Mr. Peter Goldring (Edmonton East):

Last April, the Minister of International Cooperation announced Canada would be untying food aid. In September she announced that all aid would be untied. [What are] the next steps in the government's aid effectiveness agenda?

Hon. Bev Oda (Minister of International Cooperation):

Today Canada is moving forward on another element of its aid effectiveness agenda. We will be increasing our effectiveness efforts in 20 countries, with increased resources focusing our bilateral country programs and improved coherence and coordination. This does not mean we are abandoning those in need. We will continue to respond to humanitarian crisis around the world. Today I am also pleased to announce an additional $1.5 million for shelter and protection for Sri Lankan civilians who are victimized by the conflict.

(*House of Commons Debates, 23 February 2009, p. 852*)
(*Débats de la Chambre des communes, le 23 février 2009, p. 852*)

(b) Afghanistan

Hon. Ujjal Dosanjh (Vancouver South):

The extension of our mission in Afghanistan was approved by the House expressly on the condition that NATO secure a battle group of approximately 1,000 troops to rotate into Kandahar which would be operational no later than February 2009. I have two questions. First, has NATO secured additional 1,000 troops under NATO command to rotate into Kandahar? Two, our role by February 2009 by implication was supposed to have changed significantly. Is there any anticipated change and, if so, what?

Hon. Peter MacKay (Minister of National Defence and Minister for the Atlantic Gateway):

The answer to the member's questions is yes and yes. We have secured additional battle groups. In fact, I met with defence ministers from RC (South) this past weekend in Cornwallis, Nova Scotia and we had a very frank and open discussion about this. We continue to seek other support from NATO allies with regard to troop commitments as well as equipment, as well as the development, as well as the work that is being done in aid of Afghans living in this region. I met with the defence minister from Germany today to have further discussions. So, yes, we are seeing progress. It is a difficult challenge but Canadians are making a significant contribution.

Hon. Ujjal Dosanjh (Vancouver South):

I would like to know specifically which country is adding 1,000 more troops. The Manley report and the resulting resolution asked the government to be more transparent and accountable to all Canadians on the Afghanistan issue. We now know there have been serious concerns and allegations with respect to detainee transfers which may have resulted in abuse and torture. Why is the government now moving before the courts to actually bar the Military Police Complaints Commission from conducting hearings into these matters? [20]

Hon. Peter MacKay:

[P]icking up on his latter question, nothing could be further from the truth. We are in fact co-operating. There have been over 35,000 documents. We have made officials available for discussions on the subject matter. The reality is that the only issue is one of jurisdiction, not one of disclosure. As for disclosures to the House, we have had numerous opportunities before committee to discuss the mission in Afghanistan. We have had no less than 30 technical briefings.

(*House of Commons Debates*, 25 November 2008, pp. 248–49)
(*Débats de la Chambre des communes, le 25 novembre 2008, pp. 248–49*)

---

20 Editor's note: In April 2008, the attorney general of Canada filed applications for judicial review with the Federal Court of Canada that challenged the commission's jurisdiction to investigate the subject matter of relevant complaints (see also a backgrounder at Military Police Complaints Commission, *News,* "Complaints Commission 'Surprised' by Government Law Suit," 14 April 2008, at <http://www.mpcc-cppm.gc.ca/400/nr-cp/2008–04–14–1-eng.aspx>, <http://www.mpcc-cppm.gc.ca/400/nr-cp/2008–04–14–1-fra.aspx>) and also moved to have the commission stay a public interest hearing in relation to the complaints. The Federal Court dismissed the motion to stay on 28 April 2009 on the grounds that irreparable harm would not result if the stay were not granted (*Attorney General of Canada v. Amnesty International Canada et al,* 2009 FC 426; at <http:// decisions.fct-cf.gc.ca/en/2009/2009fc426/2009fc426.html>) but granted the applications for judicial review on 16 September 2009, ruling that the MPCC acted beyond its jurisdiction with respect to the complaints (*Attorney General of Canada v. Amnesty International Canada et al,* 2009 FC 918; at <http://decisions.fct-cf.gc.ca/en/2009/2009fc918/2009fc918.html>).

Mr. Peter Goldring (Edmonton East):

The motion passed last March by the House specifically called for the government to secure medium-lift helicopters and unmanned aerial vehicles to better protect our brave men and women in Afghanistan ... [W]hen we will have these helicopters and UAVs in Afghanistan?

Hon. Peter MacKay (Minister of National Defence and Minister for the Atlantic Gateway):

Our government is committed to providing our brave soldiers with the best possible equipment. In fact, we have recently purchased six Chinook helicopters and UAVs in addition to those that were leased, all of which will be operational next year. [W]e will also deploy eight specially-equipped utility Griffin helicopters to act as escorts for these Chinooks. Most importantly, this will help reduce the risk to soldiers and civilians from ambushes, landmines and IEDs, all of this saving lives and continuing the important work of Canadian soldiers in theatre.

(*House of Commons Debates, 26 November 2008, p. 285*)
(*Débats de la Chambre des communes, le 26 novembre 2008, p. 285*)

Mr. Paul Dewar (Ottawa Centre):

According to recent reports commanders on the ground refused a NATO order to target drug traffickers in Afghanistan because they were concerned about violating international law ... Does the government believe that such military action will resolve the drug problem in Afghanistan and does the government support NATO orders that potentially put our soldiers at risk of violating international law?

Mr. Laurie Hawn (Parliamentary Secretary to the Minister of National Defence):

Alliance members, including Canada, decided at the NATO defence minister's meeting in Budapest that ISAF may carry out direct operations against the narcotics industry which could include destruction of narcotics production facilities and the apprehension of drug traffickers supporting the insurgency. Canada welcomes NATO's decision on countering narcotics. That being said, countering narcotics has not been identified as one of Canada's priorities in Afghanistan. However, let us be clear. There is a direct connection between the illicit drug trade and insurgent activity. That insurgent activity kills and wounds Canadian soldiers and Afghan civilians. All Canadian Forces operations are carried out in accordance with our legal international obligations.

Mr. Paul Dewar:

Canadians are extremely concerned about accusations that one of our agents may have been involved in torture and interrogation. Could the government confirm whether or not Sarah, the Canadian, is in fact a Canadian? Could the government confirm whether or not she was acting with the authority of the Canadian government and what actions has the government taken to ensure that Canada's reputation has not been damaged?

Hon. Lawrence Cannon:

[M]y department has no knowledge with respect to these allegations. The Government of Canada has in the past objected strongly in instances where foreign agents claimed alleged links to Canada.

(*House of Commons Debates, 6 February 2009, p. 499*)
(*Débats de la Chambre des communes, le 6 février 2009, p. 499*)

M. Paul Crête (Montmagny — L'Islet — Kamouraska — Rivière-du-Loup):

Le prochain sommet de l'OTAN devrait aussi être l'occasion pour lancer l'idée d'un sommet international sur l'Afghanistan qui déborde le seul cadre de l'OTAN. L'Organisation de coopération de Shanghai, qui regroupe la Chine, la Russie et cinq ex-républiques soviétiques d'Asie centrale, pourrait être mise à contribution. Est-ce que le premier ministre entend se faire le porteur d'une telle proposition auprès de ses partenaires de l'OTAN?

L'hon. Peter MacKay (ministre de la Défense nationale et ministre de la porte d'entrée de l'Atlantique):

Je suis confiant face à la prochaine réunion de l'OTAN. C'est une opportunité pour avoir une discussion claire et très importante pour attirer plus d'appuis pour cette mission. Cela inclut peut-être certains États dans la région pour appuyer la mission et appuyer l'approche pangouvernementale.

(*House of Commons Debates, 3 March 2009, p. 1226*)
(*Débats de la Chambre des communes, le 3 mars 2009, p. 1226*)

Hon. Bob Rae (Toronto Centre):

The government of France announced today [as did the United States, Great Britain, and Germany] that it is appointing a special envoy to Afghanistan and Pakistan. Why does the government still continue to reject an approach that ... will make sure that our political efforts are equal to the sacrifice of our troops?

Hon. Peter Kent (Minister of State of Foreign Affairs (Americas)):

We do have an envoy to Afghanistan, Mr. Ron Hoffmann. He is our ambassador. We have an envoy in the form of a high commissioner in Islamabad. We have confidence on this side of the House in our foreign affairs professionals.

(*House of Commons Debates, 4 March 2009, p. 1277*)
(*Débats de la Chambre des communes, le 4 mars 2009, p. 1277*)

(c) Africa / Afrique

Mme Johanne Deschamps (Laurentides — Labelle):

Comment le retrait de la liste de l'ACDI de pays parmi les plus pauvres de la planète va-t-il contribuer à améliorer leur situation?

Hon. Bev Oda (Minister of International Cooperation):

The facts are that 45% of CIDA's total budget goes to African countries and, in fact, we are on track to meeting our commitment to doubling aid to Africa a whole year ahead of the original commitment.

(*House of Commons Debates, 24 February 2009, p. 920*)
(*Débats de la Chambre des communes, le 24 février 2009, p. 920*)

(d) China / Chine

Mr. Colin Mayes (Okanagan — Shuswap):

Today marks the one year anniversary of the devastating earthquake in China's Sichuan province ... [H]ow much money [has] Canada contributed and how this money has been used?

Hon. Bev Oda (Minister of International Cooperation):

Canadians did show their compassion and took action, raising over $30 million, and our government matched that dollar for dollar. Because of that $60 million and our international partners, homes are being rebuilt, shelters were provided, and medical teams were on site. Some 160,000 children and women received micronutrients, and school classes continued with 60,000 schoolkids. Our government will continue to support the Chinese Canadian community and all Canadians who are showing compassion.

(*House of Commons Debates,* 12 May 2009, p. 3407)
(*Débats de la Chambre des communes, le* 12 mai 2009, p. 3407)

(e) Haiti / Haïti

Mr. Mario Silva (Davenport):

Haiti is the second largest recipient of Canadian foreign aid ... Last Friday, in a clearly disturbing development, the senate in Haiti voted to remove the country's prime minister who was just elected in 2008. [W]hat action has the government actually taken to deal with this issue?

Hon. Lawrence Cannon (Minister of Foreign Affairs):

The president ... has reassured me ... that they will be continuing to keep to the game plan that the previous government had put forward. We as well as our allies, which are not only involved in building infrastructure, building institutions, policing that country and ensuring that Haitians take over that country, are satisfied with the course of action taking place.

(*House of Commons Debates,* 6 November 2009, p. 6731)
(*Débats de la Chambre des communes, le* 6 novembre 2009, p. 6731)

(f) Latin America / Amérique latine

Mme Johanne Deschamps (Laurentides — Labelle):

Parmi les pays ajoutés sur [la] liste [de l'ACDI], on retrouve la Colombie et le Pérou. Or, nous savons que le Canada a signé des accords de libre-échange avec ces deux pays. Doit-on comprendre que pour ce gouvernement, ce sont les intérêts commerciaux qui dictent maintenant l'aide internationale?

Hon. Bev Oda (Minister of International Cooperation):

We want to ensure that Canadian dollars are being used responsibly. I must say that of the many countries I have visited, the slums in Peru are among the worst. There are needs among the people in Peru and Colombia and, like we serve all peoples around the world, we will also serve those people in Peru and Colombia.

(*House of Commons Debates,* 24 February 2009, p. 920)
(*Débats de la Chambre des communes, le* 24 février 2009, p 920.)

(g) Pakistan

Mr. Rick Norlock (Northumberland — Quinte West):

The situation in Pakistan has worsened. According to reports, up to 360,000 people have fled the fighting, with more expected in the coming weeks. This adds up to an estimated 550,000 people who have already been internally displaced since August of 2008. [Will] the Canadian government be providing any support for these victims?

Hon. Bev Oda (Minister of International Cooperation):

This government shares the concerns of Canadians with the plight of those forced to leave their homes in the Swat region of Pakistan, and the government is acting. I am announcing $5 million to provide food, proper health care and temporary shelters. The Red Cross and the World Food Programme are on the ground, working with those in need.

(*House of Commons Debates, 14 May 2009, p. 3527*)
(*Débats de la Chambre des communes, le 14 mai 2009, p. 3527*)

(h) Philippines

Mr. Rod Bruinooge (Winnipeg South):

Our government is making available up to $5 million for emergency and humanitarian assistance because of typhoon Ketsana ... in the Philippines. [W]hat is [the government] doing to help alleviate [this situation]?

Hon. Jason Kenney (Minister of Citizenship, Immigration and Multiculturalism):

Effective immediately, immigration officials will begin expediting applications from individuals directly and significantly affected by the typhoon. The special measures I am announcing include priority processing for new and existing family class applications from the Philippines for individuals affected by the typhoon. Their applications will be put to the front of the queue. In addition, Canadian visa officers will also be prioritizing temporary resident applications from Filipino nationals who can demonstrate that they are negatively affected by the typhoon. In addition to our generous aid contribution, we are doing what we can to stand by the people of the Philippines.

(*House of Commons Debates, 1 October 2009, p. 5454*)
(*Débats de la Chambre des communes, le 1 octobre 2009, p. 5454*)

(i) Sri Lanka

Hon. Bob Rae (Toronto Centre):

There are now as many as 300,000 civilians in Sri Lanka who find themselves caught in the desperate last days of fighting between the government and the Tamil Tigers. The United Nations Secretary-General and the European Union, as well as our fellow federation in Switzerland, have all called for specific action to be taken to protect the lives of these civilians, whose lives are quite desperately threatened by the events. [W]hy [has] Canada not been more forthcoming in attempting to say something and do something together with our friends [?]

Hon. Lawrence Cannon (Minister of Foreign Affairs):

[O]f course Canada does continue its efforts with like-minded countries to deliver strong messages to all parties involved in this conflict in order to protect civilians by allowing them safe and voluntary movement from combat zones and by ensuring unhindered access for humanitarian workers ... J'ai eu l'occasion de parler au ministre des Affaires étrangères de ce pays. Il faut rappeler aussi que, en tant que gouvernement, nous avons effectivement aidé les citoyens de ce pays; nous les avons aidés par l'entremise du travail qu'effectue l'Agence canadienne de développement international. Nous avons également fait des démarches auprès des Nations Unies de façon à appuyer leurs efforts humanitaires.

(*House of Commons Debates, 28 January 2009, p. 47; 3 February 2009, p. 297*)
(*Débats de la Chambre des Communes, le 28 janvier 2009, p. 47; le 3 février 2009, p. 297*)

Mr. Bob Dechert (Mississauga — Erindale):

[H]ow [is] Canada reacting ... [to] what is going on in Sri Lanka?

Hon. Bev Oda (Minister of International Cooperation):

We are very concerned with what is happening in Sri Lanka. My colleague, the Minister of Foreign Affairs, has called for an immediate ceasefire and called on the Sri Lankan government to exercise caution. We need a ceasefire to allow the evacuation of the sick and wounded and to allow safe, unhindered access to humanitarian needs for civilians. Yesterday, I announced that Canada will commit up to $3 million in humanitarian aid. We continue to call on both parties to stop the fighting [and reach] ... a durable political solution[.]

(*House of Commons Debates, 5 February 2009, p. 450*)
(*Débats de la Chambre des communes, le 5 février 2009, p. 450*)

(j) Landmines and cluster bombs / Mines terrestres et les bombes à fragmentation

Hon. Mark Eyking (Sydney — Victoria):

It has been over a decade since Canada led the way in the signing of the Ottawa treaty to ban landmines. On May 30, 2008, last year, the Convention on Cluster Munitions was adopted at the UN, including by Canada. Would [Canada] commit to be among the first 30 countries to ratify the convention?

Hon. Lawrence Cannon (Minister of Foreign Affairs):

Canada has played a leading role in the establishment and the implementation of the Ottawa convention on anti-personnel mines. Our government was also active in the negotiations of the new Convention on Cluster Munitions in 2008 and was pleased to be among the 91 countries that signed the Convention on Cluster Munitions in December 2008. Preparations are under way to seek ratification of this treaty. Ratification of protocol No. 4 of the convention, which addresses the explosive remnants of war, was approved by cabinet in November 2008. We intend to formally ratify the protocol in the future.

(*House of Commons Debates, 19 June 2009, p. 4853*)
(*Débats de la Chambre des communes, le 19 juin 2009, p. 4853*)

(k) Nuclear disarmament / Désarmement nucléaire

Mr. Paul Dewar (Ottawa Centre):

[W]here is our team Canada for nuclear disarmament?

Hon. Stockwell Day (Minister of International Trade and Minister for the Asia-Pacific Gateway):

It is very encouraging to see around the world especially in countries that are significantly developing, such as India, that they have a desire in their development to use clean energy in the years ahead. They have been pursuing an ongoing future of nuclear energy. Canada has a lot to offer in that particular aspect. We will continue to be with other countries signing nuclear cooperation agreements whereby the countries that are involved have to fully respect the International Atomic Energy Agency guidelines. This is not only helping the environment, but it discourages proliferation at the same time.

(*House of Commons Debates, 30 September 2009, p. 5376*)
(*Débats de la Chambre des communes, le 30 septembre 2009, p. 5376*)

M. Gilles Duceppe (Laurier — Sainte-Marie):

N'est-ce pas irresponsable de la part du gouvernement de vendre des réacteurs nucléaires à un pays qui n'a pas signé le Traité sur la non-prolifération des armes nucléaires, d'autant plus que l'Inde a un lourd passé en la matière?

Hon. Lisa Raitt (Minister of Natural Resources):

Canada is very proud of its technology with respect to nuclear energy. We have been very successful in selling it around the world. It is incredibly important to ensure that we not only have a marketplace around the world but that we have one in which we are following the rules that are set down by international standards, and those are the standards that we will abide by.

Hon. Peter Kent (Minister of State of Foreign Affairs (Americas)):

India has made substantial non-proliferation and disarmament commitments to achieve the trust of the nuclear suppliers group which were reiterated in a political statement on September 5. India has agreed to remain committed to a voluntary unilateral moratorium on nuclear testing ... [N]o agreement has yet been signed.

(*House of Commons Debates, 17 November 2009, p. 6856*)
(*Débats de la Chambre des communes, le 17 novembre 2009, p. 6856*)

(l) Refugees / Réfugiés

Mr. David Sweet (Ancaster — Dundas — Flamborough — Westdale):

Christians and members of other minority faith groups are often subject to severe persecution in Iraq and elsewhere in the Middle East. [What has been Canada's recent measures] to assist Iraqi refugees?

Hon. Jason Kenney (Minister of Citizenship, Immigration and Multiculturalism):

Canadians are deeply concerned about the plight of Iraqi refugees facing persecution in their homeland, which is why last year our government committed to increase by more than 50% the number of resettled refugees from the Middle East. It is also why yesterday I announced further increases. In 2009, Canada will accept approximately 3,900 refugees through our Damascus mission, representing an increase of several times since our government took office. I am pleased to say that the Canadian representative, the UN High Commissioner of Refugees, has said that Canada should be commended in continuing to uphold its humanitarian commitment to finding permanent solutions for refugees from one of the most pressing refugee situations in the world.

(*House of Commons Debates, 11 February 2009, p. 677*)
(*Débats de la Chambre des communes, le 11 février 2009, p. 677*)

Mr. Don Davies (Vancouver Kingsway):

The Sri Lankan government is making life unbearable for the Tamil population, especially those who remain in detention camps ... Will the Minister of Citizenship, Immigration and Multiculturalism ensure that this is corrected and that there is fast, fair and legal adjudication of these men's claims?

Hon. Jason Kenney (Minister of Citizenship, Immigration and Multiculturalism):

Any individual who arrives in Canada will be processed in full accordance with our Immigration and Refugee Protection Act. That means that people will undergo a screening for their admissibility and their eligibility to come to Canada. [I]f they are detained, they will have access to the IRB for detention hearings at the 48 hour, 7 day and 30 day stages and, of course, they have the right to legal counsel. [I]n this particular incident legal counsel has been offered to the 76 foreign nationals being detained in Maple Ridge, British Columbia.

(*House of Commons Debates, 20 October 2009, p. 5939*)
(*Débats de la Chambre des communes, le 20 octobre 2009, p. 5939*)

7   *Trade and Economy / Commerce et économie*

(a) A Buy Local Policy / Politique d'achat local

Mr. Michael Ignatieff (Leader of the Opposition):

The stimulus package just passed by the U.S. Congress includes protectionist clauses that are harmful to Canada. The U.S. bill states that none of the funds made available by this act may be used for a project "unless all of the iron and steel used in such project is produced in the United States." [Can Canada] not prevent protectionism language creeping into the package?

Right Hon. Stephen Harper (Prime Minister):

[T]his is obviously a serious matter and of serious concern to us. I spoke to our ambassador about it yesterday and I know that countries around the world are expressing grave concern about some of these measures that go against not just the obligations of the United States but, frankly, the spirit of our G20 discussions. We will be having these discussions with our friends in the United States and we expect the United States to respect its international obligations.

Mr. Michael Ignatieff:

What action is the government taking in Washington to ensure that Congress and the auto companies do not end up working together to suck auto sector jobs out of Canada?

Right Hon. Stephen Harper:

[T]his is precisely why in December the Premier of Ontario and I made it clear that we are working together and working with our colleagues in both the outgoing and now the incoming administration to ensure that we are on the same page in terms of helping the auto sector and to ensure that we bring our share of any restructuring package to the table and preserve those jobs in Canada ... We are doing it in lockstep. Our officials talk daily to their counterparts in the United States and we have a great partner in the Government of Ontario in this endeavour.

M. Michael Ignatieff:

Le premier ministre abordera-t-il la question du protectionnisme américain lors de la visite du président Obama, et qu'est-il prêt à dire pour défendre les intérêts de notre pays?

Le très hon. Stephen Harper:

[Q]uel que soit le pays, le protectionnisme est une grande préoccupation lors d'une période économique comme celle-ci. Je suis prêt depuis longtemps. On doit éviter le protectionnisme durant un ralentissement mondial. Le processus au Congrès continue aux États-Unis. On verra les changements, les plans et les propositions. Nous sommes unis avec tous les pays du monde pour insister afin que les États-Unis respectent leurs obligations vis-à-vis de l'Organisation mondiale du commerce.

(*House of Commons Debates, 29 January 2009, pp. 112–13*)
(*Débats de la Chambre des communes, le 29 janvier 2009, pp. 112–13*)

Mr. Brian Masse (Windsor West):

Yesterday, the U.S. House of Representatives passed its $825 billion economic stimulus bill with the pledge to support its industries and buy American iron and steel ... Why does the Prime Minister not implement our own buy-Canadian program instead of his current program that sees Navistar truck workers thrown out of their jobs and a bunch of Texans hired? Will the government look after Canadian steelworkers like their counterparts south of the border?

Hon. Stockwell Day (Minister of International Trade and Minister for the Asia-Pacific Gateway):

We are watching that legislation very carefully because history is clear that protectionism does not stimulate economies. As a matter of fact, protectionist measures are a drag on economies. We are a trading nation. We are prosperous because the products and services that Canadians make and export around the world bring those returns to our country and also benefit other countries. We are going to ensure that the United States lives up to its obligations under the WTO and under NAFTA. There are clear legal obligations there and we will engage with it to ensure it sticks with them ... The G-28ers in Washington, just at the end of last year, were very clear in their declaration that the country should not lapse into protectionist measures. We can look at history back as far as the Great Depression and we see that those protectionist measures that were followed then by the United States took what could have been a very bad one or two-year recession and made it go into a depression because of the retaliatory measures that other countries were forced to take.

(*House of Commons Debates, 29 January 2009, p. 117*)
(*Débats de la Chambre des communes, le 29 janvier 2009, p. 117*)

Mr. Tony Martin (Sault Ste. Marie):

When will the government recognize that balance is needed to ensure the longstanding viability of our steel industry and kickstart a buy Canadian strategy?

Mr. Gerald Keddy (Parliamentary Secretary to the Minister of International Trade):

There is balance in the marketplace now. [It] is absolutely false [that] ... the Canadian government is not standing up for Canadian steelworkers. There are currently more than 20 anti-dumping and countervailing duty measures in place against imports from China. Several of those measures are against Chinese steel.

(*House of Commons Debates, 6 February 2009, pp. 500–1*)
(*Débats de la Chambre des communes, le 6 février 2009, pp. 500–1*)

M. Gilles Duceppe (Laurier — Sainte-Marie):

[Q]u'on est en pleine crise économique et que plusieurs industries tirent le diable par la queue, pourquoi le gouvernement ne se dote-t-il pas d'une politique d'achat local qui respecte les règles de l'OMC et de l'ALENA?

L'hon. Stockwell Day (ministre du Commerce international et ministre de la porte d'entrée de l'Asie-Pacifique):

[L]es produits canadiens sont les plus efficaces et les meilleurs au monde, mais il appartient aux individus qui veulent les produits de décider s'ils veulent les acheter. Nous continuons à encourager les gens à considérer les produits et les services canadiens. Il y a aussi des occasions où il est nécessaire d'acheter canadien. Nous allons continuer à encourager cette direction.

(*House of Commons Debates, 2 February 2009, p. 218*)
(*Débats de la Chambre des communes, le 2 février 2009, p. 218*)

Hon. Jack Layton (Toronto — Danforth):

[T]he United States has had a buy American act for 76 years. It is perfectly legal under the World Trade Organization. In fact, under NAFTA, governments are allowed to buy at home in order to use taxpayer money to create jobs for workers and to support communities and their industries. Mexico, China, Japan and South Korea all have national procurement policies ... [W]hat is wrong with a buy Canadian policy, as permitted under continental and global trade rules?

Right Hon. Stephen Harper (Prime Minister):

We believe strongly that the proposals before the American Congress violate its trade obligations. We have a global slowdown. All the countries of the G20 have committed themselves to working together to provide stimulus packages to stimulate not just their own economies, but the world economy. The leader of the NDP suggests we respond to this by starting a trade war with the United States. This is not advice that we will be taking.

(*House of Commons Debates, 3 February 2009, p. 294*)
(*Débats de la Chambre des communes, le 3 février 2009, p. 294*)

(b) Aerospace industry / Industrie aérospatiale

M. Royal Galipeau (Ottawa — Orléans):

Les industries canadiennes ... travaillent fort pour naviguer sur la crise financière ... This is certainly true in the aerospace sector, where we have invested significantly. Further, last year's budget committed $350 million for the Bombardier C Series. [Quels sont] les résultats du secteur aérospatial grâce à nos investissements?

L'hon. Tony Clement (ministre de l'Industrie):

Notre gouvernement est fier, bien sûr, de l'appui qu'il donne au secteur aérospatial. C'est pour cette raison que, aujourd'hui, je tiens à féliciter Bombardier à l'occasion de l'annonce de la première commande d'avions Série C signée par la Deutsche Lufthansa. Cette commande de 30 avions correspond à une valeur d'environ 1,53 milliard de dollars. Elle marque une étape majeure pour Bombardier et témoigne de l'ingéniosité de l'industrie aérospatiale canadienne. Il est encore plus évident que ce gouvernement renforce l'industrie aérospatiale.

(*House of Commons Debates, 11 March 2009, p. 1595*)
(*Débats de la Chambre des communes, le 11 mars 2009, p. 1595*)

(c) Agriculture / Agriculture

(i) Beef / Boeuf

Mr. Rick Casson (Lethbridge):

Livestock producers ... across Canada have been hurting since the BSE crisis hit them in May 2003 ... [W]hat action [has] [the government] taken to open up new markets and help the bottom line for our cattle industry?

Hon. Gerry Ritz (Minister of Agriculture and Agri-Food and Minister for the Canadian Wheat Board):

We were very fortunate in January, on our trip to Hong Kong in conjunction with the livestock sector, to reopen that market to a lot of the cuts we do not make use of here in Canada, or internationally for that matter, which will double our sales to the Hong Kong market. Yesterday we received great news from a small, dynamic market in Jordan that will open its doors to complete access to us after the BSE crisis. That is the beginning of many good announcements to come.

(*House of Commons Debates, 4 February 2009, p. 342*)
(*Débats de la Chambre des communes, le 4 février 2009, p. 342*)

Ms. Candice Hoeppner (Portage — Lisgar):

Last year Canadian producers exported high-quality beef to more than 55 countries. Unfortunately, many countries continue to close their doors to Canadian beef despite Canada's cutting-edge animal health care systems. [W]hat [is] the ... government doing to stand up for Canadian producers?

Hon. Stockwell Day (Minister of International Trade and Minister for the Asia-Pacific Gateway):

On the ban on beef from Colombia alone, in fact if we did not have that ban in place right now, we would have about a $6 million access for our producers ... On the issue of Colombia's ban, the Minister of Agriculture and I have continually pursued this issue. I am pleased to announce that the country of Colombia has announced today that it is lifting that ban on beef.

(*House of Commons Debates, 16 September 2009, p. 5072*)
(*Débats de la Chambre des communes, le 16 septembre 2009, p. 5072*)

(ii) Canola

Mme France Bonsant (Compton — Stanstead):

Dans le but de convaincre les autorités chinoises de ne pas suspendre leurs importations de canola canadien aux prises avec un parasite, le ministre de l'Agriculture et de l'Agroalimentaire a affirmé qu'une limitation des importations de canola serait inutile, puisque le canola canadien est de type Terminator ... Le ministre peut-il nous dire pourquoi il a tenu de tels propos qui, en plus d'être faux, portent préjudices aux producteurs de grandes cultures?

L'hon. Jean-Pierre Blackburn (ministre du Revenu national et ministre d'État (Agriculture)):

Toute mesure qui vise à contrer l'exportation de quelque produit agroalimentaire que ce soit, également bien sûr la question du canola, est pour nous une préoccupation. Ce l'est doublement lorsque ce n'est pas une question de salubrité qui est en cause. Dans ce cas-ci, nous travaillons et discutons bien sûr avec les autorités chinoises et également avec les autorités américaines, qui ont eu certains problèmes avec le canola, afin d'en arriver à une solution qui sera bonne pour notre pays.

(*House of Commons Debates, 27 November 2009, p. 7321*)
(*Débats de la Chambre des communes, le 27 novembre 2009, p. 7321*)

(iii) Pork / Porc

Hon. Bob Rae (Toronto Centre):

Another drastic decision by the Chinese government is something on which the Canadian government needs to fight back, and that is the question of the Chinese government deciding that it will not accept importation of Canadian pork products ... [W]hy would [the government] accept the pathetic words of the Minister of International Trade, who said that the decision by the Government of China was "disappointing"?

Hon. Gerry Ritz (Minister of Agriculture and Agri-Food and Minister for the Canadian Wheat Board):

China is operating outside of sound science. China has received those assurances from the World Health Organization and the OIE. It has also received calls from the Minister of International Trade and me on that very issue. We are looking for clarification as to why it has gone as far as it has. We will have a response to that very shortly. Should China continue on, of course there is the WTO challenge which we would not hesitate to initiate.

(*House of Commons Debates, 4 May 2009, pp. 2999–3000*)
(*Débats de la Chambre des communes, le 4 mai 2009, pp. 2999–3000*)

Ms. Candice Hoeppner (Portage — Lisgar):

What is the government doing to ensure our pork producers are treated fairly?

Hon. Gerry Ritz (Minister of Agriculture and Agri-Food and Minister for the Canadian Wheat Board):

The science is clear. Canada's pork is safe. I spoke with U.S. agricultural secretary Tom Vilsack last night. The U.S. is Canada's major trading partner for pork. The Americans are doing everything they can to work with us to prove the science, to keep those borders open and pork flowing. We will defend Canada's pork producers in whatever venue necessary. The claims that are being made by some countries are absolutely outrageous. To that end, we, as the government, have organized a pork barbecue on the Hill tomorrow. I invite everyone to come and take part and enjoy some great top quality Canadian pork.

(*House of Commons Debates, 5 May 2009, p. 3080*)
(*Débats de la Chambre des communes, le 5 mai 2009, p. 3080*)

(d) Alaska Gas Pipeline / Pipeline en Alaska

Mr. Dennis Bevington (Western Arctic):

On Monday the U.S. Congress supported a bill increasing the loan guarantees for the Alaska pipeline from $18 billion to $30 billion. Yesterday, Imperial Oil's parent company, ExxonMobil struck a deal with TransCanada Corporation to develop an Alaska gas pipeline at a projected cost of $26 billion, a clear threat to the Mackenzie Valley pipeline ... How [is] [this relationship] advancing the Canadian pipeline [?]

Hon. Jim Prentice (Minister of the Environment):

The Mackenzie Valley project continues to have a four to five year lead in front of the Alaska project. Certainly positive news has been announced for the Alaska project ... It is the position of the Government of Canada that we wish to see the Mackenzie project proceed first so that a northern basin is opened up. We remain four years ahead of the Alaska project in terms of regulatory work and work with aboriginal Canadians.

(*House of Commons Debates, 12 June 2009, pp. 4556–57*)
(*Débats de la Chambre des communes, le 12 juin 2009, pp. 4556–57*)

(e) Arts

Mme Carole Lavallée (Saint-Bruno — Saint-Hubert):

L'abolition des programmes PromArt et Routes commerciales continue de faire des ravages, et c'est maintenant au tour des Grands Ballets Canadiens d'annuler des tournées prévues, faute de financement ... Le gouvernement va-t-il enfin entendre raison ... et rétablir le financement de ces programmes?

Hon. Gary Goodyear (Minister of State (Science and Technology)):

There have been no cuts to the core funding on any of these programs. [In] the budget, [there is] $5.1 billion of additional new funding. That is on top of the core programs.

(*House of Commons Debates, 9 March 2009, p. 1468*)
(*Débats de la Chambre des communes, le 9 mars 2009, p. 1468*)

Mme Carole Lavallée (Saint-Bruno — Saint-Hubert):

La coupe du programme PromArt du ministère des Affaires étrangères obligera notamment les Grands Ballets Canadiens à assumer les coûts de leurs déplacements pour se produire à Tel-Aviv, à Jérusalem et au Caire. Comment le ministre des Affaires étrangères peut-il accepter sans broncher cette coupe de son ministère alors qu'il disait, lors de son récent passage en Israël, qu'il était important de renforcer les liens diplomatiques avec ce pays, sur les plans politique, économique, social et culturel?

L'hon. James Moore (ministre du Patrimoine canadien et des Langues officielles):

Nous aidons maintenant nos artistes sur la scène internationale. Cette année, les investissements sont de 22 millions de dollars. C'est un montant sans précédent dans l'histoire de notre pays ... [Le] ministère des Affaires étrangères maintient son réseau de 171 agents chargés des affaires culturelles dans ses missions à l'étranger ... On donne 13 millions de dollars au Conseil des Arts du Canada, 4,8 millions de dollars à l'Association pour l'exportation de livres canadiens, 1,9 million de dollars à Téléfilm Canada, 1,8 million de dollars à FACTOR Music Action et 900 000 $ à l'Office national du film du Canada.

(*House of Commons Debates, 23 March 2009, p. 1795*)
(*Débats de la Chambre des communes, le 23 mars 2009, p. 1795*)

(f) Automotive industry / Secteur de l'automobile

Mr. Francis Valeriote (Guelph):

There is speculation that General Motors may pull out of Canada entirely. While the industry has struggled to meet its February 20 deadline, the Minister of Industry has been idling. The Detroit Three are working hard. The auto workers are at the table. The U.S. government is on the ball ... When exactly did the minister actually meet with his American counterpart to ensure our Canadian jobs would be protected?

Hon. Tony Clement (Minister of Industry):

This government has been working ... with officials in the United States as well as with the Government of Ontario. We have a strict set of conditions that mirror what the Americans are also looking at for the industry to restructure that industry and to preserve our 20% production capacity. The hon. member asked me to meet with my American counterpart. When President Obama appoints that counterpart, I will meet with that person.

(*House of Commons Debates, 4 February 2009, p. 335*)
(*Débats de la Chambre des communes, le 4 février 2009, p. 335*)

(g) Canada-US Border / Frontière canado-américaine

Mr. Brian Masse (Windsor West):

The U.S. passport policy, which takes effect today, will cause travel delays ... and damage our tourism industry ... Why [the government] would accept a border policy that threatens our Canadian tourism industry and jobs?

Hon. Peter Van Loan (Minister of Public Safety):

In no way did we accept the policy. We [have worked] to correct the deficiencies [of the past]. We did that in a number of ways: by putting in place a number of extensions on implementation of the western hemisphere travel initiative; by creating the opportunity to utilize alternative documents such as an enhanced driver's licence ... In doing so, we were able to significantly advance the interests of Canadians. We will continue to do that on a number of fronts because our relationship and our trade across that border is very important.

(*House of Commons Debates, 1 June 2009, p. 4000*)
(*Débats de la Chambre des communes, le 1 juin 2009, p. 4000*)

(h) Dispute settlement / Règlement des différends

M. Serge Cardin (Sherbrooke):

En fin de semaine, on apprenait que Dow AgroSciences a entrepris une poursuite en vertu du chapitre 11 de l'ALENA sous prétexte que le Code de gestion des pesticides du Québec viole son droit de vendre du 2,4-D, un puissant herbicide. Le ministre du Commerce international s'engage-t-il à défendre le Code de gestion des pesticides du Québec afin de garantir son droit de légiférer et d'adopter des règlements dans l'intérêt public?

L'hon. Stockwell Day (ministre du Commerce international et ministre de la porte d'entrée de l'Asie-Pacifique):

Oui, nous allons permettre aux provinces et aux États de défendre leurs décisions dans l'intérêt public et selon le dossier de la santé publique, et nous allons travailler avec la province de Québec pour améliorer la situation et défendre ses priorités et ses droits dans ce cas.

(*House of Commons Debates, 4 March 2009, p. 1280*)
(*Débats de la Chambre des communes, le 4 mars 2009, p. 1280*)

(i) Dumping

Mr. Ron Cannan (Kelowna — Lake Country):

Canada's Border Services Agency recently determined that foreign companies were dumping aluminum products into the Canadian market and imposing a 43% penalty on these products. [H]ow [will] this action preserve Canada's rules based trading relationship with our international partners?

Hon. Stockwell Day (Minister of International Trade and Minister for the Asia-Pacific Gateway):

If there is a situation where it is determined that imports from another country have been dumped into Canada at a cost that is below their production, or if they are subsidized, then, following our rules based system, we are able to assess a countervail or a duty for that. That has been done in this case with certain Chinese aluminum extrusion products. The Chinese officials are certainly welcome to use the dispute settlement that is there to contest it. I look forward to talking about this with my counterpart in China when I am there in April.

(*House of Commons Debates, 12 March 2009, p. 1681*)
(*Débats de la Chambre des communes, le 12 mars 2009, p. 1681*)

(j) Executive pay / Rémunération accordée aux dirigeants de compagnies

M. Jean-Yves Laforest (Saint-Maurice — Champlain):

Le président des États-Unis a fait connaître son intention de fixer des conditions aux compagnies qui recevront l'aide du gouvernement et de limiter notamment la rémunération de leurs dirigeants. Le premier ministre entend-il ... exiger des compagnies canadiennes qui reçoivent de l'aide du gouvernement fédéral, notamment les banques, qu'elles limitent la rémunération et les bonis qu'elles accordent à leurs dirigeants?

Hon. Jim Flaherty (Minister of Finance):

The G20 has looked at this issue ... [W]e are working together with our G20 partners to create mutual economic stimulus around the world because that will help relieve the global recession. This also is one of those points that was agreed on, and members will note this week that some Canadian bank executives have voluntarily restricted their compensation. The member needs to note also that we also have not put one cent of Canadian taxpayers' money into our banking system, unlike the United States and the United Kingdom.

(*House of Commons Debates, 4 February 2009, p. 340*)
(*Débats de la Chambre des communes, le 4 février 2009, p. 340*)

Mr. Brian Masse (Windsor West):

The Globe and Mail is reporting that the CEOs of Canada's six largest banks are pocketing $8.3 billion in bonuses. This comes less than one year after the government propped the banks up with $75 billion. In the United States and the United Kingdom, the governments are taking this on and restricting executive pay. Why will [Canada's] government not do the same?

Hon. Jim Flaherty (Minister of Finance):

This is not the United Kingdom [or] the United States. We did not have to ... nationalize banks. We did not have to use taxpayer money to bail out banks in Canada. That is why we have the reputation around the world as having one of the most sound financial systems. The G20 has guidelines. There are the Financial Stability Board guidelines. I have written to the financial institutions, requesting their compliance. If there is not compliance, there will be consequences in Canada.

(*House of Commons Debates, 10 December 2009, p. 7911*)
(*Débats de la Chambre des communes, le 10 décembre 2009, p. 7911*)

(k) Global recession and Canada's budget / Récession mondiale et le budget du Canada

L'hon. Stéphane Dion (chef de l'opposition):

Le [gouvernement] admettra-t-il que ses propres choix budgétaires, sa décision de dépenser plus que tous ses prédécesseurs et sa décision d'éliminer la réserve pour éventualité ont mis le Canada au bord d'un déficit?

Le très hon. Stephen Harper (premier ministre):

[A]u contraire, le Canada est un pays qui a un surplus. C'est le seul pays du G7, le seul grand pays industrialisé, qui a un surplus. Nous avons eu une bonne discussion lors d'une réunion des chefs du G20 la semaine passée. Nous sommes tous unis dans la position que nos gouvernements feront tout ce qui est nécessaire. Je parle des actions financières, des actions monétaires et même des actions fiscales pour accroître l'économie globale des Canadiens ... It is correct that the surplus is weaker than it was in the past because the government took deliberate action to provide long-term tax stimulus to the economy as the economy was slowing. That was the right fiscal decision and it was supported by Canadians. We will take additional fiscal stimulus measures, as we agreed at the G-20, if necessary. Anybody who would say that in the midst of a global recession they would turn around and raise taxes or cut essential spending, that would be an ideological position that the government has no intention of following.

(*House of Commons Debates, 20 November 2008, pp. 61–62*)
(*Débats de la Chambre des communes, le 20 novembre 2008, pp. 61–62*)

Hon. John McCallum (Markham — Unionville):

[What] policies will lead to the elimination of Canada's net debt?

Hon. Jim Flaherty (Minister of Finance):

As the International Monetary Fund noted on Friday, our government paid off about $40 billion in debt in the first three years of our mandate. As the International Monetary Fund also pointed out, this puts this country in the best position in the G7 as we enter the recession and as we weather the storm. We have the best fiscal position of all our competitors in the G7.

(*House of Commons Debates, 28 May 2009, p. 3857*)
(*Débats de la Chambre des communes, le 28 mai 2009, p. 3857*)

(l) Investments / Investissement

L'hon. Scott Brison (Kings — Hants):

On March 18, DFAIT hosted a boot camp for Canadian entrepreneurs in Ottawa, where Canadian firms were told that the best way for them to access venture capital was to incorporate in Delaware and move to the United States. Why is the government giving up on Canada's venture capital industry and telling Canadian innovators to move their intellectual property, jobs and innovation to the United States?

Hon. Stockwell Day (Minister of International Trade and Minister for the Asia-Pacific Gateway):

EDC alone in this last year has done business with over 8,600 customers. It has facilitated $85 billion worth of financial activity. That is a 22% increase over 2007. As of the end of February, it had already transacted with 400 new customers to the tune of $9.4 billion. The member should not frighten people with things that are not true ... Also in our new economic comprehensive package are millions of dollars available in a program to allow for Canadians, who want to be involved in exportation and business across the border, to learn about the abilities and the programs that are available to them. That is one of a number of products. The bottom line is this. There has been a huge increase in activity of Canadian businesses. They are being successful. It is through their involvement with EDC.

(*House of Commons Debates*, 24 March 2009, pp. 1874–75)
(*Débats de la Chambre des communes, le 24 mars 2009, pp. 1874–75*)

Mr. Brian Masse (Windsor West):

Canadians have been watching with concern as so many Canadian-owned companies are bought up by foreign firms. Now Nortel is joining the list, forced to sell off parts of its company to foreign interests ... When will the minister ... act in the national interest?

Hon. Tony Clement (Minister of Industry):

In fact, this company has gone through a court-managed process because it has sought protection under the CCAA. That process is ongoing and should not be interfered with by the Government of Canada. Our Investment Canada laws have recently changed. They have a national security provision in them so that we can defend our national security interests, but this is a country that also must trade with the world. We must be open for business. That is how we get jobs and opportunity here, as well as through our own domestic competitiveness.

(*House of Commons Debates*, 12 May 2009, p. 3406)
(*Débats de la Chambre des communes, le 12 mai 2009, p. 3406*)

Mr. Bob Dechert (Mississauga — Erindale):

The CIDA-INC program was intended to encourage private sector engagement in developing countries to promote economic growth and poverty reduction. However, a recent review of the program found it was outdated and ineffective. [What] [is] the Conservative government doing to ensure Canadian tax dollars are spent responsibly?

Hon. Stockwell Day (Minister of International Trade and Minister for the Asia-Pacific Gateway):

This is a very well-intended program and it is designed to allow private sector companies or individuals in Canada to invest in countries that are emerging in terms of their developing economies. However, it was found, upon review, that it would be more effective to have this under the international trade area, where there are some 150 trade offices around the world with over 950 representatives who can work with private sector companies in Canada to guide them and also to give resources to allow them to invest in emerging countries to help poverty issues in those countries and also benefit Canadians at the same time.

(*House of Commons Debates, 3 June 2009, p. 4115*)
(*Débats de la Chambre des communes, le 3 juin 2009, p. 4115*)

Hon. Ujjal Dosanjh (Vancouver South):

The west coast U.S. ports have accused the ports of Vancouver and Prince Rupert of receiving illegal subsidies under the WTO just because our governments in Canada have attempted to provide better roads and rail links to our ports ... What is the government doing to protect our sovereign right to make these nationally important investments in our ports?

Hon. Stockwell Day (Minister of International Trade and Minister for the Asia-Pacific Gateway):

We are getting the message out around the world that the Asia-Pacific advantages that we have put in place, including infrastructure, our very competitive tax regime and a sound banking system, are an invitation to other countries to consider investing in Canada, in the Asia-Pacific in looking at their shipping opportunities. These are clearly areas that we have taken a close look at to ensure we are not off-side in any areas of trade. We are proud of what we have done with the Asia-Pacific initiatives. It gives a great advantage to Canadians and a great advantage to people wanting to do business with Canada.

(*House of Commons Debates, 9 June 2009, pp. 4384–85*)
(*Débats de la Chambre des communes, le 9 juin 2009, pp. 4384–85*)

(m) Labelling / Étiquetage

Hon. Ralph Goodale (Wascana):

Canadian livestock producers are facing unprecedented financial trouble and this week their problem got a whole lot worse. The U.S. agriculture secretary has just relaunched the issue of country of origin labelling. In three weeks, he will impose new labelling rules that are directly anti-Canadian ... Will [the government] now relaunch Canada's WTO challenge on labelling, which they abandoned in January?

Hon. Gerry Ritz (Minister of Agriculture and Agri-Food and Minister for the Canadian Wheat Board):

Livestock industries on both sides of the border are concerned about what is being proposed. We were able to argue with the former administration for a better set of rules. Those are the ones being implemented. The Americans will seek to do some voluntary assessments of that, but let me quote Brad Wildeman, the president of the Canadian Cattlemen's Association, in regard to the challenge. He says, "We have no doubt the federal government will continue to deliver strong action to oppose any unfair implementation of COOL." We will certainly do that.

(*House of Commons Debates, 25 February 2009, pp. 964–65*)
(*Débats de la Chambre des communes, le 25 février 2009, pp.964–65*)

(n) Manufacturing industry / Secteur manufacturier

Mr. Gerard Kennedy (Parkdale — High Park):

Many of the 160,000 lost jobs [in Canada's manufacturing sector] could have been avoided ... What is it about the government ... that makes them refuse to act to help families and workers when their jobs are in jeopardy?

Hon. Jim Flaherty (Minister of Finance):

[W]e have acted, of course. We acted well over a year ago. The cumulative effect on the economy is 1.4% of GDP stimulus this year. Some of the provinces have joined us in reducing taxes on businesses. Next year the stimulus in the economy will be about 2%. To put that in context, that is among the highest in the G-7 in terms of the stimulus we have already built into the economy structurally. This is very important for businesses. We will have the federal business tax rate to 15% by 2012. Many of the provinces will get to 10% by then. That is a 25% business tax rate. That is a great way to brand Canada [and] attract investment.

(*House of Commons Debates, 20 November 2008, p. 66*)
(*Débats de la Chambre des communes, le 20 novembre 2008, p. 66*)

(o) Procurement / Marchés publics

M. Serge Cardin (Sherbrooke):

En matière de sécurité, notamment, rien n'interdit au gouvernement de faire construire au Canada, entre autres au Québec, les camions qu'il destine à l'armée. Pourquoi le gouvernement refuse-t-il de se prévaloir de ces exemptions [de l'ALENA et de l'OMC] et préfère-t-il confier ses contrats de fournitures militaires à des firmes étrangères, une décision illogique en ces temps de ralentissement économique?

L'hon. Peter MacKay (ministre de la Défense nationale et ministre de la porte d'entrée de l'Atlantique):

Avec cet enjeu, il est clair que les Forces canadiennes ont besoin d'une certaine sorte de camions. On this particular procurement, what we have done is receive, dollar for dollar, the amount for this particular contract in the range of $274 million. Much of the work on the component parts of this particular truck will be done in Canada. Much of the in-service support will of course be done in Canada, around the country at various bases where these trucks, these workhorses of the Canadian Forces, will be located.

M. Serge Cardin:

L'industrie québécoise veut sa part des retombées qui découlent des contrats militaires. Un an après l'octroi du contrat à Boeing et Lockheed, l'industrie aéronautique est incapable de confirmer si les contrats octroyés totalisent 660 millions de dollars. Est-ce que le ministre de l'Industrie reconnaît que le Québec n'a pas la part qui lui revient?

L'hon. Tony Clement (ministre de l'Industrie):

Notre gouvernement reconnaît l'importance de l'industrie aérospatiale pour l'économie. C'est évidemment une partie très importante de l'économie du Québec, mais également de l'économie de tout le pays. Nous appuyons cette industrie dans nos budgets de 2008 et de 2009. Cette industrie représente une partie de notre plan économique pour le Canada et pour le Québec aussi. Nous appuyons bien sûr un plan d'action du Canada qui pourrait investir dans les industries de l'avenir, comme c'est le cas de l'industrie aérospatiale.

(*House of Commons Debates*, 2 *February* 2009, *pp. 218–19*)
(*Débats de la Chambre des communes, le 2 février* 2009, *pp. 218–19*)

(p) Science and technology / Sciences et la technologie

M. Michael Ignatieff (chef de l'opposition):

Rafick-Pierre Sékaly, une sommité mondiale du sida, quitte l'Université de Montréal pour les États-Unis. Les 25 chercheurs de son équipe le suivent ... Où est la stratégie de ce gouvernement pour empêcher le départ de nos meilleurs scientifiques?

Hon. Gary Goodyear (Minister of State (Science and Technology)):

The ... government committed $94 million to HIV-AIDS research this year. We committed $111 million to the Bill & Melinda Gates Foundation for HIV-AIDS .... This government took the recommendations and put that money back. Not only did we do that, but we added $5.1 billion [into science and technology].

(*House of Commons Debates, 5 May 2009, p. 3073*)
(*Débats de la Chambre des communes, le 5 mai 2009, p. 3073*)

(q) Securities / Valeurs mobilières

Mr. James Rajotte (Edmonton — Leduc):

[T]he current market crisis has shown the importance of prudent financial regulations. While Canada's banking sector has been assessed as the world's strongest, our securities framework has been criticized by investors, businesses and international institutions as fragmented, cumbersome and ineffective. In the words of the IMF, "Canada is currently the only G-7 country without a common securities regulator, and Canada's investors deserve better." [W]hat our government is prepared to do to address this situation?

Hon. Jim Flaherty (Minister of Finance):

[W]hile Canada's financial system is the soundest in the world, the credit crisis, the financial crisis, certainly since last year has demonstrated one glaring deficiency in our system of regulation in Canada, and that is the absence of a national securities regulator. This is not an academic subject. This matters to seniors, to people with investments, mutual funds, to families, to Canadians from coast to coast to coast. Therefore, we are going to move forward toward a common national securities regulator for Canada with willing partners in the provinces and willing participants.

(*House of Commons Debates, 20 November 2008, p. 68*)
(*Débats de la Chambre des communes, le 20 novembre 2008, p. 68*)

M. Jean Dorion (Longueuil — Pierre-Boucher):

Lors d'une commission parlementaire tenue hier à l'Assemblée nationale, le ministre des Finances du Québec et le PDG de l'Autorité des marchés financiers ont rappelé, à l'instar du FMI, de la Banque mondiale et de l'OCDE, l'efficacité de notre système décentralisé de réglementation des valeurs mobilières et ils ont dénoncé vigoureusement le projet des conservateurs d'une commission pancanadienne unique. Est-ce que le ministre des Finances va abandonner son projet totalement contre-productif et dont personne ne veut au Québec?

Hon. Jim Flaherty (Minister of Finance):

We have the most sound financial system in the world and that is the view of the World Economic Forum. Certainly, the IMF uses our financial system as one of the most sound in the world. We have one glaring deficiency in that system. It is in the area of securities regulation, where we have 13 separate securities regulators. We will move forward, as set out in the first budget bill, with the plan for a national securities regulator with willing partners, willing provinces, and willing participants ... The intention ... is to create a national securities regulator to better serve the country, the Government of Canada acting within its area of jurisdiction and respecting the jurisdiction of the provinces. I spoke with the minister of finance in Quebec just before question period. We agreed on a plan going forward with respect to negotiations concerning harmonization.

(*House of Commons Debates, 29 April 2009, p. 2860*)
(*Débats de la Chambre des communes, le 29 avril 2009, p. 2860*)

(r) Softwood lumber and forestry industry / Bois d'œuvre et l'industrie forestière

M. Robert Bouchard (Chicoutimi — Le Fjord):

Un économiste déclarait: "C'est le rôle du premier ministre de défendre les intérêts du Canada. Et vous avez échoué de le faire. Par exemple, dans le bois d'oeuvre, depuis plus de trois ans, tous les chefs de l'opposition ont demandé des garanties de prêts pour nos compagnies forestières." Qu'attend le ministre d'État pour l'Agence de développement économique du Canada pour les régions du Québec pour agir en ce sens?

L'hon. Denis Lebel (ministre d'État (Agence de développement économique du Canada pour les régions du Québec)):

C'est très très dangereux présentement au niveau de l'industrie forestière. Étant donné que les garanties de prêts offertes par l'Ontario et le Québec sont actuellement le sujet d'une procédure d'arbitrage avec les États-Unis, il ne serait pas approprié de commenter l'interprétation de ces accords. Cependant ... l'accord fournit la certitude et la stabilité à l'industrie, aux communautés et aux travailleurs forestiers à travers le Canada ... 80 p. 100 des exportations du bois d'oeuvre canadien vont vers les États-Unis. Pour nous, il est extrêmement important de préserver cette entente et de faire en sorte que nos travailleurs continuent d'exporter leur bois vers notre principal partenaire économique que sont les États-Unis.

(*House of Commons Debates, 12 February 2009, p. 751*)
(*Débats de la Chambre des communes, le 12 février 2009, p.751*)

Ms. Joyce Murray (Vancouver Quadra):

The U.S. Southern Governors' Association has passed a motion attacking the already crippled Canadian softwood lumber industry. It calls on President Obama to take new extraordinary measures to punish a sector that has done nothing wrong and is hanging on by a thread ... Why [is the government] not standing up for Canada?

Hon. Stockwell Day (Minister of International Trade and Minister for the Asia-Pacific Gateway):

We would support [the resolution]. If there is someone who is part of the agreement who is perceived to be running afoul of the agreement, then there is a dispute mechanism in place that should be followed and we endorse that. We think it is a good motion.

(*House of Commons Debates, 23 February 2009, p. 849*)
(*Débats de la Chambre des communes, le 23 février 2009, p. 849*)

Mrs. Alexandra Mendes (Brossard — La Prairie):

Last Friday, the London Court of International Arbitration imposed a 10% tax on Quebec and Ontario softwood lumber exports to the United States ... How can the Conservatives possibly explain to unemployed Quebec and Ontario forestry workers that even before they can be rehired, $68 million in export taxes need to be paid?

Hon. Stockwell Day (Minister of International Trade and Minister for the Asia-Pacific Gateway):

Before the softwood lumber agreement was in place there were constant court battles and constant quota assessments going against Canada. We have an agreement now that has huge support from the industry. When we have an agreement like this, there is a dispute settlement mechanism. If one side goes to the referee and the referee says that the other side has to pay or is offside on it, then we must live up to the agreement. We intend to do that and we intend to work with the provinces to see how this can be repaid in a way that does not hurt them. We must keep in mind that $5 billion was returned to the Canada side of this agreement.

(*House of Commons Debates, 3 March 2009, p. 1226*)
(*Débats de la Chambre des communes, le 3 mars 2009, p. 1226*)

M. Gilles Duceppe (Laurier — Sainte-Marie):

Le ministre du Revenu national a admis qu'à première vue, les garanties de prêts respectaient l'accord sur le bois d'oeuvre ... L'industrie a besoin de liquidités et les garanties de prêts sont là pour cela. Qu'attend le gouvernement?

L'hon. Denis Lebel (ministre d'État (Agence de développement économique du Canada pour les régions du Québec)):

Exportation et développement Canada, en 2008, a aidé 534 entreprises forestières, soit 90 p. 100 des entreprises de l'industrie forestière au Canada. Plusieurs milliards de dollars ont été donnés en soutien à l'industrie forestière, et nous continuerons ainsi. Les dossiers qui ont été présentés comme étant prioritaires au comité Canada-Québec concerneront entre autres l'accès au capital qui sera vérifié par ce comité, le soutien aux travailleurs et aux communautés, ainsi que le développement de nouveaux produits et des marchés. Le problème actuel de l'industrie forestière, si on veut bien être honnête, en est malheureusement un de marché puisque 50 p. 100 du bois du Québec est exporté et 96 p. 100 de ce bois est exporté aux États-Unis.

(*House of Commons Debates, 21 April 2009, p. 2512*)
(*Débats de la Chambre des communes, le 21 avril 2009, p. 2512*)

(s) Taxation / Fiscalité

M. Robert Carrier (Alfred-Pellan):

Plusieurs pays, dont la France, l'Allemagne et le Royaume-Uni, ont dénoncé les paradis fiscaux et réaffirmé leur volonté, à l'occasion du sommet du G20, de resserrer les contrôles financiers pour contrer l'évasion fiscale. Curieusement, le Canada adopte l'attitude inverse et remet en place une échappatoire fiscale. Le gouvernement peut-il nous expliquer son raisonnement?

L'hon. Jean-Pierre Blackburn (ministre du Revenu national et ministre d'État (Agriculture)):

Toute personne qui gagne un revenu doit le déclarer, qu'il le gagne à l'étranger ou ici, au Canada. Des règles obligent ces gens à le déclarer. Lorsque des gens éludent l'impôt qu'ils doivent au Canada par des paradis fiscaux, c'est évidemment une préoccupation. Nous y travaillons afin de protéger l'assiette fiscale et d'être justes envers ceux qui paient leur part d'impôt par rapport à ceux qui tentent de ne pas le faire.

Mr. Ted Menzies (Parliamentary Secretary to the Minister of Finance):

We established a panel of experts to bring us a report on [double deduction]. We have acted on that report ... We are aligning with other countries in the world so we do not put our Canadian companies at a disadvantage.

(*House of Commons Debates, 31 March 2009, p. 2217*)
(*Débats de la Chambre des communes, le 31 mars 2009, p. 2217*)

M. Jean-Yves Laforest (Saint-Maurice — Champlain):

Le ministre mettra-t-il enfin sur pied des mesures musclées pour faire face aux problèmes des paradis fiscaux?

L'hon. Jean-Pierre Blackburn (ministre du Revenu national et ministre d'État (Agriculture)):

La question des paradis fiscaux est une préoccupation de notre gouvernement. Dernièrement, on a vu le dossier de UBS qui est revenu sur la table. [O]n constate que 12 personnes sur 38 qui ont des paradis fiscaux à l'étranger ont déjà rempli une divulgation volontaire, ce qui rapporte au gouvernement 4,5 millions de dollars. On veut progresser dans le dossier sur les paradis fiscaux.

(*House of Commons Debates, 14 September 2009, p. 4912*)
(*Débats de la Chambre des communes, le 14 septembre 2009, p. 4912*)

(t) Trade- and Trade-related Agreements / Accords commerciaux et liés au commerce

M. Steven Blaney (Lévis — Bellechasse):

[Quelles sont les] des initiatives entreprises récemment pour conserver notre leadership en matière de libre-échange canadien?

L'hon. Stockwell Day (ministre du Commerce international et ministre de la porte d'entrée de l'Asie-Pacifique):

J'ai le plaisir d'annoncer aujourd'hui que nous nous sommes entendus avec l'Union européenne sur les secteurs qui feront l'objet de négociations pour une entente économique avec celle-ci. L'Union européenne est notre deuxième partenaire économique. Un accord final pourrait à lui seul rapporter plus de 12 milliards de dollars dans l'économie canadienne. Il s'agit d'une bonne nouvelle pour les compagnies et les travailleurs canadiens. Nous espérons lancer des négociations officielles le plus tôt possible.

(*House of Commons Debates, 5 March 2009, pp. 1359–60*)
(*Débats de la Chambre des communes, le 5 mars 2009, pp. 1359–60*)

Hon. Jack Layton (Toronto — Danforth):

Will [the government] move on [the] idea [of renegotiating the environmental and labour elements of the NAFTA agreement]?

Hon. Stockwell Day (Minister of International Trade and Minister for the Asia-Pacific Gateway):

President Obama, following our Prime Minister's lead, has made a clear statement, for instance, with the buy American act to ensure that everything done on that act complies with its trade obligations. When it comes to NAFTA, the indication has been very clear that there is not an intention to have serious changes made to it. President Obama has indicated his interest in the labour and the environmental accords that are associated with that. The Prime Minister has indicated those accords are strong. We intend to talk to him about that.

(*House of Commons Debates, 30 March 2009, p. 2125*)
(*Débats de la Chambre des communes, le 30 mars 2009, p. 2125*)

Mrs. Nina Grewal (Fleetwood — Port Kells):

How [does] our government's record on trade with China and India compare to the record [in the past]?

Hon. Stockwell Day (Minister of International Trade and Minister for the Asia-Pacific Gateway):

In past months, we have had 14 members of Parliament and ministers visit China, including myself and the Minister of Foreign Affairs. We have invested $2.5 billion into the Asia-Pacific corridor to help the flow of goods to Asia. There are six new trade offices in China and three more in India, which brings us up to eight. The Prime Minister has started negotiations with the EU in terms of free trade agreements. We are having discussions with India right now in terms of trade. There is a foreign investment protection and nuclear co-operation agreement in progress. There are more FTAs on the way.

(*House of Commons Debates, 15 September 2009, p. 5028*)
(*Débats de la Chambre des communes, le 15 septembre 2009, p. 5028*)

Mr. Ron Cannan (Kelowna — Lake Country):

Today the government tabled new legislation to implement the Canada-Jordan free trade agreement ... Why [is] this agreement so important for Canada?

Mr. Gerald Keddy (Parliamentary Secretary to the Minister of International Trade):

The reality is that the potential here for jobs and opportunities is exponential. The best example is to look at how the United States was doing before it signed its free trade agreement with Jordan. It was doing 200 million dollars' worth of trade. Today it is doing two billion dollars' worth of trade. This agreement would mean increased jobs for Canadian workers and increased opportunity for Canadian consumers.

(*House of Commons Debates, 17 November 2009, p. 6862*)
(*Débats de la Chambre des communes, le 17 novembre 2009, p. 6862*)

(u) Trade in medicines / Commerce des médicaments

Hon. Carolyn Bennett (St. Paul's):

Last week, President Obama's budget signaled support to open up the cross-border medicine trade ... What is the Minister of Health doing to protect Canada's drug supply to ensure that we do not become the U.S. discount drug store?

Mr. Colin Carrie (Parliamenary Secretary to the Minister of Health):

We continue to monitor the U.S. developments. [W]e are a long way from a successful U.S. drug import bill. If future situations warrant action ... we will take a balanced approach to this issue to protect Canadians' health, while also respecting our international trade obligations.

(*House of Commons Debates, 6 March 2009, p. 1413*)
(*Débats de la Chambre des communes, le 6 mars 2009, p. 1413*)

M. David McGuinty (Ottawa-Sud):

[O]ne-third of all hospital patients in this country rely on nuclear medicine. Pourquoi, devant cette crise [de l'industrie canadienne des isotopes], la réaction du premier ministre est-elle ... de laisser tomber le monde entier?

Hon. Lisa Raitt (Minister of Natural Resources):

In 2008, AECL made the decision to discontinue the MAPLE-1 and MAPLE-2 reactors, which were to supply medical isotopes to the world. It was after 12 years, over half a billion dollars, and not one single medical isotope produced. As a result of that, the government instructed AECL to extend the licence of the NRU as best it could in order to continue to produce medical isotopes. Along with that, last week we struck an expert panel to review other options that may be made available.

(*House of Commons Debates*, 11 June 2009, p. 4501)
(*Débats de la Chambre des communes, le 11 juin 2009, p. 4501*)

Hon. Geoff Regan (Halifax-Ouest):

Is it not reasonable to expect that most of the remaining supply of cancer testing isotopes is going to be soaked up by the U.S. market?

Hon. Lisa Raitt (Minister of Natural Resources):

As we indicated yesterday through our conversations with the United States, the Minister of Health is working with the distributors of generators. We do know that next week we will have 50% of the supply that we normally have in isotopes here in Canada and that has been communicated to the medical community. [I]t is a very complex chain in which we have isotopes coming from global reactors into the Canadian marketplace. We are working with all the parties involved in that supply chain.

(*House of Commons Debates*, 11 June 2009, p. 4503)
(*Débats de la Chambre des communes, le 11 juin 2009, p. 4503*)

(v) Trade and human rights / Commerce et les droits de la personne

M. Peter Julian (Burnaby — New Westminster):

[Q]uatre des cinq grands partenaires économiques du Canada sont membres de la Coopération économique de la zone Asie-Pacifique et l'APEC compte pour plus de la moitié de l'économie mondiale. Toutefois, le [gouvernement du Canada] est sur le point de partir pour le sommet de l'APEC sans objectifs clairs. Est-ce que le ministre est d'accord pour affirmer que le commerce international doit mener au respect des droits humains, au respect de l'environnement et à améliorer les conditions des travailleurs et des travailleuses?

Mr. Gerald Keddy (Parliamentary Secretary to the Minister of International Trade):

Canada is committed to re-engagement with the Americas and part of that is free trade. [O]ur free trade agreements are complemented with provisions on labour and environmental co-operation. We need to be perfectly clear that our free trade agreements promote and reinforce the protection of human rights.

(*House of Commons Debates, 21 November 2008, p. 113*)
(*Débats de la Chambre des communes, le 21 novembre 2008, p.113*)

M. Serge Cardin (Sherbrooke):

[L]e premier ministre s'est empressé d'annoncer un accord de libre-échange avec la Colombie ... La Colombie a un des pires dossiers de l'hémisphère en matière de respect des droits de la personne. Comment le [gouvernement] peut-il justifier une telle entente avec la Colombie, lorsque l'on sait que syndicalistes et Autochtones sont assassinés en toute impunité?

L'hon. Stockwell Day (ministre du Commerce international et ministre de la porte d'entrée de l'Asie-Pacifique):

Cela a été un honneur pour moi de signer le document que mon ami a mentionné ... [I]l contient des sections exactes et très précises. Notamment au chapitre 16, je pense que ce sont les articles 16.3 et 16.4 qui sont spécifiques aux droits humains et aux droits des travailleurs. Ils sont très clairs et très forts ...[L]a Colombie a fait des progrès dans le domaine des droits humains, surtout grâce à une entente sur le travail. C'est pourquoi nous avons reconnu ces progrès. Nous voulons une entente avec ce pays pour continuer à améliorer le niveau de vie en Colombie et à renforcer les droits humains et les droits des travailleurs et des syndiqués.

(*House of Commons Debates, 24 November 2008, p.175; 11 February 2009, p. 678*)
(*Débats de la Chambre des communes, le 24 novembre 2008, p. 175; le 11 février 2009, p. 678*)

Mme Paule Brunelle (Trois-Rivières):

Un rapport inspiré des Tables rondes sur l'industrie minière en 2007 recommandait la création d'un poste d'ombudsman et l'adoption de normes sociales obligatoires sur les activités des compagnies à l'étranger. Au lieu de cela, le ministre crée un organisme bidon qui n'imposera ni règles ni conséquences aux compagnies qui polluent ou bafouent les droits des populations. Comment le gouvernement peut-il se fier aux entreprises fautives puisque, de toute façon, il n'y a aucune conséquence?

Mr. Gerald Keddy (Parliamentary Secretary to the Minister of International Trade):

We have the position of counsellor for the extractive sector. We are expecting this position to do a lot to benefit corporate social responsibility in Canada. It should be recognized that Canadian companies control around 43% of the world's mining sector. There are 8,000 Canadian companies in 100 countries around the world doing a great job in the mining and extractive sectors, and doing a great job on corporate social responsibilities.

Mme Paule Brunelle:

Malgré les inquiétudes et les critiques, le gouvernement conservateur a déposé un projet de loi pour ratifier l'accord de libre-échange avec le Pérou ... Quel message le ministre envoie-t-il en n'imposant aucune règle aux compagnies minières?

Mr. Gerald Keddy:

The free trade agreements with Peru and Colombia have some of the strongest provisions on human rights of any free trade agreement ever signed by Canada. Human rights are respected, the environment is respected and corporate social responsibility is adhered to. These are some of the best and strongest agreements we have ever signed.

(*House of Commons Debates, 27 March 2009, p. 2072*)
(*Débats de la Chambre des communes, le 27 mars 2009, p. 2072*)

(w) World Trade Organization (WTO) / Organisation mondiale du commerce (OMC)

M. André Bellavance (Richmond — Arthabaska):

À Davos, le ministre du Commerce international a déclaré vouloir demander au directeur général de l'OMC, Pascal Lamy, de remettre les négociations à l'ordre du jour. Ce faisant, il risque de faire perdre un milliard de dollars de revenus aux producteurs sous gestion de l'offre. Le ministre de l'Agriculture et de l'Agroalimentaire en est-il conscient, et va-t-il veiller à faire inclure la protection de la gestion de l'offre et des produits sensibles dans les textes?

L'hon. Jean-Pierre Blackburn (ministre du Revenu national et ministre d'État (Agriculture)):

On sait qu'il y a eu en cette Chambre, en 2005, une résolution unanime qui nous demandait de protéger la gestion de l'offre. Notre gouvernement s'est positionné très clairement en faveur de nos agriculteurs et de tous ceux également qui œuvrent dans le domaine de la G05. Oui, nous gardons le cap. Nous voulons que la gestion de l'offre soit respectée au sein de l'OMC et nous allons continuer à défendre nos gens là-dessus.

(*House of Commons Debates*, 5 February 2009, p. 447)
(*Débats de la Chambre des communes, le 5 février 2009, p. 447*)

M. Raynald Blais (Gaspésie — Îles-de-la-Madeleine):

Le Parlement européen s'est prononcé ce matin en faveur de l'interdiction de la vente des produits dérivés du loup-marin sur tout le territoire de l'Union. Cette interdiction doit prendre effet dès 2010. La ministre des Pêches et des Océans et son gouvernement ont-ils prévu un plan d'action pour contrer cette décision et comptent-ils, entre autres moyens, porter plainte auprès de l'Organisation mondiale du commerce?

Hon. Gail Shea (Minister of Fisheries and Oceans):

The EU has dealt a serious blow to the livelihoods of many of our coastal communities across the country. This is totally unacceptable and we will take whatever trade action is necessary to protect the markets for Canadian seal products. Unlike the Liberal Party, we will stand up for Canadian sealing families.

(*House of Commons Debates*, 5 May 2009, p. 3080)
(*Débats de la Chambre des communes, le 5 mai 2009, p. 3080*)

8   *Law of the Sea / Droit de la mer*

(a) Fisheries / Pêches

Hon. Gerry Byrne (Humber — St. Barbe — Baie Verte):

European factory freezer trawlers continue to plunder Canadian cod stocks inside Canada's supposed new territory. It was NAFO, however, not Canada, that resumed fishing of cod on the Flemish Cap this year after 10 years of closure and it was NAFO that set these irresponsible quotas beyond the scientifically recommended amounts. Why did the minister simply not use her new-found powers of custodial management to stop this foreign fishing activity inside the Canadian management zone?

Hon. Gail Shea (Minister of Fisheries and Oceans):

All decisions at this year's NAFO meeting were made within scientific advice and with the full participation of the province of Newfoundland and Labrador. [A]ccording to the Newfoundland industry the decisions taken at NAFO will put an additional $11 million into the Newfoundland economy.

(*House of Commons Debates, 6 October 2009, pp. 5638–39*)
(*Débats de la Chambre des communes, le 6 octobre 2009, pp. 5638–39*)

Mrs. Tilly O'Neill-Gordon (Miramichi):

Important meetings are beginning today in Recife, Brazil. Canada has long pressed the International Commission for the Conservation of Atlantic Tunas to adhere to scientific advice and enforce the rules of this organization. However, members fishing the stock in the eastern Atlantic and Mediterranean, fish recklessly, leaving environmental groups and some countries to call for a trade ban. [Will] Canada stand up for conservation and its fishers?

Hon. Gail Shea (Minister of Fisheries and Oceans):

Canada's bluefin tuna fishery is a responsible and sustainable fishery. It is worth as much as $10 million annually to Canadian fishers, not to mention significant economic spinoffs. Canada is calling on all ICCAT members to take immediate, concrete and decisive action on conservation and management at ICCAT's annual meeting, which begins today. ICCAT must put an end to the overfishing by the violating countries. If it does not take immediate action, it could have serious and long-term consequences for international trade for all of bluefin tuna.

(*House of Commons Debates, 6 November 2009, p. 6732*)
(*Débats de la Chambre des communes, le 6 novembre 2009, p. 6732*)

9   *Sports / Sports*

M. Pascal-Pierre Paillé (Louis-Hébert):

Le Défi sportif de Montréal est le seul événement sportif multi-déficience au monde. Il regroupe 15 pays, 13 sports adaptés et plus de 3 000 athlètes. En 2006, le gouvernement conservateur se dotait de la Politique sur le sport pour les personnes handicapées ... Sur les 100 000 $ demandés cette année, le Défi sportif n'a obtenu de Sport Canada que 75 000 $ malgré des besoins criants ... Pourquoi Sport Canada s'entête-t-il à refuser au Défi sportif les 25 000 $ qu'il demande, et qu'entend faire le ministre à ce sujet?

Hon. Gary Lunn (Minister of State (Sport)):

Défi sportif [has done] the great work it does [by] bring[ing] 3,000 disabled athletes from 15 different countries, with 9,000 volunteers. Our government has been supporting it. It has received the same amount for the last three years. There were $25,000 that were ineligible, but we are proudly working with it. Notre gouvernement continuera d'apporter des contributions au Défi sportif et au développement du sport au Canada.

(*House of Commons Debates, 7 May 2009, p. 3231*)
(*Débats de la Chambre des communes, le 7 mai 2009, p. 3231*)

Mme Raymonde Folco (Laval — Les Îles):

Peut [le gouvernement] assurer les Canadiens et les athlètes francophones internationaux que le Canada assurera un service adéquat dans leur langue aux Jeux olympiques?

L'hon. James Moore (ministre du Patrimoine canadien et des Langues officielles):

Oui, absolument. Cela dit, notre gouvernement et le COVAN travaillent ensemble pour que les Jeux olympiques soient complètement bilingues. Les Jeux olympiques de 1988 représentaient une grande amélioration par rapport aux Jeux olympiques de 1976, et les Jeux olympiques de 2010 représenteront une grande amélioration par rapport aux Jeux olympiques de 1988. Les Jeux olympiques de 2010 respecteront les langues officielles du Canada, point final.

(*House of Commons Debates, 4 June 2009, p. 4207*)
(*Débats de la Chambre des communes, le 4 juin 2009, p. 4207*)

M. Greg Rickford (Kenora):

Quelques 300 jeunes athlètes et artistes du Canada sont présentement à Beyrouth pour défendre fièrement les couleurs de notre pays dans des compétitions de haut calibre. Trois délégations, soit celles du Canada, du Canada-Québec et du Canada-Nouveau Brunswick participeront aux compétitions au cours des prochains jours dans diverses épreuves. La ministre de la Francophonie peut-elle nous dire ce que fait le gouvernement du Canada pour contribuer au succès de cet événement?

L'hon. Josée Verner (ministre des Affaires intergouvernementales, présidente du Conseil privé de la Reine pour le Canada et ministre de la Francophonie):

Récemment, j'ai eu le plaisir d'annoncer que notre gouvernement octroyait 1 million de dollars à l'Organisation internationale de la Francophonie pour faciliter l'organisation de la sixième édition de ces jeux à Beyrouth. Plus de 3 000 jeunes sportifs et artistes provenant des cinq continents sont présentement à Beyrouth, au Liban, dans un des plus grands rassemblements de l'histoire des Jeux de la Francophonie.

(*House of Commons Debates, 29 September 2009, p. 5332*)
(*Débats de la Chambre des communes, le 29 septembre 2009, p. 5332*)

Treaty Action Taken by Canada in 2008 / Mesures prises par le Canada en matière de traités en 2008

compiled by / préparé par

JAQUELINE CARON

I BILATERAL

Argentina

Treaty between the Government of Canada and the Government of the Argentine Republic on the Transfer of Offenders. *Signed:* Buenos Aires, 3 July 2003. *Instruments of ratification exchanged and entered into force:* 11 August 2008. CTS 2008/14.

Brazil

Treaty between the Government of Canada and the Government of the Federative Republic of Brazil on Mutual Legal Assistance in Criminal Matters. *Signed:* Brasilia, 27 January 1995. *Entered into force:* 1 November 2008. CTS 2008/4.

Framework Agreement between the Government of Canada and the Government of the Federative Republic of Brazil for Cooperation on Science, Technology and Innovation. *Signed:* Sao Paulo, 17 November 2008. *Entered into force:* 19 April 2010.

Chile

Agreement between the Government of Canada and the Government of the Republic of Chile to Amend the Free Trade Agreement between the Government of Canada and the Government of the Republic of Chile. *Signed:* Hanoi, 15 November 2006. *Entered into force:* 5 September 2008. CTS 2008/15.

China

Agreement for Scientific and Technological Cooperation between the Government of Canada and the Government of the People's Republic of China. *Signed:* Beijing, 16 January 2007. *Entered into force:* 17 July 2008. CTS 2008/6.

Colombia

Free Trade Agreement between Canada and the Republic of Colombia. *Signed:* Lima, 21 November 2008.

Agreement on the Environment between Canada and the Republic of Colombia. *Signed:* Lima, 21 November 2008.

Jaqueline Caron is Treaty Registrar in the Legal Advisory Division of the Department of Foreign Affairs / Greffier des Traités, Direction des consultations juridiques, Ministère des Affaires étrangères.

Agreement on Labour Cooperation between Canada and the Republic of Colombia. *Signed:* Lima, 21 November 2008.

Convention between Canada and the Republic of Colombia for the Avoidance of Double Taxation and the Prevention of Fiscal Evasion with respect to Taxes on Income and on Capital. *Signed:* Lima, 21 November 2008.

Gabon
Convention between the Government of Canada and the Government of the Gabonese Republic for the Avoidance of Double Taxation and the Prevention of Fiscal Evasion with Respect to Taxes on Income and on Capital. *Signed:* Libreville, 14 November 2002. *Instruments of ratification exchanged and entered into force:* 22 December 2008. CTS 2008/5.

Iceland
Agreement on Agriculture between Canada and the Republic of Iceland. *Signed:* Davos, 26 January 2008. *Entered into force:* 1 July 2009.

India
Agreement for Scientific and Technological Cooperation between the Government of Canada and the Government of the Republic of India. *Signed:* Toronto, 18 November 2005. *Entered into force:* 11 November 2008. CTS 2008/10.

Japan
Agreement between Canada and Japan on Social Security. *Signed:* Tokyo, 15 February 2006. *Entered into force:* 1 March 2008. CTS 2008/7.

Exchange of Notes between the Government of Canada and the Government of Japan Constituting an Agreement on Special Measures Concerning Supply Assistance Activities in Support of Counter-Terrorism Maritime Interdiction Activities. *Signed:* Tokyo, 7 March 2008. *Entered into force:* 7 March 2008.

Kyrgyzstan
Agreement between the Government of Canada and the Government of the Kyrgyz Republic Concerning Cooperation in the Field of Biological Security and Biological Safety. *Signed:* Bishkek, 22 August 2008. *Entered into force:* 8 April 2009.

Norway
Agreement on Agriculture between Canada and the Kingdom of Norway. *Signed:* Davos, 26 January 2008. *Entered into force:* 1 July 2009.

Peru
Free Trade Agreement between Canada and the Republic of Peru. *Signed:* Lima, 29 May 2008. *Entered into force:* 1 August 2009.

Agreement on the Environment between Canada and the Republic of Peru. *Signed:* Lima, 29 May 2008. *Entered into force:* 1 August 2009.

Agreement on Labour Cooperation between Canada and the Republic of Peru. *Signed:* Lima, 29 May 2008. *Entered into force:* 1 August 2009.

Poland
Agreement on Social Security between Canada and the Republic of Poland. *Signed:* Warsaw, 2 April 2008. *Entered into force:* 1 October 2009.

Agreement between the Government of Canada and the Government of the Republic of Poland Concerning the Promotion of Mobility of Young Citizens. *Signed:* Warsaw, 14 July 2008. *Entered into force:* 1 August 2009.

Russian Federation

Exchange of Notes between the Government of Canada and the Government of the Russian Federation Constituting an Additional Agreement to the Agreement between the Government of Canada and the Government of the Union of Soviet Socialist Republics for Cooperation in the Peaceful Uses of Nuclear Energy, done on 20 November 1989. *Signed by Canada:* Ottawa, 6 May 2008. *Signed by the Russian Federation:* Ottawa, 23 April 2008. *Entered into force:* 3 June 2009.

Switzerland

Agreement on Agriculture between Canada and the Swiss Confederation. *Signed:* Davos, 26 January 2008. *Entered into force:* 1 July 2009.

United States

Agreement between the Government of Canada and the Government of the United States of America Relating to the Establishment of Integrated Lines of Communications to Ensure Logistic Support for the Canadian Armed Forces and the Armed Forces of the United States of America. *Signed:* Washington, 23 April 2008. *Entered into force:* 5 September 2008. CTS 2008/9.

Exchange of Letters Constituting an Agreement between the Government of Canada and the Government of the United States of America Amending Appendix 6 of Annex 300-B, Textiles and Apparel Goods, of the North American Free Trade Agreement between the Government of Canada, the Government of the United States of America and the Government of the United Mexican States. *Signed by Canada:* Ottawa, 21 July 2008. *Signed by the United States of America:* Washington, 29 May 2008. *Entered into force:* 1 July 2009.

Agreement between the Government of Canada and the Government of the United States of America on Pacific Hake/Whiting. *Signed:* Seattle, 21 November 2003. *Entered into force:* 25 June 2008. CTS 2008/3.

Agreement between the Government of Canada and the Government of the United States of America on Emergency Management Cooperation. *Signed:* Washington, 12 December 2008. *Entered into force:* 7 July 2009.

Protocol Amending the Convention between Canada and the United States of America with Respect to Taxes on Income and on Capital done at Washington on 26 September 1980, as amended by the Protocols done on 14 June 1983, 28 March 1984, 17 March 1995 and 29 July 1997. *Signed:* Chelsea, 21 September 2007. *Entered into force:* 15 December 2008. CTS 2008/11.

Exchange of Letters Constituting an Agreement Expanding upon Article XXVI of the Convention between Canada and the United States of America with Respect to Taxes on Income and on Capital, signed at Washington on 26 September 1980. *Signed:* Ottawa, 21 September 2007. *Entered into force:* 15 December 2008. CTS 2008/12.

Exchange of Letters Constituting an Agreement Setting Out Various Understandings and Interpretations as They Apply to the Convention between Canada and the United States of America with Respect to Taxes on Income and on Capital, signed at Washington on 26 September 1980. *Signed:* Ottawa, 21 September 2007. *Entered into force:* 15 December 2008. CTS 2008/13.

Exchange of Notes between the Government of Canada and the Government of the United States of America Relating to Annex IV of the Treaty between the Government of Canada and the Government of the United States of America Concerning Pacific Salmon. *Signed:* Washington, 23 December 2008. *Entered into force:* 1 January 2009.

II   MULTILATERAL

Conservation
Agreement on International Humane Trapping Standards between the European Community, Canada and the Russian Federation, Brussels, 15 December 1997. *Signed by Canada:* 15 December 1997. *Ratified by Canada:* 31 May 1999. *Provisionally applied by Canada:* 1 June 1999. *Entered into force for Canada:* 22 July 2008.

Defence
Protocol to the North Atlantic Treaty on the Accession of the Republic of Albania, Brussels, 9 July 2008. *Signed by Canada:* 9 July 2008. *Accepted by Canada:* 16 January 2009. *Entered into force for Canada:* 27 March 2009.

Protocol to the North Atlantic Treaty on the Accession of the Republic of Croatia, Brussels, 9 July 2008. *Signed by Canada:* 9 July 2008. *Accepted by Canada:* 16 January 2009. *Entered into force for Canada:* 30 March 2009.

Disarmament
Convention on Cluster Munitions, Dublin, 30 May 2008. *Signed by Canada:* 3 December 2008. *Entered into force:* 1 August 2010.

Human Rights
The International Institute for Democracy and Electoral Assistance Statutes (as amended), Stockholm, 24 January 2006. *Accepted by Canada:* 12 June 2008. *Entered into force for Canada:* 21 November 2008.

Narcotics
Amendments to Annex I of the International Convention against Doping in Sport, Paris, 15 November 2007. *Entered into force for Canada:* 1 January 2008. CTS 2008/2.

Navigation
Protocol of 1996 to Amend the Convention on Limitation of Liability for Maritime Claims, 1976, London, 2 May 1996. *Signed by Canada:* 9 September 1997. *Ratified by Canada:* 9 May 2008. *Entered into force for Canada:* 7 August 2008.

Science
Agreement among the Government of Canada, the Government of the United Mexican States, and the Government of the United States of America for Cooperation in Energy Science and Technology, Victoria, 23 July 2007. *Signed by Canada:* 23 July 2007. *Entered into force for Canada:* 24 July 2008. CTS 2008/8.

Trade
Free Trade Agreement between Canada and the States of the European Free Trade Association (Iceland, Liechtenstein, Norway and Switzerland), Davos, 26 January 2008. *Signed by Canada:* 26 January 2008. *Ratified by Canada:* 30 April 2009. *Entered into force for Canada:* 1 July 2009.

Exchange of Letters Constituting an Agreement between the Government of Canada, the Government of the United Mexican States, and the Government of the United States of America, amending Annex 401 of the North American Free Trade Agreement between the Government of Canada, the Government of the United Mexican States, and the Government of the United States of America, Ottawa, Mexico, Washington, 11 April 2008.

Signed by Canada: 11 April 2008. *Entered into force for Canada:* 1 September 2009.

War

Protocol Additional to the Geneva Conventions of 12 August 1949, and Relating to the Adoption of an Additional Distinctive Emblem (Protocol III), Geneva, 8 December 2005. *Signed by Canada:* 19 June 2006. *Ratified by Canada:* 26 November 2007. *Entered into force for Canada:* 26 May 2008.

War Graves

Agreement between the Governments of Australia, Canada, India, New Zealand, South Africa and the United Kingdom of Great Britain and Northern Ireland and the Government of the Republic of Namibia Concerning the Treatment of War Graves of Members of the Armed Forces of the Commonwealth in the Territory of the Republic of Namibia, Windhoek, 27 June 2005. *Signed by Canada:* 18 June 2008.

I BILATÉRAUX

Argentine

Traité entre le gouvernement du Canada et le gouvernement de la République argentine sur le transfèrement des condamnés. *Signé:* Buenos Aires, le 3 juillet 2003. *Entrée en vigueur:* le 11 août 2008. RTC 2008/14.

Brésil

Traité d'entraide en matière pénale entre le gouvernement du Canada et le gouvernement de la République fédérative du Brésil. *Signé:* Brasilia, le 27 janvier 1995. *Entrée en vigueur:* le 1er novembre 2008. RTC 2008/4.

Accord cadre entre le gouvernement du Canada et le gouvernement de la République fédérative du Brésil sur la coopération en science, technologie et innovation. *Signé:* Sao Paulo, le 17

novembre 2008. *Entrée en vigueur:* le 19 avril, 2010.

Chili

Accord entre le gouvernement du Canada et le gouvernement de la République du Chili modifiant l'Accord de libre-échange entre le gouvernement du Canada et le gouvernement de la République du Chili. *Signé:* Hanoï, le 15 novembre 2006. *Entrée en vigueur:* le 5 septembre 2008. RTC 2008/15.

République populaire de Chine

Accord de coopération scientifique et technologique entre le gouvernement du Canada et le gouvernement de la République populaire de Chine. *Signé:* Beijing, le 16 janvier 2007. *Entrée en vigueur:* le 17 juillet 2008. RTC 2008/6.

Colombie

Accord de libre-échange entre le Canada et la République de Colombie. *Signé:* Lima, le 21 novembre 2008.

Accord sur l'environnement entre le Canada et la République de Colombie. *Signé:* Lima, le 21 novembre 2008.

Accord de coopération dans le domaine du travail entre le Canada et la République de Colombie. *Signé:* Lima, le 21 novembre 2008.

Convention entre le Canada et la République de Colombie en vue d'éviter les doubles impositions et de prévenir l'évasion fiscale en matière d'impôts sur le revenu et sur la fortune. *Signé:* Lima, le 21 novembre 2008.

États-Unis

Accord entre le gouvernement du Canada et le gouvernement des États-Unis d'Amérique concernant l'établissement de lignes de communication intégrées en vue d'assurer le soutien logistique des Forces armées canadiennes et des Forces armées des États-Unis d'Amérique. *Signé:* Washington, le 23 avril 2008. *Entrée en vigueur:* le 5 septembre 2008. RTC 2008/9.

Échange de lettres constituant un Accord entre le gouvernement du Canada et le gouvernement des États-Unis d'Amérique modifiant l'Appendice 6 de l'Annexe 300-B, Produits textiles et vêtements, de l'Accord de libre-échange nord-américain entre le gouvernement du Canada, le gouvernement des États-Unis d'Amérique et le gouvernement des États-Unis du Mexique. *Signé par le Canada:* Ottawa, le 21 juillet 2008. *Signé par les États-Unis d'Amérique:* Washington, le 29 mai 2008. *Entrée en vigueur:* le 1er juillet 2009.

Accord relatif au merlu du Pacifique entre le gouvernement du Canada et le gouvernement des États-Unis d'Amérique. *Signé:* Seattle, le 21 novembre 2003. *Entrée en vigueur:* le 25 juin 2008. RTC 2008/3.

Accord de coopération entre le gouvernement du Canada et le gouvernement des États-Unis d'Amérique concernant la gestion des urgences. *Signé:* Washington, 12 décembre 2008. *Entrée en vigueur:* le 7 juillet 2009.

Protocole modifiant la Convention entre le Canada et les États-Unis d'Amérique en matière d'impôts sur le revenu et sur la fortune, faite à Washington le 26 septembre 1980 et modifiée par les protocoles faits le 14 juin 1983, le 28 mars 1984, le 17 mars 1995 et le 29 juillet 1997. *Signé:* Chelsea, le 21 septembre 2007. *Entrée en vigueur:* le 15 décembre 2008. RTC 2008/11.

Échange de notes constituant un accord qui développe l'article XXVI de la Convention entre le Canada et les États-Unis d'Amérique en matière d'impôts sur le revenu et sur la fortune, faite à Washington le 26 septembre 1980. *Signé:* le 21 septembre 2007. *Entrée en vigueur:* le 15 décembre 2008. RTC 2008/12.

Échange de notes constituant un accord qui expose différentes perceptions et interprétations s'appliquant à la Convention entre le Canada et les États-Unis d'Amérique en matière d'impôts sur le revenu et sur la fortune, faite à Washington le 26 septembre 1980. *Signé:* le 21 septembre 2007. *Entrée en vigueur:* le 15 décembre 2008. RTC 2008/13.

Échange de notes entre le gouvernement du Canada et le gouvernement des États-Unis d'Amérique relatif à l'Annexe IV du Traité entre le gouvernement du Canada et le gouvernement des États-Unis d'Amérique concernant le saumon du Pacifique. *Signé:* le 23 décembre 2008. *Entrée en vigueur:* le 1er janvier 2009.

Gabon
Convention entre le gouvernement du Canada et le gouvernement de la République gabonaise en vue d'éviter les doubles impositions et de prévenir l'évasion fiscale en matière d'impôts sur le revenu et sur la fortune. *Signé:* Libreville, le 14 novembre 2002. *Entrée en vigueur:* le 22 décembre 2008. RTC 2008/5.

Inde
Accord de coopération scientifique et technologique entre le gouvernement du Canada et le gouvernement de la République de l'Inde. *Signé:* Toronto, le 18 novembre 2005. *Entrée en vigueur:* le 11 novembre 2008. RTC 2008/10.

Islande
Accord sur l'agriculture entre le Canada et la République d'Islande. *Signé:* Davos, le 26 janvier 2008. *Entrée en vigueur:* le 1ᵉʳ juillet 2009.

Japon
Accord de sécurité sociale entre le Canada et le Japon. *Signé:* Tokyo, le 15 février 2006. *Entrée en vigueur:* le 1ᵉʳ mars 2008. RTC 2008/7.

Échange de notes entre le gouvernement du Canada et le gouvernement du Japon constituant un Accord portant sur des mesures spéciales concernant des activités d'assistance à l'approvisionnement au soutien d'activités d'interdiction maritime antiterroristes. *Signé:* Tokyo, le 7 mars 2008. *Entrée en vigueur:* le 7 mars 2008.

Kirghizistan
Accord entre le gouvernement du Canada et le gouvernement de la République kirghize concernant la coopération en matière de biosûreté et de biosécurité. *Signé:* Bichkek, le 22 août 2008. *Entrée en vigueur:* le 8 avril 2009.

Norvège
Accord sur l'agriculture entre le Canada et le Royaume de Norvège. *Signé:* Davos, le 26 janvier 2008. *Entrée en vigueur:* le 1ᵉʳ juillet 2009.

Pérou
Accord de libre-échange entre le Canada et la République du Pérou. *Signé:* Lima, le 29 mai 2008. *Entrée en vigueur:* le 1ᵉʳ août 2009.

Accord sur l'environnement entre le Canada et la République du Pérou. *Signé:* Lima, le 29 mai 2008. *Entrée en vigueur:* le 1ᵉʳ août 2009.

Accord de coopération dans le domaine du travail entre le Canada et la

République du Pérou. *Signé:* Lima, le 29 mai 2008. *Entrée en vigueur:* le 1ᵉʳ août 2009.

Pologne
Accord sur la sécurité sociale entre le Canada et la République de Pologne. *Signé:* Varsovie, le 2 avril 2008. *Entrée en vigueur:* le 1ᵉʳ octobre 2009.

Accord entre le gouvernement du Canada et le gouvernement de la République de Pologne concernant la promotion de la mobilité des jeunes citoyens. *Signé:* Varsovie, le 14 juillet 2008. *Entrée en vigueur:* le 1ᵉʳ août 2009.

Fédération de Russie
Échange de notes entre le gouvernement du Canada et le gouvernement de la Fédération de Russie constituant un Accord additionnel à l'Accord de coopération entre le gouvernement du Canada et le gouvernement de l'Union des Républiques socialistes soviétiques concernant les utilisations pacifiques de l'énergie nucléaire, fait le 20 novembre 1989. *Signé par le Canada:* Ottawa, le 6 mai 2008. *Signé par la Fédération de Russie:* Ottawa, le 23 avril 2008. *Entrée en vigueur:* le 3 juin 2009.

Suisse
Accord sur l'agriculture entre le Canada et la Confédération suisse. *Signé:* Davos, le 26 janvier 2008. *Entrée en vigueur:* le 1ᵉʳ juillet 2009.

II   MULTILATÉRAUX

Cimetières de guerre
Convention entre le gouvernement de la République de Namibie et les gouvernements d'Australie, du Canada, d'Inde, de Nouvelle-Zélande, d'Afrique du Sud, du Royaume-Uni de Grande-Bretagne et d'Irlande du Nord relative au traitement des sépultures de guerre des membres des Forces armées

du Commonwealth sur le territoire de la République de Namibie, Windhoek, 27 juin 2005. *Signé par le Canada:* le 18 juin 2008.

Commerce
Accord de libre-échange entre le Canada et les États de l'Association européenne de libre-échange (Islande, Liechtenstein, Norvège et Suisse), Davos, 26 janvier 2008. *Signé par le Canada:* le 26 janvier 2008. *Ratifié par le Canada:* le 30 avril 2009. *Entrée en vigueur pour le Canada:* le 1er juillet 2009.

Échange de lettres constituant un Accord entre le gouvernement du Canada, le gouvernement des États-Unis du Mexique et le gouvernement des États-Unis d'Amérique, modifiant l'Annexe 401 de l'Accord de libre-échange nord-américain entre le gouvernement du Canada, le gouvernement des États-Unis du Mexique et le gouvernement des États-Unis d'Amérique, Ottawa, Mexico, Washington, 11 avril 2008. *Signé par le Canada:* le 11 avril 2008. *Entrée en vigueur pour le Canada:* le 1er septembre 2009.

Conservation
Accord sur des normes internationales de piégeage sans cruauté entre la Communauté européenne, le Canada et la Fédération de Russie, Bruxelles, 15 décembre 1997. *Signé par le Canada:* le 15 décembre 1997. *Ratifié par le Canada:* le 31 mai 1999. *Appliqué provisoirement par le Canada:* le 1er juin 1999. *Entrée en vigueur pour le Canada:* le 22 juillet 2008.

Défense
Protocole au Traité de l'Atlantique Nord sur l'accession de la République d'Albanie. Bruxelles, 9 juillet 2008. *Signé par le Canada:* le 9 juillet 2008. *Accepté par le Canada:* le 16 janvier 2009.

Entrée en vigueur pour le Canada: le 27 mars 2009.

Protocole au Traité de l'Atlantique Nord sur l'accession de la République de Croatie, Bruxelles, 9 juillet 2008. *Signé par le Canada:* le 9 juillet 2008. *Accepté par le Canada:* le 16 janvier 2009. *Entrée en vigueur pour le Canada:* le 30 mars 2009.

Désarmement
Convention sur les armes à sous-munitions, Dublin, 30 mai 2008. *Signé par le Canada:* le 3 décembre 2008. *Entrée en vigueur:* le 1er août 2010.

Droits de la personne
Statuts de l'Institut international pour la démocratie et l'assistance électorale (version modifiée), Stockholm, 24 janvier 2006. *Accepté par le Canada:* le 12 juin 2008. *Entrée en vigueur pour le Canada:* le 21 novembre 2008.

Guerre
Protocole additionnel aux Conventions de Genève du 12 août 1949 relatif à l'adoption d'un signe distinctif additionnel (Protocole III), Genève, 8 décembre 2005. *Signé par le Canada:* le 19 juin 2006. *Ratifié par le Canada:* le 26 novembre 2007. *Entrée en vigueur pour le Canada:* le 26 mai 2008.

Navigation
Protocole de 1996 modifiant la Convention de 1976 sur la limitation de la responsabilité en matière de créances maritimes, Londres, 2 mai 1996. *Signé par le Canada:* le 9 septembre 1997. *Ratifié par le Canada:* le 9 mai 2008. *Entrée en vigueur pour le Canada:* le 7 août 2008.

Science
Accord de coopération en science et technologie énergétiques entre le gouvernement du Canada, le gouver-

nement des États-Unis du Mexique et le gouvernement des États-Unis d'Amérique, Victoria, 23 juillet 2007. *Signé par le Canada:* le 23 juillet 2007. *Entrée en vigueur pour le Canada:* le 24 juillet 2008. RTC 2008/8

Stupéfiants

Amendements à l'annexe I de la Convention internationale contre le dopage dans le sport, Paris, 15 novembre 2007. *Entrée en vigueur pour le Canada:* le 1ᵉʳ janvier 2008. RTC 2008/2.

Cases / Jurisprudence

Canadian Cases in Public International Law in 2008–9 / Jurisprudence canadienne en matière de droit international public en 2008–9

compiled by / préparé par

GIBRAN VAN ERT

Refugee protection — Deserters — Military action condemned by the international community

Key v. Canada (Minister of Citizenship and Immigration) 2008 FC 838 (4 July 2008). Federal Court.

This was an application for judicial review of a decision of the Refugee Protection Division of the Immigration and Refugee Board rejecting the refugee status applications of a deserter from the United States Army and his wife and children. Key enlisted in April 2003 and served in Iraq in the 43rd Combat Engineer Company. He and his company conducted night-time raids of private Iraqi homes, during which Key alleged that he witnessed several instances of unjustified abuse, unwarranted detention, humiliation, and looting by fellow soldiers. During a furlough in the United States in November 2003, Key deserted. In March 2005, Key and his family came to Canada and initiated refugee protection claims.

The board accepted Key's allegations as truthful. It noted that the International Committee of the Red Cross reported on night-time raids of the sort described by Key in a 2003 report[1] as follows:

Gibran van Ert is an associate with Hunter Litigation Chambers in Vancouver.

[1] The Immigration and Refugee Board's reference to this report is particularly interesting given that it was a confidential document of the International Commission of the Red Cross (ICRC), which was apparently leaked to the *Wall Street Journal* in May 2004. See the press release of the ICRC, <http://www.icrc.org/web/eng/siteengo.nsf/htmlall/5yrl67?opendocument>. A copy of the report may be readily found online by searching for it by title.

Arresting authorities entered houses usually after dark, breaking down doors, waking up residents roughly, yelling orders, forcing family members into one room under military guard while searching the rest of the house and further breaking doors, cabinets and other property. They arrested suspects, tying their hands in the back with flexi-cuffs, hooding them, and taking them away. Sometimes they arrested all adult males present in the house, including elderly, handicapped or sick people. Treatment also included pushing people around, insulting, taking aim with rifles, punching and kicking and striking with rifles. Individuals were often led away in whatever they happened to be wearing at the time of the arrest — sometimes in pyjamas or underwear — and were denied the opportunity to gather a few essential belongings, such as clothing, hygiene items, medicine or eyeglasses. Those who surrendered with a suitcase often had their belongings confiscated. In many cases personal belongings were seized during the arrest, with no receipt being issued.

The board expressed the view that "the manner in which the military routinely invaded the homes of Iraqi citizens and the conduct of the soldiers may have been violations of articles 27, 31, 32 and 33 of the Fourth Geneva Convention" but also observed that "not all breaches of the Geneva Conventions are war crimes." The board found that Key was not a conscientious objector in the sense of being opposed to war generally but objected instead to the systematic violations of human rights that resulted from the conduct of the United States Army in Iraq and the requirement that he participate in them. Having found that Key was not a conscientious objector and that the abuses he complained of were not sufficiently egregious as to constitute war crimes or crimes against humanity, the Board found that Key and his family did not qualify for refugee protection.

Justice Barnes allowed the Keys' application for judicial review. He concluded that the board erred in its interpretation of paragraph 171 of the United Nations High Commissioner for Refugees (UNHCR) *Handbook on Procedures and Criteria for Determining Refugee Status*,[2] which reads:

---

2 United Nations High Commissioner for Refugees, *Handbook on Procedures and Criteria for Determining Refugee Status under the 1951 Convention and the 1967 Protocol Relating to the Status of Refugees*, Doc. HCR/IP/4/Eng/REV.1 Re-edited, Geneva, January 1992. The learned judge cited *Chan v. Canada (Minister of Employment and Immigration)* [1995] 3 S.C.R. 593 on the status of the handbook as a highly relevant authority in considering refugee admission practices.

Not every conviction, genuine thought it may be, will constitute a sufficient reason for claiming refugee status after desertion or draft-evasion. It is not enough for a person to be in disagreement with his government regarding the political justification for a particular military action. Where, however, the type of military action, with which an individual does not wish to be associated, is condemned by the international community as contrary to basic rules of human conduct, punishment for desertion or draft-evasion could, in the light of all other requirements of the definition, in itself be regarded as persecution.

Barnes J. disagreed with the board's conclusion that paragraph 171 means that refugee protection for military deserters and evaders is only available where the conduct objected to amounts to a war crime, a crime against peace, or a crime against humanity. He noted, citing English precedent, that the response of the international community to the legitimacy of a particular conflict or to the means in which it is being prosecuted has generally been seen as a relevant but not a determinative consideration. He added, pointedly:

That this is so is not surprising: there are many reasons for countries to be reticent to criticize the decisions or conduct of an ally or a significant trading partner even where the impugned actions would, in some other political context, draw widespread international condemnation. Article 171 of the UNHCR Handbook speaks of the need for international condemnation for "the type of military action" which the individual finds objectionable. Thus, even where the response of the international community is muted with respect to objectionable military conduct, the grant of refugee protection may still be available where it is shown that the impugned conduct is, in an objective sense and viewed in isolation from its political context, contrary to the basic rules or norms of human conduct.[3]

The learned judge then proceeded to review Canadian, English, and American authorities on the meaning of paragraph 171's concept of military action contrary to basic rules of human conduct. He found that *Zolfagharkhani v. Canada (Minister of Employment and Immigration)*[4] did not make a finding that the claimant would be

---

[3] *Key v. Canada (Minister of Citizenship and Immigration)*, 2008 FC 838 (4 July 2008) at para. 21 [*Key*].

[4] *Zolfagharkhani v. Canada (Minister of Employment and Immigration)*, [1993] 3 FC 540 (CA).

required to commit war crimes or crimes against humanity the *sine qua non* of a successful claim to refugee protection. Barnes J. found support for this view in the English decisions *Sepet et al v. Secretary of State for the Home Department*[5] and *Krotov v. Secretary of State for the Home Department*,[6] as well as in the US decisions *Tagaga v. INS*[7] and *M.A. A26851062 v. U.S. Immigration & Naturalization Service*.[8] Barnes J. concluded,

> [i]t is clear from the above passages that officially condoned military misconduct falling well short of a war crime may support a claim to refugee protection. Indeed, the authorities indicate that military action which *systematically* degrades, abuses or humiliates either combatants or non-combatants is capable of supporting a refugee claim where that is the proven reason for refusing to serve.[9]

That was not the end of the matter, however. Soldiers facing punishment in the United States for desertion must, as a rule, pursue the available options for state protection at home before seeking protection in Canada: *Hinzman v. Canada (Minister of Citizenship and Immigration)*.[10] By concluding that the United States was itself Key's persecutor, and therefore that insufficient state protection was available to Key and his family, the board erred. To remedy this error, Barnes J. ordered that the matter be remitted to a differently constituted Board to address fully the question of whether the Keys' fear of persecution is objectively well-founded due to the insufficiency of state protection available to them.

Kyoto Protocol — implementing legislation — justiciability

Friends of the Earth v. Canada (Governor in Council) 2008 FC 1183 (20 October 2008). Federal Court.

Friends of the Earth v. Canada (Governor in Council) 2009 FCA 297 (15 October 2009). Federal Court of Appeal; leave to appeal to the Supreme Court of Canada denied without reasons 25 March 2010.

---

5 *Sepet et al v. Secretary of State for the Home Department*, [2003] 3 All ER 304 (HL).

6 *Krotov v. Secretary of State for the Home Department*, [2004] EWCA Civ 69 (CA).

7 *Tagaga v. INS*, (2000) 228 F.3d 1030 (9th Cir.).

8 *M.A. A26851062 v. U.S. Immigration & Naturalization Service*, (1988) 858 F.2d 210 (4th Cir.).

9 *Key, supra* note 3 at para. 29 [original emphasis].

10 *Hinzman v. Canada (Minister of Citizenship and Immigration)*, 2007 FCA 17.

The applicant Friends of the Earth (FOTE) brought three judicial review applications against the Governor in Council and the minister of the environment alleging breaches by the federal government of sections of the Kyoto Protocol Implementation Act.[11] The respondents admitted the breaches but argued that they were not justiciable. In their submission, accountability for breaches of the act was a parliamentary, not a judicial, matter.

As is well known, the Harper government, under whose watch — but without whose blessing — this act became law in June 2007, has repeatedly stated that Canada does not intend to comply with its Kyoto Protocol obligations.[12] The applications judge, Barnes J., noted, unusually, that the act was introduced by a private member rather than by the government, that it was not supported by the government, and that it "thus embodies a legislative policy which is inconsistent with stated government policy."[13]

To appreciate fully the issue before the court, it is necessary to quote at length from the act.

An Act to ensure Canada meets its global climate change obligations under the Kyoto Protocol	Loi visant à assurer le respect des engagements du Canada en matière de changements climatiques en vertu du Protocole de Kyoto
Recognizing that	
...	Attendu :
Canada ratified the Kyoto Protocol in 2002 following a majority vote in Parliament, and the Protocol entered into force in 2005,	...
	que le Canada a ratifié le Protocole de Kyoto en 2002 par un vote majoritaire au Parlement et que le Protocole est entré en vigueur en 2005;
this legislation is intended to meet, in part, Canada's obligations under the UNFCCC and the Kyoto Protocol	que la présente loi vise, en partie, à assurer le respect des engagements du Canada aux termes de la CCNUCC et du Protocole de Kyoto;
...	...
3. The purpose of this Act is to ensure that Canada takes effective and timely action to meet its obligations under the Kyoto Protocol and help address the problem of global climate change.	3. La présente loi a pour objet d'assurer la prise de mesures efficaces et rapides par le Canada afin qu'il honore ses engagements dans le cadre du Protocole

---

11 Kyoto Protocol Implementation Act, S.C. 2007, c. 30.

12 Kyoto Protocol, (1997) 2303 U.N.T.S. 148; ratified by Canada 17 December 2002.

13 *Friends of the Earth v. Canada (Governor in Council)*, 2009 FCA 297 (15 October 2009) at para. 8 [*Friends of the Earth*].

4. This Act is binding on Her Majesty in Right of Canada.

5. (1) Within 60 days after this Act comes into force and not later than May 31 of every year thereafter until 2013, the Minister shall prepare a Climate Change Plan that includes

(a) a description of the measures to be taken to ensure that Canada meets its obligations under Article 3, paragraph 1, of the Kyoto Protocol...

(c) the projected greenhouse gas emission level in Canada for each year from 2008 to 2012, taking into account the measures referred to in paragraph (a), and a comparison of those levels with Canada's obligations under Article 3, paragraph 1, of the Kyoto Protocol;

(d) an equitable distribution of greenhouse gas emission reduction levels among the sectors of the economy that contribute to greenhouse gas emissions ...

(2) A Climate Change Plan shall respect provincial jurisdiction and take into account the relative greenhouse gas emission levels of provinces.

...

6. (1) The Governor in Council may make regulations

(a) limiting the amount of greenhouse gases that may be released into the environment;

(a.1) within the limits of federal constitutional authority, limiting the amount of greenhouse gases that may be released in each province by applying to each province Article 3, paragraphs 1, 3, 4, 7, 8, and 10 to 12, of the Kyoto Protocol, with any modifications that the circumstances require;

de Kyoto et aide à combattre le problème des changements climatiques mondiaux.

4. La présente loi lie Sa Majesté du chef du Canada.

5. (1) Dans les soixante jours suivant l'entrée en vigueur de la présente loi et au plus tard le 31 mai de chaque année subséquente jusqu'en 2013, le ministre établit un Plan sur les changements climatiques qui contient notamment les éléments suivants :

(a) une description des mesures à prendre afin d'assurer le respect des engagements du Canada aux termes de l'article 3, paragraphe 1, du Protocole de Kyoto...

(c) le niveau projeté d'émissions de gaz à effet de serre au Canada pour chaque année de la période de 2008 à 2012, compte tenu des mesures visées à l'alinéa a), et une comparaison de ces niveaux avec les engagements du Canada aux termes de l'article 3, paragraphe 1, du Protocole de Kyoto;

(d) une répartition équitable des niveaux de réduction des émissions de gaz à effet de serre entre les secteurs de l'économie qui contribuent aux émissions de gaz à effet de serre; ...

(2) Chaque Plan sur les changements climatiques doit respecter les compétences provinciales et tenir compte des niveaux respectifs des émissions de gaz à effet de serre des provinces.

...

6. (1) Le gouverneur en conseil peut, par règlement :

(a) limiter la quantité de gaz à effet de serre qui peut être libérée dans l'environnement;

(a.1) dans les limites des compétences constitutionnelles fédérales, de limiter la quantité de gaz à effet de serre qui peut être libérée dans chaque province en appliquant à chacune l'article 3, paragraphes 1,

(b) establishing performance standards designed to limit greenhouse gas emissions;

(c) respecting the use or production of any equipment, technology, fuel, vehicle or process in order to limit greenhouse gas emissions;

(d) respecting permits or approvals for the release of any greenhouse gas;

(e) respecting trading in greenhouse gas emission reductions, removals, permits, credits, or other units;

(f) respecting monitoring, inspections, investigations, reporting, enforcement, penalties or other matters to promote compliance with regulations made under this Act;

(g) designating the contravention of a provision or class of provisions of the regulations by a person or class of persons as an offence punishable by indictment or on summary conviction and prescribing, for a person or class of persons, the amount of the fine and imprisonment for the offence; and

(h) respecting any other matter that is necessary to carry out the purposes of this Act.

...

7. (1) Within 180 days after this Act comes into force, the Governor in Council shall ensure that Canada fully meets its obligations under Article 3, paragraph 1, of the Kyoto Protocol by making, amending or repealing the necessary regulations under this or any other Act.

(2) At all times after the period referred to in subsection (1), the Governor in Council shall ensure

3, 4, 7, 8 et 10 à 12 du Protocole de Kyoto, avec les adaptations nécessaires;

(b) établir des normes de performance conçues pour limiter les émissions de gaz à effet de serre;

(c) régir l'utilisation ou la production d'équipements, de technologies, de combustibles, de véhicules ou de procédés afin de limiter les émissions de gaz à effet de serre;

(d) régir les permis ou autorisations nécessaires à la libération de gaz à effet de serre;

(e) régir les échanges en matière de réductions des émissions de gaz à effet de serre, d'absorptions, de permis, de crédits ou d'autres unités;

(f) régir la surveillance, les inspections, les enquêtes, les rapports, les mesures d'application, les peines et les autres questions visant à favoriser la conformité aux règlements pris en vertu de la présente loi;

(g) désigner la contravention à une disposition ou une catégorie de dispositions des règlements commise par une personne ou une catégorie de personnes comme une infraction punissable sur déclaration de culpabilité par acte d'accusation ou par procédure sommaire et imposer, à l'égard de cette personne ou catégorie de personnes, le montant de l'amende et la durée de l'emprisonnement;

(h) régir toute autre question nécessaire à l'application de la présente loi.

...

7. (1) Dans les cent quatre-vingts jours suivant l'entrée en vigueur de la présente loi, le gouverneur en conseil veille à ce que le Canada honore les engagements qu'il a pris en vertu de l'article 3, paragraphe 1, du Protocole

that Canada fully meets its obligations under Article 3, paragraph 1, of the Kyoto Protocol by making, amending or repealing the necessary regulations under this or any other Act.

...

8. At least 60 days before making a regulation under this Act or, with respect to subsections 7(1) and (2), any other Act, the Governor in Council shall publish the proposed regulation in the Canada Gazette for consultation purposes with statements:

   (a) setting out the greenhouse gas emission reductions that are reasonably expected to result from the regulation for every year it will be in force, up to and including 2012; and

   (b) indicating that persons may submit comments to the Minister within 30 days after the publication of the regulation.

9. (1) Within 120 days after this Act comes into force, the Minister shall prepare a statement setting out the greenhouse gas emission reductions that are reasonably expected to result for each year up to and including 2012 from

   (a) each regulation made or to be made to ensure that Canada fully meets its obligations under Article 3, paragraph 1, of the Kyoto Protocol, pursuant to subsections 7(1) and (2); and

   (b) each measure referred to in subsection 7(3).

...

10. (1) Within 60 days after the Minister publishes a Climate Change Plan under subsection 5(3), or within 30 days after the Minister publishes a statement under subsection 9(2), the National Round Table on the Environment and

de Kyoto en prenant, modifiant ou abrogeant les règlements appropriés en vertu de la présente loi ou de toute autre loi.

(2) En tout temps après la période prévue au paragraphe (1), le gouverneur en conseil veille à ce que le Canada honore les engagements qu'il a pris en vertu de l'article 3, paragraphe 1, du Protocole de Kyoto en prenant, modifiant ou abrogeant les règlements appropriés en vertu de la présente loi ou de toute autre loi.

...

8. Au moins soixante jours avant la prise d'un règlement sous le régime de la présente loi ou, en ce qui concerne les paragraphes 7(1) et (2), de toute autre loi, le gouverneur en conseil publie le projet de règlement dans la Gazette du Canada, pour consultation, accompagné de déclarations :

   (a) énonçant les réductions d'émissions de gaz à effet de serre auxquelles il est raisonnable de s'attendre à la suite de la prise du règlement pour chaque année qu'il demeurera en vigueur au cours de la période se terminant en 2012;

   (b) indiquant les personnes qui peuvent présenter des observations au ministre dans les trente jours suivant la publication du règlement.

9. (1) Dans les cent vingt jours suivant l'entrée en vigueur de la présente loi, le ministre prépare une déclaration dans laquelle il énonce les réductions d'émissions de gaz à effet de serre auxquelles il est raisonnable de s'attendre chaque année au cours de la période se terminant en 2012 à la suite de?:

   (a) chaque règlement qui a été pris ou qui sera pris afin d'assurer que le Canada respecte tous les engagements qu'il a pris en vertu de l'article 3, paragraphe 1, du Protocole de Kyoto, en application des paragraphes 7(1) et (2);

the Economy established by section 3 of the National Round Table on the Environment and the Economy Act shall perform the following with respect to the Plan or statement:

(a) undertake research and gather information and analyses on the Plan or statement in the context of sustainable development; and

(b) advise the Minister on issues that are within its purpose…

10.1 (1) At least once every two years after this Act comes into force, up to and including 2012, the Commissioner of the Environment and Sustainable Development shall prepare a report that includes

(a) an analysis of Canada's progress in implementing the Climate Change Plans;

(b) an analysis of Canada's progress in meeting its obligations under Article 3, paragraph 1, of the Kyoto Protocol; and

(c) any observations and recommendations on any matter that the Commissioner considers relevant.

…

(3) The Commissioner shall submit the report to the Speaker of the House of Commons on or before the day it is published, and the Speaker shall table the report in the House on any of the first three days on which that House is sitting after the Speaker receives it.

(b) toute mesure visée au paragraphe 7(3).

…

10. (1) Dans les soixante jours suivant la publication par le ministre du Plan sur les changements climatiques en vertu du paragraphe 5(3) ou dans les trente jours suivant la publication par le ministre d'une déclaration en vertu du paragraphe 9(2), la Table ronde nationale sur l'environnement et l'économie constituée par l'article 3 de la Loi sur la Table ronde nationale sur l'environnement et l'économie exécute les fonctions suivantes quant au Plan ou à la déclaration :

(a) effectuer des recherches et recueillir de l'information et des données provenant d'analyses sur le Plan ou la déclaration dans le contexte du développement durable;

(b) conseille le ministre sur les questions qui relèvent de sa mission…

10.1 (1) Au moins tous les deux ans suivant l'entrée en vigueur de la présente loi, et ce jusqu'en 2012, le commissaire à l'environnement et au développement durable prépare un rapport renfermant notamment :

(a) une analyse des progrès réalisés par le Canada pour mettre en oeuvre les plans sur les changements climatiques;

(b) une analyse des progrès réalisés par le Canada pour respecter ses engagements en vertu de l'article 3, paragraphe 1, du Protocole de Kyoto;

(c) toutes autres observations et recommandations sur toute question qu'il estime pertinente.

…

(3) Le commissaire présente le rapport au président de la Chambre des communes au plus tard le jour où il est publié et le président le dépose devant la Chambre dans les trois premiers jours de séance de celle-ci suivant sa réception.

It is also useful to refer to Article 3(1) of the Kyoto Protocol:

The Parties included in Annex I shall, individually or jointly, ensure that their aggregate anthropogenic carbon dioxide equivalent emissions of the greenhouse gases listed in Annex A do not exceed their assigned amounts, calculated pursuant to their quantified emission limitation and reduction commitments inscribed in Annex B and in accordance with the provisions of this Article, with a view to reducing their overall emissions of such gases by at least 5 per cent below 1990 levels in the commitment period 2008 to 2012.

Les Parties visées à l'annexe I font en sorte, individuellement ou conjointement, que leurs émissions anthropiques agrégées, exprimées en équivalent-dioxyde de carbone, des gaz à effet de serre indiqués à l'annexe A ne dépassent pas les quantités qui leur sont attribuées, calculées en fonction de leurs engagements chiffrés en matière de limitation et de réduction des émissions inscrits à l'annexe B et conformément aux dispositions du présent article, en vue de réduire le total de leurs émissions de ces gaz d'au moins 5 % par rapport au niveau de 1990 au cours de la période d'engagement allant de 2008 à 2012.

Section 5 of the act requires the minister of the environment to prepare an annual Climate Change Plan. The minister's initial plan, published in August 2007, made clear that the government had no present intention to meet its Kyoto Protocol commitments.[14] The plan also described the government's position on the challenges it faces in complying with the Kyoto Protocol, a description from which Barnes J. quoted at length.[15] The emission reduction targets set in the plan were well above Canada's Kyoto Protocol commitments.[16]

Sections 7 to 9 of the act require the government to exercise the regulatory powers granted in section 6 to ensure that Canada meets its obligations under Article 3(1) of the Kyoto Protocol. The evidence was uncontradicted that, at the time Friends of the Earth (FOTE) commenced its applications related to those sections, the government had not carried out any of the regulatory action contemplated by these provisions.[17]

FOTE argued that the government's initial plan breached section 5 of the act by acknowledging non-compliance with the Kyoto Protocol instead of describing "measures to be taken to ensure that

14 *Ibid.* at para. 11.

15 *Ibid.* at para. 12.

16 *Ibid.* at para. 13.

17 *Ibid.* at para. 17.

Canada meets its obligations" as required by that section. Barnes J. described FOTE's argument with respect to sections 7 to 9 as "much the same."[18] He therefore turned to consider the justiciability of these provisions. He described justiciability as "a matter of statutory interpretation directed at identifying Parliamentary intent: in particular, whether Parliament intended that the statutory duties imposed upon the Minister and upon the GIC by the KPIA be subjected to judicial scrutiny and remediation."[19] He also quoted the remark of Thomas Cromwell (now Cromwell J. of the Supreme Court of Canada) that "[t]he justiciability of a matter refers to its being suitable for determination by a court."[20] Barnes J. also observed: "While the courts fulfill an obvious role in the interpretation and enforcement of statutory obligations, Parliament can, within the limits of the constitution, reserve to itself the sole enforcement role."[21]

Having framed the question as one of statutory interpretation and parliamentary intent, Barnes J. turned to the terms of the act. Astonishingly, he made no reference at all to either the preamble or section 3. The preamble declares "this legislation is intended to meet, in part, Canada's obligations under the [United Nations Framework Convention on Climate Change] and the Kyoto Protocol." Recall that section 13 of the Interpretation Act[22] provides that the preamble of an enactment shall be read as a part of the enactment intended to assist in explaining its purport and object. Section 3 of the Act explains its purpose as "to ensure that Canada takes effective and timely action to meet its obligations under the Kyoto Protocol and help address the problem of global climate change." Even if Barnes J. regarded these provisions as not determinative of the justiciability of the Act, he surely ought to have referred to them.

Instead, Barnes J. began his justiciability analysis with section 5. He observed:

If the intent of section 5 of the Act was to ensure that the Government of Canada strictly complied with Canada's Kyoto obligations, the approach taken was unduly cumbersome. Indeed, a simple and unequivocal statement of such an intent would not have been difficult to draft. Instead section 5 couples the responsibility of ensuring Kyoto compliance with a

[18] *Ibid.* at paras. 29–30.
[19] *Ibid.* at para. 31; see also paras. 22–23.
[20] *Ibid.* at para. 25.
[21] *Ibid.* at para. 26.
[22] Interpretation Act, R.S.C. 1985, c. I-21 as amended.

series of stated measures some of which are well outside of the proper realm of judicial review. For instance, subparagraph 5(1)(a)(iii.1) requires that a Climate Change Plan provide for a just transition for workers affected by greenhouse gas emission reductions and paragraph 5(1)(d) requires an equitable distribution of reduction levels among the sectors of the economy that contribute to greenhouse gas emissions. These are policy-laden considerations which are not the proper subject matter for judicial review.[23]

The learned judge is, with respect, quite right to observe that notions of a just transition for workers and equitable distribution of reduction levels among the sectors of the economy are not susceptible to judicial enforcement. Yet his premise — that is, that section 5 was intended to ensure the federal government's strict compliance with the Kyoto Protocol, is fallacious: while that intention is reflected in section 5, its chief expression occurs in the preamble and in sections 3 and 7. By focusing on section 5, which concerns the preparation and content of climate change plans and which is, as the learned judge rightly says, rather cumbersome, Barnes J. deflects attention from those other provisions. It is, in short, a straw man argument.

Turning to section 7 (requiring the governor in council to "ensure that Canada fully meets its obligations" under the Kyoto Protocol by "making, amending or repealing the necessary regulations under this or any other Act" within six months of enactment and at all times thereafter), Barnes J. held that the word "ensure," as used here and elsewhere in the act, was not an imperative statement but "reflected only a permissive intent."[24] This conclusion would surprise most dictionaries. The word occurs in its imperative conjugation in section 7 ("the Governor in Council shall ensure that Canada fully meets its obligations"), and its infinitive formulation (for example, "to ensure that Canada takes effective and timely action to meet its obligations" in section 3) seems no less compulsory. The learned judge's observation that, "[s]o far as I can determine, the word 'ensure'... is not commonly used in the context of statutory interpretation to indicate an imperative,"[25] is questionable[26] and,

---

23 *Friends of the Earth, supra* note 13 at para. 33.

24 *Ibid.* at para. 37.

25 *Ibid.* at para. 34.

26 A quick search of CANLII for "shall ensure" in federal statutes (excluding regulations) generated sixty-seven results, including the following provisions that

more importantly, seemingly at odds with the word's plain English meaning.[27]

The learned judge's conclusion that "to ensure" established only a permissive intent appears to have been heavily influenced by his admitted confusion over the relationship between subsections (1) and (2), which he described as "unclear" and "difficult to fully reconcile." But they are not unclear so much as inelegantly drafted. Section 7(1) requires the governor in council to ensure that Canada meets its obligations under Article 3(1) of the Kyoto Protocol by making, amending, or repealing the necessary regulations within 180 days after the act comes into force. Section 7(2) then provides that the governor in council shall do the same at all times after the 180 days have passed. The draftsperson responsible for the marginal notes had no difficulty seeing that subsection (1) creates an "Obligation to implement Kyoto Protocol" while subsection (2) creates an "Obligation to maintain implementation of Kyoto Protocol."[28] Yet Barnes J. concluded that the "apparent intent [of the two subsections] is to allow for an ongoing process to regulate Kyoto compliance, with the initial 180-day timeframe being merely directory or suggestive."[29]

---

must surely be imperative rather than permissive in nature: "Every owner of a vessel described in subsection (1) shall ensure that it is registered under this Part" (Canada Shipping Act 2001, S.C. 2001, c. 26, s. 46(2)); "Subject to section 10, the Minister shall ensure the destruction of all anti-personnel mines stockpiled by Her Majesty in right of Canada or that are delivered under section 8 for destruction" (Anti-Personnel Mines Convention Implementation Act, S.C. 1997, c. 33, s. 9): "Where a project is described in the comprehensive study list, the responsible authority shall ensure public consultation with respect to the proposed scope of the project for the purposes of the environmental assessment." (Canadian Environmental Assessment Act, S.C. 1992, c. 37, s. 21(1)); "Federal institutions shall ensure that employment opportunities are open to both English-speaking Canadians and French-speaking Canadians." (Official Languages Act, R.S.C., 1985, c. 31 (4th Supp.), s. 39(2)).

27 Of course, the English text is not determinative. The act is bilingual and must be interpreted according to the principles of bilingual statutory interpretation: *R. v. Daoust* [2004] 1 S.C.R. 217. Yet Barnes J. made no reference to these principles or to the French language text of the enactment, in reaching his conclusions.

28 In saying this I do not forget that marginal notes form no part of the enactment but are inserted for convenience of reference only: Interpretation Act, R.S.C. 1985, c. I-21 (as amended) at s. 14.

29 *Friends of the Earth, supra* note 13 at para. 38.

Perhaps the most unaccountable feature of Barnes J.'s interpretation of this statute is his complete disregard for the presumption of conformity with international law. This interpretive rule has featured prominently in Supreme Court of Canada jurisprudence since *National Corn Growers Assn. v. Canada (Import Tribunal)*[30] and was endorsed with especial fervour by LeBel J. for the majority of the Court in *R. v. Hape*, in which the learned judge described the rule as "a well-established principle of statutory interpretation ... based on the rule of judicial policy that, as a matter of law, courts will strive to avoid constructions of domestic law pursuant to which the state would be in violation of its international obligations, unless the wording of the statute clearly compels that result."[31] Despite this very strong recent statement from the Supreme Court of Canada, Barnes J. made no effort at all to interpret the act — which is, after all, described in its title as implementing legislation — in such a way as to conform with Canada's international legal obligations under the Kyoto Protocol.

Having interpreted section 7 as not creating a legal obligation on the government to exercise the regulatory powers granted to it by section 6 of the act to ensure Canadian compliance with the Kyoto Protocol, Barnes J. found that the regulatory and related duties described in sections 8 and 9 of the act were not justiciable either.[32] Instead, Barnes J. regarded the act as contemplating parliamentary and public accountability in the place of judicial enforcement.[33] The FOTE applications were therefore dismissed.

An appeal from Barnes J.'s decision was dismissed from the bench by the Federal Court of Appeal by means of a brief oral judgment saying, in substance, only that the court "agree[d] with the decision of Justice Barnes, substantially for the reasons he gave."[34] Leave to appeal to the Supreme Court of Canada was denied without reasons on 25 March 2010.

One can readily understand the hesitation a judge must feel when invited to order to government of Canada to implement by regulation a treaty that it publicly opposes — particularly when the treaty is as momentous in its consequences as the Kyoto Protocol. I do not

---

30 *National Corn Growers Assn. v. Canada (Import Tribunal)*, [1990] 2 S.C.R. 1324.

31 *R. v. Hape*, 2007 SCC 26 at para. 53.

32 *Friends of the Earth, supra* note 13 at para. 41.

33 *Ibid.* at para. 42.

34 *Ibid.*

mean to discount these considerations or even to diminish them. But the Kyoto Protocol Implementation Act is a law of Canada, enacted by Her Majesty by and with the advice and consent of the Senate and House of Commons. Its purpose is expressly stated. Its means, consisting chiefly of the creation of broad regulatory powers (section 6) together with an obligation to exercise them (section 7), are apt to that purpose. Surely this was a case in which Barnes J. — a judge whose judicial courage is on full display in *Smith v. Canada (Attorney General)*, noted later in this article — ought to at least have granted a declaration that the government was in violation of the act. It would then be for the government to determine how best to respond, whether by withdrawing from the Kyoto Protocol, securing repeal of the act, or simply doing nothing and facing the political consequences, if any. However, for the courts to idly tolerate flagrant disregard of an Act of Parliament and, worse, to pronounce themselves incompetent to do otherwise, is hard to reconcile with the rule of law.

Refugee protection — international human rights — role of 1966 International Covenant on Civil and Political Rights in humanitarian and compassionate applications (Immigration and Refugee Protection Act, section 25)

Okoloubu v. Canada (Minister of Citizenship and Immigration) 2008 FCA 326 (27 October 2008). Federal Court of Appeal.

The respondent Mr. Okoloubu was a Nigerian national whose refugee application was dismissed in 1999. In 2005, an inadmissibility report was issued against him on the grounds of serious criminality. This disqualified him from making an In Canada Application for Permanent Resident Status, Spouse or Common-law Partner in Canada Class. He therefore applied to the minister under section 25(1) of the Immigration and Refugee Protection Act[35] for an exemption on humanitarian and compassionate grounds. The immigration officer who heard the application refused the respondent's application. On judicial review, Harrington J. set aside the decision and referred the matter back to another officer for redetermination since the first officer had, for lack of jurisdiction, declined to consider the respondent's arguments based on the 1966 International Covenant on Civil and Political Rights (ICCPR).[36] Mr.

---

[35] Immigration and Refugee Protection Act, S.C. 2001, c. 27.

[36] International Covenant on Civil and Political Rights, [1976] Can. T.S. no. 47.

Okoloubu relied in particular on the protections of family and children in Articles 17, 23, and 24 of the ICCPR.

Harrington J. certified the following serious question of general importance pursuant to section 74 of the act:

Does an immigration officer in charge of assessing an application under section 25 of the *Immigration and Refugee Protection Act* (for an exemption from the obligation to present an application for an immigrant visa from outside Canada) have jurisdiction to consider whether an applicant's removal would breach the International Covenant on Civil and Political Rights, more specifically Articles 17, 23 and 24?

For his part, Harrington J. was of the view that section 25 of the act "is clearly the proper venue for taking [the ICCPR] into consideration," citing *Baker v. Canada (Minister of Citizenship and Immigration)* and others.

Trudel J.A. for the Court of Appeal allowed the appeal. She began by noting that the issue of whether the minister's delegate has jurisdiction under section 25(1) to consider questions of international and constitutional law is a question of law reviewable on a correctness standard.[37] She then considered section 3(3)(f) of the act, which provides:

This Act is to be construed and applied in a manner that	L'interprétation et la mise en oeuvre de la présente loi doivent avoir pour effet :
...	...
complies with international human rights instruments to which Canada is signatory.	de se conformer aux instruments internationaux portant sur les droits de l'homme dont le Canada est signataire.

Trudel J.A. noted prior decisions of the Court of Appeal holding that section 3(3)(f) does not implement international human rights instruments into Canadian law but merely directs that the act be construed as applied in a manner that complies with them. She then observed that "this principle is sufficient to set the place of the ICCPR in the section 25 application, which was in front of the officer" without considering, as the court below had suggested,

---

[37] *Okoloubu v. Canada (Minister of Citizenship and Immigration)*, 2008 FCA 326 (27 October 2008) at para. 29 [*Okoloubu*].

whether the ICCPR's principles have been incorporated into domestic law without legislation according to the "adoptionist approach to the reception of customary international law" described
by LeBel J. in *R. v. Hape*.[38] On this issue, which the judge below
had raised "on his own initiative,"[39] Trudel JA said only that *Hape*
"deals with a different matter" and "is of no assistance to the present
appeal."[40]

On the issue of the immigration officer's jurisdiction to consider
the ICCPR, the parties relied on the Court of Appeal's decision in
Covarrubias v. Canada,[41] in which it held that a pre-removal risk
assessment officer had no implied jurisdiction to consider constitutional issues. Yet Trudel J.A. noted that the practical considerations at issue in the present case are different from those in a
pre-removal risk assessment. While officers carrying out humanitarian and compassionate analyses do not generally possess legal expertise and are not empowered to hear and determine questions
of law, including questions of jurisdiction, they are routinely required to consider the protection of children's interests — a principle found in a number of international instruments — as part of
their analysis.[42] Trudel J.A. continued:

> To respect the objectives of the Act in the performance of their duties,
> H&C officers must bear in mind the "humanitarian and compassionate
> values" which are enshrined in the Charter and the ICCPR. The principles
> of non-interference in family life in Article 17, the importance of a family
> unit and protection thereof by society and the State in Article 23, as well
> as the child's "right to such measures of protection as are required by his
> status as a minor, on the part of his family, society and the State" in Article
> 24 of the ICCPR are all family-related interests and the officer must have
> those interests in mind when dealing with a section 25 application.

Applied to the H&C officer's work ... those values must inform
the decision of the H&C officer. However, "paragraph 3(3)(f) of
the [act] does not require that an officer exercising discretion
under section 25 of the [act] specifically refer to and analyze the

---

[38] *R. v. Hape*, 2007 SCC 26.

[39] *Okoloubu, supra* note 37 at para. 38.

[40] *Ibid.* at paras. 41–42.

[41] *Covarrubias v. Canada*, 2006 FCA 365.

[42] *Okoloubu, supra* note 37 at para. 46.

international human rights instruments to which Canada is signatory. It is sufficient if the officer addresses the substance of the issues raised" (*Thiara v. Canada (Citizenship and Immigration)*, [2008] F.C.J. No. 668, 2008 FCA 151 at paragraph 9).[43]

Having reached this conclusion, Trudel J.A. went on to apply it in the present case. She observed: "When scrutinizing the officer's decision, attention ought to be given to its substance rather than its form"[44] and criticized the court below for placing "much importance on the words of the officer regarding her jurisdiction, while leaving the officer's decision *per se* without careful scrutiny." In her view, the officer did "factor into her decision the substantive rights set out in the ICCPR on which the respondent based his application,"[45] despite having explicitly observed that she lacked jurisdiction to deal with international law. Trudel J.A. held that the officer "addressed in substance the different and important issues at stake, giving careful weight to the interests of the child and the importance of the family unit."[46]

The court's emphasis on substance over form in this decision is commendable. Rather than approaching the issue as an arid jurisdictional inquiry, the court confirmed that humanitarian and compassionate decisions must be informed by the protection of family and children's interests as provided for in the ICCPR and other international human rights instruments, with or without express reference to those instruments in a lawyerly way. The court was also right to decline to consider whether the ICCPR provisions at issue here have been incorporated by the common law according to the doctrine described by LeBel J. in *Hape*, though more might have been said against this suggestion. The *Hape* case was not an invitation to courts and litigants to give direct effect to treaty obligations without legislative implementation. The incorporation doctrine provides that rules of customary — not conventional — international law will be incorporated by the common law where those rules (1) are shown to have customary status in international law; (2) have some potential application to domestic law; and (3) are not inconsistent with statute. While there is no denying that norms founded in conventional international law may in principle

---

43 *Ibid.* at paras. 49–50.

44 *Ibid.* at para. 52.

45 *Ibid.* at para. 53.

46 *Ibid.* at para. 60.

pass into customary international law, the transformation of an international norm's character, from conventional to customary, is a momentous international legal event that a domestic court should not lightly declare.

Charter — extraterritorial application — Afghan detainees

Amnesty International Canada v. Canada (Canadian Forces) 2008 FCA 401 (17 December 2008). Federal Court of Appeal. (Leave to appeal to Supreme Court of Canada denied 21 May 2009.)

The appellants sought judicial review of decisions by the Canadian Forces, operating in Afghanistan, to transfer persons detained by them to the government of Afghanistan. The appellants alleged that the arrangements entered into by Canada and Afghanistan did not provide adequate substantive or procedural safeguards to ensure that transferred detainees would not be exposed to a substantial risk of torture in the hands of the Afghan authorities. The appellants appear to have relied exclusively on the Canadian Charter of Rights and Freedoms as the legal basis of their judicial review applications.[47] As the application of the Charter to Canadian Forces activities in Afghanistan was disputed, the parties put the following questions to the court under rule 107 of the Federal Court Rules:

(1) Does the Charter apply during the armed conflict in Afghanistan to the detention of non-Canadians by the Canadian Forces or their transfer to Afghan authorities to be dealt with by those authorities? and
(2) If not, would the Charter nonetheless apply if the applicants were ultimately able to establish that the transfer of the detainees in question would expose them to a substantial risk of torture?

The motion judge answered both questions in the negative and dismissed the application for judicial review. Desjardins J.A. for the Court of Appeal agreed and dismissed the appeal.

The court addressed the second question first. The appellants appear to have argued that the effect of the Supreme Court of Canada's decisions in *R. v. Hape*[48] and *Canada (Justice) v. Khadr*[49]

[47] See *Ibid.* at para. 3.
[48] *R. v. Hape,* 2007 SCC 26.
[49] *Canada (Justice) v. Khadr,* 2008 SCC 28.

was that while the Charter generally did not apply extraterritorially, this rule was subject to an exception where violations of fundamental international human rights had occurred. That does seem to be the doctrine enunciated in those cases. The motions judge decided the case before *Khadr* was decided and therefore did not have the benefit of the Supreme Court of Canada's application of the exception it conspicuously planted in *Hape*. She concluded that *Hape* did not create a "fundamental human rights exception" justifying the extraterritorial assertion of Charter jurisdiction where such jurisdiction would not otherwise exist.[50] In *Khadr*, however, the Supreme Court of Canada observed:

> In *Hape* ... the Court stated an important exception to the principle of comity. While not unanimous on all the principles governing extraterritorial application of the Charter, the Court was united on the principle that comity cannot be used to justify Canadian participation in activities of a foreign state or its agents that are contrary to Canada's international obligations. It was held that the deference required by the principle of comity "ends where clear violations of international law and fundamental human rights begin."[51]

Counsel for the appellants described this passage as dispositive of the appeal. But Desjardins J.A. gave it very short shrift:

> I understand the Supreme Court of Canada to say that deference and comity end where clear violations of international law and fundamental human rights begin. This does not mean that the Charter then applies as a consequence of these violations.[52]

> This is, with respect, a surprising conclusion given the result in *Khadr*. How, then, is one to know whether the Charter applies extraterritorially in a given situation? Desjardins J.A. tells us only that "all the circumstances in a given situation must be examined before it can be said that the Charter applies."[53]

Having answered the second question in the negative, the court turned to the first, namely whether the Charter applies to the

---

50 *Amnesty International Canada v. Canada (Canadian Forces)*, 2008 FCA 401 (17 December 2008) at para. 18 [*Amnesty International*].

51 *Canada (Justice) v. Khadr*, 2008 SCC 28 at para. 18.

52 *Ibid.* at para. 20.

53 *Ibid.*

detention of non-Canadians by the Canadian Forces or their transfer to Afghan authorities. Desjardins J.A. considered that the "key issue" here was "whether the [Canadian Forces] have 'effective control' over territory in Afghanistan so that the Charter should be given territorial application over Afghan territory and over Afghan people."[54] Desjardins J.A. then observed that Canadian Forces control of its detention facilities at Kandahar Airfields cannot be considered effective control within the meaning of that phrase as employed by the European Court of Human Rights in *Bankovic v. Belgium*.[55] She noted that the Canadian Forces are in Afghanistan at the request of that country's government and not as occupiers and that the government of Afghanistan has not acquiesced to the extension of Canadian law over Afghan nationals.[56] The learned judge then noted the evidence that Canada and Afghanistan had expressly identified international law, including international humanitarian law, as the law governing the treatment of detainees in Canadian custody.[57] Desjardins J.A. apparently regarded this state-to-state agreement as determinative, for she concluded, "Considering that the motions judge decided according to the evidence, the intervention of this Court is unwarranted."[58]

This decision is unsatisfying on at least two levels. First, it is difficult to understand why Amnesty International and the other appellants limited themselves to the Charter as their only basis for relief against government decisions to transfer detainees to Afghan authorities in circumstances where there was alleged to be substantial grounds for believing that they would be in danger of being subjected to torture. Surely the Charter is not the only basis for challenging refoulement to torture in Canadian law. By limiting themselves in this way, the appellants imply a false dilemma: either the Charter applies or the transfers are legal. A second unsatisfying feature of this decision is its lack of legal analysis. The question of how domestic courts should respond to alleged human rights violations by their agents acting abroad has prompted detailed, scholarly consideration in other courts.[59] By contrast, the Court of Appeal's treatment of this difficult issue is summary, even perfunctory.

---

[54] *Ibid.* at para. 24.

[55] *Bankovic v. Belgium*, [2001] E.C.H.R. 890.

[56] *Amnesty International, supra* note 50 at paras. 25–6.

[57] *Ibid.* at paras. 29–30.

[58] *Ibid.* at para. 33.

[59] See, e.g., *Al-Skeini v. Secretary of State for Defence*, [2007] U.K.H.L. 26.

Criminal Code — extraterritorial application — offences against children

R. v. Klassen 2008 BCSC 1762 (19 December 2008). Supreme Court of British Columbia.

The accused was indicted on thirty-seven counts including importation and possession of child pornography, sexual interference, invitation to sexual touching, making child pornography, and obtaining sexual services for consideration of a person under eighteen years. It was alleged that some of the offences occurred in Colombia, Cambodia, and the Philippines. None of the alleged victims was a Canadian citizen or resident. As the offences were alleged to have been committed outside Canada, the Crown relied on section 7(4.1) of the Criminal Code:

(4.1) Notwithstanding anything in this Act or any other Act, every one who, outside Canada, commits an act or omission that if committed in Canada would be an offence against section 151, 152, 153, 155 or 159, subsection 160(2) or (3), section 163.1, 170, 171 or 173 or subsection 212(4) shall be deemed to commit that act or omission in Canada if the person who commits the act or omission is a Canadian citizen or a permanent resident within the meaning of subsection 2(1) of the *Immigration and Refugee Protection Act.*

(4.1) Malgré les autres dispositions de la présente loi ou toute autre loi, le citoyen canadien ou le résident permanent au sens du paragraphe 2(1) de la Loi sur l'immigration et la protection des réfugiés qui, à l'étranger, est l'auteur d'un fait — acte ou omission — qui, s'il était commis au Canada, constituerait une infraction aux articles 151, 152, 153, 155 ou 159, aux paragraphes 160(2) ou (3), aux articles 163.1, 170, 171 ou 173 ou au paragraphe 212(4) est réputé l'avoir commis au Canada.

The accused challenged the constitutionality of this provision on the ground that it is *ultra vires* the Parliament of Canada or, in the alternative, that it unjustifiably infringed section 7 of the Charter.

Cullen J. began his analysis by noting that section 7(4.1) "was enacted as part of, and in response to, a significant international consensus favouring the need for measures to be undertaken to protect children," a consensus "initially expressed in the *United Nations Convention on the Rights of the Child.*"[60] His lordship then noted that, in 2001, Canada and other signatories to the Convention on the Rights of the Child ratified its optional protocol on the sale of

---

[60] *R. v. Klassen*, 2008 B.C.S.C. 1762 (19 December 2008) at para. 54 [*Klassen*]; United Nations Convention on the Rights of the Child, [1992] Can. T.S. no. 3.

children, child prostitution, and child pornography.[61] He went on to quote at length from Articles 3 and 4 of the optional protocol, under which Canada and the other states parties undertake to criminalize certain offences and to take necessary measures to establish jurisdiction over those offences in their territory, when the offender is a national or resident, when the victim is a national, or when the offender is present in the territory, and the state party does not extradite him. Cullen J. also noted that, as of October 2008, 129 states had ratified the optional protocol, including Colombia, Cambodia, and the Philippines.[62]

Turning to the constitutional challenge, Cullen J. quoted a commentator's observation that "[t]he exercise of extraterritorial prescriptive jurisdiction is not necessarily contrary to international law, but is subject to the limitation that it cannot interfere with the rights of other states, whether by involvement in their domestic affairs or by some other means."[63] Cullen J. then rightly observed that "what is at issue in the present case is prescriptive and adjudicative jurisdiction, not enforcement jurisdiction."[64] The learned judge regarded the "critical issue between the parties" as "whether, in enacting section 7(4.1), Parliament had encroached on the authority of other states to decide freely and autonomously in respect of matters occurring within their sovereign territory, or whether the reach of section 7(4.1) comports with international law."[65]

There can be no real dispute, observed Cullen J., that Canada has the authority and jurisdiction to legislate extraterritorially.[66] In support of this proposition, his lordship cited section 132 of the Constitution Act 1867[67] which, with respect, can have no application

---

[61] Convention on the Rights of the Child, G.A. Res. 54/263, Annex II, 54 UN GAOR Supp. (No. 49) at 6, UN Doc. A/54/49 (2000); ratified by Canada 14 September 2005.

[62] *Klassen, supra* note 60 at paras. 56–7.

[63] *Ibid.* at para. 61, quoting R. Currie and S. Coughlan, "Extraterritorial Criminal Jurisdiction: Bigger or Smaller Frame?"

[64] *Ibid.* at para. 64.

[65] *Ibid.* at para. 66.

[66] *Ibid.* at para. 77.

[67] "The Parliament and Government of Canada shall have all Powers necessary or proper for performing the Obligations of Canada or of any Province thereof, as Part of the British Empire, towards Foreign Countries, arising under Treaties between the Empire and such Foreign Countries."

here as the treaties at issue are not Empire treaties. Yet he also cited section 3 of the Statute of Westminster 1931 as "expressly [conferring] on Parliament the 'full power to make laws having extraterritorial operation.'"[68] Yet the learned judge noted that Parliament is presumed not to intend to enact laws having extraterritorial effect, in the absence of clear words or necessary implication to the contrary.[69] Cullen J. then turned to *R. v. Hape*,[70] the case that, it seems clear, inspired the accused's constitutional challenge in the first place. After quoting at length from *Hape* on the principles of sovereign equality and the comity of nations, the learned judge deftly rejected the accused's *vires* argument as follows:

> The principle [*sic*] thrust of the applicant's argument is, however, deflected by the fact that section 7(4.1) is not an enforcement provision implicating enforcement jurisdiction. Rather, it is prescriptive and engages prescriptive and adjudicative jurisdiction. It does not seek to intervene in "the power of each state freely and autonomously to determine its tasks or organize itself and to exercise within its territory a monopoly of legitimate physical coercion." What it does do is seek to control the conduct of Canadian nationals abroad, but only by the use of enforcement measures in Canada.

As such, section 7(4.1) does not run afoul of the principle of sovereign equality or impinge upon the concept or requirements of comity.[71]

Cullen J. noted that section 7(4.1) is not anomalous in asserting prescriptive and adjudicative jurisdiction over events which occur outside Canada, citing the Crimes Against Humanity and War Crimes Act.[72] The accused attempted to distinguish that act from section 7(4.1) on the ground that offences under the former are subject to universal jurisdiction. It is difficult to see how universal jurisdiction would make federal legislation on war crimes *intra vires* if federal legislation on child sexual exploitation were not. Cullen

---

68 *Ibid.* at para. 78. Recall that the Statute of Westminster 1931 is Item no. 17 in the schedule to the Constitution Act 1982 and, therefore, pursuant to section 52(2)(b) of that act, is part of the Constitution of Canada.

69 *Ibid.* at para. 80, quoting *Society of Composers, Authors and Music Publishers of Canada v. Canadian Assn. of Internet Providers*, 2004 SCC 45 at paras. 54-5.

70 *R. v. Hape*, 2007 SCC 26.

71 *Klassen, supra* note 60 at paras. 85-6.

72 *Ibid.* at para. 91; Crimes against Humanity and War Crimes Act, S.C. 2000, c. 24.

J.'s response to this argument is, however, equally hard to follow. He noted that some forty-four states parties to the optional protocol have legislation comparable to section 7(4.1) and observed, "this strongly augurs in favour of a conclusion that this legislation itself forms a part of customary international law under the universal principle in much the same way as the *Crimes Against Humanity and War Crimes Act* does."[73] Certainly, section 7(4.1) of Canada's Criminal Code is not itself part of customary international law. Nor can it safely be said that the principle animating this provision — that is, impunity for child sex offenders, is a customary norm, for the norm's enunciation has occurred chiefly if not entirely in conventional international law. Finally, even if the state obligations to criminalize and punish child sexual exploitation, established in the optional protocol, pass in future from conventional to customary international norms, this metamorphosis will not necessarily confer universal jurisdiction on states to prosecute child sex offences. Notably, Article 4 of the optional protocol itself does not establish universal jurisdiction over these offences.

Cullen J. concluded that section 7(4.1) was not *ultra vires* Parliament "and that its extraterritorial effect is not prohibited by any principle of international law or by the concept of comity."[74] His lordship then turned to the Charter challenge. The accused contended that section 7(4.1) was inconsistent with the trial fairness guarantees of section 7 of the Charter by extending Canada's prescriptive jurisdiction beyond the reach of the Charter which, in *Hape*, was held to be generally territorial. The learned judge rejected this argument without difficulty by invoking *Hape*'s holding that principles of fundamental justice protected by section 7 may be invoked to obtain redress for abuses abroad in gathering evidence even if the Charter itself has no extraterritorial application.[75]

The confusion between prescriptive and enforcement jurisdiction, which the *Hape* decision sought to remedy, but regrettably exacerbated, made it inevitable that some accused person would try to persuade a Canadian court that the Criminal Code's occasional tolerance of extraterritorial offences was unconstitutional. While there was little likelihood that offences under child sex tourism laws would be struck down, it is encouraging to see a trial judge reject

---

[73] *Klassen, supra* note 60 at para. 93; see also paras. 91–92.

[74] *Ibid.* at para. 101.

[75] *Ibid.* at paras. 111–13.

this argument for the right reasons, namely that the exercise of extraterritorial prescriptive jurisdiction is not necessarily contrary to international law, and that the prosecution in Canada of offences against Canadian law committed by a Canadian abroad is not an exercise of extraterritorial enforcement jurisdiction. There is a further objection to the accused's argument that does not expressly arise from this judgment. However, even if Parliament had violated international law by enacting these offences, how would that make the law unconstitutional?

Foreign affairs — justiciability — clemency policy for foreign death penalty inmates

Smith v. Canada (Attorney General) 2009 FC 228 (4 March 2009). Federal Court of Canada.

The applicant Smith was a Canadian citizen sentenced to death in Montana in 1982 for the murder of two men. For more than twenty years, previous Canadian governments assisted Smith in his bid for clemency from the governor of Montana. Then in October 2007, the new government led by Mr. Harper announced that it would no longer assist Smith in his efforts to avoid the death penalty. Smith therefore sought an order compelling the respondents (the attorney general, the minister of foreign affairs and international trade, and the minister of public safety) to assist him in pursuing commutation of his death penalty. He claimed relief under the Charter and also on the basis of administrative law principles of procedural fairness. Against the application, the government argued that its decision was one of high policy falling within the royal prerogative over foreign affairs and that the court had no authority to intervene.

In response to a reporter's question in late October 2007, officials from the Department of Foreign Affairs and International Trade advised that the government's clemency policy had not changed and that it would continue to support Smith's case on humanitarian grounds. Four days later, the same reporter was told by the Department of Public Safety that there were no ongoing efforts to seek a commutation of Smith's death penalty. This gave rise to exchanges in the House of Commons in which the minister of public safety, Mr. Day, told the house: "We will not actively pursue bringing back to Canada murderers who have been tried in a democratic country that supports the rule of law." Similar declarations were made in Parliament in the following months, the most significant of which was a March 2008 statement by the foreign affairs minister, Mr.

Bernier, that "the Government of Canada will continue to consider whether to seek clemency on a case by case basis."[76] Other than statements by government officials in Parliament and to the press, the respondents provided no evidence of a new Canadian government policy on clemency or with respect to the government's decision to deny further support for Smith. The government did not consult Smith before deciding to withdraw its support for him.[77]

Barnes J. began his analysis by acknowledging that "in some measure, the relief that Mr. Smith seeks would extend the previously recognized boundaries of Canadian law."[78] The respondents argued that the Canadian government owed no justiciable legal duties to Smith because the decision not to support him falls squarely within the Crown prerogative of foreign affairs, including the right to speak freely with a foreign state on all such matters. While acknowledging that the general principle of non-justiciability is subject to constitutional obligations and to situations where individual rights or private law interests are engaged, the respondents asserted that here the government had decided to adopt a new foreign policy on clemency for Canadians facing the death penalty in other countries and that this decision was beyond judicial review.

In support of this argument, the respondents relied heavily on the decision of the English Court of Appeal in *Abbasi v. Secretary of State for Foreign and Commonwealth Affairs.*[79] In this case, a British detainee in Guantanamo Bay sought an order compelling British officials to do more to assist him. The court declined to grant this relief and, as Barnes J. put it, "there is no question that this unwillingness to intervene was based on a recognition of the non-justiciability of executive decisions involving finely nuanced and multi-faceted political judgments."[80] Yet Barnes J. also found support in the *Abbasi* case for the applicant's position. He observed that the case "makes it quite clear ... that where the application of foreign policy requires certain criteria to be satisfied, the process of decision-making — as distinct from its content — may be subject to judicial

---

[76] *Smith v. Canada (Attorney General),* 2009 FC 228 (4 March 2009) at paras. 10–16 [*Smith*].

[77] *Ibid.* at para. 17.

[78] *Ibid.* at para. 19.

[79] *Abbasi v. Secretary of State for Foreign and Commonwealth Affairs,* [2002] E.W.C.A. Civ. 1598.

[80] *Smith, supra* note 76 at para. 24.

review."[81] Barnes J. quoted the following portions of the *Abbasi* judgment:

99. What then is the nature of the expectation that a British subject in the position of Mr Abbasi can legitimately hold in relation to the response of the government to a request for assistance? The policy statements that we have cited underline the very limited nature of the expectation. They indicate that where certain criteria are satisfied, the government will "consider" making representations. Whether to make any representations in a particular case, and if so in what form, is left entirely to the discretion of the Secretary of State. That gives free play to the "balance" to which Lord Diplock referred in *GCHQ*. The Secretary of State must be free to give full weight to foreign policy considerations, which are not justiciable. However, that does not mean the whole process is immune from judicial scrutiny. The citizen's legitimate expectation is that his request will be "considered," and that in that consideration all relevant factors will be thrown into the balance.

100. One vital factor, as the policy recognises, is the nature and extent of the injustice, which he claims to have suffered. Even where there has been a gross miscarriage of justice, there may perhaps be overriding reasons of foreign policy which may lead the Secretary of State to decline to intervene. However, unless and until he has formed some judgment as to the gravity of the miscarriage, it is impossible for that balance to be properly conducted.

...

104. The extreme case where judicial review would lie in relation to diplomatic protection would be if the Foreign and Commonwealth Office were, contrary to its stated practice, to refuse even to consider whether to make diplomatic representations on behalf of a subject whose fundamental rights were being violated. In such, unlikely, circumstances we consider that it would be appropriate for the court to make a mandatory order to the Foreign Secretary to give due consideration to the applicant's case.

...

106. We would summarise our views as to what the authorities establish as follows:

...

iv.   It is highly likely that any decision of the Foreign and Commonwealth Office, as to whether to make representations on a diplomatic level,

81 *Ibid.* at para. 25.

will be intimately connected with decisions relating to this country's foreign policy, but an obligation to consider the position of a particular British citizen and consider the extent to which some action might be taken on his behalf, would seem unlikely itself to impinge on any forbidden area.

Barnes J. found further authority for the proposition that a court may review a foreign policy decision where its subject matter directly affects the rights or legitimate expectations of an individual in the decision of the Court of Appeal for Ontario in *Black v. Canada (Prime Minister).*[82]

Having satisfied himself that the decision at issue was at least potentially justiciable, Barnes J. turned to the facts before him. He rejected the respondents' characterization of the issue as whether the court could review a change in foreign policy. Rather, it was the application of any new clemency policy to Smith which was in issue.[83] Moreover, Barnes J. found it to be "quite obvious" that there was not, in fact, any new government policy on clemency, and added that if the supposed new policy was that enunciated by Mr. Bernier, the applicant was entitled to have his case individually reviewed, and there was no evidence that such a review had occurred.[84] The learned judge forcefully observed:

Government policy is not and cannot be the sum total of contradictory public statements of its ministers and spokespersons made inside or outside of Parliament. While the Government is generally free to change its policies there must still be a tangible and intelligible articulation of any policy before it can be applied to a case like Mr. Smith's. Mr. Smith was entitled to know precisely what the new clemency policy was before it was applied to his situation. He could not be expected to discern the policy by sorting through the inconsistent versions offered by various Government representatives.

…

My concern, then, is not with the authority of this Court to tell the Canadian Government how to formulate foreign policy or how to conduct its business with the Governor of Montana but, rather, with the Court's obligation to ensure that the Government's decisions in that regard are made fairly

---

[82] *Black v. Canada (Prime Minister)*, (2001) 54 OR (3d) 215 (CA).

[83] *Smith, supra* note 76 at para. 31.

[84] *Ibid.* at paras. 32–3.

and with appropriate regard to Mr. Smith's legal interests. This is a matter which is indisputably justiciable and which attracts a duty of fairness.[85]

Barnes J. found on the evidence that, until 2007, Canada's official policy was to support clemency for Canadians facing execution in a foreign state, and that this position is "consistent with Canada's long-standing international policy to support the universal abolition of the death penalty." It is notable that this evidence came, in part, from the affidavit of a former Canadian foreign affairs minister, Mr. Graham. Barnes J. concluded that, "[i]n the absence of any other policy, this is the policy that the Government must continue to apply in good faith to Mr. Smith's case."[86]

The applicant invited the court to consider the lawfulness of the government's treatment of Smith on Charter grounds and in the light of international law. Barnes J. declined to do so. On the Charter argument, he noted that Charter decisions must not be determined hypothetically and that here had found no new government clemency policy to scrutinize against the Charter's requirements.[87] Smith's international law argument is only briefly summarized in the judgment but appears to have been that Canada was obliged by international principles of diplomatic protection and by sections 10(2)(a), (i) and (j) of the Department of Foreign Affairs and International Trade Act,[88] to take positive steps to protect Smith. Barnes J. agreed that "the Government's decision to deny clemency assistance to Mr. Smith is hard to reconcile with Canada's international commitment to promote respect for international human rights norms including the universal abolition of the death penalty" but did not agree "that this inconsistency creates a positive legal obligation to act." He noted, quite rightly, that the imposition of the death penalty in the United States is not of itself a violation of international law principles, and could not find the words of section 10 of the act to be sufficiently explicit to create positive duties of

---

[85] *Ibid.* at paras. 37 and 40.

[86] *Ibid.* at para. 49.

[87] *Ibid.* at para. 50.

[88] Department of Foreign Affairs and International Trade Act, R.S.C. 1985, c. E-22: "In exercising his powers and carrying out his duties and functions under this Act, the Minister shall (a) conduct all diplomatic and consular relations on behalf of Canada ... (i) administer the foreign service of Canada ... (j) foster the development of international law and its application in Canada's external relations."

diplomatic protection. Barnes J. observed: "While the evolution of international law may be in that direction, I am of the view that the *Charter* will provide a sufficient basis for protection such that resort to international law principles will not be required in an appropriate case."[89]

Barnes J. concluded that the government's decision to withdraw support for the applicant was made in breach of the duty of fairness, was unlawful and was set aside. He ordered the government to continue to apply the former/current clemency policy to Smith.

The contrast between Barnes J.'s two justiciability decisions, here and in the *Friends of the Earth* case (noted earlier), is hard to resist. Yet there may not be much to be gained from it, given how different the two cases are. What the *Smith* case makes clear, however, is that the finding of non-justiciability in *Friends of the Earth* did not stem from faint-heartedness on the judge's part. The *Smith* decision is audacious and, in this commentator's view, rightly so.

Génocide, crimes contre l'humanité, et crimes de guerre — Rwanda

R. c. Munyaneza 2009 QCCS 2201 (22 mai 2009).

Désiré Munyaneza, né au Rwanda, a été accusé de sept chefs d'accusation de génocide, crimes contre l'humanité et crimes de guerre en vertu de la Loi sur les crimes contre l'humanité et les crimes de guerre.[90] Sa poursuite, qui fut la première intentée en vertu de cette loi, a été entendu devant un juge seul, le juge Denis. Le procès a commencé le 27 mars 2007 à Montréal et s'est déroulé en français. La majorité des témoins ont été entendus en kinyarwanda, une des langues officielles du Rwanda, et des interprètes ont traduit en continu les témoignages à l'audience. Avant le début du procès, le juge Denis a présidé à Kigali au Rwanda une commission rogatoire où il a entendu les 14 premiers témoins de la poursuite. D'autres témoins ont été entendu à Paris, Dar es Salaam et Montréal. En total il y avait 66 témoins. L'accusé a choisi de ne pas témoigner.

Munyaneza est le fils d'un commerçant hutu de Butare. Lorsque le mouvement génocidaire s'est amorcé au Rwanda, en avril 1994, Munyaneza dirigeait le principal magasin général de la ville. Il s'est enfui au Canada en 1997 où il a été arrêté en 2005. La poursuite

---

[89] *Smith, supra* note 76 at para. 54.

[90] Loi sur les crimes contre l'humanité et les crimes de guerre, L.C. 2000, ch 24.

a affirmé que l'accusé était un chef local de la *Interahamwe*, une milice responsable d'actes de génocide contre la minorité Tutsi pendant le génocide rwandais. Les deux premiers chefs d'accusation reprochaient à l'accusé d'avoir commis un acte de génocide contre les Tutsi par meurtre intentionnel et atteinte de façon grave à leur intégrité physique ou mentale. Les chefs d'accusation trois et quatre reprochaient à l'accusé d'avoir commis un crime contre l'humanité par meurtre intentionnel et les actes de violence sexuelle contre les Tutsi. Les trois derniers chefs d'accusation alléguaient un crime de guerre au moyen de meurtre intentionnel, d'actes de violence sexuelle, et de pillage.

L'arrêt compte plus de 150 pages, la grande majorité duquel se compose d'un examen approfondi des témoignages. Les preuves contre l'accusé étaient accablantes. L'accusation établi, par des dizaines de témoins, que l'accusé était l'un des dirigeants des *Interahamwe* et qu'il s'attaquait aux personnes pour le seul motif qu'elles étaient Tutsi. Les attaques inclus l'assassinat en masse, le viol, l'infanticide et le pillage. L'accusé a fait partie des assaillants qui ont tué des centaines de réfugiés tutsi à l'église de Ngoma. Il a violé et participé à l'agression sexuelle de dizaines de femmes tutsi réfugiées à la préfecture de Butare. Il a participé au meurtre de quatre Tutsi en affirmant que: "Tous les Tutsi doivent mourir." Il a tué à coups de bâton des enfants enfermés dans des sacs. À de nombreuses reprises, au cours de ces événements, l'accusé est armé et porte, du moins en partie, une tenue militaire.

Seule une partie relativement petite de l'arrêt est consacrée aux éléments constitutifs des infractions de génocide, crimes contre l'humanité et crimes de guerre tels que mis en place (ou plutôt déclarées) par la Loi.[91] Cependant, cette observation ne vise pas à la critique. Les notes de l'arrêt démontre que l'examen du juge des infractions en cause a été fortement influencé par la jurisprudence des tribunaux pénaux internationaux pour l'Ex-Yougoslavie et le Rwanda. Le juge note également que l'objectif de la Loi canadienne est de mettre en œuvre le Statut de Rome de la Cour pénale internationale de 1998,[92] et se réfère au besoin à d'autres traités principaux de droit pénal international, tels que la Convention sur le génocide de 1948,[93] l'article 3 commun aux Conventions

---

[91] *R. c. Munyaneza*, 2009 QCCS 2201 (22 mai 2009) aux para. 58–154 [*Munyaneza*].

[92] Statut de Rome de la Cour pénale internationale, [2002] R.T.C. no. 13.

[93] Convention sur le génocide, [1949] R.T.C. no. 47.

de Genève de 1949 et le Statut du Tribunal pénal international pour le Rwanda de 1994.[94] Dans le droit pénal international comme le droit pénal interne, ce n'est pas chaque arrêt qui soulève des questions juridiques épineuses.

Le juge Denis a déterminé qu'il a existé au Rwanda dès le 7 avril 1994 un projet prévu de détruire l'ethnie tutsi, un projet appuyé par le président, les membres du gouvernement, l'armée, les *Interahamwe* et une partie de la population civile.[95] Quant à l'accusé, le juge a conclu qu'il avait l'intention spécifique de détruire l'ethnie tutsi à Butare et dans les communes environnantes. À cette fin, il a tué intentionnellement des Tutsi, en a blessé gravement d'autres, a porté atteinte gravement à leur intégrité physique et mentale, a agressé sexuellement de nombreuses femmes tutsi et de façon générale a traité les Tutsi de façon inhumaine et dégradante. Ce faisant, il a commis le crime de génocide tel que défini par la Loi.[96] En outre, il a commis intentionnellement les meurtres de nombreux Tutsi, un groupe clairement identifiable de la population civile de Butare et des communes environnantes, sachant que ses actes s'inscrivaient dans le cadre d'une attaque généralisée et systématique encouragée et supportée par le gouvernement, l'armée, les *Interahamwe* et les élites locales dont il faisait partie et une partie de la population civile. Dans les mêmes circonstances et avec la même intention coupable, il a commis de nombreux actes de violence sexuelle à l'égard des Tutsi. Ce faisant, il a commis un crime contre l'humanité tel que défini par la Loi.[97] Enfin, l'accusé, alors qu'un conflit national armé faisait rage au Rwanda, a, de façon intentionnelle, tué des dizaines de personnes à Butare et dans les communes environnantes qui ne participaient pas directement à ce conflit, a agressé sexuellement des dizaines de personnes et a pillé les demeures ou commerces d'individus qui n'avaient rien à voir avec le conflit armé. Ce faisant, il a commis un crime de guerre tel que défini par la Loi.[98]

La première poursuite réussie en vertu de la nouvelle législation canadienne des crimes de guerre revêt une importance indéniable,

---

[94] Statut du Tribunal pénal international pour le Rwanda Rés. 955 (1994) 8 November 1994, du Conseil de securité, tel qu'amendé.

[95] *Munyaneza, supra* note 91 au para. 2077.

[96] *Ibid.* aux para. 2082–3.

[97] *Ibid.* aux para. 2084–6.

[98] *Ibid.* aux para. 2087–8.

non seulement au Canada mais au plan international, étant donné le lien fort entre notre législation et le Statut de Rome. Pourtant, l'affaire *Munyaneza* ne semble pas établir des innovations importantes dans la loi. Il se peut que la valeur jurisprudentielle du présent arrêt ne réside pas dans le raisonnement du juge Denis mais dans le simple fait que la poursuite et détermination de cette affaire ont été effectués de la même manière (plus ou moins) que n'importe quel procès criminel.

Charter — Listing by the UN 1267 Committee — complicity of Canadian Security Intelligence Service (CSIS) in detention of Canadian citizen by Sudan

Abedelrazik v. Canada (Minister of Foreign Affairs) 2009 FC 580 (4 June 2009). Federal Court.

Abousfian Abdelrazik became a Canadian citizen in 1995 after being accepted as a refugee from Sudan in 1992, where he had been jailed for opposing the government of Omar al-Bashir. He lived in Montreal from 1990 to 2003 with no criminal record or charges. However, following the 2001 terror attacks on the United States, he came under scrutiny for possible terrorist connections. He was an acquaintance of Ahmed Ressam (since convicted for plotting to blow up the Los Angeles Airport) and Adil Charkaoui (held by Canada for over six years under a security certificate on the ground that he was a danger to national security).

In 2003, Abdelrazik decided — mistakenly, in hindsight — to return to Sudan for an extended stay. Some six months after arriving, he was arrested by Sudanese authorities and detained for eleven months. Agents of the CSIS took advantage of Abdelrazik's detention to interrogate him. Once released, Abdelrazik required a new Canadian passport to return to Montreal, for his current passport had expired during his detention. Foreign Affairs officials at the embassy in Khartoum made efforts in July 2004 to fly Abdelrazik home via Frankfurt on a Lufthansa flight, together with a diplomatic escort. Those efforts failed when Lufthansa refused to board Abdelrazik because his name appeared on a "no-fly" list. Serious Canadian efforts to help Abdelrazik get home appear to have ended about this time. Officials advised him that the government was not prepared to contribute to the cost of a return flight or to provide him with an escort.

Sudan detained Abdelrazik again in October 2005, this time for nine months. Upon his release in July 2006, the US government designated Abdelrazik as a person posing a significant risk of committing acts of terrorism. Within a fortnight, the UN 1267 Committee had listed Abdelrazik as an associate of the Al-Qaida terrorist organization. This committee was established under UN Security Council Resolution 1267 to implement that and subsequent resolutions aimed at controlling the Taliban and later the Al-Qaida terrorist networks. Having been listed by the 1267 Committee, Abdelrazik was subject to a global asset freeze and a global travel ban. In Canada these restrictions were implemented by regulations enacted under the United Nations Act.[99] Canada sought to have Abdelrazik removed from the list in 2007, but the 1267 Committee denied its request without reasons.

In April 2008, Abdelrazik, fearing that he might again be detained by Sudanese authorities, sought refuge in the Canadian embassy in Khartoum. He had lived there for over a year, without leaving, at the time of this application. In August 2008, Abdelrazik managed to reserve a flight home via Abu Dhabi, yet he was unable to take the flight because Canada failed to issue him the necessary travel document. In March 2009, Abdelrazik again made flight arrangements. He was to travel from Khartoum to Toronto on 3 April 2009. Two hours before his scheduled departure, he learned that the minister of foreign affairs had again refused to issue him an emergency passport. No reasons were given.

Abdelrazik applied to the Federal Court for relief under section 6(1) of the Charter:

Every citizen of Canada has the right to enter, remain in and leave Canada.	Tout citoyen canadien a le droit de demeurer au Canada, d'y entrer ou d'en sortir.

Justice Zinn concluded that the government of Canada had engaged in a course of conduct and specific acts constituting a breach of Abdelrazik's right to enter Canada. Specifically, the learned judge found: (1) that CSIS was complicit in Abdelrazik's 2003 detention by Sudanese authorities; (2) that by mid-2004 Canadian authorities had determined not to take any active steps to assist Abdelrazik to return to Canada, in spite of numerous assurances to the contrary; (3) that UN Security Council resolutions were no impediment to Abdelrazik's repatriation, even if that involved transit through

---

[99] United Nations Act, R.S.C. 1985, c. U-2.

foreign airspace; and (4) that Canada's denial of an emergency passport on 3 April 2009 was an unjustified breach of Charter section 6(1).[100]

In reaching these conclusions, Zinn J. made findings and observations that deserve a wide audience. In respect of the 1267 Committee, the learned judge quoted at length from a study by the UN Office of Legal Affairs summarizing the lack of legal procedures available to persons listed by the 1267 Committee.[101] There is no hearing or notice given prior to listing, and no effective means of challenging listing once it has occurred. Zinn J. did not hesitate to characterize the 1267 Committee regime as "a denial of basic legal remedies ... untenable under the principles of international human rights." He characterized the 1267 procedure as one in which "the accuser is also the judge."[102] He noted in particular that a listed person seeking to be de-listed is required "to prove a negative, i.e. to prove that he or she is not associated with Al-Qaida," contrary to the "fundamental principle of Canadian and international justice that the accuser does not have the burden of proving his innocence." Zinn J. concluded that the 1267 Committee regime is "a situation for a listed person not unlike that of Josef K. in Kafka's *The Trial*."[103]

The learned judge's harsh words were not reserved for the 1267 Committee. He was also very critical of CSIS and the Canadian government generally for their role in exacerbating (if not initiating) Abdelrazik's plight. He found that while Foreign Affairs played no role in Abdelrazik's detention, the same could not be said of CSIS. Rather, the evidence before the court (which did not include any direct evidence from CSIS officials) established, on the balance of probabilities, that CSIS was complicit in Abdelrazik's initial detention by the Sudanese.[104] Turning back to Foreign Affairs, Zinn J. found that, as of late July 2004, Canadian authorities did not want Abdelrazik to return to Canada and were prepared to examine avenues to prevent his return, such as the denial (without process or justification) of an emergency passport.[105] Zinn J. concluded that

---

100 *Abedelrazik v. Canada (Minister of Foreign Affairs)* 2009 FC 580 (4 June 2009) at para. 156 [*Abedelrazik*].

101 *Ibid.* at para. 50.

102 *Ibid.* at para. 51.

103 *Ibid.* at para. 53.

104 *Ibid.* at paras. 85–92.

105 *Ibid.* at paras. 107–8 and 154–5.

while there was no need to determine whether the breach of Abdelrazik's Charter right to enter Canada was done in bad faith, had it be necessary to do so "I would have had no hesitation in making that finding on the basis of the record before me."[106]

The respondents, the minister of foreign affairs, and the attorney general attempted to place the blame on Abdelrazik himself, for being foolish enough to return to Sudan, and on the United Nations, by whose Security Council resolutions Canada claimed to be bound. While acknowledging that Abdelrazik's decision to return to Sudan was "ill-advised," Zinn J. noted, "Foolish persons have no lesser rights under the Charter than those who have made wise choices or are considered to be morally and politically upstanding."[107] In response to the government's submissions on the Security Council's travel ban for listed persons, Zinn J. found that the exceptions in Resolution 1267 for entry of a state's own nationals, and for the fulfilment of judicial processes, applied. In particular the learned judge held that the obligations on states to "prevent the entry into or transit through their territories" of listed persons did not extend to excluding transit through a state's airspace. Zinn J. reached this conclusion in part by reference to international aviation conventions[108] and in part by reference to Canada's own submissions to the UN documenting its efforts to implement the travel ban — efforts that have not been directed towards persons transiting through Canadian airspace.[109] Finally, in response to Canada's astonishing submission that the Charter was "not engaged in this case" because Abdelrazik's inability to return to Canada was "the result of his listing on the 1267 list" rather than any Canadian governmental action, Zinn J. declared flatly that "the only reason that Mr. Abdelrazik is not in Canada now is because of the actions of the Minister of April 3, 2009" in refusing him an emergency passport to fly to Toronto.[110] Relying on the judgment of the Federal Court of Appeal in *Kamel v. Canada (Attorney General)*,[111] Zinn

---

[106] *Ibid.*at para. 153.

[107] *Ibid.*at para. 12.

[108] Paris Convention for the Regulation of Aerial Navigation 1919, (1922) 9 L.N.T.S. 174 (No. 297); Chicago Convention on International Civil Aviation 1944, [1944] Can. T.S. no. 36.

[109] *Abedelrazik, supra* note 100 at paras. 123–6.

[110] *Ibid.* at para. 148.

[111] *Kamel v. Canada (Attorney General)*, 2009 FCA 21.

J. held that where a citizen is outside Canada, the government of Canada has a positive obligation to issue an emergency passport to permit him or her to re-enter the country.[112]

The respondents led no evidence aimed at justifying the alleged breach of section 6(1). Having found a breach of Abdelrazik's mobility rights, and unable to find the breach justified under section 1 without evidence, Zinn J. was left to determine the appropriate remedy. As he pointedly observed, "the applicant is entitled to be put back to the place he would have been but for the breach — in Montreal."[113] Interestingly, Zinn J. invoked "the international law principle," famously declared in the *Chorzow Factory Case*,[114] that "reparation must, as far as possible, wipe out all the consequences of the illegal act and re-establish the situation which would, in all probability, have existed if that act had not been committed."[115] Zinn J. justified this reference by Dickson C.J.'s observation, *Re Public Service Employee Relations Act (Alta.)*, that the various sources of international human rights law must be relevant and persuasive sources for interpretation of the Charter,[116] to which Zinn J. added: "Similarly, I am of the view that principles of international law are helpful where it is necessary to fashion a just and appropriate Charter remedy."[117] Zinn J. ordered the government to issue Abdelrazik an emergency passport and to arrange transportation for him to Montreal within thirty days.

It is a comforting irony that, as international organizations and national governments seem to be turning away from basic international legal norms, domestic courts increasingly embrace them. Zinn J.'s observations on the gross inadequacy of the 1267 regime is not a repudiation of the UN system but an affirmation and reminder of the principles that are supposed to underlie it. Rather than asserting the pre-eminence of Canadian constitutional law over Canada's obligations as a member of the United Nations — a position for which he could not have been fairly criticized had he felt compelled to take it — Zinn J. rightly emphasized the commonality of Canadian and international law on such basic issues as

---

[112] *Abedelrazik, supra* note 100 at para. 152.

[113] *Ibid.* at para. 158.

[114] *Chorzow Factory Case*, [1928] P.C.I.J. (ser. A) no. 17 at 47.

[115] *Abedelrazik, supra* note 100 at para. 159.

[116] *Re Public Service Employee Relations Act*, [1987] 1 S.C.R. 313 at 348.

[117] *Abedelrazik, supra* note 100 at para. 159.

procedural fairness and effective remedies. In doing so, Zinn J. remind us that the flow of international law is not unidirectional. The role of domestic judges in the international legal system is not only to receive international legal norms and give effect to them according to domestic requirements but also to develop international law through its application in concrete instances.

Briefly Noted / Sommaire en bref

Charter and international law — homelessness

Victoria (City) v. Adams 2008 BCSC 1363 (14 October 2008). Supreme Court of British Columbia.

The defendants were homeless people who erected temporary shelters in a park in Victoria. The City of Victoria sought to enforce by-laws prohibiting such shelters. The defendants alleged infringements of their Charter rights, relying in significant part on Canadian international legal obligations concerning economic and social rights. Ross J. found unjustified infringements of the defendants' Charter right to life, liberty, and security of the person, relying in part on Canada's obligations under the Universal Declaration of Human Rights 1948 and the International Covenant on Economic, Social and Cultural Rights 1966.

This decision was appealed. The decision of the Court of Appeal for British Columbia will be reviewed in the next issue of the Yearbook.

Extradition — non-refoulement of refugees — Roma

Nemeth v. Canada (Minister of Justice) 2009 QCCA 99 (22 January 2009). Court of Appeal for Quebec.

The applicants sought judicial review of the minister of justice's decision ordering their extradition to Hungary. They came to Canada in 2001 and were granted refugee status based on anti-Roma (Gypsy) acts of violence against them in their country of origin. Hungary subsequently issued an international arrest warrant for the applicants on a charge of fraud, and requested their extradition. The minister signed a surrender order. The applicants argued that only the Immigration and Refugee Board was competent to withdraw its protection from them. They relied on the principle of non-refoulement of refugees. The Court of Appeal denied their application, holding that refugee status did not protect the status-holder from extradition.

This decision has been appealed to the Supreme Court of Canada. The court's decision will, if warranted, be reviewed in a subsequent issue of the Yearbook.

Canadian Cases in Private International Law in 2008–9 / Jurisprudence canadienne en matière de droit international privé en 2008–9

compiled by / préparé par

JOOST BLOM

A JURISDICTION / COMPÉTENCE DES TRIBUNAUX

1 Common Law and Federal

(a) Jurisdiction *in personam*

Attornment to the jurisdiction

Note. Attornment took the form of filing a statement of defence arguing *forum non conveniens* in *Blazek v. Blazek,* 2009 BCSC 1693. Under the British Columbia Rules of Court (Rule 14(6.4)) the defendant could have avoided this conclusion by a timely challenge to jurisdiction *simpliciter,* as distinct from arguing *forum non conveniens,* but he had not done so. In *Gemstar Canada Inc. v. George A Fuller Co.,* [2009] O.J. No. 4878 (QL), Doc. no. CV-08–00362851–0000 (S.C.J.), the defendant applied to set aside certain amendments to the statement of claim, which amounted to arguing the merits.

Non-resident defendant — claim arising out of business, investment, or professional transaction — jurisdiction simpliciter *found to exist — jurisdiction not declined*

Note. See *North America Steamships Ltd. v. HBC Hamburg Bulk Carriers GmbH* (2009), 61 C.B.R. (5th) 150, 2009 BCSC 1568, an action by a local company against a German company on freight forward swap agreement. A real and substantial connection was presumed under ssection 10 of the Court Jurisdiction and Proceedings Transfer Act, S.B.C. 2003, c. 28, because the claim was on a contract substantially to be performed in the province and in respect of a business

Joost Blom is in the Faculty of Law at the University of British Columbia.

the plaintiff carried on in British Columbia. In *Brake v. Phelps Drill-ing Co.* (2009), 78 C.P.C. (6th) 372, 2009 NLTD 91, the court held it had jurisdiction in a wrongful dismissal suit by an impoverished resident of the province against the corporation for which he had worked in Alberta. The court emphasized the unfairness of refusing to take jurisdiction as an element in determining that it had juris-diction *simpliciter.*

Non-resident defendant — claim arising out of business, investment, or professional transaction — jurisdiction simpliciter *found not to exist*

Note. The fact that the plaintiff is a local resident is by itself insuffi-cient to provide jurisdiction *simpliciter.* This was applied in *Unity Life of Canada v. Worthington Emond Beaudin Services Financières Inc.* (2009), 96 O.R. (3d) 769 (S.C.J.), in which an Ontario-headquartered corporation brought claims in breach of confidence and inten-tional interference with contractual relations against an agent that had represented it in four other provinces. None of the wrongful conduct had taken place in Ontario, and the defendants had no presence in Ontario. Likewise, in *Nelson Barbados Group Ltd. v. Com-monwealth Construction Inc.* (2009), 75 C.P.C. (6th) 58 (Ont. S.C.J.), the court held that no real and substantial connection existed be-tween Ontario and the claims of an Ontario corporation against sixty-two defendants, mostly resident in Barbados, concerning the sale of a Barbados family company and the property it owned in Barbados. The core of the action lay in Barbados, where there had already been litigation in respect of many of the same allegations.

Non-resident defendant — claim arising out of personal injury or damage to property or reputation — jurisdiction simpliciter *found to exist*

Stanway v. Wyeth Pharmaceuticals Inc. (2009), 314 D.L.R. (4th) 618, 2009 BCCA 592, leave to appeal to S.C.C. refused, 27 May 2009 (British Columbia Court of Appeal)

The plaintiff alleged that she developed breast cancer as a conse-quence of taking Progestin in combination with the defendant's hormone therapy drug, Premarin. She brought an action claiming damages from the defendants either in negligence or under a statu-tory cause of action for deceptive acts or practices. The defendants manufactured and distributed Premarin in British Columbia and elsewhere. The Canadian companies did not dispute jurisdiction, but the United States companies, which included the parent of

Wyeth Canada, applied for a dismissal of the actions against them on the basis that the court had no territorial competence over the claims under the Court Jurisdiction and Proceedings Transfer Act, S.B.C. 2003, c. 28, s. 3 (CJPTA). They contended that they carried on no activities in Canada, and the claims against them therefore had no real and substantial connection with British Columbia. The chambers judge applied the eight factors for determining jurisdiction *simpliciter* as set out in *Muscutt v. Courcelles* (2002), 213 D.L.R. (4th) 577 (Ont. C.A.). These factors included unfairness to the defendant if jurisdiction was taken and unfairness to the plaintiff if it was not. She held that in light of those factors there was a real and substantial connection with British Columbia.

The Court of Appeal affirmed her decision but disapproved of her approach to the issue of real and substantial connection. Section 10 of the CJPTA lends a degree of order and certainty for practical purposes by listing a number of circumstances in which a real and substantial connection will be presumed, including section 10(g) (the claim concerns a tort committed in British Columbia) and section 10(h) (the claim concerns a business carried on in British Columbia). Before the CJPTA was enacted, the defendant could lead affidavit evidence to challenge the correctness of the jurisdictional facts pleaded by the plaintiff, and the plaintiff had the burden of showing a good arguable case that the facts supported jurisdiction. Under the CJPTA, however, the presumption in section 10 is a mandatory presumption with basic facts. The basic facts are those set out in section 10(a) through (1), which are taken to be proven if they are pleaded. While the presumption is rebuttable, it is likely to be determinative in almost all cases.

The pleaded facts supported a claim that the defendants, including the United States defendants, committed a tort in British Columbia (section 10(g)) because they pleaded that the defendants jointly "marketed, tested, manufactured, labeled, distributed, promoted, sold and otherwise placed" the products into the stream of commerce in British Columbia when they knew or ought to have known the products were unsafe; that they failed to warn the plaintiff of the risks of using them; and that the plaintiff suffered damage in British Columbia as a result. The plea of the defendants' joint activities in relation to the stream of commerce in British Columbia was in effect a plea that they, including the United States defendants, carried on business in British Columbia, and so section 10(h) was also satisfied. The question for the chambers judge was therefore whether the defendants had rebutted the presumption created by section 10. She held that they had not and that their own evidence actually supported the real and substantial connection because it acknowledged that the United States defendants engaged in "harmonization" and "coordination" of matters involving the labeling of the products and clinical information concerning them. The chambers judge therefore had to go no further to dismiss the United States defendants' application. Her reliance on the *Muscutt* factors was misplaced. The *Muscutt* approach to jurisdiction *simpliciter* had been the subject of some judicial and academic criticism. In any case, any reliance on the *Muscutt* factors as a guide to determining the question of jurisdiction came to an end in British Columbia with the coming into force of the CJPTA.

Penny (Litigation guardian of) v. Bouch (2009), 310 D.L.R. (4th) 433, 2009 NSCA 80 (Nova Scotia Court of Appeal), leave to appeal to S.C.C. refused, 25 March 2010

The plaintiff commenced an action in Nova Scotia, both as litigation guardian for her son and in her personal capacity, with respect to the severe disabilities allegedly caused to her son by medical malpractice when he was born at a hospital in Red Deer, Alberta, in July 2004. The plaintiff had then been resident in Alberta for a year, but after three weeks in the hospital she moved back to Nova Scotia, where most of her family lived, taking the newborn and her older child. The three of them remained in Nova Scotia until July 2005, when they moved with the plaintiff's fiancé to Saskatchewan. Very shortly before the latter move, the son, who had been receiving further medical tests and treatment, was diagnosed with spastic dysplasia cerebral palsy. When the relationship with her fiancé ended in October 2007, the plaintiff and her children moved to Ontario so she plaintiff could provide support for her sick sister. It was during her residence in Ontario, in January 2008, that the plaintiff commenced the action in Nova Scotia. She returned to Nova Scotia in June 2008 so she could have the support of her family in raising her two small sons, one with a severe disability, and she intended to stay there for the indefinite future. The defendants applied for an order dismissing the plaintiff's action on the ground that the Nova Scotia court lacked territorial competence under the CJPTA because there was no real and substantial connection between Nova Scotia and the facts giving rise to the proceeding, and none of the defendants was resident in Nova Scotia or had attorned to the court's jurisdiction. Alternatively, the defendants sought a stay under section 12 of the act on the basis that Nova Scotia was *forum non conveniens*. Also at issue was whether the act applied to actions commenced before it came into force on 1 June 2008.

The chambers judge, in a decision noted in (2008) 46 C.Y.I.L. 667, held the Nova Scotia court had territorial competence under the CJPTA. None of the presumed real and substantial connections in section 11 applied, but, applying the eight factors in *Muscutt v. Courcelles* (2002), 213 D.L.R. (4th) 577 (Ont. C.A.), a real and substantial connection had been shown to exist between Nova Scotia and the facts giving rise to the plaintiff's claim. The judge emphasized particularly two of the factors. One was the fact that the boy's move to Nova Scotia meant that his ongoing medical treatment and the consequences of his disabilities had been, and for the indefinitie future would be, connected with the province. The other was that the plaintiff did not have the means to litigate in Alberta and so it would be unfair to her not to find jurisdiction *simpliciter*. The defendants appealed, arguing that the chambers judge, by applying the *Muscutt* factors, had allowed what was essentially a *forum conveniens* analysis to override the essential requirement under section 4(e) of the CJPTA of a real and substantial connection with Nova Scotia.

The Court of Appeal rejected this argument. The CJPTA was not intended to narrow the concept of a real and substantial connection as it had developed in pre-CJPTA cases in Nova Scotia and elsewhere. The court's own jurisprudence showed that, in assessing whether a real and substantial connection existed, a court was entitled to take into account the personal circumstances of the plaintiff (*Oakley v. Barry* (1998), 158 D.L.R. (4th) 679 (N.S.C.A.), leave to appeal to S.C.C. refused, 15 Oct. 1998; *O'Brien v. Canada (Attorney General)* (2002), 210 D.L.R. (4th) 668, 2002 NSCA 21, leave to appeal to S.C.C. refused, 24 Oct. 2002). The Supreme Court of Canada had said that "the assumption of and the discretion not to exercise jurisdiction must ultimately be guided by the requirements of order and fairness, not a mechanical counting of contacts or connections" (La Forest J. in *Hunt v. T & N Plc.*, [1993] 4 S.C.R. 289 at 326). The *Muscutt* factors should be endorsed as a useful, though not exhaustive, set of criteria with which to judge such matters. The chambers judge had correctly found that this was the type of case where more than one forum was capable of legitimately assuming jurisdiction and that there was a real and substantial connection between Nova Scotia and the facts on which the plaintiff's litigation was based.

The court also upheld the chambers judge's conclusion that he should not decline jurisdiction on the ground of *forum non conveniens,* as codified in section 12 of the CJPTA. It was appropriate for the judge to ask whether Alberta was clearly a more appropriate forum, even if the word "clearly" did not appear in the CJPTA. He had not imposed an unfair or improper burden of persuasion on the defendants.

Finally, the court affirmed that the judge was entitled, both on the question of territorial competence and on *forum non conveniens,* to take into account factual developments after the litigation was commenced. To hold otherwise would defeat the flexible, holistic approach urged by the Supreme Court of Canada in the *Teck Cominco* case (see below, under (b) Declining jurisdiction *in personam* — Parallel proceedings elsewhere (*lis alibi pendens*)), when describing legal principles that that Court acknowledged had not yet been fully shaped and defined. Section 4(e) of the CJPTA did not refer to the real and substantial connection existing at the commencement of the proceeding, whereas it did refer to that temporal requirement in the ordinary residence ground for territorial competence in section 4(d). This supported the conclusion that in conducting the real and substantial connection inquiry the judge is not tied to the moment the proceeding was commenced. The reviewing judge ought to be free to examine all of the facts as they exist at the time of the hearing in order that the question of jurisdiction may be decided on the totality of the evidence having regard to the analytical framework set forth in the CJPTA.

Note 1. The CJPTA is a uniform act that has been enacted in British Columbia, Saskatchewan, and Nova Scotia. If the defendant is neither ordinarily resident in the province nor has submitted to the court's jurisdiction, the court has territorial competence if there is a real and substantial connection between the province and the facts giving rise to the claim (section 3(e) of the British Columbia statute and section 4(e) of the Nova Scotia one). If any of the presumptions in section 10 applies and is not rebutted, section 3(e) is satisfied. If none of the presumptions applies, the plaintiff may still show on a good arguable case basis that its claim has a real and substantial connection with the province.

Note 2. A similar decision in favour of jurisdiction *simpliciter* was *Bartz (Guardian ad litem of) v. Canadian Baptist Bible College* (2009), 70 C.P.C. (6th) 108, 2009 NSSC 115 (accident suffered nine years earlier by child in Manitoba; family noved to Nova Scotia shortly afterwards).

Black v. Breeden (2009), 309 D.L.R. (4th) 708 (Ontairo Superior Court of Justice)

The plaintiff brought actions in Ontario against the directors of a company based in Chicago that he and his associates formerly controlled, alleging they had defamed him in press releases posted on the corporation's website. The plaintiff had long lived in Ontario and was a well-known figure in Canadian business. He had relocated to the United Kingdom in 1989, had homes in the United States, and was currently in prison in Florida after being convicted in the United States of mail fraud and obstruction of justice, charges arising out of his dealings with the corporation. Eight defendants resided in the United States, in four different states, and one each in Israel and Ontario. The defendants argued the court lacked jurisdiction *simpliciter* because no real and substantial connection existed between the claims against them and Ontario. They argued alternatively that Ontario was *forum non conveniens*.

The motion judge held the court had jurisdiction *simpliciter*. The alleged defamation was committed and damage was suffered in Ontario, where the libels were published and where the plaintiff had lived until he was forty-five, where he still had children and other close family, and where he still had many high-profile connections with Canadian business, charities, and community organizations. The publication or republication in Ontario was, if not probable, at least reasonably foreseeable to the defendants, who were sophisticated individuals and knew or ought to have known of the plaintiff's ties to Ontario. Taking jurisdiction was not rendered unfair by the fact that the press releases were made in the course of complying with court orders to report on the results of the directors' investigation of the plaintiff's dealings. The defendants did not have *carte blanche* to engage in the alleged defamation. The defendants would not enjoy the protection from liability they would have in an American forum, but it would be unfair to the plaintiff if he could not sue in Ontario because that was where he had lived most of his life and where his reputation was established. Although it was unlikely that a United States court would enforce an Ontario libel judgment, one of the defendants resided in Ontario and, in any event, it might still be important to the plaintiff to vindicate his reputation in Ontario. A real and substantial connection with Ontario was therefore established.

As for *forum non conveniens,* neither New York nor Illinois was clearly a more appropriate forum. No single jurisdiction was home to a majority of the parties. Witnesses and the bulk of documentary evidence were in the United States, but most of the documents could be presented electronically in an Ontairo courtroom. Ontario libel law would apply. There was no risk of parallel proceedings because the plaintiff had undertaken not to sue elsewhere with respect to the defamation. And declining jurisdiction would clearly deprive the plaintiff of a juridical advantage, namely the Canadian common law presumptions of falsity, injury, and malice.

Non-resident defendant — claim arising out of personal injury or damage to property or reputation — jurisdiction simpliciter *found not to exist*

Note. Paulsson v. Cooper (2009), 70 C.C.L.T. (3d) 152 (Ont. S.C.J.), held that the court had no jurisdiction in a defamation action, when the book review in question was written by an Australian and had appeared only in an American scholarly journal that had minimal circulation in Ontario. *Roed v. Scheffler* (2009), 71 C.P.C. (6th) 337, 2009 BCSC 731, held there was no real and substantial connection between British Columbia and a personal injury action arising out of an accident in the state of Washington. The fact the plaintiff suffered the consequences of the injury in British Columbia, where he lived, and might have a claim against his own insurer there, were not enough. All the other connections were with Washington.

(b) Declining jurisdiction *in personam*

Resident defendant — claim arising out of employment, business, investment, or professional transaction

Note. The court refused to stay a wrongful dismissal action by a resident of the province against a former employer that had a presence in the province and was served there, notwithstanding that the employment had been entirely in Alberta: *Critch v. Ceda-Reactor Ltd.* 2009), 286 Nfld. & P.E.I.R. 281, 2009 NLTD 41. Similarly, an insurer's action against a Saskatchewan corporation to determine coverage issues was not stayed, although the relevant loss was an Illinois judgment arising from regulatory offences the company committed while performing services in Illinois: *Saskatchewan Mutual Ins. Co. v. Homegrown Advertising Inc* (2009), 342 Sask. R. 104, 2009 SKQB 358. Compare *Teck Cominco Metals Ltd. v. Lloyd's Underwriters,* noted below under Parallel proceedings elsewhere (*lis alibi pendens*).

Non-resident defendant — claim arising out of personal injury or damage to property or reputation

Note. An Ontario lawsuit against Michigan residents for injuries suffered in a motor vehicle accident in Michigan was not stayed in *Silvestri v. Hardy* (2009), 95 O.R. (3d) 555, 2009 ONCA 400. A major factor was that an Ontario proceeding would avoid a multiplicity of lawsuits. The defendants were defending on the basis of the negligence of an unidentified driver, which required the plaintiff to claim against her uninsured motorist insurer, an Ontario corporation that could not be sued in Michigan. Jurisdiction was declined in *Mynerich v. Hampton Inns Inc.* (2009), 75 C.P.C. (6th) 199, 2009 ONCA 281, in which an Ontario resident sought to sue a Quebec corporation for injuries suffered in its hotel in Quebec.

Non-resident defendant — claim arising out of employment, business, investment or professional transaction

Re Pope & Talbot Ltd. (2009), 98 B.C.L.R. (4th) 169, 2009 BCSC 1014 (British Columbia Supreme Court)

Pope & Talbot Ltd. (PTL) was a subsidiary of a Delaware corporation with central management in Oregon. Its registered office was in Toronto but most of its business was operating pulp mills in British Columbia; it also had a pulp mill in Oregon and a wood products mill in South Dakota. PTL made an application under the Companies' Creditors Arrangement Act, R.S.C. 1985, c. C-36, in Ontario. The proceeding was transferred to British Columbia. The Ontario court, confirmed by the British Columbia court, made orders appointing Price Waterhouse Coopers as receiver and also as monitor of the Directors' Charge created by the court order out of PTL's assets. In this proceeding, the receiver asked for a determination whether any of the policies issued by PTL's directors' and officers' liability insurers would cover certain unpaid wage claims made by former employees of the company against the directors under the direct liability provisions in section 119 of the Canada Business Corporations Act, R.S.C. 1985, c. C-44. Three of the four insurers argued the court lacked territorial competence under the CJPTA or should decline jurisdiction on the ground of *forum non conveniens*. These insurers were based in the United States and had, in the United States, issued the policies in question to the Pope & Talbot parent company with coverage extending to the directors and officers of its subsidiaries.

The court held that it had jurisdiction *simpliciter* (territorial competence, in the statutory language). There was a real and substantial connection with the province under CJPTA section 3(e). The insurers' obligation to pay was on a worldwide basis. The claims arose from alleged wrongful acts arising in British Columbia from business operations of the Pope & Talbot group in that province. Claims were made under a Canadian statute against directors who were subject to that statute. Coverage under the policies was not limited to the United States parent. The insurers' obligation was to provide indemnity for claims that in this case were closely connected to British Columbia. Insolvency proceedings in the United States had effectively been transferred to British Columbia through recognition of the Canadian proceeding as the main proceeding in the insolvency. Although the policies imposed no direct obligation to defend, the insurers had to consent to the incurring of defence costs and so were in a position similar to that of a general liability insurer. The nature of the section 119 claims, the facts giving rise to them, and the insurers' effective rights and obligations in the defence of the claims connected the insurers to British Columbia. In addition, a presumed real and substantial connection existed under the act because the insurers' contractual obligations were substantially to be performed in British Columbia (section 10(e)) and because the claims concerned a business carried on in British Columbia (section 10(h)).

As for *forum non conveniens*, the factors in CJPTA section 11 were considered. Most favoured British Columbia, including expense, the location of witnesses, the fact that section 119 directors' liability was unknown in Oregon, a multiplicity of proceedings would be avoided, and a British Columbia proceeding would advance the fair and efficient resolution of an insolvency that the United States courts had effectively decided should be resolved in Canada. Oregon was therefore not a more appropriate forum.

Note. Jurisdiction was also not declined in *CKF Inc. v. Huhtamaki Amercars Inc.* (2009), 275 N.S.R. (2d) 67, 2009 NSSC 21, in which a Nova Scotia firm sought declarations and an injunction against an American company aimed at preventing the defendant from marketing in Canada products marked with a trade-mark to the use of which the plaintiff claimed to have exclusive rights in Canada. Only a Canadian court could grant relief in respect of Canadian trade-mark rights. In *Maple Trade Finance Inc. v. A & E Plumbing Ltd.* (2009), 273 N.S.R. (2d) 201, 2009 NSSC 11, a stay was refused in an action by a Nova Scotian assignee of receivables against the debtors, which were businesses in Ontario. The debtors' obligations were governed by Ontario law, but the real issue was the plaintiff's performance of due diligence before it advanced funds to the company from which it took the assignment. That issue was governed by Nova Scotia law as the law governing the assignment. *Peng v. Zhu* (2009), 97 O.R. (3d) 277 (S.C.J.), involved claims against an agent for breach of warranty of authority and intentional interference with contractual relations. The claims were brought by Ontario residents who had sold property located in China to the agent's wife, who resided in China. The court refused to stay the action. The defendant agent said he was resident in China but he had connections with Ontario, negotiations with him had taken place there, and he had used an Ontario address. It was essentially an Ontario case.

Jurisdiction was declined in *1092072 Ontario Inc. v. GCAN Insurance Co.* (2009), 74 C.C.L.I. (4th) 10, 2009 ONCA 464, in which a national company, headquartered in Quebec, sued Quebec insurance brokers for breach of contract and misrepresentation; all the relevant contracts were completed in Quebec. The fact that the claims included losses suffered by the plaintiff's customers outside Quebec did not alter the conclusion. The customers were not plaintiffs.

Non-resident respondent — claim relating to personal status

Note. See *Olney v. Rainville,* noted below under (f) Infants and children — Declaration of paternity.

Parallel proceedings elsewhere (lis alibi pendens)

Teck Cominco Metals Ltd. v. Lloyd's Underwriters, [2009] 1 S.C.R. 321, 303 D.L.R. (4th) 385, 2009 SCC 11 (Supreme Court of Canada)

Teck Cominco (TCML) sought to establish claims against various insurers, arising out of TCML's potential liability under United States law to remediate the pollution of lands in Washington State by slag discharged into the Columbia River over many years by TCML's smelter in British Columbia. TCML was being sued for the remediation costs in the United States District Court for the Eastern District of Washington by a number of Indian tribes and the state of Washington. TCML began legal proceedings against its insurers in Washington, for a declaration that they were liable to indemnify

TCML, subject to policy limits, for any award the United States court might make. The insurers wished to have the British Columbia court determine the issue of their liability under the policies. Most of the policies had been issued to TCML's predecessor, Cominco, through insurers' offices in British Columbia, and a few through offices in Ontario. The policy limits were expressed and premiums were payable in Canadian currency. The risks covered by the policies related to Cominco's operations worldwide.

After preliminary legal skirmishes, the parties agreed to a standstill agreement under which neither side would take legal proceedings against the other in respect of the policies. The agreement expired on 23 November 2005. Just after midnight on that day, TCML commenced an action in Washington State court, subsequently transferred to the United States District Court. At 9:00 a.m. on the same day, the insurers commenced an action in British Columbia. As far as the potential claim arising out of Columbia River pollution was concerned, the issues were the same in both proceedings, but the insurers' action in British Columbia also sought a declaration on the insurers' liability to TCML for other potential claims under the same policies, of which TCML had given notice. These arose out of Cominco's past operations at three sites in British Columbia.

On 1 May 2006, the United States District Court denied the insurers' applications to dismiss TCML's claims for want of personal jurisdiction and *forum non conveniens*. The court held it had specific jurisdiction because the action arose from a dispute over insurance policies that constituted the insurers' contact with Washington. The judge stressed Washington State's interest in adjudicating the dispute, given its interest in the timely remediation of pollution in the state. He also stressed TCML's interest in obtaining relief in Washington, where insurance law appeared to be "more developed" and where trying the case "would not result in piecemeal litigation of the [environmental cleanup action] and insurance coverage." As for *forum non conveniens*, public interest factors pointed strongly to Washington as the appropriate forum, including the local concern with the lawsuit, the court's familiarity with governing law, and Washington's "very compelling interest" in the coverage dispute. The court declined to engage in a lengthy analysis of which law governed the policies because it viewed choice of law as being of little weight at the *forum non conveniens* stage.

Soon afterwards, the British Columbia Supreme Court dismissed TCML's application to stay the insurers' proceedings on the ground of *forum non conveniens.* The chambers judge's decision was upheld on appeal. On further appeal, the Supreme Court of Canada affirmed the decisions below.

The courts below had applied the *forum non conveniens* discretion as set out in section 11 of the CJPTA. TCML argued that in doing so they had neglected the demands of comity as between the British Columbia court and the United States court, which had already positively asserted jurisdiction. The Supreme Court of Canada rejected both a "strong" version of this argument, in which section 11 was displaced if parallel proceedings were actually established in the other forum, and a "weaker" version in which the existence of parallel proceedings was entitled to predominant weight. The "strong" version was inconsistent with the statute, which created a comprehensive regime that applies to all cases where a stay of proceedings is sought on the ground that the action should be pursued in a different jurisdiction. The section 11 factors were to be considered in every case. It was not true that the factors were inconsistent with comity — they reflected a comity-based approach. Comity was not necessarily served by an automatic deferral to the first court that asserts jurisdiction.

As for the "weaker" version of the argument, neither the statute nor the case law was consistent with the proposition that deference to a foreign court that had already asserted jurisdiction ought generally to play a decisive role in exercising the discretion to decline jurisdiction. Nor would such deference accord with policy. It would encourage a first-to-file system, where each party would rush to commence proceedings in the jurisdiction that it thinks will be most favourable to it and try to delay the proceedings in the other jurisdiction in order to secure a prior assertion in its preferred jurisdiction. This was especially to be avoided at the international level, because, unlike at the inter-provincial level, there was no uniform and shared approach to the exercise of jurisdiction.

The court held that the *forum non conveniens* discretion had been properly exercised in the courts below. It was not true, as TCML argued, that the chambers judge had disregarded the fact that the insurance coverage sought was in relation to damages claimed in Washington state. The judge had considered that side of the case, but he determined that the central issues in the coverage actions (disclosure, risk assessment, and policy interpretation) weighed in favour of British Columbia and that the only coverage issues that were properly the substance of the United States environmental action were inconsequential. He concluded it would be unreasonable to apply Washington law because, *inter alia,* TCML's alleged wrongful actions occurred solely in Canada, the proceedings involved other British Columbia sites with no connection to Washington state, and the Washington residents were not beneficiaries to the policies. The judge was alive to the desirability of avoiding parallel proceedings and found the United States court's prior assertion of jurisdiction to be a factor of high importance, but he concluded it could not prevail in view of the fact that British Columbia was the forum most closely connected with TCML and the policies and that Washington state, a jurisdiction with at best a tenuous connection to the parties and the policies, was not an appropriate forum. There was no error in the judge's reasoning. While the Supreme Court of Canada was sympathetic to the difficulties presented by parallel proceedings, the desire to avoid them could not overshadow the objective of the *forum non conveniens* analysis, which was to ensure, if possible, that the action is tried in the jurisdiction that has the strongest connection with the action and the parties.

The Supreme Court of Canada did not express an opinion as to the enforceability in British Columbia of any eventual judgment in the United States proceeding. The question had not been fully developed in the courts below or on this appeal. The enforcement issue was disposed of by the chambers judge on the basis that he was satisfied that it was unlikely that TCML would have to resort to execution proceedings to obtain satisfaction from the insurers.

Note. This decision is of signal importance because it sets some ground rules, which have never been clear in the Anglo-Canadian common law, for *lis alibi pendens* situations. It affirms, partly on the basis of its interpretation of the CJPTA, that there is no special rule about concurrent proceedings. The problem is to be addressed by means of the usual *forum non conveniens* discretion. It also affirms — and a clearer instance could hardly be found — that mere priority in time should not always trump the other factors in the case. The two proceedings here were started only nine hours apart, and even that difference was just a consequence of the difference in court procedures in Washington and British Columbia. The case also illustrates the difficulty when the parties are fighting over where the litigation is going to take place because each of them believes that this may determine how the merits of the case will be decided. TCML, in the chambers judge's view, sought to have the United States court decide the coverage issues because TCML had reason to hope the American court would apply Washington state law, not

British Columbia law, to certain issues relating to the interpretation of the policies. Given that British Columbia law, in the eyes of the courts that decided this case, ought to apply to the policies, and given that the amounts at stake were hundreds of millions of dollars, it seemed wrong that the insurers should be deprived by jurisdictional tactics of their access to a British Columbia court and to British Columbia law.

Forum selection clause

Note. An exclusive choice of forum in favour of Texas applied to all disputes "arising out of, or in connection with" the contract. This was held not to apply to claims for breach of fiduciary duty and conspiracy: *Matrix Integrated Solutions Ltd. v. Naccarato* (2009), 97 O.R. (3d) 693, 2009 ONCA 593.

Arbitration clause

Note 1. Over the last years, courts have had to work out the relationship between arbitration agreements and class proceedings legislation. Must a class proceeding, brought on behalf of plaintiffs who entered into an arbitration agreement with the defendant, be stayed as an individual action must be when a dispute is covered by the arbitration clause? In *Seidel v. Telus Communications Inc.* (2009), 304 D.L.R. (4th) 564, 2009 BCCA 104, the court decided that the Class Proceedings Act, R.S.B.C. 1996, c. 50, being only a procedural vehicle, could not deprive arbitration agreements of their effect under the Commercial Arbitration Act, R.S.B.C. 1996, c. 55. An appeal to the Supreme Court of Canada had been heard at the time of writing but judgment had not yet been given.

Note 2. In *Sensor Technology Ltd. v. Geospectrum Technologies Inc.* (2009), 273 N.S.R. (2d) 210, 2009 NSSC 13, the arbitration clause covered some of the claims in a licensing dispute but not all. The claims within the clause were stayed on account of the clause, and the other claims were stayed on the ground that Ontario had been shown to be *forum conveniens* for them.

(c) Class actions

Non-resident plaintiffs — resident defendant — jurisdiction simpliciter

Note. The problem of including plaintiffs resident outside the province in a class action is giving rise to jurisdictional challenges and issues of the enforcement of eventual settlements or judgments. The most important decision this year was *Société canadienne des postes c. Lépine,* noted below under B. Foreign judgments / jugements étrangers, 2. Quebec — Compétence du tribunal étranger — Recours collectif en étranger — membres du groupe résidant au Québec.

A global class, not merely a national class, was approved in *Silver v. IMAX Corp.,* [2009] O.J. No. 5585 (QL), doc. no. CV-06-3257-00. The necessary connection between Ontario and the claims of non-residents of Ontario and of Canada was supplied by the fact that the claims arose out of alleged misrepresentations made in an Ontario company's press releases and Ontario regulatory filings.

(d) Claims in respect of property

Matrimonial property

Stefanou v. Stefanou (2009), 306 D.L.R. (4th) 526, 2009 ONCA 204 (Ontario Court of Appeal)

The husband and wife were originally from Greece and Japan, respectively. They married in Canada in 1979, became Canadian citizens, and during the husband's working life always regarded Toronto, Ontario, as their home base. As a result of the husband's work they lived in Nova Scotia from 1980 to 1982, Israel from 1982 to 1984, Toronto from 1984 to 1986, and Germany from 1986 to 1993. The husband retired in 1993, and the parties' primary residence became the island of Rhodes in Greece. They separated in 2004 and the husband began divorce proceedings in Greece in 2005; the divorce was granted in 2006. In 2005, the wife brought an application in Ontario for equalization of net family property and spousal support. The property consisted of a home, an olive grove, and a vineyard in Greece, and bank accounts and investments in Canada and the United States worth about $2 million. The husband obtained a stay of the wife's proceeding on the ground of *forum non conveniens.*

The Court of Appeal held the trial judge's decision had been entirely correct on the evidence before her, but new evidence was submitted to the Court of Appeal that decisively altered the complexion of the case. Before the motion judge, the husband maintained that the parties had had a good marriage for twenty-five years except for disagreements about money, that there really was no issue about the division of the North American bank accounts, and that the only dispute between the parties related to the properties in Greece, to which the wife had made contributions that needed to be valued. The trial judge had accordingly regarded Greece as the more appropriate forum to resolve the valuation questions relating to the Greek property, and even the Ontario court would have had to apply Greek law, as the law of the parties' last common habitual residence, to the division of property according to the Family Law Act, R.S.O. 1990, c. F.3, s. 15.

However, five months after the trial decision, the husband had applied for corollary relief in the Greek court, asserting that the wife caused the deterioration of the marriage and claiming that he was entitled to all of the money in the bank accounts and that the wife had made no contributions to the Greek properties. These differences were quantitatively significant and qualitatively shocking to the Court of Appeal. The fresh evidence could clearly have altered the result at trial. It did not change the requirement that Greek law applied to the division, but it radically changed the parameters of the property issues. In light of the husband's pleadings in the Greek proceeding, the North American bank accounts were now the most important property issue. If the parties could not agree on how their financial affairs in North America had been conducted, witnesses would be needed and most of them would be from Canada, where the bulk of the accounts were located. In these new circumstances, the balance tipped heavily in favour of Ontario as the appropriate forum. The wife's application in Ontario was therefore reinstated.

Note. Compare *Veder v. Veder* (2009), 69 R.F.L. (6th) 263, 2009 BCSC 428 (Master), in which the court declined jurisdiction in the husband's matrimonial property proceeding in favour of the courts of Florida, where the wife lived and proceedings were already underway. The husband's ties to British Columbia, although they existed, were not as strong as the husband asserted.

(e) Matrimonial causes

Divorce — declining jurisdiction

Note. Jurisdiction in the wife's divorce proceeding was not declined in *Smithers v. Smithers*, [2009] O.J. No. 5562 (QL), Doc. no. FC-09-1811, despite the fact that the husband had previously brought a divorce proceeding in New York. Their last matrimonial home was in Ontario, the wife and children lived there, the children went to school there, and the parties had Canadian pensions, a home in Ottawa, and a cottage property in Quebec.

Support obligations

Note. Three cases each involved a mother resident in the province who sought child support from a father resident elsewhere. The question in *Harman v. Harman* (2009), 314 D.L.R. (4th) 434, 2009 ABCA 410, was whether the Alberta court had jurisdiction to vary a child support order made in divorce proceedings by a Washington state court and registered under the Interjurisdictional Support Orders Act, S.A. 2002, c. I-3.5. The answer was no, because the act (in section 35(1)) provides for such variation only if the respondent ordinarily resides in Alberta or consents to the court's jurisdiction; here the father resided in Washington and did not consent. There was no common law right to seek variation. By contrast, in *Jasen v. Karassik* (2009), 306 D.L.R. (4th) 723, 2009 ONCA 245, leave to appeal to S.C.C. refused, 17 September 2009, the court did have jurisdiction to vary a child support agreement between a New York-resident father and an Ontario-resident mother. There was no evidence that the "domestic contract" was governed by foreign law under the choice of law rules in section 58 of the Family Law Act, R.S.O. 1990, c. F.3. Even if the contract were governed by foreign law, the court still had power to vary it under section 37 of the act. The Interjurisdictional Support Orders Act, 2002, S.O. 2002, c. 13, was not an exclusive code for the variation of foreign support orders. The jurisdiction of the court as against the non-resident father was based upon a real and substantial connection with Ontario. In *Kendregan v. Kendregan* (2009), 62 R.F.L. (6th) 82, 2009 BCSC 23, the court likewise made an original child support order against a non-resident father, jurisdiction *simpliciter* being based on the real and substantial connection the case had with the province on account of the father's part-time residence in the province with the mother up to the time their relationship ended.

(f) Infants and children

Declaration of paternity

Olney v. Rainville, [2009] 10 W.W.R. 439, 2009 BCCA 380 (British Columbia Court of Appeal)

The petitioner, a woman born and raised in British Columbia, married the respondent, a man from Quebec, in Vancouver in 1990.

After they both completed graduate study in England, the petitioner took a position with a United Nations agency in Geneva, Switzerland, in 1991. Both parties lived in Geneva at first and then made their home nearby in France. A son was born in 2000. The respondent had accepted a faculty position at a university in Quebec City in 1993 and spent the teaching terms in Quebec, where the petitioner joined him on her holidays. In 2002, the parties separated. A French court affirmed that the petitioner and the respondent both had parental authority. Since 2002, the son spent about ten weeks a year with the respondent, mostly in Quebec and lived the rest of the time with his mother in France. He never lived in British Columbia but had visited it in most years with his mother or both parents. The petitioner and the respondent were divorced in 2004. The following year, the petitioner married M, an Australian citizen who also worked in Geneva. In 2005, the petitioner informed the respondent that M, not the respondent, was the biological father of the son and provided DNA test results to that effect. In 2007, the petitioner commenced the present proceeding in British Columbia seeking a declaration that M was the boy's father. The respondent was served with process in Quebec. The respondent sought a dismissal of the proceeding on the ground that the court lacked territorial competence under the Court Jurisdiction and Proceedings Transfer Act, S.B.C. 2003, c. 28 (the CJPTA), or, alternatively, should decline jurisdiction pursuant to section 11 of the act on the ground of *forum non conveniens*. The chambers judge held that the court lacked territorial competence and, even if that were wrong, the court should decline jurisdiction.

The Court of Appeal held the court had territorial competence but affirmed the decision to decline jurisdiction. An unconditional stay was therefore substituted for the dismissal of the proceeding by the chambers judge. On the question of territorial competence (the CJPTA term for jurisdiction *simpliciter*) it made little difference whether the petition for a declaration of paternity was a "proceeding against a person," the rules for which are in section 3 of the CJPTA, or a "proceeding that is not brought against a person," governed by section 4, because given the current facts, involving a non-resident respondent, the test in both was whether a real and substantial connection exists between the province and the facts upon which the proceeding is based. However, it was not irrelevant whether the proceeding ought to be characterized as one "brought against" the respondent because the weight to be given to connections to Quebec to some extent turned on it. In the circumstances, it was appropriate so to regard the action. It was essentially adversarial in nature, with the goal of having the respondent displaced as the father of the child by M, who supported the proceeding while the respondent opposed it. The respondent did not want to lose the status of the child's father. In these circumstances, the proceeding was properly characterized as one brought against the respondent, both for the purposes of the CJPTA and for the purpose of determing the *forum conveniens.*

Territorial competence was established here; there was a real and substantial connection between the facts on which the proceeding was based and British Columbia (CJPTA section 3(e)). The material facts for this purpose were not necessarily those essential to the establishment of the claim. The catalogue of presumed connections in section 10 of the act included some in which the antecedent facts as such were not closely connected, for example, those in which it was the consequences of the decision, rather than the facts giving rise to the claim, that were closely connected with the province. This suggested that the "real and substantial connection" should be broadly interpreted. The only connection in this case was domicile. British Columbia was the mother's domicile of origin and the evidence suggested that she had never abandoned the intention of returning to the province permanently at some time in the future. She maintained minor, but not inconsequential, ties to the province. It was not seriously contended in these proceedings that her domicile was other than here. By virtue of section 28 of the Infants Act, R.S.B.C. 1996, c. 223, the son's domicile, under British Columbia law, was that of his mother as the parent with whom he usually resided. It was at least arguable that his personal status was to be decided under the law of British Columbia and that provided a real and substantial connection between the facts on which the proceeding was based and British Columbia.

Nevertheless, the chambers judge was right to decline jurisdiction. It was clear that Quebec was the more appropriate forum for these proceedings. The case had a much greater connection to that province than to British Columbia. Quebec was also likely to be a less costly and more convenient forum for the litigation, particularly from the respondent's standpoint. The genetic relationship between the child and M was a critical issue in deciding on paternity, but the court had to decide whether a declaration should be granted at all. Aside from the possibility that there were legal bars to the granting of such relief, the court would also have to wrestle with the question whether the court's discretion to grant relief should be exercised. On that issue, the court would have to evaluate the possible effect of a declaration on the established relationship between the respondent and the child and on the best interests of the child. The Quebec courts were in a much better position to evaluate those issues in a convenient and economical way than the courts of British Columbia.

The applicant argued that a stay of the proceeding would deprive her of a legitimate juridical advantage, namely the non-application of Article 530 of the Civil Code of Quebec, which prohibits a person from seeking a declaration of paternity that is contrary to that shown on a person's birth certificate if the person shown as the father has acted as, and been reputed to be, the father for a period of eighteen months. The court rejected this argument for several reasons. First, the provision was substantive, not procedural, so a court in either province might or might not apply it depending on which system of law governed the question of paternity. Second, the applicant was not a plaintiff asserting rights but an applicant for a declaration. Whatever arguments might be made in favour of a British Columbia court assuming jurisdiction over a dispute brought by a person who claimed to have suffered a legal wrong cognizable under the laws of the province, it was not apparent that they had application to a person who, while not alleging that any legal wrong had been done to her, sought declaratory relief from a British Columbia court. In any event, the court must take into account the question whether it is proper for a party to enjoy the juridical advantage on which she relies. The court was not convinced that there would be any injustice in requiring the case to proceed, if it proceeded at all, before the Quebec courts.

Custody — jurisdiction

Pichler v. Fiegehen, [2009] 10 W.W.R. 625, 2009 SKCA 101 (Saskatchewan Court of Appeal)

The mother and her three-year-old child had lived in Alberta for the first twenty months of the child's life and then moved to Saskatchewan. The mother was separated from the father. About eight months before the present proceeding, the child's paternal grandmother had, with the mother's consent, taken the child to the grandmother's home in Quebec. The visit was to be for a month, but the grandmother did not return the child and obtained two

Quebec court orders granting her custody. The mother had received no notice of the applications in Quebec. The mother now applied under the Children's Law Act, S.S. 1997, c. C-8.2, for custody. The chambers judge held that (1) the child was habitually resident in Saskatchewan; (2) Saskatchewan was the appropriate jurisdiction to deal with the issue of custody; and (3) the grandmother was ordered to return the child to Saskatchewan.

The grandmother's appeal was dismissed. The Saskatchewan court was not obliged to defer to the decisions of the Quebec courts. Essentially a *forum non conveniens* analysis had to be made. The mother had limited financial means compared to the grandmother, and it would be more onerous for her to travel to Quebec to plead her case before the Quebec courts than it would be for the grandmother to have to come to Saskatchewan. The balance of convenience and expense favoured Saskatchewan. The Quebec orders deserved respect as properly made orders of another province, but they were obtained on a default basis. It would be wrong to defer to the Quebec courts, in the name of avoiding multiplicity of proceedings, when those orders had not dealt with the merits. The grandmother had wrongfully retained the child in Quebec, conduct that should not be condoned because it results in the forum being other than the child's habitual residence. Obliging the mother to apply to set aside the Quebec orders, as on the evidence she would have to do, and to present her own defence there to the grandmother's application, would put her at a disadvantage at the outset when under the Children's Law Act she was presumed to be the custodial parent. For these reasons, the chambers judge's decision not to decline jurisdiction, and the orders she made, were correct.

Note. Pangracs v. Dick (2009), 307 D.L.R. (4th) 654, 2009 SKCA 14, held, as in the *Pichler* case earlier, that the children continued to be habitually resident in Saskatchewan although the mother had taken them without the father's consent to British Columbia, and so the court had jurisdiction in custody under section 16 of the Children's Law Act, S.S. 1997, c. C-8.2. There was insufficient reason to decline jurisdiction in favour of the British Columbia courts.

Jurisdiction in custody, when it is not corollary to a divorce proceeding, depends in some provinces on statutory rules and in others on common law rules. The common law rules were applied in *G.(J.Y.) v. T.(K.)* (2009), 75 R.F.L. (6th) 125, 2009 ABQB 603. The court lacked jurisdiction. The mother and child lived in Quebec, and there was no ongoing real and substantial connection between them and Alberta. The family had effectively left Alberta before the marriage broke up. In *Carabelea v. Carabelea* (2009), 72 R.F.L. (6th) 219, 2009 BCSC 933, the court refused a declaration that the court had jurisdiction in a custody proceeding brought by the husband, resident in the province, against a wife who resided with the child in Romania. The question of custody was before the Romanian courts as part of the wife's divorce proceeding there, commenced before the husband began a divorce proceeding in British Columbia. The Romanian proceedings were stayed, but that was because the husband was pursuing a Romanian order for the return of the child under the Hague Convention on the Civil Aspects of International Child Abduction. It would be wrong to let his own Hague Convention application in Romania be grounds for ignoring the jurisdiction of the Romanian courts to deal with custody.

Zaman v. Khan (2009), 70 R.F.L. (6th) 95 (Ont. S.C.J.), involved a mother's application for divorce and custody made in Ontario. The court held that it had no jurisdiction under section 3 of the Divorce Act, R.S.C. 1985, c. 3 (2nd Supp.), because the mother had been ordinarily resident in Ontario for less than a year when she commenced the proceeding. It also lacked jurisdiction under the custody provisions of the Children's Law Reform Act, R.S.O. 1990, c. C.12, because the child was habitually resident with his father in Qatar and all the evidence as to his best interests was there.

(g) Anti-suit injunctions

Class action — defamation action in other province brought by class action defendants against plaintiffs

Speers Estate v. Readers' Digest Association (Canada) ULC (2009), 73 C.P.C. (6th) 281 (Ontario Superior Court of Justice)

Since Quebec law does not regard statements made for the purposes of ligitation as absolutely privileged, the defendants in an Ontario class action, most of whom resided in Quebec, commenced an action in Quebec claiming that the representative plaintiffs had defamed the defendants by accusing them of preying on the elderly by using illegal marketing techniques. The court refused the plaintiffs an injunction to delay the Quebec proceeding pending the outcome of the Ontario class action. There was jurisdiction to issue such an injunction, either under the class proceedings legislation or as an anti-suit injunction. However, the plaintiffs had not sought to persuade the Quebec court to decline jurisdiction and the Quebec court should be given that opportunity. Nor was there evidence that the Quebec action was instituted as a strategy to discourage participation in the Ontario class proceeding. The plaintiffs were not prejudiced by the defamation proceeding in Quebec as they would be able to argue the thrust of their allegations as defendants in that proceeding and, if they succeeded, would be relieved of having to fight the same issue in Ontario because it would be covered by issue estoppel.

2   Québec

(a) Action personnelle

Compétence territoriale — élection de for

9163–2802 Québec Inc. c. Pioneer Steel Pre-Febricated Buildings, 2009 QCCS 1010 (Cour supérieure du Québec), confirmé 2009 QCCA 2072 (Cour d'appel du Québec)

La demanderesse, 9163, a poursuivi la défenderesse, Pioneer, en dommages à la suite de l'effondrement d'une structure d'acier acquise de Pioneer par 9012 (une compagnie qui est subséquemment acquise par 9163) et installée par 9012 dans St-Eugène, en Ontario. Pioneer présente un moyen d'irrevabilité plaidant la présence au contrat liant les parties d'une clause d'élection de for en vertu de laquelle le tribunal du district de Mississauga en Ontario a seul compétence pour entendre la litige. La demanderesse plaide, s'appuyant sur l'article 1436 C.c.Q., que la clause doit être considérée nulle puisque le contrat qui la lie à Pioneer est un contrat d'adhésion et la clause est illisible.

La Cour supérieure a accueilli la requête en irrevabilité. Les seules règles particulières de droit international privé édictées concernent le contrat de consommation ou le contrat de travail (art. 3149 C.c.Q.), le contrat d'assurance (art. 3150), le recours en responsabilité liée à l'exposition à une matière première provenant du Québec (art. 3129) et certaines actions réelles ou en matière successoriale ou de régime matrimonial (art. 3152 *et ss.*). Il n'existe aucun règle visant le contrat d'adhésion. S'il fallait examiner le caractère illisible ou incompréhensible de la clause selon l'article 1436 C.c.Q., malgré l'absence de règles de droit international privé propres au contrat d'adhésion, on se trouverait à appliquer le droit québécois au contrat, ce que les parties ont expressément exclu. Le contrat ici incluant une clause d'attribution à un autre for constitutive d'une élection de for impérative, seul le tribunal en Ontario a compétence pour entendre la présente affaire. La Court d'appel a rejetté l'appel.

Compétence territoriale — forum non conveniens

Bil'in (Village Council) v. Green Park International Inc., [2009] R.J.Q. 2579, 2009 QCCS 4151 (Québec Superior Court)

The plaintiffs in this case were the village council of a village in the West Bank and members of a Palestinian family that owned property in the village. They brought this action against two Quebec corporations and an individual domiciled in Quebec who was said to be the principal of these corporations. The plaintiffs claimed that the defendants on their own behalf, or as agents of the state of Israel, were engaged in constructing and selling condominiums in the village exclusively to Israeli civilians, thus participating in war crimes by Israel through its violation of the obligations of an occupying power under the Fourth Geneva Convention. The plaintiffs sought declarations that the defendants were in violation of these international obligations, punitive damages, an immediate cessation of the wrongful activities, the demolition of the buildings in dispute, and an accounting. The defendants argued, among other points, that the action should be dismissed because the alleged wrongs had already been the subject of judgments of the High Court of Justice of Israel and were thus *res judicata;* that the action was unfounded in law even if the facts alleged were true; and that the Québec court was *forum non conveniens* under Article 3135 C.c.Q. because the Israeli High Court was in a better position to decide the action.

The court held on the first point that the claims in the action were not *res judicata* on account of the Israeli judgments. The only common object between those judgment and the present claims was the stoppage of construction on the lands. The cause differed as between them and the present action, and there was therefore no risk of contradictory judgments.

On the second point, the court held that it could not be said that the plaintiffs' pleadings disclosed no claim. The Superior Court had jurisdiction over defendants domiciled in Quebec regarding a civil action based on extracontractual liability for an injury caused and suffered in a foreign country. The law that normally applies in such case is the *lex loci delicti*. That law must be proven. In the absence of proof, the law of Québec applied. Under Québec law, a defendant will incur civil liability if he causes damages to another by his fault. Knowingly favouring a breach by a state party of its undertakings under a convention, and knowingly assisting a state in the perpetration of a war crime, were both civil faults. A generous reading of the action, considered as a whole, did not lead to the inescapable conclusion that it was unfounded in law even if the facts alleged were true, which was the standard for summary dismissal under Article 165(4) C.C.P.

On the third point, the court held it should decline jurisdiction. The Israeli High Court was clearly the preferable venue, given the residence of the parties and the witnesses; the location of the evidence; the place where the injuries were allegedly suffered; the court's ability to assess the significance of the previous proceedings between the plaintiffs and the corporations; the location of the defendants' assets, which so far as the corporations were concerned were apparently all in the West Bank; the need to have an eventual Québec judgment enforced overseas; and the applicability of the law of the West Bank. The court considered at length a submission that the law that an Israeli court would apply excluded the Fourth Geneva Convention and so should be regarded as contrary to the public policy of Québec. On the basis of evidence as to the practice of the Israeli courts, the Superior Court concluded that the courts of Israel did not apply international instruments unless they were incorporated into Israel's domestic law. This could not be said to be contrary to public order because a similar requirement existed in Canada. The fact that Canada, contrary to Israel, had approved the Fourth Geneva Convention by statute was insufficient to conclude that the application of the law of the West Bank would be "manifestly inconsistent with public order as understood in international relations" contrary to Article 3081 C.C.Q.

It was noteworthy that the plaintiffs did not allege that the High Court of Justice of Israel is not an independent tribunal or that it would try the action fairly and impartially or, more specifically, that it would not be prepared to reconsider, in light of fresh evidence or the current practice of states, the issue of whether Article 49(6) of the Fourth Geneva Convention, the provision relevant to the plaintiffs' claims, has now become customary international law. By choosing the Québec forum, the plaintiffs were avoiding the necessity of discharging their onus of proving before the High Court of Justice in Israel that Article 49(6) is indeed customary international law as they allege, thus ensuring for themselves a juridical advantage based on a merely superficial connection of the action with Québec.

The Superior Court's judgment was under appeal at the time of writing: see 2009 QCCA 2470.

B   FOREIGN JUDGMENTS / JUGEMENTS ÉTRANGERS

I   *Common Law and Federal*

(a) Conditions for recognition or enforcement

Meaning of judgment — in personam *money judgment — fixed sum*

Magellan Morada Investment LP v. Miller, [2009] 8 W.W.R. 506, 2009
ABCA 124 (Alberta Court of Appeal)

The plaintiff, an Arizona corporation that developed real estate in
San Diego, California, obtained summary judgment in Arizona
against three defendants for US $1.65 million. Two of them, M and
W, were principals in corporations and limited partnerships that
provided management services to the plaintiff; the third was W's
wife. The liability arose out of a bad investment the management
entities had made on the plaintiff's behalf. The wife was included
as a defendant pursuant to Arizona's community property laws. The
defendants appealed the judgment, but their appeal was dismissed.
The plaintiff brought an action on the Arizona judgment in Alberta
and the chambers judge granted summary judgment against all
three defendants while staying execution of the judgment until the
Arizona appeals were concluded, which at the time they had not
yet been. The Court of Appeal upheld the judgment as against M
and W, because against them there was no doubt that the Arizona
judgment was a final judgment for a fixed sum. The matter was
remitted to the chambers judge in respect of W's wife.

Although an enforcing court is not entitled to delve into the merits
of the foreign judgment, it still falls to the enforcing court to ensure
that the necessary preconditions are met for recognizing and enforcing a foreign judgment. The purpose of the fixed sum requirement is to ensure that a foreign *in personam* money judgment
clearly sets out the debt obligation to be enforced without the need
for further investigation or clarification from the enforcing court.
Aside from that, however, there is the threshold requirement that
the judgment be a personal judgment against the named defendant
for the full amount of the fixed and final sum. In this case, the cause
of action against Ms. W seemed to be based on her marital status
only and not on any alleged improper actions on her part. This
raised a concern about whether the Arizona judgment was actually
a judgment against her personally for the face amount of the judgment. In light of the wording of the Arizona community property
legislation, the court was unable to determine whether the Arizona

judgment against Ms. W was an *in personam* judgment for the full amount of the fixed sum in the judgment; an *in personam* judgment limited to the value of the couple's community property, whether at the time of judgment or otherwise; or some form of *in rem* judgment against their community property only. In these circumstances, the question whether the Arizona judgment met the *in personam* fixed sum requirement *vis-à-vis* Ms. W ought to have been determined by the chambers judge and the matter had to be remitted to the lower court so this could be done. Both sides might be required to adduce additional evidence on this missed issue.

Jurisdiction of the originating court — by defendant's submission

Litecubes LLC v. Northern Light Products Inc., 2009 BCSC 181 (British Columbia Supreme Court)

The plaintiff sued the defendant in United States District Court in Missouri, alleging trade-mark and copyright infringement through the defendant's exporting lighted artificial ice cubes into the United States. The defendant pleaded that venue was improper in the district and that there was no personal jurisdiction either under Missouri's long-arm statute or under the constitutional standard of the due process clause. The defendant pleaded various defences, including no infringement and invalidity of the plaintiff's patent. The defendant also counterclaimed for declarations of patent invalidity and non-infringement, and requested a jury trial. The jury held for the plaintiff on most but not all points and awarded damages that totaled more than US $600,000. The defendant filed a motion for judgment with the original court essentially challenging the jury verdict on grounds of sufficiency of evidence. It was clear that the defendant's principal had testified at trial, that experts testified for both sides, and that the defendant participated in and conducted numerous pre-trial depositions. The defendant also filed a motion to dismiss for want of subject-matter jurisdiction, arguing that it had not infringed in the United States because all sales took place in Canada. This argument failed although the issue was held on appeal to go, not to subject matter jurisdiction, but to the merits. The jury's findings were upheld on appeal. The plaintiff now sought to enforce the United States judgment in British Columbia.

The court held it was enforceable. The defendant had attorned to the foreign court's jurisdiction by participating fully in the proceedings. The defendant argued that what constituted attornment was a question for British Columbia law, and that under the circumstances the defendant's participation would not have constituted attornment under the British Columbia rules of court because of an exception (in Rule 14(6.4)) if the defendant challenges jurisdiction *simpliciter.* The judge doubted whether one could simply transpose the local rules of court onto the foreign proceeding. A straight application of the British Columbia rules in an enforcement proceeding, if the foreign rules were different, would mean that the defendant could not be sure what steps to take in order to avoid an enforceable judgment. However, in this case, the point did not need to be decided because the defendant's participation would have constituted attornment even if one applied Rule 14(6.4).

The judge also rejected an argument that attornment by itself did not give a foreign court jurisdiction because it did not necessarily create a real and substantial connection between the litigation and the foreign court. The judge acknowledged that some of the expressions used in Supreme Court of Canada cases left obscure the relationship between the long-standing rule that consent gives jurisdiction, and the new rule that a real and substantial connection gives jurisdiction. However, she concluded that it made sense to treat consent as a stand-alone ground of jurisdiction; that made conceptual sense and it was consistent with the drafting of the territorial competence rules in section 3 of the CJPTA, which treat consent and real and substantial connection as alternative grounds. Even if that were wrong, she held that the defendant's participation did create a real and substantial connection between the litigation and the United States court in Missouri.

Jurisdiction of the originating court — class action — jurisdiction to bind non-resident plaintiffs

Note. See *Société canadienne des postes c. Lépine,* noted immediately below.

2   *Québec*

(a) Compétence du tribunal étranger

Recours collectif en étranger — membres du groupe résidant au Québec

Société canadienne des postes c. Lépine, [2009] 1 R.C.S. 549, 2009 CSC 16 (Cour suprême du Canada)

En septembre 2000, la Société canadienne de postes commercialise un service d'Internet à vie sur le marché canadien, mais met fin à son engagement en septembre 2001. Cela provoque des plaintes et des recours divers. Au Québec, un client de ce service dépose une requête en autorisation d'exercer un recours collectif au nom de toute personne physique résidant au Québec qui avait acheté le service. Plus tard, en Ontario, la Cour supérieure de justice certifie un recours collectif puis entérine une transaction aux termes de laquelle les consommateurs canadiens pourront se faire rembourser le prix d'achat du cédérom et recevoir trois mois de service Internet gratuit. Selon le jugement ontarien, la transaction lie tous les résidants du Canada qui ont acheté le service, sauf ceux de la Colombie-Britannique. Le lendemain, la Cour supérieure du Québec autorise le recours collectif au Québec pour un groupe incluant seulement les résidants du Québec. La Société tente alors d'obtenir la reconnaissance du jugement ontarien en vertu de l'article 3155 C.c.Q. La Cour supérieure du Québec rejette sa demande au motif que l'avis de la certification du recours ontarien était inadéquat au Québec et créait de la confusion avec le recours collectif entamé au Québec, ce qui violait les principes essentiels de la procédure (l'art. 3155(3) C.c.Q.). La Cour d'appel du Québec confirme le jugement sur cette question et ajoute que bien que la cour ontarienne avait compétence à l'égard du recours, elle aurait dû décliner compétence sur les résidents québécois en application de la doctrine du *forum non conveniens* (l'art. 3155(1) et les art. 3164 et 3135 C.c.Q.). Enfin, il y avait litispendance entre les deux recours collectifs, la procédure québécoise ayant été engagée la première (l'art. 3155(4) C.c.Q.).

La Cour suprême a rejeté le pourvoi de la Société.

En appliquant la doctrine du *forum non conveniens,* la Cour d'appel ajoute un élément non pertinent dans son analyse de la compétence du tribunal étranger. Bien que le libellé très large du renvoi au titre troisième relatif à la compétence internationale des autorités québécoises figurant à l'art. 3164 C.c.Q. invite à première vue à cette application, une telle interprétation néglige le principe premier de l'aménagement juridique de la reconnaissance de l'exécution des jugements étrangers dans le Code civil du Québec. Dans le cas d'une demande de reconnaisance d'un jugement étranger, le tribunal québécois n'a pas à se demander comment la cour d'une autre province ou d'un pays étranger aurait dû exercer sa compétence ni, en particulier, comment elle aurait pu utiliser un pouvoir discrétionnaire de ne pas se saisir de l'affaire ou de suspendre son intervention. L'*exequatur* du tribunal québécois dépend de l'existence de la compétence du tribunal étranger, et non des modalités de l'exercice de celle-ci, hormis les exceptions prévues par le Code civil du Québec. Le recours au *forum non conveniens* dans ce contexte fait donc fi de la distinction de base entre la détermination de la compétence proprement dite et son exercice. En général, le recours aux règles spécifiques prévues aux art. 3165 à 3168 C.c.Q. permet de statuer sur la compétence des tribunaux étrangers. Il se peut qu'une situation juridique complexe exige d'appliquer le principe général de l'art. 3164 C.c.Q. et d'établir la présence d'un lien important entre le litige et le tribunal d'origine. Même s'il a recours à cette règle générale, le tribunal de l'*exequatur* ne peut s'appuyer sur une doctrine incompatible avec la procédure de reconnaissance. Dans la présente affaire, l'existence même de la compétence de la Cour supérieure de justice de l'Ontario ne fais pas de doute selon l'art. 3168 C.c.Q., puisque la Société, défenderesse à l'action, a établi son siège social en Ontario. Ce facteur de rattachement justifiait à lui seul la reconnaissance de la compétence du for ontarien.

Dans le contexte où ils ont été publiés, les avis prévus par le jugement de la Cour supérieure de justice de l'Ontario ne respectaient pas les principes essentiels de la procédure au sens de l'art. 3155(3) C.c.Q. En matière de recours collectif, il importe que la procédure de notification soit conçue de telle manière qu'elle rende probable la communication de l'information à ses destinataires. La rédaction des avis doit prendre en considération le contexte dans lequel ils seront diffusés, et, en particulier, la situation du destinataire de l'information. Le respect de ces exigences constitue une manifestation de la courtoisie nécessaire entre les différents tribunaux et une condition de sa préservation dans l'espace juridique canadien. Dans la présente affaire, le clarté de l'avis importait particulièrement dans un contexte où, à la connaissance de tous les intéressés, des procédures collectives parallèles avaient été engagées au Québec et en Ontario. L'avis ontarien était de nature à créer de la confusion chez ses destinataires, car il n'explicitait pas adéquatement la portée du jugement de certification pour les membres québécois du groupe national établi par la Cour supérieure de justice de l'Ontario. Il pouvait amener le lecteur québécois à conclure qu'il n'était tout simplement pas concerné.

La litispendance empêchait aussi la reconnaissance du jugement ontarien vu l'art. 3155(4) C.c.Q. L'interprétation voulant que l'action en recours collectif n'existe qu'à compter du moment de son dépôt, après autorisation, ne respecte pas le texte de l'art. 3155(4) ni les modalités de son application dans le contexte d'un recours collectif. La demande d'autorisation du recours collectif constitue une forme de débat judiciaire engagé entre les parties pour déterminer précisément si le recours collectif verra le jour. À l'étape de cette demande, les trois identités se rencontraient dans la présente affaire. Les faits essentiels au soutien des deux procédures étaient les mêmes quant aux résidents du Québec, l'objet était le même et l'identité juridique des parties était établie.

La Cour ajoute que la formation de groupes de réclamants provenant de plusieurs provinces peut poser le problème délicat de la constitution de sous-groupes en leur sein et de la détermination du régime juridique qui leur serait applicable. Le contexte de ces instances impose aussi au tribunal saisi de la demande le devoir de s'assurer que la conduite de la procédure, le choix des réparations et l'exécution des jugements prennent effectivement en compte les intérêts particuliers de chaque groupe et il leur commande de veiller à la communication d'une information claire. Le création des groupes nationaux pose aussi le problème des rapports entre tribunaux supérieurs égaux, mais différents, dans un système fédéral où la procédure civile et l'administration de la justice relèvent des provinces. Les législatures provinciales devraient porter plus d'attention au cadre des recours collectifs nationaux et aux problèmes posés par ceux-ci. Des méthodes plus efficaces de gestion des conflits de compétence devraient être établies dans l'esprit de courtoisie mutuelle qui s'impose entre les tribunaux des différentes provinces dans l'espace juridique canadien.

D CHOICE OF LAW (INCLUDING STATUS OF PERSONS) / CONFLITS DE LOIS (Y COMPRIS STATUT PERSONNEL)

1 Common Law and Federal

(a) Characterization

Substance and procedure — bar on recovery of fees for unlicensed services

Note. Although they are often worded in terms that "no action shall be brought" for fees if the claimant was not licensed to perform the services, such rules are treated as substantive. Therefore, in *Douglas v. Pointe of View Condominiums* (2009), 13 Alta. L.R. (5th) 206, 2009 ABQB 289 (Master), a claim by an Alberta firm, not licensed as a real estate agent, for a "finder's fee" from its Alberta client depended on whether the agreement between it and the client was governed by the law of Alberta, where the agreement was made, or the law of British Columbia, where the land was located that the client purchased. The services were caught by the licensing rule in Alberta as real estate services, but the definition of such services in the British Columbia licensing statute was narrower and so arguably did not lead to recovery of the fee being barred.

(b) Contracts

No express choice — proper law

Re Pope &Talbot Ltd. (2009), 66 B.L.R. (4th) 58, 2009 BCSC 1552 (British Columbia Supreme Court)

The jurisdiction phase of this litigation is noted above under 1. Jurisdiction (b) Declining jurisdiction *in personam* — Non-resident defendant — claim arising out of employment, business, investment, or professional transaction. In the present phase, the court had to determine the law applicable to the officers' and directors' liability policies that were the subject of the action. The policies had been issued by United States insurers to the Pope and Talbot parent company, which was headquartered in Oregon. The court held, upon construction of the terms of the policies, that the intention of the parties was to have coverage in respect of a particular claim determined by the court that was adjudicating the substance of the claim against the directors or officers. This was an intended *dépeçage* of the proper law, so far as the insurability and coverage of certain specific types of claims were concerned. This did not mean that the contracts existed in a vacuum or that their proper law "floated." The policies in this case were, in fact, connected to more than one jurisdiction and legal regime, for example, British Columbia, Ontario, Delaware, Oregon, Indiana, New Jersey, Pennsylvania, New York, and Connecticut. This was an extraordinary case, one where the parties intended that a court having taken jurisdiction over the claim or matter in dispute would determine the proper law of the policy according to its own rules in order to determine coverage.

The court therefore had to apply British Columbia choice of law rules in determining the law applicable to the coverage issues. The place where the policies were issued was presumed to be British Columbia under section 5 of the Insurance Act, R.S.B.C. 1996, c. 226, because they insured persons resident in British Columbia. The insurers had not rebutted this presumption. The form of the policies was not tied to any particular jurisdiction. The insurers' head offices were respectively in five different American states. The decision to accept the risk was made in various locations in the

United States. Although it was the group that was insured, the bulk of the group's business was located in British Columbia, which favoured British Columbia law. Most of the claims likely to arise would arise from the Canadian operations of PTL (the Canadian subsidiary). The court inferred that under all the circumstances, the parties expected British Columbia law to apply to claims flowing out of the operations of PTL and, specifically, the claims based on directors' liability for unpaid wages pursuant to the federal Canadian corporations statute.

Note. For a settlement reached subsequently, which covered most of the unpaid wage claims, see *Re Pope & Talbot Ltd.*, 2009 BCSC 1823. Another case on the proper law of an insurance policy was *American Home Assurance Co. v. Temple Ins. Co.* (2009), 94 O.R. (3d) 534 (S.C.J.). An umbrella policy was held, under the circumstances, to be governed by Ontario law, the same law as governed the primary policy, although the insured was based in Quebec and operated a hotel in Florida.

(c) Torts

Note. Green v. State Farm Mut. Automobile Ins. Co. (2009), 76 C.C.L.I. (4th) 277 (Ont. S.C.J.), held that the Ontario no-fault insurance régime, including its verbal and monetary thresholds, did not apply where the accident took place in Florida. Such no-fault systems were substantive liability rules, not procedural rules relating to quantum. Florida also had a no-fault scheme that would have deprived one plaintiff of her claim because it was below the relevant threshold, but the scheme only applied to insureds that carried a Personal Injury Protection endorsement, which the Florida driver did not.

(d) Property

Matrimonial property — validity of prenuptial contract — division of assets

Friedl v. Friedl (2009), 95 B.C.L.R. (4th) 102, 2009 BCCA 314 (British Columbia Court of Appeal)

The wife applied for a division of family assets. The parties lived in Germany when they were married in 1997. The wedding took place in the United States but they had, shortly before, made a prenuptial agreement in Germany that excluded the provisions of German law providing for an equal division of propery acquired by either spouse during marriage. The husband worked as a surgeon; the wife had been a physiotherapist before they married. She looked after the household and the children. They moved to British Columbia in 2001. Before the marriage, the husband had acquired property in Michigan, Germany, and Switzerland. After the marriage, he purchased additional property in Michigan, homes in Germany and Kamloops, British Columbia, two other properties in British Columbia, and an interest in a business. The parties separated in 2006. The wife petitioned in British Columbia for divorce. The husband attempted to begin divorce proceedings in Germany, but the court held the British Columbia court had jurisdiction.

The wife also sought a division of the family assets, none of which were in her name, under the Family Relations Act, R.S.B.C. 1996, c. 128. The husband relied on the prenuptial agreement, which provided it was governed by German law. An expert in German law provided two reports to the effect that the German courts would assess the validity of the prenuptial agreement in light of the circumstances leading up to its execution, including the fact that the wife was four months pregnant at the time. The judge noted that the wife was first shown the agreement on the day she signed it and could not review it with her family or a lawyer of her choosing. The husband was more sophisticated in business matters and had directed the drafting of the agreement and orchestrated its execution to prevent the wife from fully reviewing it before she signed. The judge said that the wife's pregnancy at the time was a significant factor placing the wife under duress. The judge held the agreement void both under German law and under British Columbia law, for duress, coercion, and undue influence. Since that also rendered void a clause in the agreement to the effect that German law would apply to a termination of the parties' marriage, the judge proceeded to apply British Columbia law to divide the assets, given the family's substantial property ties and other links to the province.

The Court of Appeal affirmed the decision, rejecting various challenges to the judge's handling of the expert reports on German law. The court refused to admit fresh evidence that the husband wanted to introduce. A court can examine the sources of foreign law where there is conflicting expert evidence and the sources are those that have been referred to by the experts. In this case, however, the expert's two reports were consistent with each other on the issue the judge found he had to resolve, and there was no reason to refer to other sources of German law. Hence, the Court of Appeal rejected the submission of fresh evidence. Findings of foreign law, like other findings of fact, could be impeached only for palpable and overriding error. The judge made no such error in dealing with the expert's reports on the issues of the process a German court would undertake in reviewing a marriage agreement, the function of a *notar* in German law (one was present when the agreement was made), and the German concepts of coercion, duress, or undue influence.

Book Reviews / Recensions de livres

The Human Dimension of International Law: Selected Papers of Antonio Cassese. Edited by Paola Gaeta and Salvatore Zappalà. Oxford: Oxford University Press, 2008. 624 pages.

Introduction

War, its conduct, and consequences, commands the interest of many and sometimes for very personal reasons. My father was a prisoner of war during the 1939–45 conflict and my first childhood memories are of my attempts to understand the reasons for his absence in that distant "war overseas." As a university student, the post-war creation of the United Nations with its avowed purpose "to save succeeding generations from the scourge of war" was the focus of an intellectually challenging course in international law given by a brilliant Canadian political scientist, the Honourable Jean Luc Pépin (with whom I subsequently served in the cabinet of a government led by Pierre Trudeau). Later, as Canada's minister of defence, I pursued a professional interest in my country's contribution to the maintenance of international peace and security. This personal and professional background led me to undertake post-graduate studies in international law and, in that context, to read with great interest and delight *The Human Dimension of International Law,* a collection of writings by Antonio Cassese previously published in the 1970s, 1980s, and 1990s.

The Human Dimension of International Law also includes biographical notes on Cassese written by a number of his colleagues. According to these, Antonio Cassese has spent his professional life in the service of international law and in its development as a practitioner, a scholar, and a jurist. In addition to teaching international law, Cassese has acted as the Italian government's representative at many international conferences, negotiating and advocating advancements in international law. A crowning achievement of this remarkable career was certainly his appointment as the first president of the International Criminal Tribunal for the Former Yugoslavia (ICTY), serving in that capacity from 1993 to 1997. In 2004, Cassese was appointed by the United Nations Secretary-General to be the chairperson of the International Commission of Inquiry on Darfur. Since March 2009, he has acted as judge and president of the Special Tribunal for Lebanon. He continues to be a professor of international law at Florence University.

The publication of the book was timed so as to mark Cassese's seventieth birthday. It was edited by an editorial committee composed of students and friends who sought to bring together a collection of Cassese's most important writings. Selecting from a huge body of work (the list of publications attributed to Cassese covers seven pages of the text), the editors chose those of Cassese's writings that centre on the "human dimension of international law."[1] The articles in the collection remain surprisingly timely. They should be required reading for all students of the law as well as that part of the broader public interested in understanding the international legal order and the increasing importance of human rights in its evolution.

FORM AND CONTENT OF THE COLLECTION

Omitting preliminary materials, the substantive content of the book comprises 527 pages in twenty-five chapters, each of which comprises a standalone text. These span over twenty-five years of Cassese's writings from 1974 to 2001. The inclusion of the original publication date of the selected pieces is significant in that they reveal Cassese's ongoing contribution to the evolution of international law. The clear and intelligible style of the author in all articles is welcome and helps to demystify complex international legal issues, as the author evidently intended. The collection includes a wide variety of topics, clearly selected for their continued relevance to today's events, ranging from the prohibition of torture and inhuman or degrading treatment or punishment to state criminality and its prosecution, crimes against humanity and the resulting

---

1 Paola Gaeta and Salvatore Zappalà, eds., *The Human Dimension of International Law: Selected Papers of Antonio Cassese* (Oxford: Oxford University Press, 2008) at xxxvii-xliii.

liability of individuals, and the International Criminal Court. The editors, however, have included two chapters that do not quite fit with the remainder of the collection: chapter 18 on the notorious "Nestlé Affair," related to corporate greed; and chapter 24 on the doctrine of *respondeat superior,* which was contested at the post-war Nuremberg trials. Although of interest in themselves, these two pieces do not add much to the collection's themes. The confines of this review do not allow for an examination of each individual chapter in the collection. This review will rather attempt to describe and examine a number of important themes that weave their way through several of the chapters.

CASSESE'S THOUGHTS ON THE HUMAN DIMENSION OF INTERNATIONAL LAW

Cassese contributes an opening essay written specifically for this publication, entitled "Soliloquy." He sets the stage for the following chapters by giving a reflective and insightful summary of his career path, his personal philosophy, and the individuals and events that have played roles in his professional life. He also identifies the intellectual underpinning of the collection — Cassese's interest in the individual and the increasing attention paid to the individual by international law. He claims to have been professionally motivated by the maxim *hominum causa omne jus constitutum est,* explaining that "I still believe that only those problems that dramatically affect the daily lives of human beings are worth studying."[2] Given the humanitarian content of the collection, it would appear that Cassese held true and fast to that maxim throughout his career.

Towards the end of his introductory essay, Cassese presents a pessimistic assessment of the international community — a view grounded in the lack of enforceability of legal norms. Indeed, he questions the very existence of an international community. He accepts that some of the trappings of a community exist, such as legal standards and institutions that attempt to regulate international activity and the United Nations Charter that acts as a "sort of Constitution."[3] He regrets, however, the insistence by states on their Westphalian sovereignty, anchored solidly in the right to use force. In his view, states do not readily accept limitations on that sovereignty when presented with enforceable treaties, in large part

[2] *Ibid.* at lxx.

[3] *Ibid.* at lxxviii.

because of an absence of international collegiality. He writes: "What however is lacking is a *'community sentiment,'* the feeling in each member state that it is part of the whole and must pursue common goals; a shared conviction that each member not only must comply with existing legal and moral standards, but is also bound to call upon and even demand that other members do likewise in the interest of the whole community."[4]

The absence of a "community sentiment" is a concern that underlies the body of work chosen for the collection. Cassese suggests that in the absence of a degree of enforceability of legal norms in the municipal environment, one is obliged to focus on the quality of the content of international legal standards. At one point in his "Soliloquy," Cassese recounts having been taken to task by B.V.A. Röling, the well-known Dutch international lawyer and former judge of the International Military Tribunal for the Far East, whom Cassese befriended. Röling reacted to Cassese's suggestion that it is pointless to struggle to bring about unenforceable legal principles in the field of international humanitarian law (IHL) with which states and individuals would never comply. In rebuking Cassese's arguments, Röling argued that international principles were important as legal standards "even when they are unheeded. International principles ... may lie dormant for a time; but they are there and sooner or later they may be used by one or more international actors to curb violence."[5] Cassese clearly found much wisdom in that view and has contributed significantly to the formulation of international legal standards, all the while struggling to advance stronger enforcement mechanisms.

The first article in the collection, entitled "Current Trends in the Development of the Law of Armed Conflict," is an example of that struggle. It was written when Cassese was a member of the Italian delegation to the 1971, 1972 and 1974 international conferences on IHL. The article deals with the advancement and development of this area of international law in light of the armed struggles against colonial rule in the 1960s and highlights the author's participation in the process. In the concluding paragraph, Cassese optimistically refers to "new means of ensuring strict compliance with international law ... being devised" in the proposals that ultimately led to Protocols I and II Additional to the 1949 Geneva

---

4 *Ibid.* at lxxviii.

5 *Ibid.* at lxxiii.

Conventions.[6] This optimism was to prove unjustified. In Chapter 7, an article that initially appeared in 1981 dealing with Additional Protocol II of 1977 on non-international conflict, Cassese states that the provisions he had hoped would allow for the enforcement or supervision of the protections provided by the protocol were not in the end retained.[7] Ultimately, states refused to grant international status to rebels since they believed this would weaken state sovereignty.

In Chapter 9, "Means of Warfare," Cassese again raises the issue of enforcement, this time in relation to Article 23(e) of the 1899 and 1907 Hague Regulations on Land Warfare. The provision provides for limits on the use of weapons of war "calculated to cause unnecessary suffering," yet it does not identify specific weapons. Cassese contrasts this approach with the one that had previously dominated in the early 1800s, where the banning of weapons of excessive cruelty had been achieved by specifically identifying the prohibited armaments. He provides examples, including the ban on poisoned bullets, projectiles filled with glass and caustic lime, and minced lead and chain-bullets.[8] The practice of banning specific weapons has been revived more recently. The banning of land mines by the Ottawa Convention on Land Mines is a recent example. However, it is clear that Cassese favours the approach adopted in the Hague Regulations. It is more difficult to prohibit the use of weapons of war that are increasingly devastating because of technology if bans have to be negotiated on a case-by-case basis. The banning of nuclear weapons is a case in point. Cassese supports the use of a more general provision that could more effectively prevent the use of cruel weaponry without the need for individual treaties every time new weapons of barbaric cruelty are introduced.

Much to his dismay, Cassese considers Article 23(e) a valiant but unsuccessful attempt to achieve the goal he favours: "The principle laid down in Article 23(e) is to a great extent couched in such vague and uncertain terms as to be barren of practical result."[9] He goes on to add that:

Its limited prohibitory scope would be further eroded by the present condition of enforcement procedures in the international community. When

[6] *Ibid.* at 38.
[7] *Ibid.* at 151.
[8] *Ibid.* at 193.
[9] *Ibid.* at 211.

there exists no authority capable both of stating with binding effect that the use of a weapon in a certain instance is contrary to Article 23(e) and of enforcing such statement, scant practical value can be attributed to any contention that a specific means of combat inflicts unnecessary suffering.[10]

Yet, faithful to his Röling-inspired ambition to forge legal standards, even where enforcement is a problem, he writes:

What is needed is a principle which, being couched in not too vague terms, could provide some standard of conduct, however general it may be. The major role of such principle should be to fill the gaps of existing specific prohibitions, by at least covering extreme cases of new weapons which while they are patently cruel, do not fall under specific bans.[11]

He then proceeds to offer, in two pages of text, creative suggestions as to how that could be done.

It is the same dedication to the creation of international legal standards that motivates, in Chapter 2, his review of the origins and relevance of the controversial "Martens Clause," first included in the Hague Convention of 1899 and now reflected in the preamble of Additional Protocol II. The clause introduces "[l]es principes de l'humanité et [l]es exigeances de la conscience publique," as suggested sources of IHL in the absence of agreed-to treaty provisions. If given effect, the "Martens Clause" would impose an obligation on states engaged in armed conflict to accept as valid legal standards and principles found in practices among civilized nations and the dictates of public conscience.[12] He discusses the origins of the clause, its author, and the circumstances of its adoption, and reviews through copious footnotes its jurisprudential travels. I would have preferred that Cassese advocate the clause more strenuously, which he favours, and he certainly had the opportunity to do so. He refers to a 1950 Belgian Military Court decision where the Martens Clause was used to apply the principles of the Universal Declaration of Human Rights (UDHR).[13] He approves of the decision but goes no further. Readers would have benefitted from his applying his expertise to a discussion of the opportunities and potential pitfalls

[10] *Ibid.* at 213.

[11] *Ibid.* at 215.

[12] *Ibid.* at 39.

[13] *Ibid.* at 59.

to be found in the application of the principles of the UDHR to IHL using the Martens Clause as the door opener. One issue that comes to mind is Article 3 of the UDHR on the right to life, liberty, and security of the person and its relevance to IHL's acceptance of the destruction of human life.

Cassese does engage in advocacy in two articles in the collection dealing with the Israeli occupation of Palestine. In Chapter 11, published in 1992, he considers the application of the law of belligerent occupation to the Israeli occupation of Arab territory after 1967. He argues that, contrary to the Israeli claim, principles found in the 1907 Hague Regulations and Geneva Convention IV of 1949 do apply to the occupation. He uses the occupation of Palestine as a helpful illustration of international rules restraining an occupying force. He is assisted in his analysis by judgments of the Israeli Supreme Court on the issues. He nevertheless criticizes the Court, stating: "[I]n spite of its important contribution to the scrutiny of military action by Israel in the Occupied Territories, the Court has frequently shown excessive self-restraint towards the other Israel authorities, or has indulged in some sort of legal formalism that ultimately diminishes its bearing on the action of the occupying forces."[14] He illustrates clearly the difficulty of an ostensibly independent judiciary applying international legal principles in the face of dominant military force and political realities: the rule of law suffers.

The relationship between the law and force is also the subject of Chapter 12 dealing with the international status of Jerusalem, an article written in 1986. In the piece's introduction, Cassese underlines the dominance of the use of force in relation to international legal norms. Referring to Sir H. Lauterpacht's and his description of IHL as constituting law's "vanishing point," he writes: "I shall start from the assumption that even where international law has reached its 'vanishing point' in matters *directly impinging upon force,* one should not *a priori* discount the possible role of legal standards."[15] The article suggests that Israel, under existing customary rules, cannot claim sovereignty over any part of Jerusalem without the involvement of the United Nations. "In the case of Jerusalem, we come face to face with a striking phenomenon: a *de facto* situation brought about *by force of arms* and now solidly implanted in the daily life of the city, not recognized by any other member of the world

[14] *Ibid.* at 271.

[15] *Ibid.* at 273 [emphasis added].

community, and consequently not validated either under general international law or conventional law."[16] Cassese's message is clear: force may empower Israel to occupy territories to which it has no legal claim but that occupation cannot endure in its illegality. Cassese is convincing in his determination to persuade his reader that the strength and excellence of the legal principles at play will ensure that Israel will ultimately accept their primacy over political and military force.

CONCLUSION

Few individuals have the extensive experience of Antonio Cassese in a discipline upon which international peace and security depends. This collection lucidly records the experience and views of Antonio Cassese by providing a collection of writings from his many years of exemplary service and dedication. It is a fascinating and absorbing tale told via an assemblage of various articles, all of which bring to life the evolving universe of international law, with all its challenges, strengths, and shortcomings. At a time when globalization has made the strengthening of international law a *sine qua non* of human progress, this collection is a must read by all who take to heart Cassese's humanitarian values.

JEAN JACQUES BLAIS, P.C., Q.C.
Ph.D. Candidate, University of Ottawa

International Criminal Law and Philosophy. Edited by Larry May and Zachary Hoskins. New York: Cambridge University Press, 2010. 268 pages.

International Criminal Law (ICL) serves as a beacon of hope for a new world order for many around the world. Those who commit the greatest atrocities can now be met with criminal sanction. The value of this option is clear. However, this burgeoning field is ripe with philosophical puzzles that are of pressing practical relevance. *International Criminal Law and Philosophy,* edited by Larry May and Zachary Hoskins, invites the reader to reflect on a myriad of deep, potentially intractable problems that lie just beneath the

---

[16] *Ibid.* at 290.

surface of ICL. The over-arching aim of the volume is to grapple with issues pertaining to the moral foundations of ICL as they arise in a variety of contexts.

The book begins with Win-chiat Lee's fresh theoretical account of what counts as an international crime. In "International Crimes and Universal Jurisdiction," he argues that it is "neither the egregiousness of a crime nor the universality of the values protected" that brings an act within the ambit of international criminal law.[1] Instead, his account hinges on a formal quality: the nature of universal jurisdiction is the distinctive feature of ICL. Next, we enter into a nuanced discussion of sovereignty wherein Kristen Hessler wants us to continually reflect on the meaning of sovereignty in a changing world. In "State Sovereignty as an Obstacle to International Law," she urges us not to treat sovereignty as an all-encompassing quasi-mysterious trait of states. Rather, we should reflect on particular cases in order to determine whether the state's sovereignty interest must cede to other more pressing interests. Later in the volume, the consideration of issues raised by ICL becomes more specific still when the reader is treated to Larry May's careful analysis of what qualifies as a "group" in the legal definition of genocide. May argues for an *intersubjective* approach that avoids the descriptive and normative pitfalls of the purely subjective and purely objective alternatives.

Additional chapters present the reader with probing reflections on topical issues. For instance, in "Postwar Environmental Damage: a Study in *Jus Post Bellum*," Doug Lackey puts forward the timely argument that "participants in war have an affirmative obligation to restore the environmental damage by their military operations."[2] Steve Viner tackles another key question that has troubled many: Can the United States rely on the defence of self-defence in reference to the Guantanamo Bay detainees? While he answers this question in the negative, it is only after he sets out a fourth criterion for the use of this defence — the due diligence principle — which emerges from reflection on the "epistemic obligations" that must be present if an individual is to rely on this particular defence.[3] Joanna Kyriakakis wades into the philosophical debate about the possibility of criminalizing the behaviour of corporations in "Prosecuting Corporations for International Crimes: The Role for

---

[1] Larry May and Zachary Hoskins, eds., *International Criminal Law and Philosophy* (New York: Cambridge University Press, 2010) at 37.

[2] *Ibid.* at 141.

[3] *Ibid.* at 162.

Domestic Criminal Law." Here she sets out a strong case for the inclusion of private corporations within the jurisdictional domain of the International Criminal Court (ICC) that relies on complex arguments about territoriality and collective responsibility. Finally, in "Politicizing Human Rights (Using International Law)," Anat Biletzki urges human rights organizations to utilize international criminal law in order to protect victims. While she maintains that ICL is legal in form, she contends that it is fundamentally a political phenomenon. This is not, however, a detriment given that politics "is the engine of current affairs."[4]

After canvassing a mere selection of chapters, it becomes clear that this book covers a wide range of subject matter. While some might feel that the diversity of topics covered undermines the unity of the volume, I would argue that this is one of the virtues of this collection: one can identify a given problem that arises in ICL and then mine the various essays to arrive at a complex understanding of the issue at hand. Consider, for instance, the familiar dichotomy between law and politics from the perspective of the legitimacy of international law. ICL is often conceived of as apolitical — law is able to exist in the realm of principle, hovering above the messy world of politics. Legal institutions promise justice and the hope of peace when domestic politics prove to produce only conflict. Conversely, a common critique of ICL is that it merely represents "victor's justice" — law is not a neutral instrument, but a political tool. While there is certainly a partial truth on both sides of this familiar argument, the argument, when stated at this level of abstraction, remains unhelpful. Understanding law through an overly idealistic lens will not help practitioners navigate the complex realities on the ground. Conversely, the phrase "victor's justice" has become a cliché that offers little by way of advice. When we consider the relationship between law and politics as it is addressed in some of the remaining chapters of *International Criminal Law and Philosophy*, what emerges is a complex picture that promises to be more helpful to practitioners and fruitful for further philosophical reflection.

Ideally, international law brings with it the ideals that accompany the rule of law more generally — and it brings these ideals to the places that need it most. In "Political Reconciliation and International Criminal Trials," Colleen Murphy urges us not to underestimate the ability of ICL to promote reconciliation: International criminal tribunals introduce the values of "agency, reciprocity and

---

4 *Ibid.* at 196.

justice" into communities much in need of the stabilizing force of the rule of law.[5] Murphy gives content to the familiar phrase "rule of law" by following Lon Fuller, who sees law's central function as maintaining a "sound and stable framework (or baselines) for self-directed action and interaction."[6] As a result of ICL's "deep level of involvement" in the community, Murphy argues that this allows those involved to "affect the norms, practices, and patterns of inter-action within transitional societies in a much more profound man-ner than [in] nontransitional contexts."[7] It can do so by "restoring confidence and faith in law among ordinary citizens."[8] Part of ICL's reconciliatory function is educative:

Seeing norms of international law enforced, and seeing officials held ac-countable for failing to respect the constraints that law imposed, can restore confidence in the fact that law will be enforced and declared rules will provide an accurate picture of what the actual practice of law enforcement will be.[9]

Murphy notes, however, that obstacles emerge once it becomes clear that the rule of law, if adhered to too rigidly, will impede this goal. After all, there is no guarantee that those most responsible will actually be found guilty. If, for instance, the standard of due process is "too high, then it appears that the legacy of impunity, far from being successfully countered, will in fact be continued through international criminal trials."[10] The general public will likely lose trust in the legal process and ICL, and the goal of healing the frac-tured society will be undermined. Ultimately, Murphy advocates that we loosen strict procedural safeguards.[11]

This comes at a price, however. If key tenets of the rule of law are loosened, we move towards the "show trial" end of the spectrum. Law becomes a mere instrument of politics. Moreover, law's educa-tive function may also be undermined in the process. The balance that Murphy tries to strike between legal form and political purpose

5 *Ibid.* at 225.

6 *Ibid.* at 227.

7 *Ibid.* at 238.

8 *Ibid.* at 240.

9 *Ibid.* at 241.

10 *Ibid.* at 243.

11 *Ibid.* at 243–4.

is a delicate one. Insofar as practitioners seek to help rebuild transitional societies, they must tread this particular line with great care.

Deirdre Golash, in "The Justification of Punishment in the International Context," is less hopeful that ICL can play a reconciliatory role. Golash contends that it is likely that punishment will be viewed in partisan terms and not as an occasion for reconciliation.[12] This likelihood is exacerbated given the manner in which the legal forum categorizes people as either "guilty" or "innocent." While Murphy is worried about a guilty party being declared "innocent," Golash is concerned about those who are deemed innocent by default. The law will label certain people or groups as "criminals," often leaving those on the other side of the conflict untouched by criminal proceedings, even if they have blood on their hands. She argues that this shortcoming is not easily amended given the fact that the ICC needs the cooperation of states, making it difficult to indict those on whom it depends for such assistance. Golash also notes that the ICC takes a hands-off approach with respect to its primary benefactors.[13] It is not surprising, therefore, to find that those on the "losing" side may view the criminal proceedings as "political victimization."[14] As a result of these political factors, Golash is skeptical about the "expressive" value of legal punishment. In short, she fears that international legal trials might solidify political partisanship instead of playing a curative role.

Golash also articulates a deep concern about the ability of ICL to prevent future atrocities. According to Golash, one of the primary difficulties with ICL is the fundamental difference in the relationship between the political and the legal when we shift from the domestic to the international contexts.[15] Domestically, the focus is on "deviant" behaviour. In the world of ICL, such so-called deviant behaviour becomes the norm. The social pressure to conform pulls us towards and not away from performance of the condemned acts. By exploring the kind of psychological dispositions that characterize the perpetrators of genocide and crimes against humanity, Golash casts doubt on the ability of international criminal trials to deter in any meaningful way: "It is not realistic to think that the threat of punishment by an international body can counter the psychological, situational, and social pressures that induce individuals to

[12] *Ibid.* at 202–3.

[13] *Ibid.* at 219.

[14] *Ibid.* at 221.

[15] *Ibid.* at 202.

engage in atrocities, even those individuals who do so without being coerced."[16] When her attention is turned to leaders, Golash's message remains pessimistic: the psychological profile of such individuals is likely impervious to the consequences that the ICC may potentially impose.[17] With this in mind, the question we must ask needs to be sharpened: "For punishment to be justified on the grounds of deterrence we need to know not simply whether punishment has some tendency to prevent crime (as presumably it does), but also how much crime it prevents, and at what cost."[18] Golash is doubtful that this cost/benefit analysis will yield favourable results for ICL. If we are truly interested in deterring crimes, perhaps the millions of dollars spent on the various international criminal tribunals would be better spent in efforts to intervene before lives are lost.[19] What law can do in normal political situations, it seems less able to do in extreme social conditions. The complex interaction of political realities and international legal bodies makes the justification for punishment more difficult.

Leslie G. Francis and John P. Francis draw a similar conclusion in their chapter "International Criminal Courts, the Rule of Law, and the Prevention of Harm: Building Justice in Times of Injustice." They argue that prevention is the most important purpose that the ICC can serve. However, they are quite cynical about the ability of ICL to serve this function. In their analysis they turn to Rawls's theory of "partial compliance" rather than his more familiar "ideal theory." The former is aimed at thinking about principles of justice in "contexts in which people lack basic assurances of stability."[20] Once we inquire into what justice requires from this perspective, it becomes clear that "protecting the most vulnerable individuals" is of central concern, and this means it is of the utmost importance to prevent re-occurrence of the gravest atrocities.

Once the primacy of prevention is established, Francis and Francis turn their attention to the role of ICL. They argue that if ICL is going to act as a deterrent, it must address one of the primary causes of atrocities. The introduction of the legal form is not, however, the clear path to peace given the fact that "[i]t is difficult to

[16] *Ibid.* at 215.

[17] *Ibid.* at 216–17.

[18] *Ibid.* at 217.

[19] *Ibid.* at 217, citing Rwanda by way of illustration.

[20] *Ibid.* at 65.

sort out whether sanctions, military intervention, or the quality of internal politics constrain mass violence."[21] The worry is not simply that the law might fail in its efforts to prevent future atrocities in the region. Rather their fear is that "when nonlocal courts are brought into play, attention and resources are diverted from the broader social, economic and political context," where many of the key causes of atrocities may reside.[22] Note that theirs is a reversal of the traditional critique of ICL: it is the apolitical, not the political, nature of ICL that is problematic. Their analysis raises a pressing practical question: Can the ICC work to integrate law and local political realities in a way that can better enable the goal of prevention to be realized?

Helen Stacy is pre-occupied with a similar question, but from a slightly different angle. In her chapter "Criminalizing Culture," she focuses on the use of domestic criminal law to translate international human rights violations into domestic crimes. Stacy's concern is not simply with the re-emergence of a kind of legal imperialism. Rather, she also worries about the effectiveness of this top-down method of implementation. Stacy illustrates her worry with the graphic example of female genital cutting, arguing that criminal prohibitions do not eradicate the practice. Instead, the practice simply "goes underground" where infant girls are exposed to riskier procedures that place them in an even more vulnerable position.[23] We need not slip into cultural relativism in order to understand that criminal prohibitions may produce unintended consequences that threaten to harm the very people the law seeks to protect. Her analysis also "raises the question of how cultural practices ought to be viewed by the international community, and whether criminal law is the best tool for changing human rights."[24] More generally, Stacy is led to question the legitimacy of legal norms that "do not reflect any consensus of even a small percentage of the domestic polity."[25] Like Murphy, Stacy views the legitimacy of law not simply in terms of form or content — legitimacy is at least partly a function of the manner in which legal norms interact with the broader political community.

[21] *Ibid.* at 69.

[22] *Ibid.* at 71.

[23] *Ibid.* at 81–84.

[24] *Ibid.* at 84.

[25] *Ibid.* at 85.

At the end of this brief overview of this volume, two conclusions emerge: ICL seems to be both too political and too apolitical. It seems, therefore, that ICL needs to become both more political and less political if it is to be legitimate. Can law become less political? That is, can the ICC "rise above" the politics of money and power and prosecute individuals in a more even-handed way? Second, can law become more political? Can legal institutions be more sensitive to the complex political and cultural needs of the communities where the tribunals are located? These are tough questions, but they are the kinds of tough questions that make this book worth reading.

MARGARET MARTIN
Assistant Professor, University of Western Ontario

The End of Reciprocity: Terror, Torture and the Law of War. By Mark Osiel. Cambridge: Cambridge University Press, 2009. 676 pages.

Examining the conduct of "America's conflict with Al Qaeda and kindred groups," Mark Osiel asks a deceptively simple question in his fifth book on the law of war: "[I]f the enemy will not exercise a similar forbearance, at what point (and in what ways) is the law-abiding state released from its normal legal duties, to restore a tactical and moral symmetry in confrontation?" *The End of Reciprocity* provides his answer and assesses its challenging implications with a nuanced multidisciplinary review of legal, ethical, social science, and public policy issues arising from the "war on terror."

Recognizing that expectations of reciprocity — in particular, the "tit-for-tat" variety — underlie much of the humanitarian regime applicable in war (unlike human rights law), Osiel argues that both international law and moral theory permit considerable ill treatment of Al-Qaeda detainees. This is a provocative argument, particularly in its justification of ill treatment during armed conflict on the basis of a customary legal right of reprisal. Despite highlighting this theoretical freedom, Osiel nevertheless submits that the United States should refrain from such ill treatment so as to maintain its soft power and thereby advance its "ambitions to global influence" — a strategy informed by, and consistent with, a non-reciprocal "professional ethic of honor derived from military culture." In doing so, he heralds the end of bilateral reciprocity in the application of humanitarian norms in (counter-terrorist) warfare.

Osiel expressly acknowledges his focus on the counter-terrorism efforts of the United States itself. While warranted, given its lead role in the conflict with Al-Qaeda, this has important substantive legal implications. The United States is not a party to Additional Protocol I, which expressly prohibits civilian reprisals in Article 51(6), nor has it accepted the customary status of this provision. Although arguments concerning the continued legality of civilian reprisals nonetheless remain controversial, they are much easier for the United States — either in opposition to a customary norm itself or in support of persistent objector status — than for most other states (particularly to justify activities not characterized as *jus cogens* prohibitions, to the extent that such status exists).

For Canada's counter-terrorism efforts, Osiel's legal arguments therefore carry less weight. Unlike the United States, Canada is a party to Additional Protocol I and its prohibition on civilian reprisals. Further — and in contrast to many of its allies within the North Atlantic Treaty Organization, including the United Kingdom, France, and Italy — Canada did not enter a reservation to this provision for the purpose of protecting (at least as a matter of treaty law) its right to reprisal against prior deliberate enemy targeting of its civilians.

Nonetheless, Osiel's advocacy of restraint above and beyond legal requirements also applies to Canada (and other states). In some respects, such soft power arguments are more compelling for Canada since, unlike the United States, there is far less hard power for it to fall back on in the event that its moral suasion is lost. Inherent "martial restraint" also applies in Canada where, like the United States, the profession of arms is founded on anti-reciprocal principles promoting honourable conduct regardless of the conduct of the enemy (although these principles are arguably shaped by accepted international legal standards of combat, perhaps more so than is acknowledged by Osiel).

Understanding specific legal obligations is, in any case, important for determining whether restraint is indicated as a matter of law or solely for other reasons. Here, Osiel highlights necessary and substantial differences between humanitarian and human rights law, raising serious concerns about uncritical deference to the latter to resolve legal ambiguities in the former. Too often in Canada, as elsewhere, arguments for restricting wartime conduct have described the law in aspirational, rather than in actual, terms.

The End of Reciprocity focuses on the ill treatment of Al-Qaeda detainees constituting torture or cruel, inhuman, or degrading treatment. This is not surprising in the wake of the scandal at Abu Ghraib and officially sanctioned mistreatment — including torture — at detention facilities in Guantanamo Bay and elsewhere. Given this recent context, Osiel's suggestion that such mistreatment may be acceptable as a matter of both law and ethics is controversial. In making such a suggestion though, Osiel generally advances a stronger justification of policies implemented under President George W. Bush than the administration itself offered publicly (as Osiel himself notes, citing comments from reviewers of an earlier draft of his book).

Nonetheless, this remains a challenging position. Osiel recognizes that reciprocity (in this case, fairness) does not explain the application of Common Article 3 of the 1949 Geneva Conventions to the conflict against Al-Qaeda. This provision establishes minimum standards of humane treatment for persons not (or no longer) taking an active part in hostilities, including protections against "cruel treatment and torture," applicable "at any time and in any place whatsoever." Although an expectation of enemy reciprocity may underpin Common Article 3, it is not expressly reflected in its actual formulation. However, Osiel argues that this provision may not govern the conflict against Al-Qaeda at all, for reasons including its ambiguous threshold — namely, the existence of "an armed conflict not of an international character." While Osiel offers some persuasive moral and legal arguments in support of his position on this and related questions, and a strong general critique of absolute non-reciprocal norms during times of war, he nonetheless concedes that military lawyers in the United States (and elsewhere) have themselves argued the applicability of this provision to the conflict against Al-Qaeda, as has the Supreme Court of the United States.

Osiel further suggests that the prohibition on torture may not be absolute and that coercive interrogation of Al-Qaeda detainees involves conflicting *jus cogens* norms — on the one hand, the prohibition on torture and, on the other hand, the requirement to investigate, prevent, and prosecute crimes against humanity. This comparison will not be accepted by all. Characterizing the prohibition on crimes against humanity as *jus cogens* does not (necessarily) extend such status to their prevention, let alone to their investigation and prosecution, which appears to weight the legal balance against torture even in such circumstances.

In contrast to these rather permissive arguments concerning mistreatment, Osiel may not offer a sufficiently vigorous legal defence of the targeted killing of terrorist leaders, particularly during armed conflict. There is certainly a greater justification for this tactic than for torture or cruel, inhuman, or degrading treatment, without requiring resort to reprisal. For example, while there is considerable debate concerning its exact scope, there are strong legal arguments that direct participation in hostilities — activity that may permit lawful military targeting of otherwise protected civilians — extends beyond circumstances where the targeted individual poses an immediate or imminent violent threat (although this argument is strengthened considerably when the targeted killing itself is conducted by military rather than civilian personnel).

This provides an important basis for distinguishing targeted killing from mistreatment of detainees, and a significant explanation for its greater acceptance by the international community as well as the Obama administration (which has overseen a substantial recent increase in the tactical use of targeted killing, notably in Pakistani territory abutting Afghanistan). As a result, specific discussion of targeted killing may distract unnecessarily from the broader theme of *The End of Reciprocity*, particularly given its substantially more detailed discussion of specific moral and legal issues applicable to coercive interrogation.

While occasional disparaging comments in this volume provide a welcome personal touch, the more extreme statements also serve at times to distract from and undermine its arguments. For example, Osiel rightly raises serious questions concerning the growing influence and role of the International Committee of the Red Cross (ICRC) in humanitarian law development. However, to characterize it as a "semi-private spin-off" of the Swiss government that does not "contribute significantly *per se* to binding international custom" seems a tad unfair. This is particularly true in light of the ICRC's significant (albeit admittedly indirect) recent role in facilitating and contributing to multilateral "deliberative" reciprocity on customary law applicable to some of the very activities discussed by Osiel (notably direct participation in hostilities and the lawful targeting of civilians).

While warranted with respect to differences in applicable law, the American focus of *The End of Reciprocity* also manifests itself in other more controversial ways. For example, Osiel argues that the lack of continued ill treatment of Guantanamo Bay detainees should properly be viewed by American allies as a "gift" requiring (or at least indicating) a need for reciprocal future support of its ongoing war against terror. Some individuals outside the United States would balk at this rather one-sided characterization.

The End of Reciprocity is a rich and thorough volume, drawing on deep multidisciplinary research. However, by providing lengthy citations in endnotes rather than footnotes, it has sacrificed the ease of academic reference for more general readability. This is significant, as the book includes almost 250 pages of detailed citation and explanatory notes, including definitions of key terms. Clear headers in the endnote section correspond to specific pages in the text (for example, "Notes to pages 127–129"), which helps to mitigate, though not eliminate, this concern.

That said, dwelling too long on specific critiques of its arguments (whether warranted or not) misses the larger point and expected impact of *The End of Reciprocity*. This volume provides a reasoned, albeit provocative, examination of many aspects of American counter-terrorism policy that too often are politicized in public debate — or avoided altogether. The present review has only just skimmed its surface, necessarily simplifying the complex ethical, legal, and public policy positions advanced by Osiel with considerable subtlety, depth, and candour.

Clear, compelling rationales are required to justify resort to — or restraint of — particular counter-terrorism policies, rather than ill-informed polemics. The law alone does not and cannot tell us what we *should* do or why. In assessing America's ongoing conflict with Al-Qaeda, Osiel clearly situates the law of war in its broader moral and practical context, highlighting the potential value of restraint whether it is reciprocated or not. Whatever one may think about his specific arguments, *The End of Reciprocity* is an important book, contributing to a more nuanced and rational understanding of one of the major security challenges of our time.

CHRISTOPHER K. PENNY
Assistant Professor, Norman Paterson School of International Affairs,
Carleton University

On the Interpretation of Treaties: The Modern International Law as Expressed in the 1969 Vienna Convention on the Law of Treaties. By Ulf Linderfalk. Dordrecht, The Netherlands: Springer, 2007. 440 pages.

INTRODUCTION

Ulf Linderfalk's book *On the Interpretation of Treaties* is an important contribution to scholarship on the interpretation of treaties as well as an ambitious attempt to influence its practice. Linderfalk states that his primary concern is with practice and, more particularly, with the justification of correct outcomes by judicial authorities. As he points out, treaty disputes arise because states have different views about what a treaty means, and these disputes often prove difficult to resolve, resulting in separate and dissenting opinions, because arbitrators and judges also reach different conclusions about what the treaty means. In his view, such differences should be minimized because they complicate the dealings between states and undermine the legitimacy of judicial decisions.[1]

Linderfalk begins by staking his ideological ground. On the one hand, he is not a radical legal skeptic. He believes that legal rules are capable of constraining political judgment. Indeed, one of the goals of the book is to enhance the constraining capacity of the rules set out in Articles 31–33 of the Vienna Convention on the Law of Treaties. On the other hand, Linderfalk does not subscribe to the other extreme in interpretive theory, the single right answer thesis. He acknowledges that even interpreters who are faithful to the rules may be left with "a certain freedom of action."[2] There are thus two questions to be addressed: first, what is the content of the existing system of rules for interpreting treaties and, second, given that this system allows some freedom of action to interpreters, how should that freedom be used?[3]

Linderfalk focuses almost exclusively on the first question. He devotes ten chapters and more than 300 pages to elaborating the content of the system of rules codified in Articles 31 to 33. In the final chapter of the book, in thirteen pages, he identifies three sources of open-texturedness in the system that, in his view, give rise to a degree of freedom of action and the need for value judgments. The issue of how that freedom should be used — what values might govern those judgments — is never reached. As he explains,

[i]n this work, attention will be focused on operative interpretation of treaties. The idea is to make an attempt to create some assumedly greater

---

[1] Ulf Linderfalk, *On the Interpretation of Treaties: The Modern International Law as Expressed in the 1969 Vienna Convention on the Law of Treaties* (Dordrecht, The Netherlands: Springer, 2007) at 1–2.

[2] *Ibid.* at 5.

[3] *Ibid.* at 4–5 and 373–75.

certainty among the appliers of international law with regard to the content of the currently existing regime for the interpretation of treaties.[4]

Readers looking for practical guidance in interpreting a particular treaty or treaties in general may or may not find this book useful. Certainly, there is no shortage of guidance. However, for a number of reasons, mentioned in the following discussion, the practical value of this guidance is difficult to assess. For me, an academic lawyer with an interest in statutory interpretation, the chief value of the book lies in its original, sometimes surprising, approach to the theory of interpretation.

THE SYSTEM OF LEGAL RULES

In the introductory chapter, Linderfalk explains that Articles 31 to 33 of the Vienna Convention on the Law of Treaties "tell appliers how to proceed to determine what they shall regard as the correct meaning of an interpreted treaty provision, considered from the point of view of international law."[5] Chapter 2 then defines "the correct meaning" and sets out the methodology for determining that meaning. This methodology consists first in reading the text to determine its ordinary meaning. If that meaning is clear, there is no need for interpretation. However, should it turn out to be ambiguous, resort must be had to the first order and possibly the second order rules of interpretation set out in Articles 31 to 33. First order rules tell interpreters how to identify the correct meaning when the ordinary meaning of the text is unclear. Second order rules tell interpreters how to identify the correct meaning if applying the first order rules produces conflicting results.

By the end of the book, Linderfalk has produced a massive gloss on Articles 31–33 of the convention and has codified this gloss in forty-four rules, many with definitions and sub-rules.[6] Each rule is the result of painstaking analysis and is justified by Linderfalk's interpretation of Articles 31–33 in accordance with those articles as glossed by him as well as the decisions of international courts and the commentary of recognized international law scholars. Here are some examples of first order rules:

---

4 *Ibid.* at 12.

5 *Ibid.* at 7.

6 *Ibid.* at 387–95.

Rule 1, based on Article 31 and dealing with ordinary meaning, provides:

(1) If it can be shown that in a treaty provision, there is an expression whose form corresponds to an expression of conventional language, then the provision shall be understood in accordance with the rules of that language.
(2) For the purpose of this rule, "conventional language" means the language employed at the time of the treaty's conclusion, except for those cases where paragraph (3) applies.
(3) For the purpose of this rule, "conventional language" means the language employed at the time of interpretation, on the condition that it can be shown that the thing interpreted is a generic referring expression with a referent assumed by the parties to be alterable.
(4) For the purpose of this rule, "parties" means any and all states for which the treaty is in force at the time of interpretation.

Rule 18, also based on Article 31 and dealing with purpose and object, provides:

(1) If, by using the preparatory work of a treaty, a concordance can be shown to exist, as between the parties to said treaty, and with regard to the norm content of an interpreted treaty provision, then the provision shall be understood in such a way that it logically agrees with the concordance.
(2) For the purpose of this rule, "the preparatory work" of a treaty means any representation produced in the process of drafting the treaty, whether textual or not.
(3) For the purpose of this rule, "parties" means any and all states for which the treaty is in force at the time of interpretation.

Rule 36 is an example of a second order rule:

(1) If it can be shown that a treaty provision prohibits an act or a state of affairs which — from the point of view of the parties — can be considered more tolerable than another generically identical act or state of affairs, then the provision shall be understood to prohibit this second act or state of affairs too.
(2) For the purpose of this rule, "parties" means any and all states for which the treaty is in force at the time of interpretation.

These examples give a taste of what in my view is an unfortunate feature of the book — it is written in the style of monographs in analytic philosophy. Writers in this tradition strive to ensure that every claim or hypothesis is precisely stated, its terms are carefully defined, and its validity or truth is demonstrated through logical argument. Such a style makes for difficult reading but is worth the trouble if it facilitates clear and accurate communication. In this book, at least some of the time, I questioned the value of this style. Consider, for example, the following definition of "correct meaning":

The correct meaning of a treaty should be identified with the pieces of information conveyed by that treaty with regard to its norm content, according to the intentions of the treaty parties ... insofar as these intentions can be considered mutually held.[7]

It is hard to see how this formulation improves upon the assertion that the correct meaning of a treaty should be identified with the rules or norms that the parties mutually intended to adopt. Similarly, Rule 1 is said to be based on the following communicative standard (a concept explained below): "if a state makes an utterance taking the form of a treaty provision, then the provision should be drawn up so that every expression in the provision whose form corresponds to an expression of conventional language, bears a meaning that agrees with that language."[8] So far as I can tell, this amounts to saying that treaties are presumed to be drafted using the conventions of ordinary language. It is hard to see what value is added by the more formal and elaborate formulation.

A related problem with the book is its frequent reliance on technical language drawn from disciplines other than law. To fully understand Rule 1, for example, a reader must master the concept of "generic referring expression." This involves first mastering general and singular referring expressions, which may be definite or indefinite, all of which are time-bound: "[W]hen a singular or general referring expression is uttered, a (temporal) relationship is established between the occasion of utterance and the point in time or time period at or during which the referent is presumed to exist."[9] These time-bound expressions contrast with generic

---

[7] *Ibid.* at 33.

[8] *Ibid.* at 61.

[9] *Ibid.* at 77.

referring expressions, which do not establish a temporal relationship because they are timeless. At the end of the day, the analysis captured by paragraphs (2) and (3) of Rule 1 is original and persuasive, and it offers helpful, well-reasoned guidance. However, one wonders whether Linderfalk's insights could not have been communicated in more user-friendly language. While an opaque writing style may put off a casual reader or a lawyer looking for practical guidance, readers familiar with the "interpretive turn" in legal theory will find themselves in familiar terrain.

THE UNDERLYING THEORY

Most systems of legal interpretation begin by directing the interpreter to establish the ordinary meaning of the text to be interpreted, and Article 31 is no exception — treaties are to be interpreted "in accordance with the ordinary meaning to be given to the terms of the treaty." Most commentaries on ordinary meaning do not seriously address the issue of how ordinary meaning is established. Most assume — without attempting to analyze or defend the assumption — that meaning results from reliance on a code that is shared by the competent speakers of a language. This is the code-based theory of communication. It posits that the communication of meaning involves three steps: it begins when person A relies on a code to translate his or her thoughts into a message; the message is then transmitted to a listener or reader B who, if competent, is privy to the code; upon receiving the message, reader B applies the code to extract A's thoughts.

Linderfalk reviews this model and rightly rejects it because it is inaccurate and misleading. Despite considerable effort, linguists have found it impossible to describe a code that is capable of accounting for successful communication. They have shown that semantic, grammatical, and pragmatic meanings can be coded and decoded, and this can take listeners or readers part of the way to the goal of successful communication — but never all the way. No code is capable of bridging the gap between sentence meaning (the meaning of the text derived from semantic, grammatical, and pragmatic rules) and utterance meaning (the message that the speaker or writer wishes to communicate).

Linderfalk embraces the more recently developed inferential model of communication. According to this model, person A signals his or her intention to communicate by producing an utterance; upon receiving the utterance, person B considers what has been said in context and, based on what is relevant in the context, infers the message that A probably wanted to send. Context, for this purpose, consists of the entire set of assumptions about the world that person B has access to when listening to person A's remark or reading A's text — a set that is clearly countless if not infinite.[10]

The key question to be addressed by an inference model of communication is the following: given all the assumptions available to listener or reader B when interpreting A's utterance, how can he or she know which ones are likely to lead to successful communication? The answer, Linderfalk explains, is that B relies on a second order assumption: B assumes that when A produced the utterance to be interpreted, he or she conformed to certain communicative standards. Given this answer, the key challenge for linguists committed to the inference model is to identify those communicative standards.

The inferential model of communication was developed by linguists to explain how ordinary meaning is established. That is not how Linderfalk uses the model. He adapts it to his own purposes by suggesting that Articles 31 to 33 of the Vienna Convention are properly understood as establishing the communicative standards that identify the assumptions that can legitimately be relied on in interpreting a treaty. He writes:

[I]t appears that in order to distinguish between correct and incorrect interpretive results, we would have to single out some contextual assumptions as being acceptable and some as unacceptable ... The provisions of the [*Vienna Convention*] do not address so much the idea of acceptable and unacceptable contextual assumption; rather, they address the idea of acceptable and unacceptable means of interpretation. However, on closer inspection, this must be seen to amount to very much the same thing ... Of all those contextual assumptions that can possibly be made ... the only ones that may be used, according to the *Convention,* are ... the means of interpretation recognized as acceptable.[11]

At the end of this analysis, Linderfalk adopts the following principle as the basis for his exposition of Articles 31 to 33:

If it can be shown that between an interpreted treaty provision and any given means of interpretation M, there is a relationship governed by the communicative standard S, then the provision shall be understood as if the relationship conformed to this standard.

10 *Ibid.* at 34ff.
11 *Ibid.* at 48–49.

In other words, the means of interpretation mentioned in articles 31 to 33 are grounded in or express particular shared assumptions about how the meaning of a treaty is to be understood.[12]

The rest of the book then examines the means of interpretation identified as acceptable by Articles 31–33 of the convention (such as conventional language, context, object and purpose, and supplementary means of interpretation) by exploring the communicative standards underlying these means. This approach yields many insights. I particularly liked the way Linderfalk draws attention to the difference between standards grounded in linguistics and standards grounded in logic (see, for example, the discussion of redundancy later in the book)[13] — a distinction that is often blurred in interpretive practice. The former depends on drafting conventions, the latter on the relationship between norms.

To my mind, Linderfalk's recognition that every system of legal interpretation presupposes a theory of communication is an important contribution to the scholarship on legal interpretation, as are his concise accounts of the code-based and inference-based theories. I would have liked to see him use his adoption of the inference-based theory as a basis for evaluating, not just glossing and recodifying, existing law. After all, the methodology and rules of Articles 31 to 33 are themselves grounded in a code-based theory of communication. A major (false) assumption of that theory — that language is either clear or ambiguous — is perpetuated in Linderfalk's account rather than challenged. It is found in the distinction between meaning and interpretation with which the book begins, in the belief that the means of interpretation are appropriately applied in fixed sequence and in the fundamental notion, found throughout the book, that once clarity has been achieved the work of interpretation is done:

As observed earlier, interpreting a treaty, according to the terminology of the *Vienna Convention,* is tantamount to clarifying the text of a treaty that has been shown to be unclear. From this definition two norms of interpretation can be derived ... According to the first of the two norms, a process of interpretation shall be concluded when one arrives at a point where the interpreted treaty provision can be regarded as clear. According

12 *Ibid.* at 51.
13 *Ibid.* at 110.

to the second norm, a process of interpretation shall *not* be concluded, as long as the interpreted treaty provision *cannot* be regarded as clear.[14]

No doubt this understanding of Articles 31 to 33 accords with the ordinary meaning of the text and is shared by many international law scholars. It is so fundamentally at odds with the insights of inference-based theory, however, that one is surprised by Linderfalk's willingness to accept and defend it. The distinctions between various aspects of context and purpose, some of which are assigned to the primary means of interpretation, while others to supplementary means, strike me as particularly ripe for reform. For example, the principle that within a text the same words should be given the same meaning is treated as an aspect of context, which is a primary means of interpretation. Conversely, the principle of *ejusdem generis* is treated as a supplementary means. Since both principles are grounded in conventions of legal drafting, one would expect them to be analyzed and classified in the same way.

Conclusion

To be fair to Linderfalk, he did not write this book to advance legal theory or engage in law reform. He was looking for a way to improve the predictability and legitimacy of outcomes of interpretation disputes in the context of existing international law. Ironically, perhaps, his efforts to achieve this goal take the form of a code — a complete and fully explicated code, in which all terms are carefully defined and relations among the rules clearly set out. It is very likely that if the practitioners and judges to whom the book is addressed were to internalize and apply this code, the outcomes of disputes would be easier to predict, justification for the outcomes would be more transparent, and legitimacy would be enhanced. In particular, it would be easier to distinguish the rule-governed portions of a justification from those in which the judge enjoyed a certain freedom of action and was forced to resort to values. This would allow a judge to identify and try to justify the values on which he or she relied. In other words, in my view, Linderfalk largely succeeds in setting out a full description of the modern law of treaty interpretation in the form of rules that lead to a correct answer. In this respect, the book is a *tour de force,* and those who are willing to master the vocabulary and style of the book will be amply rewarded.

---

[14] *Ibid.* at 326.

I am less certain about the practical impact of the book. The limitation of codes is that they are successful only in so far as their content is sound *and* they are shared by all of the parties to the enterprise. Unfortunately, the vocabulary and style considered necessary to ensure sound content in this case creates some barriers to easy comprehension and internalization.

RUTH SULLIVAN
Professor, Common Law Section, Faculty of Law,
University of Ottawa

The International Law of Investment Claims. By Zachary Douglas. New York: Cambridge University Press, 2009. 684 pages.

International investment law suffers from the deficiencies one might expect of an area of law without appellate review — no rule of *stare decisis* and inconsistent treaty language. Jurisprudence on the same obligation can be contradictory. Tribunal decisions are often based on contrived legal analysis (presumably to arrive at a desired result) or even avoid issues entirely. Further, the limited grounds for judicial review (or for setting aside proceedings) that exist tend to be applied with great deference by domestic courts. *The International Law of Investment Claims* by Zachary Douglas confronts the resulting deficiencies in international investment law in unapologetic fashion. Flawed and lazy legal reasoning is exposed, while divergent or conflicting jurisprudence is synthesized pragmatically. In doing so, Douglas has successfully distilled and justified legal rules in this evolving area of law in a way that will provide academics, practitioners, and arbitrators with important touchstones.

Leaving substantive investment obligations aside for another day, *The International Law of Investment Claims* synthesizes principles only with respect to choice of law, jurisdiction, and admissibility. The author codifies each principle as one of fifty-four legal propositions. Each proposition is supported through extensive justification. Some propositions are so plain as to raise questions about the merits of their inclusion (for example, Rule 15, which holds that for an investment treaty tribunal to adjudge the merits of a claim arising out of an investment it must have jurisdiction over the parties and the claims and the claim submitted to the tribunal must be admissible).

However, once the leading jurisprudence on even the most obvious of principles is thoroughly examined, one is immediately struck by the power and necessity of this approach.

By codifying rules of law, the reader is forced to *confront the rules.* Given that many of the principles enunciated are either inadequately pleaded by counsel or inadequately addressed by arbitrators, the need for a plain articulation of even the most obvious propositions is manifest. More complex propositions are likewise presented in a plain and simple manner. Douglas's chosen methodology creates a resource that is both easily referenced and, perhaps more importantly, easily subjected to criticism, debate, and future adaptation. These virtues of his approach are best illustrated through a few telling examples. Douglas first deals with the juridical foundations of investment treaty law. His first rule is simple enough — where the contracting parties have agreed by treaty to a procedure for the settlement of disputes between an investor and the host state, the claim advanced is that of the investor, while its home state has no legal standing in the claim (Rule 1). The basic premise here is that claims made under international investment treaties are those of the claimant investor exercising its own right. They are not a claim of the investor's home state, which merely permits the investor to exercise the claim on the home state's behalf.

The inherent difficulties in reconciling a "derivative" model for a juridical foundation in investment claims are then dealt with. After thoroughly discussing why diplomatic protection's rules of admissibility do not generally apply in investment disputes (Rule 2), Douglas concludes that the juridical foundation for investment treaty arbitration is based on a "direct model." Under a derivative model, such as diplomatic protection, the international legal obligations are owed to the contracting states. In the investment treaty law context, this means that contracting states merely confer standing on their private national investors to enforce these obligations. However, the relevant features of diplomatic protection are contrasted with that of international investment law to support Douglas's assertion that it is actually a "direct model" that governs in the investment world. For instance, with respect to functional control over claims, Douglas observes that control over diplomatic protection claims resides with the contracting state, while in international investment law it lies with the investor. Similarly, with respect to nationality of claims, in diplomatic protection some genuine connection is required for a state to press a claim whereas under typical investment treaties the mere location of incorporation is generally sufficient.

By examining such factors, the author concludes that investors bring claims as of their own right and not in place of their contracting home state. In a broader demonstration that the investment treaty itself, supplemented by general international law, is the applicable law in investment claims, it is proposed that legal principles rather than policies should inform a tribunal's interpretation of the relevant investment treaty standards (Rule 10). Again, this seemingly obvious proposition begs the question of why it is necessary. As the author points out in his commentary, tribunals have been guilty of transforming *policies* found in preambular text into *principles* of law purporting to give content to the substantive application of investment protection standards. The author's discussion of Rule 10 chastises these tribunals for using preambular text, as evidence of an investment treaty's "object and purpose" under the guise of determining the ordinary meaning of treaty terms, to actually determine the *substantive content* of treaty obligations.

The danger in such an approach is made explicit: it is not the role of an arbitral tribunal to determine whether a particular interpretation of an investment treaty obligation will fulfil the policy objectives of the contracting parties. Such an approach can lead to egregious results. For example, in *SGS v. Philippines,* the tribunal used the preambular text of the Switzerland/Philippines bilateral investment treaty (BIT) as evidence of its object and purpose — that of creating and maintaining favourable conditions for investment in the territories of the contracting parties. The tribunal reasoned that uncertainties in interpretation of substantive obligations should, therefore, be resolved in favour of the protections in the BIT — that is to say, in favour of the investor.

The author reasons that the risk is that, since all substantive investment treaty obligations are uncertain because they take the form of general concepts, any interpretative uncertainties will *always* be resolved to favour the claimant. Favouring the claimant based on policy considerations is not the role of an investment tribunal. Rather, a tribunal should make legally principled decisions. While unstated by Douglas, it is apparent that he is here advocating generally for a more principled international investment law than currently exists. In fact, this seems to be a central thesis of the entire work.

Of critical importance to any discussion of preliminary issues is the tribunal's finding of its own jurisdiction over the parties and the claims (Rule 15) based on the inherent *quid pro quo* between a contracting party's guarantee of minimum standards of treatment and the making of an investment by a third party in the territory of that contracting party (Rule 16). The author quite rightly reasons that if this *quid pro quo* is a fundamental underpinning of investment treaties, then it must bear on the principles governing a tribunal's jurisdiction over a dispute.

Particularly useful in making a determination of jurisdiction is the clarification of terms or "taxonomy of preliminary issues" offered to the reader. Such precision is welcome because, as Douglas points out, terms such as "jurisdiction," "consent to arbitrate," "competence," and "admissibility" are often used too loosely and without regard to their foundations.

In laying out this taxonomy, Douglas distinguishes between the existence, scope, and exercise of adjudicative power. With respect to the *existence* of adjudicative power, the question is whether the conditions for granting the tribunal adjudicative power have been met (*l'attribution de la juridiction*). The *scope* of adjudicative power determines which categories of parties and disputes come within the tribunal's adjudicative reach (*l'étendue de la juridiction*). The existence and scope of adjudicative power together comprise the jurisdiction of the tribunal. Whether the tribunal can *exercise* its adjudicative powers relative to the specific claims raised (*les conditions de recevabilité*) is a matter of admissibility.

Having defined the terms of the discussion, Douglas then turns to highlighting the importance of a tribunal properly finding its jurisdiction by focusing on the consent of the contracting party and the making of an investment by a national of another contracting party. For example, Douglas shows how the existence and scope of an investment are critical to each phase of an investment dispute. In particular, a tribunal's jurisdiction *ratione materiae, ratione personae,* and *ratione temporis* are all dependent on the existence and scope of an investment. Findings of a host state's liability are necessarily dependent on the linkage between the alleged prejudice and the rights comprising the investment. And, obviously, any finding of damages and their quantification depends on an assessment of the investment itself and how much it has earned or lost.

Douglas exposes the folly of not examining the investment with respect to each aspect of a claim through criticism of the majority decision in *Feldman v. Mexico*. In the course of its finding on expropriation, the majority in *Feldman* held that the only significant assets related to the US investor's investment (an enterprise known as CEMSA) was an alleged right to receive tax rebates upon exportation of cigarettes and the profits arising from this endeavour. It went on to find that the claimant never possessed a "right" to obtain these tax credits on cigarette exports. As a result, the right to obtain tax rebates could not have been part of the bundle of rights making up the investor's investment. Obviously, where there is no investment (the alleged right to export tax credits), there could be no expropriation.

Yet, the majority in *Feldman* also held that Mexico had breached its national treatment obligation to Feldman by forcing CEMSA to return these tax rebates after an audit, while a Mexican-owned company in like circumstances was not forced to do so. It is obviously untenable to hold that national treatment has been violated in respect of an investment right which the investor does not possess.

Having pointed out the inconsistency of the *Feldman* majority decision, Douglas then uses the decision in *Tecmed v. Mexico* to show how a tribunal should deal with such matters. In *Tecmed,* the tribunal had to determine whether the purchased rights to a landfill for hazardous industrial waste included an operating license of unlimited duration. The tribunal made this determination as a preliminary matter of determining the scope of the subject investment. Douglas commends the *Tecmed* tribunal's "meticulous examination" of all of the relevant evidence in coming to its holding. It is on the basis of this key preliminary finding that the tribunal then determined that Mexico had expropriated this right on the merits.

Another example of the author's enunciation of useful principles is his discussion of defining the quality and extent of "the nexus between the measure and the investment" in the essential task of determining a tribunal's jurisdiction *ratione materiae*. Here, Douglas focuses on a common formulation that a state measure must "relate to" the investment — that is to say, the measure attributable to the host state must be connected to the rights and interests making up the claimant's investment.

First, Douglas disposes of the *Methanex v. United States* tribunal's finding that the phrase "relating to" requires a legally significant connection between a measure and an investor or an investment. In *Methanex,* the tribunal, in its preliminary ruling, held that there was no significant connection between California's two measures and Methanex's investment in methanol production. Thus, the measures did not "relate to" the investment. Nevertheless, the tribunal still heard Methanex's claims on the merits but only to the extent they were based on the United States's alleged intent to favour domestic producers at the expense of foreign producers. Such intent, according to the tribunal, would constitute evidence providing the requisite legally significant connection between the measure and the investment.

The *Methanex* tribunal's "eloquent justification" for this requirement that the requisite nexus must be legally significant was that limits must be imposed to restrict the liability consequences to which conduct may give rise. Analogizing to the law of tort, the tribunal reasoned that there must be a reasonable connection between the complainant, the tortfeasor, the tortious conduct, and the harm and that the limits are imposed by legal rules on duty, causation, and remoteness.

Again, the inherent problem with the *Methanex* tribunal's reasoning is evident. It was dealing with the required nexus between the host state's impugned measure and the claimant's investment in the context of determining its own jurisdiction *ratione materiae* (that is, a preliminary jurisdictional, not substantive, issue). Yet, the formulation developed in *Methanex* necessarily involves determinations of substantive legal rules (that is, duty of care, causation, and remoteness). As the author points out repeatedly, this is not the duty of the tribunal at this stage. A determination of a tribunal's jurisdiction should not involve adjudicating substantive claims.

Instead, a more principled assessment of the required nexus is suggested. Douglas proposes that the inquiry should be a factual one focused on the concept of property. In particular, he distinguishes between "property-limitation rules" and "property-independent prohibitions" in attempting to discern a threshold for the required nexus. The suggestion is that the nexus establishing that a measure "relates to" an investment can be satisfied if the measure is a "property-limitation rule" but not a "property-independent prohibition."

Property-limitation rules are rules fettering a property holder's rights in some manner. By contrast, a property-independent prohibition does not depend on whether a person or entity has an interest in property at all. Douglas uses the example of a measure declaring a three-day national holiday causing financial losses to a foreign investment. This is a property-independent prohibition because it is directed to both owners and employees. It does not merely limit the owners' property rights. This is an example of the useful and principled analytic tools presented by the author to deal with fundamental yet often poorly examined preliminary issues in investment treaty law.

Rule 27 states that the legal foundation of claims submitted to a tribunal must be objectively determined in a preliminary ruling on its jurisdiction *ratione materiae*. Douglas cautions that the claimant investor's characterization of its own claims (a subjective test) cannot simply be accepted by a tribunal to find jurisdiction. Rather, an objective assessment is necessary. Once again, the power of enunciating a rule (even an apparently obvious one) is in forcing the reader to confront it. Douglas's commentary demonstrates that many tribunals do not conduct an objective assessment of this basic jurisdictional test.

Douglas demonstrates the mischief a subjective test can create using the *Azurix Corp. v. Argentina Republic* case as an example. In *Azurix*, the claimant and the province of Buenos Aires were parties to a concession agreement. The agreement included an exclusive jurisdiction clause favouring local courts and a waiver by the parties of any other forum. Argentina argued that because the claim arose out of the concession agreement, the claimant was bound by its terms. Douglas shows that the tribunal conducted no analysis of the claimant's claims but, instead, upheld its jurisdiction by adopting the claimant's characterization of its own claims. He does not comment on the motives behind avoiding an objective assessment. However, his point is clear here as it is throughout this volume — international investment law often suffers from unprincipled decision making.

A final issue worthy of note is the author's treatment of the controversial practice of some tribunals that use most-favoured nation (MFN) provisions to incorporate by reference provisions from investment treaty relating to the jurisdiction of the tribunal. Douglas's position is summed up by Rule 43 — unless there is an unequivocal provision to the contrary, an MFN clause in a basic investment treaty does not incorporate by reference provisions from a third investment treaty relating to jurisdiction.

In a discussion highly critical of the tribunal's decision in *Maffezini v. Spain* and the several other cases relying on it, Douglas characterizes the issue as a "false question." In *Maffezini*, the tribunal had to determine whether the investor could rely on the MFN clause in the Argentina/Spain BIT to avoid the modified rule on exhaustion of local remedies and rely on more favourable rules in other BITs to which Spain was a party. The tribunal took jurisdiction, reasoning that because "dispute resolution arrangements" such as the modified local remedies rule are inextricably tied to the protection of foreign investors and because MFN clauses protect foreign investors, the investor should be able to invoke provisions more favourable to the protection of its rights from a third treaty.

Douglas points out that this should not be a question of whether there is an inextricable link between protecting foreign investors and dispute settlement arrangements. Rather, the issue is whether the contracting parties somehow derogated from the "dispute resolution arrangements" by including an MFN clause. So, the tribunal here conflates "dispute resolution arrangements" such as the modified local remedies rule with the treatment accorded to investors and wrongly assumes jurisdiction.

By synthesizing legal propositions through careful and critical analysis of the jurisprudence, the *International Law of Investment Claims* provides a very useful reference on fundamental issues relating to choice of law, jurisdiction, and admissibility in international investment law. The author promises that "[t]he next volume will address the substantive obligations of investment protection that are common to the majority of investment treaties." If that next volume is as unforgiving in its criticism of jurisprudence and as principled and well reasoned in its synthesis of the law, it will be as useful a legal resource as its predecessor.

RAAHOOL WATCHMAKER
*Counsel, Trade Law Bureau, Foreign Affairs and
International Trade Canada*

Analytical Index / Indexe analytique

—

THE CANADIAN YEARBOOK OF INTERNATIONAL LAW

2009

ANNUAIRE CANADIEN DE DROIT INTERNATIONAL

(A) Article; (NC) Notes and Comments; (Ch) Chronique;
(P) Practice; (C) Cases; (BR) Book Review

(A) Article; (NC) Notes et commentaires; (Ch) Chronique;
(P) Pratique; (C) Jurisprudence; (BR) Recension de livre

Al-qaeda, 106, 107, 110, 111, 117, 127, 132, 136
armed conflict, and customary international law, 99-159
bilateral investment treaty, 197-259; Canada's program, 203-59; China's program, 207-59; comparison of Canadian and Chinese programs, 213-59; and expropriation, 235-43; and human rights and sustainability, 250-57; and minimum standard of treatment, 217-22; and most-favoured nation treatment, 229-35; and national treatment, 222-29; and procedural protections, 243-50
biological diversity, risks of causing damage to, 331-41
Blais, Jean Jacques, review of *The Human Dimension of International Law: Selected Papers of Antonio Cassese*, edited by Paola Gaeta and Salvatore Zappalà (BR), 643-49
Blom, Joost, *Canadian Cases in Private International Law in 2008–9 / La jurisprudence canadienne en matière de droit international privé en 2008–9* (C), 607-42

Canada-China Foreign Investment Promotion and Protection Agreement, 197-259
Canada-Colombia Agreement on Labour Cooperation, 187-90
Canada-Colombia Free Trade Agreement: Colombian reservations to, 184-87; corporate social responsibility, 180-84, 193-94; expropriation, 179-80; and gender mainstreaming, 191-93; and a human rights impact assessment, 193; investment provisions of, 174-75; labour provisions, 187-90; national treatment and most-favoured nation treatment, 175-78; performance requirements, 178-79; and women's rights, 161-95
Canadian Cases in Private International Law in 2008–9, Joost Blom (C), 607-42
Canadian Cases in Public International Law in 2008–9, Gibran Van Ert (C), 567-606
Canadian Practice in International Law: At the Department of Foreign Affairs in 2008–9, Alan Kessel (P), 411-48

679

Index of Cases /
Index de la jurisprudence

———